OXFORD MODERN LANGUAGES
AND LITERATURE MONOGRAPHS

The Origins of Modern Literary Yiddish

DOV-BER KERLER

CLARENDON PRESS · OXFORD

OXFORD

UNIVERSITY PRESS

Great Clarendon Street, Oxford OX2 6DP

Oxford University Press is a department of the University of Oxford.
It furthers the University's objective of excellence in research, scholarship,
and education by publishing worldwide in

Oxford New York

Athens Auckland Bangkok Bogotá Buenos Aires Calcutta
Cape Town Chennai Dar es Salaam Delhi Florence Hong Kong Istanbul
Karachi Kuala Lumpur Madrid Melbourne Mexico City Mumbai
Nairobi Paris São Paulo Singapore Taipei Tokyo Toronto Warsaw

and associated companies in Berlin Ibadan

Oxford is a registered trade mark of Oxford University Press
in the UK and certain other countries

Published in the United States
by Oxford University Press Inc., New York

British Library Cataloguing in Publication Data

Data available

Library of Congress Cataloging in Publication Data
Kerler, Dov-Ber, 1958–
The origins of modern literary Yiddish / Dov-Ber Kerler.
Includes bibliographical references and index.
1. Yiddish language—Grammar, Historical.   2. Yiddish
language—18th century—Style.   3. Yiddish language—18th century—
Dialects.   I. Title.
PJ5116.K43   1995   437'.947—dc20   94-45337
ISBN 0-19-815166-7

1 3 5 7 9 10 8 6 4 2

Typeset in Photina
by Regent Typesetting, London
Printed in Great Britain
on acid-free paper by
Biddles Ltd.,
Guildford and King's Lynn

ACKNOWLEDGEMENTS AND DEDICATION

This book wouldn't have come to fruition if it weren't for the tremendous help extended to me by many friends, colleagues, and a number of institutions. Hence my deep gratitude to them all.

My greatest indebtedness is to the two individuals whose constant assistance, wise counsel, and constructive criticism were readily available at each and every stage: Dovid Katz—with whom I was privileged to study from 1984 and later to become a colleague at Oxford University—was and continues to be an inexhaustible source of inspiration and of intellectual, linguistic, and scholarly sustenance; my wife Didi Kerler repeatedly and not always unsuccessfully instructed me on both common sense and stylistic coherence and lucidity. Likewise I owe a great debt to my mother Anna Kerler, who has taught me Volhynian Yiddish and folklore, and my father, the Yiddish poet and editor Josef Kerler, for teaching me his native Podolian dialect, literature, and the craft of Yiddish poetry.

For providing me with an atmosphere of collegiality, tolerance, and friendship my thanks are due to my colleagues at the Oxford Centre for Hebrew and Jewish Studies, in particular to its founding president David Patterson, and to the Fellows and staff of Lincoln College where the final draft of the book was completed during my tenure there as Porter Research Fellow in Yiddish Studies (1989–93). Among the many individuals who were kind enough to offer me help and support at various stages I would also like to express my gratitude to Marion Aptroot, Sonia Argyle, David Djanogly, the late Naki Doniach, Daniel Frank, Christopher Hutton, Richard Judd, Eliyakum Klepfish, Wolf Moskovich, Varun Sahni, Nick Thomas, Nigel Wilson, and Constantine Zuckerman. Special thanks are also due to the staffs of Judaica collections of the Bodleian Library (Oxford), the Jewish National and Hebrew University Library (Jerusalem), and the British Library (London). Last but not least my gratitude also goes to Oxford University Press and in particular to George Tulloch and Frances Whistler, thanks to whose unreserved dedication and thorough professionalism this book is being published.

It was a privilege to be assisted and supported by all these people and it is my unavoidable duty to take full responsibility for the book's errors of fact and interpretation.

This book is a study of the eighteenth-century linguistic origins of modern literary Yiddish in Eastern Europe. The recurrent predictions and the 'enlightened' prescription of the impending demise of Yiddish originate in roughly the same period as the rise of the Jewish Enlightenment movement in Germany. The twentieth century witnessed both the meteoric rise of modern Yiddish culture and the murderous destruction of its creators, its people and their natural habitat. It is none the less my deep conviction that despite all odds even the most recent forebodings concerning the fate of Yiddish need not be proven true. After all, Yiddish language and literature were created by and for people with great dedication to memory for the sake of the future. It is in this spirit of remembering for the sake of the future that this book is humbly dedicated to the memory of my mother's immediate family:

my great grandmother Henye Gluzman	מרת העניע גלוזמאַן הי״ד
my grandmother Miriam bas Itsye Barshap	מרת מרים בת איציע באַרשאַפּ הי״ד
my grandfather Moyshe bereb Ahrn Shenker	ר׳ משה ב״ר אהרן שענקער הי״ד

and their children:

Avrom ben Moyshe	אברהם בן משה הי״ד
Pesye bas Moyshe	פּעסיע בת משה הי״ד
Shmerl (Shmaryohu) ben Moyshe	שמריהו (שמערל) בן משה הי״ד
Freyde bas Moyshe	פֿריידע בת משה הי״ד
Ite bas Moyshe	איטע בת משה הי״ד
Khatskl (Yekhezkl) ben Moyshe	יחזקאל (כאצקל) בן משה הי״ד
Simkhe ben Moyshe	שמחה בן משה הי״ד
Ahrn ben Moyshe	אהרן בן משה הי״ד

ת נ צ ב ״ ה

They together with 19,000 other Jewish inhabitants of Kremenets (Krzemieniec, Poland, now Ukraine) were brutally murdered by the Nazis and their collaborators in the years 1941–2.

CONTENTS

LIST OF TABLES

LIST OF APPENDICES

ABBREVIATIONS AND LISTING OF PRIMARY SOURCES

Full abbreviation refers to the title, place, and year of publication; in the shorter form the year is omitted. Place-names and years given in square brackets are missing from the identified edition.

AH1795   *(Seyfer) Avkes roykhl*, Horodne [= Grodno], 1795

BF1769   *Ben hameylekh vehanozir*, Frankfurt am Main, 1769

BZ1771   *Ben hameylekh vehanozir*, Zholkve, 1771

B[L1798]   *Bove mayse*, [Lemberg], *c.*1798

DtZ1723   *Derekh tomim*, Zholkve, 1723

DkZ[1723]   *Derekh khayim*, Zholkve, *c.*1723

EP1790   *Eyzer Yisroel*, Poritsk [= Poryck], 1790, by Moyshe Markuze of Slonim

KF1705   [= KF1] *Kav hayosher*, Frankfurt am Main, 1705-6, 2 vols. (H. and Y.), by Tsvi-Hirsh Koidonover

KF1709   [= KF2] *Kav hayosher*, Frankfurt am Main, 1709-10, 2 vols. (H. and Y.)

KN1788   *Kav hayosher*, Novidvor, 1788, 2 vols. (H. and Y.)

KZ1777   *Kav hayosher*, Zholkve, 1777, 1 vol. (H. and Y.)

MF1783   *Mayse gdoyle min k[ehilo]"k[disho] Uman bimdines Ukrayne*, Fürth, 1783

M[N1783]   *Mayse gdoyle min Uman umin Ukrayne*, [Novidvor], *c.*1783

*MS1834   *Mayse gdoyle min Uman umin Ukrayne*, Sadilkov, 1834 (as reprinted in Dubnov, 1929)

*MV1845   *Mayse gdoyle min Uman umin Ukrayne*, Vilna, 1845 (as reprinted in Dubnov, 1929)

SA1723   *Simkhes hanefesh*, Amsterdam, 1723

SF1707   *Simkhes hanefesh*, Frankfurt am Main, 1707, by Elkhonon Kirkhhahn

SS1718   *Simkhes hanefesh*, Sulzbach, 1718

SSh1796   *Simkhes hanefesh*, Shklov, 1796

SZ1776   *Seyfer khsidem*, Zholkve, 1776

TA1726   *Tsene rene*, Amsterdam, 1726, by Yankev ben Yitskhok Ashkenazi of Yanev

TH1622   *Tsene rene*, Hanau, 1622

TL1786   *Tsene rene*, Lemberg, 1786

TV1827   *Tsene rene*, Vilna–Grodno, 1827

TY1845   *Tsene rene*, Yozefov, 1845

VS[1783]   *Vikuekh yeytser tov im ben odem*, Shklov, *c.*1783 (H. and Y.)

Introduction

1 Objectives

The stage at which a language discards the conventions of its older literary monuments and develops a new form is one of the most interesting in the history of written languages (see M. Weinreich 1940b: 105; 1950: xii). A whole gamut of linguistic, social, and cultural issues underlie the process of a radical and sometimes rapid transformation of a literary language. The various socio-linguistic and historical correlates of this process can help to elucidate the motivations of individual users, as well as the societal forces that contribute to the reshaping and establishment of a new supraregional literary language.

The emergence of Yiddish as a modern literary language is in many respects analogous to the rise of other national literary languages of Europe. Yet, at the same time, its extra-linguistic setting is strikingly unique. Unlike other European languages, Yiddish had little to do with the Western grammatical tradition which, when coupled with rising nationalism in Europe, was applied to moulding the linguistic behaviour of the users of various European national languages (see Harris 1980: 128; 1981: 9). Traditional Jewish education in its various pedagogic and ideological phases and guises was in no way oriented towards the standardization of the everyday spoken language, either oral or written (see Ben-Sasson 1976: 717; J. Katz 1978: 217 ff.). In fact, its main concern was with the source languages (Hebrew and Aramaic), rather than the vernacular in which studies were conducted. In the realm of language study, its main didactic purpose was to ensure the preservation and proper understanding of the unspoken languages of the sacred source-texts and liturgy. The use of Yiddish was not at stake. The major objectives were knowledge of Hebrew and Aramaic texts and the ability to make them intelligible according to the traditionally established conventions of translation into Yiddish.

Devoting their studies to Hebrew, the early medieval Spanish (Sephardic) Jewish grammarians were chiefly motivated by the same didactic considerations (see Hirschfeld 1926: 7; Kukenheim 1951: 89; Fishman 1973: 296-7). This grammatical tradition was not directly continued by Central and

Eastern European (Ashkenazic) Jews. Still, the primary educational concern of the Ashkenazim continued to focus upon the proper understanding of the source languages. At the time when linguistic interest in European vernaculars was beginning to emerge (cf. Robins 1967: 99; Ol'khovikov 1985: 125-9, 136 ff.), the linguistic efforts of Central and Eastern European Jews were generally limited to Hebrew and Yiddish lexicography (see D. Katz 1990). This lexicography was designed to assist in the comprehension of Hebrew and Aramaic words via translation into Yiddish.

This explicit orientation towards the comprehension of the source languages, Hebrew and Aramaic, rather than the systematic study and conscious standardization of the vernacular, is sometimes seen as the principal factor in the emergence of Jewish languages. The primary structural distinction between a new Jewish language and its non-Jewish co-territorial cognate is, according to Fishman (1981: 11), determined by the fact that it 'shadows' the linguistic patterns of the Hebrew and Aramaic 'sanctified model texts'. However, even without delving into the socio-linguistic universals of Jewish interlinguistics (see Wexler 1981a; Fishman 1985b; cf. D. Katz 1991c), it is apparent that this very orientation was responsible for some of the most fundamental perceptions of language underlying the use of Yiddish as a written medium. Scriptism, by definition inherent in every written language (see Harris 1980: 7 ff.), was genuinely influenced by the orthographic tradition of the Jewish source languages (see Fishman 1981: 12). The word-based and sometimes morph-based approach, manifested in spelling habits and realized in lexicography, mirrored the traditional perception of Hebrew and Aramaic (cf. Fishman 1973: 195-6). The stylistically determined selection of certain lexical items for use in the written language was partly conditioned by the more concervative convention of rendering the language of the sacred texts into Yiddish. It was also reinforced by the stylistic standards introduced from Middle High German literary usage (see M. Weinreich 1960: 109 ff.; cf. below §3.1).

The same orientation towards the language of the sacred texts and liturgy contributed to the relegation of Yiddish to a lower societal value by most of the literary and religious leadership of the pre-modern European Jewish community (cf. Fishman 1973: 191). Such an attitude towards the everyday language was a serious obstacle to the full-fledged development of the modern literary language. Nevertheless, Modern Literary Yiddish did emerge in spite of the indifference and, indeed, in some circles, the hostility to its use as a pan-European literary medium. Throughout the nineteenth and early twentieth centuries literary Yiddish was further developed into a modern literary language with stable norms of usage. The language was then rapidly acquiring new literary and educational, as well as ideological and political, functions. Before long it emerged as a modern standard language. The fact that a standard language was developed without state support is in itself not all that exceptional or remarkable. In pre-modern times—that is prior to the rise of Nationalism—a number of written or literary languages functioned either as geographically and ethnically more localized or as supraregional standard languages. However, with the advent of modernity, the notions of national language and nation state emerged, and became interlinked in both theory and practice. Since then, governmental support and national language policy have become the order of the day. The rise of modern Standard Yiddish, however, occurred in the complete absence of governmental or institutional coercion or authority to codify its grammar, to develop a language-planning policy, and to ensure its implementation (see M. Weinreich 1950: xii; U. Weinreich 1972: 789–90; Herzog 1978: 55; D. Katz 1983: 1033). Modern Literary Yiddish appears to have been the result of a more general endeavour to employ Yiddish as a written language to serve all East European Jewry. Its success as a standard language 'must be attributed to the sheer centripetal, nation-forming will of the speech community' (U. Weinreich 1972: 790). Its emergence is one of the most remarkable socio-cultural achievements of the modernization of Eastern European Jewish society.

The first known attempts to repattern literary usage on the model of the spoken language and the earliest efforts to employ the modern vernacular in a literary form did not occur in a vacuum. Until then, the latest form of Old Literary Yiddish served the traditional Western, Central, and Eastern European Jewish communities. Literary Yiddish is a historical category that may be divided chronologically, sociologically, and above all linguistically into two major formations: the old and the modern literary languages.

Throughout the first half of the nineteenth century various ideological, stylistic, and linguistic tendencies gave rise to different types of written Yiddish. It is traditionally believed that these types are the 'transitional written languages' (D. Katz 1983: 1032) or 'literary dialects' (Roskies 1974a: 21 ff., 1974b) preceding the rise of Modern Literary Yiddish per se, which was masterfully developed by Mendele Moykher Sforim (Shmuel-Yankev Abramovitsh c.1836–1917), who was affectionately crowned the 'grandfather of modern Yiddish literature', and his followers. However, between the two extremes of writing in '"pure" native dialectal Yiddish' on the one hand and 'remodelling literary Yiddish on the model of New High German' on the other (D. Katz 1983: 1033), there were many compromising tendencies in usage (see M. Weinreich 1940a: 68), which resulted, ultimately, in the creation of a pan-East-European written medium. These compromising tendencies served, in fact, to develop the nascent Modern

Literary Yiddish in the first half of the nineteenth century, while the rising 'self-conscious literature in [the] 1860s' (U. Weinreich 1972: 796) introduced consciously developed norms and patterns for further standardization of modern supraregional literary usage (see M. Weinreich 1940a: 43; 68–9).

In view of the striking 'statelessness' of Yiddish, the emergence and consolidation of its modern literary form offers a challenging case for a constructive clarification of such concepts as 'standard' or 'supraregional written/ literary language' (see Guchmann 1955: 8–17; Vinogradov 1967: 69–82; Jedlička 1976: 17 ff.; 1983; Barnet 1976: 58–61; Akhunzyanov 1978: 201–5; Leith 1983: 32–4, 38–44; Bartsch 1987), as well as their relation to 'normativism', 'purism', 'language planning', and 'perspective intervention' (see Wexler 1974a: 1 ff.; 7 ff.; Kirkness 1975; Schaechter 1977; Thomas 1991). Moreover the case of Yiddish may prove to be of particular value for the further exploration of the so-called 'linguistic' and 'ideological standardization' (Devitt 1989: 2 ff).

This book examines the hitherto unexplored eighteenth-century origins of Modern Literary Yiddish. The narrowing down of the period under investigation allows for a more detailed linguistic examination of the two earliest known books from the first half of the eighteenth century and of most of the known printed literary texts written or linguistically re-edited in the last three decades of the eighteenth century (1771–c.1798). The eighteenth century constitutes the period in which Hebrew and Yiddish printing were re-established and further developed in Eastern Europe. As a result, many subsequent developments in Modern Literary Yiddish originated in this period. This study aims to contribute also to our knowledge of the crystallization process of a literary language without the usual governmental support and above all as a result of a natural linguistic, as yet ideologically undefined, drive for language change and standardization.

2 The Structure and History of Yiddish

Yiddish served for centuries as the language of Ashkenazic (Central and Eastern European) Jewry. In modern popular parlance 'Yiddish' usually refers to the language spoken by the Jews of Eastern Europe and their descendants around the world. It is also the case that at least since 1864 (the year when Mendele Moykher Sforim started his literary career in Yiddish), the language has enjoyed the prestige of a modern literary language. However, when put into historical perspective, the subject appears far more complex. It therefore seems appropriate to outline some basic issues of Yiddish synchronic and historical linguistics, paying special attention to their immediate relevance to our subject. First we shall focus on the specific fusion nature of Yiddish, then extract the main historical and socio-linguistic factors that conditioned its emergence and development, and finally offer a summary of the major aspects of its history.

2.1 The Fusion Nature of Yiddish

The history of analyses of Yiddish as a 'mixture' (or in Max Weinreich's more refined terminology, a 'fusion') begins with sixteenth-century attempts to outline some of the main features of the language (see Dovid Katz 1982: 18). However, it was the early twentieth-century founders of modern Yiddish philology and linguistics who laid the conceptual and methodological basis for the structural description of Yiddish as a fusion language (ibid. 22–3). The most systematically developed model of fusion was that of Max Weinreich, the late historian of Yiddish. The conceptual framework he introduced has now become standard in contemporary Yiddish linguistics, and is of special value for the general study of 'mixed' languages (ibid. 15, 17; 1985: 85). Max Weinreich (1973: i. 32–3) distinguishes three structurally and historically distinct, though interrelated, concepts. These are (1) STOCK LANGUAGES, from which the raw linguistic material of the fusion language is drawn; (2) DETERMINANTS, which are those elements of the stock languages that could have potentially entered the language by chance of 'historical time and space (contemporality and coterritoriality)' (D. Katz 1982: 16); and (3) COMPONENTS, which are the actual synchronic elements (or principal genetically disparate ingredients) of the fusion language at any stage in its history.

At first sight the definition of Yiddish as a fusion language might seem loose and even truistic. The more one studies the history and dynamics of any language, the more one becomes aware of such phenomena as borrowing or language/dialect mixing (see Bloomfield 1933: 361, 444 ff.; Deroy 1956: 23 ff.; Bynon 1977: 216 ff.; D. Katz 1982: 2 ff.), as well as of interference in the speech of bilinguals (U. Weinreich 1953: 11 ff.; Bynon 1977: 239–44). All these may at times introduce drastic changes into the structure of the recipient language, and even result in the emergence of new languages (see U. Weinreich 1953: 69–70; Lehiste 1988: 76 ff.). However, it is its emergence as a new language that historically justifies the definition of Yiddish as a fusion language. Viewed in retrospect, this language 'includes as two *panterritorial* and *pantemporal* elements the Germanic and Semitic Components' (D. Katz 1984: 91, my emphasis). It is also important to bear in mind the constant interplay between the socio-linguistic and structural aspects. The average Yiddish speaker is far more likely to be aware of the heterogeneous components of his language than, say, the average English speaker (see M. Weinreich 1969: 109; 1973: iv. 362; Fishman 1973: 295; D. Katz 1982: 24; on 'foreign' components of English see Leith 1983: 61 ff.; Strang 1970: 188–92). In the literary language this awareness has been stabilized symbolically by traditional orthography, which has preserved the original spelling of the Semitic component, while adopting a more Western type of 'phonetic'-based system for the non-Semitic elements. Moreover, the Semitic component, at the lexical and phraseological levels, is closely associated with the internal multilingualism of Ashkenazic Jewry (see M. Weinreich 1973: ii. 319). Component awareness continues to play a prominent role in modern Yiddish stylistics and normativism (see Hutton 1984: 5 ff.; cf. Harshav 1990: 39 ff., 43 ff.; D. Katz 1993a). The various 'prescriptive' attitudes towards the vitality, productivity and cultural worth or historical validity of the Semitic component in Modern Literary Yiddish were all questions at the centre of heated ideological debates, primarily among Soviet Yiddish linguists between the two world wars (e.g. Shtif 1929; Zaretski 1931: 21–91; Spivak 1934; cf. Peltz 1981; Hutton 1984: 20–30). These debates surfaced again to some extent in the Soviet Union in the 1960s and early 1970s (see Moskovich 1984: 41–2).

With the addition of the Slavonic component to Eastern Yiddish, the 'expanding' fusion nature of Yiddish becomes directly relevant to the emergence of the modern literary language. Although this component is not pan-chronic or pan-territorial, it has obviously become one of the three major socio-linguistically and stylistically significant elements of modern Yiddish, alongside the Semitic and Germanic components. The introduction of this new productive component into written Yiddish is one of the most decisive developments in the formation of the modern literary language (see M. Weinreich 1973: i. 256–7. On the Slavonic component as an essential structural feature of modern Yiddish see Landau 1927–9; Joffe 1928; Shtif 1932a: 5; 1932b: 37 ff.; U. Weinreich 1958a: 412–13; 1972: 795).

2.1.1 *Phonology*

As to the structural aspect, the fusion nature of Yiddish is evident in a number of ways. Most obviously, the same phonological system serves all the heterogeneous components, and can be verified by consistent diaphonemic correlation, as is evident from modern Yiddish dialectology. Thus, for example, the phonemic realizations of the Semitic חלום xɔləm 'dream' and the Germanic נאָדל nɔdḷ 'needle' are synchronically integrated in the extant Yiddish dialects, as are those of the Semitic חודש xɔjdəš 'month' and the Germanic ברויט brɔjt 'bread' (see Table 1, based on the examples in D. Katz 1985: 95).

Table 1 Diaphonemic correspondences in Yiddish dialects

Mideastern Yiddish	Northeastern Yiddish	Northwestern Yiddish	Standard Eastern Yiddish
xuləm	xɔləm	xōləm	xɔləm
nudļ	nɔdļ	nōdļ	nɔdļ
xɔjdəš	xejdəš	xoudəš	xɔjdəš
brɔjt	brejt	brout	brɔjt

This remarkably consistent diaphonemic correlation between all Yiddish dialects allows us to consider them historically and socio-culturally as geographical varieties of one linguistic continuum.

The correlation between the reconstructed proto-Yiddish vowel system and its diaphonemic correspondences across *all* Yiddish dialects is accommodated in modern Yiddish linguistics by a specially adopted system of notation. The following presentation adheres to Dovid Katz's revision of the diaphonemic system of pan-Yiddish vocalism (see D. Katz 1983: 1021–4). Each stressed vowel is assigned a double-digit designation, whereby the first digit alludes to a presumed reconstructed proto-vowel (1 = the historical *a*; 2 = *e*; 3 = *i*; 4 = *o*; 5 = *u*) and the second represents the vowel's historical quantity (1 = historically short vowels; 2 = long; 3 and 5 = lengthened; 4 = diphthongs). Thus, for example, the historical vowels 12 and 42 yield [u] and [ɔj] as in xúləm and brɔjt in the Mideastern and Southeastern dialects; [ɔ] and [ej] as in xɔ́ləm and brejt in Northeastern; and [ō] and [ou] as in xṓləm and brout in Northwestern and so on (cf. Table 1). A representative sample of diaphonemes across major Yiddish dialects is offered in Table 2.

Table 2 Sample of proto-Yiddish vowels and their diaphonemic correspondences across major Yiddish dialects

Dialect	Proto-vowel								
	11 *a	31 *i	51 *u	12 *ɔ	22 *ē	42 *ō	13 *a	24 *əj	25 *ɛ
Northwestern	[ă]	[ĭ/ɛ]	[ŏ/ŭ]	[ō]	[ɛj]	[ou]	[ō]	[ā]	[ē]
Midwestern	[ă]	[ĭ]	[ŭ]	[ŭ]	[ē]	[ō]	[ā]	[ā]	[í]
Southwestern	[ă]	[ĭ]	[ŭ]	[ū/ou/ō]	[ɛj]	[ou]	[ā]	[ā]	[i/ē]
Mideastern	[ă]	[ĭ]	[ĭ]	[u]	[aj]	[ɔj]	[u]	[aj]	[ej]
Southeastern	[ɔ/a]	[i/ĭ/ɪ]	[i/ĭ/ɪ]	[u]	[ɛj/ej]	[ɔj]	[u]	[ɛj/ej]	[i/ĭ/ej]
Northeastern	[a]	[i]	[u]	[ɔ]	[ej]	[ej]	[ɔ]	[ej]	[ɛ]

The double-digit labelling avoids any direct reference to a supposed phonetic value of a proto-Yiddish vowel. Instead, the phonetic notation is used to show the actual dialectal realization. Hence the notation *Mideastern* u_{12} meaning 'the proto-Yiddish [*ɔ] which appears in Mideastern Yiddish as [u]'. The following combined notation shows a number of historically disparate vowels that synchronically merged in different Yiddish dialects (and which can be conveniently contrasted with the corresponding vowels in other dialects): $\bar{o}_{12/13}$ in Northwestern Yiddish; $\bar{a}_{13/24}$ in Midwestern and Southwestern Yiddish; $aj_{22/24}$ and $u_{12/13}$ in Mideastern Yiddish; $i/\bar{\imath}/I_{31/51}$ and $\varepsilon j/ej_{22/24(/25)}$ in Southeastern Yiddish; and $ej_{22/42/24}$ in Northeastern Yiddish (see Table 2, cf. also Tables 8, 12, 13, 26). On dialects of Yiddish see §2.3.2.

2.1.2 *Morphology*

A striking degree of fusion can also be observed at the morphological level. In many cases, the Semitic component is fully integrated in accordance with the productive derivational patterns of Yiddish, as can be seen from the following examples:

> געגנבט gəganvət 'stole' /gə+ganve+t/
> (cf. געקויפט gəkɔjft 'bought' /gə+kɔjf+t/);
> באלעבאטישקייט [בעל־הביתישקייט] baləbátiškajt 'household' /baləbat+iš+kajt/
> (cf. נאַרישקייט náriškajt 'foolishness' /nár+iš+kajt/);
> בתולהשאַפט bsúləšaft 'virginity' /bsulə+šaft/
> (cf. מוטערשאַפט mútəršaft 'motherhood' /mutər+šaft/);
> פשטל pšɛtļ 'quibbling' /dim. of פשט pšat 'literal meaning' → pšɛt+ļ/
> (cf. בלעטל blɛtļ 'leaflet' /dim. of בלאַט blat 'leaf' → blɛt+ļ/).

The structural impact of the Slavonic component upon the patterns of modern Yiddish is especially noticeable in the case of the pejorative male and female agentivizing suffixes -ák/-áčkə and -nik/-nicə (see Gitlic 1940: 50–1; U. Weinreich 1958*a*: 378; cf. Mieses 1924: 110–12, 135, 164) and to a lesser degree with respect to the 'emotive' adjective-qualifying suffix -ink- or the adjective formant -əvátə (on the former cf. M. Weinreich 1956: 628). These are equally productive with items of non-Slavonic derivation (see Table 3; for more examples of morphological fusion in modern Yiddish see Falkovitsh 1966: 608–9, 624–6; 1984: 688–9, §16; 712–13, §60; Stankiewicz 1985). In a number of cases the original plural marker -(ə)n was reanalysed as, or levelled with, the etymologically Semitic plural marker ־ים -əm, as in the following lexical items:

> דאָקטוירים dɔktójrəm 'physicians' /dɔktər (sing.) → dɔktɔrṇ (old pl.) → dɔktójr+əm/
> (cf. חברים xavéjrəm 'friends' /xávər (sing.) → xavéjr+əm/);

Table 3 Productive Slavonic component morphemes in Modern Yiddish

Pejorative nominal suffixes	
-ák	-áčkə
צבֿוּעק cvuák 'hypocrite';	צבֿוּעטשקע cvuáčkə 'hypocrite' (fem.)
פֿרומאַק frumák 'pious' (pej.);	פֿרומאַטשקע frumáčkə 'pious' (fem., pej.)
(cf. פּראָסטאַק prɔsták 'ignoramus';	פּראָסטאַטשקע prɔstáčkə 'ignorant' (fem.))
-nik	-nicə
שלימזלניק šliməzálnik 'unlucky man'	שלימזלניצע šliməzálnicə 'unlucky woman'
(cf. נודניק núdnik 'bore, "pest"';	נודניצע núdnicə 'bore' (fem.))

Adjective diminutive infix

-ink-

טייער tajər 'dear' → טייערינקער tájərinkər 'dear [fellow]' (masc.)

גרויס grɔjs 'large; big' → גרויסינקער grɔ́jsinkər 'big' (masc., about a little child)

Adjective qualifying suffix

-əvátə

תם tam 'simpleton' → תמעוואַטע taməvátə '[somewhat] stupid; idiotic'

נאַריש nárish 'foolish' → נאַרישעוואַטע narishəvátə 'not terribly bright'

קאָלטן kɔltṇ 'elflock' → קאָלטנעוואַטע kɔltənəvátə 'with elflocks'

שניידאָרעם šnajdɔ́rəm 'bad tailors' (pej.) /šnájdər (sing.) → šnajdɔ́r+əm/
  (cf. ספרים sfɔ́rəm 'books' /séjfər (sing.) → sfɔ́r+əm/);

פּויערים pɔ́jərəm 'peasants' /pɔjər (sing.) → pɔjərṇ (old pl.) → pɔjər+əm/
  (cf. בוררים bɔrərəm 'arbitrators' /bɔ́jrər (sing.) → bɔ́rər+əm/);

נאַראָנים narɔ́nəm 'fools' / nar (sing.) → narṇ (old pl.) → nar+ɔ́n+əm/
  (cf. רבנים rabɔ́nəm 'rabbis' /rɔv (sing.) → rab+ɔ́n+əm/).

These examples should not, however, obscure the fact that the Semitic component in Yiddish enjoys an 'overall morphological autonomy' (D. Katz 1985: 94; on 'internal' productivity of Hebrew and Aramaic formants within the Semitic component see Mark 1958b). Many Semitic derivational patterns do not fit into the fusion formula, thus remaining available for use only within the Semitic component. It seems that the same observation can be made with regard to each of the three main components of Yiddish, and it would be interesting to explore the extent to which the Slavonic component has had an impact on the overall structure of modern Yiddish (see especially Stankiewicz 1985).

Moreover, it seems that in general the Germanic derivational machinery sets the major patterns for the morphological and to some degree syntactical integration of the other components (cf. Lincoff 1963: 158; Harshav 1990:

43) even in the heavily Slavonicized Eastern varieties of Yiddish. Thus, on the morpho-syntactic level the following word-order pattern appears to be the 'grammatical' one in the modern literary language with regard to periphrastic verbs: ער וועט חתונה האָבן ɛr vət xasənə hɔbn̥ 'he'll get married' or איך האָב מסכים געווען ix hɔb máskim gəvɛn 'I agreed', whereas איך האָב* ‏געווען מסכים ix hɔb gəvɛn máskim and ער וועט האָבן חתונה* ɛr vət hɔbn̥ xasənə are felt to be unacceptable, if not wholly agrammatical (cf. Besten and Moed-van Walraven 1986: 119–20; Taube 1987: 14).

2.2 Historical and Socio-linguistic Factors

Each of the three main components of modern Yiddish reflects retro-spectively the different historical factors that determined its development. According to D. Katz (1982: 37–8; 1984: 90, 100), the Semitic component is ultimately derived from the language of the Jews who settled in German-speaking territories some thousand years ago (for a different view see M. Weinreich 1940a: 35–6; 1973: ii. 394; cf. also D. Katz 1982: 32–51; 1985: 88–9). The Germanic component reflects the shift in the actual speech of those Jews (cf. Hiley 1990: 110 ff.). This shift subsequently 'gave birth to Yiddish'. The Slavonic component reveals the increasing migration of Yiddish speakers into the Slavonic regions of Eastern Europe.

2.2.1 *External Bilingualism*

Each of the consecutive stages in the history of Yiddish was conditioned by an appropriate situation of external bilingualism (see M. Weinreich 1973: iii. 253–4) in which a Jewish language existed alongside a non-Jewish language or languages (ibid. 1973: i. 251; Fishman 1971: 77–8). The chain of external Jewish bilingualism is illustrated in Table 4.

Table 4 External Jewish bilingualism and the history of Yiddish

Chronology . . . periodization		Input (languages in contact)	Output
±1000	Early	Semitic – Germanic	Yiddish
		Yiddish – Germanic	
			Western Yiddish
±1250	Old		
±1500	Middle	Yiddish – Slavonic	Eastern Yiddish
±1650	New		
±1800	Modern		

2.2.2 Internal Jewish Multilingualism

The major socio-linguistic factor that conditioned the development of Yiddish is the internal Jewish multilingualism of traditional Ashkenaz (on the latter see §2.3.2). It consisted of one spoken language—Yiddish—and three written languages—Hebrew, Aramaic, and Yiddish (D. Katz 1985: 98). The first two are usually described as one merged written language: namely, 'Hebrew–Aramaic' or *loshn-koydesh* 'language of holiness' (see M. Weinreich 1973: i. 74–5; Wexler 1981a: 119; on Ashkenazic Hebrew see D. Katz 1993b). It is interesting to note, however, that although traditional Hebrew has an Aramaic component of its own and although Jewish Aramaic was in its turn considerably influenced by Hebrew, these distinct written languages were in fact employed in a 'functionally complementary distribution' (D. Katz 1985: 98). Hebrew, for example, was used for commentary on the Bible and for medieval Hebrew literature (see Dan 1974: 5–7), and Aramaic for Talmudic and Kabbalistic literature (see M. Weinreich 1973: i. 72). The issue of the functional correlation between these two languages on the one hand and Yiddish on the other is more complicated. The obvious temptation to describe the situation in terms of diglossia is met here by the peculiar complexity of the socio-linguistic situation in Ashkenaz (see M. Weinreich 1973: i. 260–1, 284; Fishman 1973; 1976; 1980: 43; 1981: 12–14). In this respect, internal Jewish multilingualism can be compared paradigmatically with other socio-cultural formations in which both the literary form of the spoken idiom and the unspoken language of culture and liturgy were employed (see Zhirmunsky 1940: 135–6; M. Weinreich 1973: i. 253–4; Wexler 1974b). However, in terms of the sociology of language, the societal allocation of macro-functions to Hebrew (and Aramaic) on the one hand and to Yiddish on the other was far more complex (Fishman 1976: 39, 44–5). Hebrew served consistently not only as a literary language, but also as a quasi-official medium for intra-community use. As the language of the sacred texts and of liturgy, it benefited from a very high status. Yiddish was employed not only as the vernacular, but also as the language of prayer among women (see D. Fishman 1991), traditional education, instruction, preaching (see Fishman 1973; 1980: 44), and learned oral discussions amongst Ashkenazic Talmudic scholars and rabbinic authorities (see M. Weinreich 1973: i. 259; for a different opinion see Breuer 1989: 467–8, where the author maintains that Hebrew was the language of instruction in early Ashkenazic academies until the fourteenth century).

The mutual influence of Hebrew and Yiddish in traditional Ashkenazic society was substantial, and in many instances overwhelming. Usage of Hebrew was conditioned by the everyday spoken language (cf. Noble 1958), while Yiddish was open to accepting new borrowings from *loshn-koydesh* which intensified the 'component awareness' of Yiddish speakers (see Noble 1964; M. Weinreich 1973: i. 256 ff., 311 ff.; cf. Wexler 1974b: 36). Certain older and to a large extent modern styles of literary Yiddish show a great deal of openness to imports from the Semitic *determinant*. Conversely, the Ashkenazic Hebrew that was employed in communal and professional protocols (*pinkósim*) and in private communication was in many cases saturated with loans and calques from Yiddish. Starting with the sixteenth century, we find an ever increasing number of communal, professional, and quasi-official documents written in the various forms of mixed Hebrew–Yiddish scribal language (see Dubnov 1909: 27–39; U. Weinreich 1958d; M. Weinreich 1973: i. 262; 313–14, Kahan-Newman 1990).

Certain diglossia-upsetting trends from earlier times (mostly from the Yiddish end) can be brought forth. There were some marginal attempts to use *loshn-koydesh* (or, more precisely, post-exilic Hebrew) as a spoken language, and at least from the sixteenth century on there was a tendency to introduce Yiddish as a liturgical language, though with very limited success (see M. Weinreich 1973: i. 261, 264 ff., 284; iii. 268–9). More significantly, Yiddish was also used as a literary language, for both popular and quasi-secular consumption as well as for traditionally approved ends. In the latter case it was 'justified' as a medium intended mainly (but not exclusively) for women and uneducated men (see Niger 1913b and Tsinberg 1935: 144; cf. M. Weinreich 1973: i. §§67 ff.).

The conventional semiological and stylistic legitimization of traditional Yiddish literature in Ashkenaz boldly symbolizes the socio-linguistic interrelationship between Hebrew and Yiddish as literary languages. Yiddish books printed in traditional Ashkenaz normally appeared under a Hebrew, or in some cases a compound Hebrew and Yiddish, title. As for the stylistic aspect, an important method of legitimization was offered via traditional Yiddish translations from Hebrew, in which a paragraph usually opened with the original Hebrew word or phrase. To begin a paragraph with a Hebrew phrase or gloss implied that the book was either a translation or a compilation based upon the traditionally approved *loshn-koydesh* sources (see M. Weinreich 1973: i. 279–80, iii. 288–9). This practice was soon turned into a stylistic device of legitimization even for books written originally in Yiddish. Of course, not all older Yiddish literary works fully complied with these patterns of legitimization. Yet the very fact that such legitimization took place on a large scale means that Yiddish as a written language was not only accepted or tolerated, but that it was in fact fully incorporated into the multilingual traditional system of Ashkenazic literacy.

The traditional configuration of *loshn-koydesh* and Yiddish in the realm of

Figure 1 Old, New and Modern Yiddish Type-Fonts		

Modern — Unpointed Square since c.1913

ו) איך חזר איבער: מע דארף זיך קלאר מאכן דעם חילוק צ
וון סילא לא ג נ י ע. לינגוויסטיק איז אן אלגעמיינע היסנשאפס. סילא־
לינגוויסטיק קאן זיך באשעטטיקן אויך מיט לחלוטין טויטע אדער ל
ײ סילאלאגיע זעצט אבער פאראויס, אז א שפראך. מיט העלבער ווי גי
ן קולטור־היסטאריש ן וװערט לסחות סאר דעם עבר. נע
ווילאלאגיע נאך היימער און סטיצט זיך אויף דער איבערצײגונג, א
אציאנאלן הערס אין דער ציקינס. חזר ס'גלייבט ניט אינעם ק
ופראר, קאן אפשר נאך זיין א ײדישער לינגוױסס, אבער ניט ׳

New — Pointed Square since the 19th century

מילא וּיראׇמעריקֿא אונ נֿאׇרדׇאׇמעריקֿא וֶעִנֶין נֿאׇר פּ
קֶיִןְ הׇאׇנדריל אונ קֶיִן מֿלֿאָכֿה גֿילֿט רֿאׇרט ניט, נֿאׇר אֿפֿילו א
לֿאׇרט אוֹיךֿ וֶויֿער פּיֿעֿל, בֿעׇואׇגֿערֶעם רֿיֿא פֿאׇבֿריקֿן פֿין בֿ
סֿחֿורֿוֹת.—רֿאֿבֿֿט וֶעךֿ עֿם וֿאׇלֿט שֿוֹן צֿיֿיט גֿעֿוֶוֶעֶוֶין אֿו רֿי׳
צֿרֿדֿיֿם וֶאׇלֿשֶֿן וֶעךֿ אֿֿיֿמֿוֹשֶֿן אֿנ אֿֿיטֶלֿעֿבֿֿער וֶאׇל אֿבֿֿיֿסֿיֿל נ
אונ וֶֿיֿיֿא וֶֿאׇלֿיֿן וֶעךֿ אֿויֿסֿנֿגֿֿלֿיֿיֿבֶֿֿן. נֿאׇר רֿאׇם אֿיֿוֹ רֿֿֿער ע
פֿיֿן נֿצֿחֿוֹן אֿיֿטֶֿלֿיֿבֶֿֿער וֿיֿל וֶֿיֿיֿן פּֿיֿן אֿֿויֿבֿֿין, אֿיֿן רֿיֿא הֶערֿצֶֿ

Old — Plain Mashkit c.17th–18th centuries

אונ׳ טׄאׄר נֿרׄב דש עֶֿלֿט אֿין אֿֿיֿן קֿׄיֿרֿן לֿׄוֹךֿ דֿׄא אֿֿן פֿֿס
אֿיֿן טׄׄ הֿֿיֿבֿֿן אֿֿובֿׄ אֿיֿבֿֿר יֿׄאׄר טׄׄ הֿׄאׄלֿֿטֿֿין דֿׄא וֿׄאׄר עֿֿבֿֿן
דֿשֿ לֿוֹךֿ וׄׄ אׄר אֿֿונֿׄ אֿׄךֿ וׄׄ יׄ א דֿֿער דֿֿש עֿֿלֿֿט טֿׄאׄר בֿֿםֿ אׄ
דֿֿר סֿֿוֹחֿֿר אֿֿיֿן וֶֿעֿֿךֿ נֿֿֿיֿנֿֿן זֿֿֿא נֿֿֿאֿׄס דֿֿער וׄׄ אׄן דֿֿש עֿֿ
סֿֿוֹחֿֿר וֶֿֿידֿֿר קֿׄאׄס אֿֿובֿׄ וֿׄאׄלֿֿטֿֿ וֿֿין עֶֿלֿֿטֿֿ וֶֿֿידֿֿר נֿֿֿשֿֿין דֿֿאׄ
אֿֿן דֿֿא שֿׄרֿֿיֿׄא ער נֿׄאׄר דֿֿער אֿֿובֿׄ שֿֿֿטֿֿרֿֿאׄךֿ אֿֿֿךֿ אֿֿֿֿרֿֿֿֿיֿׄר ׳
בֿׄ אׄן אֿֿֿֿ הֿֿֿיֿבֿֿן דֿֿֿֿעֿֿן אֿֿֿֿךֿ אֿֿֿֿֿֿן אֿֿֿֿֿֿךֿ נֿֿֿ אֿׄר וֶֿֿֿאֿׄל אֿֿֿֿֿֿס נֿֿֿֿׄעֿֿהֿֿֿן אֿ
דֿֿֿא נֿֿֿ עֿֿֿֿֿׄשֿֿֿֿֿֿֿֿט בֿֿֿוֹֿךֿ אֿֿֿֿז אֿֿֿֿֿֿֿֿֿֿֿ דֿֿֿֿֿֿֿֿֿֿֿֿ אֿֿֿֿֿֿֿֿֿ עֿֿֿֿֿֿֿֿֿׄלֿֿ ׳

Old — Mashkit with brackets c.16th–18th centuries

דאס דיׄא לֿֿיׄט גֿׄיֿט זֿֿמֿֿן זֿֿאׄגֿֿן עֿֿר הֿֿאֿֿׄט דֿֿֿֿֿֿם דֿֿֿֿֿֿ׳
בֿֿֿֿן אֿֿֿֿֿֿֿן סֿֿֿֿֿֿֿֿֿֿֿֿֿֿ אֿֿֿֿֿֿֿֿֿֿֿֿֿֿֿ

/ literary usage was symbolically reflected by typographical convention. From
the first printing of Yiddish books in the 1540s, Hebrew and Aramaic texts
were set in the traditional square characters (*oysyes-meruboes*), whereas the
Yiddish text of both bilingual publications and of books wholly written in
Yiddish was printed in the special type-font known as *meshit* or *mashkit* (later
also dubbed *vayber-taytsh*, see Figure 1). For almost three centuries this
practice was a well-established Ashkenazic tradition. It is believed to have
started to decline at the beginning of the nineteenth century with adoption
of the square characters for the printing of Yiddish in Eastern Europe (see
Shtif 1928: 37, 41; Joffe 1940: 87, 88; Reyzen 1965: 121; M. Weinreich
1973: iii. 275; 289).

The earliest dated pre-nineteenth-century Yiddish book printed in square
characters is probably Aron ben Shmuel's prayer-book *Liblikhe tfile oder
artsnay far guf un neshome* (Hergershausen, 1709; note its Yiddish title). This
book was exceptional for its time in more than one respect. Retrospectively,
Aron ben Shmuel can be seen as an early proponent of radical educational
and liturgical reforms that did not go down well in the pre-Enlightenment
era of traditional Ashkenazic Jewry (see Erik 1928: 212–4; Tsinberg 1935:
255–8; M. Weinreich 1973: i. 267–8). His choice of square characters was
clearly intentional, and even demonstratively radical. Otherwise, Yiddish
texts continued to be printed in all parts of Ashkenaz in the traditional *meshit*
font until the early nineteenth century. (For another possible exception,
Seyfer tikuney shabes, printed in Eastern Europe in 1742(?) see Liberman
1980: i. 404–5.)

Precisely when, and in what circumstances, the change in the traditional
typographical practice occurred remains unclear (cf. Fishman 1973). Many
of the early nineteenth-century texts closely connected with the rise of
Modern Literary Yiddish were printed in the square letters hitherto used only
for printing Hebrew texts. The replacement of the conventional *meshit* type-
font with square letters in the late 1820s was accompanied by a significant
reorganization and modernization of the older Yiddish orthographic conventions, which included the use of a diacritical vocalization system for Yiddish
spelling (see Joffe 1940: 98–9; cf. Shtif 1928: 40; Roskies 1974*a*: 9; 1974*b*:
31; Mashbitz 1970: 20 ff., 39). It may be that the change of type-font was
primarily due to some unknown, possibly even technical, factors that
emerged in the rapidly developing Yiddish printing centres of Eastern Europe
in the first half of the nineteenth century. However, in retrospect this major
semiological change seems to be of special significance from the viewpoint of
the sociology of modern Yiddish. One of the main socio-linguistic features of
the rise of the modern literary language is the tendency to employ Yiddish
not as a subcategory in a functionally complementary distribution with

Hebrew and Aramaic, but rather as an independent written medium within the general system of internal Jewish multilingualism (cf. Fishman 1973). The full adoption of square characters for the printing of Yiddish may be seen retrospectively as an external symbolic expression of the general drive towards modernization and the more independent development of Yiddish as a literary language.

2.3 Basic Premisses

Modern Yiddish is the direct heir of only one younger branch of the language. A brief statement of its major historical periods and major dialectal branches will provide the basic premisses upon which the present work is based.

2.3.1 The Periodization of Yiddish

Periodization is one of the central issues of the linguistic and cultural history of Yiddish and it seems that it should occupy an important place in the historiography of Ashkenazic Jewry. Modern Yiddish linguists have offered a number of different scenarios for the periodization of Yiddish. Max Weinreich's periodization plan, which crowns the final chapter of his *Geshikhte fun der Yidisher shprakh* (see 1973: ii. 397), provides the best integrated scenario which enlists the geographical, historical, and cultural aspects, as well as the linguistic and literary manifestations of the language.

Without entering into the controversies over the original nature, the early stages, and the developmental mechanisms of Yiddish, or even the different proposals for its division into periods (see M. Weinreich 1940a: 29-30; Süsskind 1953; Lincoff 1963: 4-5; Mark 1967: 125; Bin-Nun 1973: 61-77; D. Katz 1988c) we shall present simplified versions of (1) the most widely accepted periodization plan proposed by Max Weinreich (see Table 5A based on M. Weinreich 1973: i. 11; ii. 383-9; cf. Herzog 1974: 26; 1978: 49) and (2) the more recent plan offered by Dovid Katz (1988c: 5). The latter (see Table 5B) adapts Yudl Mark's suggestion (see Mark 1967: 125); its distinction between Early New Yiddish period and the New Yiddish period

Table 5A Max Weinreich's periodization of Yiddish

Early Yiddish	to ±1250
Old Yiddish	±1250-±1500
Middle Yiddish	±1500-±1700
New Yiddish	±1700-present

Table 5B Dovid Katz's periodization of Yiddish

Old Yiddish	to ±1350
Middle Yiddish	±1350-±1650
Early New Yiddish	±1650-±1800
New Yiddish	±1800-present

proper is in part suggested by the present study (see §37). These periodization schemes provide us with a schematic framework for further discussion of some basic issues in the history of Yiddish.

2.3.2 *Western and Eastern Yiddish*

As mentioned at the outset, the modern notion of 'Yiddish' is usually restricted to the language spoken by Eastern European Jews and their descendants. Yet, historically, Yiddish arose in Central Europe, and both its history and its major dialect groups must be seen within the broader historical context of Ashkenaz.

Following Max Weinreich (1973), we distinguish between Ashkenaz I (the original Jewish communities of Western and Central Europe) and its latter-day extension in Eastern Europe, Ashkenaz II. Jewish migration eastwards began in the thirteenth century (see M. Weinreich 1973: ii. 391; Shmeruk 1981: 14–15). Initially and throughout the Old Yiddish period, Ashkenaz II was no more than a peripheral extension of Ashkenaz I (cf. M. Weinreich 1973: ii. 392). From the very start, the language became co-territorial with Slavonic languages. Thus the emergence of Ashkenaz II was the first step in the development of a fundamentally new variety of Yiddish. Its linguistic structure was significantly reorganized under the impact of the Slavonic determinant, which became one of the three modern productive components. (On the Slavonic component cf. Joffe 1928; Shtif 1932*b*; M. Weinreich 1956; U. Weinreich 1958*a*.) Subsequently, the language split into the two major dialect groups: Western Yiddish with its major dialects in Ashkenaz I and Eastern Yiddish in Ashkenaz II (see Landau 1896: 46–7; M. Weinreich 1940*a*: 37–9; D. Katz 1983: 1020–1). During the Middle Yiddish period, Ashkenaz II became an important centre in its own right. The origins of Eastern Yiddish and its chronology still await further research. Jacob Willer (1915: 399) noticed that the major division between the Northern and Southern Eastern Yiddish dialects corresponds to the geopolitical and ethnic border between Poland and Lithuania prior to the Union of Lublin of 1569. On the other hand, Joffe (1954: 116–21), on the basis of some interesting but wholly insufficient observations, suggested a much later (and unrealistically 'precise') dating of Eastern Yiddish dialects *circa* 1730. It is none the less generally accepted that by the middle of the seventeenth century, Eastern Yiddish had developed into a distinct system with its own dialectal varieties (cf. Tsinberg 1935: 54–5; Weinreich 1973: i. 16, 386; ii. 390–1; iv. 390; Shmeruk 1981: 18; Kerler 1990: 278–9 and §4.4.2 below). These major varieties comprise MIDEASTERN, SOUTHEASTERN, and NORTHEASTERN dialects. In popular parlance they are often referred to as 'Polish' (for MIDEASTERN YIDDISH), 'Ukrainian' (for SOUTHEASTERN YIDDISH), and 'Lithuanian' (for NORTHEASTERN YIDDISH). (For a synoptic analysis of Western and Eastern Yiddish dialects and their classification see D. Katz 1983.)

3 Yiddish as a Literary Language

As pointed out above, Yiddish was employed both as the everyday oral medium and as a written language with various educational, social, and literary functions. It thus falls into the category of languages with an older tradition of literary usage. (For the distinction between languages with and without written traditions see Guchmann 1977: 42–3.) This is especially important in the historical account of Modern Literary Yiddish. Its beginnings are to be found in texts that from the viewpoint of style and genre directly continue the Old Yiddish literary conventions. The stylistic, and to a certain extent the linguistic, legacy of the older written tradition (Old Literary Yiddish) can still be encountered in all the earliest works that were either largely based on, or for the first time wholly written in, modern Eastern Yiddish. Some Old Yiddish features survived as stylistic archaisms even in the modern literary language, which has, from the middle of the nineteenth century onwards, been exclusively based on modern Eastern Yiddish.

3.1 The Old Literary Language

Originating in the Old Yiddish period, the old literary language was employed for centuries as the medium for older Yiddish literature. In the middle of the fourteenth century it was developed into a supraregional written language based exclusively on Western Yiddish (see Süsskind 1953: 106; M. Weinreich 1955: 12; see also idem 1953: 39; 1973: ii. 389, 392; D. Katz 1983: 1032).

During the Middle Yiddish period this written language was further developed as a supraregional literary standard serving both Western and Eastern European Yiddish speakers and readers (see D. Katz 1983: 1025; Schaechter 1977: 37). Not only did the literature published in the West and distributed for Eastern consumption follow the old literary standard, but the language of Yiddish books printed in Poland deliberately used it as well, thereby facilitating distribution among Western European Jews (see Borokhov 1915: 209; Birnbaum 1954: 69; Shmeruk 1978: 81, 85; 1981: 24–5). Indeed, Yiddish printing in general originated in the 1530s in Cracow (see Rosenfeld 1987: 111–12).

3. 2 Literary and Spoken Yiddish

The diverse genres and stylistic conventions of Old Yiddish literature were determined by either the Jewish tradition developed internally or by the adopted models of contemporary non-Jewish literature and folklore. (On politics and ideologies underlying the modern research and perceptions of Old Yiddish texts see Frakes 1989, cf. also Miller 1987.) It is fascinating that some of the finest achievements of Old Yiddish literature appear to be a unique synthesis of both these sources (see Erik 1926: 31–2, 54–9, 91 ff.; 1928: 51–6, 77–81, 106–29, 219 ff.; Tsinberg 1935: 33–8, 41–53, 61–4, 82–102, 123–35, 138 ff.; M. Weinreich 1960: 109; Shmeruk 1978: 40–56, 57–71; 117 ff.). Yet both the conventional translation of Biblical books and prayers (the so-called *taytsh* tradition), as well as the stylistic standards of Yiddish authors, imposed severe restrictions on the language of Old Yiddish literature.

As a matter of principle, the *taytsh* tradition tried to avoid the use of the Semitic component (see D. Katz 1990: 165–70), following the logic that a Hebrew word cannot properly be rendered into itself even when it is normally used in the relevant sense in the colloquial language (see Shmeruk 1978: 125–6). On the other hand, the language and style of Old Yiddish Biblical epic literature were 'patterned after the M[iddle] H[igh] G[erman] model' (M. Weinreich 1960: 109; cf. idem 1973: ii. 319, iv. 363). Its authors regarded the Semitic component as unacceptable for elevated poetic language.

Throughout its long history, Old Literary Yiddish underwent many important changes, and M. Weinreich in an earlier article on Yiddish (1940a: 42) even elaborated on the old and middle stages of written Yiddish, defining them diachronically as two distinct written languages. Nevertheless, it is obvious that the old literary language could not adequately represent the spoken language of its time (see Tsinberg 1935: 26–8). In addition to the general disparity of spoken and literary languages and the general conservatism of the latter (see M. Weinreich 1940a: 43, 78; Birnbaum 1954: 69) the old literary language soon evolved into a highly stylized literary medium that in its various genres kept to the restrictions imposed either by the *taytsh* tradition or by the poetic language standards of Old Yiddish literature. Secondly, it was based in principle on Western Yiddish, which by definition could not reflect the language spoken in Eastern Europe. Above all, it intentionally avoided any outright dialectisms (even of the Western dialects) in order to assure its supraregional or interdialectal character (see M. Weinreich 1940a: 39–45; 1953: 38–9; Beem 1954: 124–5).

There are several reasons why the old literary language is an unreliable source for the study of Western Yiddish *per se* as a linguistic entity (see M. Weinreich 1940*a*: 42; 1953: 39; D. Katz 1983: 1025), let alone for the study of Eastern Yiddish. It cannot be doubted that the linguistic situation in Eastern Europe was clearly one of an ever increasing discrepancy between the spoken and written languages.

3.3 The Historical Factors

The growing linguistic and socio-cultural differences between eighteenth-century Ashkenaz I and Ashkenaz II (see Shmeruk 1978: 178), as well as the developments internal to East European Jewry, are among the most important factors that spurred the rise of Modern Literary Yiddish. The whole traditional cultural macro-system of Ashkenazic Jewry was undergoing change and restructuring. In Western and Central Europe (hitherto Ashkenaz I) the modernization of traditional Jewish society resulted in rapidly increasing linguistic and cultural assimilation. Consequently, an essentially new type of German Jewish subculture, formally patterned on the German model, emerged in Western Europe (see Sorkin 1988: 5–8; 122–3; 174–8). In Eastern Europe the socio-political and ideological frameworks of traditional Jewish society were also changing radically with the rise of a new religious movement: Hasidism. At the same time, the first Eastern European proponents of the Jewish Enlightenment had to modify the Western model of cultural modernization to meet the specific needs of East European Jewry.

3.3.1 *The Decline of Western Yiddish*

The tendencies towards assimilation that took root among eighteenth-century West European Jewry (see Ettinger 1976: 781), coupled with the rise of the Haskala (Jewish Enlightenment) movement in Germany in the 1780s, presented a practical example, as well as an ideological rationale for learning the 'proper' language of the country for many Jews (see Shmeruk 1978: 147). The traditionally lower status of the everyday language was exacerbated by the explicit hostility of Moses Mendelssohn (1729–86), founder of the Haskala, and his disciples towards Yiddish, both in theory and in practice (see Reyzen 1923: 11–22). The general decline of Western Yiddish, the result of growing assimilation, was further augmented by the rise of the Jewish Enlightenment amid high hopes of full emancipation. Though as an oral medium Western Yiddish actually survived in vestigial traces until late into the twentieth century (see M. Weinreich 1940*a*: 61; 1973: i. 286 ff.; Guggenheim-Grünberg 1950; 1954; 1964; Shy 1990; Matras 1991), it had begun to decline drastically as a literary language in the last decades of the eighteenth century (see Borokhov 1915: 209; 1926: 24; Dinse 1974: 146–7; Shmeruk 1978: 176–8). Consequently, the Western European Yiddish book market collapsed and Old Literary Yiddish began to disintegrate; or as Beem (1954: 128) has put it, 'as the eighteenth century was ending, the all-European writing convention was breaking down'. The ever increasing assimilation to New High German in Western Europe led to a significant Germanization of written and printed Western Yiddish. This Germanization was effectively supported by contemporary attempts to write and print (Jewish) New High German or 'Ashkenazic German' works with Yiddish characters (see Paper 1954; Wexler 1981b). In Holland too there was a significant *rapprochement* between spoken Dutch Yiddish and the literary language (Beem 1954; Aptroot 1988; 1989: 86–7). However, the most significant development from the viewpoint of productive continuity of oral and literary Yiddish culture took place in Eastern Europe, where spoken Eastern Yiddish served as the direct source of the modern literary language.

3.3.2 *The Rise of Hasidism and Haskala in Eastern Europe*

The rise of the popular religious movement Hasidism, founded in the eighteenth century by Rabbi Yisroel Bal Shem Tov (c.1700–60), as well as the varieties of the East European version of the Haskala (or Haskole, Jewish Enlightenment), were the central forces reshaping the socio-cultural and ideological settings of East European Jewry in the late eighteenth and nineteenth centuries. Both movements, while bitterly opposed to each other, did much to promote the rise of Modern Literary Yiddish (see M. Weinreich 1928: 276–7; Viner 1940b: 26–7; 29–30).

Some factions of Hasidism contributed to the changing status of the everyday language, and the movement as a whole played an important role in the adoption of modern Eastern Yiddish as a literary language. (On the role of Hasidism in the rise of modern Yiddish literature see Reyzen 1923: 107–10; Niger 1932: 112–7; 1944: 210 ff.; Tsinberg 1937: ii. 203–27; Viner 1940b: 29–38; Shmeruk 1978: 175–6.) But it was the leaders and proponents of the East European Jewish Enlightenment who actually developed it into a written language with an ever expanding range of didactic, educational, ideological and literary functions (see Erik 1935: 35–7; Viner 1940b: 30; 58–60).

4 The Origins of Modern Literary Yiddish: Concepts, Sources, and Strategies

The major division between Western and Eastern Yiddish coincides roughly with the two distinct dialectal infrastructures of the old and the modern literary languages, or in Max Weinreich's terms WRITTEN LANGUAGE A and WRITTEN LANGUAGE B, respectively (see M. Weinreich 1973: ii. 386, 389-90; cf. Moskovich and Wolf 1981: 60-1). The old literary language was primarily and, until its decline in the late eighteenth century, almost exclusively based on Western Yiddish. The earliest conscious attempts to introduce Eastern Yiddish features into literary usage and the increasing reorientation of some late eighteenth-century East European writers towards the spoken varieties of Eastern Yiddish mark the actual beginnings of the modern literary language. By the end of the first half of the nineteenth century, the modern literary language was largely based on Eastern Yiddish.

The choice of the designation Modern or nascent Modern Literary Yiddish (as opposed to Old Literary Yiddish) is motivated by the retrospective perception of the tremendous socio-linguistic transformation that modern Yiddish underwent in the late nineteenth and early twentieth century. This transformation may be summed up as an overall modernization whereby the 'popular' or socially lower status language acquired new educational, ideological, and even political functions (cf. Kerler 1990: 274-5), becoming in the eyes of many of its speakers a modern national language.

Modern Yiddish literature as we now know it (e.g. see Shtif 1919; Viner 1940b; Niger 1944) emerged several decades after these pioneering attempts to employ Eastern Yiddish as a literary medium. The claim that a literary language is older than the literature itself may sound paradoxical at first, but it is substantiated by a twofold distinction: first, between Old and Modern Literary Yiddish, and, second, between Modern Literary Yiddish and the self-consciously developed language of modern Yiddish literature (see Viner 1928: 102-4; 125-6). Here Birnbaum's (1953: 115) famous claim that 'Yiddish orthography is older than the language itself' may be taken, with all necessary caution, as a working metaphor for the present assertion that Modern Literary Yiddish is older than modern Yiddish literature itself. In this connection I quote Max Weinreich's general evaluation:

מענדעלעס געוואַלדיקער אויפֿטו איז דאָס וואָס ער האָט געשאַפֿן די **נאָרמע**;
אין אירע עלעמענטן איז זיין שפּראַך שוין געווען פֿאַרטיק ביי אַזוינע שרייבערס
ווי אַקסנפֿעלד, עטינגער און פּערל און אפֿילו נאָך פֿריִער.

The tremendous achievement of Mendele was that he created the *norm*; in its elements, however, his language in fact existed in the works of such authors as Aksenfeld, Etinger, Perl and earlier still. (M. Weinreich 1940a: 43)

The emergence of the modern literary language and the shift from Old to nascent Modern Literary Yiddish in the late eighteenth and early nineteenth centuries have been major concerns of philologists and historical dialectologists of Yiddish (see M. Weinreich 1928: 27–8; Viner 1928; Shtif 1932a; 1932b; Joffe 1940; Mark 1967; Shmeruk 1964a; 1964b; 1979b; Roskies 1974a). The fact that the earliest manifestations of nascent Modern Literary Yiddish can be traced to certain late eighteenth-century works has been variously acknowledged by many scholars (e.g. Prilutsky 1917; Reyzen 1920: 27; Shtif 1932a: 34–6; Joffe 1940: 98–9; Viner 1940b: 15; Roskies 1974a: 4). It was repeatedly stated by M. Weinreich who also urged a systematic linguistic examination of eighteenth-century books that were linguistically re-edited or written in Eastern Yiddish (e.g. M. Weinreich 1928: 27–8; 1940a: 62; 64–5; 1973: ii. 385–6; iv. 389). However, most studies in the field have been devoted to the various Eastern Yiddish literary works written or printed during the first half of the nineteenth century (e.g. Kalmanovitsh 1937; Shlosberg 1936, 1937; Lerner 1939; Shmeruk 1964b; 1969: 70–5; 1977; Herzog 1965b; Mashbitz 1970), since the most decisive developments in the field of Modern Literary Yiddish did not come to fruition until that period.

Moreover, some scholars were primarily interested in works that were Eastern Yiddish in language and novel ('modern') in literary form and content. Thus Shtif (1932a: 1–4) declaratively concentrates on the early popular educational works and 'modernizing' *belles-lettres* of the period, though he has to resort to 'traditional' literary texts to illustrate the actual dynamics of the linguistic modernization of literary Yiddish (1932a: 4–7; 1932b: 34–6). Viner, too, repeatedly states that modern Yiddish literature originated in the late eighteenth and early nineteenth centuries (Viner 1940b: 11, 26; cf. also Remenik's (1971) attempt at a socio-historical periodization of modern Yiddish literature). However, Viner's primary interest in modern Western-style Yiddish literature in effect restricts all his literary and stylistic studies (e.g. Viner 1928; 1940a; 1940b) to those works written or published during the first half of the nineteenth century. In this respect, Niger's (1944: 209) argument that one of the major direct sources of modern Yiddish literature was the Hasidic oral and folk culture which evolved between the mid-eighteenth and mid-nineteenth centuries seems to be chronologically more realistic.

The earliest phase in the history of modern Yiddish literature, beginning in the second decade of the nineteenth century, is undoubtedly a central issue still awaiting further study. It is important to stress, however, that the language itself had an older literary tradition. The continuous and, in Eastern Europe, uninterrupted history of literary Yiddish (Old and Modern alike) is also the living literary and linguistic link between old and modern Yiddish literature, although they are worlds apart in many respects. Thus there is every reason to look for the origins of the modern literary language in works that are chronologically and semiotically still part of old Yiddish literature. (Cf. Reyzen 1932 on this literature in the first half of the nineteenth century.)

4.1 The Point of Departure

Although many of its features can be traced back to fourteenth-century Yiddish manuscripts, the old literary language owes its existence to the impact of Yiddish printing that was launched on a pan-European scale in the 1540s. (On the direct correlation between the introduction of printing and language standardization in general see Harris 1980: 130–1; Zhuravlev 1982: 121 ff.; within the pan-European context see Fevre and Martin 1984: 319–2; on German see Zhirmunsky 1936: 266 ff.; Guchmann 1959: 78 ff; Bach 1961: 202–3; Waterman 1966: 127–8; see also Vachek 1967 for an attempt to establish a distinction of principle between written and printed varieties of literary language.) As a relatively homogeneous written language based on, and related to, the varieties of spoken Western Yiddish, the old literary language merits a separate study. It is known, however, that its originators were often speakers of Western Yiddish whose literary and commercial objectives were to serve the entire Yiddish-speaking community, both Western and Eastern.

While the modern literary language has undergone radical stylistic changes over the past two hundred years, it none the less lies closely in the background of today's late twentieth-century standard written Yiddish. Arising sometime in the late eighteenth and early nineteenth centuries and coinciding for decades, in ever changing proportions, with the old literary language, the modern literary language is based on dialects of Eastern Yiddish (co-territorial with the Slavonic and Baltic languages). By the time the modern literary language had come into its own, there was virtually no longer a community of motivated Western-Yiddish readers, and, in sharp contrast to the objectives of the creators of the old literary language centuries before, its purpose was to serve the entire Yiddish-speaking population of Eastern Europe.

4.2 Causation

It is assumed that the primary cause of the radical shift from the old literary language to the nascent modern literary language was the increasing unintelligibility of the old literary language. Conscious awareness of the problem is evident from the prefaces in which editors and publishers, when reissuing an older classic work in Eastern Europe in the late eighteenth or the early nineteenth century, advertise their editions as making the work more intelligible (see Weinreich 1928: 27–8; 1940a: 64). This by now traditional explanation is probably true in a broad sense, but should be further investigated, and other possible factors should be taken into consideration: e.g. (1) the decline of Yiddish publishing in the West, (2) the subsequent remapping of the European Yiddish book market, (3) the rapid growth of Yiddish printing in Eastern Europe (see Shmeruk 1964a: 332; 1981: 151; Kon 1936; Bernshteyn 1975), (4) the emergence of new socio-cultural and ideological orientations in late eighteenth- and early nineteenth-century Ashkenaz II (Hasidism, Haskole), and, possibly, (5) the need for authors of radically different genres, previously unknown in Yiddish literature, to present a commercially viable 'exciting new product' (see Shtif 1932a: 4 ff.; 1932b; Shmeruk 1972: 799).

4.3 Literary Correlates

The emergence of the modern literary language coincides with a dramatic growth in the thematic scope and number of genres to which Yiddish was applied in writing and publishing. The rise of proto-modern Yiddish literature did not take place until the first decades of the nineteenth century, and it was to a large degree initiated by authors who were closely associated with the East European Jewish Enlightenment movement in its many phases and guises. This has been a subject of scholarly investigation since the 1930s (e.g. Shtif 1932a: 4, 17–27; Viner 1940b: 26–9; Reyzen 1965: 222; 229 ff.; Mark 1967: 129). However, the only right way to approach the historical development of literary Yiddish is to examine *all* the available texts from the period in question, whatever their genre and literary, educational, or ideological orientation may be. Moreover, in the case of the Eastern Yiddish texts from the late eighteenth century, the linguistic modernization of literary Yiddish occurred before the actual beginnings of modern Yiddish literature.

4.4 Linguistic Aspects

The primary goal of the present study is to analyse and categorize the linguistic changes manifest in the shift from Old to nascent Modern Literary Yiddish. To define this change in linguistic terms involves tracing the innovations introduced into the corpus of extant texts from the perspective of their phonological, morphological, and syntactic features. The linguistic investigation of the late eighteenth-century origins of Modern Literary Yiddish will prepare the groundwork for a future study of the principal phases in the crystallization process of the modern literary language which took place in the first half of the nineteenth century, when a number of competing stylistic trends and transitional types of literary language prevailed.

4.4.1 *Transition and Shift from Old to Nascent Modern Literary Language*

Bearing in mind the continuity of literary Yiddish, we may evaluate its transformations in late eighteenth-century Eastern Europe within the conceptual framework of TRANSITION and SHIFT from old to nascent modern literary language.

The term TRANSITION refers to the reprinting, re-editing, and linguistic revision of old Yiddish literary works that began in the late eighteenth century. In many cases the original language of these works was linguistically updated by anonymous East European 'style-editors'. The linguistic re-editing and revision of most of the conventional old Yiddish books continued well into the second half of the nineteenth century. By the middle of the nineteenth century, this linguistic transition had in many cases brought about a wholesale shift from the old to the new literary language, though certain archaic features survived as stylistic peculiarities of traditional ('non-secular') Yiddish literature. Some of these features were later adopted in the modern literary language as stylistic archaisms or as elements of a more formal or stylistically elevated usage (cf. Shmeruk 1978: 180).

The term SHIFT is used to describe the linguistic characteristics of the earliest Eastern Yiddish books from the last three decades of the eighteenth century. These comprise some entirely new translations, one new Eastern Yiddish version of an older literary work, as well as two original works written in Eastern Yiddish. All these texts mark the actual change-over from the old literary language to nascent Modern Literary Yiddish. These texts exhibit various gradations of approximation to spoken Eastern Yiddish. The extent of emancipation from the Old Yiddish linguistic and stylistic features was different in each text. But it is clear that the most remarkable grammatical innovations in the literary language were often introduced systematically into these books, and that the general direction of change was towards an increasing *rapprochement* of the spoken and the literary languages.

4.4.2 *Dialectological Sources*

Once the essential linguistic correlates of the transition from Old to Modern Literary Yiddish have been systematized, we shall proceed to determine the dialectological sources and correlates of nascent Modern Literary Yiddish.

This is a risky undertaking, because our knowledge of Yiddish dialectology implicit in this phase derives largely from twentieth- rather than eighteenth- or nineteenth-century varieties of Yiddish, and any presumptions or conclusions must rest on the shaky premiss of 'relative continuity' in each dialectal region. However, the sharp divergence in certain aspects of phonology, morphology, and possibly syntax between the three major Eastern Yiddish dialects can be dated as substantially earlier than the late eighteenth—perhaps even well before the mid-seventeenth—century (see M. Weinreich 1973: ii. 386; iv. 389, 390). The radical linguistic alterations introduced in the extant texts constitute the primary evidence for the change in the literary language. On the other hand, much earlier attestations (from the sixteenth century onwards) of distinctly Eastern Yiddish features can be gleaned from non-literary documents (e.g. community protocols; see Balaban 1916; Dubnov 1909: 27–39; U. Weinreich 1958d; M. Weinreich 1973: i. 262, 313–14) as well as from some non-Yiddish sources (e.g. rabbinical responsa collections; see Dubnov 1909: 10–26; Rubashov 1929 and later Shazar 1971; Shtif 1932b: 33–4; Joffe 1940: 91–3; Kosover 1967) and even from casual Eastern Yiddish 'outbursts' in some of the old Yiddish literary monuments written by Eastern Yiddish speakers (e.g. M. Weinreich 1927: 203–4; 1928: 193; Shmeruk 1978: 80–2; 1981: 24; 34; 58). The use of the empirical findings of modern Yiddish dialectology in order to ascertain the geo-linguistic composition of Modern Literary Yiddish at its inception is thus a conceptually viable and legitimate step.

4.4.3 *The Correspondence of Speech and Writing*

Whatever the variations inherent in modern or pre-modern varieties of vernacular Yiddish, it will be demonstrated that the shift from the old to the modern literary language is, from the perspective of Yiddish speakers in Eastern Europe, a consistently growing set of correspondences between the written and the spoken language. Old Literary Yiddish was far from being identical with the declining varieties of spoken Western Yiddish, and was certainly more remote from the blossoming varieties of Eastern Yiddish. Modern Literary Yiddish arose largely from conscious attempts to write in a language primarily based on the contemporary vernacular. The same literary and commercial motives (together with that of didactic enlightenment in the East) that had once incited authors and publishers to create a written language for the pan-European market now served to move the pioneers of a new literary language in Eastern Europe towards a more localized consumption.

4.5 General Plan of the Book

The origins of Modern Literary Yiddish are traced and analysed within the following framework:

Part I offers an overview of some of the most important Eastern Yiddish features that can be recovered from earlier old Yiddish works. Two early eighteenth-century books from Eastern Europe (1723) are examined textually and linguistically in Chapter 1. Both books, while directly based on contemporary Western Yiddish literary sources, introduce a significant number of Eastern Yiddish features. It is possible that these two texts were printed for a more localized readership in Eastern Europe. In any event, they may be considered to be the most significant early manifestations of modern Eastern Yiddish in the old literary language.

Part II (Chapters 2–5) examines the linguistic mechanism of *transition* from Old to nascent Modern Literary Yiddish whereby the language of the late eighteenth-century East European printed works (re-editions of 1771 and 1788, Chapter 2; one revision of 1786, Chapter 3; one reprint of 1796, Chapter 4) is contrasted with that of their respective old Yiddish source texts. Chapter 5 provides a synoptic summary of the linguistic Easternization (and ultimately the modernization) of literary Yiddish.

Part III is devoted to all the accessible Eastern Yiddish books (1771–c.1798) in which the shift from the old to the nascent modern literary language was initiated or effected. Chapter 6 discusses the major orthographic, phonological, and morpho-syntactic features of the earliest known Eastern Yiddish text (1771). Chapter 7 examines both textually and linguistically the earliest original work written in modern Eastern Yiddish (c.1783). Finally, all the extant Eastern Yiddish books are dialectologically and linguistically analysed in Chapter 8. The major dialectal features of the extant texts and some early tendencies towards a supraregional literary usage are abstracted. This is followed by a comparative survey of the major pan-Eastern Yiddish grammatical features characteristic of all these books. The main patterns of the shift from the old to the nascent modern literary language are summarized.

Finally, Chapter 9 sums up the major linguistic, historical, and sociolinguistic implications. A more detailed internal periodization of the New Yiddish period is offered on the basis of the known literary works from the late eighteenth and early nineteenth century. The interface between Eastern Yiddish dialects and the emerging modern literary language is summarized and the essential early trends of standardization are summed up.

PART I

Eastern Yiddish in the Old Literary Language

5 Preface

Virtually every scholar concerned with the origins of Modern Literary Yiddish has eagerly searched for the earliest texts containing significant traces of Eastern Yiddish. Although such texts are hardly reliable sources for the linguistic reconstruction of the chronological development of Eastern Yiddish dialects, they nevertheless provide some of the earliest written manifestations of the distinctly Eastern Yiddish features that infiltrated the old literary language at a certain stage. The closer such a pre-modern text is to our period, the more realistic are the chances that it was written primarily for a more localized Eastern Yiddish readership.

5.1 Pre-eighteenth-century Yiddish Books from Eastern Europe

Naturally, all earlier books with some distinct traces of Eastern Yiddish were written by authors from Eastern Europe. Among the earliest works of this kind that are especially noteworthy we find Binyomen Arn ben Avrom's *Seyder mitsves noshim* (Cracow, 1577; cf. Shmeruk 1981: 53-6; 81-2, no. 10; 86 no. 18; 96 no. 34), Yitskhok Sulkes's *Seyfer shir hashirim* (Cracow, 1579; cf. Shmeruk 1981: 33-7; 83-4 no. 12), Yankev Kopelman's *Targum shel khomesh megiles bloshn ashkenaz* (Freiburg, 1584; cf. Shmeruk 1981: 31-3), Yitskhok ben Eliezer's *Seyfer hagan* (Cracow, [1571 or 1579]; cf. Shmeruk 1981: 113 no. 59) and Avrom Ashkenazi Halperin's bilingual (Hebrew and Yiddish) *Sam khayim* (Prague, 1590; cf. Tsinberg 1929: 177-80; 1935: 176-9; Erik 1928: 286-7; Shmeruk 1981: 48-53; Turniansky 1985a: 169 no. 12). To these we may add Rivke Tiktiner's *Meynekes Rivke* (Prague, 1609; cf. Shmeruk 1981: 56-63, 101-2 no. 44) and the unpublished manuscript of Yitskhok Kopserlish's 'Tsemakh Dovid' dating from 1669 (see Turniansky 1985b: 572, 587-603, 605-20).

These and other Yiddish works emanating from sixteenth- and seventeenth-century Eastern Europe require a separate linguistic examination. The few specifically Eastern Yiddish features of these works will have to

be analysed in the context of a broad linguistic reconstruction of the chronological development of Eastern Yiddish dialects. But it is clear even at this
stage that until the second half of the eighteenth century the grammatical
and stylistic patterns of the pan-European Old Literary Yiddish prevailed in
most works written by native speakers of Eastern Yiddish.

5.2   Traces of Eastern Yiddish in Old Yiddish Literature

The frequently cited earliest manifestations of Eastern Yiddish in the old
literary language are usually restricted to a handful of well-known lexical
items such as the pan-Eastern Yiddish דֿבֿנן dáv(ə)nən 'pray' (cf. pan-Western
Yiddish אָרן ɔrņ) and the interjection of compassion נ(ע)בוך / נעביך nébəx
'unfortunate(ly); alas; oh dear!' According to Max Weinreich (1973: iii. 86)
דֿבֿנן dáv(ə)nən appears eight times in Yitskhok ben Eliezer's *Seyfer hagan*
(Cracow, [1571 or 1579]), whereas its Western Yiddish equivalent אָרן ɔrņ
appears there only twice. Both nébəx and dáv(ə)nən were employed in
Yitskhok Sulkes's *Seyfer shir hashirim* (Cracow, 1579; cf. Shmeruk 1981: 34
nn. 57-8) and in Rivke Tiktiner's *Meynekes Rivke* (Prague, 1609; cf.
Shmeruk 1981: 58 n. 94). Another distinctly Eastern Yiddish word that
occurs in *Meynekes Rivke* is זײדֿא zéjdə 'grandfather'. In *Seyfer shir hashirim* we
also find such remarkably 'modern' forms as גיווען gəvɛn 'was' and אונזרי
יודליך undzərə jidələx 'our fellow Jews', the latter being a contextually
ambiguous employment of an Eastern Yiddish diminutive.

In fact, both the conjunction חאָטשי xɔ́čə 'although' and the interjection
נעבוך nébəx (or nébax) 'alas' are the only two items unusual for Western
Yiddish that became acceptable in the old literary language at various stages
and in certain genres (see M. Weinreich 1928: 23; 1973: ii. 256). Thus
nébəx occurs in a number of early and otherwise stylistically conservative
works (cf. ibid. ii. 201); e.g. in an early sixteenth-century manuscript, in the
Yiddish Biblical epic poems *Shmuel bukh* (*editio princeps*, Augsburg, 1544; see
Falk 1961) and *Mlokhim bukh* (*editio princeps*, Augsburg, 1543; see Fuks
1965: i. 7 n. 1). This may mean that either this form penetrated into
Western Yiddish from Eastern Yiddish already in the late fifteenth century
(or earlier still) or, alternatively, that nébəx is not necessarily of exclusively
Eastern Yiddish or even Slavonic origin. The latter may be suggested by its
peculiar function as a psycho-ostensive adverb in modern Yiddish. (For
standard Slavonic and other etymologies of nébəx see M. Weinreich 1973: ii.
201-2, iv. 271; Bloomfield 1933: 472; Wexler 1987: 159.) Conversely, the
conjunction xɔ́čə does not have such a distinguished attestation in the old
literary language (cf. Wexler 1987: 155 n. 14). It may be suggested that in
the wake of the Khmelnitski massacres of 1648-9 which brought waves of

Table 6 Eastern Yiddish lexical items from *Khinekh kotn* (1640; 1658)

| Hebrew | Yiddish | | Gloss |
	Cracow 1640	Amsterdam 1658	
1. בתי ידיים	הענטשקם hɛnčkəs	האנטשוך hántšux	gloves
2. צימוקים	ראזינקם rɔ́žinkəs	ראזינקם וויינפרלך rɔ́žinkəs [;] vajnpərləx	raisins
3. אבי זקני	מיין זדה majn zejdə	זידה העראי zejdə [;] hɛrlə	[my] grandfather
4. אמי זקנתי	מיין באבא majn bɔbə	באבא פֿראלי bɔbə/babə[;] fralə	[my] grandmother
5. התפלל	דאבֿן davn̦	דאבֿן אודר אור davn̦ ɔdər ɔr	pray

Jewish refugees into Central and Western Europe, this form (possibly with some other Eastern Yiddish words such as dáv(ə)nən) penetrated into Western Yiddish dialects. Hence its use in Glikl Hamil's memoirs written in 1691–1715 in Western Yiddish (printed in 1896; cf. Landau 1901; Fridberg 1961: 88–9; Aptroot 1991: 44–7; for more details on this important work see Turniansky 1992 and 1993*b*).

The earliest work in which the conjunction כאטשי xɔčə appears seems to be *Tikuney tshuve erets Tsvi* (Cracow, 1666; see §7.2.3). In all three subsequent Western re-editions of the book the conjunction remained unaltered, although in the third re-edition (Amsterdam, 1701) the original and for its time remarkably 'modern' language of *Tikuney tshuve erets Tsvi* was radically changed in accordance with the linguistic and stylistic norms of the old literary language. If certain Eastern Yiddish lexical items did become more familiar among Western Yiddish speakers, especially since the massacres of 1648–9, then this may also provide a partial explanation for the way in which the distinctly Eastern Yiddish items of the anonymous Hebrew–Yiddish dictionary *Khinekh kotn* (Cracow, 1640; cf. Shmeruk 1981: 111 no. 54) were treated in its later Western re-editions. These items were often replaced by their Western Yiddish equivalents in the latest Western re-edition (Amsterdam, 1761; see D. Katz 1990: 199–201). However, in the earlier re-editions (Amsterdam, 1658; Dessau, *c.*1698; Jesnitz, *c.*1726) some of them were orthographically and morphologically Westernized (see

D. Katz 1990: 200; also Table 6, no. 1). For many others, the Western
Yiddish equivalent was simply added (see Table 6, nos. 2–5). These items
(some already used by earlier authors from Eastern Europe; e.g. דבֿנן
dáv(ə)nən 'pray'; זײדא zéjdə 'grandfather') were thus potentially made
known to contemporary speakers of Western Yiddish, thereby enabling a
possible interdialectal confluence in the domain of lexicon.

5.3 Eastern Yiddish Features in the Seventeenth Century

The closer we come to the eighteenth century the more likely we are to find
traces of Eastern Yiddish morphology and syntax in texts written and printed
in Eastern Europe. However, very rare occurrences of Eastern forms can
sometimes be spotted in even the least plausible works written or stylized by
Western Yiddish speakers. Thus we find that the modern Eastern Yiddish
form of the future-tense auxiliary appears (of all places!) on the title-page of
the *editio princeps* of *Mayse bukh* (Basle, 1602):

[...] אך [אויש] רבי יהודה החסיד מעשים וועט אייך אך קיינש טון פֿעלין [...]
ax [ojs] rábi jɛhúdə (h)akhósəd májsəm vət ajx ax kajns tun fɛlṇ
'also you will not miss any of the stories [also: deeds] of rabbi Judah Hasid'

[...] וויא איר וועט הינטון אין מיינן סמנים טון זעהן [...]
vi ir vət híntən in májnən simónəm tun zɛn
'as you will see below in my table of contents'

[...] אזו וועט איר האבן כל התורה כולה גאר.
azó vət ir hɔbn kɔl (h)atójrə kúlə gɔr
'thus you will have the whole Torah in its entirety [available to you in Yiddish]'

This triple vət (once for 3rd pers. sing. and twice for 2nd pers. pl.) surfacing
instead of the then standard Western Yiddish vərt on the title-page of one the
most important (and from our perspective 'archaic') old Yiddish literary
monuments, is a remarkable and at that time rare 'slip of print'. The title-
page also announces that this [first] edition of *Mayse bukh* was printed 'at the
initiative' of one *Yankev bereb Avrom mik[ehiles] k[oydesh] Mezritsh deLita*
('Jacob son of Abraham from the Holy Community Międzyrzec of Lithuania').
A native speaker of Eastern Yiddish from Poland, he was a wandering
bookseller who moved to Western Europe, where he was responsible for
printing a number of Yiddish books (see Shmeruk 1981: 71 and n. 110). It
seems quite possible that he, Yankev bereb Avrom, was also personally
responsible for providing us with one of the earliest known attestations of a
distinctly modern Eastern Yiddish feature, one which was rather successfully
suppressed in old literary Yiddish throughout the seventeenth and most of
the eighteenth century. However, in certain works emanating from Eastern

Table 7 Section of *Tikuney tshuve erets Tsvi* in two editions (1666 and 1701)

	[*Cracow*] 1666	Amsterdam 1701
1	איין אשה דז זיא איר קינד	ווען איין אשה ליגט בייא נבֿט אויף
	דער קווע̆טש[ט] אין שלאָף	איר קינד אונ׳ דר דרוקט עש צו טוט
	דא מוז זי פֿסטן איין גנץ יאר	איז איר תשובה זי מוז איין גנץ יאר
	אונ׳ טאר אויף די נבֿט	פֿשטן אונ׳ זאל
5	קיין פֿלייש ניט עשין אונ קיין וויין	קיין פֿלייש עשן אונ אך קיין
	ניט טרינקן נישׁט מין שבת אונ יום טוב	וויין טרינקן זיי׳דען שבתֿות וויו׳ טובי׳
	חנוכה אונ פורים וואָרום די טעג	חנוכ׳ ופורים דען די זעלביגן טעג
	טאר זי ניט פֿסטן כלל וכלל ניט	דארף זיא גאר ניט פֿשטין
	אבר זיא מוז צילן וויאפֿיל די טעג	אבר זיא מוז צילין די טעג
10	אן טרעפֿין פֿון שבתֿות אונ׳ יומים טובֿים	
	אז זי האט ניט גפֿסט	דיא זי ניט גפֿשט האט

1	an išə dɔs zi ir kind	vən an išə ligt ba naxt af
	dərkvečt in šlɔf	ir kind un dərdrukt əs cu tɔjt
	dɔ muz zi fastṇ a ganc jɔr	iz ir tšuvə zi muz a ganc jɔr
	un tɔr af di naxt	fastṇ un zɔl
5	kejn flejš nit ɛsṇ un kejn vajn	kejn flejš ɛsṇ ɔjx kejn vajn
	nit trinkən ništ mein šabəs un jɔntev	trinkən zajdən šabɔ́səs vəjɔntɔ́jvəm
	xanəkə un púrim vɔ́rəm di tɛg	vəxanəkə vəpúrim den di zélbikṇ tɛg
	tɔr zi nit fastṇ klal uxlal nit	darf zi gɔr nit fastṇ
	ɔbər zi muz cejlṇ vifil di tɛg	ɔbər zi muz cejlṇ di tɛg
10	ɔ́ntrɛfṇ fun šabɔ́səs un jɔntɔ́jvem	
	az zi hɔt nit gəfast	di zi nit gəfast hɔt

1	A woman who squeezes	When a woman lies at night on
	her child to death while asleep	her child and presses him to death
	[she] has to fast a whole year	then her penance is to
	and is not allowed before night	fast a whole year and [she] should
5	to eat meat or to drink	not eat meat nor drink
	wine. Except on Sabbath and holiday,	wine. Except on Sabbath [day]s and
	[on] Hanuka and Purim, for in those	holidays, [on] Hanuka and Purim, for
	days she is not allowed to fast at all.	in those days she does not have to
	However, she has to count how many	fast at all.
	Sabbath days and holidays altogether	However, she has to count the
10	[during which] she did not fast.	days [during which] she did not fast.

Europe, namely in *Tikuney tshuve erets Tsvi* and *Tfile minkhe umayrev* ([Cracow?], 1666), the Eastern Yiddish future-tense auxiliary וועט *vət* (3rd pers. sing.) is used predominantly in place of the usual Western Yiddish וערט *vərt*, which was the norm in the old literary language.

Some of the most striking lexical, phraseological, and syntactic differences between Western and Eastern Yiddish can be gleaned from a comparison of *Tikuney tshuve erets Tsvi* (Cracow, 1666; on this small but remarkable book see Balaban 1935: 32–3; 1936: 43; Scholem 1973: 593; Weinryb 1972: 228) with its later Western European re-edition (Amsterdam, 1701). Thus the original edition, in sharp contrast to the later one, often prefers (or possibly slips into using) the more colloquial form vət. In fact, many changes that were effected in the Amsterdam (1701) edition point towards the major stylistic and dialectal differences between the Western-based old literary language and the pre-modern varieties of Eastern Yiddish. It is evident from the following passage that the double negation, characteristic of the original text, was consistently avoided in the later re-edition (see Table 7, lines 5–6, 8). Similarly, the place of the finite verb in the subordinate clause was reordered (see line 11). The differences in the choice of lexical items (e.g. דער קוועטשן[ט] dərkvéčt vs. דר דרוקט dərdrúkt 'squeeze (to death)'; נישט מיין ništ mejn vs. זיי'דען zájdən / zájdṇ 'unless' (cf. mod. Y. niš(t)mɛr and sajdṇ); טאָר ניט tɔr nit vs. דארף ניט darf nit 'not allowed, forbidden') show that the more conspicuous Eastern Yiddish features of the original text were systematically neutralized in the later edition. In fact, the whole text of *Tikuney tshuve erets Tsvi* was by and large rewritten in accordance with the linguistic and stylistic norms of the old literary language.

5.4 The Seventeenth-century Commemorative Poems

A number of important manifestations of Eastern Yiddish can be found in the three Yiddish commemorative poems (*kines*) from the second half of the seventeenth century (see Shtif 1932a: 34–5; Turniansky 1989). The first poem, *Kine al gzeyres hakehiles dek[ehile]"k[oydesh] Ukrayne* (Prague, 1648, and Amsterdam, c.1649), describes Khmelnitski's massacres of 1648–9. It was written by Yoysef ben Eliezer Lipman of Prostits (Prosnitz), a native speaker of Western Yiddish, and was printed almost simultaneously in Prague and Amsterdam (see M. Weinreich 1928: 193–4 and his critical edition of this poem, ibid. 198–214). The two Eastern Yiddish lexical items of Slavonic origin that appeared in the Prague edition were stylistically neutralized in Amsterdam. (For a detailed discussion see Shmeruk 1978: 81–2; 1988: 129–30; cf. Turniansky 1989: 51–2 n. 8.) Thus קאָסים kɔ́səs 'scythe' (pl.) was replaced by a paraphrase, and פּאָסטליז póstələs 'sandals' by שטיפליז ⟨štifliz⟩ 'boots' (cf. mod. Y. שטיוול štivl 'boot(s)'). However, morphologically the latter form too is apparently characteristic of Eastern Yiddish (cf. mod. Y. שטיוואל(י)עם štivál(y)əs or štivɔ́l(y)əs '[large, clumsy] boots'). Otherwise this, as well as the other two commemorative poems, are written in the stylistic tradition of similar Old Yiddish contemporary accounts (see M. Weinreich 1928: 197–8).

The second poem is a shorter, anonymous description of the events of 1656 that followed Khmelnitski's massacres (cf. M. Weinreich 1928: 194–6 and his critical edition of this poem, ibid. 215–18). It was possibly written in Eastern Europe. Such distinctly, though not exclusively, Eastern Yiddish forms as זענן zɛnən 'are'; אז az 'that' (conj.; cf. Timm 1987: 423); ארויז גישר(י)בן arójsgəšrìbņ 'wrote (perf.); announced in writing' occur.

The third poem, *Dray kdoyshem bek[ehiles] k[oydesh] Vilne* (Amsterdam, 1692), describes the Vilna blood libel of 1690 (see M. Weinreich 1927: 204–9, and his edition of this poem, ibid. 210–20). It was either written by a native speaker of Eastern Yiddish or based on his authentic testimony, and a number of important Eastern Yiddish features can be traced in its phraseo-logy, lexicon, and morphology: e.g. אלי דריי אין איינן álə draj inéjnən [or inéjnəm] 'all three together'; זייט וויושן zajt visņ 'you (pl.) should know'; זייער zejər 'their' (instead of the then standard איר ir); זעטיגה zétikə 'such' (pl.); האטשי xočə 'although'; ע(ט)ץ ɛ(t)c 'you' (pl. nom.) and ענק ɛnk 'you' (pl. acc./dat.; cf. Mideastern Yiddish עץ ɛc and ענק ɛnk). Of these, inéjnəm, zejər and zajt visņ are pure and simple modern Eastern Yiddish. The forms ɛ(t)c and ɛnk were also current in some Western dialects; however, since the mid-nineteenth century they seem to have become particularly characteristic of some varieties of Mideastern Yiddish (see §34.1.2). Finally the form zétikə corresponds directly to the distinctly Northeastern form אזעטיקע azétikə 'such' (cf. M. Weinreich 1927: 203).

However, the most significant Eastern Yiddish features can be found in the two earliest known books from the eighteenth century, both of which were only recently discovered. They are *Derekh tomim* (Zholkve, 1723) and *Derekh khayim* (Zholkve, c.1723). Their language testifies to the increasing direct impact of spoken Eastern Yiddish upon the old literary language at one of its later stages.

Two Early Eighteenth-Century
East European Texts

6 Two Books from the Early Eighteenth Century

6.1 *Derekh tomim* (Zholkve, 1723)

In 1979 a unique copy of a book called *Derekh tomim* was discovered by Ch. Shmeruk in the Jewish National and University Library of Jerusalem (Shmeruk 1979*a*). It had been printed in Zholkve in 1723. Comprising fifty-six pages, of which ten are missing, the book belongs to the *muser* genre. (On this genre in Old Yiddish literature see Shulman 1913: 86-105; Sosis 1926: 13 ff.; Erik 1928: 245-319; Tsinberg 1935: 162-96; Minkov and Joffe 1942: 30-64; Maitlis 1958: 18-29; Dinse 1974: 91-5, 116 ff.; Shmeruk 1981: 43-63.)

The traditional ethical literature (*muser*) was, in its various forms and guises, one of the most popular genres of Old Yiddish literature from the sixteenth to the eighteenth centuries. With the advent of the seventeenth century the so-called *muser* monographs in Yiddish became very popular (see Dan 1975: 9, 146, for a broad definition of this form within the historical and literary framework of the Jewish literary tradition in Hebrew). These monographs were written in prose, in a sequence of thematically arranged moral instructions usually interlaced, in varying proportions, with proverbs, parables, and longer narratives (see Tsinberg 1935: 235 ff.). The most famous of them, including the *Brantshpigl* (Cracow, 1597?), *Lev tov* (Prague, 1620), and *Simkhes hanefesh* (Frankfurt am Main, 1707, = SF1707), are sometimes called 'muser-encyclopaedias' (Erik 1928: 247; Turniansky 1985*a*: 60; cf. Elbaum 1990: 227-9).

Although designed as a shorter work, *Derekh tomim* belongs to the category of seventeenth- and early eighteenth-century Yiddish *muser* monographs. Shmeruk has discussed its literary and bibliographic background (1979*a*: 121-2, 125), and has also outlined some of its most striking Eastern Yiddish linguistic features (ibid. 123). The astonishing quantity and frequency, for this period, of certain Eastern Yiddish features suggest that the anonymous author was himself a speaker of Eastern Yiddish. In addition to these outbursts of Eastern Yiddish, the book also makes a few references to early eighteenth-century East European Jewish customs, manners, and practices (ibid. 125). Could all this mean that the book was written primarily for an Eastern Yiddish readership? Although it is not possible to give a definitive answer, there is another closely related text that may reinforce the possibility.

6.2 *Derekh khayim* (Zholkve, c.1723)

The Jewish National and University Library of Jerusalem also holds a book that is the more 'practical' companion volume of *Derekh tomim* (= DtZ1723). It has 104 pages, of which the title-page, as well as pages 1–16, 25–32, 79–80, 86–7 and 89–90, are missing. Fortunately the final page, with the name of the book and its printer, remains intact. The book is *Derekh khayim* (= DkZ[1723]), and it was printed by the *zetser* ('type-setter') Yehude Zelig b[en] mo[reynu] h[orav] r[eb] Eliezer Lipman Katz z[ikhroyne] l[evrokhe], who worked in the Zholkve printing shop between 1721 and 1749 (see Friedberg 1950: 67). The same page includes the anonymous author's final statement, in which he mentions the 'other part of this book called "Derekh tomim"'. He also discloses his main Hebrew sources: namely, *Shulkhn orukh oyrekh khayim* (or *Shulḥan arukh oraḥ ḥayyim*) and *Shulkhn orukh yoyre deye* (or *Shulḥan arukh yoreh de'ah*). These are parts of the classic codification of Jewish Law, the שׁלחן עָרוּך (*Shulḥan arukh*) compiled by Rabbi Joseph Caro (1488–1575) in 1555.

As for a more precise dating of this book, there is good reason to believe that *Derekh khayim* was compiled and written before *Derekh tomim*, which is referred to as 'the other part of this book' (in *Derekh khayim*, p. 104). In *Derekh tomim* (p. 11) the author clearly says 'in this book the first part of which was compiled [from] the *Shulkhn Orukh Oyrekh Khayim* and from *Yoyre Deye*'. In any case, both works appear to have been seen by their author as two parts of one larger work, the first being *Derekh khayim*.

Like *Derekh tomim*, *Derekh khayim* was written for women and simple men, where 'simple' is the traditional designation for the majority of the adult Ashkenazic male population who did not read Mishnaic or rabbinical Hebrew, let alone Talmudic Aramaic (see D. Katz 1985: 98). No doubt this book, like other older Yiddish works of its kind, deserves the special attention of social historians. The traditional rabbinic attitude towards Yiddish translations of halakhic and related texts was often far from favourable (see M. Weinreich 1973: i. 270–1; iii. 277–9; Liberman 1952: 306; 1980: i. 402; Shmeruk 1978: 13 ff.; 1981: 53; Carmilly-Weinberger 1977: 180–2; on the halakhic and related literature in Yiddish see Shulman 1913: 74 ff.).

6.3 Textual Sources

The question of the immediate textual sources of these two books is crucial
for our understanding of their direct linguistic and stylistic models. Once
these sources are established, the detection of the most important Eastern
Yiddish features becomes philologically verifiable. The way in which these
sources were utilized can also tell us something about the possible readership
for which these two books were directly intended.

Even at first reading, the language of *Derekh tomim* seems to be uneven.
The two stories reprinted by Shmeruk (1979*a*: 126–8), as well as some other
parts (e.g. the parable of the king and his servants on pp. 23–4) and certain
general moralistic passages (e.g. pp. 8–9, 11, 12) differ sharply in their
language from the rest of the book. This linguistic heterogeneity apparently
resulted from the stylistically unlevelled blend of the sources used with the
actual 'speech' of the anonymous author and with the handful of textually
unprecedented stories, which may have been his own or Eastern Yiddish in
origin.

The *muser* genre in Yiddish, which was primarily dependent on Hebrew
musar and various Midrashic sources, was of a compilative nature. Not only
were most of the Yiddish *muser* monographs self-referential in advising their
readers to read other Yiddish *muser* collections, but some of them did in fact
use these other, in many cases Hebrew, collections. The most striking
example is the bilingual Hebrew and Yiddish *Kav hayosher* (Frankfurt am
Main, 1705–6, see §9). In the case of *Derekh tomim*, however, there seems to
be more than the usual share of borrowings from other Yiddish *muser*
monographs. In the conventional passage referring to these other collections, the author mentions the books *Lev tov*, *Kav hayosher*, and *Simkhes
hanefesh* (DtZ, 10, 11, repr. in Shmeruk 1979*a*: 125; see also ibid. 121–2).
But he fails to name one of the major sources of *Derekh tomim*: namely
Yekhiel Mikhl Epshteyn's *Derekh hayosher leoylem habe* (Frankfurt am Main,
1704; see Noble 1951; Liberman 1952; Piekarz 1964).

The first three of the six chapters of *Derekh tomim* (see Shmeruk 1979*a*:
124) have almost the same titles as the first, sixth, and sixteenth chapters of
Derekh hayosher leoylem habe. The beginning of the first chapter is a drastically shortened version of the first and second chapters of *Derekh hayosher
leoylem habe*. Similarly, the longer story of 'two servants of the king' included
in the first chapter (DtZ, 3–7) can be found in Chapter 8 of Yekhiel Mikhl
Epshteyn's book. Apparently there are also other substantial borrowings
from this source still awaiting further textual clarification. The author of
Derekh tomim usually shortened, at times beyond recognition, the passages
borrowed from *Derekh hayosher leoylem habe*, and also interwove them into

his own text. All this does not make the task of comparative textology any easier.

Another important source of *Derekh tomim* was Elkhonon Kirkhhahn's *Simkhes hanefesh* (see §14). A few of the stories incorporated here (e.g. *Derekh tomim*, pp. 20–1, 22–4(?), 37, 50–3) can be traced back to the narratives found in Kirkhhahn's book. Fortunately, in this case, there are more deviations from earlier parallel texts (see one of these narratives in Appendix 1, pp. 263–4). The fact that these deviations are usually purely linguistic is crucial to further discussion of the language of *Derekh tomim*. At the same time it may indicate that *Simkhes hanefesh* was the most likely direct source of these and other stories.

One might ask whether the anonymous author mentioned his direct Yiddish source on the missing title-page of *Derekh khayim*. On the last page he preferred to mention only the more prestigious Hebrew sources *Shulkhn orukh oyrekh khayim* and *Shulkhn orukh yoyre deye*. His most direct Yiddish source-text was the final part of *Simkhes hanefesh*, consisting of a selection of *dínim* 'laws' and *minhógim* 'rituals; customs'. Not everything in *Simkhes hanefesh* made its way into *Derekh khayim*. Certain parts were omitted or shortened and many new passages were added. However, the main arrangement in chapters, with further subdivision into paragraphs, and many of the passages are common to both. Once again, the linguistic differences evident in these passages are most illuminating.

Whereas *Derekh tomim* is an abridged collection of general ethical preachings and moral parables and narratives (*muser*), its more practical counterpart, *Derekh khayim*, is a more comprehensive selection of codified instructions on some of the most essential religious laws and customs (*dinim* and *minhogim*; on the latter cf. Dinse 1974: 90–1). Thus the two books, taken together, constitute a forgotten, but significant, attempt to provide contemporary Yiddish readers with a handy compilation of general *muser* and of the most essential *dinim*. It is possible, however, that the text of *Derekh khayim* was reprinted later. Two quotations from *Shulkhn orukh oyrekh khayim veyoyre deye* given in the *Great Dictionary of the Yiddish Language* are identical with the sentences found in *Derekh khayim*, on pages 72 and 42 respectively (see Mark 1971: 1258, s.v. אימאנט *ímant* 'always', and 1980: 1859, s.v. אָפּשנייצן *ópšnàjcṇ* 'blow one's nose'). In both instances the source of the *Great Dictionary of the Yiddish Language* is identified as '*Shulkhn orukh oyrekh khayim veyoyre deye*, Lemberg, beginning of the nineteenth century'. Tsinberg (1935: 246) argued that the later text was an Eastern reprint of the second part of *Simkhes hanefesh* presented under a different and more prestigious title (*Shulkhn orukh oyrekh khayim veyoyre deye*). The possible thematic and textual affiliations of these three texts (i.e. *Simkhes hanefesh, Derekh khayim*, and *Shulkhn orukh oyrekh khayim veyoyre deye*) and their possible thematic relation to the popular Yiddish *Khayey odem* of 1809 (see M. Weinreich 1973: i. 271; iii. 278) require further clarification. It is note-worthy that in the 1796 Shklov edition of *Simkhes hanefesh* (SSh1796) the final part containing *dinim* was omitted (cf. Tsinberg 1935: 246–7 n. 14 and Shulman 1913: 74 n. 2; for more on this edition see below §14).

This brings us back to the question of the intended readership of both books. Their anonymous author often directly employed the actual language of the contemporary Yiddish *muser* monographs printed in Western Europe, and thus seems to have written them with Western and Central European readers in mind. It is reasonable to suggest, however, that his more immediate readership consisted of Eastern Yiddish speakers. It is difficult to prove this claim now, but it is clear that in the language of both books we find some of the earliest significant features of Eastern Yiddish.

7 The Language of *Derekh tomim* and *Derekh khayim*

7.1 Phonology

Phonology, and above all the stressed-vowel system, provide one of the most revealing criteria in the analysis of the language of written Yiddish texts. In both texts we find a few give-away exceptional spellings that point to the underlying Eastern Yiddish phonology. On the whole, the spelling system employed in both texts does not differ much from the broadly defined conventions of the older Yiddish orthography of the period (see Shtif 1928: 37–40; on graphemic conventions of old and particularly of early seventeenth-century Yiddish see Timm 1987). This is especially evident in the conventional spelling of the consonants and in the varying, often incomplete, representation of the unstressed vowels. (The notation system of stressed vowels is explained in §2.1.1.)

7.1.1 *Merger of the Historical Vowels* 51/52 *and* 31/32

The most significant deviant spellings are those representing stressed vowels. The lexeme úndzərə 'our' (pl.) with historical short vowel 51 is spelled once with the ⟨י⟩ grapheme; e.g. אינזרי índzərə (DtZ1723: 10), denoting the u → i shift characteristic of Southeastern and Mideastern dialects of Yiddish (see Herzog 1965a: 165–70; D. Katz 1983: 1029–30). Similarly, the verb banúgn(ən) zəx 'to be content' is also spelled with ⟨י⟩ where it represents the historical long vowel 52; e.g. דען ער לאָזט זיך בניגן dən ər lɔzt zəx baníg̊n 'for he lets himself be satisfied' (DtZ1723: 46). The adverb vi 'as' (cf. the MEY and SEY vi for standard Y. vu 'where', with vowel 52) is in one case spelled with a combination of three *vov* graphemes ⟨װֹא⟩ (ibid. 8) which is extremely unusual, for that period. These spellings are among the earliest known examples of Eastern Yiddish spelling hypercorrections that resulted from the merger of vowels 5_1 and 3_1 into unitary $i_{31/51}$ and of vowels 5_2 with 3_1 into unitary $i \sim \hat{i}_{32/52}$ in Mideastern and Southeastern Yiddish (in the latter with the eventual loss of distinctive vowel-length).

7.1.2 *Evidence for the* ɔ → u *Shift*

Another possibly dialectal spelling is ⟨װֹאיש⟩, representing the pronoun vɔs 'that' (DkZ[1723]: 54, here meaning 'something'; cf. mod. Y. עֶטװֹאָס ɛtvɔs). This spelling may mark the realization vus or vūs. We must remember that in these texts the ⟨ו⟩ grapheme was also used to represent vowels 4_1 (NEY ɔ ‖ MEY ɔ̄/ɔ ‖ SEY ɔ), 4_2 (NEY ej ‖ MEY and SEY ɔj), and 4_4 (NEY ej ‖ MEY and SEY ɔj). However, it seems possible that this spelling reflects the author's u realization of the vowels 1_2 and 1_3 (both yielding NEY ɔ ‖ MEY and SEY u), as we know from Mideastern and Southeastern dialects (see U. Weinreich 1958*b*: 242; D. Katz 1983: 1030).

7.1.3 *Merger of the Historical Vowels* 22 *and* 25

A more precise pinpointing of the author's dialect may be deduced from the spelling ⟨צײן⟩ of the lexeme cejn 'teeth', which appears twice (DkZ[1723]: 51) and of the past participle gəvén (e.g. מתּפֿלל גיװעין mispáləl gəvéjn 'prayed', DkZ[1723], p. 54). Unless the latter spelling is a misprint (cf. מתּפֿלל גיװעזן mispáləl gəvézn̦ on the following line and elsewhere in both texts), it may be viewed as a dialectally 'more phonetic' representation of vowel 25 (NEY ɛ ‖ MEY ej ‖ SEY i/ej). The first spelling, being the representation of vowel 22 (NEY cejn ‖ MEY cajn ‖ SEY cejn), could reflect the author's confusion of vowel 22 with 25. This could have occurred only in some varieties of Southeastern Yiddish (e.g. in 'Bessarabian' Yiddish), where 22 and 25 have merged (see U. Weinreich 1958*b*: 235–6, 240; 1958*c*: 230–1; D. Katz 1983: 1030). The prevailing realization of vowel 25 in the 'Podolian' regions of Southeastern Yiddish was i (see Prilutski 1920*a*: 19–22; Herzog 1969: 62–4). Socio-linguistically the ej realization of this vowel was the preferable one in nineteenth- and twentieth-century Southeastern Yiddish. It is impossible, on the basis of this single case, to determine whether this spelling was motivated by a variety that had ej_{25} or, alternatively, by his socially motivated choice of the more prestigious (already in the eighteenth century?) ej realization.

The number of Eastern Yiddish spellings in these texts is limited to a handful of cases. This may be explained by the author's strong adherence to the general conventions of older Yiddish orthography. No doubt some of the texts that he actually used and that were printed earlier in Western Europe presented him with quite stable patterns of conventional spelling norms.

7.1.4 *Avoidance of Western Spellings of Vowels* 24 *and* 44

It is nevertheless remarkable that both texts avoided the distinctly Western Yiddish orthographic treatment of vowels 24 (NEY ej ‖ MEY aj ‖ SEY ɛj ‖‖ WY ā) and 44 (NEY ej ‖ MEY ɔj ‖ SEY ɔj ‖‖ WY ā). Motivated by their phonemic value in Western Yiddish (see Prilutski 1924*a*: 72–109, 152, 128–30, M. Weinreich 1958: 164 ff.), these vowels were often spelled with the ⟨א⟩ grapheme. This spelling was quite acceptable in the old literary language (see Joffe 1954: 112–14; Sand 1965: 39–40; Timm 1987: 193 §14.3.9; D. Katz 1990: 185). The spelling of kléjdər 'clothes' (vowel 24) was altered from the original dialectal קלאדר klādər (in SF1707) to the interdialectally more agreeable קלײדר /klādər ~ klejdər ~ klajdər ~ klɛjdər/, already found in the Western European re-editions of this book that pre-date our two texts—e.g. *Simkhes hanefesh*, Sulzbach (1718); Amsterdam (1723); Prague [1720–30?] (note, however, that the spelling ⟨ײ⟩ was often used to represent ā or a in pre-eighteenth-century texts; see Timm 1987: 187–8). Similarly, the spelling of lɔjfṇ 'run' (vowel 44) was changed from ⟨לאֿפֿן⟩ /lāfṇ/ to ⟨לוֿיֿפֿן⟩ /lejfṇ ~ lɔjfṇ/ only in the relevant portions of *Derekh tomim* and *Derekh khayim*.

7.1.5 *The Stressed-Vowel System*

The deviant spellings found in both books allow for the following reconstruction of their underlying stressed-vowel system (see Table 8). Vowels in square brackets could not be directly deduced from their graphemic representation in the texts.

Table 8 Reconstruction of the stressed-vowel system in *Derekh tomim* (1723) and *Derekh khayim* (c.1723)

i $_{31/32/51/52}$		u $_{12/13}$
ej $_{22/[24]/25}$		ɔj $_{[42]/44}$
[e $_{21}$]		[ɔ $_{41}$]
	a $_{11/[34]}$	

7.2 Lexicon

7.2.1 Dialectal Forms

Perhaps the most striking Eastern Yiddish feature in both texts is the frequently used dialectal form אילץ ilc for the pronominal adjective אלץ alc 'everything' (Old Literary Yiddish אל(י)ז al(i)s ~ אל(י)ש al(i)z; on אילץ ilc see M. Weinreich 1923: 33; Landau 1924: 57). This dialectal form is discussed in detail by Shmeruk (1979a: 123). Because of its dialectological significance and, for this period, unexpected frequency, Shmeruk commissioned a map, courtesy of Columbia University's *Language and Culture Atlas of Ashkenazic Jewry* (Shmeruk 1979a: 123 n. 5).

Interestingly enough, אילץ ilc and other related forms like אילע ilə 'all; every', אילעמען iləmən 'all; everyone (oblique case)' and their derivatives (see Mark 1971: 1256, 1257; Schaechter 1986: 129–30) can also be found in some locations outside the Southeastern territory, especially in Mideastern Yiddish (see Prilutski 1924b; Shmeruk 1979a: 123) and even in North-eastern Yiddish in Zamut (see Mark 1954: 442) and in Belorussia (see Veynger 1926: 186 on the dialect of Mozyr, close to the border line between NEY and SEY). However, the most important stronghold of this feature was in the Southeast, particularly in the Podolian part of the Southeastern territory. Thus, according to Shmeruk (1979a: 123), a closely related form אילע ilə was 'until recently a distinctly characteristic feature of the Yiddish dialect in the vicinities of Berdichev and Brod'. Likewise the map 'confirms that the most significant concentration of the form אילץ and of its cognates is in the Eastern regions of Poland' (ibid. 123 n. 5).

Other phonetically related and apparently forgotten dialectal forms are the adverbial superlative prefix אים im (cf. mod. Y. אם am ~ צום cum) and the adverb איליין ilajn or ilejn 'alone' (DkZ[1723]: 21; cf. אליין NEY and SEY alejn ‖ MEY alajn). And although the form אים was found only once, the sentence in which it appears leaves little doubt as to its contextual and functional 'meaning':

un hɔt gəgɛbṇ ejnəm šif man un	אונ' האט גינעבן איינם שיף מאן אונ'
hɔt im bəfɔjlṇ vən du kumst	האט אים ביפֿולין ווען דוא קומשט
in jam vu ɛs im tifstṇ iz	אין ים וואו עש אים טיפֿשטן איז
dɔ varf dɔs fas in jam arájn	דא ווארף דאש פֿאס אין ים אריין

'And he gave [it] to the ship captain and urged him: When you come to the sea at its deepest then throw this barrel into the sea.' (DtZ1723: 45; repr. in Shmeruk 1979a: 127)

It is possible that the form אים is semantically related to the preposition אום um (MEY and SEY im; see Mark and Joffe 1966: 509 no. 5). In any case, the existence of the earlier-mentioned dialectal alternation /alə, aləmən, alc, alcdíng/ ~ /ilə, iləmən, ilc, ilcdíng/ in Eastern Yiddish dialects certainly sets a possible pattern for the variations /am tifstņ/ ~ /im tifstņ/ and /alejn/ ~ /ilejn/. It is also possible, however, that the latter two forms are just orthographic variants that follow this pattern. Unlike the case of ilc, the vowels in question are proclitic.

7.2.2 Eastern Yiddish Lexical Items

Another distinctly Eastern Yiddish word is dáv(ə)nən 'pray' that lacks a sound Slavonic or any other etymology (see M. Weinreich 1973: iii. 85–7; Birnbaum 1987; cf. §5 above). This verb was apparently quite well known and perhaps even used in late seventeenth-century Western Europe; however, in works emanating from the West we normally find its Western Yiddish equivalent ɔrņ. In Derekh khayim we find דאַבֿ(ע)ן dáv(ə)nən exclusively, including the passages identical with those of Simkhes hanefesh, in which א(ו)רן ɔrņ was originally used.

In Derekh tomim (p. 54) we also find אַן נמעניש án(n)ɛməniš ~ ɔ́n(n)ɛməniš 'remedy, medicine', which may be a characteristic Eastern Yiddish form (cf. mod. Y. איינ(ג)עמעניש ajn(n)ɛməniš). No attestations from Old Literary Yiddish were given for this item in the Great Dictionary of the Yiddish Language (see Mark 1971: 1186, 1606). But this alone is hardly proof that the word is exclusively of Eastern Yiddish provenance.

7.2.3 Lexical Items of Slavonic Origin

The more discernible and specifically Eastern a feature is, the less likely it is to be found in the older literary language. This is especially evident in the case of items of Slavonic origin. In fact, it took a long time for these to become fully or almost fully acceptable in most styles of the modern literary language in the second half of the nineteenth century. In the early eighteenth century, even in the texts under discussion, lexical items of Slavonic origin are extremely rare. The anonymous author of these texts was apparently only too well aware that these items, otherwise acceptable in his speech, were barred from literary usage.

The apparent absence of such words as xɔčə and nɛbəx from other books belonging to the muser genre (e.g. Simkhes hanefesh and Derekh hayosher leoylem habe; see §6.3) is particularly striking, since both lexical items, though distinctly Eastern, are claimed to be at least partially acceptable in the old literary language (see M. Weinreich 1928: 23; 1973: ii. 256; cf. §5 above). In this context it is remarkable that in both Derekh tomim and Derekh khayim the conjunction האטשי xɔčə 'although' is used quite frequently.

Derekh khayim also contains a few other lexical items of Slavonic origin that the author either failed to avoid or alternatively felt impelled to use in order to be more precisely understood, on the assumption that his more immediate readership was one that *spoke* Eastern Yiddish. Thus kɛšənəs 'pockets' (cf. Pol. *kieszeń*, Ukr. кишеня), spelled קעשנוש and קעשונוש, occur in *Derekh khayim* (p. 40), whereas the Western Yiddish טעשן tɛšn̩ (cf. mod. Yiddish טאשן tašn̩) was used in the parallel portion of the source-text (SF1707: 132). A sample of lexical items of Slavonic origin that were found in *Derekh khayim* is provided in Table 9.

Table 9 Lexical items of Slavonic origin in *Derekh khayim* (c.1723)

		Transcription	Gloss	Page
1	לאטי	latə	patch	57
	לאטום	latəs	patches	57
2	לולקי	lulkə	smoking pipe	84
3	סמעטני	smɛtənə	sour cream	63
4	קוליטשן	kɔjləčn̩	twisted loaves	64
5	קעשונוש/קעשנוש	kɛšənəs	pockets	40
6	רוזינקש	rózinkes ~ róžinkes	raisins	82

(1) cf. Pol. *łata*, Ukr. лата, St.Y. לאטע latə; לאטום replaces ⟨פלינג⟩ flɛkn̩ 'stains'(?) or flikn̩ 'tears, breaches'(?) of *Simkhes hanefesh* (SF1707: 143 a).

(2) cf. Pol. *lulka*, Ukr. люлька; St.Y. לולקע lulkə.

(3) cf. Pol. *śmietana*, Ukr. сметана; St.Y. סמעטענע smɛtənə.

(4) cf. Pol. *kołacz*, Ukr. калач; St.Y. קוילעטש kɔjləč 'twisted loaf'; see also Kosover 1958: 123–5.

(5) cf. Pol. *kieszeń*, Ukr. кишеня; St.Y. קעשענעס kɛšənəs; replaces טעשן tɛšn̩ of *Simkhes hanefesh* (SF1707: 132).

(6) cf. Pol. *rodzinki*, Ukr. родзинки; St.Y. ראזשינקעס róžinkes.

In *Derekh tomim* (p. 8) we also find another, etymologically disguised Slavism firárbət 'he earns; deserves', spelled פֿר ארבייט. This is apparently a calque from Slavic (cf. Pol. *zapracować*, Ukr. заробляти). Although the modern Yiddish fardínən is used far more often than firárbətn̩, the latter is attested in Lifshits's *Yiddish–Russian Dictionary* (1876: 146; פֿאראַרביטן farárbətn̩ 'earn'), which is usually a good indication that it was used in Southeastern Yiddish of the mid-nineteenth century and earlier.

7.3 Morphology

Many important morphological features peculiar to these two texts point to underlying Eastern dialectal forms, although it is difficult to say which one of the dialects (e.g. Southeastern or Mideastern Yiddish) was the actual source for given usages.

7.3.1 *Past Participles*

In contrast to *Simkhes hanefesh*, the past participle of strong verbs usually receives the gə- prefix in *Derekh tomim*. Thus, where the source-text, *Simkhes hanefesh*, has גאנגן gángən 'went' and געבן gɛbn̩ 'gave', *Derekh tomim* (p. 22) replaces them with גיגאנגן gəgángən and גגעבן gəgɛbn̩.

7.3.2 *Diminutive Forms*

Another striking difference between our two texts and their Western Yiddish antecedents is evident in the morphology of diminutive forms. The form שטיקלי štikxə or štikjə 'piece' that was used earlier in *Simkhes hanefesh* was replaced by the Eastern Yiddish שטיקל štikl̩ (DtZ, 22). The same variation is found in *Derekh khayim*, where the diminutives שפעלטלי špɛltxə 'slot' and לעכלי lɛxlxə 'little hole' (of SF1707: 143a) were replaced by שפעלטל špɛlt̩l and לעכל lɛxl̩ (DkZ, 57). Likewise, all other diminutives found in *Derekh khayim* consistently follow the Eastern Yiddish pattern of diminutive formation: e.g. ליכטל lixtl̩ or lɛxtl̩ 'candle' (ibid. 56); שנירל šnir̩l 'string, lace' (ibid. 57); קערנדיל kɛrn̩dl̩ 'kernel' and קערנדלך kɛrn̩dlax 'kernels' (ibid. 58); קערבלך kɛrblax 'small baskets' (ibid. 82).

7.3.3 *Forms Introduced from the Spoken Language*

The form האפֿונג hófung 'hope' in *Derekh tomim* (p. 22) that replaces האפנונג hóf(ə)nung in SF1707 is levelled on the pattern {stem + *ung*} (cf. mod. Y. שרייבונג šrájbung 'writing'; לערנונג lérnung 'learning; instruction'). This formation was apparently introduced from the author's spoken language. Other Eastern Yiddish forms found in both texts are בלייט baléjt 'he accompanies' (DtZ, 22) and בילייטן bəléjtn̩ 'accompany' (DkZ, 39). They conform with modern spoken Yiddish באלייטן baléjtn̩ ~ balájtn̩ (see Lifshits 1876: 53; Schaechter 1986: 283), although in modern literary usage באגלייטן bagléjtn̩ became far more frequent.

7.3.4 *The Definite Article: Merger of Accusative and Dative*

The total merger of dative neutral with accusative and dative masculine forms of the definite article, yielding unitary dəm, occurred in Eastern Yiddish dialects long before it became attested in the literary language. There is significant variation that itself testifies to the fact that in the author's spoken language both forms became syncretic. It seems that his choice to employ דען dən rather than דעם dəm for the accusative depended on his varying degree of faithfulness to the actual source-texts that he had at hand. At times he is less faithful to his textual sources, and as a result replaces the older Western Yiddish accusative dən with its Eastern Yiddish equivalent dəm; thus the original זיצן אויף דען מישט zicn̩ af dən mist 'sitting on garbage' and פֿארלאַנגט דען טויט farlángt dən tɔjt 'wished to die' in SF1707 turn up in *Derekh tomim* (p. 22) as זיצן אויף דעם מישט zicn̩ af dəm mist and פֿאַרלאַנגט דעם טויט farlángt dəm tɔjt.

7.3.5 *Old and New Forms*
The same may be said of the present third-person singular forms of the verbs געבן gɛbn̩ 'give' and זען zɛn 'see'. Whereas the forms גיבט gibt '(he) gives' and זיכֿט zixt '(he) sees' can often be found in both texts, the more modern variants (and the only possible ones in Modern Literary Yiddish) גיט git and זעהט zɛt / zejt (e.g. DtZ, 22; DkZ, 34) in fact replace the original גיבט gibt and זיכֿט zixt of *Simkhes hanefesh* (e.g. SF1707: 128a).

7.3.6 *The Relative Pronouns*
In both texts the older types of relative pronouns (דער/די/דעם(ע)ר/דיש/דש (דא) dər /di /dɔs (dɔ) 'that; which; who', are often employed alongside the newer indeclinable general relative pronoun וואָש vɔs (on the latter see M. Weinreich 1973: ii. 278). But in both books, especially when compared with their Western Yiddish textual sources, there is a further expansion in the employment of vɔs as a general relative pronoun; e.g.

dər májnstər zɔl dəm zélbikn̩	דער מיינשטר זאל דעם זעלביגן
mɛnč vɔs im vərt ɔ́pgɛbn̩	מענש וואש אים ווערט אב געבן
dəm briv in káləx ɔjvn̩ varfn̩	דעם בריוו אין קאלך אויבן ווארפֿין

'the craftsman should throw into the lime kiln the person who will deliver to him this very letter'. (DtZ, 35)

For early manifestations of the undeclining relative pronoun in the literary language, Max Weinreich (1973: iv. 326) refers to early nineteenth-century Eastern Yiddish literary texts (see also Joffe 1940: 97–8). However, vɔs as a relative pronoun can be found in much earlier texts, as far back as in the late seventeenth century. Considerable competition between the older and the newer types of relative pronouns can also be traced in these two texts from the early eighteenth century.

7.3.7 *Verbal Aspect*

Among the most significant Eastern Yiddish features found in both texts are the aspectually differentiated verbal forms (see Schaechter 1951; U. Weinreich 1952*b*; Lockwood-Baviskar 1974; Wexler 1964; 1972; Rothstein 1990). A preliminary examination of *Derekh khayim* and parallel portions in *Simkhes hanefesh* revealed that *Derekh khayim* often replaced neutral (simple) verbs with their aspectually marked, perfective forms. For example, קליִאן מן מוז muz mən klíən 'one must make (it) glow' (SF1707: 143 a) is rendered גליִאן אויס מן מוז muz mən ɔ́jsgliən (DkZ, 57; cf. modern Yiddish אָנגליִען מען מוז muz mən ɔ́ngliən).

The following are samples of some of the more distinct aspectually marked forms:

1 **With the prefix** אויש ɔjs
   1.1 וואַשׁן אויש ɔ́jsvàšn̩ 'wash' (perf.) (DkZ, 56)
   1.2 ווישׁן אויש ɔ́jsvìšn̩ 'dry, wipe' (perf.) (ibid. 48)
   1.3 קוועטשׁין אויש ɔ́jskvɛtšn̩ 'squeeze out' (ibid. 46).

2 **With the prefix** אב ɔp
   2.1 גיגעשׁן אב ɔ́(p)gəgɛsn̩ 'ate' (perf.) (ibid. 56);
   2.2 געבן צו אב ɔ́pcugɛbn̩ 'to give (perf.); return' (ibid. 57);
        אב גיב gib ɔ́p 'return' (imper.) (ibid. 35);
   2.3 כשׁרן צו אב ɔ́pcukašern̩ 'to prepare [utensils] for Passover', also in past tense
        גיכשׁרת אב ɔ́(p)gəkašərt (ibid. 57);
   2.4 וואַשׁן אב ɔ́pvašn̩ 'to wash off' (ibid. 59).

3 **With the prefix** פֿר far-
   3.1 *זיך רעדן פֿר *farédn̩ zəx 'forget oneself, blunder (in speaking)'; e.g.
        ניט זיך מן רעט פֿר שוויִיגן מיט mit švajgn̩ farét mən zəx nit 'he who keeps silent does not forget himself in chatter' (DtZ, 40).

Some of these prefixed verbs could have been employed at that time in Western Yiddish dialects as well. However, in Eastern Yiddish the whole aspect system was drastically restructured due to the overwhelming semantic and morpho-syntactic impact of the co-territorial Slavonic languages (cf. §§28.3.3.5 and 35.10). It is also evident from the context that in both books, *Derekh khayim* and *Derekh tomim*, the prefixed verbs are employed as aspectually marked perfective forms, in opposition to the simple, unprefixed, and thus imperfective forms of the same verbs (e.g. *kvɛtšn̩ vs. ɔ́jskvɛtšn̩; vašn̩ vs. ɔ́jsvašn̩ vs. ɔ́pvašn̩; ɛsn̩ vs. ɔ́pɛsn̩; gɛbn̩ vs. ɔ́pgɛbn̩; kášərn̩ vs. ɔ́pkašərn̩). As for spoken Yiddish in Eastern Europe, it is reasonable to suppose that by the eighteenth century the verbal aspect system had by and large reached its present stage. It is even possible that for some Eastern Yiddish speakers the employment of verb prefixation for aspectual marking was also acceptable with the periphrastic or 'inherently analytic' verbs (on these verbs see D. Katz 1987a: 172–5):

un mə gəhɛrt gəvɔrn̩t cu zajn	אונ׳ מן גיהערט גיוואַרנט צו זיין
nit cu rejdn̩ fun dər brɔxə ɔn biz	ניט צו רידן פֿון דר ברכה אן ביז
ər hɔt ɔ́jsbɔjdək gəvézn	ער האָט אויש בודק גיוועזין

'And one should be careful not to speak from the time he said the blessing until he completed the [ceremonial] search [for leavened dough, on the day before Passover]'. (DkZ, 56)

Such prefixation did not become acceptable in modern Yiddish, where this device is productive only with simple verbs. Thus the modern equivalent of the above-mentioned periphrastic perfective ɔ́jsbɔjdək zajn is the prefixed simple form אויסבדקנען ɔ́jsbadkə(nə)n. On the other hand, the very fact that so-called aspectual stem constructions (i.e. forms such as *a šrajb tɔn or *gɛbn̩ a kuk to express instantaneous action) are absent from both these texts may indicate their relatively late development (see Taube 1987; below §35.9.1). It is possible that the grammaticalization of the 'stem construction' took place in Eastern Yiddish at a later stage (perhaps in the late eighteenth century) after aspectual verb prefixation became fully developed. If so, then a formation such as *ɔ́jsbɔjdək gəvɛzn̩ might have been structurally more viable in the period when the *Aktionsart*, or aspect of instantaneous action, was not yet paradigmatically expressed by special stem constructions. This, of course, is no more than speculation, based on just one case of aspectual periphrastic verb prefixation. Moreover, the absence of aspectually marked stem constructions in the texts discussed does not necessarily mean that these did not exist in the spoken Eastern Yiddish of that period.

7.4 Semantic Change

Both texts, when compared with their Western Yiddish sources, will reveal a few lexical replacements indicating some of the fundamental variations in meaning and subsequently in vocabulary. Perhaps the most striking among these is the systematically effected replacement of the verb דארפֿן (ניט //ניקש) (nit//niks) darfn̩ 'allowed; (with negation) forbidden' with מעגן mɛgn̩ and with its anomalous negative ניט טאָרן nit tɔ́rn̩. Whereas דארפֿן darfn̩ is often employed in *Simkhes hanefesh* (e.g. SF1707: 131, 136) in the sense of 'to be allowed, permitted', the anonymous author of *Derekh khayim* insists on replacing it with מעגן mɛgn̩ (DkZ, 40 and elsewhere) and ניט טאָרן nit tɔrn̩ (ibid. 50 and elsewhere) respectively. On the other hand, he does use dárfn̩ (or dafn̩) in its modern sense 'have to' (ibid. 42).

7.5 Syntax

One of the most salient features of the changing grammar of literary Yiddish in the eighteenth century is the restructuring of word-order patterns in certain types of main clauses and in most of the subordinate clauses. In this respect both texts show significant variation by employing both the older literary standard and the emerging more flexible types of syntactic constructions characteristic of modern Eastern Yiddish.

7.5.1 *Verb First Place*

The origins of the 'consecutive' main clauses with the finite verb in first place remain unclear. (On this type of main clause see Zaretski 1929: 235; Falkovitsh 1940: 294; Mark 1978: 377–9; D. Katz 1987*a*: 236.) Each one of the stock languages has constructions with verbs taking first place in the main clause. However, in High German (see Henzen 1954²: 74; Lockwood 1968: 265–8; Scaglione 1981: 177; Wells 1985: 252–3) such main consecutive clauses are far from frequent in literary usage, and are often felt to be 'incorrect' or left unobserved by the grammarians (see Faucher 1984: 50 ff.; cf. also his discussion of Yiddish apropos verb first place in German, 59–61). Hebrew and the relevant Slavonic languages, while offering many possible patterns for such word order, do not share the much more rigorous Germanic 'verb second place' conventions. In this context modern Yiddish developed an important syntactic device for higher-level text organization that exceeds the limits of a single sentence. Within the framework of generative grammar it has been analysed as topicalization (see Waletzky 1980 for a generative analysis of Yiddish word order; cf. also Besten and Moed-van Walraven 1986).

Although such main clauses can be found in older Yiddish literary texts (e.g. *Lev tov*, 1620; *Kav hayosher*, 1705–6), it seems that on the whole the only 'correct' pattern to follow was the consecutive construction with the initial adverbs דא do, אזו azó(j) or זו zo, נון nun, and their likes (cf. especially such classical narrative texts as the *Mayse bukh* (Basle, 1602), and *Tsene rene* (Hanau, 1622). In fact, we find that in the eighteenth-century re-editions of *Lev tov* (Amsterdam, 1705 and 1723) these adverbs (usually דא do, and less frequently זו zo) were inserted in most of the main consecutive clauses by the anonymous 'style-editor'. My contention is that such clauses with the finite verb in first place were often used in the spoken language in Western and Eastern Europe, but were generally suppressed in literary usage.

It is thus not surprising that the increasing introduction of such main clauses, often replacing the older, standard construction with the initial adverb (see Shmeruk 1981: 154; cf. below §13.6), became one of the central syntactic hallmarks of nascent Modern Literary Yiddish. Naturally, such constructions can be found mostly in the more narrative *Derekh tomim*. However, having before his eyes other Western Yiddish texts, as well as apparently being aware of the older general convention to avoid such clauses in writing, the anonymous author usually employed consecutive main clauses with an initial adverb אזו azó(j), דא dɔ, or נון nun. Yet, we find in this book several main clauses starting with the finite verb, three times on page 28, once each on pages 36 and 45, and twice on page 55. Main consecutive clauses are also found in the two stories from *Simkhes hanefesh* (DtZ, 20-1 and 22) where these appeared already in the original text.

7.5.2 *Subordinate Clauses*

Some of the most significant examples of the restructured word order of subordinate clauses can easily be found in *Derekh khayim* in comparison with its main source. Here are two examples:

1 װען איינר קומט אין איין שטאט װאו מן טראגן דארף
 vən ejnər kumt in a štɔt vu mən trɔgṇ darf (SF1707: 131a) →
װען איינר קומט אין איין שטאט װאו מן מאג טראגן
vən ejnər kumt in a štɔt vu mən mɛg trɔgṇ (DkZ, 40)
'when one comes to a town where it is allowed to carry [on the Sabbath]';

2 אפֿילו װען מן געלט גיפֿינד דארף מן ניט אויף נעמן
afilə vən mən gɛlt gəfind darf mən nit úfnɛmən (SF1707: 131a) →
אפֿילו װען מן גיפֿינד געלט טאר מן אוך ניט אויף הייבן
afilə vən mən gəfind gɛlt tɔr mən ɔjx nit úfhejbṇ (DkZ, 40)
'even if one finds money [on the Sabbath] he is not allowed to pick [it] up'.

In another syntactic 'improvement' the author of *Derekh khayim* replaces the relative clause with a noun phrase complementing the direct object. At the same time he leaves intact the verb of the original clause, which in the context of modern Yiddish can be reinterpreted as the general 'fictitious' or 'blank' copular form איז iz that introduces, and syntagmatically belongs to, the main clause (see Zaretski 1927: 79-82; Kahan-Newman 1988).

3 װען מן זיכֿט איין רבֿ דר א איין גרושר תלמיד חכם איז מאכֿט מן ברכה [. . .]
vən mən zixt a rɔv dər a grɔjsər tálməd xóxəm iz [,]maxt mən bróxə (SF1707: 1b) →
װען מן זעהט איין רבֿ איין גרושן תלמיד חכם איז מאכֿט מן דיא ברכה [. . .]
vən mən zɛt a rɔv a grɔjsṇ tálməd xóxəm [,] iz maxt mən di bróxə (DkZ, 34)
'when one sees a rabbi who is a great learned man he shall say the [following] benediction [. . .]'.

In modern Yiddish this type of איז iz can hardly be viewed as a verb. It does not change according to number or person, and may even come immediately before a finite verb (cf. Kahan-Newman 1988: 81, 89 no. 5). Falkovitsh

(1940: 293–4) regards it more properly as a 'particle', although he does not recommend using it immediately before the finite verb.

7.6 Summary

Both books, *Derekh tomim* and *Derekh khayim*, introduce many Eastern Yiddish features into literary usage. These are features that were by and large stylistically unacceptable in the old literary language. On the other hand, the anonymous author of these texts was working within the literary framework of the older Yiddish *muser* and *minhogim* genre. His most direct textual sources were the early eighteenth-century *muser* collections written and printed primarily in Western Europe. Therefore we are in a fortunate position in being able to contrast large portions of these texts with the language of their immediate sources. At present it is possible to gauge the most significant linguistic changes by dividing them into two principal groups, each of which is conditioned by the varying degree of the author's faithfulness to his textual sources.

The first group consists of the few sporadic linguistic changes that usually appear in the passages in which the author remained more faithful to his sources at hand. The most important of these changes are a number of dialectally motivated deviations from Old Yiddish spelling conventions. These exceptional spellings (see §7.1) are significant indications of the direct impact that the phonology of Eastern Yiddish (most likely of Southeastern or Mideastern Yiddish) had on the written language of the anonymous author of that time and place.

More illuminating is the second group of changes. It consists of the numerous, often systematically effected, alterations and, from the point of view of literary Yiddish, innovations in the realms of lexicon (see §7.2), morphology (§7.3), semantics (§7.4), and syntax (§7.5). These changes often conform to the various Eastern Yiddish features characteristic of those passages that may be considered original, or at least textually unprecedented in the direct textual sources of *Derekh tomim* and *Derekh khayim* (see §6.3).

The question as to whether the author aimed primarily at an Eastern European readership and was therefore more likely to introduce many Eastern Yiddish features into literary usage must remain open. However, the significance of these features in both books which were compiled, written, and printed in Eastern Europe of the 1720s cannot be overestimated. These two books substantially pre-date the actual rise and subsequent flourishing of Yiddish printing in Eastern Europe, which began only in the last quarter of the eighteenth century.

One may thus ponder whether the actual rise of Modern Literary Yiddish would have evolved sooner, had the conditions for the revival of Yiddish printing in Eastern Europe been more favourable in the first half of the eighteenth century or earlier.

The fact remains, however, that *Derekh tomim* and *Derekh khayim*, the two Eastern European Yiddish books from the early eighteenth century, already introduce some of the most significant elements of Eastern Yiddish into literary usage. Retrospectively, these are the earliest known printed texts in which we find the origins of what was later to evolve into Modern Literary Yiddish.

PART II

Transition: Easternization of Old Literary Yiddish

8 Preface

The changing literary Yiddish of eighteenth-century Eastern Europe may be described in terms of transition, and of shift from the old literary to the nascent modern literary language. The shift is evident in the new Eastern Yiddish translations of *Ben hameylekh vehanozir* (Zholkve, 1771; see Chapter 6) and *Seyfer khsidem* (Zholkve, 1776), as well as in the 'Eastern version' of *Mayse gdoyle min Uman* (Novidvor(?), c.1783; see Chapter 7) and *Avkes roykhl* (Horodne, 1795), that are written wholly in Eastern Yiddish. (On the language of the extant late eighteenth-century Eastern Yiddish books see Chapter 8.)

Another significant group of texts that mark the transition from the old to the modern literary language was subjected to increasing linguistic modernization. In terms of Yiddish dialectology they may be viewed as literary monuments of 'Easternized' Yiddish. These are the late eighteenth-century Eastern European reprints, re-editions, and revisions of works originally published in Old Literary Yiddish. The original language of these works was revised by the anonymous printers, typesetters or publishers who saw these re-editions into print (see Shmeruk 1978: 178-9). The most salient feature of these linguistic revisions was the increasingly systematic replacement of many Western and Old Literary Yiddish forms by their Eastern Yiddish equivalents.

This process of linguistic modernization of Old Yiddish works did not reach its peak until the first half of the nineteenth century, when many of the Eastern Yiddish revisions became more and more systematic and far-reaching, to the point that their linguistic make-up was principally based on modern Eastern Yiddish. At this stage these re-editions were also supported by some newly issued translations of traditional Jewish literary texts directly into modern Eastern Yiddish (e.g. *Khoyves levoves* (Sadilkov, 1820); cf. Yaari 1936; Roskies 1974a: 5; the *Makhzer* (Berditshev, 1818); cf. Shtif 1928: 41 n. 8, 43-6; Liberman 1980: ii. 148). However, the actual initiation of this process can be traced clearly to the last quarter of the eighteenth century.

The earliest known eighteenth-century Eastern European reprints of older literary texts started to appear from the 1750s; e.g. *Nakhles Tsvi* (Zholkve, 1750); *Khoyves halevoves* (Zholkve, 1759); *Seyfer hayire* (Zholkve, 1760) and *Lev tov* (Zholkve, 1777). Many of these reprints are linguistically, although not always systematically, revised versions of older texts previously published from the sixteenth century onwards elsewhere in Eastern, Central, and Western Europe. The extent to which the original language was updated or Easternized allows us to classify all Eastern European editions into (a) EASTERN REPRINTS with minimal linguistic changes; (b) EASTERN RE-EDITIONS with many more systematic linguistic changes and alterations; (c) EASTERN REVISIONS in which the original old literary language was substantially revised in accordance with the morphological and syntactic patterns of modern Eastern Yiddish.

The earliest Eastern European linguistic revision of an older Yiddish text to have been examined is the Lemberg (1786) edition of the popular Yiddish collection of homiletic prose *Tsene rene*. The need for a systematic comparative linguistic examination of these texts has often been enunciated in the field of Yiddish philology (e.g. Reyzen 1932: 176–9; Shtif 1932a: 5 ff.; M. Weinreich 1940a: 62; Joffe 1940: 88 ff.). These Eastern reprints, re-editions, and revisions are of paramount importance for research on the origins of Modern Literary Yiddish, not least because they provide us with the unique opportunity of following the transition in action.

There has been no exhaustive examination of these Eastern editions of Old Yiddish texts from the late eighteenth and early nineteenth centuries. (A summary of linguistic comparison between the Western and Eastern editions of *A sheyne vunderlekhe historye fun a fisher zayn zun* ⟨AT 400⟩ is provided in Timm 1988: 57–60.) It is hoped that Part II of this book will contribute towards establishing the framework for such an examination. More specifically, Part II is devoted to a close linguistic study of four representative eastern editions from the late eighteenth century:

(a) the two Eastern re-editions of *Kav hayosher* (*editio princeps*, Frankfurt am Main, 1705) that appeared in Zholkve in 1777 (KZ1777) and in Novidvor in 1788 (KN1788) (see Chapter 2);

(b) the earliest Eastern revision of an old Yiddish literary work, the Lemberg (1786) edition of *Tsene rene* (TL1786) (see Chapter 3);

(c) the Eastern reprint of *Simkhes hanefesh* (*editio princeps*, Frankfurt am Main, 1707) that was published in Shklov in 1796 (SSh1796) (see Chapter 4).

2

The Late Eighteenth-Century Eastern Re-editions
of *Kav hayosher*

9 The Original Work and its Language

Kav hayosher is one of the larger *muser* collections that were published in the first decades of the eighteenth century. (On this genre in the older Yiddish literature see §6.1.) Its author, the famous kabbalist Tsvi-Hirsh Koidonover (d. 1712), was himself a native speaker of Eastern Yiddish, born in Vilna. He wrote *Kav hayosher* in both Hebrew and Yiddish, and published it in a bilingual edition in Frankfurt am Main, the first volume appearing in 1705, the second in 1706. (On this book see Erik 1928: 309–11; Tsherikover 1932; Zfatman 1987: 82–3.) Like many other bilingual texts of the pre-modern period, this work merits a separate study of the various discrepancies between the Hebrew and the Yiddish versions and of their possible socio-linguistic implications (cf. the discrepancies cited in Zfatman 1987: 83–6 nn. 4, 9–10, 12–15, 17, 19–21).

Despite the underlying Eastern Yiddish of its author, *Kav hayosher* is written in the Old Literary Yiddish of its day. This may be explained by the vitality of the old literary language in the early eighteenth century, as well as by the fact that for various periods Tsvi-Hirsh Koidonover lived in Germany, where he became acquainted with Western Yiddish. It is noteworthy that his son-in-law Elkhonon (Henele) Kirkhhahn (born in Kirchhahn), a native speaker of Western Yiddish, was the author of another important *muser* collection, *Simkhes hanefesh* (see Chapter 4). It is also important to note that Tsvi-Hirsh Koidonover was apparently well read in other classics of the Old Yiddish *muser* genre, and that some of the principal sources of *Kav hayosher* were works written in Old Literary Yiddish (e.g. *Mayse bukh* (Basle, 1602) and *Derekh hayosher leoylem habe* (Frankfurt am Main, 1704); on this book see §6.3).

It is therefore not surprising that the language of *Kav hayosher* is so well shielded from Eastern Yiddish. Indeed, whatever Eastern features can be safely discerned in the original language of *Kav hayosher* must be considered as unintended deviations from the old literary norm. A separate examination of such features, especially on the morphological level, would elucidate the possible influences of the author's spoken Eastern Yiddish upon his literary language (some observations to this effect are offered in §§11.3.1.1, 11.3.1.3, 11.3.2.1, 11.3.3.8, 11.6.1, 28.3.2.1). Such an examination, however relevant to the subject, lies outside the scope of the present study, for *Kav hayosher* was not intended primarily for speakers of Eastern Yiddish, as was apparently the case with *Derekh tomim* and *Derekh khayim*, and its style and language remained principally unreceptive to most of the fundamental Eastern Yiddish features found in these two books.

In his general bibliography of Hebrew books Friedberg (1951: 882 no. 26) lists ten bilingual (Hebrew and Yiddish) editions of *Kav hayosher*. To these we may add those published in Frankfurt am Main in 1705–6 (KF1705; cf. Joffe 1934), Zholkve in 1777 (KZ1777), and Novidvor in 1788 (KN1788). Friedberg also lists seven monolingual Yiddish editions of the book printed between 1713 and 1817. Of these only the last is known to have been printed in Eastern Europe, in Lashchov.

The Zholkve re-edition of 1777 contains a somewhat abridged version of the first volume of *Kav hayosher*. It ends with Chapter 43, whereas the original and the Novidvor editions of 1788 of the first volume end with Chapter 53. The Novidvor re-edition of the first volume usually follows the text, orthography, and language of the earlier Zholkve re-edition. However, in the second volume Novidvor is closer to the second edition of the book (Frankfurt am Main, 1709–10 (KF1709)). So it seems that the Novidvor publisher relied primarily on the earlier Zholkve re-edition for the printing of the first volume, while for the second volume he had to use one of the Western European editions independently.

The text sequences used in our examination show that certain passages of the original *Kav hayosher* were abridged in the Zholkve and Novidvor re-editions (on later East European editions see Zfatman 1987: 83 n. 4). The sequences examined comprise parts of both volumes, as well as Chapters 25 and 69 in their entirety; references are to lines (see Appendix 2, pp. 265–72 for Chapter 25, and pp. 272–8 for Chapter 69) unless specified otherwise. KF alone refers to both Frankfurt editions. These two Chapters were photomechanically reproduced from the Frankfurt am Main (KF1709) edition by Zfatman (1974: 28–31 and 34–5). More recently Chapter 69 was published as 'Mayse Pozna' on the basis of the first bilingual edition of *Kav hayosher* (KF1705) in Zfatman (1987: 131–7; the original is reproduced there on pp. 168–71).

10　The Early Western Editions

The changes found in KF1709 are mainly in orthography and morphology. The number of lexical and syntactic alterations is minimal. The second edition appeared only four years after the first, when Tsvi-Hirsh Koidonover was still alive; but the changes introduced are particularly characteristic of the language of Western Yiddish prints of the eighteenth century.

10.1　Orthography

KF1709 tends towards a more regular orthographic representation of most of the unstressed vowels, the spelling of which is optional in KF1705 (the changes shown are: KF1705 → KF1709); e.g. דער שראקן → דר שראקן dəršrəkn̩ 'frightened' (73); בהיטן → ביהיטן bahítn̩ 'guard; keep safe' (7); דרייסג → דרייסיג drájsik 'thirty' (44). The same applies to most of the inter-consonantal stressed a/ɔ vowels; e.g. צוונציג → צוואנציג cváncik 'twenty' (44); האב → הב hɔb 'have' (1st pers. sing.; 191); האט → הט hɔt 'has'.

The orthographic representation of posttonic shewa and of the posttonic interconsonantal ə vowels was by and large abolished in KF1709; e.g. גיווזין → גיווזן gəvézn̩ 'was; been' (p.p., 33, 35, 47); גיטראגן → גיטראגין gətrɔgn̩ 'bear; bore' (p.p., 14); זיינין → זיינן zájnən 'are' (3rd pers. pl., 208, 382); אליז → אלז alz 'constantly' (adv., 168, 221; cf. mod. Y. אלץ alc) or 'that; as' (conj., 252, cf. mod. Y. אז az).

Finally, the employment of the grapheme ⟨ו⟩ for stressed ɔ (vowel 41) was discontinued in KF1709: זולט → זאלט zɔlt 'shall' (2nd pers. pl., 131, 245); זולבי → זאלבי zɔlxə 'such' (193, 215; cf. mod. Y. azélxə).

With regard to consonant representation KF1709 sometimes substitutes ⟨פ̄⟩ for the older spelling convention ⟨פֿפ⟩ representing the syllable initial f: פפערד → פ̄ערד fɛrd 'horse' (90).

10.2　Phonology

The peculiar spelling ⟨אוי⟩ of vowel 54 that often occurs in KF1705 apparently reflects the author's efforts to represent this vowel in line with its modified New High German realization. In KF1709 this spelling was normally replaced by the more conventional ⟨וי⟩ grapheme:

לאויטר → לויטר lɔjtər 'whole', 129, 189, 197, 207
(cf. Western Yiddish lɔutər, NHG *lauter*);

מאויל → מויל mɔjl 'mouth', Ch. 6, KF1705: 23; KF1709: 27
(cf. Western Yiddish mɔul, NHG *Maul*);

פֿראוי → פֿרוי frɔj 'Mrs, wife', 424, 432
(cf.Western Yiddish frɔu ~ frā, NHG *Frau*);

זאוימט זיך → זוימט זיך zɔjmt zəx 'tarries', 431
(cf. Western Yiddish zɔumt zəx, NHG *säumen*).

By contrast, the orthographic representation of the stressed vowel in the following past-participle forms shows that their preferred underlying phonemic realization in KF1709 was influenced by the New High German pattern: ביפֿולין → בפֿאלן bafɔjlņ 'ordered', 126 (cf. NHG *befohlen*); גיצאגין gəcɔjgņ 'moved', 338, 346 (in both editions, cf. NHG *gezogen*).

The Western Yiddish dialectal spelling of vowel **24** often remained intact in KF1709, at least in the case of the past-participle form ⟨גיקֿאֿפֿט⟩ gəkāft (WY) ‖ gəkɔjft (EY) 'bought' (e.g. 497 and in Ch. 6, KF1705: 24; KF1709: 28).

In neither edition do historically front-rounded vowels have special orthographic representation. As can be seen from the case of the verb kušņ 'to kiss', the vowel in question could be represented by one of two graphemic alternants, ⟨ו⟩ or ⟨י⟩: ⟨קישט⟩ 'kisses' (478); ⟨קושט⟩ '(he) kisses'; ⟨קיסטין⟩ 'they kissed' (last two examples from Ch. 6, KF1705: 23; KF1709: 27).

10.3 Morphology

The changes in morphology, though not as numerous, are often systematic. They point clearly to underlying Western Yiddish and New High German models. Thus almost all the third-person plural possessive adjectives, zejər 'their' (sing.) and zejər(ə) 'their' (pl.), were replaced by the Western Yiddish or New High German equivalents ir and irə; e.g. זיער אייגיני zejər ejgənə → איר אייגיני ir ejgənə, 'their own' (sing.) (238); זיער מעשים zejər majsəm → אירע מעשים irə majsəm, 'their deeds' (128). Similarly, in most instances איז iz, the third-person singular form of the verb zajn 'to be', was replaced by איזט izt, which is closer to its New High German parallel *ist* (e.g. 18, 42, 56, 75, 258). However, the form איזט is sometimes found in the first edition as well (e.g. 53, 252).

Other alterations in morphology are less frequent, though by no means less significant. These include the following changes:

גיפֿונן gəfunən → גיפֿונדן gəfundņ 'found' (p.p., 331);
גיפֿינן gəfinən → גיפֿינדן gəfindņ 'find' (1st pers. pl., Ch. 6, KF1705: 23; KF1709: 27);
גיווארין gəvɔrņ → גיוווארדן gəvɔrdņ 'became' (Ch. 6, KF1705: 23; KF1709: 27);
האט hɔt → האבט hɔbt 'have' (2nd pers. pl., 184).

10.4 Lexicon

In the chapters under discussion only one lexical change is found. It is גאויל
(KF1705, WY *gɔul/gōl; cf. NHG *Gaul*, non-existent in modern Yiddish),
which is replaced in KF1709 by what seems to be the more common Yiddish
equivalent פֿערד fɛrd 'horse' (64). The spelling of the noun kin(d)pət 'childbirth, labour' is apparently more 'phonetic' in the first edition (cf. mod. Y
קימפּעט kimpət). In the second it was replaced by the more etymological and
apparently more conventional spelling, i.e. ⟨קינדפּעט⟩ → ⟨קינדבעט⟩ (53; cf.
קינדבעטרי[ן] kin(d)bətərn̩ 'woman in childbirth', 100, 124; mod. Y.
קימפּעטאָרן kímpətɔrn̩).

10.5 Syntax

Changes in syntax were minimal. This may be explained by the fact that as
regards main clauses, the original text of *Kav hayosher* is written in line with
the main requirements of word order current in the literary Yiddish of that
period. The only syntactic change is the introduction of the 'inflected' form
of the indefinite article, which apparently mirrors a New High German
pattern: אײן ראײיה נעמן a rajə nɛmən → אײין ראײיה נעמן ajnən rajə nɛmən 'to
take an example' (275).

Unlike the Eastern re-editions, KF1709 tends to normalize the language of
Kav hayosher in accordance with the general requirements of Yiddish literary
usage that prevailed in the late seventeenth and eighteenth centuries in
Western Europe. The number of dialectal Western Yiddish features introduced into, or preserved in, KF1709 is minimal. On the other hand, almost
all alterations made in KF1709 reflect the growing impact of contemporary
New High German upon the literary Yiddish of that place and period.

The Eastern re-editions, on the other hand, are much more extensively
revisionist in morphology and, up to a point, in syntax. Together with
some Eastern Yiddish dialectal spellings, they point towards the increasing
influence of Eastern Yiddish on the older literary language.

11 The Eastern Yiddish Re-editions

The Eastern European re-editions of *Kav hayosher* afford an important insight
into the nature and scope of the linguistic revision that the original text
underwent in the late eighteenth century. The most significant changes were
those introduced in the realms of morphology, lexicon, and, to a lesser
degree, syntax. The changes in orthography are particularly systematic, and
reflect the orthography of many other contemporary Eastern Yiddish texts

that were printed before the early nineteenth-century adoption of the square-letter type-font (cf. §2.2.2).

The primary aim of the following analysis is to clarify the extent of the linguistic revision. Older Yiddish forms that remained unaltered or were more resistant to modernization (see §§11.3.1–2) are no less important for an adequate evaluation of the actual Easternization process of the older literary language.

11.1 Orthography

In retrospect, the spelling system of the second edition of *Kav hayosher* (KF1709) is closer to modern Yiddish orthography than the one employed in Zholkve (1777) and Novidvor (1788). This is evident in the orthographic representation of most of the unstressed and certain stressed vowels. As to the orthographic representation of the consonants, these re-editions by and large follow the older Yiddish spelling conventions. A number of exceptional spellings of certain stressed vowels reveal the underlying dialectal Eastern Yiddish phonology of the anonymous editors or printers of Zholkve and Novidvor. The orthographic conservatism of these re-editions (i.e. no graphic representation of many unstressed and some stressed vowels (see §11.1.1), the old graphemic treatment of sibilants and shibilants (see §11.1.3)) is characteristic of many books printed in Eastern Europe since the eighteenth century. The radical modernization of Eastern Yiddish spelling apparently occurred together with the replacement of the conventional type-font with the 'modern' square letters. This important typographical change took place later, probably during the first decades of the nineteenth century (cf. §2.2.2). The orthographic modernization of Eastern Yiddish was in all likelihood Western-inspired; for in many respects it mirrors the way in which the old Yiddish spelling was adapted for writing and printing German and Germanized Western Yiddish texts by the late eighteenth-century proponents of Jewish Enlightenment and by Western and Central European publishers.

11.1.1 Unstressed Vowels

The traditionally acceptable graphic representation of certain unstressed vowels in Western Yiddish editions was almost completely abandoned in many late eighteenth-century Eastern Yiddish prints. In this respect both re-editions show a high degree of consistency. As can be seen from Table 10, the unstressed vowels are not graphically represented in verbal prefixes bə-/ba-, gə-, dər- (see Table 10, nos. 1–3), the nominal prefix gə- (see no. 4), and the masculine definite article dər (and subsequently in other forms

entailing dər; see no. 5). The posttonic vowels too are significantly less frequently represented in both re-editions. This is true of most of the verbal, as
well as the adjectival and nominal, suffixes (see nos. 6–10).

In many instances the orthographic representation of these unstressed
vowels was optional in the original *Kav hayosher* (e.g. nos. 1, 3, 7–10; cf.
above §10.1). However, in both KF1705 and KF1709 there was an increase
in their orthographic representation, whereas in Eastern re-editions the
general trend was in the opposite direction. The number of graphemically
represented unstressed vowels is minimal in the Zholkve and Novidvor re-
editions of the first volume. Occasionally the original spelling was preserved;
e.g. גיבויאט gəbɔj(ə)t 'built' (in all four editions, see line 83).

Table 10 Orthographic representation of unstressed vowels in three
editions of *Kav hayosher* (1705 vs. 1777 and 1788)

	KF1705	KZ1777, KN1788	transcription and gloss
		Pretonic vowels	
1	ביפֿוילין	בפֿוילן	bafɔjln̩ 'ordered' (p.p.; 126)
2	גימיינט	גמיינט	gəmejnt 'thought' (10)
	גיפֿוֹרכֿטן	גפֿאָרכֿטן	gəfɔrxtn̩ 'was afraid' (p.p.; 29)
3	דער שראָקן	דר שראָקן	dəršrɔkn̩ 'frightened' (73)
4	גישטאַלט	גשטאַלט	gəštalt 'shape; figure' (51, 136)
5	דער זעלביגר מאַן	דר זעלבגר מאַן	dər zélbikər man 'the same man' (23)
	דער נאָך	דר נאָך	dərnɔx 'afterwards' (68, 205)
		Posttonic vowels	
6	נעמין	נעמן	nɛmən 'take' (58)
	קענין	קענן	kɛnən 'can' (235)
7	עסין	עשן	ɛsn̩ 'eat' (inf.; 143, 162)
8	קאַרגיר	קאַרגר	kargər 'greedy' (24; cf. no. 5 above)
9	קיטין	קיטן	kejtn̩ 'chains' (99)
10	הייזיר	הייזר	hajzər 'houses' (319–20)

Only in the second volume of KN1788, where its editor could not follow
KZ1777 (cf. above §9), we find that the spelling is usually closer to the earlier
Frankfurt editions; e.g. זיך ביהעפֿט zəx bahéft 'communicates; copulates'
(309); גיוואוּשט gəvúst 'knew' (p.p.); גישעדיקט gəšédikt 'hurt, destroyed;
spoiled' (358); אויש גיוואָרצלט ójsgəvɔrclt 'uprooted' (520). However, even
here the unstressed vowels remain mostly unrepresented, especially in
certain frequently used forms, such as גוועזן gəvɛzn̩ 'was' (318, 320, 334,
376, 377, 412, 416, 443, 445).

The spelling of the unstressed vowel in the nominal and adjectival -ik/-ig suffixes remained optional in both Eastern re-editions, and it is usually represented when the suffix occupies an ultimate position; e.g. צוואנציג דרייסיג cváncik drájsik 'twenty, thirty' (in both re-editions, 44, 82). Yet this vowel sometimes remains unspelled; e.g. וויניק (KF1705) → ווינינ'ג (KF1709) → וויינג (KZ1777; KN1788) véjnik 'a bit' (81), especially in the penultimate position; e.g. דער זעלביגר מאן (KF1705; KF1709) → דער זעלבנגר מאן (KZ1777, KN1788) dər zélbikər man 'the same man' (23).

The representation of the shewa before syllabic ļ and of the vowel in the plural marker -əx/-ax is also optional; e.g. נאגיל nɔgļ 'nail' (227); פעריל pɛrļ 'pearl' (99; but note שליסל šlisļ 'keys', 211, 219, 245); פערליך pérləx 'pearls' (204).

In all editions of *Kav hayosher* the grapheme ⟨ע⟩ is employed to represent the posttonic vowel following a diphthong: זייער zejər 'very' (141); 'their' (238). This spelling was introduced in both Western and Eastern eighteenth-century Yiddish printed works alongside the older conventional ⟨א⟩ grapheme (cf. נייאי מויארן najə mɔjərn̩ 'new walls', 256).

The unstressed vowel of the plural marker -ən (normally not spelled; see Table 10, no. 9) is represented once in Zholkve by the grapheme ⟨ו⟩: שלוסלון šlislən 'keys' (207). This spelling is apparently an innovation introduced into late eighteenth-century Eastern European printed works. It was probably modelled on the shewa realization of certain reduced posttonic vowels etymologically spelled with ⟨ו⟩ in forms belonging to the Semitic component (e.g. עשירות ašírəs 'wealth', 96; ניצול ווערן nicļ vɛrn̩ 'to be saved', 111). Two other spellings with a ⟨ו⟩ grapheme for an unstressed vowel are פֿעניג (KZ1777) fénig 'Pfennig' (30) and גוהער (KN1788) gəhɛr 'has to' (522). As in the first example, the ⟨ו⟩ in these two items is orthographically interchangeable with ⟨י⟩. These spellings can also be related to the merger of the stressed u and i vowels in Southeastern and Mideastern dialects (where the historical vowels 51/52 and 31/32 merged in a unitary i; cf. below §11.2.3.2).

The employment of the so-called silent alef (mute ⟨א⟩) after final vowels, mostly in monosyllabic words (e.g. דיא di 'the' (pl./fem. sing.), דוא du 'you', זיא zej 'they'/ zi 'she'; וויא vi 'as; like') is drastically reduced in both Eastern re-editions of the first volume of *Kav hayosher*. This silent alef was retained in the various traditional Eastern Yiddish reprints and re-editions until the early twentieth century (see Reyzen 1920: 115 §37). However, in comparison with the earlier eighteenth-century Western Yiddish editions, the use of this archaic spelling convention became increasingly obsolete.

11.1.2 *Stressed Vowels*

The Old Yiddish convention of optional representation of the inter-consonantal historical a was changing in eighteenth-century Western and Central European printed works in favour of the full spelling of all stressed a vowels. This development is akin to the increasing trend towards the full orthographic representation of the unstressed vowels as well. Both these tendencies are found in KF1709 (cf. above §10.1). However, in KZ1777 and KN1788 the change is once more reversed.

The examples provided in Table 11 show that in contrast to the second edition of *Kav hayosher* (KF1709), the spelling of certain interconsonantal stressed vowels was abolished in KZ1777 and especially in KN1788. It is usually vowel 11, and less frequently 41, that remain orthographically unrepresented in the Zholkve edition (see Table 11, nos. 1–2). In the Novidvor edition this also applies to vowel 12 (see no. 3).

Table 11 Orthographic representation of stressed a/ɔ vowels in four editions of *Kav hayosher* (1705, 1709, 1777, and 1788)

	KF1705	KF1709	KZ1777	KN1788	Transcription and gloss
1	גאנץ	גנץ	גנץ	גנץ	ganc 'whole' (20, 25)
	בלד	באלד	באלד	בלד	bald 'soon; shortly' (79)
	לאנג	לאנג	——	לנג	lang 'long' (423)
	לנד	לאנד	לנד	לנד	land 'land; country (68)
	מאכט זיך	מאכט זיך	מכט זיך	מכט זיך	maxt zəx 'pretends' (140)
	שאפֿן	שאפֿן	שאפֿן	שפֿן	šafn̩ 'govern; possess' (8)
2	זאלין	זאלן	זלן	זאלן	zɔln̩ 'shall' (3rd pers. pl.; 7)
	האט	האט	האט	הט	hɔt 'has' (28, 31, 38, 42, 47, 54)
	הט	האט	——	האט	" " (325, 330, 334, 343, 352)
3	האבן	האבן	האבן	הבן	hɔbn̩ 'have' (3rd pers. pl.; 8)
	הבין	האבן	הבן		" "

Only in a handful of cases were the changes from the Frankfurt edition to the Zholkve and Novidvor editions reversed; i.e. from zero to full graphemic representation of the stressed interconsonantal vowel:

מרק (KF1709) → מארק (KZ1777, KN1788) mark 'market' (49);

ברנט וויין (KF1709) → בראנטוויין brántvajn 'spirit; liquor' (152; cf. mod. Y. בראָנפֿן bronfn̩);

גס (KF1709) → גאס (KN1788) gas 'street' (311).

The following chains of spelling alterations: הט (KF1705) → האט (KF1709) → האט (KN1788); האט (KF1705) → האט (KF1709) → האט (KZ1777) → הט (KN1788); זאלין (KF1705) → זאלן (KF1709) → זלן (KZ1777, see Table 11, no. 2) may indicate that in Novidvor, and to a lesser degree in Zholkve, the older Yiddish spelling convention was in some cases continued, rather than directly copied, from KF1705.

Both re-editions usually continue to employ the older Yiddish spelling convention ⟨י⟩ for vowels 25 (ביט bɛt 'ask' (1st pers. sing.), 54, 115), 22 (גין ארײן צו arájncugèjn 'enter, come in', 147), and 24 (אפ לינג óplèjgn̦ 'postpone', 409). It is used alongside the graphemes ⟨ע⟩ for vowel 25 and ⟨יי⟩ for vowels 22 and 24.

11.1.3 Consonants

Little change was introduced in the spelling of consonants. The old Yiddish spelling, which did not mark the Eastern Yiddish phonemic opposition between sibilants and shibilants, remained basically intact in both editions (i.e. ⟨ש⟩ is employed for the majority of both, whereas ⟨ס⟩ represents only a minority of sibilants). However, the employment of the ⟨ס⟩ grapheme for sibilants seems to have increased generally in eighteenth century books, as can be seen by comparing the original *Kav hayosher* with its later Eastern re-editions. Sometimes, as was the case with the representation of the unstressed and some of the interconsonantal stressed vowels, the Zholkve and Novidvor re-editions are more conservative than the Frankfurt am Main editions; e.g. עסין (in both KF) → עשן (KZ, KN) ɛsn̦ 'eat' (inf. 109, 143, 157, 162); בעסר (in both KF) → בעשר (KZ, KN) bɛsər 'better' (60). However, there is no consistent trend. At times the later Eastern re-editions prefer to spell the voiceless sibilant with a ⟨ס⟩ grapheme; e.g. פֿאשט (both KF) → פֿאסט (KZ, KN) fast 'fast' (153).

A number of graphemic substitutions point to more phonetic spelling from the viewpoint of modern Eastern Yiddish. In KF1709 there seems to have been an effort to maintain an orthographic and possibly a phonemic distinction between ד(א)ש dɔs 'the' (neut. sing.), 'this' (e.g. 65, 80, 208, 264, 268) and ד(א)ז daz 'that' (e.g. 41, 112, 120, 165, 168, 421, 505). It is possible that in the Western Yiddish of that time the two forms were also phonemically differentiated as dɔs vs. daz/dɔz (cf. modern Eastern Yiddish forms דאָס dɔs and אז az). In the later Eastern re-editions, however, this differentiation could not be preserved. Most of the conjunctions dɔs were spelled ⟨דש⟩ in Zholkve and Novidvor. Both forms, of the neuter definite article and the conjunction, apparently became homophonic in the Eastern Yiddish of that period (cf. dɔs 'that' synonymous with modern אז az in the archaic and traditional styles of Modern Literary Yiddish).

The same change towards a more 'phonetic' consonantal representation is evident in the following replacements of the older conventional variant spellings (found mostly in KF1709): עם (KF1705) → עז (KF1709) → עש (KZ, KN) ɛs 'it' (9); אויז ריד ; אויש ריד (KF1705) → אויז ריד (KF1709) → אויש ריד (KZ, KN) ɔjsrejd 'pretext' (142, 175).

The older spelling conventions ⟨פֿפ⟩ and ⟨פּף⟩, which represented syllable-initial f and syllable-final p, were usually replaced in the Zholkve and Novidvor re-editions with ⟨פֿ⟩ and ⟨פ⟩ respectively; e.g. פֿפֿעֶרד (KF1705) → פֿעֶרד (KF1709) → פֿעֶרד (KZ, KN) fɛrd 'horse' (90); פֿפֿעֶניג (KF) → פֿעֶניג (KZ, KN) fénig 'Pfennig' (30). Syllable-final p was spelled in the Frankfurt editions either with ⟨פֿ⟩ or with ⟨ב⟩. The first is apparently a remnant of the older Yiddish spelling convention ⟨פֿפ⟩, whereas the second is an adoption of the New High German model (cf. NHG *ab*); e.g. אב ליגֿן (KF, 160–1); אב ליגין (KF, 417) → אפ ליגֿן (KZ and KN) ɔplejgṇ 'postpone'.

Another case of more 'phonetic' spelling is the substitution of the original ⟨טשט⟩ with ⟨טץ⟩ in the forms גוטשט (KF1705) → גוטש (KF1709) → גוטץ (KZ and KN) guts 'good deeds' (257); 'goods' (272). Here the phonetic value of the cluster ts is more realistically reinterpreted as tc, where ⟨ט⟩ is possibly morpho-phonemic and ⟨ץ⟩ is the outcome of the affrication t + s → c. The spelling ⟨גוטשט⟩, which also appears elsewhere in KF1705, is apparently a word-final dental accretion, which was partially abandoned in KF1709 and systematically avoided in both Eastern re-editions (on dental accretion cf. §§11.3.3.1 and 13.3.2).

11.2 Phonology

Both Eastern re-editions of *Kav hayosher* replace the Western Yiddish and New High German-based spellings of certain stressed vowels found in KF1705 and KF1709. These changes anticipate the reorganization of the supradialectal modern orthography on the basis of Eastern Yiddish phonology. Moreover, a few deviant spellings reveal the underlying Eastern Yiddish phonology of the Zholkve and Novidvor re-editions. These spellings happen to be narrowly dialectal; i.e. they represent features not common to all Eastern Yiddish dialects. They do testify, however, to the direct impact of spoken Eastern Yiddish upon the literary language.

11.2.1 *Apocope Maintained*

The growing impact of New High German on Western Yiddish in the eighteenth century resulted *inter alia* in the restoration of many word-final reduced vowels ('de-apocopation'). This is evident in the first-person singular form ix badánkə məx 'I reckon' found in both Western editions. Such forms

remained structurally unusual for Eastern Yiddish. So in the Zholkve and
Novidvor re-editions it was changed back to the apocopated form ix badánk
məx, in line with the general Yiddish paradigm of the first person singular
forms of verbs derived from the Germanic component: hence איך בידאנקי מיך
ix badánkə məx (KF) → איך בידאנק מיך ix badánk məx (KZ, KN) 'I reckon'
(203).

11.2.2 From Western Yiddish and New High German to Eastern Yiddish

A few Western Yiddish and New High German-based spellings of the stressed
vowels found in KF (cf. above §11.1) were replaced in the Zholkve and
Novidvor re-editions by the more interdialectal alternative spellings which
were to become hallmarks of Eastern Yiddish:

vowel 44

גיקאָפֿט gəkāft (KF) → גיקױפֿט gəkɔjft 'bought' (KZ, KN; 497);

גיקאָפֿט (KF) → גקופֿט (KZ) → גיקױפֿט (KN; Ch. 6, KF1705: 24, KF1709: 28).

vowel 42

ביפֿולן (KF1705), ביפֿאָלן bəfɔln (KF1709) → בפֿולן bafɔjln 'ordered' (KZ, KN, 126);

גיצאָגן gəcɔgn̩ (KF) → גיצוגן gəcɔjgn̩ (KZ, KN) 'moved' (346).

The spelling ⟨ו⟩ in Zholkve and Novidvor in these forms is interdialectal in
so far as it does not entirely match either of the Eastern Yiddish dialectal
realizations of the vowels in question. At the same time, it is closer to any of
the Eastern Yiddish varieties than the spelling it replaces. In Eastern Yiddish
this use of ⟨ו⟩ was later modified to ⟨וי⟩ (cf. Novidvor גיקױפֿט), which subsequently became the orthographic norm for vowels 42 (NEY ej ‖ MEY, SEY
ɔj), 44 (NEY ej ‖ MEY, SEY ɔj), and 54 (NEY ɔj ‖ MEY ou ‖ SEY ou/u). Vowels
42 and 44 are merged in all forms of Eastern Yiddish. The orthographic
merger of 42, 44, and 54 is not matched by any dialectal merger, but did in
fact develop in the standard language.

11.2.3 Eastern Yiddish Phonology

A few deviant spellings found in the Zholkve and Novidvor re-editions enable
us to detect some of the most salient Eastern Yiddish dialectal features. These
point towards Mideastern or Southeastern dialects. There are no further
indications of a more precise dialectal location than that suggested by the
place of publication of each of these editions; i.e. Southeastern for Zholkve,
Mideastern for Novidvor.

11.2.3.1 The Loss of Functional [h]   In one instance the Novidvor edition
has a form that testifies to the loss of functional h: היברייא (KZ) → איברייא (KN)
(h)ibəráj(?) (129–30). This word is unknown to me; in KZ1777 and

KN1788 it replaces the more common נרירייא narəráj 'deception' (KF). It is clear, however, that the variation ⟨היברייא⟩ → ⟨איברייא⟩ is a clear indication of the facultative loss of the organic or functional h in one of these re-editions. This loss is especially characteristic of Southeastern Yiddish and the Southeastern regions of Northeastern Yiddish (see §31.2.1).

11.2.3.2 *Merger of Vowels* 51 *and* 31 The following cases testify to the merger of vowels 31 and 51, yielding unitary i in Southeastern and Mideastern Yiddish. The merger is most evident in the dialectal spelling of vowel 51 with the grapheme ⟨י⟩ instead of ⟨ו⟩. This spelling is phonetically more viable from the viewpoint of Southeastern and Mideastern Yiddish: פֿול ful (KF) → פֿיל (KZ) fil 'full' (209); גטרונקן gətrunkən (KF) → גטרינקן (KZ) gətrinkən 'drank; drunk' (p.p., 184); פֿר שוונדן פֿר (KF1705) → פֿר שוואונדן faršvúndņ (KF1709) → פֿר שווינדן faršvíndņ 'disappeared' (KZ, Ch. 6).

Another indication of the merger is the hypercorrect spelling of vowel 31 with the ⟨ו⟩ grapheme instead of the conventional ⟨י⟩: שליסלן (KF) → שלוסלון (KZ, KN) šlislən 'keys' (207, 209).

The well-attested merger of vowels 31 and 51 suggests the parallel convergence of vowels 32 and 52 among the long vowels.

11.2.3.3 *Vowels* 12 *and* 13 *Yield* [u] In both re-editions the stressed u vowel of the lexeme gəšmuk 'jewelry' was spelled with the grapheme ⟨א⟩, which replaced the original spelling with ⟨ו⟩: גישמוקין (KF) → גישמאקן (KZ, KN) gəšmukņ 'jewelry' (pl., 199); גישמוק (KF) → גישמאק (KN) gəšmuk 'jewelry' (299). This rare example indicates that u was one of the possible realizations of the ⟨א⟩ grapheme in Mideastern and Southeastern Yiddish of that time. This realization coincides with the modern Mideastern and Southeastern u realization of vowels 12 and 13. We may infer that in the Zholkve and Novidvor re-editions the realization of vowels 12 and 13 was u.

11.2.3.4 *Vowel* 34 *Yields* [a] In one case Novidvor has a dialectal spelling of vowel 34 with ⟨א⟩: גלייך (KF, KZ) → גלאך (KN) glajx 'straight' (adv., 223). Vowel 34 was monophthongized into ā in Mideastern Yiddish, and further shortened into a in Southeastern Yiddish. In certain varieties of Southeastern Yiddish, vowels 11 and 34 merged in a unitary a. The spelling ⟨גלאך⟩ suggests that in Novidvor vowel 34 was perceived as a monophthong. Another explanation may be that the anonymous printer of Novidvor was a speaker of Southeastern Yiddish, where the merger of vowels 11 and 34 occurred.

11.2.3.5 *The Stressed-Vowel System* The following reconstruction of the stressed-vowel system of the Zholkve and Novidvor re-editions of *Kav hayosher* constitutes a summary of most of their Eastern Yiddish phonological features (see Tables 12 and 13). Vowels which could not be directly identified from their graphemic representations in the texts are given in square brackets. They have been inferred from the structural criteria provided by the respective dialects. The merger of vowels 11 and 34 can be identified only in Novidvor.

Table 12 Reconstruction of the stressed-vowel system in *Kav hayosher* (Zholkve, 1777)

$i_{31/32/51/52(/25)}$	$u_{12/13}$
$[ej_{22/24}]$	$[ɔj_{42/44}]$
$[ɛ_{21}]$	$[ɔ_{41}]$
$[a_{11/34}]$	

Table 13 Reconstruction of the stressed-vowel system in *Kav hayosher* (Novidvor, 1788)

$i_{31/32/51/52}$	$u_{12/13}$
$[ej_{25}]$	$[ɔj_{42/44}]$
$[ɛ_{21}]$	$[ɔ_{41}]$
$[aj_{22/24}]$	
$a_{11/34}$	

11.3 Morphology

The most systematic changes introduced in the Eastern re-editions of *Kav hayosher* are in the realm of morphology. They are the hallmark of the linguistic modernization, and testify to the extent and intensity of the early Easternization of the older literary language.

Nevertheless, many features remained resistant to change in varying degrees. These features cannot be viewed as vestiges of the older literary language or as archaic forms in the given context, for even in its later Eastern re-editions *Kav hayosher* remains by and large a product of older literary Yiddish. Occasionally even some of the most resistant categories underwent Easternization in the re-editions under discussion.

The morphological changes effected in KZ and KN fall into two main groups. The first consists of forms that were only partially (i.e. inconsistently) substituted and is therefore characterized by varying degrees of morphological instability (see §§11.3.1–2). The second comprises all the systematic (or nearly systematic) replacements of the older and Western Yiddish forms by their Eastern Yiddish equivalents (see §11.3.3).

11.3.1 *Forms and Categories Resisting Easternization*

The degree of resistance varies from one category to another. The most resistant are Western Yiddish relative pronouns, the forms of the future tense auxiliary, and the past tense of modal verbs. We may also include here the preterite, although a number of cases indicate that for the Eastern re-edition this category was in a state of decline.

11.3.1.1 *Relative Pronouns* Both forms of relative pronouns, the Western Yiddish dər (dɔ)/di (dɔ) 'that, who' and the Eastern Yiddish invariant vɔs, are employed in the original text of the book. The indeclinable vɔs (e.g. 17–18, 223, 315, 326, 371, 445, 474) possibly reflects the underlying Eastern Yiddish of the author. At the same time, *Kav hayosher* makes extensive use of the declinable relative pronouns that prevailed in the older literary language:

איין עושר דער ווֹאר גאנץ רייך
an ɔ(j)šər dɛr vɔr ganc rajx
'a prosperous man who was rather rich' (19–20);

דיא מוטיר פֿון דיא שידים דיא דא הייסט מחל״ת
di mutər fun di šejdəm di dɔ hejst mɔ́xlas
'the mother of the demons who is called Mokhlas [= Maḥălath]' (294–6);

גווינן קינדר פֿון מענשין דיא זיינין הלבי מענשן אונ׳ הלבי מזיקים
gəvinən kindər fun mɛnčn̩ di zajnən halbə mɛnčn̩ un halbə mazíkəm
'[they] give birth to children of people who are half human and half demons' (304–6).

In late eighteenth-century Eastern Yiddish printed works there was an ever increasing tendency to replace these Old Yiddish pronouns by the indeclinable vɔs (e.g. in *Ben hameylekh vehanozir* (Zholkve, 1771); *Tsene rene* (Lemberg, 1786); *Avkes roykhl* (Horodne, 1795)). However, in KZ1777 and KN1788 they remained intact (see 375, 408, 456; 233, 296, 304, 443). This is probably related to the fact that the syntactic changes in these re-editions were on the whole limited (see below §11.6), since in some cases the replacement of dər/di/dɔs by vɔs would have involved changes in the word order of the subordinated clause (e.g. the insertion of the personal pronoun).

11.3.1.2 *Future Tense Auxiliary* The paradigmatic instability of the future-tense auxiliary is characteristic of the original language of *Kav hayosher*. Here again we find Western Yiddish forms; e.g. (ו)ווערשט vərst(u) (2nd pers. sing., 263, 269, 270); ווערט vərt (3rd pers. sing., 4, 6, 110, 261, 262); ווערין vern̩ (3rd pers. pl., 312) alongside the Eastern Yiddish forms וויל vəl (1st per. sing., 58, 59, 229); ווְעלין vɛln̩ [or vəln̩?] (1st pers. pl., 160); ווילן vəln̩ [or viln̩?] (3rd pers. pl., 391, 393). First-person singular and first- and third-person plural forms that attracted ווְעלן vɛln̩ (e.g. וויל vil and ווילן viln̩) rather than ווערן vərn̩ were also part of the older Western Yiddish suppletive paradigm of the future-tense auxiliary (see Lincoff 1963: 144–5 §§9.22–4). However, the fact that there is variation between vərņ and vəlņ for the third-person plural may indicate an interference from New High German. Alternatively, the form ווערין vərņ can be explained as a hypercorrection. A native speaker of Eastern Yiddish who had to Westernize vəst to vərst and vət to vərt for the second- and third-person singular and for the second-person plural could have by analogy Westernized her or his native vəlņ into vərņ. At all events, this text in all the editions under discussion is far from presenting the full Eastern Yiddish paradigm for the future auxiliary.

Only once is a Western Yiddish form of the future auxiliary replaced by its Eastern Yiddish equivalent in Zholkve and Novidvor (e.g. ווערט vərt (KF) → וועט vərt (KZ, KN, 262)). The survival of the Old Yiddish future auxiliary in KZ1777 and KN1788 indicates some of the basic limitations of the Easternization process in its earlier stages.

11.3.1.3 *Past Tense of Modal Verbs*   The older periphrastic past tense of the modal verbs constructed on the pattern {past-tense auxilary + infinitive} was almost exclusively employed in *Kav hayosher*; e.g.:

האט ער קיין עני קענן פֿר זיך זעהן hot ər kin óni kenən far zix zɛn 'he refused to pay attention to the poor' (31–2; cf. 343, 410);

האבן זיך מוזן אויש ציהן hobņ zəx muzņ ójscìən 'had to move out' (362–3; cf. 416, 512, 513);

האט זעלן שטאַרבן hot zɛlņ štarbņ 'had to die' [=was about to die] (472).

The only exception is the past tense of the verb וועלן vɛlņ 'to want', which was constructed on the more regular (in modern Yiddish) pattern {past tense auxilary + past participle}; e.g., האט גיוועלט hot gəvɛlt 'wanted' (414). The form גיוועלט gəvɛlt appeared only in the first edition (KF1705), and was changed in KF1709 and KN1788 to גיוואלט (cf. St.Y. gəvɔlt). It may well be that gəvɛlt, which is especially characteristic of the Northeastern dialect, is a genuine feature of the author's native Eastern Yiddish.

The pattern {past tense auxilary + infinitive} remained unaltered in the KZ and KN re-editions. It is possible that both constructions, one with infinitive, the other with past participle, were at that time equally acceptable for modal verbs in Eastern Yiddish. In passing, we may note that in modern Yiddish one of the two forms, infinitive or past participle, may accompany the auxiliary וואָלטן vɔltņ 'would' to form the periphrastic conditional construction; e.g. איך וואָלט וועלן/געוואָלט וויסן ix vɔlt vɛlņ / gəvɔlt visņ 'I would like to know' (see Zaretski 1929: 128–9 §§339–42; Falkovitsh 1940: 196–7 §254; Mark 1978: 290 §3; D. Katz 1987a: 160 §9.1.5).

In Modern Literary Yiddish the past tense of modal verbs was levelled with all other verbs in accordance with the pattern {past-tense auxilary + past participle}. Thus already in the Lemberg (1786) edition of the *Tsene rene* (see Chapter 2) the preferred past tense of modal verbs was the one containing the past participle.

11.3.1.4 *The Preterite*   Neither KZ1777 nor KN1788 totally rejected the preterite. Such forms as וואר vɔr 'was' (19, 20, 101, 133, 175, 442, 483); ווארי(ן) vɔrṇ 'were' (82); גינג ging 'went' (48, 430, 432, 447, 455); שפּראך šprɔx (or šprax) 'spoke' (57, 77, 103); גאב gɔb 'gave' (87), אריין קאם arájn kɔm (?) 'entered' (210); קאם kɔm 'came' (428), נאם nɔm (?) 'took' (249); and העט hɛt (?) 'had' (280) appear in all editions of *Kav hayosher*, including Zholkve and Novidvor. The frequency of some of these forms (viz. וואר vɔr, גינג ging, and שפּראך šprɔx) ensured the continuing existence of the preterite in the later Eastern re-editions.

At the same time a number of cases show that in both KZ1777 and KN1788 the preterite as a category was in a state of decline. The forms גאב gɔb 'gave' (103) and שיקטן šiktṇ 'sent' (3rd pers. pl., 370) were omitted. In other cases the stem vowels of the original forms were re-spelled; e.g.:

דער שראק (KF) → דער שרעק (KZ) dǝršrɛk '(got) frightened' (122);
קאם kɔm(?) (KF) → קום (KZ, KN) kum/kim(?) 'came' (252);
שטערב štɛrb (KF) → שטארב (KN) štarb 'died' (483);
אן [. . .] פּינג fing ón (KF) → פֿאנג (KN) fang ón 'began' (380).

This re-spelling suggests that phonetically the forms in question were altered to conform to the more comprehensible present-tense forms; e.g. דערשרעקט זיך dǝršrékt zǝx '(got) frightened'; קומט kumt/(SEY and MEY kimt) 'arrives'; שטארבט štarbt 'dies'; פֿאנגט אן fang ón 'begins'. As we shall see later (§13.3.3) present-tense forms, along with those of the regular past tense, became the usual candidates to replace the preterite forms in Easternized Old Literary Yiddish. This is amply illustrated by the few cases where the original preterite was replaced altogether, either by the present tense or by regular past-tense forms; e.g.:

העטין hɛtṇ '(they) had' (KF) → האבן hɔbṇ '(they) have' (KN, 389);
וואר vɔr 'was' (KF) → איז iz 'is' (KZ, KN, 91);
קאם kɔm (KF) → איז געקומן iz gǝkúmǝn 'came' (KZ, KN, 134);
שיקטן šiktṇ '(they) sent' (KF) → שיקן šikṇ '(they) send' (KN, 374).

11.3.2 *Morphological Instability*

All other morphological categories were altered with varying degrees of consistency in the Zholkve and Novidvor re-editions. The changes, which were

only partially effected, further unbalanced the somewhat unstable morphological make-up of the original *Kav hayosher*. Both re-editions introduced
many more variant Eastern Yiddish forms to the original and far from consistent use of the dative forms of the neuter definite article, the dative and
accusative forms of the masculine definite article, and the dative and accusative forms of the masculine personal pronoun. The same applies to the
changing morphology of Yiddish possessive pronouns, where the alterations
introduced in KZ1777 and KN1788 favour the Eastern Yiddish 'short' (i.e.
indeclinable) possessive pronouns.

In addition, the editors of both re-editions often preferred to replace one
type of plural formation by an Eastern Yiddish form that has a zero plural
marker. All this results in still more morphological instability, which singles
out Zholkve and Novidvor as texts increasingly affected by the process of
creeping Easternization.

11.3.2.1 *The Merger of Dative and Accusative Forms*   In the original
language of *Kav hayosher*, there is ample evidence of the merger of the dative
and accusative forms of the masculine definite article. We often encounter
functionally dative or prepositional case forms of the neuter and masculine
definite articles which formally equal the historical or Western Yiddish
masculine accusative form. The clearest evidence of this is to be found in the
hypercorrect employment of דען dən for דעם dəm; e.g.:

פֿון דען יאר fun dən jɔr 'from the year' (486–7);
אויז דען הויז ɔjs dən hɔjz 'from the house' (449–50);
מיט דען דרוש mit dən druš 'with this parable [= exegesis]' (10);
דען מוהל צו גיפֿאלין dən mɔjəl cu gəfélṇ 'to suit the circumciser' (dat. 159).

These are a number of hypercorrections from which we may deduce that in
the author's native Eastern Yiddish the form dən was either disappearing or
had disappeared altogether (cf. also 76, 84, 187, 206, 384). A few cases of
the merger of word-final -(ə)n and -(ə)m into unitary -(ə)m may be attested
in some varieties of earlier Western Yiddish (see Herzog 1965b: 53 §2.11).
However, in Eastern Yiddish this merger had far-reaching morphological
and syntactic implications, and subsequently became one of the major
features of the nascent modern literary language (cf. §§11.5.5, 35.6).

Both Eastern re-editions introduce changes that either favour the Eastern
Yiddish form (דעם dəm instead of דען dən) or result in additional hypercorrections (דען dən instead of דעם dəm). These features testify to the printer's
or editor's uncertainty as to the actual use of the Western Yiddish form דען;
e.g.:

accusative case

דען בונט שליסלן dən bunt šlislən (KF) → דעם בונט שליסל dəm bunt šlisļ (KZ, KN)
'the bundle of keys' (acc., 244–5).

prepositional case

אין דען וועג in dən vɛg (KF) → אין דעם וועג in dəm vɛg (KZ, KN) 'on the road' (76);

אויז דען הויז ɔjs dən hɔjz (KF) → אויז דעם הויז ɔjs dəm hɔjz (KN)
'[to move out] of the house' (363);

אויז דען בית החיצון ɔjs dən béjsxìcņ (KF)→ אויז דעם בית החיצון ɔjs dəm béjsxìcņ (KN)
'[came out] of the outdoor toilet' (449–50);

אויז דען פרק ɔjs dən pejrək (KF) → אויז דעם פרק ɔjs dəm pejrək (KZ, KN)
'from this chapter' (272–3).

additional hypercorrections

אין דעם הויז (KF) in dəm hɔjz → אין דען הויז (KN) in dən hɔjz 'in the house' (loc. 320);

צו דעם מוהל cu dəm mɔjəl (KF) → צו דען מוהל (KZ, KN) cu dən mɔjəl
'to the circumciser' (138, 182);

פֿון דעם מוהל fun dəm mɔjəl (KF) → פֿון דען מוהל (KZ, KN) fun dən mɔjəl
'from the circumciser' (275);

ביי דעם וייב ba dəm vajb (KF) → ביי דען וייב (KN) ba dən vajb, 'with his wife' (444);

נאך דעם nox dɛm (KF) → נאך דען (KZ; KN) nox dɛn 'afterwards' (272, 509).

It may be that some of the additional hypercorrections stem from the later Western Yiddish editions of *Kav hayosher*. Their very existence in KZ1777 and KN1788, as well as the many instances in which דען dən remained unaltered, testify to the continuing predominance of the Western Yiddish pattern, even in the Easternized old literary language of the last decades of the eighteenth century (cf. 10, 49, 60, 84, 100, 138, 187, 200-1, 211, 246, 426-7).

By contrast, the Western Yiddish accusative form אין in 'him' of the masculine personal pronoun is far less frequent even in the original language of *Kav hayosher* (e.g. 36-8, 69, 74, 151, 170, 188, 195, 205, 331, 334, 478 where אים im is used as accusative in KF1705 and KF1709). In the Zholkve and Novidvor re-editions the form אין was either omitted (e.g. on line 164) or replaced by the Eastern Yiddish אים (e.g. 311). Only in one instance was the original אים replaced by אין (see 213). However, this replacement seems to have originated in one of the earlier Western Yiddish editions upon which the Eastern re-editions were based.

11.3.2.2 *The Loss of Declinable Possessive Pronouns*   The treatment of possessive pronouns in the original *Kav hayosher* generally conforms with the morphology of Old Literary Yiddish. The indeclinable forms appear in the nominative and accusative cases, the declinable in the prepositional and dative cases (see Lincoff 1963: §5.2). However, as can be seen from the following examples (see Table 14), the indeclinable forms were also employed with feminine and neuter nouns in the prepositional case. More-over, the inflection of the pronouns preceding feminine nouns in the prepositional case was reduced from -ər to -ə, and it is possible that these forms were reinterpreted as special cases of gender agreement (see Table 14, nos. 1, 2, 6).

Table 14 Attributive possessive pronouns in *Kav hayosher* (1705)

Declinable	Indeclinable
fem.	
1 מיט זײני פֿראוי mit zajnə frɔj 'with his wife' (424)	מיט זיין משפחה mit zajn məšpɔxə 'with his family' (528)
2 אין אירי שטוב in irə štub 'in her room' (448)	
3 זײנר נשמה zajnər nəšomə 'his soul' (dat., 285)	
neut.	
4 מיט זיינים רעכטין וױיב mit zajnəm rextṇ vajb 'with his real wife' (419)	אן זיין וױיב on zajn vajb 'with his wife' (530)
5 אין זיינם הויז in zajnəm hɔjz 'in his house' (482)	
6 מיט זײני גיזינד mit zajnə gəzind 'with his household' (521)	
masc.	
7 ביז זיינים טוט biz zajnəm tɔjt 'until his death' (257)	
8 פֿון זיינם גרושין עשירות fun zajnəm grɔjsṇ ašírəs 'from his great wealth' (279–80)	
9 געגין אירם מאן kɛgṇ irəm man 'against her husband' (452–3).	

The variation between declinable and indeclinable possessive pronouns in *Kav hayosher* may be seen as another example of competition between older and more recent features in the eighteenth-century literary language. In spoken Eastern Yiddish the loss of the declinable possessive pronouns was apparently completed before the late eighteenth century. Both Eastern re-editions clearly point to further decline of the inflected forms in literary usage (but cf. §35.5). Once more, the changes introduced in the KZ and KN re-editions of the first volume are more frequent and more consistent than those in the latter re-edition of the second volume. Thus numbers 2, 4, 5, and 9 (see Table 14) remained unaltered in Novidvor, whereas in all other cases cited the inflected masculine possessive pronoun was replaced; e.g.:

מיט זייני פֿראוי mit zajnə frɔj (KF) → מיט זיין פֿראוי mit zajn frɔj (KN, 424);

זיינר נשמה zajnər nəšɔmə (KF) → זיין נשמה zajn nəšɔmə (dat., KZ, KN, 285);

מיט זייני גיזינד mit zajnə gəzind (KF) → מיט זיין גיזינד mit zajn gəzind (KN, 521);

ביז זיינים טוט biz zajnəm tɔjt (KF) → ביז זיין טוט biz zajn tɔjt (KZ, KN, 257);

פֿון זיינם [. . .] עשירות fun zajnəm ašírəs (KF) → פֿון זיין [. . .] עשירות fun zajn ašírəs (KZ, KN, 279).

Our texts demonstrate that all inflected forms of the third-person singular possessive pronoun were replaced in KZ and KN re-editions of the first volume. This replacement may be viewed as a paradigmatic levelling of the uninflected masculine possessive pronoun, which is fully in line with the prevalent Eastern Yiddish pattern.

By contrast, the few cases of older forms of short possessive pronouns in the plural that disagree in number with the noun—the historical genitive forms—remained unaltered in the Novidvor re-edition of the second volume; e.g. אין זיין זאבֿן in zajn zaxn̩ 'in his efforts' (378); זיין קינדר zajn kindər 'his children' (406); מיט איר כיתות mit ir kitəs 'with her cliques' (296).

11.3.2.3 *Older and Modern Forms* A number of older verbal forms were replaced in the Novidvor re-edition of the second volume, although the same or related forms remained unaltered in both Eastern re-editions of the first volume. These include the following forms:

וואו זומפֿן זיין vu zumpn̩ zajn (KF) → וואו זומפֿן זענן vu zumpn̩ zɛnən (KN) 'where swamps are' (387);

זיבֿט zixt (KF) → זעהט zɛt (KN) 'sees' (434, 437);

גיוועשן gəvešn̩ (KF) → גיוואשן gəvašn̩ (KN) 'washed, bathed' (467).

The short form זיין zajn is believed to be the regular form for the first- and third-person plural present in the older Yiddish inflectional paradigm of the verb זיין zajn 'be' (see Lincoff 1963: 129 §§8.43–4). In *Kav hayosher* this form is substantially less frequent than its 'newer' variant זיינ(ע)ן zajnən, and it was still less frequent in late eighteenth-century Eastern Yiddish. But it remained unaltered in KZ1777 (see 92), and in one case the original זיינין zajnən turned up as זיין zajn (see 231).

Similarly, the older Yiddish form זיבֿט zixt 'sees' (85, 95; cf. modern Yiddish זעט zɛt) and the Western Yiddish וועשין vešn̩ 'wash' (138, 173; cf.

modern Yiddish vašṇ) remained unchanged in the Eastern re-editions of the first volume.

11.3.2.4 *Preference for the Eastern Yiddish Plural Form*   In two cases, KZ and KN re-editions preferred to replace the plural forms שליסלן šlislən 'keys' and פּערל(י)ך pɛrləx 'pearls' with their Eastern Yiddish equivalents שליסל šlisḷ and פּערל pɛrḷ. The form šlislən remained unaltered twice when it first appeared in the text (cf. 207, 209). In all other instances it was replaced by šlisḷ (cf. 211, 219, 222, 223, 245, 249, 266). The form pɛrləx appeared twice in the original *Kav hayosher* (99, 204), and in the first instance it was replaced by pɛrḷ in both KZ and KN.

This instability *vis-à-vis* plural formation of nouns ending with a syllabic -ḷ reflects the increasing morphological and possibly semantic confluence of first diminutives and 'quasi-diminutive' forms in Eastern Yiddish. This confluence in many cases defies the normative principle according to which the plural of all diminutive forms ending with a syllabic -ḷ should be formed with the -əx suffix (e.g. for 'table': tišḷ → tišləx), whereas the plural form of nouns with the same ending but which are not diminutives is formed with the -ən suffix (e.g. for 'bowl': šisḷ → šislən; cf. Falkovitsh 1940: 162 n. 1; Zaretski 1926: 51 §83; 1929: 70–1 §162; Mark 1978: 164 no. 5.1; Birnbaum 1979: 231 §56). Thus Zaretski (1926: 51; 1929: 71) lists some exceptions to this rule: e.g. hitḷ '[small] hat' → hitlən '[small] hats', an actual diminutive, but knejdḷ → 'kneidl; dumpling' → knéjdləx 'kneidls; dumplings'; and ɔjringḷ 'earring' → ɔjringləx 'earrings', two 'quasi-diminutives'. He also lists lɛfḷ and lɛflən 'spoon' among nouns that can have two plural forms (see Zaretski 1926: 56 §87; 1929: 72 §167). Mark (1978: 164 no. 5.3) offers a separate category of 'some nouns belonging to the neuter gender and ending with the syllabic ḷ' that form plural with -əx. Most of these, it seems, were either reanalysed as, or levelled with, the first diminutive forms. It seems that some uncertainty and variation with regard to these types of plural formation still exists in the modern language, given the overpowering productivity of the diminutive forms in Eastern Yiddish and the exclusively semantic (and therefore unsatisfactory) principle offered by the normativist grammarians (cf. Zaretski 1929: 71 §163, which states that the two types of plural formation, that with -ən and that with -əx 'are often confused').

Each one of the morphological and morpho-syntactic changes discussed above clearly points to the overall Easternization of the older literary language. In the case of the merger of dative and accusative forms of the masculine and neuter definite article, the changes were far from systematic, though they often betray the underlying Eastern Yiddish. The replacement of inflected possessive pronouns and of the old plural forms of nouns by their

Eastern Yiddish equivalents was, by comparison, far more frequent and consistent.

11.3.3 *Systematic Changes*

All other changes in morphology were systematically carried out in both Eastern re-editions. A sizeable number of Western Yiddish forms were entirely replaced. As a result, certain older (then contemporary Western Yiddish) forms were completely abandoned in favour of their Eastern Yiddish equivalents. These changes are in part supported by a number of similar lexical shifts in which certain Western Yiddish lexical items were avoided (see §11.4 below).

11.3.3.1 *The Loss of Word-Final Dental Accretion*   A number of forms used in the original *Kav hayosher* have dental accretion; e.g. מאלט אײן amɔ́lt 'once'; היפשט hipšt 'beautiful'; גוטשט gutst 'goods'. (For a brief examination of dental accretion in German and Yiddish see Birnbaum 1979: 56.) In some cases the final ⟨ט⟩ had already been omitted in KF1709. However, in Zholkve and Novidvor all these forms were replaced. Dental accretion was not generally sustained in most Eastern Yiddish dialects in these forms (see §13.3.2; cf. Herzog 1965a: 225 §5.24):

1 אײן מאלט a(jn) mɔ́lt (KF) → אמאל amɔ́l (KZ, KN) 'once' (19);
  אײן מאלט a(jn) mɔ́lt (KF) → אײן מאל amɔ́l (KN) 'once' (425);
2 היפשט hipšt (KF) → היפש hipš (KN) 'beautiful' (443);
3 גוטשט gutst (KF1705) → גוט gut (KF1709) → גוטש guts (KZ, KN) 'goods' (235, 272);
  גוטשט gutst (KF1705) → גוט gut (KF1709, KZ, KN) 'goods' (226);
  גוטשט gutst (KF1705) → גוטש guts (KF1709, KZ, KN) 'goods' (257).

11.3.3.2 *Adverbial Prefixation*   In the original *Kav hayosher* the adverbial prefix a- was either missing in some forms or conventionally spelled אײן a(jn) (sharing this spelling with the indefinite article). In KZ and KN all relevant adverbs and adverbial complements received this prefix, and it was usually spelled phonetically and morphologically as part of a given form:

אײן הײם (KF) → אהײם (KZ, KN) ahéjm 'home' (adv., 251–2);
אײן מאלט amɔ́lt (KF) → אמאל (KZ, KN) amɔ́l 'once' (19);
שטערבין אלי װעק štɛrbn̩ alə vɛk (KF) →
שטארבן אלי װעק (KN) štarbn̩ alə avék 'all die out' (522);
קומט װעק kumt vɛk (KF) → קומט אװעק (KN) kumt avék 'dies' (perf.), (527);
װעק װערפין (KF) → אװעק װארפן (KN) avékvàrfn̩ 'throw away' (Ch. 70, KF1709: 29b).

To this we may add the Western Yiddish adverb דא הין dɔhín 'there' (cf.

NHG *dahin*) which was replaced in the Zholkve and Novidvor re-editions by
the Eastern Yiddish prefixed adverb אהין ahín (72). The prefix a- (historically
an indefinite article) was also inserted before the Western Yiddish adverb זו
zɔ ~ זוא zɔ (KF) → אזו azój (KZ, KN) 'so' (158). The more 'phonetic' spelling
of the indefinite article איין a (e.g. זו איין a(jn) zó (KF) → אזו azój (KN) 'such',
309) and of the adverbial prefix a- (cf. the first two adverbs cited above) is
another important Easternizing feature in both re-editions.

11.3.3.3 *The Levelling of Past Participles*   In a departure from the original
Kav hayosher all past participles of strong verbs receive the prefix gə- in both
KZ and KN re-editions:

אריין גאנגן arájngàngən (KF) → אריין ג(י)גאנגן arájngəgàngən (KZ, KN)
'entered' (28, 324);
גאנגן gángən (KF) → גיג(א)נגן gəgángən (KN) 'went' (395, 418);
אויף געסין úfg(ə)ɛsŋ (KF) → אויף גגעסין úfgəgɛsŋ (KZ, KN) 'ate' (perf., 181);
געבין gɛbŋ (KF) → ג(י)געבין gəgébŋ (KZ, KN) 'gave' (254, 505).

In fact, this is one of the very first, one could say 'mechanical' features of
Easternization, found in even the least Easternized editions of that period.
(For earlier eighteenth-century attestation of the prefixation of past parti-
ciples see §7.3.1.) Systematic prefixation of past participles was also effected
in some earlier eighteenth-century Western printed works such as the
Amsterdam 1726 and 1736 re-editions of *Tsene rene*. In late eighteenth-
century books printed in Eastern Europe this prefixation became the norm.
The prefix gə- is added to most of the past participles of strong verbs in the
Shklov (1796) edition of *Simkhes hanefesh,* although linguistic changes were
kept to a minimum in that edition (see Chapter 3).

11.3.3.4 *The Loss of the Subjunctive*   Subjunctive forms are rare in the
original language of *Kav hayosher*. This reflects the general loss of the
subjunctive that occurred in the Middle Yiddish period as a result of the
general levelling of stressed stem vowels (see Lincoff 1963: 109–10 §7.3).
The only subjunctive form found in our text in KF1705 and KF1709 was
apparently inspired by New High German usage. In KZ and KN the subjunctive was abandoned in favour of the 'regular' indicative form: דען איר
וואוסט דען וועג dɛn ir vust dən vɛg (KF; cf. NHG *wüsstet*) → איר ווייסט דען וועג ir
vejst dən vɛg (KZ, KN) 'you know the way, (don't you)' (60).

11.3.3.5 *The Negation Adverb*   The Western Yiddish negation adverb ניקש
niks (see Hutton 1987: 34–5) was replaced by the Eastern Yiddish forms
נישט ništ (8) and ניט nit in both Eastern re-editions of *Kav hayosher* (see 117,
169, 186, 248). Also the Western Yiddish pronoun ניקש niks 'nothing' (cf.

modern Yiddish גאָר(ני)שט (gɔ́r)ništ) is replaced twice by ניט nit (see 108, 183). But in a number of instances (126, 143, 452) the pronoun ניקש niks remains unchanged.

11.3.3.6 *The Diminutivization Pattern*   The Western Yiddish diminutives used elsewhere in the original *Kav hayosher* were replaced in the Zholkve and Novidvor re-editions by their Eastern Yiddish equivalents; e.g.:

שיפֿליין šíflejn (KF) → שיפֿל šif] (KZ, KN) 'small boat' (Ch. 8, KF1705: 12b);

פֿינגרליין fíngərlejn (KF) → פֿינגרל fingər] (KZ, KN) 'finger ring' (Ch. 70, KF1709: 30a, b);

אײן ביסכין abísxən (KF) → אײן ביסל abís] (KZ) → אביסל abís] (KN) 'a bit; slightly' (adv., Ch. 8, KF1705: 11a).

The noun fingər] 'finger ring' and the verb modifier abís] 'a bit; slightly' are in Eastern Yiddish synchronically levelled with, or reanalysed as, diminutive forms (see §11.3.2.4).

11.3.3.7 *The Easternization of Forms Derived from* al(ə)s   All functional words that shared the stem אל(י)ס ál(ə)s in the original *Kav hayosher* were replaced in both Eastern re-editions by their appropriate Eastern Yiddish equivalents:

conjunctions

אלזו alzɔ (KF) → אזו azɔ́j (KZ, KN) 'so' (45, 329, 397 420, 467, 492, 504, 519);

אליז al(ə)s (KF1705) → אלז als (KF1709) → אז az (KZ, KN) 'that' (90, 141 167, 223, 252, 423, 437).

adverbs

אליז al(ə)s (KF) → אלץ alc (KZ, KN) 'constantly; continually' (65, 221).

The invariant adjective אל(י)רלייא álərlej 'various; all kinds of', historically derived from the same root, was replaced in one case in the Novidvor re-edition by a distinctively Eastern Yiddish dialectal form, איילירלייא ílərlej (300). (On related dialectal forms see §§7.2.1 and 27.3.3.)

11.3.3.8 *The Easternization of Nominal Forms*   The adjectives גולדן/גאָלדן gɔ́ldṇ 'golden' and זולכי/זאָלכי zɔlxə 'such' (pl.) were systematically replaced in both re-editions by the Eastern Yiddish גילדן gildṇ (see 98, 196, 201, 439, 441) and זעלכי zɛlxə (see 193, 215, 237, 304; cf. modern Yiddish אַזעלכע azɛ́lxə 'such' (pl.)). The original בערג bɛrg 'mountain' was, in accordance with Eastern Yiddish morpho-phonology, re-spelled as ⟨באַרג⟩ in KZ and ⟨ברג⟩ in KN, both yielding Eastern Yiddish barg.

Some of the changes 'brought back' the original Eastern Yiddish forms used in KF1705. For the third-person plural possessive pronouns, KF1705 usually employed the forms זיר/זירי zejər/zejərə 'their' (sing./pl.). In KF1709 these were altered to איר/אירי ir/irə (see §§5.4, 10.3, 28.3.2.1, and 35.5.3).

Zholkve and Novidvor, on the other hand, returned to the original Eastern Yiddish form זייער (e.g. 128, 238). But the Western Yiddish forms איר/איר ir/irə remained unchanged in the KN1788 re-edition of the second volume of *Kav hayosher*, which apparently remained faithful to an earlier, intermediary Western edition: e.g., זיערי זכיות zejərə zxíəs (or zɔxjəs) (KF1705) → אירי זכיות irə zxiəs (KF1709 and KN) 'their rights' (393).

11.3.3.9 *Easternization of Verbal Forms*   The same type of change from Eastern to Western and back to Eastern Yiddish is evident in the case of the third-person singular present form of the verb זיין zajn 'to be'. Both forms איז iz and occasionally איזט izt were employed in KF1705. The most frequent form in KF1709 was איזט. KZ and KN systematically replace it by Eastern Yiddish איז.

Both Eastern re-editions preferred to replace the original characteristically Northeastern first- and third-person plural present form זיינ(ע)ן zajnən 'are' with its Southeastern and Mideastern variant זענן zenən (e.g. 129, 196, 207, 233, 300, 305, 335, 336, 345, 382, 396, 406, 493, 518). The original זיינ(ע)ן zajnən remained unchanged in only two instances (viz. 209, 230). Similarly, the second-person plural present form זייט zajt was replaced in both Eastern re-editions by the Southeastern and Mideastern form זענט zent (e.g. Ch. 6, KF1705: 11a, KF1709: 13a), although the form זייט zajt is once found unaltered in KN1788 (120).

The variant forms employed in KF1705 and KF1709 for the third-person singular and plural forms of the verb ענטפֿערן entfərṇ 'answer' reveal an ongoing competition between the patterns of Eastern Yiddish, New High German, and Western Yiddish.

en(t)fərt 'answers':
ענוורט (KF1705) → ענטפֿרט (KF1709) → ענטפֿרט (KZ) → ענפֿרט (KN, 192);
ענטוואָרט (KF1705) → ענטפֿרט (KF1709) → ענטפֿרט (KZ) → ענפֿרט (KN, 220);
ענטוואָרט (KF1705) → ענטוואָרט (KF1709) → ענפֿרט (KZ, KN, 267);

entfərṇ 'answer' (3rd pers. pl.):
ענטוואָרטין (KF1705) → ענטפֿרן (KF1709) → ענפֿרן (KN, 389).

The forms ⟨ענוורט⟩ in KF1705 and ⟨ענפֿרט⟩ in KN apparently represent the Eastern Yiddish dialectal variant enfərt (see Shmeruk 1981: 154), whereas the spelling of the post-nasal or post-dental f with the ⟨וו⟩ grapheme, as well as the morphological structure of ⟨ענטוואָרט⟩ in both KF editions and ⟨ענטוואָרטין⟩ in KF1705 denote the impact of the New High German pattern (cf. NHG *antwortet, antworten*). On the whole, KF1709 and KZ1777 prefer the interdialectal forms ⟨ענטפֿרט⟩ and ⟨ענטפֿרן⟩, which were equally acceptable in Western and Eastern Yiddish and remain the acceptable forms in Modern Literary Yiddish. Novidvor, on the other hand, clearly preferred the dialectal Eastern Yiddish ⟨ענפֿרט⟩ and ⟨ענפֿרן⟩. Forms that were patterned on the New High German model in the earlier Frankfurt editions were abandoned in both Eastern re-editions of *Kav hayosher*.

Other alterations of verbal forms in KZ and KN concern changes of the stem vowel in accordance with the phonological and morphological patterns of Eastern Yiddish; e.g.:

גיפֿאָלט gəfalt (KF) → גפֿעלט gəfɛlt (KZ, KN) 'like' (191; but note 159 where גיפֿאלין gəfaln remains unchanged);

ווערפֿין vɛrfn̩ (KF) → וואָרפֿן (KZ, KN) varfn̩ 'throw' (30);

פֿינגין ... אן fingən ón (KF) → אן ... פֿאָנגן (KN) fangən ón 'start' (3rd pers. pl., 313, 472, 521);

פֿראָגט frɔgt (KF and KN) → פֿרעגט (KZ) frɛgt 'asks' (73);

שטערבן štɛrbn̩ (KF) → שטאָרבן (KN) štarbn̩ 'die' (313, 472, 521).

Aspectually marked verbs characteristic of the further developed aspect system of modern Eastern Yiddish were not found. This applies to the original text of *Kav hayosher* as well as to its Eastern re-editions. We note, however, that in two instances the stressed verbal prefix ɔp- was omitted in KF 1709, thereby yielding an aspectually unmarked verb. In Novidvor the original forms aspectually marked with the prefix ɔp- were restored; e.g.:

אב ליגין óplejgn̩ (KF 1705) → ליגין lejgn̩ 'put, lay' (KF 1709) → אפ לינג (KN) óplejgn̩ 'put aside, put off' (417);

אב ווייכין ópvajxn̩ (KF 1705) → ווייכין vajxn̩ 'depart from; keep away' (KF 1709) → אפ ווייכין (KN) ópvajxn̩ 'leave (perf.); deviate (from)' (512).

11.4 Lexicon

Not too many specifically Western Yiddish lexical items can be found in *Kav hayosher*. Those that were employed were the ones usually acceptable in the old literary language. The author himself was apparently well aware of the lexical differences between contemporary Western and Eastern Yiddish. At one point he supplies the Western Yiddish term for 'the night before a circumcision' with its Eastern Yiddish equivalent, ווייץ נאָכט (אָדר וואַכט נאַכט) vájcnaxt (ɔdər váxtnaxt) '"váytsnakht" or "vákhtnakht"' (144; see also M. Weinreich 1928: 354; Kosover 1967: 260-1). In KZ and KN, however, only the further modified Eastern Yiddish form was used; i.e. וואַך נאַכט váxnaxt (cf. modern Yiddish וואַכנאַכט váxnaxt; see also 134). Other lexical alterations, in which the original Western Yiddish words were replaced by their Eastern Yiddish variants are:

1 אין דיזן הויז in dizn̩ hɔjz (KF) → אין דעם הויז in dɛm hɔjz (KN), 'in this house' (384);

2 גיפֿאטר gəfátər (KF) → קוואטר kvátər (KZ, KN) 'godfather' (151, 155);

3 גיצוגן gəcɔgṇ(?) (KF) → גפֿארן gəfɔrṇ (KZ, KN) 'travelled' (337);

גיצאג(י)ן gəcɔgṇ(?) 'moved' (KF) → גינגגן gəgangən 'went' (KN, 338);

4 דאנרשטאג dónərštɔg(?) (KF) → דאנרשטיג dónərštik (KZ, KN) 'Thursday' (27);

5 מאנטאג móntɔg(?) (KF) → מאנטיג móntik (KZ, KN) 'Monday' (26);

6 לעקוכ(י)ן lékùxən(?) (KF) → לעקח lékax (KZ), לעקוך (KN) lékəx 'cake' (151-2);

7 קיסט(י)ן kistṇ (KF) → קסטן kastṇ (KZ, KN), 'trunk' (225, 235); קימט kist (KF) → קסטין kastṇ (KZ, KN), 'trunks' (238).

It is remarkable that only two words were replaced with etymologically different forms: viz. דיזן dizṇ → דעם dɛm; גיצוגן gəcɔgṇ → גפֿארן gəfɔrṇ; גיצאג(י)ן gəcɔgṇ → גינגגן gəgangən (see above nos. 1 and 3). Moreover, these replacements were not consistently supplied (cf. 230 and 346, where דיזן dizṇ and גיצוגן gəcɔgṇ remained unchanged). Other words were replaced by their Eastern Yiddish morpho-phonetic variants (see nos. 2, 4, 5, and 6). In the case of קיסט(י)ן kistṇ → קסטן kastṇ (no. 6) the Western Yiddish doublet קיסט(י)ן kistṇ (cf. NHG *Kiste, Kisten*), including its (apocopated?) plural form קיסט kist, was rejected in both Eastern re-editions, although the Eastern Yiddish form קסטן kastṇ is used there as a plural form as well (cf. MHG *Kasten, Kasten ~ Kästen*, modern Yiddish קאסטן kastṇ, קאסטנס kastṇs).

In addition, the Western Yiddish word פֿארט fart 'ride; fare' (81; cf. NHG *Fahrt*, modern Yiddish יאָזדע jazdə , נסיעה nəsiə) was not employed in either Eastern re-edition. The more formal ברית מילה brismílə 'circumcision' is replaced at one point by the modern colloquial ברית bris (see 44).

All this points to the dual nature of the Eastern re-editions of *Kav hayosher* with regard to the lexicon. Some of these Western Yiddish words (see nos. 3, 4, and 5) were replaced by their Eastern Yiddish variants, clearly upsetting the inherent conservatism of the written language, which would be expected to preserve the older spelling. In some cases (e.g. nos. 5 and 6) there was probably no real need to alter the spelling, since the same graphic form could be 'read' equally by speakers of Western and Eastern Yiddish (e.g. 〈דאנרשטאג〉 can be read as dónərštɔg or dónərštik, and 〈לעקוק(י)ן〉 as lékùxən/lekəxṇ or lɛkəx → lékax, and so forth). Alterations in all other cases (e.g. nos. 1, 2, and 6) actually exceed the surface level of spelling. At the same time, these replacements also mark the limits of the Easternization of the lexicon. The colloquial plural form קאסטנס kastṇs was apparently barred from literary usage. Similarly, no distinctly Eastern Yiddish words (with the sole exception of קוואטר kvatər 'godfather') and, more specifically, no words of Slavonic origin were employed in the Eastern re-editions. Therefore we do not find here נסיעה nəsiə or יאָזדע jazdə, which would be the plausible Eastern Yiddish equivalents of פֿארט fart. It is also possible that spoken Eastern Yiddish of the period simply did not have one common noun meaning 'journey'.

This limitation of the Easternization of the lexicon is clearly shown in the case of the following three Western Yiddish words, which were replaced by dialectally neutral forms:

8 הקדש ביקס hɛkdəš biks 'charity box' (KF) → צדקה cdɔkə 'charity (box)' (KZ, KN), where 'box' is apparently implied; cf. mod. Y. צדקה פושקע cdɔkə puškə;

9 אורן(י) ɔrṇ (KF) → מתּפּלל זיין mispáləl zajn (KZ, KN) 'pray' (147);

10 יידשן jitšṇ (KF) → מל זיין mal zajn (KZ, KN) 'circumcise' (130).

Here the anonymous 'style-editors' of Zholkve and Novidvor seem to have been careful not to employ the distinctly Eastern Yiddish words צדקה פושקע cdɔkə puškə 'charity box' (of Slavonic origin, cf. Pol. *puszka* 'tin can'), דאַוו(ע)נען dav(ə)nən 'pray', and יידישן jídišṇ 'circumcise'. The forms chosen to replace the last two words are puzzling, for dav(ə)nən had long been known and was at least partially acceptable in the old literary language (see §7.2.2), and jitšṇ was, at least in its graphemic appearance, ⟨יידשן⟩, close enough to the Eastern Yiddish variant jídišṇ, which was usually spelled ⟨יוד(י)שן⟩ during the period in question (on יידיש jídišṇ and יידשן [=ייטשן] jitšṇ cf. Harkavy 1928: 254).

In lexicon, then, there is considerable variation. Some of the replacements broke away from the older orthographic representations of certain words, whereas others introduced and almost exclusively used Eastern Yiddish variants. Nevertheless, the scope of the Easternization of the lexicon remained quite limited, since both Eastern re-editions still follow the Old Yiddish stylistic convention according to which most of the distinctly Eastern Yiddish words, especially those of Slavonic origin, were barred from literary usage (see §§7.2.2-3).

11.5 Morpho-syntax

Morpho-syntactical changes are not as numerous as the morphological ones. Nevertheless, both Eastern re-editions of *Kav hayosher* were consistent in inserting subject pronouns before finite verbs. Similarly, the omission or insertion of the definite article in Zholkve and Novidvor largely comply with the morpho-syntactical, semantic, and phraseological patterns of modern Yiddish. Other less systematic changes entail such characteristic Easternizing features as the use of the prepositional case of the definite article after certain prepositions, the introduction of full declension of the attributive adjective, the replacement of a noun compositum with the construction {attributive adjective + noun}, and the occasional use of short forms of adjectives as nominal modifiers. A few phrases were morpho-syntactically and lexically repatterned on the model of Eastern Yiddish phraseology.

11.5.1 *Insertion of Subject Pronouns*

The subject pronoun of co-ordinated or subordinate clauses was sometimes omitted in the original edition of the work. This omission is a grammatical convention in 'consecutive' subordinate or co-ordinated clauses, as long as these refer to the same agent, which was pronominally or otherwise marked in the first 'opening' clause (e.g. 345–58; and see below, nos. 1 and 2). In other cases the formally unmarked agent can be pragmatically inferred from the context and the given finite verbal form (see nos. 3, 4, and 5).

In all these cases the subject pronoun was reinstated in both Eastern re-editions of *Kav hayosher*:

1 איך בין איין מענש [. . .] בין אוף גיפֿאָנגין גיוואָרין
   ix bin a mɛnč [. . .] bin úfgəfàngən gəvɔrṇ (KF) →
   איך בין איין מענש [. . .] איך בין אויף גפֿאָנגן גיוואָרן
   ix bin a mɛnč [. . .] ix bin úfgəfàngən gəvɔrṇ (KZ, KN)
   'I am a human being (not a demon) [. . .] I was captured' (112–13);

2 אבר האבין קיין כלי ניט צו בראכין
   ɔbər hɔbṇ k(e)jn kejlə nit cəbrɔxṇ (KF) →
   אבֿר(!) זיא האבן קיין כלי ניט צו בראָבן
   ɔbər zej hɔbṇ k(e)jn kejlə nit cəbrɔxṇ (KN)
   'but they did not break any dishes' (356–7);

3 [. . .] ע״כ ביט איך זאלט מיין קינד מל זיין אונ׳ ביט אייך זאלט ניקש זאגין
   a[l]k[éjn] bɛt ix zɔlt majn kind mal zajn un bɛt ajx zɔlt niks zɔgṇ [. . .] (KF) →
   [. . .] ע״כ ביט איך אִיר זאלט מיין קינד מל זיין אונ ביט איר זְ[אָ]לט ניט זאגן
   a[l]k[éjn] bɛt ix ir zɔlt majn kind mal zajn un bɛt ajx ir zɔlt nit zɔgṇ [. . .] (KZ, KN)
   'therefore I ask you to circumcise my child and not to reveal a thing [. . .]'
   (115–16);

4 אזו ביט איך אייך זאלט מיין קינד מל זיין
   azɔj bɛt ix ajx zɔlt majn kind mal zajn (KF) →
   אזו ביט איך איר זאלט מיין קינד מל זיין
   azɔj bɛt ix ir zɔlt majn kind mal zajn (KZ, KN)
   'so I ask you to circumcise my child' (54–5);

5 אונ׳ שוועֶר בייא גאָט   un švɛr ba gɔt (KF) →
   אונ איך שוועֶר בייא גאָט   un ix švɛr ba gɔt (KZ, KN)
   'and I swear by God' (247).

Far more extensive omissions were observed in certain 'business-like' styles of written Early New High German of the second half of the sixteenth century (see Wells 1985: 234–5). However, in the original edition of the book, subject pronouns are less often omitted, and this applies only to first- and second-person pronouns. In all these cases the agent is sufficiently indicated by the given finite verb form. It is possible that this more economical employment of subject pronouns in *Kav hayosher* is one of the morpho-syntactic features of the older literary language. Yet this suggestion needs to be verified by other studies of contemporary and earlier Yiddish texts.

Conversely, the employment of subject pronouns is obligatory in modern Eastern Yiddish, although in a sequence of subordinate or co-ordinated consecutive clauses it remains optional. The systematic instalment of the subject pronoun in both Eastern re-editions of *Kav hayosher* clearly conforms with the modern usage.

11.5.2 *The Definite Article*

In both re-editions of *Kav hayosher*, the use of the definite article was often repatterned on the morpho-syntactic models of modern Eastern Yiddish. As a result, in a number of cases the definite article was omitted (see below, nos. 1–6) or alternatively inserted (see nos. 7–8). These changes are very frequent, and most of them were effected in full agreement with the morpho-syntactic patterns of Modern Literary Yiddish:

definite article omitted

1 אונ' איז קיין מאנטאג אונ' דאנרשטאג ניט אין דיא שול אריין גאנגין
un iz k(e)jn móntɔg un dónɔrštɔg nit in di šul arájngangɔn (KF) →
אונ איז קיין מאנטיג אונ דאנרשטיג אין שול אריין גגאנגין
un iz k(e)jn móntik un dónɔrštik in šul arájngɔgàngɔn (KZ, KN)
'and he did not usually go to the synagogue on Mondays and Fridays' (26–8);

2 מיר קומין בלד אין דאש דארף mir kumɔn bald in dɔs dɔrf (KF) →
מיר קומן ב[א]לד אין דארף mir kumɔn bald in dɔrf (KZ, KN)
'we shall soon arrive at the village' (79–80);

3 קאם דיא צייט אין דער שול אריין צו גין
kɔm di cajt in dɔr šul arájncugèjn (KF) →
קאם דיא צייט אין שול אריין צו גין
kɔm di cajt in šul arájncugèjn (KZ, KN)
'it was time to go (in)to the synagogue' (146–7);

4 דיא מלחמה האט גיווערט פֿון דַעַן יאר ת״ח [. . .] ביז [. . .]
di milxómɔ hɔt gɔvɛrt fun dɔn jɔr tax [. . .] biz [. . .] (KF) →
די מלחמה האט גיווערט פֿון יאר ת״ח ביז [. . .]
di milxómɔ hɔt gɔvɛrt fun jɔr tax biz [. . .] (KN)
'the war continued from the year 1648 until [. . .]' (486–7);

5 וועלין מיר דיא סעודת מילה אפ ליגן
vɛln mir di súdɔs mílɔ ɔ́plejgn̩ (KF) →
וועלן מיר סעודות(!) מילה אפ ליגן
vɛln mir súdɔs mílɔ ɔ́plejgn̩ (KZ, KN)
'so we shall postpone the [festive] meal [after] the circumcision' (160);

6 קומט צו אים איין שד אין דיא גישטאלט פֿון איין מענשן

kumt cu im a šed in di gəštalt fun a mɛnčṇ (KF) →

קומט צו אים איין שד אין גשטאלט פֿון איין מענש

kumt cu im a šed in gəštalt fun a mɛnč (KZ, KN)

'a demon in human appearance came to him' (50–1);

definite article inserted

7 ווען דער גאלד שמיד איז אין שול גיוועזן

vən dər góldšmid iz in šul gəvɛzṇ (KF) →

ווען דער גאלד שמיד איז אין דר שול גוועזן

vən dər góldšmid iz in dər šul gəvɛzṇ (KN)

'when the goldsmith was in the synagogue' (415–416);

8 ווען מן זיך צו טיש גיזעצט הט

vən mən zəx cu tiš gəzéct hɔt (KF) →

ווען מן זיך צום טיש גיזעצט האט

vən mən zəx cum tiš gəzéct hɔt (KN)

'when everybody sat at the table' (352).

The morpho-syntactic rules of the three-component article system, which in Eastern Yiddish consists of the definite, indefinite, and 'zero' degrees, need separate treatment. Previous discussions of this system have been almost exclusively based on the semantic analysis of the various noun groups for which the employment of the definite and/or indefinite article is obligatory, optional, or unacceptable (see Veynger 1913: 20–2 §§20–3; Zaretski 1926: 60–4 §§113–28; 1929: 85–91 §§208–36; Falkovitsh 1940: 154–7 §§190–3; Mark 1978: 118–21).

At present we may note that in modern Yiddish a certain group of semantically marked nouns appears with 'zero' article in the following prepositional cases in the singular: lative and locative after the preposition אין 'in' and, in some cases, ablative after the preposition פֿון 'from; of' (see examples in Mark 1978: 120 §12; D. Katz 1987a: 80 §5.3.3.2). This group was characterized by Mark (ibid.) as comprising nouns denoting a 'concrete place'. On the morpho-syntactic level a noun that belongs to this group stands in opposition to any inanimate, animate, or indeclinable human object for which 'zero' article in the prepositional cases is unacceptable. Moreover, for this group of nouns the option of 'zero' article after the prepositions אין and פֿון is the least marked one. This correlation can be tentatively and partially exemplified by the following oppositions, which may be encountered in modern Yiddish:

with 'zero' article		without 'zero' article
ער זיצט אין {Ø/אַ/דער} שול	vs.	ער זיצט אין {אַ/דעם} קאַפּעלוש
ər zict in {Ø/a/dər} šul		ər zict in {a/dəm} kápəluš
'he sits in {Ø/a/the} synagogue'		'he wears a hat',
		lit.: 'he sits in {a/the} hat';
		ער זיצט ביי {אַ/-ם} טיש
		ər zict ba {a/-m} tiš
		'he sits by {a/the} table';
ער גייט אין {Ø/אַ/דעם} פּאַרק	vs.	ער גייט אין {אַ/דעם} מאַנטל
ər gejt in {Ø/a/dəm} park		ər gejt in {a/dəm} mántl
'he goes to {Ø/a/the} park'		'he wears a coat';
		lit.: 'he walks in {a/the} coat';
		ער גייט מיט {אַ/דעם} פֿריינד
		ər gejt mit {a/dəm} frajnd
		'he goes with {a/the} friend'.

Some of the changes that were introduced in Zholkve and Novidvor clearly conform to the morpho-syntactic pattern prevalent in modern Yiddish. Hence the omission of the definite articles of such nouns as דאָרף dorf 'village' and שול šul 'synagogue' in the lative case (after the preposition אין; see nos. 1–3 above). By the same token, the definite article is inserted before a noun of the type טיש tiš 'table' (see no. 8). In the prepositional case it cannot be employed with 'zero' article. On the other hand, the employment of the definite article in two other phrases (nos. 4 and 5) remained optional, athough their omission from the Eastern re-editions, especially that of no. 5, does not agree with modern Yiddish usage. The alteration אין די גישטאַלט → אין גישטאַלט (see no. 6) apparently anticipates the modern Yiddish semantic differentiation between אין געשטאַלט in gəštalt 'in appearance, form, image' and אין דער געשטאַלט in dər gəštalt 'in the character, gestalt'. The insertion of the definite article in no. 7 in KN1788 is not obligatory in modern Yiddish. But it is possible that in late eighteenth-century Eastern Yiddish such usage was conditioned by a possible morpho-syntactic distinction between the locative (cf. nos. 1–3 with 'zero' article) and the lative cases (cf. no. 7 with the definite article).

11.5.3 *Short Adjectives as Noun Modifiers*

In two cases the full inflected adjective is replaced by a short form, which may be analysed as an indeclinable noun modifier:

1 פֿר גרוישׂן פֿורכיט far grojsṇ forxət (KF) →
    פֿר גרוש פֿאָרכט far grojs forxt (KZ, KN) 'of great awe' (178);

2 האט גרושי צדקה געבין hɔt grɔjsə cdɔkə gɛbn̩ (KF) →
האט גרוש צדקה גגעבין hɔt grɔjs cdɔkə gəgɛbn̩ (KZ, KN)
'gave much [to] charity' (253–4).

The first change shows that the adjective was reanalysed as a qualifier of an abstract noun with 'zero' article as in modern Eastern Yiddish (see Birnbaum 1979: 296 §193c). The choice of the short form in the second change apparently anticipates the modern Yiddish use of other indeclinable noun qualifiers (e.g. אַ סך asáx 'much, plenty'; פֿיל fil 'much') in the same syntactic environment (e.g. ער האט {אַ סך/ פֿיל} צדקה געגעבן ɛr hɔt {asáx/fil} cdɔkə gəgɛbn̩).

In another instance the short form of the adjective היפש hipš 'large; massive' was preferred in KN1788:

3 אײן היבשר גימאוירטר קעליר a hibšər gəmɔjərtər kɛlər
'a nice[ly] paved cellar' (KF) →
אײן היפש גימויארטר קעליר a hipš gəmɔjərtər kɛlər
'a massively built cellar' (KN, 321).

Here the replacement does reflect the modern Yiddish pattern {modifier + base} (e.g. שטאַרק רײַך štárk ràjx 'very rich'; cf. Zaretski 1929: 109 §274), in which the short adjective היפש hipš carries the main stress of the compound adjective היפש גימויארטר hípšgəmɔjərtər. The change from attributive adjective hibšər to an invariant adjective qualifier hipš corresponds to the semantic shift from the old Western Yiddish hibš 'beautiful' to the modern Eastern Yiddish hipš 'massive; substantial'.

11.5.4 *Full Declension of the Attributive Adjective*

In contrast to the latter changes, two short adjectives were replaced in KZ and KN by morphologically co-ordinated attributive forms:

1 אונ׳ דאש גאנץ חדר un dɔs ganc xejdər (KF) →
אונ דאש גאנצע חדר un dɔs gancə xejdər (KZ, KN) 'and the whole room' (208);
2 גולדן כלי gɔldn̩ kejlə (KF) → גילדני כלי gildənə kejlə (KZ, KN) 'golden dish' (201).

Similarly the noun compositum {modifier (adj.) + base (noun)} was re-analysed in KN in accordance with the more modern usage as a noun phrase with a full attributive adjective:

3 דער קאַרג מאַן dər kárgman (KF, KZ) →
דער קאַרגר מאַן dər kargər man (KN), 'the stingy man' (49).

In principle, the replacement of the compositum with {attributive adjective + noun} may be attributed to the Slavonic influence on Eastern Yiddish (see M. Weinreich 1973: ii. 191 §147). Nevertheless, the predominance of constructions with attributive adjectives does not seem to be an entirely Eastern Yiddish innovation.

11.5.5 *The Case System*

As we have seen (§11.3.2.1), both re-editions provide plenty of evidence for the morphological merger of dative neutral with accusative and dative masculine forms of the definite article. This merger did not result in the levelling of the case system in the written language, however. On the contrary, the substantial hypercorrect employment of דעז dən may serve as evidence that the 'editors' of Zholkve and Novidvor were at pains to preserve the older morphological pattern. On the morpho-syntactic level the case system of both editions appears to be even more conservative. Hence the following usages that remained mostly unchanged in the KN1788 re-edition of the second volume of *Kav hayosher*; e.g.:

1 מיט דאש עשין שפּייז mit dɔs ɛsṇ špajz 'with [all] the food' (354–5);

2 פֿון דיא קינד בעטרין fun di kímpetɔrṇ 'from the woman in childbirth' (421–2);

3 אין דיא מדבר in di midbər 'in the desert (locative)' (386, 507);

4 אויף דיא זייט af di zajt 'to this side (lative)' (132);

5 אויף דיא ערד גיוואֿרפֿין af di ɛrd gəvɔrfṇ '(they) threw on the floor', (348–9, 355–6; cf. 350–1);

6 אויף דיא וועלט af di vɛlt (KF) → פֿון די וועלט fun di vɛlt (KZ, KN) 'in/from this life' (278).

The prepositional case, especially of the feminine definite article, was far from being as uniform and 'neat' in the spoken varieties of Eastern Yiddish as it later became in Modern Literary Yiddish. The case and gender systems of Eastern Yiddish dialects were in some respects fundamentally different from that of the modern literary language. (For a structural analysis of case and gender variation in Eastern Yiddish see Wolf 1969.) It may well be that some, if not most, of these cases (cf. nos. 2–5 and especially 6 above) did match the morpho-syntactic pattern of Eastern Yiddish dialectal usage.

However, both re-editions occasionally preferred to replace the historical accusative forms of the definite article of all three genders by the dative forms after the preposition אין 'in'. After the preposition אויז 'out' the change from accusative to dative is consistent at least for the masculine definite article. These changes probably anticipate the rise of the modern Yiddish prepositional case (see §35.6.3):

neuter

אויז דען הויז ɔjs dən hɔjz (KF) → אויז דעם הויז (KN) ɔjs dəm hɔjz '[to move out] of the house' (363).

masculine

אין דען וואלד in dən vald (KF) → אין דעם וואלד (KZ, KN) in dəm vald 'in the forest' (loc.) (76);

אויז דען בית החיצון ɔjs dən béjsxìcṇ (KF) → אויז דעם בית החיצון ɔjs dəm béjsxìcṇ (KN) '[came out] of the outdoor toilet' (449–50);

אויז דען פרק ɔjs dən pejrək (KF) → אויז דעם פרק (KZ, KN) ɔjs dəm pejrək 'from this chapter' (272–3).

feminine

אין דיא תורה הקדושה in di tɔjrə (h)akdɔ́jšə (KF) →

אין דער תורה הקדושה in dər tɔjrə (h)akdɔ́jšə (KN),
'in the holy Torah' (loc.) (307);

אין יידשי גאס in jidəšə gas 'on the Jewish street' (KF) →

אין דר גאס in dər gas 'on the street' (loc.) (KN, 318–19).

11.5.6 *Phraseology*

Only a few phraseological changes were introduced in the Eastern re-editions. Nevertheless, these point to further linguistic modernization on the morpho-syntactic level. The older expression גיט אין הויז הין און׳ ווידר gejt in hɔjz hin-un-vidər '(he) goes into the house hither and thither' (93–4) was replaced in Zholkve and Novidvor with גיט אין הויז הין און הער gejt in hɔjz hin-un-hɛr. The expression ⟨הין און׳ ווידר⟩ had been used in the mid-seventeenth-century poem about Khmelnitski's massacres (see M. Weinreich 1928: 202). It was employed there as a locative, meaning 'here and there' (= everywhere). Conversely, ⟨הין און הער⟩, although still unprefixed, is employed in KZ1777 and KN1788 as a lative. This change in form and function has its parallel in modern Yiddish, where the differentiation between the lative אַהין און אַהער ahin un ahɛr 'hither and thither' and the locative דאָ און דאָרט(ן) dɔ un dɔrt(ṇ) 'here and there' is generally maintained.

Phraseological and, more broadly speaking, morpho-syntactic alterations sometimes affect the original meaning of the syntagm in question; e.g.:

1   און זאגט אלי דיא אויש ריד un zɔgt alə di ɔ́jsrejd
'and [he] gives all kinds of excuses' (KF) →
און זאגט איין אויש ריד un zɔgt an ɔ́jsrejd
'and [he] gives an excuse' (KZ, KN, 142);

2   איך פֿר וואונדר מיך אל(י)ז דא איין בונט שליסלן הינגין [. . .]
ix farvúndər zəx al(ə)s dɔ a bunt šlislən hɛngən [. . .]
'I am surprised that a bundle of keys hang here [. . .]' (KF) →
איך פֿר וואונדר מיך אלין דא איין בונט שליסל העננט [. . .]
ix farvúndər zəx alc dɔ a bunt šlisḷ hɛngt [. . .]
'I am indeed surprised, a bundle of keys hangs here [. . .]' (KZ, KN, 220–2).

The combination ⟨אלי דיא⟩ (see no. 1 above) was not uncommon in late eighteenth-century literary usage. However, in Modern Literary Yiddish it has become an archaism, and is employed as such, usually with the uninflected form אַל al 'all' (e.g. אַל די áldi 'all' (pl.); see Mark 1971: 1353). The disappearance of this combination from the Zholkve and Novidvor re-editions may well mean that its use in this context was already felt to be outdated. In the other case (no. 2) the conjunction אַלי(ו)ז al(ə)s 'that; how; as' was reanalysed as an adverb אַליץ alc 'constantly, continually'. This re-analysis apparently stems from the fact that both forms were often spelled identically in Old Literary Yiddish.

Other morpho-syntactic changes include the insertion of the preposition of time אין (see no. 3 below), which surfaces in the modern Yiddish expression of time אַרום — אין in — arúm 'in — time', and the restructuring of the morpho-syntactic pattern אַיין אַזו an azó 'such a' (see no. 4 below) into the more modern אַזוי אַיין azój a (cf. modern Yiddish אַזאַ azá and אַזאַן azán):

3 אלזו איין קלייני פֿירטיל שעה נאך זיין אריין גין
alzó a kléjnə firtļ šɔ nɔx zajn arájngèjn (KF) →

אזו אין איין קליני פֿירטל שעה נאך זיין אריין גין
azój in a kléjnə fɛrtļ šɔ nɔx zajn arájngèjn (KZ, KN)
'so in less than a quarter of an hour after he entered [there]' (329-30);

4 [. . .] דו איין שין אזו הויז זאל dɔs an azó šejn hɔjz zɔl [. . .]
'that such a nice house should [. . .]' (KF) →

[. . .] דש אזו איין הויז זאל dɔs azój an hɔjz zɔl (KZ, KN)
'that such a house should [. . .]' (366).

11.6 Syntax

The syntactic changes found in KZ1777 and KN1788 include the occasional introduction of double negation and the infrequent deletion of the initial 'consecutive' adverb, which resulted in a main consecutive clause with the finite verb in first place. Finally, the word order of a few subordinate clauses was restructured according to the syntactic pattern of Eastern Yiddish.

Each of these changes is an important feature of linguistic Easternization. However, in both re-editions syntactic changes are less frequent, and less systematic than alterations effected in morphology and morpho-syntax. It seems that whoever was responsible for the linguistic changes in these re-editions was not too daring in restructuring the original syntactic patterns, which fully comply with Old Literary Yiddish usage.

11.6.1 *Double Negation*

Double negation was occasionally used in the original edition of this work (e.g. 108-10, 356-8; for another quotation from the same source see

Hutton 1987: 32). This feature is sometimes believed to be distinctively characteristic of Eastern Yiddish, and is attributed to the Slavonic impact (see M. Weinreich 1973: ii. 191 §147; Lockwood-Baviskar 1975). It has recently been shown on the basis of Old Yiddish works that double negation was one of the possible syntactic devices of negation in older Western Yiddish (see Hutton 1987). However, from the perspective of early modern Yiddish and of some older Yiddish texts, double negation is one of the most characteristic syntactic features of Eastern Yiddish. In Western Yiddish printed works of that period, double negation was becoming increasingly obsolete through the ever growing impact of New High German. At the same time it was gradually becoming the prevailing form of negation in the written Eastern Yiddish of the late eighteenth century.

Double negation is by no means the most frequent syntactic feature of the original *Kav hayosher*. However, when considered alongside other negative phrases, it may be analysed as a semantically marked form of negation. Its employment in the work itself is restricted to what we may call a generic negation, one that negates all objects generically represented by the given noun; e.g.:

1 אבר האבין קיין כלי ניט צו בראבין און׳ האבין קיין מענש גישעדיקט
ɔbər hɔbṇ k(e)jn kejlə nit cəbrɔxṇ un hɔbṇ k(e)jn mɛnč gəšédikt
'and they did not break any dishes and did not harm any human' (356–8);

2 איר זולט בייא אונש ניקש עסין און׳ ניקש טרינקין און׳ קיין מתנה ניט נעמין
ir zɔlt ba undz niks ɛsṇ un niks trinkən un k(e)jn matónə nit nɛmən
'you should eat nothing and drink nothing at our place and [you should] not accept any presents' (KF) →

איר זאלט בייא אונז ניט עסן אונ טרינקין אונ קיין מתנה נעמן
ir zɔlt ba undz nit ɛsṇ un trinkən un k(e)jn matónə nɛmən
'you should not eat [n]or drink at our place and [you should] not accept present[s]' (KN, 108–10).

In modern Yiddish, on the other hand, where double negation is the regular form, 'generic' negation is marked by special particles שום šum '(not) any' or איין ejn '(not) one', and less emphatically by the negation of the plural form of the object without the definite article. Hence the modern Yiddish equivalents of the sentences cited above would be:

1.1 זיי האָבן קיין {שום/איין} כלי ניט צעבראָכן
zej hɔbṇ k(e)jn {šum/ejn} kejlə nit cəbrɔxṇ;

2.1 און קיין מתנות ניט נעמען un k(e)jn matónəs nit nɛmən, or
און קיין שום מתנה ניט נעמען un k(e)jn šum matónə nit nɛmən.

As for the treatment of these cases in the Eastern re-editions of *Kav hayosher*, it is important to note that the insertion of שום šum or איין ejn in the first phrase (no. 1 above) is not obligatory, even in Modern Literary Yiddish. However, the deletion of double negation in the second phrase (no. 2 above) may indicate that the construction was still stylistically unwelcome in literary usage. This reluctance was apparently motivated by the New High German pattern that prevailed in contemporary Yiddish printed works in Western Europe, a hypothesis supported by the fact that a number of negative phrases remained unaltered in both re-editions; e.g.:

3 דען ער קען קיין תירוץ אונ׳ אויז ריד מער זאגין
dən ər kɛn k(e)jn tɛrəc un ójsrèjd mər zɔgŋ
'then he cannot give an excuse or a pretext' (174–5);

4 וֹוען מיר קיין מאבֿט דאריבר האבין
vən mir k(e)jn maxt daríbər hɔbŋ
'if we do not have the power to use it' (264–5);

5 דז ער קיין הנאה הט גיהאט פֿון זיינם גרושין עשירות
dɔs ər k(e)jn hanóə hɔt gəhat fun zajnəm grɔjsŋ ašírəs
'then he [would] have not enjoyed his great richness' (278–80);

6 אונ׳ האבין טאג אונ׳ נאבֿט קיין רוא גיהט
un hɔbŋ tɔg un naxt k(e)jn ru gəhat
'and did not have peace by day or by night' (360–1).

However, in the Novidvor edition of the second volume, double negation was introduced in the following phrases:

7 אונ׳ קיין מזיק הט מאבֿט צו וואונן בייא לייט
un k(e)jn mazək hɔt maxt cu vɔjnən ba lajt (KF) →
אונ קיין מזיק האט ניט מאבֿט צו וואונן בייא לייט
un k(e)jn mázək hɔt nit maxt cu vɔjnən ba lajt (KN)
'no demon has the right to dwell with humans [= where humans dwell]' (387);

8 אבֿר זיי האבין קיינם גיזעהין ɔbər zej hɔbŋ kejnəm gəzen (KF) →
אבר זיא האבן קיינם ניט גיזעהן ɔbər zej hɔbŋ kejnəm nit gəzen (KN),
'but they did not see anybody' (399–400);

9 אונ׳ ער האט קיין שעה קענין אן איר זיין
un ər hɔt k(e)jn šɔ kɛnən ɔn ir zajn (KF) →
אונ ער הט קיין שעה ניט קענין אן איר זיין
un ər hɔt k(e)jn šɔ nit kɛnən ɔn ir zajn (KN),
'and he could not spend a [single] hour without her' (409–10).

In another negative phrase the verb remained unnegated. However, the indefinite article of the direct object was replaced by the negative particle קיין k(e)jn. This replacement is an important morpho-syntactic feature of modern Yiddish; e.g. אַ מענטש a mɛnč → קיין מענטש k(e)jn mɛnč 'a person' (unmarked) → 'a person' (marked as negated; see Zaretski 1929: 90–1 §233; Falkovitsh

1940: 154–5 §191; Mark 1978: 119 §5; Birnbaum 1979: 254 §103; D. Katz 1987a: 240 §14.5.3.4):

10 ‏וואו קיין מאל איין מענש דא הין קומט‎ vu kéjnmɔl a mɛnč dahín kumt (KF) →
‏וואו קיין מאל קיין מענש אהין קומט‎ vu kéjnmɔl k(e)jn mɛnč ahín kumt
(KZ, KN), 'where no human [foot] treads' (71–2).

Double negation has not become a regular pattern of negation in the Eastern re-editions. Moreover, it was apparently felt to be undesirable for literary usage, since it sharply diverged from the pattern of negation that prevailed in Western Yiddish printed works of that period. In spite of this, double negation was occasionally introduced into the Novidvor re-edition. This testifies to the limited, but none the less significant, impact of Eastern Yiddish syntax on the older literary language.

11.6.2 *Word Order*

The restructuring of word-order patterns is one of the major syntactic features of the Easternization of literary Yiddish. It affected the placement of the finite verb in certain types of main clauses and in most subordinate clauses. It also affected the position of the uninflected parts of periphrastic verb forms and of infinitives and past participles governed by modal verbs.

11.6.2.1 *Past Participle* The predominant trend in *Kav hayosher* is to place past participles in a clause-final position. This remained virtually unchanged in the Eastern re-editions. The following two cases, in which the word order was Easternized, are exceptions:

1 ‏אונ׳ דער זעלביגר מאן איז איין קארגיר מאן גיוועזן וואש מאן אין גאנצין‎
un dər zélbikər man iz a kargər man gəvɛzn̩ vɔs mən in gancn̩
(‏עולם אזו איין קמצן ניט גיוועזן(!)‎
ɔjləm azój a kamcn̩ nit gəvɛzn̩
'and this man was a stingy person, so that in the whole world there was not another such miser' (KF) →

‏אונ דר זעלבנגר מאן איז איין קארגר מאן גוועזן וואש מן אין גנצן עולם‎
un dər zélbikər man iz a kargər man gəvɛzn̩ vɔs mən in gancn̩ ɔjləm
‏גפֿינט ניט אזו איין קמצן‎
gəfint nit azój a [= aza(n)?] kamcn̩
'and this man was a stingy person, so that in the whole world another such miser [could not be] found' (KZ, KN, 23–6);

2 ‏אונ׳ איז נפטר בשם טוב גיווארין‎ un iz niftər bəšémtɔv gəvɔrn̩ (KF) →
‏אונ׳ איז נפֿטר גווארין בשם טוב‎ un iz niftər gəvɔrn̩ bəšémtɔv (KN)
'and [he] died leaving a good reputation' (228).

As in Eastern Yiddish, the clause-final position of the past participle was abandoned in both these sentences. In the second sentence (no. 2 above) the change also resulted in the reanalysis of the expanded periphrastic verb ניפֿטר בשם טוב ווערן niftər bəšémtɔv vɛrn̩ 'pass away leaving a good reputation' into a combination {periphrastic verb + invariant adverb} preceding infinitive and past participle of the auxiliary verb (i.e. ניפֿטר ווערן niftər vɛrn̩ 'pass away' + בשם טוב bəšémtɔv 'with a good reputation').

The fact that all other past participles remained in their original final position in Zholkve and Novidvor may be explained by the general syntactic conservatism of these re-editions. In Modern Literary Yiddish the use of the past participle in final position (whenever grammatically optional) is reserved for more formal or elevated styles (see Mark 1978: 384 §3).

11.6.2.2 *Deletion of Consecutive Adverbs*   The occasional deletion of the initial consecutive adverb, so characteristic of older literary Yiddish, is one of the most important syntactic features of *rapprochement* between literary and spoken Yiddish in the seventeenth and eighteenth centuries (see §7.5.1). This deletion introduced into literary usage so-called consecutive main clauses with the finite verb in first place. Yet, in general, such clauses were a rarity, because the use of the initial consecutive adverbs (e.g. דא dɔ 'then; thus' and זו zɔ ~ אז(ל)זו alzɔ́/ azɔ́j 'so; thus') conventionally prevailed in the narrative styles of Old Literary Yiddish. This fully applies to the original *Kav hayosher*, where the consecutive main clauses are relatively rare (e.g. 2, 9, 50, 107, 263). As for the Eastern re-editions of this work, our texts show that no substantial changes were introduced. Deletion of the consecutive adverb was very rare; it was found twice in KZ1777 and once in KN1788.

1 מיין ווייב [. . .] האט איין זון אזו ביט איך איר זאלט מיין קינד מל זיין
   majn vajb [...] hɔt a zun azɔ́j bɛt ix ajx ir zɔlt majn kind mal zajn (KF) →
   מיין ווייב [. . .] האט איין זון ביט איך איר זאלט מיין קינד מל זיין
   majn vajb [...] hɔt a zun bɛt ix ajx ir zɔlt majn kind mal zajn (KZ, KN)
   'my wife [. . .] had a son so I ask you to circumcise my child' (53–5);

2 אונ׳ צום אנדרין טאג דא פֿאריט דער בעל ברית אויף איין וואגין
   un cum andərn̩ tɔg dɔ fɔrət dər balbrís af a vɔgn̩ (KF) →
   אונ צום אנדרן טאג פֿארט דר בעל ברית אויף איין וואגן
   un cum ándərn̩ tɔg fɔrt dər balbrís af a vɔgn̩ (KZ)
   'thus the next day the *balbrís* [= father] travels in a carriage' (61–2).

In the second sentence (see no. 2 above) deletion of the adverb דא did not result in a true main consecutive clause. Rather, it was apparently felt to be superfluous in the sentence, as it certainly would be in modern literary usage (although the original sentence is still possible in some oral narrative styles).

In general, main consecutive clauses remained suppressed in both Eastern
re-editions, a result once again of their general syntactic conservatism.

11.6.2.3 *Subordinate Clauses*   In nearly a third of the subordinate clauses
of the original *Kav hayosher* the finite verb occupies the final position in the
clause. Most of these clauses remained unaltered in the Eastern re-editions
(e.g. 5–6, 92, 232–3, 352–3, 378–80). Only in the following three cases
was the word order of subordinate clauses Easternized by abandoning the
verb's clause-final position:

1 מוז מן דאך פֿרשטין וואש אונזרי חכמים מיט דען דרוש גימיינט האבין
   muz mən dɔx farštéjn vɔs undzərə xaxóməm mit dən druš gəmejnt hɔbṇ
   '[so] we have to understand, then, what our sages meant [to say] with this
   homiletic extrapolation' (KF) →
   זאל מן דאך פֿר שטין וואש [הבן] אונזרי חכמים מיט דען גמיינט
   zɔl mən dɔx farštéjn vɔs [hɔbṇ] undzərə xaxóməm mit dən gəmejnt
   '[so] we have to understand, then, what our sages meant [to say]
   by [claiming] this' (KZ omits the verb, KN inserts it in a new place, 9–10);

2 [. . .] וויא עם צו וויין דיא נאכט קאם vi əs cu vajc di naxt kɔm (KF) →
   [. . .] ווי עש איז גקומן די וואך נאכט vi əs iz gəkumən di váxnaxt (KZ, KN),
   'when it was *vaxnaxt* (= the vigil before circumcision)' (134–6);

3 דז דיא שידית אין ממית איז dɔs di šejdəs in mejməs iz (KF) →
   דז דיא שידית איז אים ממית dɔs di šejdəs iz im mejməs (KN)
   'that the she-devil kills him' (311).

The few syntactic changes introduced in Zholkve and Novidvor are
replacements of syntagms prevalent in the old literary language by their
Eastern Yiddish equivalents. In one case deletion of the initial 'consecutive'
adverb transformed the given phrase into a main consecutive clause with the
finite verb in first place. The word order of a few subordinate clauses was
restructured on the syntactic patterns of Eastern Yiddish, and double
negation was sometimes introduced. However, these changes remain rare
and unsystematic. In both re-editions syntax proves to be much more
resistant to Easternization than other levels. To some extent this syntactic
conservatism restricts the modernization of morphology. Hence the preference to replace the preterite forms with present-tense or 'quasi-present'-
tense forms. Otherwise the replacement of the preterite with the regular
periphrastic past tense would have caused additional syntactic complications
(cf. above §11.3.1.4). The most significant morpho-syntactic changes did not
involve a drastic restructuring of the original word-order pattern of *Kav
hayosher*. Thus the word order remains otherwise unaffected by the insertion
of the subject pronoun (cf. §11.5.1) or the omission or insertion of the
definite article (cf. §11.5.2).

The changes effected on the syntactic level offer one of the most decisive criteria by which the overall extent of language change can be evaluated. The limited success of Easternization of the syntax of *Kav hayosher* shows some of the most fundamental limitations of the overall linguistic modernization of the old literary language in the late eighteenth century.

3
The Eastern Revision of *Tsene rene*

12 Introduction

A principally new stage in the Easternization of Old Literary Yiddish was achieved in the 1786 Lemberg re-edition of the *Tsene rene* (= TL1786). Of all known late eighteenth-century Eastern reprints and re-editions of pre-modern Yiddish texts, this is the earliest one in which the language was systematically and substantially revised and restructured on the patterns of modern Eastern Yiddish. Moreover, TL1786 represents the first eighteenth-century Eastern re-edition of this work. In view of the extent and the quality of linguistic Easternization in this and subsequent re-editions of the *Tsene rene* they will be referred to as the Eastern Yiddish linguistic revisions.

It is hardly a coincidence that the text of *Tsene rene* should have played a key role in the late eighteenth-century Easternization and linguistic modernization of the old literary language. This extensive Yiddish collection of popular Biblical exegesis and homilies was written by Yankev ben Yitskhok Ashkenazi of Yanev, and was published around the turn of the seventeenth century. The earliest preserved edition is that of Hanau (1622). For the last three and a half centuries it has been one of the most popular and influential Yiddish books of traditional Ashkenazic society (see Shatzky 1928; Erik 1928: 223–30; Tsinberg 1935: 150–7; Shmeruk 1964a; 1978: 115–17; 1986: 62–4; Turniansky 1971: 835; 1977: 165).

The outstanding popularity of the *Tsene rene* (sometimes also referred to as *Zeuno uReuno* or *Zeunah uReunah*) is amply reflected in the numerous reprints and re-editions, although many have been lost, and many were not even recorded. Shmeruk (1964a; 1981: 148) lists sixty-three editions between the early seventeenth century and 1785, almost all of which appeared in Central and Western Europe, and at least another 110 editions printed mostly in Eastern Europe between the years 1786 and 1900. The linguistic and textual variation displayed by these Eastern editions led to Shmeruk's pioneering study, 'The Eastern European editions of *Tsene rene*' (Shmeruk 1964a; 1981: 147–64). Because of its popularity and traditionally approved educational status, *Tsene rene* served as the basis of a number of ideologically motivated adaptations into Yiddish and New High German in nineteenth-century Western and Central Europe (see Turniansky 1971; 1977: 169–76;

Shmeruk 1978: 152-4). In Eastern Europe, starting in the early 1840s, it was subjected to two ideologically oriented re-editions. The 'Maskilic edition', prepared by an anonymous proponent of the Eastern European Jewish Enlightenment movement, appeared in Vilna in 1842; and the alternative 'Hasidic edition', revised and re-edited in a distinctly traditional vein by an unidentified Hasidic editor, was published in Yozefov in 1845 (see Shmeruk 1981: 159-62; 163-4).

This later development was preceded by the drastic linguistic moderniza-tion, already evident in the TL1786 re-edition of the book. However, this process of modernization continued well into the first half of the nineteenth century. Thus *Tsene rene* was not only the first and most important vehicle of Easternization for the old literary language; it was also one of the most significant indicators of the continuous progressive linguistic modernization of literary Yiddish between the years 1786 and 1845.

According to Shmeruk, the extant Eastern European texts of *Tsene rene* prior to 1845 comprise three principal linguistic revisions, each of which was prepared independently. TL1786 was reprinted in Zholkve in 1790 and 1799, in Lemberg *c.*1800 and in Lashchov in 1816; the Sadilkov revision of 1819 was reprinted in Sadilkov in 1824, in Slavita in 1827, and in Yozefov in 1827; and the Vilna–Grodno revision of 1827 was reissued with various modifications in Vilna in 1836, 1842, and 1848 (see Shmeruk 1981: 156-7).

We still lack proper clarification regarding the direct textual sources of each of the four principal Eastern revisions: Lemberg (1786), Sadilkov (1819), Vilna–Grodno (1827), and Yozefov (1845). In other words, it is unclear which earlier edition or editions of *Tsene rene* served as the basis of each of these revisions. A comparison of the text sequence published by Shmeruk (1964*a* and 1981) with other early to mid-eighteenth-century Western and Central European editions reveals that neither of the Eastern Yiddish revisions could have been based on the distinctly modified Prague edition of *c.*1695, later reprinted in Prague in 1709. This comparison also points to the possibility that the seventeenth-century Amsterdam editions, especially those printed in 1722, 1726, and 1736, may be viewed as the standard editions of *Tsene rene* prior to 1786 (see Shmeruk 1981: 149). In this connection, we note that the earliest Amsterdam edition appeared in 1648. And we now know of fifteen subsequent Amsterdam editions (see ibid. 148).

The linguistic changes introduced into TL1786 and the other two Eastern Yiddish revisions of *Tsene rene* have been discussed in detail by Shmeruk (ibid.). The present chapter offers a systematic linguistic reassessment of a text sequence selected from the weekly 'portion of Noah' (*parshes noyakh*), published and examined by Shmeruk (1964*a*: 330, 327, 326–5; 1981: 153–4; 156–7; 158; line numbers refer to Appendix 3, pp. 279–85). Additional eighteenth-century Central and Western European editions of the *Tsene rene* that were consulted include the Amsterdam editions of 1726 (= TA1726) and 1736 (= TA1736; TA alone refers to both these Amsterdam editions). The earliest accessible edition of *Tsene rene* was printed in Hanau in 1622 (= TH1622). The comparison of these four editions (TH1622, TA1726, TA1736, and TL1786) will be the basis for summing up the essentials of one of the earliest and most advanced attempts to Easternize Old Literary Yiddish in the last quarter of the eighteenth century.

13 Linguistic Easternization of *Tsene rene* (Hanau, 1622; Amsterdam, 1726; Lemberg, 1786)

Most of the linguistic changes in TL1786 were systematically carried out. This suggests that the linguistic revision of the text was a conscious editorial undertaking. During that period, the previous model of one supradialectal literary language for both Western and Eastern Yiddish communities had become ever more untenable. In the new configuration, Eastern Europe had begun to emerge as the new, rapidly growing, and linguistically increasingly autonomous centre. Therefore TL1786 may be considered one of the landmarks of the growing linguistic independence of Yiddish printing in late eighteenth-century Eastern Europe, and there is a good reason to suggest that it was primarily, or even exclusively, aimed at an Eastern Yiddish readership.

In our text sequence we find that in TL1786, Easternization has affected almost every major facet of morphology, morpho-syntax, and syntax. Linguistic changes had also been effected in the earlier eighteenth-century re-editions of *Tsene rene* in Central and Western Europe. These, however, were far less drastic morphological modifications, reflecting aspects of change and innovation with respect to older Literary Yiddish (see §13.3.1 below; cf. Shmeruk 1981: 152, 155 n. 14).

13.1 Orthography

The spelling system of TL1786 is typical of late eighteenth-century Eastern European Yiddish books. Its major features include the non-representation of most unstressed vowels, as well as certain interconsonantal stressed vowels, and the conventional graphemic representations of stressed vowels, of sibilants, shibilants, and syllable-initial f and syllable-final p (for a full discussion of these features see §11.1).

On the orthographic level we note that TL1786 virtually abandoned the Old Yiddish convention of the silent alef (mute ⟨א⟩) after certain word-final vowels. In our text sequence the silent alef has disappeared from all forms in which it was previously used; e.g.:

דיא (TH, TA) → די (TL) di [pl. or fem. sing. definite article] (6, 16, 22, 25, 34, 51);

דר בייא (TH, TA) → דר ביי (TL) dərbaj 'at that; nearby (adv.)' (4, 38);

זיא (TH, TA) → זי (TL) zej 'they' (28, 29, 31, 32, 50).

In contrast to its orthographic conservatism, this edition fully implements the abandonment of the silent alef which was only partially carried through in many other contemporary and much later Eastern Yiddish printed works (cf. §11.1.1).

In addition to the frequent omission of interconsonantal a vowels, TL1786 also adheres to optional orthographic representation of stressed vowels **21** and **13** in interconsonantal position:

vowel **21** (ɛ in all Yiddish dialects)

זעלבציג (TA) → זכציג (TL) zéxcig 'sixty' (9);

דער זעלביגר (TA) → דר זלבגר (TL) dər zɛlbikər 'the same' (11);

vowel **13** (NEY ɔ ‖ MEY and SEY u)

זאגט (TA) → זגט zɔgt (TL) 'says' (15, 22, 23, 29, 34)

זגן zɔgṇ 'say' (inf.) (TL, 45);

האבן (TA) → הבן (TL) hɔbṇ 'have' (3rd pers. pl., 29).

13.2 Phonology

Of all aspects, phonology remained least affected in TL1786. This can be explained by the general orthographic conservatism of this revision. Neither of the above-mentioned orthographic changes could substantially affect the conventional graphemic representation of consonants or stressed vowels. Therefore dialectal spellings, which would point to underlying Southeastern or Mideastern Yiddish phonological features, are still quite rare in this edition. Only three examples were found in the given text sequence, all testifying to the Southeastern or Mideastern merger of vowels **51** and **31** into a unitary i. The preposition אין 'in' and the conjunction און 'and', both yielding *in* in Southeastern and Mideastern dialects, are confused twice. Thus at one point ⟨אין⟩ was printed instead of ⟨און⟩, and vice versa (ll. 30 and 34). Analogously, the form git 'gives' (l. 34) is spelled ⟨גוט⟩ instead of the expected ⟨גיט⟩.

13.3 Morphology

A number of important morphological changes had already been introduced into the earlier Western re-editions of *Tsene rene*. These are surveyed in §13.3.1. An analysis of some prominent morphological changes introduced in TL1786 is offered in §13.3.2.

13.3.1 *Changes Introduced in the Western and Eastern Re-editions*

Certain older forms were morphologically and grammatically modernized in the Amsterdam re-edition of 1724. A number of nouns, verbs, past participles, and adverbs were replaced by their newer or more modern equivalents (see nos. 1–3 below). Accusative and dative forms of the third-person singular masculine pronoun usually merged into a unitary אים (no. 4); the inflected form of the attributive possessive pronoun was replaced by an indeclinable form (no. 5). Conversely, the short form of a substantivized attributive adjective was substituted for a full form (no. 6).

1 זעלבֿציג zéx(t)cik (TH) → זעלבֿציג zéxcik (TA) → זו(ע)לבֿצ(י)ג zéxcik (TL) 'sixty' (8, 9);
    פֿונבֿציג fú(n)fcik (TH) → פֿופֿציג fúfcik (TA, TL) 'fifty' (7);

2 אישט ist (TH) → איז iz (TA, TL) 'is' (5);
    איזט izt (H) → איז iz (TA, TL) 'is' (36, 53);

3 הרויש גאנגן (h)arójsgangən (H) → ארוי(י)ש ג(י)ג(א)נגן arójsgəgangən
        (TA, TL) 'went out' (46–7);
    הרויש טאן ווארפֿן (h)arójs tɔn varfṇ (TH) → ארויש גיווארפֿן arójsgəvɔrfṇ
        (TA, TL) 'expelled' (54);

4 אינן inən (TH) → אים im (TA, TL) 'him' (50);
    אין in (TH) → אים im (TA, TL) 'him' (54, 33);

5 זיינם פֿאטר zájnəm fɔ́tər (TH) → זיין פֿאטר zajn fɔ́tər (TA, TL) 'his father' (55);

6 דר זעלביג dər zélbig (TH) → דר ז(ע)לב(י)גר dər zélbigər (TA, TL) 'the same' (11);

7 זיין zajn (TH, TL) → זיינן zajnən (TA) 'are' (past auxiliary) (51).

Shmeruk (1981: 155 n. 14) observes that in the Metz edition of 1768 the preterite forms were sometimes replaced by present-tense forms; e.g. נאם nam 'took' (TH, TA) → נעמט nɛmt 'takes' (Metz, 1768), and וואושט vust 'knew' (TH, TA) → וואשט vāst 'knows' (Metz, 1768); vāst is a distinctly Western Yiddish form, its Eastern Yiddish equivalent being ⟨וויישט⟩, vajst in MEY and vejs(t) in NEY and SEY. In one case, TA editions were more 'modern' than TL1786 in replacing the old short form of the past-tense auxiliary זיין zajn 'are' with זיינן zajnən (see no. 7).

These alterations arose from morphological changes common to both Eastern and Western Yiddish dialects. However, in the literary language of eighteenth-century Western Europe many of these changes remained optional. The newer forms often remained interchangeable with the older ones (e.g. TA1726, ll. 42, 50) or, alternatively, were increasingly suppressed by forms modelled on the morphological and morpho-syntactic patterns of New High German. In Eastern Europe, on the other hand, the newer forms eventually became the only norm. The orientation towards Eastern Yiddish as the primary basis of literary usage ultimately prevailed over the inertia of the old literary language and over the models presented in contemporary Germanized Yiddish books written and printed in Western Europe.

However, the most important morphological changes are those uniquely characteristic of TL1786. Most of them were systematically carried through; others reveal other essentially Eastern features. All in all, the morphology of the Lemberg revision is considerably restructured on the patterns of modern Eastern Yiddish.

13.3.2 *Changes Introduced in Lemberg (1786)*

The characteristic Easternizing features of TL1786 include the omission of word-final dental accretion (no. 1 below), the modernized orthographic treatment of adverbial prefix a- (no. 2), Easternization of certain verbal forms (nos. 3–6) and of the oblique case of the interrogative and relative pronoun (no. 7), and, finally, Easternization or omission of certain past participle forms (nos. 8–9). Many of these changes (e.g. nos. 1–4) have already been observed and singled out as essential Easternizing features characteristic of the KZ1777 and KN1788 re-editions of *Kav hayosher* (see §11.3.3).

1 איין מאלט ejn molt (TH, TA) → איין מאל ejn mol (TL) 'once' (13);

2 איין וועק גאנגן avé(k)gangən (TH) → איין וועק גיגאנגן (TA) → אוועק גגנגן (TL) avé(k)gəgàngən 'left' (12);

3 אנטוורט entfərt(?) (TH) → ענטפרט ɛntfərt (TA) → ענפרט ɛnfərt (TL) 'answers' (7, 49);

4 ווערפֿן vɛrfn̩ (TH, TA) → וואַרפֿן varfn̩ (TL) 'throw' (37);

5 ער זאלט ər zolt (TH, TA) → ער זאל ər zol (TL) 'he shall' (39–40);

6 זאלן מיר zoln̩ mir (TH, TA) → זאל מיר zólmir (TL) 'should we' (32);

7 וועם vɛm (TH, TA) → וועמן vɛmən (TL) 'whom' (acc.) (39, 48);

8 גשטאנדן gəštandn̩ (TH, TA) → גשטאנן gəštanən̩ (TL) 'stood' (4, 39);

9 וואָרדן vordn̩(?) 'became' (TH, TA) → Ø (TL, 52).

Most of these alterations introduced forms that were eventually to become the norm in Modern Literary Yiddish. Thus the forms אוועק גגנגן avé(k)gəgàngən 'left', וואַרפֿן varfn̩ 'throw', גשטאנן gəštanən̩ 'stood', זאל zol '(he) should', and וועמן vɛmən 'whom' came to be the norm in modern literary usage. And although the form איין מאלט ejnmólt 'once' can still be encountered in Eastern Yiddish dialects, and is sometimes considered to be a colloquialism (cf. Mark 1971: 1178), it was almost totally suppressed in the modern literary language in favour of איין מאל ejn mol and אַמאָל amól 'once'.

This was motivated at least in part by the general Eastern Yiddish trend against sustaining word-final dental accretion (cf. §11.3.3.1; note, however, the residual of accretion in the modern Yiddish form דעמאָלט dém(ɔ)lt 'then'). Similarly, ענפֿרט ɛnfərt '(he) answers' and זאָל מיר zɔ́lmir 'should we' are distinctively Eastern Yiddish forms, which are occasionally encountered in the nineteenth-century literary language. The form zɔ́lmir is an assimilated variant of zɔln̩ mir (this and similar assimilations are cited by Prilutski 1924a: 15–16 §24). As to ɛnfərt, it was apparently the prevailing form in Southeastern Yiddish (see Shmeruk 1981: 154). Lifshits (1876: 140) gives ענפֿער ɛnfər 'answer' (noun) and ענפֿערן ɛnfərn̩ 'answer' (verb) as the main variants, though ענטפֿער ɛntfər and ענטפֿערן ɛntfərn̩ eventually became the predominant forms in Modern Literary Yiddish.

The most decisive morphological changes testify to the drastic restructuring of tense categories. The original preterite forms were overwhelmingly replaced by present- or quasi-present-tense forms, which in the given context can be analysed as 'narrative' or 'historical' present (see Shmeruk 1981: 157). Similarly, the various forms of the future-tense auxiliary are by and large based on the Eastern Yiddish paradigm.

13.3.3 Replacement of the Preterite

It is not clear whether the anonymous style-editor of TL1786 failed to understand the original preterite forms or did not know how to replace them 'correctly' (see Shmeruk 1981: 154–5). At that period the preterite was still not outdated for many narrative Yiddish texts (cf. §11.3.1.4), and it is not likely that the editor would have no knowledge of this category, as it was still employed in the older literary language. In our text sequence of eleven original preterite forms, only one, בראכט braxt 'brought' (l. 14), remained unchanged.

preterite → present tense

1 גאב gɔb 'gave' (TH, TA) → גוט git 'gives' (TL, 34);

2 וואר vɔr 'was' (TH, TA) → איז iz 'is' (TL, 38);

3 וואושט vust 'knew' (TH, TA) → ווייסט vejst 'knows' (TL, 39);

4 נאם nam 'took' (TH, TA) → נעמט nɛmt 'takes' (TL, 18);

5 פֿרוגט (TH) → פֿראגט frɔg(ə)t 'asked' (TA) → פֿרעגט frɛgt 'asks' (TL, 6).

preterite → 'quasi-present' tense

6 גאב gɔb 'gave' (TH, TA) → גיב gib 'give[s]' (TL, 21);

7 ליש (TH) → ליס lis 'let' (past tense) (TA) → לאז lɔz 'let[s]' (TL, 20);

8 נאם nam 'took' (TH, TA) → נעם nɛm 'take[s]' (TL, 16, 33);

9 קאם kɔm 'came' (TH, TA) → קום kum/kim 'come[s]' (TL, 22).

This consistent replacement of preterite forms indicates that the anony-

mous style-editor made a conscious attempt to modernize the text linguistically. By replacing preterite with present-tense forms (cf. nos. 1–5 above) he
did not alter too drastically the original function of the preterite as a narrative tense. Likewise, his preference for the present tense over the regular
periphrastic past can be explained on morphological grounds. Whenever the
replacement does not alter the meaning too drastically, it seems more
reasonable to replace the simple forms of one tense category by those of
another than by periphrastic forms.

On the other hand, the numerous cases of quasi-present-tense forms
which do not receive the third-person present suffix (nos. 6–9 above) leave
open the question as to whether the editor intended to preserve something of
the original flavour of the preterite, or whether his revisionary goal was not
fully implemented. These quasi-present-tense forms do not seem to have
existed in the spoken language. Such forms were also common to other
contemporary Eastern re-editions and revisions of older Yiddish narrative
texts (e.g. KZ1777, KN1788, and the *Seyfer Yosifun* printed in Lemberg in
1801). It may therefore be suggested that what we call 'quasi-present-tense
forms' are a special morphological contamination characteristic of the
transitional texts, in which the gradual replacement of the preterite can be
schematically summed up in the following chain of progressive alterations
(although the ultimate change may remain optional):

{preterite} → {'quasi-present'} → {present} → {periphrastic past} .

13.3.4 *The Future-Tense Auxiliary*

In TL1786 the first-person singular form of the future-tense auxiliary is often
orthographically identical with the first-person singular of the modal verb
וועלן vɛln 'want' (see ll. 37, 41, 44–5 where ⟨וויל⟩ represents ⟨וועל⟩). But it is
significant that the Old Yiddish future-tense auxiliary (1st pers. sing.) וויל
was replaced by the modern Eastern Yiddish וועל (e.g. 42). Moreover, the
old third-person singular form ווערט was systematically replaced by its
Eastern Yiddish equivalent וועט (e.g. 41, 44). TL1786 is therefore far more
advanced than the Eastern re-editions of *Kav hayosher* in introducing the
modern Yiddish paradigm of the future auxiliary into literary usage (cf.
§11.3.1.2).

13.4 Lexicon

In the TL1786 revision of our text sequence only two lexical changes were
effected (see Shmeruk 1981: 155). The form צלמים cləməm 'idols' was either
omitted (l. 2) or systematically replaced by the collective term עַ[בֿודה] זָ[רה]

avójdə zɔrə 'idol worship' (ll. 16, 18, 25). Similarly, the noun פסל pɛsļ '(hewn) image, statue' was consistently deleted (ll. 20, 27).

Both changes were motivated by certain lexical and semantic shifts that occurred in modern Eastern Yiddish. The lexeme פסל pɛsļ '(hewn) image, statue' was apparently felt to be somewhat too learned. This possibility is supported by the fact that פסל pɛsļ, although recorded in Harkavy's dictionary (1928: 374), is not found in Lifshits's dictionary (1876), which was based primarily on spoken usage, especially that of Southeastern Yiddish. Moreover, this word does not generally occur in modern Yiddish. As to the replacement of צלמים clɔmǝm, it may be relevant that in Western Yiddish the noun צלם cejləm had both meanings 'image' and 'cross' (see Beem 1975: 136). In modern Eastern Yiddish it came to designate 'image of crucifixion; cross' exclusively. In the modern language, there is a potential differentiation between the plural forms צלמער cejləmǝr 'crosses' and צלמים clɔmǝm 'images; crosses'. In the singular, צלם cejləm 'cross' is distinguished from צלם=אלוקים cɛləm-ɛlɔj(k)ǝm 'the image of God'. However, such differentiation, even if it could have been sustained in late eighteenth-century Eastern Yiddish, was far beyond the editorial intentions of the anonymous style-editor of TL1786. He did not aim to introduce subtle semantic and stylistic differentiations. Rather, his revision was intended to update the original language of *Tsene rene* by revising it on the patterns of spoken Eastern Yiddish, thereby making it clearer and more accessible to its contemporary and presumably Eastern European readership.

13.5 Morpho-syntax

The few important morpho-syntactical changes effected in TL1786 include the replacement of the old compound relative pronoun, the occasional omission of the definite article, and one omission of the preposition מיט 'with'. These last two changes are in accordance with the morpho-syntactic patterns of modern Eastern Yiddish. Likewise, the full declension of the attributive adjective was introduced.

13.5.1 Relative Pronouns

The second component (דא dɔ) of the Old Yiddish compound relative pronouns דאס דא dɔs dɔ 'that' (10) and וואס דא vɔs dɔ 'which' (49) was omitted from TL1786, thereby yielding דאס and וואס respectively. In many Easternized texts of older Yiddish literature, the form דאס sometimes remained interchangeable with the relative pronoun וואס 'that; which', and more often with the subordinating conjunction אז 'that'. The fact that דאס

sometimes survived as a relative pronoun possibly originates in the confusion between the two distinct functions of the Old Yiddish *dɔs* and modern
Yiddish *vɔs*. As a relative pronoun, the modern *vɔs* fully replaces the old
relative pronoun *dɔs* as a subordinating conjunction; *vɔs*, on the other hand,
functions in modern Yiddish in a semantically stipulated complementary
distribution with *az* (see Taube 1994). In many Easternized texts, as well as
in Mideastern Yiddish, the old subordinating conjunction *dɔs* often remained
interchangeable with the modern Yiddish subordinating conjunctions *az* and
vɔs. This interchangeability occasionally resulted in far less frequent
variation between the relative pronouns *vɔs* and *dɔs*.

The ultimate outcome of Easternization, however, was the complete
replacement of the old machinery of the relative pronouns *dər* (*dɔ*) 'that'
(masc. nom. sing.), *di* (*dɔ*) 'that' (pl.; fem. nom. and acc. sing.), *dəm* (*dɔ*)
'that' (neut. dat. sing.; masc. dat. and acc. sing.) and *dɔs* (*dɔ*) 'that' (neut.
nom. and acc. sing.) by the modern Yiddish indeclinable relative pronoun *vɔs*
(cf. §§28.3.2.5 and 35.7; see Shtif 1932*b*: 56–7; Fridberg 1968; M.
Weinreich 1973: ii. 191 §147, iv. 255; Taube 1994). The old relative
pronoun דאָש *dɔs* (l. 10), which survived in all earlier Eastern revisions of
Tsene rene, was thus eventually replaced by וואָש *vɔs* in the latest and most
modernized Yozefov revision of 1845. A similar replacement was also
effected in TL1786:

1 דא וויל איך זאָגן איך דין דעם גוט דעם אברהם דינט
dɔ vəl ix zɔgn̩ ix din dəm gɔt dəm avrɔ́m dint 'so I shall say [that] I worship the God
that [= whom] Abraham worships' (TH) →
וועל איך זאָגן איך וויל דעם גאָט וואָש אברהם דין
vəl ix zɔgn̩ ix vil dəm gɔt vɔs avrɔ́m dinən '[so] I will say I want to worship the God
that [= whom] Abraham [will] worship' (TL, 42–3).

Similarly, the older compound relative pronoun וואָש דא *vɔs dɔ* is replaced
by the modern relative personal pronoun וועמן *vɛmən* 'whom' (acc.):

2 דא וויל איך דינן וואָש דא נמרוד דינט
dɔ vəl ix dinən vɔs dɔ nímrɔjd dint
'so I shall worship what [= the deity that] Nimrod worships' (TH) →
וויל איך זגן איך וויל דינן וועמן נמרוד דינט
vəl ix zɔgn̩ ix vil dinən vɛmən nímrɔjd dint
'[so] I shall tell I want to worship whom Nimrod worships' (TL, 45).

13.5.2 *Omission of a Preposition*

There is a single omission of the preposition מיט 'with' in the phrase די
שיסל מיט זעמיל מעל di šis‖ mit zém‖mɛl 'bowl with best flour' (l. 17) which
becomes די שיסל מעל di šis‖ mɛl 'bowl of flour' in TL1786. This alteration is
not repeated in the later Eastern revisions of the *Tsene rene*. Nevertheless, it
is hardly an arbitrary omission. It seems to have been based on the morpho-
syntactic pattern of the so-called noun parallelism or noun compounds. This
important morpho-syntactic feature of modern Eastern Yiddish has been
discussed and analysed by modern Yiddish linguists (Veynger 1913: 22-4
§24; Birnbaum 1918: 65, 66 §133; 1979: 299-300 §202; Zaretski 1929:
191-2 §§578-82; Shtif 1932*b*: 59; Falkovitsh 1940: 152 §188; Mark
1978: 180ff.; D. Katz 1987*a*: 70 §4.4), but no detailed analysis or
agreement on terminology has been achieved.

13.5.3 *Omission of the Definite Article*

Deletion of the definite article after certain prepositions in modern Yiddish
was discussed earlier (§11.5.2). In this revision, the definite article of the
noun פייאר fájər 'fire' is consistently omitted after the preposition אין 'in(to)',
in compliance with the morpho-syntactic patterns of Eastern Yiddish:

1 ווערפֿן אין דז פייאר vɛrfn̩ in dɔs fajər (TH) →
   ווארפֿן אין פייאר varfn̩ in fajər (TL) 'to throw into the fire' (38);
2 אין דש וייאר היניין גיווארפֿן in dɔs fajər hinájngəvɔrfn̩ (TH) →
   אין פייאר אריין גווארפֿן in fajər arájngəvɔrfn̩ (TL) 'threw him into the fire' (50).

13.5.4 *The Full Declension of the Attributive Adjective*

One case demonstrates that the anonymous style-editor of TL1786 preferred
the full declension of an attributive adjective (cf. also §13.3.1 no. 6),
although the noun to which this adjective was originally attached was
omitted for lexical reasons (see above §13.4; cf. Shmeruk 1981: 155-6):

איין גרוש פסל ליש ער שטיין ejn grɔjs pɛs‖ lis ər štejn (TH) →
איין גרושן לאז ער שטיין ejn grɔjsn̩ [sc. pɛs‖] lɔz ər štejn (TL)
   'he left one idol unbroken' (20).

13.5.5 *Phraseology*

In our text sequence the Old Yiddish adverb דא dɔ 'so; then; thus' is deleted
eighteen times. This deletion had the most decisive impact on the phraseological and syntactic make-up of this revision (cf. below §§13.6.1-3).
Another Old Yiddish adverb avoided in TL1786 is נון nun 'now' (9).
Similarly, the adverbial combination דא נון dɔ nun 'and now/then' was

replaced by its modern equivalent ווען vən 'when' (45–6). This replacement
also marks the syntactic change from parataxis to hypotaxis (see §13.6.2).

Perhaps the most obvious change in phraseology is the replacement of the
more archaic combination אלי דיא צלמים alə di clɔməm 'all the idols' (pl. acc.)
by the more colloquial juxtaposition זיא אלי zej alə 'them all [= all of them]'
(l. 19). This substitution is parallel to the phraseological alteration in the
Eastern re-editions of *Kav hayosher* (cf. §11.5.6).

13.6 Syntax

Almost all the syntactic changes in TL1786 are the direct outcome of the
massive deletion of the Old Yiddish 'consecutive' adverb דא dɔ 'so; then;
thus'. The only change not conditioned by this deletion had already found
precedents in the earlier Amsterdam re-editions of the *Tsene rene* in which the
word order of TH was grammatically normalized according to the requirements of older and, retrospectively, also of Modern Literary Yiddish:

I דא תרח קאם dɔ térax kɔm (TH) → דא קאם תרח dɔ kɔm térax (TA) →
דא קום תרח dɔ kum térax (TL) 'Then Terah came' (22).

We note, however, that in contrast to changes in morphology (cf. above
§13.3.1), not every syntactic alteration introduced into the Amsterdam re-
editions is automatically found in this Eastern revision, even when the
changes significantly modernize the syntactic patterns of the text; e.g.:

2 אונ׳ ווען איינר קומן אישט un vən ejnər kumən ist (TH) →
אונ׳ ווען איינר איז גיקומן un vən ejnər iz gəkumən (TA) →
אונ ווען איינר גקומן איז un vən ejnər gəkumən iz (TL)
'So when one [person] came [. . .]' (5).

Leaving aside the unresolved question of whether the editor of TL1786
consulted the Amsterdam re-editions, we conclude that the most fundamental syntactic differences between the earlier editions of the *Tsene rene*
(starting with Hanau, 1622) and the Lemberg revision of 1786 originate
from the massive (see nos. 7–10 below) and in certain cases systematic (nos.
3–6) deletion of the Old Yiddish adverb דא dɔ 'so; then; thus'. As a result,
this revision radically modernized the syntactic organization of the whole
text by restructuring the 'if–then' clauses (§13.6.1), by replacing the
paratactical arrangement of clauses with a hypotactical construction
(§13.6.2), and by introducing the main consecutive clauses with finite verb
in first place (§13.6.3). All these changes are closely related. The place of the
finite verb is in each case conditioned by the preceding subordinate or main
clause. All in all, these changes show the overall shift from the paratactical

(i.e. lexical-syntactical) organization of the text towards the strictly syntactical subordination of main clauses and of main and subordinate clauses.

13.6.1 *The Restructuring of the 'If–Then' Clauses*

With the omission of דא dɔ the original {adv.–verb–subject} pattern of the main clause in the 'if–then' construction was consistently transformed into {verb–subject}:

3 ווילשטו דיך בוקן צו דעם פֿייאר דא איז(ט) עש גוט
vílstu dəx bukņ cu dəm fajər dɔ iz(t) əs gut
'[If] you will bow to the fire then it is fine' (TH, TA) →
ווילשטו דיך בוקן צו דען פֿייאר איז גוט
vílstu dəx bukņ cu dən fajər iz gut
'[If] you will bow to the fire—fine' (TL, 35–6);

4 ווילשטו דען ניט דא וויל איך דיך לאזין ווערפֿן [. . .]
vílstu dən nit dɔ vil ix dex lɔzņ vɛrfņ [. . .]'
[If] you, however, will not [bow] then I shall let you be thrown [. . .]'
(TH, TA) →
ווילשטו ניט וויל איך דיך לאזין וואָרפֿן [. . .]
vílstu nit vəl ix dex lɔzņ varfņ [. . .]
'[If] you will not [bow then] I shall let you to be thrown [. . .]' (TL, 36–7);

5 ווערט אברהם הרויש גין דא וויל איך זאגן [. . .]
vərt avróm (h)arójsgèjn dɔ vəl ix zɔgņ [. . .] (TH, TA) →
וועט אברהם ארוש גין וועל איך זאגן [. . .]
vət avróm arójsgèjn vəl ix zɔgņ [. . .] (TL)
'[If] Abraham walks out [alive from the fire then] I shall say [. . .]' (TL, 41–2);

6 אבר ווערט אברהם דרינן בלייבן דא וויל איך דינן [. . .]
ɔbər vərt avróm drinən blajbņ dɔ vil ix dinən [. . .]
'but [if] Abraham will stay there then I shall worship [. . .]' (TH, TA) →
אבר וועט אברהם דרינן בלייבן וויל איך זגן [. . .]
ɔbər vət avróm drinən blajbņ vəl ix zɔgņ [. . .]
'but [if] Abraham will stay there [then] I shall say [. . .]' (TL, 43–5).

This change in the word order of the main clause from {adverb–verb–subject} to {verb–subject} is directly based on the phraseological and syntactic pattern of spoken Eastern Yiddish. In modern literary usage the construction {{subordinate clause} + {verb–subject–object}} became one of the regular patterns of compound sentences (see Veynger 1913: 59–60 §86; Birnbaum 1918: 68–9 §§141–2; 1979: 305–6 §212; Zaretski 1926: 170, §394; 1929: 255–256, §797; Falkovitsh 1940: 336–7 §472; Mark 1978: 65 §4; Katz 1987a: 234–5 §14.4.5).

13.6.2 *From Parataxis to Hypotaxis*

The replacement of parataxis by hypotaxis is another significant trend in the syntactic modernization of the Lemberg (1786) revision of the *Tsene rene*:

אונ' דא נון אברהם וואר גאנץ הרויש גאנגן אויש דעם פֿייאר 7

דא פֿרעגט מן הרן [. . .] un dɔ nun avrɔ́m vɔr ganc (h)arɔ́js

gàngən ɔjs dəm fajər dɔ frɛgt mən hɔrɔn

'And since Abraham came out of the fire unharmed; so Haran was asked [. . .]' (TH, TA) →

אונ ווי אברהם וואר גנץ ארוש גגנגן אוש דעם פֿייאר פֿרעגט מן צו הרן

un vi avrɔ́m vɔr ganc arɔ́jsgəgàngən ɔjs dəm fajər frɛgt mən hɔrɔn

'And when Abraham came out of the fire unharmed, Haran was asked [. . .]' (TL, 45–7).

It may be added that the clauses cited below (see §13.6.3 no. 8) may also be analysed as a compound sentence. So the second-in-line syntagm in that example, האבן זיך די ע״ז מיט אננדר גקירגט hɔbn̩ zəx di avɔ́jdə-zɔ́rə mitanándər gəkrigt, can be analysed as either a main consecutive clause or a main clause to which the previous syntagm is subordinated (hypotaxis). In speech, such borderline cases would normally be resolved by suprasegmental means, i.e. by distinctive intonation patterns.

The replacement of parataxis by hypotaxis is sometimes seen as a more advanced level of syntactic organization stemming from the literary and allegedly more 'cultivated' or 'refined' syntactic patterning (see Falkovitsh 1940: 339 §477; Mark 1978: 70–2; Scaglione 1981: 7–8). In modern Yiddish, as in High German, certain types of hypotaxis are expressed by word order alone. In the case of High German the preference for hypotaxis is usually considered to be a characteristic trend of literary Early New High German (cf. Hensen 1954: 187; Lockwood 1968: 265–70). The possible influences of Latin grammar or of the vernacular upon Early New High German literary usage are variously acknowledged and assessed (see e.g. Bach 1961[7]: 232–4 §142; Scaglione 1981: 10; Wells 1985: 259). Speech and spoken dialects, however, are often observed, or at least strongly believed, to be principally paratactical in opposition to literary High German (see Hensen 1954: 191, 272, 273; Wells 1985: 259–60).

In modern Yiddish, however, hypotaxis is mainly restricted to the subordinating word order of the 'second in line' main clause. The main pattern, as in the earlier case, is {{subordinate clause} + {verb–subject–object}}. It is possible that the literary language could 'by itself' encourage the replacement of parataxis by hypotaxis as early as in the Lemberg edition of 1786. This issue has not yet been examined in relation to Old Literary Yiddish. However, the primary factor in this shift from co-ordination to subordination seems to stem from the general impact of spoken Eastern Yiddish. So if we were to accept the claim that literary usage is more likely to involve hypotaxis, we must still agree that the kind of hypotaxis found in Modern Literary Yiddish is also (if not to say primarily) one of the major syntactic models of the spoken language. Moreover, given the direct correlation between hypotaxis and 'verb first' consecutive main clauses, it should be noted that some modern Yiddish writers (e.g. Bashevis-Singer) often avoid consecutive main clauses even when they choose the form of monologue or try to emulate various speech styles.

13.6.3 *Main Consecutive Clauses*

Perhaps the most effective syntactic change has been achieved by the massive introduction of consecutive main clauses with the finite verb in first place (see nos. 8–10 and ll. 7, 8, 16, 31, 33, 34, 47, 50). This has radically modernized the syntactic and stylistic organization of most of the text of TL1786:

8 אײן פֿרויא האט גיבראַכֿט זעמיל מעל צו קרבן דא ה(א)בן זיך דיא צלמים מיט אנגדר גיקריגט

ejn frɔj hɔt gəbraxt zemḷ mɛl cu kɔrbn̩ dɔ hɔbn̩ zəx di clɔmɔm mitanándər gəkrigt

'a woman brought the best flour to sacrifice, so the idols quarrelled with each other' (TH, TA) →

אײן פֿרוי הט גברכט זעמל מעל צו קרבן האבן זיך די ע″ז מיט אנגדר גקירגט

a frɔj hɔt gəbraxt zemḷ mɛl cu kɔrbn̩ hɔbn̩ zəx di avójdə-zórə mitanándər gəkrigt

'a woman brought the best flour to sacrifice. [Thus] the idols quarrelled with each other' (TL, 24–5);

9 אונ׳ וועם דינשטו דא אנטוֹורט [ענטפֿרט] ער [. . .]

un vɛm dínstu dɔ ɛntfərt ər [. . .]

'And whom do you worship? So he answered [. . .]' (TH, TA) →

וועמן דינשטו ענפֿרט ער [. . .]

vɛmən dínstu ɛntfərt ər [. . .]

'Whom do you worship? [So] he answered [. . .]' (TL, 48–9);

10 דא איז(ט) אײן מלאַך (גי)קומן אונ׳ האט [. . .]

dɔ iz(t) a malɔx gəkumən un hɔt [. . .]

'Then came an angel, and he [. . .]' (TH, TA) →

איז אײן מלאך גקומן אונ האט [. . .]

iz a malɔx gəkumən un hɔt [. . .]

'[Then] came an angel, and he [. . .]' (TL, 53).

By deleting the consecutive adverb דא dɔ 'so; thus; then', this revision does away with an important stylistic and lexical device in Old Literary Yiddish, a particular convention in 'narrative' or 'epic' style. Its conventionalism can be illustrated by the fact that דא was usually retained in the later Eastern revisions of *Tsene rene* (e.g. in Sadilkov, 1819, and Vilna–Grodno, 1827). Moreover, this adverb was not replaced in the Lemberg revision by another, less archaic, and by then quite popular adverb אזו azó(j) 'so; then', as was sometimes the case in the Yozefov revision of 1845 (see ll. 8, 25, 53, where דא is replaced by אזו). Instead, the connection between main clauses is often expressed by the syntactic means of inverted word order in the consecutive main clauses (see D. Katz 1987a: 236 §14.4.8). This is no doubt one of the most significant features of linguistic modernization found in this revision (see Shmeruk 1981: 154). Hitherto consecutive main clauses with the finite verb in first place were apparently felt to be too colloquial, and were thus rarely, if ever, welcome in the older literary language (cf. §7.5.1). In this respect TL1786 took a significant step towards the general *rapprochement* of the spoken and literary languages. Retrospectively, this *rapprochement* is one of the major characteristic trends of the modern literary language.

4

The Eastern Reprint of *Simkhes hanefesh*

14 Introduction

Of the three texts under discussion in this Part, the Shklov (1796) reprint of
Simkhes hanefesh (=SSh1796) is the latest, following the Zholkve re-edition
of *Kav hayosher* (KZ1777) and the Lemberg revision of *Tsene rene* (TL1786).
It is also the least Easternized. Hence its classification as a reprint rather than
a re-edition (which would entail considerably more sizeable linguistic
changes, as in KZ1777) or a new linguistic revision (which would often
systematically modernize the language of the original text, as in TL1786).
Nevertheless, linguistic changes were effected in it, and their examination
will serve to demonstrate some of the most basic features of Easternization,
which were bound to be introduced even into what is the least Easternized
older Yiddish text.

Three works, Yekhiel-Mikhl Epsteyn's *Derekh hayosher leoylem habe*
(1703), Tsvi-Hirsh Koidonover's *Kav hayosher* (1705), and Kirkhhahn's
Simkhes hanefesh (1707), constitute the major corpus of early eighteenth-
century Yiddish *muser* literature, although each bears the distinctively
individual stamp of its author. (On the striking differences between *Kav
hayosher* and *Simkhes hanefesh* see Shatzky 1926: 40; Erik 1928: 301, 311;
Tsinberg 1935: 236.) Originally the first volume of *Simkhes hanefesh* consisted of two parts: the first is the main collection of ethical tales, parables,
and preachings (*muser*), the second a compilation of codified instructions on
some of the most essential religious laws, practices and customs (*dinim* and
minhogim). So the anonymous Eastern Yiddish *muser* collection comprising
Derekh tomim and *Derekh khayim* not only borrowed much of its content from
Simkhes hanefesh, but was also modelled directly on Kirkhhahn's book by
adopting its original structure (see §6.3).

Originally published in Frankfurt am Main in 1707, the first volume of
Simkhes hanefesh was reprinted at least eleven times during the eighteenth
century. This alone testifies to its popularity. (For full bibliographic details see
Shatzky 1926: 23–56.) By contrast, the second volume of *Simkhes hanefesh*
turned out to be far less successful. It is basically a collection of fifteen
Sabbath and holiday songs (*zmires*), written by Kirkhhahn to various
borrowed tunes. Musical notations often accompany the songs (see Fleiss

1912; Shatzky 1926: 21–50; Erik 1928: 304–9; Tsinberg 1935: 323–9). As far as we know, the second volume was printed only once, in Frankfurt am Main in 1727, and almost 200 years later was reproduced photo-mechanically by Shatzky in 1926. Only the first volume of *Simkhes hanefesh* will be considered here.

14.1 The Language of *Simkhes hanefesh*

It stands to reason that Kirkhhahn, a native speaker of Western Yiddish, was familiar with Eastern Yiddish. He mentions in his book that he used to live in Poland. Apparently while there, he married Tsvi-Hirsh Koidonover's daughter (see Shatzky 1926: 19–20; Erik 1928: 302; Tsinberg 1935: 236). Naturally Kirkhhahn's native Western Yiddish had a decisive impact on his writing. But he himself could not have been completely unaware of spoken Eastern Yiddish, and it is possible that a detailed dialectological analysis of the original *Simkhes hanefesh* would unearth Eastern Yiddish influences.

One of Kirkhhahn's ambitions was to write in a language intelligible to all (see Shatzky 1926: 42). From a linguistic point of view, *Simkhes hanefesh* is an outstanding realization of this ambition. On the one hand, it is written in a clear, syntactically well-organized style; on the other, it is enriched with various Western Yiddish idioms and expressions. Its language was to a large degree modelled on the spoken Yiddish of its time and place. Thus Kirkhhahn almost completely abandons the 'consecutive' adverb דא dɔ 'so; thus; then', which was so conventional in the epic and narrative styles of Old Literary Yiddish. Instead, he often employs the adverb אזו azó(j), which at the time seems to have been its more colloquial equivalent. On the syntactic level Kirkhhahn's frequent use of consecutive main clauses with the finite verb in first place is noteworthy. No less instructive are the morphological features of *Simkhes hanefesh*. A whole tense category, the preterite, was all but abandoned, and the archaic, as well as the Germanized, variants of Yiddish איז iz 'is' (e.g. אישט ist and איזט izt) do not occur, whereas the general relative pronoun וואָס vɔs 'which; that; who' appears to be employed at least as often as the older type of relative pronouns. By comparison, the more archaic of these features are still characteristic of *Kav hayosher*, written and printed by Kirkhhahn's father-in-law only two years earlier.

15 Linguistic Easternization of *Simkhes hanefesh* (Shklov, 1796)

Before long the first volume of *Simkhes hanefesh* became popular in Eastern Europe as well. However, the earliest known Eastern edition is SSh1796. Significantly, this edition lacks the second part of the original first volume.

This was apparently due to rabbinical opposition to the publication of halakhic and related texts in Yiddish (see Shulman 1913: 74; Tsinberg 1935: 246–7). Otherwise the Shklov edition is based on one of the later eighteenth-century Western editions. Thus the few textual omissions characteristic of the Sulzbach edition of 1718 (SS1718) and the Amsterdam edition of 1723 (SA1723) are repeated in SSh1796.

The texts chosen for the present discussion consist of a parable (see Appendix 4, pp. 286–7) and a story (ibid., pp. 287–92). The line numbers cited refer to Appendix 4. Both the parable and the story were also incorporated into *Derekh tomim* (see §6.3). In certain respects the versions included in *Derekh tomim* are more Easternized than those of SSh1796 (cf. below §15.3.2). But in *Derekh tomim* the story and the parable borrowed from *Simkhes hanefesh* (apparently from its first edition) were freely retold, whereas SSh1796, being itself an Eastern reprint of *Simkhes hanefesh*, is textually more dependent on one of the intermediary Western re-editions of this book.

This work was also re-edited in the nineteenth century; e.g. in Warsaw in 1848 and 1865. These two re-editions were apparently independent of SSh1796, and certain stories and parables were omitted or altered by the Czarist censor. (For a detailed discussion of the Warsaw editions of 1848 and 1865, see Prilutski 1931: 220–7.) The most puzzling detail about these and other later re-editions of *Simkhes hanefesh* is that, in spite of the many linguistic changes, the original language of the book remained relatively less modernized. Whereas the Yozefov (1845) revision of *Tsene rene* was remarkably Easternized, the Warsaw (1848) edition of *Simkhes hanefesh* retained most of its original syntactic and some of its lexical and morphological features.

15.1 Orthography

The spelling system of SSh1796 does not differ much from that characteristic of most late eighteenth-century Eastern Yiddish books. The omission of most of the unstressed vowels (e.g. גיטאן → גטאן gəton 'did', 8, 19, 21; דימאנטן → דימנטן dímantṇ 'diamonds', 20) and certain of the stressed vowels (e.g. גימאכט → גימכט gəmaxt 'made', 248; האט → הט hot 'has', 6, 15, 98, 141, 186, 210) and the conventional representation of the sibilants by ⟨ש⟩ and markedly less frequently by ⟨ס⟩ are among the most salient orthographic features of this system, and have been discussed in detail in connection with the orthography of *Kav hayosher* (see §§10.1 and 11.1).

Other more progressive orthographic features common to SSh1796 and Eastern re-editions of *Kav hayosher* and the *Tsene rene* are the substantial deletion of the silent alef after word-final open syllables, hence דיא → די di 'the' (sing. fem., pl.) and בייא ← בײ ba 'at' (e.g. 7, 31; 189, 251). Similarly, the apostrophe conventionally used in the Old Yiddish spelling of the conjunction *un* 'and' was in this reprint systematically deleted; hence ⟨אונ'⟩ ← ⟨אונ⟩.

In the realm of stressed-vowel representation, SSh1796 employed the digraphic representation ⟨יי⟩ of diphthong aj more consistently than the previous Western re-editions of *Simkhes hanefesh*:

אין גיבראבֿן (SF) ← איין גיבראבֿן (SS, SA, SSh) ájngəbrɔxn̩ 'burgled' (l. 1);

אין זאמליט (SF, SS, SA) ← איין זמלט (SSh) ájnzamļt 'collects' (46);

אין צו קויפֿן (SF, SS, SA) ← איין צו קויפֿן (SSh) ájncəkɔjfn̩, 'to buy' (perf., l. 50).

The same can be said of the replacement of the older spelling convention ⟨ו⟩ by ⟨א⟩ for the graphemic representation of vowel 41 (the universal Yiddish ɔ vowel); e.g.:

זורג zɔrg (SF) ← זאריג zɔrəg (SS) ← זארג zɔrg (SA, SSh) 'worry' (46, 49);

זורגן (SF, SS) ← זארגן (SA, SSh) zɔrgn̩ 'to worry' (50, 52, 58);

הוט (SS) ← האט (SF, SA, SSh) hɔt 'has' (17, 20);

הוט (SA) ← האט (SF, SS, SSh) hɔt 'has' (87).

To these we may add the following analogous re-spelling: טון (SF, SS, SA) ← טאן (SSh) tɔn 'to do' (184, 205; cf. 130, 233). In one case, however, the editor of SSh1796 preferred to employ the ⟨ו⟩ grapheme to represent the ɔ vowel: האשט (SF, SS, SA) ← הושט (SSh) hɔst '(you) have' (202). The same spelling of the form הוט hɔt 'has' is sometimes found in the SS1718 edition (e.g. 258, 259). This spelling was for the most part obsolete by the late eighteenth century in Eastern printed works, although it was often used in the Eastern Yiddish *Mayse gdoyle min Uman* (M[N1783]; see §31.2.1).

The diphthong ɔj (vowels 42 and 44) is sometimes represented in SSh1796 by the single ⟨ו⟩ grapheme; e.g. לויפֿט (SF, SS, SA) ← לופֿט (SSh) lɔjft 'runs' (l. 33); ביפֿאלן (SF) ← ביפֿולן (SA, SSh) bafɔjln̩ 'ordered' (206). This orthographic representation was conventional in many other contemporary Eastern Yiddish books, and is also consistent with Old Yiddish orthography; e.g. גרוש grɔjs 'large; big' (60, 135, 156); טוטי tɔjtə 'dead' (pl.) (142); לון lɔjn 'reward' (129). Similarly, the conventional spelling of the preposition af 'on' and of the stressed verbal prefix uf was in most cases changed from ⟨אויף⟩ to ⟨אוף⟩ (e.g. 81, 93, 157, 176, 207).

With regard to consonantal representation, SSh1796 adopts a number of spelling conventions especially characteristic of Eastern Yiddish. It replaces the spelling of the syllable-final plosive in the perfectivizing stressed preverb ɔp with a voiceless ⟨פֿ⟩; e.g. אב ציהן ɔbcign̩ ~ ɔpcign̩ (SF) ← אפ ציהן ɔpciən (SSh) 'draw aside; take off' (179); אבגישנידן ɔbgəšnidn̩ ~ ɔpgəšnidn̩ (SF) ←

אפ גישניטן (SSh) ɔpgəšnitṇ 'cut off' (p.p., 260). The spelling ⟨אב⟩, which was retained in the later Western re-editions of the book, was modelled on the orthographic patterns of New High German. On the other hand, in many Eastern Yiddish prints of the late eighteenth century, the spelling ⟨אפ⟩ becomes the orthographic norm, and the two phonemes p and f are orthographically distinguished as ⟨פ⟩ and ⟨פֿ⟩ respectively.

Another Eastern Yiddish spelling convention is the use of the ⟨צ⟩ grapheme for a more 'phonetic' representation of the affricated spirant c; e.g. פינשטר (SF, SS, SA) → פינצטר (SSh) finctər 'dark(ness)' (42), and with c in the postliquid position:

אליש (SF) → אליז (SS, SA) aləs → אליץ alc (SSh) 'everything' (39);
אלז aləs (SS, SA) → אליץ alc (SSh) 'constantly' (adv., 224).

Such spellings were observed in the Prague edition of *Hamagid* (1675). The graphemes ⟨צ⟩ and ⟨טש⟩ were also systematically employed for the postliquid affricated sibilants and shibilants in one of the earliest Eastern Yiddish texts, *Ben hameylekh vehanozir*, printed in Zholkve in 1771 (= BZ1771; cf. Prilutski 1924a: 106–7 §§159–60; see below §28.1.2). It appears, however, that in SSh1796 only the spelling of the postliquid sibilants was modernized. Hence the old conventional spelling מענטש mɛnč (e.g. 57, 143) remains unchanged. In one case the word-final cluster ts was re-spelled more 'phonetically' in SSh1796 as c; e.g. גוטש guts (SF, SS, SA) → גוץ (SSh) guc 'good (deeds)' (130).

15.2 Phonology

Judging by the text sequences under discussion, SSh1796 has no dialectal spellings that would betray a particularly Northeastern Yiddish phonology. On the contrary, the few dialectal spellings that are found point to Mideastern or Southeastern Yiddish. These spellings indicate the apparent merger of vowels 31 and 51 (cf. §15.2.2), the lowering of stressed vowels before x (cf. §15.2.3), the loss of stem-final r (cf. §15.2.4), and the possibility of word-final devoicing (cf. §15.2.5). All this suggests that SSh1796 was prepared or printed by a native speaker of Mideastern or Southeastern Yiddish. Available information about the printing shop in which this edition was printed neither supports nor rules out such a possibility (cf. Friedberg 1950: 90).

15.2.1 *From Western to Eastern Yiddish Vocalism*

A number of dialectal Western Yiddish spellings are found in the first edition of *Simkhes hanefesh*. The past participle gəlɔfṇ 'ran' is spelled ⟨גילויפֿן⟩ (26).

This apparently stems from the confusion between the ⟨א⟩ representation of vowel 41 (pan-dialectal Yiddish ɔ) and the ⟨וי⟩ and ⟨א⟩ representations of vowel 44 (WY ā ‖ NEY ej ‖ MEY and SEY ɔj). This spelling had previously been 'corrected' to ⟨גילאָפֿן⟩ in the SS1718 and SA1723 editions.

The use of the ⟨א⟩ grapheme for vowels 24 and 44 is a distinctly dialectal spelling, which testifies to the Western Yiddish merger of these two vowels into a unitary a. Not surprisingly, this spelling is found in the original edition of *Simkhes hanefesh*; e.g. ⟨ביפֿאַלן⟩ 'order' (206) and ⟨האַשט⟩ '(is) called' (132). These dialectal spellings were replaced, however, by the standardized interdialectal ⟨ביפֿולן⟩ in SA1723 and by ⟨הייסט⟩ in SS1718 and SA1723. The forms ⟨ביפֿולן⟩ and ⟨הייסט⟩ yield bəfāln and hāst in Western, bafejln and hejst in Northeastern, bafɔjln and hajst in Mideastern, and bafɔjln and hɛjst in Southeastern Yiddish.

In SSh1796 the Western Yiddish adverb אך āx 'also' (with vowel 44) is consistently replaced by its Eastern Yiddish equivalent ɔjx, spelled either ⟨אוך⟩ or ⟨אויך⟩ (e.g. 27, 211, and 246, 250). Our edition was apparently printed from one of the later Western editions of the book. So the alterations of the original Western Yiddish spellings must be credited to the earlier editions (e.g. SS1718 or SA1723).

15.2.2 *Merger of Vowels 31 and 51*

One orthographic variant found only in SSh1796 may indicate the underlying Mideastern or Southeastern i realization of vowel 31:

ביפֿינדן bəfindn̦ (SF, SS, SA) → בפֿונדן bafindn̦ (SSh) 'be; exist' (189).

Though this item is hardly characteristic of Eastern Yiddish, its spelling in SSh1796 as בפֿונדן ⟨bfundn⟩ apparently testifies to the Mideastern or Southeastern merger of vowels 31 (NEY i ‖ MEY and SEY ĭ ‖ i) and 51 (NEY u ‖ MEY and SEY i). By virtue of this merger, the original i vowel could be either represented by ⟨ו⟩ or mistakenly reanalysed as u (i.e. a hypercorrection).

15.2.3 *Vowel Lowering before* [x] *and* [r]

The lowering of stressed vowels before x and r is another characteristic Eastern Yiddish feature (cf. Herzog 1965a: 191–7 §5.3.5). In some late eighteenth-century Eastern Yiddish printed works lowering is quite often encountered in the spelling of certain words. The following two cases of the lowering of vowel 31 to ɛ before x were found in SSh1796:

זיכר zixər (SF, SS, SA) → זעכר zɛxər (SSh) 'sure, certain' (37);

אום גירילט umgəríxt (SF, SS, SA) → אום גרעלט umgəréxt (SSh) 'unexpectedly' (38).

A possible secondary lowering (see Herzog 1965a: 192–7 §5.13.52 and maps 5.60–1) of historical vowel **21** (the pan-dialectal Yiddish ɛ) before r may have been a supporting factor in the retention of the Western Yiddish form שטערבן štɛrbn̦ 'die', which replaces the original שטארבן štarbn̦ in the Sulzbach and Amsterdam editions; e.g. שטארבן štarbn̦ (SF) → שטערבן štɛrbn̦ (SS, SA) → שטערבן štɛrbn̦ (SSh). In SSh1796 štɛrbn̦ is more likely to be a survival from earlier Western editions of the book.

15.2.4 *Word-final Devoicing and Regressive Devoicing*

Word-final devoicing is especially characteristic of Mideastern Yiddish (see Herzog 1965*a*: 220–3 §5.22; King 1980; cf. also King 1968: 47–8, 202; Bynon 1977: 125–6). The following spelling testifies to the editor's or printer's uncertainty with regard to the etymological distribution of word-final voiced and unvoiced dentals: פֿאלט (SF, SS, SA) → פֿאלד (SSh) falt 'falls' (255). In the same line we find the following misspelling: שטייגט štajgt (SF, SS, SA) → שטקיים štajkt (?) (Sh) 'reaches'. Here ⟨שטקיים⟩ stands for ⟨שטייגט⟩. The latter form is indicative of the pan-Eastern Yiddish regressive devoicing; i.e. gt → kt (cf. King 1980: 381–2).

15.2.5 *The Loss of Post-vocalic [r]*

The loss of post-vocalic r is divulged in SSh1796 by the etymologically unjustified reinstatement of r in the following case:

טרויאט trɔjət 'trusts' (SF, SS, SA) → טרוייארט trɔjərt 'grieves' (SSh, 227).

This type of hypercorrection was observed in Mideastern Yiddish (see Herzog 1965*a*: 223 §5.23). In the Shklov reprint, this spelling makes the original rhymed saying somewhat nonsensical:

ווער צו גאט טרויאט דער האט וואל גיבויאט
ver cu gɔt trɔjət der hɔt vɔjl gəbɔjət
'he who puts his trust in God does well' (SF, SS, SA) →

ווער צו גאט טרוייארט (!) דער האט וואל גיבויאט
ver cu gɔt trɔjərt der hɔt vɔjl gəbɔj(ɛ)t
'he who grieves [sic!] to God does well' (SSh, 227–8).

15.3 Morphology

As in the Eastern re-editions of *Kav hayosher*, the most systematic changes in SSh1796 were in morphology. A number of changes are specific to this reprint. However, on the whole, the extent of Easternization is markedly less advanced in this text.

15.3.1 *Systematic Changes*

Most of the systematic changes had already been introduced on a much larger scale in other, earlier Eastern reworkings of older Yiddish works (cf. e.g. §7.3.3). These changes include the consistent replacement of such Western Yiddish forms as גי)ענטפֿערט gəentfərt 'answered', זאָללש zɔlxs 'such' (sing.), and זאַללי zɔlxə 'such' (pl.) by their Eastern Yiddish or Easternized equivalents גיענטפֿרט gəenfərt (see 55, 134, 197), זיעלב(י)ש zɛlx(ə)s, and זיעלבי zɛlxə (47–8, 56, 79, 183, 188, 224).

Among the most striking morphological changes specific to SSh1796 are the introduction of Eastern Yiddish אַרבט arbət 'work; (he) works' instead of the older literary or Western אַרבייט arbə(j)t (63, cf. 33) and the consistent replacement of האָפֿנונג hɔfnung 'hope' by its Eastern Yiddish equivalent האָפֿונג hɔfung (e.g. 92, 140, 141, 204). The first case reflects the full integration of the item into the sound pattern of the language by the consistent application of posttonic reduction. The second reflects the Eastern Yiddish intolerance of medial nasal clusters.

In addition, the phonetically integrated form פֿר גיעלשט fargɛ́lst 'reward, repay' (2nd pers. sing.) is changed to the morphologically differentiated פֿר גיעלטשט fargɛ́ltst (130). The original ⟨פֿר גיעלשט⟩ is apparently a result of the assimilation *tst → st* (cf. modern Yiddish וואָלסט vɔlst 'you would' as a legitimate variant of וואָלטסט vɔltst), and its replacement by ⟨פֿר גיעלטשט⟩ could have been effected to avoid a possible homonymy with פֿאַרגיעלסט fargɛ́lst 'make yellow' (2nd pers. sing.).

Similarly, the Western Yiddish forms of negation (see below, no. 1) and of diminutive formation (no. 2) were replaced in SSh1796 by their Eastern Yiddish equivalents; e.g.:

1 ניקש גיבט niks gi(b)t 'does not give anything' (SF, SS, SA) →
   ניט גינעבן nit gəgɛbn̩ 'did not give' (SSh, 106);
   גאָר ניקש gɔr niks (SF, SS, SA) → גאָר נישט gɔ́rništ (SSh, 26) 'nothing';
2 שטיקלי štikxə (SF, SS, SA) → שטיקל štikl̩ (Sh, 87) 'piece'.

These two changes, as well as the use of Eastern Yiddish האָפֿונג hɔfung 'hope' for האָפֿנונג hɔfnung, were noted among the Eastern Yiddish features characteristic of the *Derekh tomim* of Zholkve 1723 (§§7.3.2–3).

15.3.2 *Forms and Categories Resistant to Easternization*

In many other respects the Shklov reprint is far less Easternized than the language of *Derekh tomim* (DtZ1723). Such Western Yiddish forms as גיפֿונדן gəfundn̩ 'found' (176), גיבט gibt 'gives' (100), בארים הערציג bar(ə)mhɛ́rcik 'merciful' (117), and שטיערבט štɛrbt 'dies' (SS, SA, 38) remained unaltered in SSh1796. By contrast, most of them were Easternized to גיט git 'gives',

באָרים האַרציג bár(ə)m̩hárcik 'merciful', and שטאַרבט štarbt 'dies' in *Derekh tomim* (cf. §2.3.5). Moreover, the 'modern' form גיפֿינן gəfinən can be found in the early and remarkably Eastern work *Tikuney tshuve erets Tsvi* (Cracow, 1666, cf. §5.3).

The following assorted changes were far from systematic in SSh1796:

3 אָן קומן ɔ́nkumən (SF, SS, SA) → אָן גקומן ɔ́ngəkùmən (SSh) 'arrived' (22);
   גאַנגן gangən (SF, SS, SA) → גגאַנגן gəgangən (SSh) 'went' (85, 157);

4 ארליזן ərlejzn̩/arléjzn̩ (SF, SS) → דער ליזן dərlejzn̩ (SA) →
   דר לייזן dərlejzn̩ (SSh) 'redeem' (125);
   בידאַרף bədárf (SF, SS, SA) → בדאַרף badárf (SSh) 'requires' (49, 51);
   ביגראָבן bəgrɔbn̩ (SF, SS, SA) → בגראָבן bagrɔ́bn̩ (SSh) 'bury' (147);

5 אויף דען מישט איז גילעגן af dən mist iz gəlɛgn̩ (SF, SS, SA) →
   אוף דעם מישט איז גילעגן af dəm mist iz gəlɛgn̩ (SSh),
     'lay on the garbage' (166–7);

6 אליש (SF) → אליז (SS, SA) ál(ə)s → אלין alc (SSh) 'everything' (39);
   אלז al(ə)s (SA) → אלין alc (SSh) 'everything' (224);
   אלז al(ə)s (SF, SS, SA) → אז az (SSh) 'that' (conj.) (230);

7 איך בין דער עני דער [. . .] ix bin dər ɔ́ni dər [. . .] (SF, SS, SA) →
   איך בין דער עני וואָש [. . .] ix bin dər ɔ́ni vɔs [. . .] (SSh)
   'I am the poor man who [. . .]' (199–201);

8 ווערט vərt (SF, SS, SA) → וועט vət (SSh) 'will' (fut. aux., 3rd pers. sing., 24).

The Eastern Yiddish merger of the dative and accusative forms of the definite article had very little effect on this Eastern reprint of *Simkhes hanefesh*. Only in one case was the original דען dən replaced by דעם dəm (see no. 5 above). The Easternization of the Old Yiddish form אליש ~ אל(י)ז ál(ə)s 'everything (pron.); that (conj.); constantly (adv.)' into אלין alc and אז az (see no. 6) was remarkably rare. And not all previously unprefixed past participles (no. 3) were consistently prefixed (e.g. 82, 97, 243).

As to the Easternization of the unstressed preverbs bə- and ər-/ar- into ba- and dər- (see no. 4), the spelling of ba- often remained unchanged (e.g. 89, 103, 194, 211, 244), and ər-/ar- had already been modified earlier in SA1723.

By comparison, all these changes were systematically effected in the Zholkve (1777) and Novidvor (1788) re-editions of *Kav hayosher*. The only exception is the accidental, but no less significant, replacement of the Western Yiddish relative pronoun דער dər by the Eastern Yiddish invariant וואָש vɔs (see no. 7 above). Elsewhere in our text sample, SSh1796 preserves the original older relative pronouns. We may thus assume that this alteration, as well as the singular replacement of the future-tense auxiliary ווערט vərt (see no. 8 above), were effected in SSh1796 in spite of its general reluctance to consistently modernize the original language of *Simkhes hanefesh*. These changes are, nevertheless, evidence of the growing impact of Eastern Yiddish in the 1790s, even on less Easternized older Yiddish texts.

15.4 Lexicon and Phraseology

It is very rare for distinctly Eastern Yiddish lexical items to be used in Easternized texts. It would appear that words not acceptable in the old literary language were not deemed fit for Easternized texts (cf. §7.2.2). In this respect the printer or editor of SSh1796, like those of the Eastern re-editions of *Kav hayosher* (cf. §11.4), is cautious not to introduce Eastern Yiddish lexemes of Slavonic origin.

Nevertheless, a number of Old Yiddish and Western Yiddish lexemes were either omitted or replaced. The adverb עבין ɛbn 'fast, quickly' (160) was deleted from SSh1796, and other words were replaced by Eastern Yiddish forms; e.g.:

1 אורב(ל)יצלינג urb(l)icling (SF, SS, SA) → פלוצים plucəm (SSh) 'suddenly' (36);
2 בישעפֿנים bəšéfənis (SF, SS, SA) → בשעפֿניש bašéfəniš (SSh) 'creatures' (118);
3 קיסן kisn̩ (SF, SS, SA) → קושן kušn̩ (SSh) 'kiss' (verb) (205);
4 רענט rɛnt 'runs' (SF, SS, SA) → ארביט arbət 'works' (3rd pers. sing.) (33);
  רענן rɛnən 'run' (SF, SS, SA) → רייז rajz[n̩] (SSh) 'travel' (verb) (234).

These words would appear not to have been sufficiently intelligible to the average speaker of Eastern Yiddish. And whereas one of the replacements (no. 2) can be viewed as morphological, the replacement of the distinctly archaic אורב(ל)יצלינג urb(l)icling 'suddenly' (cf. Mark and Joffe 1966: 820) and of the exclusively Western Yiddish קיסן kisn̩ 'kiss' and רענט rɛnt 'runs' are important features of Easternization and modernization in the lexicon. These replacements suggest that the words in question had become unintelligible, or at least less familiar in contemporary Eastern Yiddish.

With regard to phraseology, we find that only one significant change was introduced in our text segment:

נון עש האט איין צייט לאנג אן גישטאנדן
nun əs hɔt a cajt lang ɔ́ngəštandn̩ (SF, SS, SA) →
נון עש האט איין צייט לאנג אן גטראפֿן
nun əs hɔt a cajt lang ɔ́ngətrɔfn̩ (SSh)
'now, after a long time' (152–3).

The use of the verb ɔ́nštējn̩ in such expressions of time was apparently characteristic of Western Yiddish (cf. the examples cited in Mark 1971: 1663, viz. אָנשטיין, no. 4), but possibly not very familiar in Eastern Yiddish.

Hence its replacement in SSh1796 by ɔ́ntrɛfn̩, which seems to be idiomatically more acceptable in Eastern Yiddish.

15.5 Morpho-syntax

A number of changes effected in SSh1796 testify to continuous Easternization on the morpho-syntactic level. Hence the avoidance of the inflected form of the indefinite article, the introduction of the full declension of the attributive adjective (see below no. 1), and the use of the short adjective as an abstract noun qualifier (no. 2). These last two changes are also found in the Eastern re-editions of *Kav hayosher* (cf. §§11.5.3–4).

1 **full declension of the attributive adjective with uninflected indefinite article**
   פֿון איינר הױכֿי משפחה fun ejnər hɔjxə mišpɔ́xə (SF, SS, SA) →
   אונ פֿון איין הױכֿר משפחה fun a hɔjxər mišpɔ́xə (SSh)
   'from a high(ly reputed) family' (170–1).

2 **short adjective as an abstract noun qualifier**
   האט גרושן דוחק מוזן לײדן hɔt grɔjsn̩ dɔjxək muzn̩ lajdn̩ (SF, SS, SA) →
   האט גרוש דוחק מוזן לײדן hɔt grɔjs dɔjxək muzn̩ lajdn̩ (SSh)
   '(he) had to suffer from great poverty' (156–7).

3 **deletion of the -(ə)n suffix in the syntagm {adjective + noun}**
   צינן גיפֿעס cínən gəfɛ́s (SF, SS, SA) → צין גפֿעס cíngəfɛ́s (SSh) 'tin dishes' (28).

4 **the case system:**
   a—the dative case
   העלפֿן [. . .] מיך mix [. . .] hɛlfn̩ (SF, SS, SA) →
   העלפֿן [. . .] מיר mir [. . .] hɛlfn̩ (SSh) 'help [. . .] me' (64–5).
   b—the prepositional case
   הינטר מיך לאזן hintər mix lɔzn̩ (SF) →
   הינטר מיר לאזן hintər mir lɔzn̩ (SS, SA, SSh) 'to leave behind me' (68).

The deletion of the adjectival -(ə)n suffix in a syntagm of the type {adjective + noun} (see above no. 3) can also be seen to have been motivated by Eastern Yiddish. Indeed, the morpho-syntactic restructuring of the syntagm cínən gəfɛ́s 'dishes of tin' also yields cínərn̩ gəfɛ́s in modern Eastern Yiddish, where cínərn̩ remains an attributive adjective. It is possible that the variants cínərn gəfɛ́s ~ cíngəfɛs could have had a different distribution in Eastern Yiddish dialects.

From the dialectological point of view, the introduction of the dative case with hɛlfn̩ 'to help' (see above no. 4a) is most likely a feature of Northeastern Yiddish. In any case, the original מיך mǝx 'me' (acc.) in this position would seem to have been acceptable in Southeastern Yiddish as well. In Modern Literary Yiddish מיר mir 'me' (dat.) would normally be expected (cf. Mark

1978: 175 §6). The other change of case (see above no. 4b) conforms fully with the Eastern Yiddish requirements of the so-called prepositional case. This change, however, cannot be credited to SSh1796, since it was introduced into the earlier Western re-editions of the book.

In spite of all these changes, the overall Easternization of the original *Simkhes hanefesh* on a morpho-syntactic level remained limited. It seems that this reprint would have benefited from the insertion of a few subject pronouns (e.g. 15, 26, 51) and from some other morpho-syntactic 'improvements'. Syntactic changes were even more marginal.

15.6 Syntax

In our texts only two important syntactic changes were found. One of these seems to have arisen spontaneously as a result of the direct impact of the printer's spoken language. The finite verb in the subordinate clause jumps to the second position, but is none the less repeated in its original final position:

1 אזו האט דער עשיר אים דר צילט דיא שבֿועה וואש ער גיטאן האט

azój hɔt dər ɔ(j)šər im dərcejlt di švuə vɔs ər gətɔn hɔt (SF, SS, SA) →

אזו האט דער עשיר אים דר צילט די שבֿועה וואש ער האט גיטאן האט

azój hɔt dər ɔ(j)šər im dərcejlt di švuə vɔs ər hɔt gətɔn hɔt (SSh)

'then the rich man told him about an oath that he took' (103–5).

In the second case, the original word order with the past participle in final position was reordered in accordance with the stylistically neutral pattern of Eastern Yiddish:

2 אזו האבן דיא שטאט לייט אים צו איין שר גימאכֿט

azój hɔbn̩ di štótlàjt im cu a sar gəmaxt (SF, SS, SA) →

אזו האבן אים די שטאט לייט גמאכֿט צו איין שר

azój hɔbn̩ di štótlàjt im gəmaxt cu a sar (SSh)

'[and] so the citizens chose him to be a dignitary' (171–3).

The fact that these are the only syntactic changes may indicate that whoever saw this edition through the press had little intention of Easternizing or modernizing *Simkhes hanefesh*. It may well be that he perceived this book as an example of syntactic 'well-formedness'.

5

Easternization: A Comparative Overview

16 Introduction

The three Eastern editions of older Yiddish works examined represent markedly different degrees of linguistic adaptation of the original text. In terms of Yiddish dialectology, this adaptation is described as Easternization. From the viewpoint of the history of literary Yiddish, it may be perceived as linguistic modernization. The Shklov (1796) reprint of *Simkhes hanefesh*, chronologically the latest of the three editions, is a striking example of 'poor Easternization'. Even in its later nineteenth- and early twentieth-century Eastern revisions, Kirkhhahn's book has remained a remarkable example of linguistic anachronism. On the other hand, the Zholkve (1777) edition of the first volume of *Kav hayosher* is one of the earliest Easternized re-editions known to date, and the extent of Easternization in it is somewhat limited. Still, it underwent systematic revision of many significant morphological and morpho-syntactic features. The earliest and most radical, and therefore the most advanced, degree of Easternization was achieved in the Lemberg (1786) revision of the *Tsene rene*.

This chapter will contrast and evaluate the extent of the linguistic changes effected in these three texts (§§17–23). It will be claimed that Easternization can be qualitatively evaluated in terms of the most and the least affected levels of the linguistic structure of a given text (§24). Thus the morphological level is the one at which Easternization will be clearly manifested even in a little-Easternized text. However, the qualitative breakthrough is fully achieved only when the syntactic make-up of the given text is systematically restructured on the patterns of modern Eastern Yiddish.

17 Orthography and Phonology

In the realm of orthography, Easternized re-editions may generally be characterized as conservative. They do not exhibit traces of the orthographic innovations that became the semiological hallmark of nineteenth-century Eastern Yiddish texts. On the contrary, our texts clearly tend towards the total omission of most of the unstressed and of certain stressed vowels. None of them adopted the ⟨ע⟩ or ⟨י⟩ graphemes to represent postdiphthongal or word-final ə vowels. The clear-cut orthographical distinction between sibilant ⟨ס⟩ and shibilant ⟨ש⟩ is as absent as it was in conventional Old Yiddish orthography (cf. §§11.1, 13.1, 15.1).

Full representation of all stressed and unstressed vowels (including shewas) and graphemic distinction between sibilants and shibilants were originally introduced into eighteenth-century Western Yiddish books and into contemporary New High German texts printed with Yiddish characters (cf. Paper 1954; Wexler 1981b). These conventions originate from the radical adaptation of the Old Yiddish spelling system, an adaptation that was designed to mirror the orthographical (and ultimately phonological and morphological) models of New High German (see e.g. §§27.1 and 31.1; cf. also §§31.2.1 and 31.3.1). However, in Eastern Europe only some of these features can be found in late eighteenth-century Eastern Yiddish texts (e.g. in *Ben hameylekh vehanozir* (Zholkve, 1771); see §28.1.3; and in *Mayse gdoyle min Uman* ([Novidvor], c.1783); see §32.1.1). The earliest Eastern Yiddish text to adopt many of these orthographical features, *Eyzer Yisroel* (Poritsk, 1790), is also the first to introduce *daytshmerish* into Eastern-based literary language in general (see §25). It is, therefore, an exception among other Easternized and Eastern Yiddish books published during the last decades of the eighteenth century. Moreover, orthographical innovations based on New High German spelling conventions still had no effect on the re-editions examined and on most other late eighteenth-century Easternized texts.

On the other hand, we do find in our texts a limited number of Eastern Yiddish spellings. A degree of dialectal interference can be observed in the hypercorrect or dialectal spellings of certain stressed vowels. These clearly reveal the Mideastern or Southeastern merger of vowels **51** and **31** (see §§11.2.3.2, 13.2.2, 15.2.2) and the Southeastern merger of vowels **11** and **34** (cf. §11.2.3.4). Other variant spellings reveal Mideastern or Southeastern phonological features such as the loss of functional h (see §11.2.3.1), the lowering of certain stressed vowels before x and r (see §15.2.3), word-final devoicing (see §15.2.4), and the loss of postvocalic r (see §15.2.5). Similarly, these texts consistently replace the Old Yiddish ⟨פֿפ⟩ and ⟨פֿף⟩ graphemes with ⟨פֿ⟩ for syllable-initial f and with ⟨פ⟩ for syllable-final p. The word-final cluster ts ⟨טש⟩ was sometimes re-spelled more 'phonetically' as ⟨טץ⟩ tc or c ⟨ץ⟩. (On the last two see §§11.1.3 and 15.1.) Other orthographic changes that anticipate the modernization of Yiddish orthography are the total deletion of the apostrophe in the spelling of the conjunction un 'and'—i.e. ⟨און'⟩ → ⟨און⟩—and the frequent deletion of the conventional word-final silent alef— e.g. ⟨דיא⟩ → ⟨די⟩; ⟨זיא⟩ → ⟨זי⟩, which is systematic in TL1786.

The orthography of these re-editions was largely shared by contemporary late eighteenth-century Eastern Yiddish texts (see §§28.1 and 32.1), and it by and large continued to adhere to the fundamental features of the older Yiddish spelling system. Later books printed in the nineteenth century tended towards far more frequent graphemic representation of the unstressed vowels and towards more phonetic spelling of consonants. Therefore, the evolution of Yiddish orthography is best treated separately, as an essential, but none the less principally external, aspect of the Easternization and modernization of the literary language. Suffice it to say that the most Easternized text, the Lemberg (1786) revision of the *Tsene rene*, introduced no revolutionary reforms of spelling. Conversely, after the rapid transformations in Yiddish spelling during the first half of the nineteenth century, even the linguistically least Easternized re-edition of *Simkhes hanefesh* (Warsaw, 1865) had to modernize its spelling in accordance with the new norms and conventions of contemporary Yiddish orthography.

Paradoxical as it may sound, the late eighteenth-century Eastern revisions, re-editions, and reprints of older Yiddish works did not adopt any major orthographic conventions of the contemporary Germanized Western Yiddish editions of the same works. At the same time, a number of mainly exceptional spellings, clearly deviating from the older Yiddish orthographic conventions, testify to the direct impact of Eastern Yiddish dialects. While in principle preserving the older spelling system, these texts were not totally shielded from the increasing impact of Eastern Yiddish phonology. The Easternization of orthography was limited, but none the less significant; whereas the adoption of certain orthographical models from New High German had not yet surfaced. All this is fully in keeping with the very nature of the linguistic change that was carried out in our texts: the language was modified according to the morphological and syntactic patterns of modern Eastern Yiddish, while the parallel New High German patterns so dominant in contemporary Western Yiddish books had virtually no effect on these Eastern re-editions.

The late eighteenth-century transition from Old to the nascent Modern Literary Yiddish did not begin with radical spelling reform. The transition occurred in the language itself, as it were, with morphological and some morpho-syntactic features being often consistently Easternized, and with syntax as well as lexicon being to various degrees modernized on the basis of modern Eastern Yiddish.

18 Lexicon

There is only marginal lexical change in our texts, and only a few lexemes were Easternized; e.g. לעקוכין lékuxn̩ → לעקח lɛkəx / lékax 'cake'; קימטין kistn̩ → קסטן kastn̩ 'trunk' (see §11.4); קימן kisn̩ → קושן kušn̩ 'to kiss' (see §15.4).

Some of the older, as well as some of the contemporary, Western Yiddish lexemes were replaced by their Eastern Yiddish equivalents; e.g. גיפֿאָטר gəfatər → קװאָטר kvatər 'godfather'; אורין ɔrŋ → זײן מתּפלל mispáləl zajn 'pray' (see §11.4); רענט rɛnt 'runs; is occupied' → אַרבּיט arbət 'works'; אורבליצלינג urblícling → פלוצים plucəm 'suddenly' (see §15.4).

However, the number of lexical replacements is relatively small. All three re-editions seem to have been reluctant to introduce any distinctive Eastern Yiddish lexemes, especially those belonging to the Slavonic component. Even those that were acceptable in the older literary language—e.g. the conjunction xɔčə 'although' and the interjection nɛbəx 'unfortunately; oh dear!; poor thing'—were not used.

This reluctance to modernize the lexicon too radically may partly be explained by the fact that the basic lexical inventory of the original texts was largely common, or at least intelligible, to Eastern Yiddish speakers. Yet, on the whole, this reluctance also served to preserve the archaic character of these re-editions. During the first half of the nineteenth century the tendency to preserve most of the original vocabulary of the older Yiddish texts, coupled with the convention not to enrich it too freely with lexical items of Slavonic origin, became a major factor in the crystallization of the archaic style of Modern Literary Yiddish (see §22).

19 Morphology

Morphology is the major arena of linguistic modernization. All three re-editions share a number of systematically effected changes (§19.1). The most revealing are those introduced in SSh1796, for there is little reason to suspect its printer in being too zealous in matters of linguistic modernization. In retrospect, however, some of the basic limitations of complete transition to Eastern Yiddish are revealed by those forms and categories that, with various degrees of success, continue to survive in the KZ1777 re-edition and in the TL1786 revision (§19.2). Some of them continued to survive until the first decades of the nineteenth century; none of them, however, was inherited by the modern literary language as a stylistically marked archaic feature (cf. §22).

19.1 Systematic Changes

Even SSh1796, the least Easternized re-edition, shows a number of systematic morphological changes. Some of these are common to all three texts. They include the levelling of the past participles of strong verbs, the adoption of the Eastern Yiddish diminutivization pattern, and the Easternization of such forms as ענטוו(א)רט ɛntfərt → ענפֿרט ɛnfərt 'answers'; ג(י)ענטפֿרט gɔɛntfərt → גיענפֿרט gɔɛnfərt 'answered'; זאלכ- zɔlx- → זעלכ- zɛlx- 'such'. The number of systematic changes is considerably greater in KZ1777 and TL1786 than in SSh1796. It is possible that some of these were automatically introduced into the KZ1777 re-edition of *Kav hayosher*. However, the very existence of these systematic changes allows us to qualify both KZ1777 and KN1788 as re-editions, rather than as mere editions or reprints. It seems very unlikely that their anonymous printers, style-editors, or proof-readers were totally unaware of the introduction of these changes. On the other hand, the Shklov (1796) edition of *Simkhes hanefesh* is more likely to be viewed as a reprint, the very few systematic changes introduced there being in all probability unintentional. As to the Lemberg (1786) revision of the *Tsene rene*, the extent and intensity of its linguistic modernization clearly testify to the fact that its morphological, as well as its syntactic, changes were the product of a conscious 'style editing' effort.

19.2 The Easternization of Resistant Forms

Certain categories remained more resistant to change. These comprise the preterite, the forms of the future-tense auxiliary, the older relative pronouns, and the Western Yiddish accusative and dative forms of the masculine definite article. However, these too were affected in different ways. KZ1777 often replaced preterite forms either with the regular past tense or with present-tense and quasi-present-tense forms. In TL1786 replacement of the preterite became the norm. Eastern Yiddish forms of the future-tense auxiliary were still exceptional in KZ1777 and SSh1796, but were more frequently, and in some cases consistently, used in TL1786. The Eastern Yiddish indeclinable relative pronoun וואָס vɔs 'that; which; who' was apparently not favoured in KZ1777. However, occasionally in SSh1796 and more frequently in TL1786, it replaced the Old Yiddish relative pronouns דער dər 'that' (masc. nom.) and דעם dəm 'that' (masc. dat./acc.). The Eastern Yiddish merger of accusative and dative forms of the masculine definite article resulted in many cases in which דען dən was hypercorrectly installed in both KZ1777 and SSh1796. In TL1786, however, דען dən was almost unthinkable.

20 Morpho-syntax

Both KZ1777 and TL1786 exhibit salient morpho-syntactic features of linguistic modernization. These comprise the deletion of the definite article of certain nouns after the preposition אין 'in' (see §§11.3.2.1 and 13.3.1), the introduction of the pronoun subject (see §11.5.1), the omission of the definite article after certain prepositions (see §§11.5.2 and 13.5.3) and of the full attributive adjective declension (see §§11.5.4 and 13.5.4), and the use of the short adjective גרוי(ס)ש grɔjs 'large; big' as an abstract noun modifier (see §11.5.3). In this, as in almost all other cases, SSh1796 is far less advanced. On the whole, however, Easternization at the morpho-syntactic level is somewhat limited in KZ1777 because of the general syntactic conservatism of this re-edition. It seems that this syntactic conservatism prevented the editors from introducing aspectually marked verbs. The Eastern Yiddish system of verbal aspect appears to have had no influence on these re-editions, not even on TL1786. By contrast, aspectually differentiated verbal forms were introduced into the latest and fully Easternized Yozefov (1845) revision of *Tsene rene*.

21 Syntax

The most significant changes are found in the realm of syntax. The restructuring of the word-order patterns of certain main clauses and of most subordinate clauses may be considered the most decisive feature of the more advanced stage of Easternization.

21.1 Double Negation

In general the original pattern of negation remained hardly affected. Double negation, one of the syntactic hallmarks of Eastern Yiddish, often remained optional, even in TL1786. On the whole, however, double negation was more frequently introduced there and in the later Novidvor (1788) re-edition of *Kav hayosher*. In some of the nineteenth-century Eastern re-editions, resistance to double negation was still strong, and can be explained as deliberate retention of an Old Yiddish literary convention, possibly enhanced by the general increase in the 'normativist' influence of New High German. In the most Easternized later re-editions the tendency to favour double negation grew. Thus in the latest Yozefov (1845) revision of the *Tsene rene* the original rhetorically emphasized pattern of negation was restructured as double negation (see below no. 2c in §24).

21.2 Placement of the Past Participle

The most remarkable changes with regard to the placement of the past participle occur in the KZ1777 and KN1788 re-editions (see §11.6.2.1). Similarly, one of the two syntactic changes found in SSh1796 is the relocation of the past participle from final to third place (see §15.6). Similar changes can be detected also in TL1786, though not in the text sequence analysed.

The place of the past participle remains variable in Modern Literary Yiddish. However, the past participle in final position is a marked construction in the modern literary language. It is reserved for the more elevated, 'literary', or formal registers (see Mark 1978: 384; cf. below §22). Relocations of past participles in late eighteenth-century Eastern re-editions are the direct result of syntactic Easternization primarily based on the prevalent pattern of spoken Eastern Yiddish. The frequency of past-participle relocation increased significantly in nineteenth-century Easternized re-editions and revisions.

21.3 Main Consecutive Clauses

Main consecutive clauses with the finite verb in first place are occasionally encountered in the original text of *Simkhes hanefesh* (Frankfurt am Main, 1707) and more often in *Kav hayosher* (Frankfurt am Main, 1705), but none of their later Eastern publishers was daring enough to further extend this usage. In this respect, the Lemberg (1786) revision of the *Tsene rene* achieved the most advanced degree of syntactic Easternization (see §13.6.3).

The subsequent Eastern revisions of the *Tsene rene*, however, were considerably less Easternized. Neither of the later revisions, Sadilkov (1819) and Vilna–Grodno (1827), show any radical restructuring of the word-order patterns of the original *Tsene rene*. Both preserve the frequently used 'consecutive' adverb דא do 'so, then, thus'. As a result, the more 'colloquial' syntactic co-ordination between main clauses—i.e. the main consecutive clause with finite verb in first place—continued to be suppressed in the Sadilkov (1819) and Vilna–Grodno (1827) revisions.

Significantly, it was the most Easternized and the latest revision of the *Tsene rene*, Yozefov (1845), that gave a new lease of life to main consecutive clauses with the finite verb in first place. In some cases the original 'consecutive' adverb דא do was replaced by the more modern אזוי azój (cf. Shmeruk 1981: 158). In most cases, however, stylistically more natural main consecutive clauses were introduced in the Yozefov revision of 1845.

21.4 Subordinate Clauses

The place of the finite verb in subordinate clauses is another major aspect of syntactic modernization. In Old Literary Yiddish of the late seventeenth and eighteenth centuries the finite verb often occupied the final or penultimate position in a subordinate clause. Later eighteenth-century Western Yiddish texts tended to further standardize this syntactic pattern in line with the requirements of literary German (see Scaglione 1981: 109-13, 173-5, 179; Wells 1985: 256-7). Hence the apparent increase in subordinate clauses with the finite verb in final position in such Western Yiddish books as *Seyfer ben hameylekh vehanozir* (Frankfurt am Main, 1769, and Fürth, 1783; see §27.3) and *Mayse gdoyle min k[ehilo]"k[disho] Uman* (Fürth, 1783; see §31.5). By contrast, the option of placing the finite verb at the end of a subordinate clause was totally rejected in Eastern Yiddish dialects. (See Lockwood 1968: 265 on the less rigorous word-order patterns of subordinate clauses in spoken New High German.)

The restructuring of the word order of subordinate clauses can thus be credited directly to the impact of spoken Eastern Yiddish. Traces of this restructuring are found in each of our Eastern re-editions. In SSh1796 we find one such case. The change was apparently made in spite of its editor's or printer's intention not to alter the original syntactic patterns of *Simkhes hanefesh* (cf. §15.6). More cases were found in the KZ1777 and KN1788 (see §§11.5-6). In TL1786, subordinate clauses were often restructured in accordance with the Eastern Yiddish pattern, though these are not found in our text sequence.

22 Archaic Features

The various late eighteenth- and nineteenth-century Eastern re-editions and revisions of older Yiddish works not only introduced and eventually implemented the wholesale transition from the old to the modern literary language, they also retained and, by extention, made stylistically productive a number of 'archaic' features (cf. Shmeruk 1978: 180). The way in which these features became organically incorporated into most varieties of Modern Literary Yiddish deserves a separate study. It is clear, however, that their major function in the modern literary language may be summed up as that of marked 'formal', 'elevated', and in some cases 'more literary' styles.

These features, so it seems, are in the main restricted to the lexical and syntactic levels: e.g. (1) the reluctance to employ too many etymologically transparent lexical items of Slavonic origin (cf. §§7.2.3 and 18); (2) the possible retention of the old conjunction dɔs 'that' instead of, or in addition to, az; (3) the avoidance of double negation (cf. §§11.6.1 and 21.1); and (4) the clause-final placing of the past participle and to a lesser degree of infinitives (cf. §§21.2 and 35.11). Most of these features as archaic elements of Modern Literary Yiddish can be traced, though not directly credited, to the Eastern re-editions examined. Even the most Easternized work, TL1786, remains a text in a state of linguistic transition; for it continues to employ, with varying degrees of success, a number of residual older forms and categories (residual in the sense of forms still resistant to full linguistic modernization; cf. §19.2). Future analysis of archaic features will have to focus primarily on the later nineteenth-century revisions and new 'translations' of older Yiddish books and on various contemporary Eastern Yiddish works.

23 Schematic Comparison

The extent of linguistic Easternization in the re-editions discussed can be summarized in a schematic diagram (see Figure 2). The morphological (m) and syntactic (s) axes are chosen as the two major parameters of linguistic change. Whatever factual or statistical data on other contemporary Eastern re-editions will be added in future, the present examination indicates that the principal correlation between these two major levels of linguistic change is significant for an overall evaluation of the various stages of transition from Old to nascent Modern Literary Yiddish.

Figure 2
The extent of Easternization of three eighteenth-century
editions of older Yiddish texts

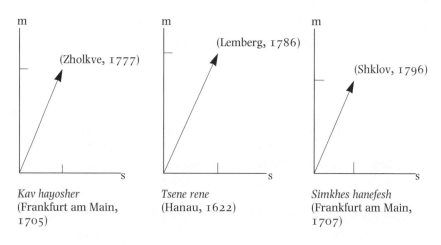

Kav hayosher   Tsene rene   Simkhes hanefesh
(Frankfurt am Main,   (Hanau, 1622)   (Frankfurt am Main,
1705)   1707)

The correlation between morphological and syntactic change will ideally be even and furthest from the original in the most Easternized re-edition. None of the late eighteenth-century re-editions reached the ideal state of full or nearly complete Easternization, which is so characteristic of the later

Yozefov (1845) revision of the *Tsene rene*. The TL1786 revision comes closest. This is chiefly due to its more advanced syntactic modernization. None of the three re-editions achieved a full Easternization of morphology, and some resistance to morphological change was found even in TL1786.

24 The Extent of Easternization and the Levels of Linguistic Change

The present investigation indicates that morphology and syntax are the most revealing aspects of linguistic change in literary Yiddish. The morphological changes, which are often systematic, mark the onset of linguistic Easternization. These changes are supported by a number of lexical alterations. On the whole, morphological changes do not necessarily result in a radical modification of the original text. The role of the anonymous 'style-editor' may be still quite limited if his intervention remains by and large confined to updating certain forms (e.g. SSh1796 and parts of KN1788).

On the other hand, syntactic changes indicate a qualitatively higher level of Easternization. When the linear syntactic make-up of the original text is restructured, a higher level of linguistic change is achieved. In TL1786 we may discern a significant, possibly conscious attempt at linguistic modernization. Even without involving the potentially confusing characterization 'conscious', the overall extent of Easternization is amply reflected in the degree of change that was introduced on the syntactic level. Conversely, the least Easternized text, SSh1796, is also the most resistant to syntactic change, whereas the more Easternized, KZ1777, is marked by a higher degree of syntactic change.

The suggestion that syntactic change indicates a higher level of linguistic modernization may be illustrated by the later nineteenth-century re-editions. The Warsaw (1865) re-edition of *Simkhes hanefesh*, although more Easternized than SSh1796, is remarkably archaic for its period, since the distinctly Western Yiddish syntax remains largely intact. As may be seen from the following examples, the morphology, morpho-syntax, and lexicon of the Warsaw (1865) edition were significantly Easternized, whereas the syntax remained largely untouched:

1   בלייב דא איבר נאכֿט ווערשטו זעהן וויא זיך

blajb dɔ ibər naxt vərstu zɛn vi zəx

ד(ע)ר בעטלר אונ' זייני פֿרויא משמח זיינן

dər bɛtlər un zajnə frɔj məsaméjax zajnən (SF1707, SSh1796) →

בלייב דא איבר נאכט ווערסטו זעהן וויא זיך

blajb dɔ ibər naxt vəstu zɛn vi zəx

דר בעטליר אונ זיין פֿרוא משמח זענין

dər bɛtlər un zajn frɔj məsaméjax zɛnən (Warsaw, 1865, p. 8b)

'stay here for the night and you will see how the beggar and his
wife pass their time in fun';

2 מן הענגט איינם חזיר איין גילדן קעט אן וועלגרט עש זיך פֿארט אין דרעג

mən hɛngt ejnəm xazər a gildṇ kejt ón vɛlgərt əs zəx fərt in drɛk

(דרעג SSh1796) ארום דר וייל עש אזו גיוואונט איז

arum dərvajl əs azɔj gəvɔjnt iz (SF1707, SSh1796) →

מען הענגט אַיין חזר איין גילדן קײַטיל אן וועלגירט ער זיך פֿארט אין דיא

mən hɛngt a xazər a gildṇ kejtḷ ón vɛlgərt ər zəx fərt in di

בלאטעם ארום וייל עַר אזו געוואונט איז

blɔtəs arúm vajl ər azɔj gəvɔjnt iz (Warsaw, 1865, p. 26b)

'when one hangs a golden chain (= charm) on the pig's neck, he [the pig]
still [keeps] roll[ing] in dirt since this is his nature'.

In sharp contrast to the Warsaw (1865) re-edition of *Simkhes hanefesh*, the
Yozefov (1845) revision of the *Tsene rene* was not only morphologically and
lexically, but also syntactically, fully Easternized. Even in our relatively small
text sequence we find ample evidence of full syntactic modernization of this
revision. Double negation (cf. below no. 2) as well as main consecutive
clauses were introduced in Yozefov (1845). Similarly, the past participle was
more frequently removed from its final position (cf. below no. 1), and the
word order of the subordinate clauses was fully restructured on the syntactic
pattern of modern Eastern Yiddish (cf. nos. 2–3):

1a דא הוט דז גרעשטי פסל איין שטעקן גינומן

dɔ hot dɔs grɛstə pɛsḷ a(jn) štɛkṇ gənumən (Hanau, 1622; Amsterdam, 1726) →

b דא האט די גרעשטי איין שטעקן גנומן

dɔ hot di grɛstə [*sc.* avójdə zɔrə] a štɛkṇ gənumən (TL1786) →

c דא האט דש גרעשטר בילד איין שטעקן גינומן

dɔ hot dɔs grɛstər bild a štɛkṇ gənumən (Vilna-Grodno, 1827) →

d אזו האט דר גרעסטער אפ גאט גינומן איין שטעקין

azój hot dər grɛstər ópgɔt gənumən a štɛkṇ (Yozefov, 1845)

'then the largest idol took the cane' (ll. 27–8);

2a וען זיא יוא קיין שכל הבין ven zej jɔ k(e)jn sɛjxḷ hɔbṇ

(Hanau, 1622; Amsterdam, 1726; Vilna-Grodno, 1827) →

b וען זי קיין שכל האבן ven zej k(e)jn sejxḷ hɔbṇ (TL1786) →

c אז זיי האבן יוא קיין שכל ניט az zej hɔbṇ jɔ kejn sejxḷ nit (Yozefov, 1845)

'if they [the idols] do not have mind [= spirit]' (ll. 31–2);

3a אונ' דוא וװילשט דיך בוקין צו איינם דאש דא איין טאג אלט איז

un du vilst dəx bukṇ cu ejnəm dɔs dɔ ejn tɔg alt iz

(Hanau, 1622; Amsterdam, 1726; Vilna-Grodno, 1827) →

b אונ וװילשט דיך בוק צו אינם דש איין טאג אלט איז

un vilst dəx bukṇ cu ejnəm dɔs ejn tɔg alt iz (TL1786) →

c אונ וװילשט דיך בוקין צו איינים וואש איז איין טאג אלט

un vilst dǝx bukŋ cu ejnǝm vɔs iz ejn tɔg alt (Yozefov, 1845)
'and you want to bow to someone who is one day old?' (ll. 9–11).

It is still not known whether Yozefov (1845) was the first edition of the most Easternized revision of the *Tsene rene* (cf. Shmeruk 1981: 163 n. 23). But it is significant that soon after Yozefov (1845), this revision apparently became the standard Eastern Yiddish text of the *Tsene rene* (cf. Shmeruk 1981: 159; the most recent newly updated linguistic revision of this work appeared in 1988 in Jerusalem). Since it was one of the most popular books, its fully Easternized revision also marks the final outcome of the long process of transition from the old to the nascent modern literary language.

PART III

Shift: The Emergence of Nascent Modern Literary Yiddish

25 Preface

Whoever looks for the first modern Yiddish *literary* texts in the eighteenth century will be disappointed. Both reprints and original works of the period are traditional texts that are semiotically part of older Yiddish literature. Yet it would be equally inappropriate to assume that the texts written and published in late eighteenth-century Eastern Europe are, linguistically speaking, a continuation of the old literary language. Some of the Yiddish books printed in the last three decades of the eighteenth century were either based on, or largely written in, modern Eastern Yiddish. They mark the very beginnings of what was later, during the nineteenth century, to become the modern literary language. Within the broader context of the changing literary Yiddish of the eighteenth century, these earliest attempts to write and publish in modern Eastern Yiddish are among the first, and sometimes most decisive, manifestations of the general shift from the Old to the nascent Modern Literary Yiddish.

The actual birth of modern Yiddish literature can safely be placed in the nineteenth century, when its major socio-cultural setting was rapidly approaching its modern stage. Hasidism (the popular religious movement) and Haskole (the Eastern European Jewish Enlightenment), the two modern rival movements, were directly involved in the rise of modern Yiddish literature in the nineteenth century (cf. §3.3.2; see also Niger 1944; Shmeruk 1988: 211–91). In the late eighteenth century, however, we find only a few literary monuments that indirectly reflect the contemporary growth of Hasidism; e.g. *Seyfer khsidem* (Zholkve, 1776) and, possibly, *Avkes roykhl* (Horodne, 1795). Analogously, Moyshe Markuze's *Eyzer Yisroel* (Poritsk, 1790), a collection of popular medical writings, is apparently the earliest stylistically disguised manifestation of the Eastern European Jewish Enlightenment (see Shmeruk 1977: 368–9).

Although many of the late eighteenth-century Eastern Yiddish prints were not preserved, or even recorded, we can still recover a substantial body of texts. Among the most important early Eastern Yiddish monuments are the following (arranged in chronological order):

1 *Ben hameylekh vehanozir* (Zholkve, 1771) = BZ1771
2 *Seyfer khsidem* (Zholkve, 1776) = SZ1776
3 *Vikuekh yeytser tov im ben odem* (Shklov, c.1783) = VS[1783]
4 *Mayse gdoyle min Uman umin Ukrayne* ([Novidvor], c.1783) = M[N1783]
5 Moyshe Markuze's *Eyzer Yisroel* (Poritsk [= Poryck], 1790) = EP1790
6 *Seyfer Avkes roykhl* (Horodne [= Grodno], 1795) = AH1795
7 *Bove mayse* ([Lemberg], c.1798) = B[L1798].

All seven texts fit into the various conventional genres of Old Yiddish literature. The rhymed ethical novel (late medieval Hebrew *maqama*) *Ben hamelekh vehanazir*, by Abraham Ibn Hasdai, had been translated into Old Literary Yiddish in the fifteenth century or earlier (see Tsinberg 1935: 45–7; Prilutski 1931). *Seyfer khsidem*, the translation of the late medieval Hebrew collection of ethical instructions and exemplary narratives (*Sefer Ḥasidim*), was apparently welcome as part of the conventional hagiographic and *muser* genres of Old Yiddish literature (cf. §6.1). The bilingual poem *Vikuekh yeytser tov im ben odem* continues the well-established literary tradition of bilingual *contest* poems, a tradition that can be traced to the fifteenth century (see Turniansky 1985a: 134–44).

From the literary point of view, the anonymous account *Mayse gdoyle min Uman* follows the stylistic conventions of many earlier accounts of anti-Jewish persecutions. In Old Yiddish literature there are many analogous accounts both in prose (see Zfatman 1983: i. 201–12) and in verse (see M. Weinreich 1923: 140–92; 1927: 203–10; 1928: 192–218; Turniansky 1989). Even Moyshe Markuze's *Eyzer Yisroel*, which may be considered the earliest important attestation to socio-cultural and linguistic modernization, is presented in the style of the well-established contemporary *muser* collections (see Shmeruk 1977: 375–7; Roskies 1974b: 13–15, 53). Thematically, it continues the Old Yiddish genre of the more conventional collections of popular or practical medical writings (cf. Erik 1928: 44–5; Dinse 1974: 101–5; Shmeruk 1977: 365).

The two remaining texts, *Avkes roykhl* and *Bove mayse*, are the new Eastern Yiddish equivalents of Old Yiddish literary monuments. The first part of the eschatological collection *Avkes roykhl* (Horodne, 1795) contains the small Hebrew Midrash on 'Ten Signs of the Messiah' (for various Hebrew versions see Jellinek 1938: ii. 58–63; vi. 117–20; Even-Shmuel 1954: 289–301, 318–23, 345–6). This Midrash appeared earlier in two separate translations in Old Literary Yiddish; viz. *Der royzn gortn* (Prague, 1568) and *Avkes roykhl taytsh apteyk* (translated by Naphtali Pappenheim and printed in

Amsterdam in 1647). Similarly, *Bove mayse*, the new adaptation of the *Bove bukh*, is one of the latest linguistically modernized transformations of the early sixteenth-century Yiddish rhymed novel *Buovo d'Antona*, written in 650 *ottava rima* stanzas by Elye Bokher (= Elijah Levita, 1469–*c*.1549) and first published in Isni in 1541 (see Joffe 1949).

In spite of their close association with the conventions and genres of Old Yiddish literature, these works were linguistically oriented towards modern Eastern Yiddish. The shift to Eastern Yiddish was not always complete. Many features of the old literary language may still be encountered in *Ben hameylekh vehanozir* (Zholkve, 1771) and to a lesser degree in *Seyfer khsidem* (Zholkve, 1776). There are fewer or in some cases no features of this type in *Vikuekh yeytser tov im ben odem* (Shklov, *c*.1783), *Bove Mayse* ([Lemberg], *c*.1798), and *Avkes roykhl* (Horodne, 1795). In effect, these later works were written *in* Eastern Yiddish, so that the few evident features of Old Yiddish may be viewed in some cases as stylistic archaisms and in many others as marginal survivals. Only a handful of these archaisms survived in the modern literary language as important features of 'archaic', (more) formal, or more 'elevated' styles (cf. §22).

The earliest known and perhaps the most remarkable literary monument of modern Eastern Yiddish is the original work *Mayse gdoyle min Uman* ([Novidvor], *c*.1783). The language of Moyshe Markuze's *Eyzer Yisroel* (Poritsk, 1790) was almost as Eastern and modern in its morphological, lexical, and phraseological elements. At the same time, Markuze introduced an important new component into written Eastern Yiddish. Both in popular parlance as well as in contemporary puristic nomenclature this component is termed *daytshmerish* (see Katz 1993a: 166–85). The term applies to the adoption of New High German as one of the major models for lexical, morphological, and syntactic repatterning of the literary usage. *Daytshmerish* was instrumental in the subsequent development of the modern literary language, and its impact persisted throughout the nineteenth and early twentieth centuries in many literary texts, especially in the language of scholarship and the press (see M. Weinreich 1973: ii. 115–17 §128.1, ii. 162–3; Schaechter 1969; 1977: 52–5; D. Katz 1983: 1033, §9.2 no. 3, 1993a: 40–1, 162–3; Moskovich 1984: 42–3; Hutton 1984: 6–20). As a new functionally and semantically integrated component it continues to play a significant role in the stylistic make-up of Modern Literary Yiddish (cf. Katz 1993a: 219–28).

While the shift to Eastern Yiddish was not complete in some texts, it is remarkable that their language is nevertheless based primarily on Eastern Yiddish. By contrast the language of the earliest known Eastern Yiddish printed works of the early eighteenth century—e.g. *Derekh tomim* (Zholkve,

1723) and *Derekh khayim* (Zholkve, *c.*1723)—is still directly and more heavily dependent on the older literary usage. The text of *Ben hameylekh vehanozir* (Zholkve, 1771), however, was not only intended for readers who *spoke* Eastern Yiddish; it was also largely translated *into* Eastern Yiddish.

These works do not necessarily show a chronological progression from less to more Eastern or modern Yiddish. Not all earlier texts are more archaic, and a number of Old Yiddish features were retained in the latest. The translation and the writing or re-writing of these texts were probably carried out by different anonymous authors with different individual stylistic preferences. It is possible that the translator of *Ben hameylekh vehanozir* (Zholkve, 1771) was more 'progressive' in his choice of grammatical forms, but 'conservative' with regard to lexicon, word-order patterns, and to some extent morphology. On the other hand, his colleague, who was responsible for the translation of *Seyfer khsidem* (Zholkve, 1776), combined more archaic grammar (e.g. by retaining more frequently the older case system) with more modernized syntax and many genuine Eastern Yiddish forms and expressions. Retrospectively, however, both these authors can be seen to have been pioneers. As far as is known, they were the first to write in Eastern Yiddish, despite the tremendous pressures exerted by the grammatical and, above all, the stylistic conventions of the old literary language.

Certain genres were linguistically more conservative. Narrative prose seems to have been especially marked as a more archaic genre. *Bove mayse* ([Lemberg], *c.*1798), chronologically speaking, is the latest Eastern Yiddish work of this period. Yet a few Old Yiddish features (e.g. the preterite) were intentionally preserved in it. The same applies to some of the later Eastern Yiddish narrative texts from the first decade of the nineteenth century, e.g. *Seyfer Yosifun* (Lemberg, 1801; see Joffe 1940: 93; Yaari 1940: 104 no. 31), *Gdules Yitskhok* (Vilna, 1801; see Zfatman 1985: 164–5 no. 171), *Igeres bale khayim* (Lemberg, 1805; see Yaari 1940: 105–6 no. 36).

In most of these works, certain Old Yiddish forms and categories appear alongside their Eastern Yiddish equivalents. From the perspective of spoken Eastern Yiddish, the coexistence of older and newer features can best be described as an ongoing competition. The well-established conventions of the old literary language imposed the partial retention of a number of forms and categories. On the other hand, new forms, categories, and patterns of usage were directly introduced from contemporary Eastern Yiddish. For the literary language these were certainly innovations. However, the massive and, in most cases, systematic introduction of these forms into the printed works under discussion soon resulted in a progressive restructuring of the literary language on the basis of modern Eastern Yiddish.

The term 'competition' implies a certain stylistic and grammatical instability. It is natural, however, that a literary language, while undergoing drastic transformation, should be marked by instability. In the case of literary Yiddish, the reorientation towards the spoken language had to interfere with the original grammatical and stylistic balances of the old literary language. Nevertheless, none of the texts under discussion can be viewed as a stylistic hotchpotch. To evaluate the style of these works in terms of Old Literary Yiddish alone would be inadequate. To judge it by the standards of Modern Literary Yiddish would be anachronistic. From the literary viewpoint these works belong to older Yiddish literature, hence their traditional, and from the modern perspective, archaic style. Yet, their linguistic make-up is in most cases essentially modern. The features introduced from the spoken language update these texts linguistically, and thus mark them as the earliest literary works written in modern Eastern Yiddish. It is important to assess the nature of the ongoing competition between Old Yiddish and Eastern Yiddish features. The overall shift from the old literary to the nascent modern literary language originated from this competition (cf. §28.3.2 and 35.11).

6

The Earliest Eastern Yiddish Work: *Ben hameylekh vehanozir* (1771)

26 The Two Eighteenth-Century Translations

The late medieval Hebrew *maqama Ben hamelekh vehanazir* was written in the thirteenth century by Abraham Ibn Shmuel Hasdai. An early Yiddish translation of it is preserved in a fifteenth-century manuscript (see Tsinberg 1935: 45-7; cf. Timm 1987: 557 for Birnbaum's dating of the manuscript as *c.*1460-90). In the eighteenth century, *Ben hamelekh vehanazir* was translated by Reuven Halevi (see Prilutski 1931: 422; Schischa 1986: 113, 118-23) into a remarkably Germanized Yiddish. It was first printed in Frankfurt am Main in 1769, and later in Fürth in 1783.

The printing of the Frankfurt am Main (1769) edition of Reuven Halevi's translation was apparently not completed before 1771 (see Schischa 1986: 120). At that time another Yiddish translation of *Ben hamelekh vehanazir* appeared in Zholkve (see Prilutski 1917*b*: 176, 231, 239; 1931: 417-19; Yaari 1934). The latter translation, *Ben hameylekh vehanozir* (Zholkve, 1771) is the earliest known literary monument of Eastern Yiddish to date.

The striking linguistic difference between Reuven Halevi's translation and the anonymous Eastern Yiddish translation is only one example of the widening linguistic and socio-cultural gaps that started to divide the Western from the Eastern European Jewish communities in the eighteenth century. Halevi's translation, devised in the traditional context of older Yiddish literature, is, from a linguistic point of view, totally oriented towards New High German as the basis of 'correct literary' usage. By contrast, the language of the anonymous Zholkve translation of 1771 was to a large degree based on Eastern Yiddish. In fact, there were also other books that were printed almost simultaneously in heavily Germanized Western Yiddish in Germany and in markedly Easternized Yiddish in Eastern Europe in the late eighteenth and early nineteenth century (cf. Timm 1988: 56-61; Kerler 1990: 285). Other well-known manifestations of this widening linguistic gap between Western and Eastern Yiddish prints are the original Eastern Yiddish text of *Mayse gdoyle min Uman* ([Novidvor], *c.*1783) and its short Germanized version printed in Fürth in 1783 (see §§29-30), and the two contemporary versions of *Bove mayse*, one abridged in a Germanized Western Yiddish (Frankfurt an der Oder, 1796), the other rewritten in modern Eastern Yiddish ([Lemberg], *c.*1798; for bibliographic details on *Bove mayse* see Zfatman 1985: 161–3, nos. 167 and 168).

Linguistic examination of the Zholkve (1771) translation is the main objective of this chapter. The interplay between the underlying Eastern Yiddish and the inherited Old Yiddish features, characteristic of this text, reveals some of the most essential grammatical and stylistic tensions that preceded and accompanied the early stages of the nascent modern literary language. A preliminary assessment of Reuven Halevi's translation will be instrumental in placing the achievements of Zholkve (1771) into the broad perspective of the rapidly changing forms of the literary language in eighteenth-century Western and Eastern Europe. Excerpts from the Zholkve (1771) *Ben hameylekh vehanozir* are presented alongside Reuven Halevi's translation printed in Frankfurt am Main in 1769 (see Appendix 5, pp. 293–6; references are to lines in Appendix 5, specified page references are to BZ1771).

27 Reuven Halevi's Translation (Frankfurt am Main, 1769)

Even a brief comparison of the two translations of *Ben hamelekh vehanazir* reveals the individual approaches of the translators. Reuven Halevi's translation is shorter, and its style is usually less emotive. He also left untranslated the short poems that are interwoven into the rhymed prose of the original text (cf. Schischa 1986: 113). By comparison, the Zholkve (1771) translation is much more elaborate (e.g. cf. 1–15, 25–60). The originally rhymed narrative is here rendered in prose, and the poems are usually translated in rhyme (e.g. cf. 16–23, 66–70, 137–47).

The most striking linguistic differences between these two translations are in morphology, lexicon, and syntax. The following brief account surveys some of the most dominant New High German features characteristic of Reuven Halevi's translation.

27.1 Morphology

The apocopated unstressed final vowels of both Western and Eastern Yiddish are systematically restored in Reuven Halevi's translation, giving such forms as פֿריידע frejdə 'happiness' (24, 28, 35; cf. mod. Y. פֿרייד frejd vs. NHG *Freude*) and שפּייזע špajzə 'food' (29; cf. mod. Y. שפּייז špajz vs. NHG *Speise*).

Reinstatement of the lost final vowels was mainly due to the important role played by final vowels in the morphological machinery of New High

German. A whole category, the simple past tense (the imperfect), became a regular feature of this translation; e.g. פֿר מעהרטי farmɛ́rtə 'grew more' (72–3); האטי hɔtə/hɛtə 'had'; ליבטה libtə 'loved' (82). Similarly, German plural and oblique case forms were adopted; e.g. פֿריינדי frajndə 'friends' (57); העני hɛndə 'hands' (129); אויזר דעם וועני ojsər dəm vɛgə 'on a side of the road' (109).

Other New High German forms regularly employed in this translation include the following:

איזט izt 'is' (35, 27, 55, 122, 131; cf. mod. Y. אי iz, NHG *ist*);

אנטוואַרטי antvɔrtə 'answered' (impf., 116;

    cf. mod. Y. ענטפֿערט ɛntfərt, NHG *antwortete*);

וואורדי vurdə 'became' (imperf., 90; cf. NHG *wurde*);

ווירט virt 'will' (fut. aux., 3rd pers. sing., 33;

    cf. Western Yiddish ווער vər, Eastern Yiddish ווע vət, NHG *wird*);

ניכט nixt 'not' (adv.; 28; cf. Western Yiddish ניקש niks 'nothing',

    Eastern Yiddish ניש ~ ניט nit ~ *ništ*, NHG *nicht*);

עפּפֿיל ɛpf(ə)l 'apple' (132; cf. mod. Y. עפּל ɛpḷ, NHG *Apfel*);

צור cur 'to the' (fem. sing., 29, 72, 100; cf. NHG *zur*).

Another regular feature is the use of the genitive case, which was directly introduced from New High German; e.g. דו ענד אלר פֿריידי dɔs ɛnd alər frejdə 'the outcome of all happiness' (25–6); דו ענד אונזרש לעבן dɔs ɛnd un(d)zərs lɛbṇ 'the end of our life' (41); דעם מענשן לעבן dəs mɛnšṇs lɛbṇ 'the life of a human being' (54–5); די פֿיינדשאַפֿט דעם קיניגם di fájndšaft dəs kínigs (or kénigs) 'the king's hatred' (73–4). Genitive case forms also occur in some of the earlier translations into Yiddish; e.g. in Naphtali Pappenheim's translation of *Avkes roykhl* (Amsterdam, 1647). On the whole, however, the genitive is relatively rare in Old Yiddish literature of the late seventeenth century, with the exception of those works textually based on books originally written in German. In Reuven Halevi's translation the use of the genitive is a standard feature, directly modelled on German morphology (e.g. דעם dəs) and morpho-syntax (e.g. די פֿיינדשאַפֿט דעם קיניגם di fájndšaft dəs kínigs).

27.2 Lexicon

The consistent avoidance of Semitic component lexical items is another striking characteristic of this translation. The aversion apparently stems from the translator's stylistic 'code' dictating that words of Hebrew or Aramaic origin should not be used in the literary language. Of course, these words abounded in the translator's spoken Western Yiddish (e.g. see Noble 1964). Many, though not most, were even acceptable in some contemporary and earlier Yiddish books. These were obviously absent, however, from the New High German that was Reuven Halevi's primary model of literary usage.

The absence of words of Hebrew or Aramaic origin is especially evident when this translation is contrasted with the Zholkve (1771) translation into Eastern Yiddish. A number of samples from each translation is provided in Table 15.

Table 15 Lexical discrepancies between two eighteenth-century translations of *Ben hameylekh vehanozir* (1769) and (1771)

FRANKFURT AM MAIN, 1769	ZHOLKVE, 1771
פֿריידי frejdə (24, 35)	שמחה simxə 'happiness' (25, 35)
וויזר vajzər (46)	חלם xɔxəm 'sage' (47)
קיניג kínig (74, 80, 100)	מלך mejləx 'king' (73, 81, 100)
פֿרומי frumə 'pious (pl.)' (74)	נזיר nɔzir 'hermit' (74)
קיניגרייך kínigrajx (88)	מלכות malxəs 'kingdom' (85)
שטראס štrɔs 'road' (104)	מחנה maxnə 'camp' (104)

In sharp contrast to Reuven Halevi's translation, words of Hebrew origin are an important and stylistically fully admissible lexical component in the Zholkve (1771) translation. Many nouns, verbs, conjunctions, and adverbs, some of which were previously seldom or never allowed in many varieties of the older literary language, were regularly used in Zholkve (1771). It seems also that some lexical items in Reuven Halevi's translation were directly imported from New High German; e.g. פֿאלגי fɔlgə 'consequence' (29; cf. NHG *Folge*); שווערצי švɛrcə 'blackness' (126; cf. NHG *Schwärze*); טריבזאלן tríbzɔln̩/tríbzaln̩(?) 'worries' (25, 27, 118; possibly a Yiddishized plural form of the NHG *Trübsal*).

27.3 Syntax

The direct impact of New High German patterns on the syntactic organization of Reuven Halevi's translation is especially evident in the final position assigned to the finite verbs in almost all subordinate clauses; e.g.:

1 אונ׳ איזט קייני פֿריידי דיא ניכֿט אייני טרויר צור פֿאלגי האט
un izt kajnə frejdə di nixt ajnə trɔjər cur fɔlgə hɔt
'and [there] is no happiness that is not followed by mourning' (27–9);

2 דער קיניג האטי איינן פֿירשטן דען ער הירצליך ליבטי
dər kínig hɔtə ajnən firštn̩ dən ər hɛrcləx libtə
'the king had a duke whom he dearly loved' (81–2).

These are just two examples of many (cf. also 85–7, 92–3, 99–103). The same applies to the clause-final placement of past participles (cf. 87–9, 101–3) and infinitives (cf. 48–50, 60–1, 77–8, 79). In the literary Yiddish of eighteenth-century Western Europe there was a trend towards accepting these syntactic patterns. However, in such strongly Germanized Yiddish texts as this, the trend turned into a dominant syntactic feature. In other words, the final position of the verb in a subordinate clause and the clause-final placement of past participles and infinitives in main clauses became obligatory in this and in other Germanized Western Yiddish texts of the late eighteenth century.

28 Ben hameylekh vehanozir (Zholkve, 1771)

This work exhibits a variety of features comprising elements of the old literary language, the conventional archaic form of Yiddish (= *taytsh*, see §28.4), and above all forms and phraseological as well as syntactic patterns of modern Eastern Yiddish. The following analysis of the work's orthography, phonology, and morphology focuses on the ongoing competition between the older literary and the modern Yiddish forms, categories, and morpho-syntactic patterns (§§28.1–3.2). Certain major aspects of the work's essentially Eastern Yiddish morphology and morpho-syntax are discussed separately (§28.3.3).

28.1 Orthography

Many Old Yiddish orthographic conventions were preserved in *Ben hameylekh vehanozir* (1771). These include the optional representation of most of the unstressed and certain stressed vowels, as well as the absence of clear graphemic differentiation between sibilants and shibilants. At the same time, a number of effectively Eastern Yiddish spellings of stressed vowels and of some consonants are introduced. Several spelling conventions were also adopted from contemporary Germanized Western Yiddish texts.

28.1.1 *Eastern Yiddish Features*

As a result of the many dialectal spellings of stressed vowels (cf. §28.2 below), the graphemes ⟨י⟩ and ⟨ו⟩ feature as variant representations of some of the unstressed posttonic vowels and shewas; e.g. פלוביּנג ⟨fluxing⟩ (mod. Y. flúxung) 'curse' (p. 7b); צירינג ⟨ciring⟩ (mod. Y. círung) 'jewelry' (p. 46a); שפראצונג ⟨šprocung⟩ šprócung 'sprouting' (p. 9a); וועגין ⟨vegin⟩ ~ וועגון ⟨vegun⟩ vɛgn̩ 'for; about' (pp. 7b, 16a). A more 'phonetic' Eastern Yiddish spelling of postdiphthongal reduced vowels is occasionally encountered; e.g. שרייאין ⟨šrajin⟩ šrájən 'shout' (p. 12a).

In the realm of consonant representation, this text consistently employs the grapheme ⟨טש⟩ to represent the alveolar č. Because of the notable absence of words of Slavonic origin, this spelling is restricted to only two lexical items: מענטש mɛnč 'man; human being' (p. 10b) and בענטשן bɛnčṇ 'bless' (p. 34b; cf. Prilutski 1924a: 106 §160.2). In both cases the use of the ⟨טש⟩ grapheme is largely restricted to shibilant affricated in post-nasal position. Nevertheless, it is a significant step towards a more adequate orthographic representation of the Eastern Yiddish consonant system. By the same token, the post-nasal sibilants are consistently represented here in the more 'phonetic' modern fashion by the grapheme ⟨צ⟩; e.g. פינצטרניש fînctərniš 'darkness' (p. 12b; cf. Prilutski 1924a: 106 §160.1). Another Eastern Yiddish orthographic trait is the regular employment of the ⟨פ⟩ grapheme for the syllable-final p: e.g. קאפ kɔp 'head' (pp. 14b, 17a); אפ שיידין ɔpšejdṇ 'divide, separate' (p. 8a). The older spellings ⟨פפ⟩ and ⟨פף⟩ become very rare; e.g.: קאפ kɔp 'head' (p. 14b); טאפ tɔp 'pot' (p. 37a). Note, however, the following spellings: קאפף kɔp 'head' (p. 29a); צו קאפ פֿין cu kɔp(f)in 'at one's head' (p. 7b; cf. mod. Y. cukɔpṇs).

28.1.2 The Impact of New High German

A number of orthographic conventions may be indirectly attributed to the impact of New High German on the contemporary Western Yiddish printed works. The silent postvocalic ⟨ה⟩ is introduced into the spelling of many lexical items; e.g. איהם ⟨ihm⟩ im 'him' (pp. 7b, 17b); שװעהר ⟨švehr⟩ švɛr 'heavy' (p. 11b); אהן ⟨ohn⟩ ɔn 'without'; איהר ⟨ihr⟩ ir 'her' (poss. pron., p. 12b). However, these spellings are not consistent, and the more traditional אים ⟨im⟩, אן ⟨on⟩, and איר ⟨ir⟩ seem to prevail (on the silent postvocalic ⟨ה⟩ cf. §31.1.2).

The orthographic contraction between the finite verb and the following second-person-singular pronoun was conventional in Old Yiddish orthography, and became obligatory in modern Yiddish (see Timm 1987: 327 §40.3). However, in this text such contractions are exceptional; e.g. זאלסטו zólstu/zɔlstə 'you should' (p. 22b). Almost everywhere else the translator spelled the verb and the following (hence normally enclitic) personal pronoun separately (e.g. זאלסט דוא zɔlst du 'you should' (p. 22b); קאנסט דוא kɔnst du 'you can', p. 17a). This lexicalized orthographic treatment was undoubtedly suppressing the contraction (i.e. the actual loss of word boundary) that most likely persisted in the translator's speech.

Far more significant for the subsequent development of modern Yiddish orthography was the adoption of the ⟨ע⟩ grapheme for the postdiphthongal ə vowel; e.g. זייער zejər 'their' (pp. 7a, 19a, 20b); זייער zejər 'very' (pp. 11b,

19b); אײַער ajər 'your' (pl., p. 31b). However, the traditional employment of the ⟨א⟩ grapheme prevails in the spelling of other lexical items; e.g. נײַארט najərt 'only' (p. 7b); גיטרײַאן gətrajən 'trustworthy' (masc. acc., p. 17a); פֿײַאר fajər 'fire' (p. 16a).

Another important orthographic innovation, apparently inspired by the contemporary Germanized Western Yiddish books, was the more regular representation of many posttonic vowels (cf. §17), frequently including the posttonic shewa; e.g. אײַלינדיגי ájlṇdikə 'speeding' (pl., p. 7a); שלאַנגין šlangən 'snakes' (p. 16a); פֿר זיכֿירט farzíxərt 'fixed' (p. 8a).

28.2 Phonology

The conventional spelling of the stressed vowels and most consonants largely masks the underlying Eastern Yiddish phonology of this text. There are, however, a number of dialectal spellings that point towards Mideastern Yiddish phonology.

A number of spellings testify to the word-final devoicing which is especially characteristic of Mideastern Yiddish (cf. §15.2.4); e.g. גים גאַלט gímgɔlt (mod. Y. gíngɔld) 'fine gold' (p. 43b); פֿרײַנט frajnt (St.Y. frajnd) 'friends' (pp. 15a, b, 17b). A fair number of hypercorrections reveal that the anonymous translator often tried to 'restore' word-final voiced stops; e.g. ווײַד ⟨vajd⟩ vajt 'far' (p. 21a); פֿאַלג ⟨folg⟩ fɔlk 'people' (pp. 33a, 43a).

Many dialectal spellings reveal the Southeastern or Mideastern Yiddish merger of the historical vowels 51/52 and 31/32 in a unitary i; e.g. גפֿינין gəfínən (NEY and St.Y. gəfúnən) 'found' (p. 7a); גוויסט gəvíst (NEY and St. Y. gəvust) 'knew' (pp. 9b, 48b); פֿין fin (NEY fun) 'from; of' (pp. 8b, 9b; 15b, 36a); מיז miz (NEY and St.Y. muz) 'must' (3rd pers. sing., p. 41a). Much less frequent is the hypercorrect use of ⟨ו⟩ for etymological i; e.g. גימוט ⟨gimut⟩ gəmít 'mood' (p. 34a).

Most of the rhymes in the poems that are interwoven into the main text do not reveal any specific Eastern Yiddish vocalism. Thus the rhymes ⟨גרוב⟩ grub 'ditch; grave': ⟨שטוב⟩ štub 'house' with historical vowel 52 (cf. p. 37b) and ⟨גראָבן⟩ grɔbṇ 'grave': ⟨האָבן⟩ hɔbṇ 'have' with the historical vowel 13 (cf. p. 33b) are equally sustained as grub:štub and grɔbṇ:hɔbṇ in Northeastern Yiddish, grip:štip and grubṇ:hubṇ in Mideastern Yiddish, and grib:štib and grubṇ:(h)ubṇ in Southeastern Yiddish. Some rhymes are phonologically incongruous in any Eastern Yiddish dialect; e.g. ⟨פֿר שפּרייטין⟩ 'spread': ⟨לייטין⟩ 'people' (cf. p. 52b) , where the rhyming stressed vowels 22 and 34 yield faršpréjtṇ:lajtṇ in Northeastern, faršprájtṇ:lātṇ in Mideastern, and faršpréjtṇ:latṇ in Southeastern dialects.

However, one rhyme פֿר לאָרין farlórṇ 'lost': יאָרין jɔrṇ 'years', used more than once (cf. pp. 11a, 35a) reveals the matching of historical vowels 12 and 41. This match-up is phonologically viable only in Northeastern Yiddish; e.g. farlɔ́rṇ:jɔrṇ (cf. MEY and SEY farlɔ́jrṇ:jurṇ). Similarly, the past participle form farlɔ́rṇ is characteristic of Northeastern Yiddish (cf. M. Weinreich 1973: ii. 378). In some of the rhymes the stressed vowels do not necessarily seem to have been phonologically equal (e.g. the rhyme שפרייטין פֿר faršpréjtṇ 'spread': לייטין lajtṇ 'people'). Everything other than this rhyme—e.g. the frequent dialectal spelling of historical vowels 51 and 52, the loss of word-final voicing, and the distinctly Mideastern or Southeastern forms of past participles (cf. §28.3.3)—testifies to the underlying phonology of the text being of Mideastern or Southeastern provenance. It seems plausible, however, that the anonymous author of this translation was familiar with Northeastern Yiddish, allowing him to occasionally exploit its phonology and forms for rhyming purposes. This suggestion is supported by an analogous case of non-native dialectal rhyming found in the Yiddish text of the bilingual poem *Vikuekh yeytser tov im ben odem* (Shklov, c.1783). Its author, apparently a native speaker of Northeastern Yiddish, employed a couple of 'Mideastern' or 'Southeastern' rhymes (see §34.2.1). Similarly, non-native dialectal rhyming can be encountered in modern Yiddish poetry from the early nineteenth and twentieth centuries (see U. Weinreich 1959; Altbauer 1965; Goldberg 1986).

28.3 Morphology and Morpho-syntax

The morphology of this work is largely based on modern Eastern Yiddish usage. Some forms are even narrowly dialectal, being distinctly characteristic of Mideastern or Southeastern dialects. Others are clearly 'general' Eastern Yiddish, in contrast to Old Yiddish and Western Yiddish. A significant number of forms and categories were inherited from the old literary language. Yet many of these are challenged by their modern alternative equivalents.

There is very little influence of New High German or of Germanized Western Yiddish upon the morphology. The only relevant form which occasionally appears is ווירט vərt (or virt), which sometimes replaces ווערט vɛrt (or vərt), the regular third-person singular present form of the modal verb vɛrṇ (or vərṇ) 'become' (e.g. on pp. 14b, 15a, 21b), and in a few cases is found instead of the third-person form of the future auxiliary ווערט vət (on p. 12a; cf. §28.3.3.4). However, the spelling ⟨ווירט⟩ can also be interpreted as an orthographic variant of ⟨ווערט⟩, since vowel 21 (pan-Yiddish ɛ) is occasionally represented by the ⟨י⟩ grapheme (e.g. שליכטי šlɛ́xtə 'bad' (pl.), p. 45b; רייכנין réxənən 'count for', p. 46b).

28.3.1 Forms Inherited from Old Literary Yiddish

Old Yiddish morphological features found in this text comprise the occasional use of a few surviving preterite forms, the frequent periphrastic construction {tɔn + infinitive}, and the consistent employment of the historical genitive forms of personal pronouns.

28.3.1.1 The Preterite

Preterite forms are restricted to a limited number of verbs; e.g. וואר vɔr 'was' (pp. 5a, 6a, 7a, 20b, 26a, 45a); וואורין vɔrn̩ 'were' (p. 21a); שיק šik 'sent' (p. 27a); קאם kɔm(?) 'came' (pp. 6a, 48b, 45a). Of these וואר vɔr 'was' is the only one frequently used. The employment of the preterite as a category seems to be restricted to the more narrative passages. There it is often accompanied by other stylistic markers of a conventional narrative, also inherited from the old literary language, e.g. the 'consecutive' adverb דא dɔ ' then; thus; so' (cf. pp. 27a, 33b, 37b, 40b, 48b).

28.3.1.2 The Construction {tɔn + infinitive}

More frequent is the employment of the construction {tɔn + infinitive}; e.g. פֿיל דוא ערד טושט דען מענטשין dú ɛrd tust dən mɛnčn̩ fil gɔb gɛbn̩ 'Earth, you give many presents to man' (p. 14b); גאב געבין טוט עש פֿר לענדין tut əs farléndn̩ '[he] destroys it' (p. 12b); זי טואן מיר דינן zej tuən mir dinən 'they serve me' (p. 17a).

In our text, this construction is one of the most characteristc features of the old literary language. In the modern literary language {tɔn + infinitive} is sometimes described as an analytic construction reserved for marking the iterative or habitual aspect (e.g. Mark 1978: 293 §3; Birnbaum 1979: 272 §149). However, in spoken and in Modern Literary Yiddish its function seems, to a certain degree, to have been overtaken by another construction {haltn̩ in (ejn) + infinitive} (cf. English {keep + -ing}: see D. Katz 1987a: 160 §§9.1.3–4), whereas {tɔn + infinitive} survived mostly as a stylistically 'higher' construction in the traditional literature, especially in the so-called *tkhine* style in which the conventional (at least since the mid-sixteenth century) Yiddish prayers for women (i.e. *tkhines*) are written (cf. M. Weinreich 1973: i. 26 §6.9). In the modern literary language it may be considered as an infrequently used 'archaism'. It is possible, however, that this construction was still used in the spoken Mideastern Yiddish of the eighteenth and nineteenth centuries (see §35.11; cf. Max Weinreich 1973: iv. 252 §145).

28.3.1.3 The Genitive of Personal Pronouns

The historical genitive of personal pronouns was lost in modern Eastern Yiddish (for a different view see Joffe 1964). As a result, its function was taken over by possessive pronouns, which inflect only by number in attributive position (cf. §35.5.2). This development apparently began before the second half of the eighteenth century. Genitive forms of personal pronouns are remarkably rare in *Mayse gdoyle min Uman umin Ukrayne* ([Novidvor], *c*.1783; cf. §32.4.1), which may be considered the earliest original work written altogether in Eastern Yiddish. However, in this translation of *Ben hameylekh vehanozir* these forms are still regularly employed; e.g.:

מיין העגט majn hɛnt 'my hands' (p. 21a);
צו דיין טעג tsu dajn tɛg 'to your days' (p. 12a);
פֿון זיין אויגן fun zajn ɔjgṇ 'from his eyes' (p. 42b);
זיין סודות zajn sɔjdəs 'his secrets' (p. 28a);
זייער מעשים zejər majsəm 'their deeds' (p. 15a);
אויף זייער לעפֿצין af zejər lɛfcṇ 'on their lips' (p. 20b).

The fact that genitive forms of the personal pronoun are a regular feature of this text does not necessarily mean that they were still current in the spoken Eastern Yiddish of the time. It seems that they were relics of the old literary language. Moreover, the use of possessive pronouns seems to be more frequent in this text; e.g.:

מייני העגט majnə hɛnt 'my hands' (p. 21b);
מייני ברידר majnə bridər 'my brothers' (p. 17a);
פֿון דייני חיילות fun dajnə xajɔ́ləs 'from your armies' (p. 16b);
דייני מנהגים dajnə minhɔ́gəm 'your customs' (p. 55b);
אירה מעשים irə majsəm 'her deeds' (p. 18a);
אין אילי אירה זייטין in ilə irə zajtṇ 'in all its corners' (p. 18a).

28.3.2 *Old versus New Forms*

Competition between old and new forms is one of the most salient features of this and some other late eighteenth-century Eastern Yiddish texts. The new forms and categories did not always become dominant, and the anonymous translator of *Ben hameylekh vehanozir* (1771) sometimes clearly preferred to adhere to the morphological and morpho-syntactic patterns of the old literary language. However, even in these instances the alternative Eastern Yiddish forms that are occasionally employed mark the decline of the older usage in favour of modern Eastern Yiddish. Thus the very coexistence of גיט git 'gives' (p. 14a) and גיבט gibt 'gives' (pp. 21b, 14a), irrespective of statistical frequency, seems to indicate that the newer form was making its way into literary usage at the expense of the older.

In some cases the competing forms coexist in a kind of complementary distribution. There seems to be a tendency to employ the imperfective older passive voice construction {vɔrṇ + past participle/adjective} as the unmarked counterpart of the newer perfective construction {past participle/ adjective + gəvɔrṇ} (see Table 16). As a result of this coexistence, the newer construction can often, though not always, be interpreted as the marked perfective member of the opposition {vɔrn̩ + past participle/adjective} (unmarked) ~ {past participle/adjective + gəvɔrn̩} (perfective). In the older construction the finite verb is optional.

Table 16 The older and newer passive-voice constructions in *Ben hameylekh vehanozir* (1771)

imperfective	perfective
זיין כבֿוד איז װארין גנידרט	דוא ביזשט אויף זייא גיזעצט גװארין
zajn kɔvəd iz vɔrn̩ gənidərt	du bist af zej gəzɛct gəvɔrn̩
'he was humiliated' (p. 7a)	'you are put to [rule] over them' (p. 16b)
lit. 'his honour was lowered'	
זייא װארין מיד	דיא רפֿואה איז [. . .] פֿרטיג גװארין
zej vɔrn̩ mid	di rəfuə iz [. . .] fártıg gəvɔrn̩
'they were tired' (p. 43b)	'the remedy is [. . .] ready' (p. 15b)

In a similar way certain competing forms may be used in a complementary way according to stylistic and prosodic requirements. The usual plural form of the noun טאג tɔg 'day' is the same as in modern Yiddish; i.e. טעג tɛg (e.g. pp. 11a, 12a, 25a, 32b). The older form טאגין tɔgn̩, however, is used to make a rhyme with another more archaic form פֿראגין frɔgn̩ 'ask' (p. 11b). The rhymed passages are not the only ones in which the more archaic forms occur. The text opens with a more formal narrative introductory passage, in which the translator chooses, once more for stylistic reasons, to use the archaic טעגין tɛgn̩ in the opening sentence (note also the use of the preterite and of the more formal קיניגן kénign̩ instead of the usual מלכים mlɔxəm 'kings'):

אין די ערשטי טעגין אין אן פֿאנג פֿון די ערשטי קיניגן װאר אין לנד הודו [. . .]
in di ɛrštə tɛgn̩ in ónfang fun di ɛrštə kénign̩ vɔr in land hójdu [. . .]
'in the first days during the early times of the first kings there was in the land of India [. . .]' (p. 5b).

28.3.2.1 *The Third-Person Plural Possessive Pronouns*   The modern Eastern Yiddish third-person plural possessive pronoun זייער zejər 'their' replaced the older form איר ir (see §§5.4, 10.3, 11.3.3.8, and 35.5.3; cf. Lincoff 1963: 77–8), which nevertheless survived in twentieth-century vestiges of Western Yiddish (cf. e.g. Guggenheim-Grünberg 1969: 10). In spoken Eastern Yiddish, the competition between איר and זייער must have started before the eighteenth century. In the original edition of *Kav hayosher* (Frankfurt am Main, 1705–6) written by a native speaker of Eastern Yiddish, both forms are used, with זייער usually functioning as the genitive of the personal pronoun and איר as a possessive pronoun. In *Ben hameylekh vehanozir* (1771) both זייער and איר are employed in much the same way. Morpho-syntactically, זייער often functions in this work as a genitive of the personal pronoun. (On the genitive forms of personal pronouns cf. §28.3.1.3.) It remains uninflected in the plural, whereas איר inflects in the plural, as do the other possessive pronouns (see Table 17).

Table 17 The third-person plural possessive pronouns in *Ben hameylekh vehanozir* (1771)

איר ir	זייער zejər
מיט אירה לעפֿצין mit irə lɛfcn	אויף זייער לעפֿצין af zejər lɛfcn
'with their lips' (p. 14a)	'on their lips' (p. 20b)
אירה מדריגות irə madréjgəs	זייער משלים zejər məšɔləm
'their types' (p. 15b)	'their parables' (p. 22a)
אירה תענוגים irə tajnúgəm	זייער פֿליגל zejər fligl̩
'their pleasures' (p. 5b)	'their wings' (p. 17a)
אירה מעשים irə majsəm	זייער מעשים zejər majsəm
'their deeds' (p. 18a)	'their deeds' (p. 15a)

It is possible that the Eastern Yiddish זייער zejər originally occurred as the genitive form of the personal pronoun. As a result of the loss of the genitive, it may subsequently have been reinterpreted as the third-person plural possessive pronoun, and then morpho-syntactically levelled with other possessive pronouns yielding the singular זייער zejər and the plural זייערע zejərə. In *Ben hameylekh vehanozir* זייער zejər is the prevailing form with singular nouns:

זייער מלאכה zejər mlɔxə 'their work' (p. 16b);

פֿאר זייער ארבית far zejər arbət 'for their labour' (p. 16b);

זייער פנים און זייער געשטאלט zejər pɔnəm un zejər gəštalt
'their face and their form' (p. 17a).

28.3.2.2 *The Periphrastic Possessive* The periphrastic possessive construction {noun (= possessor) + possessive pronoun + noun} can be found in the old literary language from the seventeenth century (cf. Lerner 1937: 128–9). This construction is also known in German dialects (cf. Wells 1985: 372 and literature listed in Lerner 1937: 132 n. 6). In Yiddish it was apparently introduced into literary usage from late sixteenth- and seventeenth-century Western and Eastern Yiddish dialects.

In the late eighteenth century, this construction may still have existed in the spoken language. Even so, it would probably have coexisted with the regular possessive case. Thanks to Carl Friedrich's testimony on Northern Transitional (or 'Prussian') Yiddish (see D. Katz 1988*b*; 1990: 187–92), we know that the possessive case in its modern form was already a regular feature of his dialect in the late eighteenth century (see Friedrich 1784: 54 §2). In the modern literary language, the periphrastic construction was completely replaced by the regular possessive case. The only well-known vestige of this construction in modern Yiddish is the archaic expression מיט גאָט זיינ(ער) הילף mit gɔt zajn(ər) hilf 'with God's help' (cf. Lerner 1937: 132). Until the late eighteenth century, the periphrastic construction prevailed in the old literary language, apparently becoming the 'more literary' form (cf. Lerner 1937: 148; Shmeruk 1964*a*: 328). This is in sharp contrast to contemporary literary New High German, where an analogous construction remained unacceptable (cf. Wells 1985: 233). The wide use of the periphrastic possessive in many late eighteenth- and some nineteenth-century Eastern Yiddish texts (cf. Lerner 1937: 129–31) may be explained as a stylistic adherence to the 'more literary' form of expressing possession.

In this respect *Ben hameylekh vehanozir* (1771) is not exceptional, and the periphrastic construction appears to be the most frequent:

דען מלך זיין הארץ dən mejlǝx zajn harc 'the king's heart' (p. 7a);
פון זיין בלוט fun zajn blut 'from his blood' (p. 8a);
דען מלך אויף זיין הארץ dən mejlǝx af zajn harc 'on the king's heart' (19b);
אז צו איין הערין זיין קנעכט az cu ajn hɛrn̩ zajn knɛxt
'as to the master's slave' (p. 20a).

However, the regular possessive is also frequently used:

וועגין גאטש פֿארכט vɛgn̩ gɔts fɔrxt 'for the fear of God' (p. 7b);
מיט גאטש הילף mit gɔts hilf 'with God's help' (p. 28b);
זייער קינדרש קינדר zejǝr kindǝrs kindǝr 'their children's children' (p. 32a);
דיין גזלינש הויז dajn gǝzɛln̩s hojz 'your friend's house' (p. 44b);
דען מענטשינש וועג dən mɛnčn̩s vɛg 'the way of a human being' (p. 35b);
גאטש וואראהפטיגהייט gɔts vɔrhaftikajt 'God's truth' (p. 18b).

There are also a considerable number of instances in which the periphrastic construction is 'mixed' with the genitive case (cf. Lerner 1937: 129); e.g.:

פֿון דען מארשליקש זיין גלויבן fun dən máršəliks zajn glɔjbn̩
'from the marshal's convictions' (p. 25a);
גאטש זיין וויסן שאפט gɔts zajn vísnšȧft 'God's knowledge' (p. 20a);
דען מענטשינש זיין לעבין dən mɛnčn̩s zajn lɛbn̩
'the life of a human being' (p. 44a);
פֿון דען שטרווילירש זיין הנט fun dən štrɔjxlǝrs zajn hant
'from the hand of the tempter' (p. 43a).

There is no apparent semantic differentiation between these three morpho-syntactic means of expressing possession, and none of them is marked as a form of the so-called inalienable possession. All three constructions compete for the same position of morpho-syntactic marking of the animate possessor. (On the opposition animate vs. inanimate in modern Yiddish see Mark 1978: 179 §4; D. Katz 1987a: 100–2 §5.15.) The frequent use of 'mixed' constructions may well indicate that the periphrastic possessive was beginning to give way to the regular possessive case, which ultimately became the norm in both spoken Yiddish and the modern literary language.

28.3.2.3 *Accusative Case of the Masculine Definite Article* There is ample evidence of the merger of the accusative and dative in eighteenth-century Eastern Yiddish. However, in some Western Yiddish dialects of the early seventeenth century the historical accusative דעֿן dən was apparently extended to the dative case (see Lincoff 1963: 54 §4.211). This is fully supported by the forms cited in Friedrich (1784: 53 §1). On the other hand, the increasing Germanization of some eighteenth-century Western Yiddish printed works strengthened the principal differentiation between accusative דעֿן dən and dative דעם dəm.

The anonymous translator of *Ben hameylekh vehanozir* (1771) apparently made every effort to sustain this differentiation. The accusative form of the masculine definite article is usually represented by דעֿן; e.g. דעֿן מענטשין dən mɛnčņ 'the man' (acc. sing., p. 5b); דעֿן שׂבר dən sxar 'the reward' (acc. sing., p. 6b); דעֿן מלך dən mejləx 'the king' (acc. sing., p. 20a). However, occasionally he 'slips' and uses דעם for the accusative; e.g. דעם סוד dəm sod 'the secret' (acc. sing., p. 34a); דעם תענוג dəm tajnəg 'the pleasure' (acc. sing., p. 34a). In some instances the translator's eagerness to use דעֿן results in hypercorrections; e.g. דעֿן קראנקין dən krankņ 'to the ill person' (dat. sing., p. 13a); דעֿן מענטשין dən mɛnčņ 'to the man' (dat. sing., p. 14b); דעֿן אנדרין dən andərņ 'to the other one' (dat. sing., p. 11b).

Another consequence of the Eastern Yiddish merger of the accusative and dative forms of the masculine definite article was the loss of morphological opposition between accusative and dative cases after prepositions. Similarly, the neuter definite article after prepositions was also fully levelled to דעם dəm. So if we find מיט דעֿן מלכֿות mit dən malxəs 'with the kingdom' (p. 26a), it is an indication of another type of hypercorrection. The noun מלכֿות malxəs is neuter, and in the older literary language the expected form would be *mit dos malxəs. However, in spoken Eastern Yiddish its equivalent is mit dəm malxəs, because דעֿן and דעם merged into unitary דעם, and the prepositional case for neuter and masculine singular was subsequently levelled. Another case, which appears to be a hypercorrection, is נאֿך דעֿן nox dən 'afterwards',

(p. 19b). The contracted Eastern Yiddish variant of these two forms—i.e. נאָך nɔx and דעם dəm—is נאָכן nɔxn̩ 'after the'. However, only the uncontracted variant became an adverbial construction (cf. mod. Yiddish נאָך דעם nɔxdəm 'afterwards, later'), and it seems most unlikely that its actual realization in the translator's spoken Yiddish was other than nɔxdəm.

All in all, the preferred form of the masculine and neuter definite article after a preposition is דען; e.g.:

פֿון דען פֿיינט fun dən fajnt 'from the enemy' (p. 15b);

פֿון דען מלך fun dən mejləx 'of the king' (p. 26b);

אויף דען גוטן מענטשין af dən gutn̩ mɛnčn̩ 'for the good person' (p. 22a);

צו היטן פֿר דען דת cu hitn̩ far dən das 'to guard from religion' (p. 20a);

צו דען מענטשין cu dən mɛnčn̩ 'to the person' (p. 10a);

ארום דען עשין וואָרג arum dən ɛsn̩varg 'with concern to food' (p. 11a);

איבר דען קראַנקין íbər dən krankn̩ 'about the ill [person]' (p. 13a).

On the other hand, דעם dəm is less frequently employed after a preposition; e.g.:

פֿר דעם מלך far dəm mejləx 'for the king' (p. 7b);

פֿן דעם תכלית fun dəm taxləs 'for the outcome' (p. 11a);

צו דעם משא ומתן cu dəm másəmàtn̩ 'for the business' (p. 10b);

אויף דעם פנים af dəm pɔnəm 'on his face' (p. 12b);

אויף דעם לייב af dəm lajb 'on his body' (p. 12b).

The prevailing use of דען after prepositions is a further indication that the translator was attempting to employ in writing a form that was already defunct in his spoken language. The effort to maintain the difference between the accusative and dative of the masculine definite article and to preserve דען is characteristic of many late eighteenth- and some nineteenth-century Eastern Yiddish texts (see e.g. §§11.3.2.1, 35.6.2). However, in the modern literary language, the whole case system was fundamentally restructured on the basis of the grammatical features of spoken Eastern Yiddish.

28.3.2.4 *The Place of Separable Verbal Prefixes*   One of the morpho-syntactic features of Old Literary Yiddish was the occasional placement of stressed adverbs (the modern separable verbal prefixes) in front of the finite verb. Our text did not completely abolish this feature. The separable prefix sometimes appears before the finite verb in subordinate clauses (and in one case in an interrogative phrase, no. 3); e.g.:

1 אז עש אן הייבט צו שפּראָצין az əs ɔn hejbt cu šprɔcn̩
'when it begins to sprout' (p. 9a);

2 [. . .] וואָש אַרויש טרייבט vɔs arɔjs trajbt [. . .]
'[a power] that drives outward [. . .]' (p. 13a);

3 [. . .] אונ׳ וואס ארויש קומט un vɔs arɔjs kumt [. . .]
'and what is the advantage [. . .]?' (p. 21b).

In most cases, however, the text adopts the modern Yiddish pattern of
placing the stressed separable prefix after the finite verb. As in modern
Eastern Yiddish, the stressed prefix normally occupies third place, unless the
given clause has a pronominal subject or object (see no. 8 below); e.g.:

4 הייבט אן צו שרייאין מיט גאנצן קראַפֿט hejbt ɔn cu šrajən mit gancṇ kraft
'[he] begins to shout with all his might' (p. 20a);

5 אונ הייבט אן צו זינגן un hejbt ɔn cu zingən
'and [he] begins to sing' (p. 17a);

6 אונ הייבט אויף זיין קול un hejbt uf zajn kɔl
'and [he] raises his voice' (p. 21a);

7 דיא נשמה גייט אויף אונ דער גוף גייט אין גרוב אריין
di nəšomə gejt uf un dər guf gejt in grúb aràjn
'the soul rises and the body goes to the grave' (p. 25b);

8 הייבט ער זיך אן צו רירן hejbt er zəx ɔn cu rirṇ
'he begins to move' (p. 48b).

As in modern Yiddish, the stressed prefix is always placed immediately after
the finite verb in the imperative.

28.3.2.5 *Functional Words*   One of the most prominent Eastern Yiddish
features of this work is the systematic use of modern Yiddish functional
words. The subordinating conjunction אז az 'that', the final conjunction כדי
kədej 'so that; in order to', and the general relative pronoun וואס vɔs 'that;
which; who' prevail. The effectiveness with which אז and וואס contribute to
the morpho-syntactic organization of most of the text can be exemplified in
the following sentence:

דא האב איך ערשט פֿר שטאנין אז דיא וואס איך האב גידאלט
dɔ hɔb ix ɛršt farštánən az di vɔs ix hɔb gədaxt
אז זיא זענין מיין פֿריינט אז [. . .] דיא וואָרין צו מיר אז ברעננדיגי
az zej zenən majn frajnt az [. . .] di vɔrṇ cu mir az brénəndìke
שלאַנגין [. . .] וואָס זיא זענען ניט אָנגשפראָכין זיא זאָלין ניט שעדיגין
šlangən [. . .] vɔs zej zenən nit ɔ́ngəšprɔxṇ zej zɔlṇ nit šɛ́dikṇ

'Only then did I understand that those whom I considered
to be my friends [. . .] were [as friendly] to me as burning snakes on
which no spell had been put so that they would not harm' (p. 15b).

However, the modern forms אז, כדי, and וואס are occasionally rivalled by
their Old Yiddish equivalents. The older forms, inherited from the old literary
language, are used alongside the new (see Tables 18 and 19). These older

forms are as follows: the subordinating conjunction דז das ∼ dɔs 'that'; the final conjunctions דר ווארטז(י)ן dərvɔrtn̦ 'in order to' and דז das ∼ dɔz 'so that'; and the relative pronouns דר (דא)/ די (דא)/ דש (דא) dər (dɔ)/ di (dɔ)/ dɔs (dɔ) 'that' (masc./fem./neut.). It is nevertheless significant that the older forms are less frequent.

Ben hameylekh vehanozir (1771) may be one of the earliest literary texts in which the conjunction כדי kədej occurs repeatedly. Since it belongs to the Semitic component, its admission to the literary language may be seen as part and parcel of the general, and proportionately unprecedented influx of Yiddish lexical items of Hebrew or Aramaic origin so characteristic of this and other contemporary Eastern Yiddish texts.

Table 18 The old and new conjunctions in *Ben hameylekh vehanozir* (1771)

New	Old
Subordinating Conjunctions	
אז az	דז dɔs
דו זאלשט ווישן אז איך בין	ח זאלשט ווישן דז דר מענטש מיט זיין
גוועזין [. . .] מלך פֿון מיין יוגנט אז	הארץ און זיין שפראך איז איין מענטש
du zɔlst visn̦ az ix bin gəvɛzn̦ [. . .]	du zɔlst visn̦ dɔs dər mɛnč mit zajn
mejləx fun majn jugn̦t ɔn	harc un zajn šprɔx iz a mɛnč
'you should know that I was [a . . .]	'you should know that the man is
king since my youth' (p. 28a)	judged by his heart and his speech' (p. 32b)
Final Conjunctions	
כדי kədej	דר ווארטז(י)ן dərvɔrtn̦
כדי איך זאל אויך ווישן [. . .]	דר ווארטן איך זאל פֿר שטיין דיין רייד
kədej ix zɔl ɔjx visn̦ [. . .]	dərvɔrtn̦ ix zɔl farštéjn dajn rejd
'so that I too shall know [. . .]' (p. 49b)	'so that I shall understand your words' (p. 35a)
כדי kədej	דז dɔz
כדי מען זאל שוין קיין בייז פֿון	קלויבט אייך אויש איינים דר זאל ריידן
דיר זעהן אודר הערין	דז מיר זאלן פֿר שטיין
kədej mən zɔl šɔjn kən bejz fun	klajbt ajx ɔjs ejnəm dər zɔl rejdn̦
dir zɛn ɔdər hɛrn̦	dɔz mir zɔln̦ im farštéjn
'so that no one will see or	'choose yourself someone to speak
hear evil from you' (45a)	so that we [can] understand him' (p. 32b)

Table 19 The old and new relative pronouns in *Ben hameylekh vehanozir* (1771)

Old	New
וואס vɔs	דר/די/דש (דא) dər/di̯/dɔs (dɔ)
דער מאן וואס דו טושט זוכין זיין	פרעגט ער אויף איינים פֿון זייני לייט
נארהייט ווער צו אים איין שטרויכלונג	דער דא פֿלעגט צו זיין [. . .]
dər man vɔs du tust zuxn̩ zajn	frɛgt ər af ejnəm fun zajnə lajt
nárhajt vɔr cu ima(jn) štrójxlung	dər dɔ flɛgt cu zajn [. . .]
the man who you are looking for	so he asked for one of his men [for the
his foolishness was his failing (p. 7a)	one] who used to be [. . .] (p. 7a)
זי זענן מייני ברידר און גזעלין וואש	אונ האט איין גזאמילט די חכמים [. . .]
איך האב מיך איבר ענטפֿערט צו זי	די דא צייטין פֿר שטייאין
zej zɛnən majnə bridər un gəzɛln̩ vɔs	un hɔt ájngəzaməl̩t di xaxómem [. . .]
ix hɔb mix ibər ɛntfərt cu zej	di dɔ cajtn̩ farštéjən
they are my brothers and friends	and [he] assembled the sages [. . .]
to whom I entrusted myself (p. 17a)	who can read the future (lit. 'who
	understand the time'; p. 19b)

By contrast, the anonymous translator was careful not to use forms or lexical items from the Slavonic component. He did not employ the concessive conjunction כאטשי xɔčə 'although' (cf. mod. Y. כאָטש(ע) xɔč(ə)). Instead, when necessary, he used the older conjunctions; e.g. וויא וואול דז vi vɔjl dɔz 'although' (p. 6b); ווען גלייך vən glajx '(even) though' (pp. 41b, 47a). The absence of כאטשי betrays stylistic sensitivity on the part of the translator, for this Eastern Yiddish form was frequently used in earlier Yiddish texts from Eastern Europe (cf. §§5.2 and 7.2.3). It can also be found in some earlier Western Yiddish monuments; e.g. in the memoirs of Glikl Hamlin (cf. Fridberg 1961: 88–9).

28.3.3 *Eastern Yiddish Morphology*

In the context of literary Yiddish, this text provides some of the earliest attestations of many Eastern Yiddish forms. Several unmistakably dialectal features testify to the immediate impact of the spoken language upon literary usage. Numerous forms conform with modern knowledge of Southeastern and Mideastern morphology.

Sometimes the dialectal form (as described from the vantage-point of modern Standard Yiddish) is dominant, as in the case of the principally Southeastern pronominal adjective אילה ilə 'all' (e.g. on pp. 6a, 6b, 14a, 18a, 20b, 22b, 33a) and its variants; e.g. אין איל זייני דינגן in il zajnə dingən 'in all his deeds' (p. 28a); מיט אילר מיגליך הייט mit ilər míglix(k)àjt 'with every effort'

(p. 14b); and מיט אילם mit iləm 'with every thing' (p. 26a; on אילה ilə and related forms cf. §7.2.1). The same is true of dialectal forms with pretonic or posttonic cluster breaking; e.g. צו ווישׁן cəvišn̩ 'between' (e.g. on pp. 7a, 21b, 44a; cf. mod. Y. צווישׁן cvišn̩) and בילעך biləx 'better' (p. 47b; cf. mod. Y. בילך bil̩x).

In many instances dialectal Southeastern or Mideastern forms are the norm in *Ben hameylekh vehanozir* (1771). The consistent employment of זענ(ע)ן zenən 'are' (1st or 3rd pers. pl.), as well as the repeated use of the comparative adjective ארגיר argər 'worse' (pp. 24a, 37b, 46a, 48b), are characteristic cases. A significant number of past participles that appear in this text are also of Southeastern or Mideastern vintage; e.g.:

גפֿינין gəfinən (NEY gəfúnən) 'found' (pp. 7a, 10a, 21b);
גוויסט gəvist (NEY gəvúst) 'knew' (pp. 9b, 48b);
גקרינ(ע)ן gəkrign̩ (NEY gəkrogn̩) 'received' (pp. 21a, 33a, 43a);
גשׁענקין gəšɛnkən (NEY gəšɔnkn̩) 'presented' (pp. 46a, 47a);
גברענגט gəbrɛngt (NEY gəbraxt) 'brought' (pp. 34a, 38b, 51b).

Finally, certain consistently occurring forms are characteristically Eastern Yiddish, and differ pronouncedly from Old Yiddish and Western Yiddish forms; e.g. בלייטין baléjtn̩ 'accompany' (pp. 43b, 55a; on this form see §7.3.3); אלמץ and אליץ alc 'everything' (pp. 14a, 15a, 26b, 49b); האָפֿונג hófung 'hope' (pp. 19b, 20b, 29a); and ארביט arbət 'work' (pp. 6b, 7a, 11a, 45a; on the last two forms see §15.3.1).

28.3.3.1 *Plural Formation*   As we have seen in the case of tɔg 'day', the modern pattern of plural formation, tɛg 'days', prevails in this work; although in certain stylistic conditions the more archaic plurals tɔgn̩ and tɛgn̩ are preferred (see above §28.3.2). To this may be added the consistent use of the plural marker -s for agentives, one of the pluralizing allomorphs characteristic of modern Southeastern Yiddish (cf. Rekhtman 1952; Katz 1993a: 261-2). In the case of feminine agentives, this marker is typical of all Eastern Yiddish dialects.

masculine agentives
זינגרס zingərs 'singers' (p. 14b);
לויפֿרס lɔjfərs 'runners; messengers' (p. 36b);
פֿיררס firərs 'drivers' (p. 11b);
קלעגירס klɛgərs 'mourners' (p. 45a);
שרייבירס šrajbərs 'scribes' (p. 38b).

feminine agentives
זינגרינס zingərn̩s '(female) singers' (p. 14b);
קלעגרינס klɛgərn̩s '(female) mourners' (p. 14b).

This plural marker, often after stem-final r or n, was apparently productive in both Western and Eastern varieties of earlier times (see M. Weinreich 1973: ii. 63–6 §§118–118.2; for the earliest attestations of this marker cf. ibid. iv. 91–4 §§118–118.1; see also King 1990). In the old literary language, however, this marker seems to have been avoided (cf. Lincoff 1963: 50–1).

28.3.3.2 *Nominal Suffixes* The most productive and regularly employed nominal suffixes (mostly for abstract and often for deverbative nouns) are -(ə)niš, -ung, -hajt, and -šaft; e.g. בדערפֿניש badérfəniš 'necessity' (p. 12b); פֿינצטרניש fínctərniš 'darkness' (p. 12b); שפּראצונג šprócung 'sprouting' (p. 9a); שטאַרקהייט štárk(h)ajt 'strength' (p. 12b); ליב שאַפֿט líbšaft 'love' (pp. 17a, 29b); ווישן שאַפֿט vísņšaft 'knowledge' (p. 20a). These suffixes were also recurrent in the traditional *taytsh* (see below §28.4). The marked productivity of these suffixes is supported in *Ben hameylekh vehanozir* by the large-scale introduction of certain forms and lexical items from *taytsh*. The abstract suffixes -šaft, -ung, and -(ə)niš are also productive in Modern Literary Yiddish (cf. Falkovitsh 1940: 149 §183; Zaretski 1929: 50–1, 56–7, 58–9; Mark 1978: 196–7 §§3–4, 200–1 §3; Birnbaum 1979: 233, 234, 238).

Still, the actual use and distribution of these suffixes differ markedly from their modern usage. In certain cases some of these abstract suffixes were eventually replaced in modern Yiddish by other nominal constructions. Thus in the modern literary language the form זיין ברומונג zajn brúmung 'his scream' (p. 13a) is replaced by a fully nominalized infinitive זיין ברומען zajn brúmən 'his screaming'. The form בוועגניש bavégəniš 'movement' (p. 13a) is replaced by the modern באַוועגונג bavégung (introduced from NHG *Bewegung*). Moreover, the suffix often came as a 'package', together with the given *taytsh* construction, which has not gained wide use in modern Eastern Yiddish. The form זילברהייט zíxərhajt 'bond, covenant' was in this text directly introduced from *taytsh* (p. 12b; cf. Noble 1943: 64 no. 208), and its modern Yiddish semantic equivalents, ברית bris 'covenant' (p. 14b) and בונט bund 'bond' (p. 34a) also occur. In the modern language, however, zíxərkajt can only mean 'certainty' or 'security'. The fact that זילערקייט zíxərkajt is the modern morphological equivalent of the *taytsh* form זילברהייט zíxərhajt 'bond, covenant' illustrates an important change in abstract noun formation. Of the two suffixes -hajt and -kajt, only the latter became productive in the modern language (see Mark 1978: 199 §2). Subsequently, almost all nouns with -hajt were eventually replaced with -kajt.

The following abstract nouns formed with -hajt and -kajt were found in our text:

1 ארום קייט ˈórəmkajt (p. 9b);
   ארמקייט ˈórəmkajt (p. 12a) ~ ארים הייט ˈórəmhajt (?) 'poverty' (p. 41a);

2 קראנקהייט kránkajt 'sickness' (pp. 23a, 41a);
   שטארקהייט štárkajt 'strength' (p. 12b);

3 טרוויארדהייט trójərhajt (?) (p. 10b) ~ טרוויריגהייט trójərik(h)ajt 'sadness;
mourning' (p. 13a);

4 מינגליך הייט mígləxhajt (?) 'possibilities; means; efforts' (p. 14b);

5 פייכטיקייט fájxtikajt (p. 11b) ~ פייכטיגהייט fájxtik(h)ajt (?)
'moisture' (p. 13a);
   בלינדיקייט blíndikajt, 'blindness' (p. 6a);

6 זיסיגהייט zísik(h)ajt (?) 'sweetness' (pp. 26a, 47a);
   לוסטיגהייט lústik(h)ajt (?) 'desire; lust' (p. 17b).

Because of the morphological impact of *taytsh* forms—e.g. וואָרהייט vórhajt
'truth' (p. 17a); פאלש הייט fálšhajt 'hypocrisy' (p. 16a)—the suffix -hajt still
appears to be very productive in this text (see nos. 3–4 above). The variation
טרוויריגהייט trójərik(h)ajt ~ טרוויארדהייט trójərhajt (no. 3 above) apparently
illustrates that some stems at that stage did not yet have a fixed derivational
pattern in the literary language. On the other hand, the employment of the
suffix -kajt on its own (no. 1 above) is very rare. The anonymous translator
seems to have preferred to replace it with -hajt. Hence the variation ארמקייט
ˈórəmkajt (p. 12a) ~ ארים הייט ˈórəmhajt(?!) 'poverty'.

It appears, however, from the variation פייכטיקייט fájxtikajt ~ פייכטיגהייט
fájxtik(h)ajt 'moisture' (see no. 5 above) that -kajt began to replace -hajt
after the final k, be it after a stem-final consonant or after the suffix -ik. Such
spellings as קראנקהייט ⟨krankhajt⟩ 'illness' and שטארקהייט ⟨štarkhajt⟩
'strength' (no. 2), as well as זיסיגהייט ⟨zisighajt⟩ 'sweetness' and לוסטיגהייט
⟨lustighajt⟩ 'desire' (no. 6), were in all probability morphological; i.e. the
disappearing suffix -hajt was only orthographically preserved. In the spoken
Yiddish of that period their actual realization apparently matched that of
ארמקייט ⟨ormkajt⟩ ˈórəm*kajt* or פייכטיקייט ⟨fajxtikajt⟩ fájxti*kajt*. We may
reasonably suggest that the actual forms were krán*kajt*, štár*kajt*, zísi*kajt*,
and lústi*kajt*. It is also possible that in the spoken language the following
change had already occurred:

{STEM} + {-ik} + {-hajt} → {STEM} + {-ikajt} → {STEM} + {-kajt}.

In modern Yiddish the suffix -ikajt was usually abandoned in favour of -kajt
in all cases in which the derivational base did not require an adjective with
an -ik suffix (e.g. שוואך švax 'weak' → שוואכקייט šváxkajt 'weakness', in
contrast to רו ru 'rest' → רואיק rúik 'calm' (adj.) → רואיקייט rúikajt 'calmness';
but note שווער švɛr 'heavy; difficult' → שוועריקייט švérikajt 'difficulty'). Such

forms as fájxtikajt, blíndikajt, and zísikajt were subsequently levelled to fájxtkajt, blíndkajt, and získajt.

It is evident that in the literary language the suffix -hajt continued to be productive, possibly due to the impact of *taytsh*. At the same time, it was apparently being replaced in the spoken language by -kajt. The beginnings of the expansion of -kajt at the expense of -hajt in the literary language can be detected in the following types:

{STEM} + {-ik} + {-hajt} → {STEM} + {-ikajt}
פֿייכטיגהייט fájxtikhajt (p. 13a) → פֿייכטיקייט fájxtikajt (p. 11b)

{STEM ##k} + {-hajt} → {STEM} + {-kajt}
שטאַרקהייט štárkhajt (p. 12b) → *štárkajt;

{STEM} + {-hajt} → {STEM} + {-kajt}
מיגליך הייט mígləxhajt (p. 14b) → *mígləxkajt;

{STEM} + {-kajt} ← {STEM} + {-hajt}
אַרום קייט órəmkajt (p. 9b) ← אָרים הייט órəmhajt (p. 41a).

(Note that the last case is analysed as a back formation; i.e. as a morphological restructuring of the spoken form on the model of the 'more literary' derivational pattern with -hajt.)

The variation טרוייריגהייט trójərik(h)ajt ∼ טרוייארהייט trójərhajt is not the only one in this text. In other cases there is competition between the suffixes -hajt/-ik(h)ajt, and -(ə)niš. The same stem can sometimes receive any of these suffixes without a noticeable change of meaning; e.g.:

מאַגירנוש mógərniš (p. 12a) ∼ מאַגיר הייט mógərhajt 'slimness' (p. 9b);
פֿייכטיקייט fájxtikajt (p. 11b) ∼ פֿייכטניש fájxətniš 'wetness' (p. 12b).

These variations in derivational patterns are characteristic of a literary language that is not yet morphologically and stylistically stabilized. The older *taytsh* formant -hajt is still often employed, in spite of its apparent disappearance from the spoken language. The same stem sometimes received more than one suffix, since a firm derivational pattern had not yet been fully established.

28.3.3.3 *Adjective and Gerundive Formation* One of the remarkable innovations of *Ben hameylekh vehanozir* (1771) is the introduction of the suffix -dik as a productive adjective formant. This suffix became especially prominent in the derivational machinery of Modern Literary Yiddish. With verbal stems it became the formant of the potential present-participle forms and especially of the modern Yiddish gerundive.

The suffix -dik and the gerundive formant -(ə)ņdik are usually described separately (e.g. Zaretski 1929: 100–1, 104–5; Mark 1978: 223–5, 334–8).

However, the traditional distinction between -dik and -(ə)ndik in modern Yiddish is not entirely satisfactory. The suffix -dik may be described as a morpheme or an underlying unitary formant of adjectives derived from (a) verbal stems where its allomorph is -(ə)ndik, and (b) non-verbal stems where its allomorph is -dik. The traditional separation of allomorph -(ə)ndik is no more than a convenient metanalysis, since in modern Yiddish this morpheme as a deverbative is in most cases operative with the infinitive. Hence the actual pattern: {[STEM] + [-(ə)n]} + { -dik}; e.g.:

{[לויֿפ lɔjf] + [נ ņ]} + {דיק dik} for lɔjfņdik 'while running'.

In our text the suffix -dik occurs with both verbal and non-verbal stems. Verbal stems appear more frequently, and in some cases (see nos. 2.1, 2.2, 2.5 below) the adjectives in question may functionally be interpreted in the spirit of modern Yiddish grammar as present-tense participles (cf. D. Katz 1987a: 122 §7.2):

1 **with non-verbal stem**
    1 אייטירדיגה מכות éjtərdike makəs 'suppurating wounds' (p. 10a);
    2 דריננדינא dríngņdikə 'urgent' (pl., p. 7a);
    3 צארנדיג cɔrņdik 'wrathful; angry' (p. 17a);
    4 שמייבלדיגי לעֿפצין šméjx|dikə lɛfcņ 'smiling lips' (p. 23a);
2 **with verbal stem**
    1 איילינדיגי לויֿפֿר ájləndikə lɔjfər 'hurrying messengers' (p. 7a);
    2 זידנדיגר טאֿפ zídņdikər tɔp 'boiling pot' (p. 37a);
    3 די מעלה ֿפון לעבנדיגן di majlə fun lébņdikņ 'the virtue of a living person' (p. 24a);
    4 דען לעבנדיגן dən lébņdikņ 'the living person' (acc. sing., p. 40b);
    5 דען צערנדיגן מאן dən cérņdikņ man 'the angry man' (acc., p. 8a);
    6 שרעקינדיגי זיילין šrékņdikə zajlņ 'awesome pillars' (p. 6a).

Yet, the present participle is hardly a regular feature even of the modern literary language (cf. Birnbaum 1979: 262 §118 n. 1). Its short form, the gerundive, on the other hand, is distinctively popular in modern Eastern Yiddish (cf. Falkovitsh 1940: 226–7 §292–4). The use of the short deverbative adjective is very infrequent in this text, and in only one case can we suggest that it functions as a modern Yiddish gerundive (cf. no. 5 below):

3 אונ טוט [. . .] עש ארויש שטוסין איילנדיג
   un tut [. . .] əs arɔjsštɔjsņ ájlņdik
   'and throws it out hastily' (p. 12b);

4 זאלשטו דוא מיך אויש ציהן ֿפון דען ארט איילנדיג
   zɔlstu məx ɔjscian fun dən ɔrt ájlņdik
   'take me away from this place immediately' (p. 36a);

5 זיפֿצנדיג [. . .] אוּן קערט ווידר אין זיין הויז

un kɛrt vidər in zajn hɔjz [. . .] zífcṇdik

'and [he] returned to his house [. . .] with a sigh' (p. 38a).

28.3.3.4 *Future-tense Auxiliary and Modal Verbs* *Ben hameylekh vehanozir* is the earliest known text in which the three-way Eastern Yiddish morphological distinction between future-tense auxiliary vəlṇ, modal verb vɛlṇ 'want', and vɛrṇ 'become' is established and systematically maintained. The various finite forms of these verbs, consistently employed throughout the text, are provided in Table 20.

Table 20 Future-tense auxiliary vəlṇ, vɛlṇ 'want', and vɛrṇ 'become' in *Ben hameylekh vehanozir* (1771)

	vəlṇ (fut. aux.)	vɛlṇ 'want'	vɛrṇ 'become'
singular			
1st pers.	וועל vəl	וויל vil	—
2nd pers.	וועסט vəst	ווילסט vilst	—
3rd pers.	וועט vət	—	ווערט vɛrt
plural			
1st/3rd pers.	וועל(י)ן vəlṇ	—	ווער(י)ן vɛrṇ
infinitives	וועל(י)ן vəlṇ	ווער(י)ן vɛrṇ	

In the case of vɛlṇ 'want', the blank slots in the table may be explained by the lack of any need to use third-person singular in this text (first- and third-person plural forms remain orthographically and pragmatically indistinguishable from those of the future-tense auxiliary). However, all these forms are attested in earlier monuments, primarily in Western Yiddish (cf. Lincoff 1963: 125–7 §8.3). The same may apply to the missing second-person singular form of the verb vɛrṇ 'become'. The absence of the first-person singular of vɛrṇ is apparently related to the fact that the stem vɛr still functions as a subjunctive form in this text; e.g.:

1 וואָרום ווען עש ווער אמתֿ דא ווער איך עש דיר מוחל גיוואוזין

vɔrəm vən əs vɛr ɛməs dɔ vɛr ix əs dir mɔjxḷ gəvezṇ

'if this were true then I would forgive you' (p. 30a).

Occasionally the form ווירט vərt/vɛrt/virt (?) takes the place of the future-tense auxiliary וועט vət (3rd pers. sing.) before the infinitives זיין zajn 'to be' (nos. 2–4) and vɛrṇ (no. 5):

2 עש ווירט ניט זיין קיין עַנד צו דיין טעג əs vərt nit zajn kejn ɛnd cu dajn tɛg

'there will be no end to your days' (p. 12a);

3 דש ווערט זיין צו מיר איין שטרויכלונג dɔs vərt zajn cu mir a štrɔ́jxlung
'this will be my temptation' (p. 33a);

4 ווירט זיין דיין לוֹיאָן פֿיל vərt zajn dajn lɔjn fil
'your reward will be great' (p. 42b);

5 ווען דאָס וויילן ווערט פֿר לאָרין ווערן vɛn dɔs vajlṇ vɛrt farlɔ́rṇ vɛrṇ
'when the enjoyment will vanish' (p. 10a).

However, these cases are relatively rare, and given the verbal form in question, ווירט vərt/vɛrt/virt (?), they may be viewed as occasional interferences that stem from the Germanized Western Yiddish books of that period. On the whole, the clear-cut distinction between the future-tense auxiliary and the modal verb ווערן vɛrṇ is preserved. By comparison, ווער(י)ן is still occasionally employed alongside ווֹעל(י)ן as a future-tense auxiliary in the much later *Avkes roykhl* (Horodne, 1795), which is otherwise far more modern and more balanced in its style and language.

28.3.3.5 Verbal Aspect   Aspectually marked verbs seem to be employed more frequently in *Ben hameylekh vehanozir* than in the average printed non-Eastern Yiddish text of the period. In general, these forms do not appear to be distinctly Eastern Yiddish. The same preverbs and stressed prefixes often functioned as lexicalized *Aktionsart* markers in Western Yiddish. These prefixed verbs usually have closely matching cognates in New High German. This may be viewed as the ultimate (though not always reliable) indication that the forms in question are not specific to Eastern Yiddish (cf. M. Weinreich 1973: ii. 353 §145.5; Wexler 1964: 87). The following are samples of some of the prefixed forms:

1 אויש ɔ́js
אויש גישטרעקט ɔ́js gəštrɛkt 'stretched out' (past part., p. 10a;
   cf. NHG *ausstrecken*);

2 איבר íbər
איבר גבליבן íbərgəblibṇ 'was left' (past part., p. 29a;
   cf. NHG *überbleiben* [= *übrigbleiben*]);

3 אוועק avék
אוועק קומין avék(k)umən 'vanish; disappear' (inf., p. 29a;
   cf. NHG *wegkommen*);
אוועק געשיקט avékgəšikt 'sent away' (past part., p. 14b;
   cf. NHG *wegschicken*);

4 דר dər-
דר ציטרן [. . .] טושט דו דיך [. . .] tústu dəx [. . .] dərcítərṇ 'you tremble'
   (pf., p. 8a; cf. NHG *erzittern*);
ווער עש דר שלאָגט זיך vər əs dəršlɔgt zəx 'whoever kills himself'
   (p. 8a; cf. NHG *erschlagen*);

5 צו cə-

צו מאַלין cəmóln̩ 'ground' (past part., p. 10a; cf. NHG *zermahlen*).

These cases constitute a modest sample of prefixed forms in this text. The form אויס גישטערעקט ójsgəštrɛkt (see no. 1 above) is an example of *Aktionsart* rather than of aspect proper (cf. also nos. 2, 3, 5). The addition of the reflexive pronoun in דיך דר ציטרן dəx dərcitərn̩ (see no. 4) may be an Eastern Yiddish feature. The employment of dər- is in this case characteristically Germanic. The morphological reflexivization, however, has an underlying Slavonic pattern (cf. Ukr. здригнутися, Russ. содрогнуться).

An interesting verbal form is אַוועק גנבֿנ זיך avé(k)gànvənən zəx 'sneak away', where the stressed prefix אַוועק avék is productive with the Semitic component verb גנבֿנן gánvənən 'steal'; e.g. ער גנבֿת זיך אַוועק פֿון אים ər ganvət zəx avék fun im 'he sneaks away from him' (p. 40a). The simple infinitive גנבֿנן gánvənən 'steal' is also present (e.g. on p. 12a). The stressed prefix avék functions here primarily as an *Aktionsart* marker. This form was apparently possible in Western Yiddish as well. However, the earliest example with אַוועק גנבֿענען זיך avé(k)gànvənən zəx 'sneak away' cited in the *Great Dictionary of the Yiddish Language* is from modern Eastern Yiddish (cf. Mark and Joffe 1966: 73). In Eastern Yiddish this form becomes aspectually marked as perfective. It also has close semantic and aspectual affinity with such forms as the Polish *zakraść się* 'to sneak into' (cf. Ukr. закрастися, Russ. закрасться). The form may well have originated in Eastern Yiddish.

With the increasing impact of Slavonic patterns of aspectualization, most of the Yiddish preverbs and verbal prefixes were reinterpreted as productive markers of a remarkably Slavonicized aspect system, exclusively characteristic of Eastern Yiddish (see §35.10; also M. Weinreich 1956: 628; 1973: ii. 187–9 §145.1, iv. 252–4 §145.1). *Ben hameylekh vehanozir* has a number of forms that point to a distinctly Eastern Yiddish aspect system. All preverbs and verbal prefixes mentioned above are also employed as Eastern Yiddish aspect markers. The following forms have direct Slavonic parallels, further supporting their Eastern Yiddish provenance:

1.1 אויס ójs

דאָס טריקנט אויס אין איטליכן אבֿר דאָס פֿײַכטיגהייט
dɔs triknt̩ ójs in itləxn̩ ejvər dɔs fájxtikajt
'this dries out the liquids in every organ' (p. 13a; cf. Pol. *wysuszyć*, Ukr. висушити, Russ. высушить);

2.1 איבר íbər

איבר לײַד מיט גוטן ווילן ibər lajd mit gutn̩ viln̩
'may you overcome the suffering in good faith',

(lit. 'suffer through with good will'; p. 20a

cf. Pol. *przemagać, przetrwać,* Ukr. перетерпити, Russ. перетерпеть);

3.1 אַוועק avék

די אויפֿה עוֹפֿוֹת האָפּן עש אַוועק di ɔjfəs xapṇ əs avék

'the birds snatch (perf.) it away' (p. 50a, cf. p. 49b;

cf. Pol. *zabrać,* Ukr. захопити, Russ. захватить);

4.1 דר dər-

דר בן מלך האָט אים דר זעהין dər bɛn mejləx hɔt im dərzɛn

'the prince saw (perf.) him' (p. 43a; cf. p. 43b;

cf. Pol. *dojrzeć,* Ukr. добачити);

5.1 צו cə-

צו גראָבין און צו אקרין cəgrɔbṇ un cəákərṇ

'to dig (perf.) and to plough (perf.)' (p. 36b;

cf. Pol. *rozkop(yw)ać, rozorywać,* Ukr. розкопати, розорати,

Russ. раскопать, распахать).

The stem האָפּין xapṇ 'catch' (no. 3.1) is the only lexical item of Slavonic origin found in this text. (On the possibly older origin of xapṇ, cf. U. Weinreich 1955: 608.) Its grammatical bond with the stressed prefix אַוועק avék apparently legitimized its admission into literary usage. The stressed prefix in this form retains its primary function as an *Aktionsart* marker. However, in the context of the Eastern Yiddish aspect system it also functions as an aspect marker. Thus אַוועק האָפּין avékxapṇ is the marked perfective member of the opposition *xapṇ 'catch; snatch' (imperf.) vs. avékxapṇ 'catch; snatch' (perf.).

As to the other aspectually marked verbs, such oppositions as lajdṇ vs. íbərlajdn 'suffer' (no. 2.1), zɛn vs. dərzɛn 'see' (no. 4.1) and grɔbṇ vs. cəgrɔbṇ 'dig' (no. 5.1) can be discerned. Both sets of forms occur in the text as imperfective and perfective respectively. The same imperfective vs. perfective aspectual differentiation can be inferred *vis-à-vis* *trikənən vs. ɔ́jstrikənen 'dry' (no. 1.1) and *akərṇ vs. cəakərṇ 'plough' (no. 5.1).

These forms do not exhaust the list of aspectually marked Eastern Yiddish forms that may be detected. They do, however, provide ample evidence of the Eastern Yiddish nature of the aspect system of *Ben hameylekh vehanozir.*

28.3.3.6 *Postpositive Adverbs*   In Eastern Yiddish certain prepositional groups end with the postpositive adverbs אַרײַן arájn 'inside' or אַרױס arɔ́js 'outside'. Each group of this type is governed by a motion verb, and functions as a closed syntagm. The adverb marks the location or motion implicit in the governing verb. The most frequent type is

{אין in 'in' (prep.)} + {noun (location)} + {אַרײַן arájn}.

Other types are:

{אין in 'in' (prep.)} + {noun (location)} + {אַרוים arɔ́js};

{פֿון fun 'from' (prep.)} + {noun (location)} + {אַרוים arɔ́js};

{אוים ɔjs 'out of' (prep.)} + {noun (location)} + {אַרוים arɔ́js}.

This morpho-syntactic feature is especially characteristic of spoken Eastern Yiddish and of the modern literary language (see Falkovitsh 1940: 271–2 §372; 1984: 708–9 §51; Mark 1946: 85–6; 1971: 1272; 1980: 2069, 2236). From a dialectological point of view it is considered an innovation of Eastern Yiddish which was especially productive in many parts of Mideastern and Southeastern Yiddish (see below §34.1.3; Herzog 1965a: 135 §4.2.4; 139 Figs. 4:59–61).

Prepositional groups with a postpositive adverb are a regular morpho-syntactic feature of *Ben hameylekh vehanozir*. Almost all belong to the most frequent type {אין in} + {noun} + {אַרײַן arájn}. In addition, one instance of a syntagm of the type {אוים ɔjs} + {noun} + {אַרוים arɔ́js} is found (see no. 5 below).

1 ביז ער קומט אין גרוב אַרײַן
biz ər kumt in grúbaràjn
'until he descends into the grave' (p. 11a);

2 וויא דער מלך קומט אין זיין הויז אַרײַן
vi dər méjləx kumt in zajn hɔ́jzaràjn
'when the king arrives in his house' (p. 44a);

3 דיא נשמה גייט אויף און דער גוף גייט אין גרוב אַרײַן
di nəšɔ́mə gejt uf un dər guf gejt in grúbaràjn
'the soul rises and the body goes to the grave' (p. 25b);

4 דער וועט גיין [. . .] אין זיין רוא אַרײַן
dər vət gejn [. . .] in zajn rúaràjn
'he will go [. . .] to his rest' (p. 33b);

5 און גייאין אלבײדי אויש דר מחנה אַרויש
un gejən álbejdə ɔjs dər máxnəarɔ̀js
'and both of them walk out of the camp' (p. 21a).

The frequent employment of the syntagm {אין in} + {noun} + {אַרײַן arájn} in this early text is especially significant, for it subsequently became an important morpho-syntactic and idiomatic feature of Modern Literary Yiddish.

28.3.3.7 *Adverbs* One of the remarkable innovations of *Ben hameylekh vehanozir* is the intensified use of various adverbs, many of which were less frequently used in the old literary language. (See Falk 1961: ii. 131–206; Fuks 1965: ii. 74–135; and especially Maitlis 1978: 221–6, and Timm

1987: 506–12 for samples of lexicographic data on the Semitic component in the old literary language.) Most of these adverbs belong to the Semitic component; e.g. באמת bəɛməs 'truly; as a matter of fact' (pp. 23a, 29b, 47b); חלילה xəlílə 'God forbid!' (p. 26a); מכל שכן məkəlškṇ 'all the more so' (pp. 25a, 29b); תמיד tómid (or tɔməd) 'always; invariably' (p. 29b). Often these adverbs are not found in the same form in the original Hebrew text of *Ben hameylekh vehanozir*. Their appearance in the Yiddish text is necessitated by the lexical, morphological, and phraseological requirements of modern Eastern Yiddish. The 'explanatory' adverbs כלומר klɔjmər 'that is' (pp. 7b, 12a, 16b, 17b, 21b, 54a) and דהיינו dəhajnə 'for instance; namely' (pp. 11a, 12a, 15b, 23b, 24a) are particularly popular. These often introduce various added explanations and specifications supplied by the translator for less clear passages. Another especially frequent adverb is רק rak 'only; nothing but' (pp. 7b, 10b, 19a, 25a, 52b). It occurs at least twice with its more recent Eastern Yiddish connotation 'continuously (from only, exclusively)'; e.g.:

1 רק ער וועט זעהן פֿיל ארלייא זיפֿצונג אונ׳ טרוויארהייט
rak ər vət zen filərlej zífcung un trójərhajt
'he will continuously (← only) see much groaning and sorrow' (p. 10a);

2 דו האשט פֿון אילה קיין גוטן בגלייבטין פֿריינט רק אילה זענין דיך מקנא
du hɔst fun ilə k(e)jn gutṇ baglέjbtṇ frajnd rak ilə zɛnən dir məkanə
'you have no good reliable friend among [them] all, every one is only (→ continuously) jealous of you' (p. 16b).

This extension from 'only; solely' to 'continuously' is also found in the co-territorial Slavonic languages (e.g. Pol. *li, tylko*, Ukr. лише, тільки; cf. Russ. лишь, только). Eventually in some forms of modern Yiddish the adverb רק became fully reinterpreted as 'continuously' or 'persistently'.

One of the most popular adverbs in this text is שוי(י)ן šɔjn 'already' (e.g. pp. 6a, 9a, 25a, 10b, 13b, 14a, 15a, 18b, 23a, 40a). It is generally used in a characteristically Eastern Yiddish manner, as is shown in the following examples:

3 דר זעלבבגיר מאן קען שון ניט נידריג ווערין
dər zɛlbikər man kɛn šɔjn nit nídərik vɛrṇ
'[the status of] that man cannot ever be lowered [again]'
(lit. the same man cannot already be lowered; p. 6b);

4 דא וועל איך אים שוין מער נישט פֿרעגין
dɔ vəl ix im šɔjn mər ništ frɛgṇ
'then I will not ask him anything any more' (p. 25a);

5 ווען ער מיך מאבֿט גירעבֿט ווער קען מיך שוין צו שולד אנשרייבין
vən ər məx maxt gərext vɛr ken mix šɔjn cu šuld ónšrajbṇ

'when He approves of my righteousness, who can then claim that I am guilty?',
lit. 'when He makes me right who can then write me down as guilty?' (p. 18b).

The potential for the semantic extension of שוין šɔjn already existed within
the confines of the Germanic component of Yiddish (cf. the various functions
of NHG *schon*). In Eastern Yiddish, however, its semantic properties and
morpho-syntactic functions were extended through the direct impact of co-
territorial Slavonic languages. By way of semantic matching it acquired such
additional meanings as 'by this time', 'by now', '[long] since', '[long] ago',
'by then', 'at once', 'as early as', 'now' (cf. the parallel polysemy of the Pol.
już, Ukr. вже, уже, and Russ. уже). Moreover, in modern Eastern Yiddish
šɔjn may be analysed as a general phrase modifier, which marks the action
in all tenses and aspects as perfective, as may be seen in Table 21 (only the
phrases with שוין šɔjn are included, but not their unmarked counterparts).

Table 21 The adverb šɔjn 'already' as a perfectivizing phrase modifier in
Modern Literary Yiddish

Tense	Imperfective	Perfective
Past	זי האָט שוין געלייענט דאָס בוך zi hɔt šɔjn gəlejənt dɔs bux She has read the book.	זי האָט שוין איבערגעלייענט דאָס בוך zi hɔt šɔjn íbərgəlèjənt dɔs bux She has read the (whole) book.
Present	זי לייענט שוין דאָס בוך zi lejənt šɔjn dɔs bux She is already reading the book.	זי לייענט שוין איבער דאָס בוך zi lejənt šɔjn ibər dɔs bux She is already reading the book. (She is finishing the book.)
Future	זי וועט שוין לייענען דאָס בוך zi vət šɔjn lejənən dɔs bux She will read the book.	זי וועט שוין איבערלייענען דאָס בוך zi vət šɔjn íbərlèjənən dɔs bux She will read the book. (She will read the (whole) book.)

The distinction between (a) zi hɔt íbərgəlejənt 'she has read', (b) zi hɔt šɔjn
gəléjənt 'she has read', and (c) zi hɔt šɔjn íbərgəlejənt 'she has read already'
lies in the varying emphasis (or markedness) of perfectivity. The use of an
aspectually marked verb (see right-hand column in Table 21) specifies the
extent to which the action was completed in relation to the direct object.
Hence zi hɔt šɔjn gəléjənt dɔs bux 'she has read the book', as opposed to zi hɔt
šɔjn íbərgəlejənt dɔs bux 'she has read the (whole) book'.

The ways in which the adverb šɔjn are employed throughout this text
reflect its increasing polysemy in modern Eastern Yiddish. It can frequently

be analysed as a general perfectivizing phrase modifier (e.g. on pp. 9a, 10b, 13b, 14a, 15a, 40a).

28.3.3.8 *Choice of Forms*   In spite of its morphological instability, *Ben hameylekh vehanozir* appears to be stylistically more advanced than many other literary texts of the period. A wealth of idiomatic expressions and of stylistic sophistication can be found in the best monuments of Old Yiddish literature. However, in many genres, morphology, phraseology, and lexicon were conventionally restrained. The relatively fixed norms of literary usage and the consciously preserved distance between the written and the spoken languages left many expressive resources of the latter unrepresented and unexploited in Old Literary Yiddish. Conversely, the expressive resources of Modern Literary Yiddish were enriched remarkably through the increasing *rapprochement* between the written and the spoken languages. Numerous expressive and emotive elements of spoken Eastern Yiddish were adopted and then further developed within the various registers of the modern literary language.

Several features characteristic of the modern literary language are found in *Ben hameylekh vehanozir*. This is especially evident in the rich arsenal of forms and usages many of which appear to be far less frequent or even absent in older literary texts. These include the more frequent use of attributive adjectives, the increasing employment of past participles as adjectives (see nos. 1 and 2 below) and nominalizations (see no. 3), and the extended use of infinitives and participles as nominalizations (see no. 4).

1 **Past participles as attributive adjectives**

   1. 1 אז איין [. . .] בצוונגנר מאן

       az a [. . .] bacvúngənər man 'as a [. . .] subjugated man' (p. 25a);

   1. 2 מיט איין צו בראלכין הארץ

       mit a cəbrɔxn̩ harc 'with a broken heart' (p. 33a);

   1. 3 מיט אפגריסני קליידר

       mit ópgərisənə klejdər 'with clothes torn off' (p. 43b).

2 **Past participles as predicative**

   2. 1 אונ ער איז אויף גשטאנין פֿר ביטרט אונ מיד

       un ər iz úfgəštanən farbítərt un mid

       'and he stood up bitter and tired' (p. 38a).

3 **Nominalized past participles**

   3. 1 איטליכר בשלאגניר

       ítləxər bašlógənər 'every defeated [person]' (p. 36b);

   3. 2 די גיפֿאנגינע

       di gəfángənə 'the captives', lit. 'those taken in captivity' (p. 35b).

4 Nominalizations

4.1 דורך האנדלין וועט פֿון דיר פֿיל גוטש אװעקרינן

durx handlən vət fun dir fil guts avékrinən

'through business you will lose many goods',

lit. 'through selling many goods will escape you' (p. 41a);

4.2 דאש האנלדין טוט דיך ברענגין צו גרוײשי זינדן

dos handlən tut dix brɛngən cu grɔjsə zindṇ

'business brings you to grave sins' (p. 41a);

4.3 דאש בינדן וועט אים מער ניט געבין אז פֿארכֿט

dos bindṇ vət im mər nit gɛbṇ az fɔrxt

'captivity (lit. binding) will only frighten him' (p. 36a);

4.4 דאש אװעק גגאנגני וועט אים אויך גקערט וערין

dos ávəkgəgangəne vət im ɔjx gəkɛrt vɛrṇ

'[things that were] lost will be returned to him' (p. 29a).

All these features significantly enrich and, retrospectively speaking, modernize the stylistic and morpho-syntactic make-up of *Ben hameylekh vehanozir*. Their use is a hallmark of the allegedly 'better' organized literary language. Their ultimate source seems to have been spoken Eastern Yiddish. However, in this work such forms are still far less frequent than in the nineteenth-century literary language. Still, these and many other grammatical, lexical, and idiomatic features are among the earliest significant manifestations of the expressive registers of Eastern Yiddish folklore. (For an important sample of oral texts see Cahan 1931; 1938; 1975.) And although the old literary language still plays a central role in the linguistic fabric of this translation, the *rapprochement* achieved in it between the written and the spoken languages reaches unprecedented dimensions.

28.4 Summary

The language of *Ben hameylekh vehanozir* (Zholkve, 1771) has been singled out as one of the earliest known printed monuments of modern Eastern Yiddish (cf. Prilutski 1920a: 339, 409; 1920b: 90 §135.2; 1924a: 93 n. 150; 106–7 §160; Reyzen 1932: 178; Shtif 1932a: 36; Roskies 1974b: 4). Compared with Eastern re-editions of older Yiddish works (e.g. *Kav hayosher* printed in Zholkve, 1777) on the one hand and Reuven Halevi's earlier translation of this book on the other, this work displays a considerably more advanced stage of linguistic Easternization. In effect it has to be considered the earliest known work written by and large *in* Eastern Yiddish.

Nevertheless, the text contains a number of features inherited from the old literary language. In addition, certain spelling conventions were apparently introduced from contemporary Germanized Western Yiddish books. The features inherited from Old Literary Yiddish can be discerned in orthography, morphology, and especially phraseology and lexicon. Their prominence in this translation may be explained by the continuing influence of the old literary language. This influence was semiotically and stylistically justified in a late eighteenth-century Yiddish text of this kind. The original Hebrew of *Ben hamelekh vehanazir* is stylistically and lexically closer to Biblical rather than to early post-Biblical Hebrew. As a result, one of the major linguistic resources of this translation was the so-called *taytsh* tradition. *Taytsh* was based on the age-old conventional oral renderings of the sacred, primarily Biblical Hebrew texts into archaic Yiddish (cf. Leibowitz 1931; Noble 1943; Mark 1944*a*; Turniansky 1988; Aptroot 1989). It was one of the major lexical and phraseological components of the old literary language. Later it became an important source of stylistic archaisms in Modern Literary Yiddish (cf. Spivak 1939: 185–7; Noble 1943: 27–8; Shmeruk 1978: 180; Schneider 1988: 114–16). The numerous *taytsh* forms systematically employed in this translation strengthened the linguistic and stylistic association of the text with earlier works written in Old Literary Yiddish.

This work is clearly marked by competing older and newer forms (§§28.3.1–2). It provides the earliest known attestation for many Eastern Yiddish features (§§28.1.2, 28.3.2.5, 28.3.3). The modern Eastern Yiddish forms of the future-tense auxiliary and of the modal verbs vɛln 'want' and vɛrn 'become' are employed with a remarkable degree of consistency (§28.3.3.4). The Eastern Yiddish paradigm of periphrastic verbs and the more developed system of verbal aspect can often be detected (on the latter see §28.3.3.5). The plural marker -s becomes fully acceptable (§28.3.3.1), and the deverbative suffix -dik becomes productive in the formation of secondary nouns and to a lesser degree of the Eastern Yiddish gerundive (§28.3.3.3). The genitive case virtually disappears (see however §28.3.1.3), and the conscious effort to resuscitate the Western Yiddish accusative form of the masculine definite article dən results in numerous hypercorrections (§28.3.2.3). A number of abstract noun suffixes, possibly introduced from or reinforced through the *taytsh* lexicon, are especially productive as in Modern Literary Yiddish (§28.3.3.2). Another important feature is the translator's choice of various forms which were stylistically 'unpopular' (hence either suppressed or hitherto unprecedented) in the old literary language. These forms and usages resulting from the increasing impact of the spoken language enrich and significantly modernize the style and diction of this work (§28.3.3.8).

Lexical items of Slavonic origin are still excluded from this work. However, the frequent employment of the adverb šɔjn 'already' as an aspectual phrase qualifier is a distinctive feature of modern Eastern Yiddish, and may be regarded as a result of Slavonic impact. Perhaps the most decisive innovation in the lexicon is the massive admission into literary usage of lexical items of Hebrew origin (cf. §§27.2, 28.3.3.7). It is noteworthy that a considerable number of these lexical items do not appear in the original Hebrew text of *Ben hamelekh vehanazir*, but nearly all of them are included in the basic lexical fund of modern Eastern Yiddish. The remarkable increase in the Semitic component, also characteristic of other contemporary Eastern Yiddish texts, had important repercussions for the stylistic and semantic development of the modern literary language.

On the syntactic level this work often appears to be modelled on the patterns of Old Literary Yiddish, and possibly on that of contemporary Germanized Western Yiddish texts. However, the final position of the finite verb in subordinate clauses remains optional. And it seems that the Eastern Yiddish word order in main consecutive clauses and in subordinate clauses prevails. Likewise, the clause-final position of the infinitive and the past participle is largely restricted to the same stylistically and structurally conditioned syntagms as in the modern literary language. The Eastern Yiddish pattern of double negation prevails, though a few instances indicate that the anonymous translator occasionally tries to suppress it.

The shift from the old literary language towards a new one wholly based on Eastern Yiddish is not complete in this text. Nevertheless, *Ben hameylekh vehanozir* (Zholkve, 1771) marks a significant beginning in this overall shift, a shift that was fully achieved only a decade later in the Eastern Yiddish version of *Mayse gdoyle min Uman umin Ukrayne* ([Novidvor], *c.*1783).

The First Original Work in Modern Eastern Yiddish: *Mayse gdoyle min Uman umin Ukrayne* (*c*.1783)

29 Introduction

Few Yiddish books were printed in Eastern Europe before the closing decades of the eighteenth century, and it was a long time before Hebrew and Yiddish printing recuperated from the aftermath of Khmelnitsky's massacres of 1648–9. Many books of that region and period were apparently lost. Therefore almost every surviving Yiddish text printed in Eastern Europe during that period is a priori an important document of the literary language before the nineteenth-century rise of modern Yiddish literature.

The few surviving books from the late eighteenth century offer ample material for tracing the origins and the earliest stages of the nascent modern literary language. One of them, *Mayse gdoyle min Uman umin Ukrayne* , is the earliest known original work written in modern Eastern Yiddish. The work comprises an account of the Zhelezniak and Gonta massacres of 1768 (so named after the two Cossack leaders) and a commemorative poem, the *kine*. (On these events see Dubnov 1953: 369–77 §50; Ettinger 1972; 1976: 752; Mahler 1971: 431–2; Schohetman 1972; Weinryb 1972: 204–5). A unique copy of what appears to be the earliest known edition of this account is found in the British Library. While this edition has neither date nor place of publication, its textual, linguistic, orthographic, and above all typographic characteristics suggest the last third of the eighteenth century as its probable time of publication (cf. §30.2 below).

One must be wary of anachronistically misapplying twentieth-century notions of 'originality' in a discussion of pre-modern literature. In the case of Yiddish literature, 'pre-modern' may designate that of the eighteenth and even the early nineteenth centuries. For that period, virtually every linguistically and textually or contextually innovative translation or adaptation from other literary sources (or from other languages) may be qualified as original from the point of view of Yiddish literary history (cf. Zfatman 1983: i. 155–9, and for a blatant example of an anachronistic devaluation of the originality of the Old Yiddish *Mayse bukh* (*editio princeps*, Basle, 1602) see Gaster 1934: xxxix). Moreover, the pre-modern concept of originality had a strikingly different connotation of 'being faithful to', or 'following sources' (i.e. the underlying originals). The authors of some works such as *Derekh tomim* and *Derekh khayim* (cf. §6.3) used other older and contemporary Yiddish books as their direct sources. Their intention was apparently to convey the 'true' (hence 'original') spirit of older canonized texts (ultimately the Bible). *Mayse gdoyle min Uman umin Ukrayne*, however, was probably written originally in Yiddish. And although there was no paucity of accounts of pogroms and persecutions in older Yiddish as well as in Hebrew literature, *Mayse gdoyle min Uman umin Ukrayne* is no doubt the earliest known literary monument written entirely in modern Yiddish. (On this genre in Yiddish see M. Weinreich 1923: 140–92; 1927; 1928: 192–213; Zfatman 1983: i. 201–12; Turniansky 1989; in Hebrew, Bernfeld 1926).

This work is also 'one of the very few Jewish sources about the massacres of 1768' (Weinryb 1972: 365 n. 63; cf. also Gurland 1886: 6–8; Dubnov 1929: 31–2). It is often referred to by Jewish historians dealing with this grim chapter of modern European history (cf. Skomorovski 1889; Litinski 1894; 1895; Dubnov 1929; Weinryb 1972: 205; cf. also Schohetman 1972).

Among Yiddish philologists concerned with the beginnings of Modern Literary Yiddish, Noyakh Prilutski (1931: 227–31) and Nokhem Shtif (1932*a*: 35–6) singled out this account as an important literary document, not only from the historical but also from the linguistic point of view. Since then the text has remained virtually unexamined by Yiddish linguists.

We do not know by whom, where, or precisely when *Mayse gdoyle min Uman umin Ukrayne* was originally written. And there seems to be room for further historical and socio-linguistic clarification of the fact that the anonymous author wrote it in Yiddish. The most authoritative accounts and chronicles of Khmelnitsky's massacres of 1648–9 were written in Hebrew by prominent rabbinical and intellectual leaders of contemporary East European Jewry (see Izraelson 1929; Rosman 1981: ix; Shmeruk 1990). If there had been a Hebrew parallel, it would be rather unlikely for the Hebrew text not to have been preserved and reprinted. However, no such text is known. Similarly, the extant Yiddish texts do not provide sufficient internal evidence for any direct Hebrew model or source. Hebrew idioms and phrases that may exceed the usual limits of the Semitic component in Yiddish function in these texts either as stylistic markers of authentication or as quotations (sometimes quasi-quotations) alluding to canonic Hebrew texts.

30 The Two Versions

Mayse gdoyle min Uman is extant in two different versions, one written in modern Eastern Yiddish, the other in Germanized Western Yiddish. These two versions have not yet been systematically contrasted with each other, and not much has been done to trace their textual history.

30.1 The Western Version

The earliest known dated edition presents us with a very short version of the account, entitled *Mayse gdoyle min k[ehiles]"k[oydesh] Uman bimdines Ukrayne* (= MF1783; references are to line numbers of the text reprinted in Kerler 1988b: 591-8; page references are to the original edition). It was printed in Fürth in 1783 as a smaller addition to another Yiddish booklet called *Seyfer poykeyakh ivrim vehu seyfer goyroles*, a twenty-three-page tract on fortune telling (see Timm 1988: 40). The account of the Uman massacre occupies the following eight pages, with a separate title-page printed on the reverse of the last page of *Seyfer poykeyakh ivrim vehu seyfer goyroles*.

This edition, designed as a report on the then recent tragic events in Eastern Europe, may have been limited by its format. The publisher apparently allocated only a limited number of spare pages for the account to come after the main book. We shall refer to this edition (= MF1783), as the 'Western version'.

30.2 The Eastern Version

Three other dated editions of *Mayse gdoyle min Uman* appeared in the first half of the nineteenth century, in Sadilkov in 1834 and 1838 and in Vilna in 1845. In addition Reyzen (1932: 191) mentions another edition of 1848. These contain the larger, far more detailed Eastern Yiddish version written in prose with occasional rhymes. A commemorative poem (*kine*), partly in rhyme, with its paragraphs arranged in alphabetical order according to the first letter of the paragraph, follows the actual account. These as well as other Eastern Yiddish editions of the work will be referred to as the 'Eastern version'.

Prilutski (1931) has given a valuable description of another undated edition of the Eastern version, which he had in his possession. It may come from the Ukraine in the first half of the nineteenth century. Linguistically, it has many dialectal Mideastern and Southeastern features (Prilutski 1931: 228-9). Textually it occupies an intermediate position between Sadilkov

(1834 and 1838) and Vilna (1845). Prilutski (1931: 229) suggested that it must have been published sometime between 1834 and 1845.

In addition, there are two undated editions in the British Library (cf. van Straalen 1894: 244, s.v. *Uman*). One of them is apparently identical with the one described by Prilutski, the other deserves special attention because it seems, on typographical, textual, and linguistic grounds, to be the earliest, hitherto unnoticed edition of the Eastern version. This edition will be referred to as M[N1783]. Unless the page of the original edition is specified, all references are to line numbers of the Eastern version reprinted from three editions in Kerler (1988*b*: 545-90).

30.2.1 *The Earliest Known Edition of the Eastern Version*

This edition was printed with the *mashkit* font, which is based on a modified variant of Ashkenazic cursive letters. From the sixteenth century until perhaps the middle twenties of the nineteenth century this font was used specifically for the publication of Yiddish texts (see §2.2.2). The format of this small booklet is 14.5 x 8.9 cm. It has twenty-four pages, of which the first seventeen (including the title-page) contain the account. The remaining seven pages contain the commemorative poem, the *kine*.

This edition is undated. However, its typographical, orthographic, and some linguistic peculiarities support our assertion that this is possibly the earliest edition of the Eastern version.

A number of spellings suggest that it was printed in the late eighteenth century. The frequent employment of the ⟨ו⟩ grapheme for interconsonantal ɔ—e.g. הוט hɔt 'has' (pp. 6, 14, 19, 23); הובן hɔbṇ 'have' (pp. 3, 5, 15, 19)—was somewhat unusual or archaic even in Eastern Yiddish printed works of the last decades of the eighteenth century (cf. §15.1; on this spelling in Old and Middle Yiddish see Timm 1987: 109-21). Other frequent spellings consistently replaced in the later nineteenth-century editions indicate that M[N1783] was most likely printed earlier, possibly in the late eighteenth century; e.g. טאר tɔ(jə)r (?) 'gate' (p. 4; cf. in later editions טויער tɔjər); טארן tɔ(jə)rṇ (?) 'gates' (p. 8; cf. in later editions טויערן tɔjərṇ); תאמר tɔmər 'if' (p. 3; cf. in later editions טאמער tɔmər).

As for linguistic evidence, the strikingly modern Eastern Yiddish of M[N1783] certainly does not indicate an early date. On the contrary, what we need in order to establish the chronological significance of this edition is the missing date of publication. Unlike other editions, M[N1783] contains a number of morphological archaisms which may be viewed as residual survivals of Old Literary Yiddish (cf. §32.4.1). This may well mean that the Eastern version of the account was written immediately or shortly after the events of 1768, and that M[N1783] is its earliest known edition. In the nineteenth-century editions all these forms were either omitted or replaced by modern equivalents; e.g. וואָרן vɔrn̩ → גיוואָרן gəvɔrn̩ 'became' (past. part., pp. 14, 21); זיין zajn → זיינין zajnən 'are' (3rd pers. pl., p. 5); האַרמטאָ harmátə → האַרמאָט harmát 'cannon' (pp. 3, 4); האַרמטוֹת ~ האַרמטום harmátəs → האַרמאָטין harmátn̩ 'cannon' (pl., pp. 12, 15); גשׁיׁ gəšíc 'arms' → גוטץ gutc 'goods' (p. 14). (For a comprehensive list of archaic forms see below §32.4.1.)

Above all, the suggestion that M[N1783] is older than the other known editions of the Eastern version is supported by typographical and textual evidence. All three types of ornaments that appear in M[N1783] can be traced unmistakably to those of the Novidvor printing shop, which was active between 1781 and 1816 (see Friedberg 1950: 76–82). The pattern on the title-page of M[N1783] (see Fig. 3, no. 1) also appears on the last page of the first volume of *Kav hayosher* (1788), on the opening page (p. 3) of *Drishas hazohov* (*Drishat hazahav*, 1794), and on the title-page of *Seyfer mivkhar hapninim* (1794). A modified version of this pattern is found on the last page of *Talmid tsakhkan musari* (1806). The second pattern in M[N1783], which decorates page 17 at the end of the account (see Fig. 3, no. 2), is also found on the last page of the first volume of *Kav hayosher* (1788), as well as on the final page of *Drishas hazohov* (*Drishat hazahav*, 1794). The third pattern, which appears at the end of the *kine*, on the last page of of this edition (p. 24; see Fig. 3, no. 3), is one of the most widely used ornaments in the Novidvor Yiddish prints (confirmed by Rosenfeld in a personal communication of 1988). It can be seen on the title-pages of *Sheeris Yisroel* (1785), *Seyfer tam veyosher* (1786), both volumes of *Kav hayosher* (1788), as well as in *Seyfer mivkhar hapninim* (1794, p. 3), and on the final pages of *Drishas hazohov* (*Drishat hazahav*, 1794) and *Seyfer sod adoynoy* (1794).

In addition, a comparison of the extant editions suggests that M[N1783] is the older, and probably the original, printed text of *Mayse gdoyle min Uman umin Ukrayne*, or the Eastern version. The second half (pp. 10–18) differs significantly from all other editions. Some passages are found only in M[N1783] (e.g. on pp. 11, 15–16). Other editions add nothing substantially new to the narration. It seems that all other editions, starting with Sadilkov (1834), contain a thorough linguistic and stylistic revision of M[N1783]. This drastic re-editing resulted in the omission of the passages mentioned above and in the reformulation of most of the second half of the account (cf. ll. 253–83, 290–319, 323–53, 361–76, 386–92, 403–17, 436–43, 455–72, 477–83, 486–8, i.e. the later changes to the text sequences on pp. 10–11, 11–12, 12–13, 13–14, 14–15, 15, 16, 16–17, 17). Subsequently, this reformulation resulted in a few minor textual insertions (e.g. ll. 266–7, 353, 425–7).

Figure 3 The ornaments used in *Mayse gdoyle min Uman umin Ukrayne* [Novidvor, *c.*1783]

1 Title-page

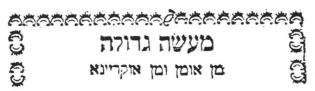

2 Page 17

3 Page 24

In a few cases, the nineteenth-century editions seem to correct a number of contextually obvious errors in M[N1783] (e.g. p. 16, where פוחזים pɔxzəm 'thugs' was appropriately replaced by סוחרים sɔxrəm 'merchants'). However, in most instances M[N1783] appears to be more precise. Thus the same episode reported in M[N1783] and the Western version was distorted in the later editions of the Eastern version (see Table 22; M[N1783], p. 6, ll. 139–40; MF1783, p. 4, ll. 99–102). Even the name of the woman described, ברײנה ⟨brajnh⟩ Brájnə or ברײנלי ⟨vrajnli⟩ Brájn(d)alə, was wrongly reported as בריאה ⟨briah⟩ and ברײה ⟨briih⟩ in Sadilkov (1834) and in Vilna (1845) editions.

Similarly, in the *kine* accompanying the Eastern version of the account we find another distortion in the Vilna (1845) edition, which apparently stems from misreading the word צאראוני carɔvnə 'the Russian empress' (see Table 22; ll. 611–12), which is missing in Sadilkov (1834).

We may conclude that M[N1783] was apparently printed in Novidvor, between 1781 and 1816. It is the earliest known edition of the Eastern version. The possibility that it was printed in the late eighteenth century is

Table 22 Two episodes from the extant texts of *Mayse gdoyle min Uman*

M[N1783]	Sadilkov, 1834 [Vilna, 1845]	Fürth, 1783
איין אשה ברײנה	[איין אשה בריאה [ברייה	איין אשה וואהר ושמה
האט גיװוארפֿן אירי	האט גילאפֿין פֿון אירע	בריינלי דיא פֿערילבֿט
קינדר אין וואשר	קינדר אין וואשער	זיך וואן זיא גטימ ווירד
אריין כדי די קינדר	אריין כדי די קינדר	מעלבֿטין איר קינדער
זאלן חלילה ניט	זאלן חלילה ניט	גשמאד װערין נעממ זיא
בלייבן אין דר	בלייבין באיי די	איר אייגני קינדר אונד
שמאד	פוחזים	טרענקט זיא צו טוט
		אין וואסיר

ejn išə brajnə	ejn iša ⟨briə⟩ [⟨brajə⟩]	ejn iša vɔr ušmə
hɔt gəvɔrfn̩ irə	hɔt gəlɔfn̩ fun irə	brajnələ di férixt
kindər in vasər	kindər in vasər	zəx vən zi gətejt vird
arájn kədej di kindər	arájn kədej di kindər	mɛxtn̩ ir kindər
zɔln̩ xólilə nit	zɔln̩ xólilə nit	gɛšmad vɛrn̩ nɛmt zi
blajbn̩ in dər	blajbn̩ ba di	ir ejgənə kindər und
šmad	pɔxzəm	trɛnkt zej cu tɔjt
		in vasər

| A woman [called] Brayne threw her children into water so that her children would not, heaven forbid, become Christians. (lit. 'remain in conversion') | A woman [called] Bray(n)e ran away from her children into water so that her children would not, heaven forbid, stay with the rakes. | There was a woman called Brayn(d)ale who was afraid that, after she is murdered, her children might be converted [so] she took her own children and drowned them to death in water. |

M[N1783]	Vilna, 1845
אונ אויך כמה אלפֿים בחורים	אונ אויך כמה אלפֿים בחורים
ובתלות האט מן צו דר צאראווני	ובתלות האט מען צו די צוואנציג
אין דיא מאסקוויא אריין גפֿירט	אין דער מאסקווא אריין גיפֿירט

un ɔjx kamə alɔfəm bɔxərəm	un ɔjx kamə alɔfəm bɔxərəm
ubsúləs hɔt mən cudər carɔ́vnə	ubsúləs hɔt mən cu di cváncig
in di mɔsk(ɔ)via arájngəfirt	in dər mɔskvə arájngəfirt

| And also a few thousand young men and maidens were taken to the empress in Moscow. | And also a few thousand young men and maidens were taken to the twenty(!) in Moscow. |

also endorsed by M. Rosenfeld's evaluation of this edition (Rosenfeld, pers. comm. 1988). We cannot rule out the possibility that it was printed even before the 1783 Fürth edition of the Western version. Rosenfeld suggests that M[N1783] is a reprint of Fürth (1783) that appeared in Novidvor *c*.1783-4. Although M[N1783] can hardly be considered a 'reprint of Fürth (1783)', its dating at *c*.1783 seems to be plausible.

30.2.2 *Later Publications of* Mayse gdoyle min Uman umin Ukrayne

The Eastern version, based on one of the nineteenth-century editions, was included in Gurland's collection of testimonies, accounts, and commemorative prayers (*kines/kinot*) dedicated to the persecutions of Jews in Poland and the Ukraine in 1648-9 and 1768 (Gurland 1892: 67-79; cf. also *idem* 1886: 17-18). It was later published in a Hebrew translation in Bernfeld (1926: 291-7).

In 1929 Dubnov published a more critical edition of the two main versions. His Eastern version was published from a handwritten copy of the Sadilkov (1834) and Vilna (1845) editions. This copy was originally commissioned in 1888 by Sholem Aleichem, who intended to republish it in his literary yearbook *Yidishe folksbibliotek*. But the full publication of this text was banned by Russian censorship (cf. Dubnov 1929: 31), and only a few censored quotations were allowed into Skomorovski's (1889) survey of written testimonies about the Zhelezniak and Gonta massacres of 1768. Sholem Aleichem seems to have been interested in republishing this text not only because of its historical and ethical value, but also because of its possible significance for documenting the earlier stages of popular literary creativity in Eastern Yiddish. It is well known that Sholem Aleichem's efforts to publish the *Yidishe folksbibliotek* (only two volumes appeared, in Kiev in 1888 and 1889; for a detailed survey see Dresner 1981, cf. Shmeruk 1980: 14-17) were motivated by his general zeal to organize and in some sense 'create' modern Yiddish literature (cf. Miller 1991). This meant establishing earlier periods of modern Yiddish literature prior to the second half of the nineteenth century, by collecting material about previous generations of Yiddish writers and by publishing their works. The Eastern Yiddish version of *Mayse gdoyle min Uman umin Ukrayne*, even if it was not published earlier than 1834, would have been especially significant to Sholem Aleichem, for it pre-dated most of the works written by the older generations of Yiddish authors, and was at the same time linguistically close to the language in which he and many of his contemporaries wrote.

In the wake of the Holocaust two anthologies on Jewish history and martyrdom appeared, one by E. Lipschitz in 1944, the other by Shmuel Niger in 1948. Lipschitz included in his anthology an abridged and orthographically modernized version based on Dubnov's edition of the Eastern Yiddish account (see Lipschitz 1944: 245-9). It seems also that the Eastern version was one of the sources which Niger used for the section on the events of 1769 in his collection entitled *Kidesh hashem* (see Niger 1948: 841-4).

30.3 The Two Versions

There are two views as to the genealogy of *Mayse gdoyle min Uman umin Ukrayne*. According to one, the Fürth (1783) edition is presented as the first (see Dubnov 1929: 30, 32) or even the original version of the account. Accordingly the Eastern version is viewed as its later expansion (see Roskies 1974b: 46 n. 69; Shmeruk 1978: 188 n. 62; Zfatman 1983: ii. 131-2 n. 221; Timm 1987: 40).

Given the known dates of publication of the extant versions, Roskies's view might at first appear plausible. However, the Eastern version is substantially larger. The same events are described in a livelier manner and in more detail, and, more importantly, it contains a number of episodes not reported in the Western version (cf. Prilutski 1931: 229-30). The gap of some fifty years between the 1783 and 1834 editions does not necessarily mean that all the additional details and episodes were incorporated only in the later edition of 1834.

Both these considerations were instrumental in forming the second view, according to which the Eastern version is much earlier than 1834. Prilutski (1931: 229-30) implicitly claimed that it must have been written soon after the events of 1768, while Shtif (1932a: 36) suggested that both versions stem from a third, original text, which was apparently much closer in its language and content to Sadilkov (1834). He also suggested that the original version must have been written in rhyme, since a number of rhymes can be found or restored in the Eastern version.

Each of these two views awaits further clarification. However, it is clear that the primary philological concern must rest with the textual origins of the events reported, rather than with their actual historical validity. Therefore Roskies's claim that 'the additions in the second [version] seem to be of a formulaic and embellishing nature rather than of an historic one' (1974a: 46 n. 69, cf. 1974b: 10 n. 40) is not only inaccurate—certainly not all the additions can be dismissed as formulaic or stylistic embellishments— but is also irrelevant to the actual textual genealogy of *Mayse gdoyle min Uman*. The outstanding Yiddish translator, style-editor, and printer of Sadilkov, Moyshe Bloshtern, cannot be considered the creator of the Eastern version on the basis of 1783 Fürth edition (as suggested by Roskies 1974b: 32, cf. 1974a: 9-10); but it is very likely that he was responsible for the thorough linguistic and stylistic re-editing of the second half of M[N1783] (cf. above §30.2.1).

I am inclined to the view that the Eastern version is considerably older than its earliest known date of publication, viz. 1834. The relation between the two should probably be reversed. That is to say, the additional details were not inserted later in the Eastern version. Rather, they were omitted in the version printed in Fürth in 1783.

In comparing the two versions, there is a temptation to consider Fürth (1783) as a drastic abridgement of the Eastern version. First, all the descriptions of events in it are also found in the Eastern version, which offers many additional and substantial details. Secondly, MF1783 omits many episodes reported in the Eastern version. These omissions comprise not less than two-thirds of the second half of the Eastern version (see Prilutski 1931: 229). By and large the Western version is restricted to the account of the atrocities that took place in Uman itself (the only exception being the brief mention of the pogroms in Balta; see MF1783, p. 5), whereas the Eastern version also describes the events that occurred in other locations—e.g. in the surrounding villages (see pp. 9-10, 247 ff.), in Balta (see pp. 11 ff.) and in Brod (= Brody; see p. 15). The general framework of the account is by and large the same in both versions: some of the paragraphs open, and some-times close, with the same phrases or key words (usually in Hebrew). This is especially evident in the first part of both M[N1783] and MF1783, as well as in the concluding remark that appears at the end of both versions (see Table 23). Curiously enough, the concluding remark in M[N1783], unlike that in the later editions of the Eastern version, is much closer to the final passage of Fürth (1783). The underlined words and phrases in the right-hand column (see Table 23) were omitted or altered in the subsequent re-editions, starting with Sadilkov (1834; cf. M[N1783]: p. 16, ll. 485-8).

It is difficult to prove that MF1783 is a drastic abridgement of the Eastern version, although it is chronologically possible, since M[N1783] could have appeared before 1783. Only in a few cases does MF1783 add certain details missing from the Eastern version (cf. MF1783, p. 3, ll. 77-9 and 92-4, vs. M[N1783], p. 5, ll. 106-7 and 125-9, respectively). However, even in those two episodes the description is far more detailed in the Eastern version (see one of them in the Appendix 8). Another possibility is a slight modification of Shtif's suggestion (1932a: 36): that both versions stem from an original Eastern Yiddish text, of which M[N1783] is the earliest known printed edition and MF1783 is a drastic abridgement, thoroughly rewritten in the heavily Germanized Western Yiddish of the time. The fact that Fürth (1783) has a number of residual Eastern Yiddish forms and phrases also testifies to its textual dependence on the Eastern version (see below §31.3.3).

Table 23 The final passage of *Mayse gdoyle min Uman* in both versions

Fürth (1783)	Eastern version (M[N1783])
מיר וועלין וויטער ניקש שרייבן .	נוא מיר וועלן וויטער ניט שרייבן
אונד וועלין ביא דען בלייבן :	אונ מיר וועלן בי דעם בלייבן
שפוך חמתך על הגוים גאט האט	(שפוך חמתך על הגוים) גאט זאל
פֿר גאסין זיין צארין אויף דיא	אונזר שונאים שלאגן מיט נגעים
שונאים. זיא צו שטראפֿין מיט נגעים	רעים אונ פֿר דיא צרות פֿון
געגין דיא צרות פֿון אוקריינא און	אוקריינה אונ אומן זאלן מיר זוכה
ק״ק אומן : כן יאבדו כל אויביך	זיין אז אונזר גואל צדק זאל
ה׳ און מיר זאללין זוכה זיין דען	במהרה קומן אמן :
גאול צדק צו זעהן במהרה בימינו אמן :	

mir vəln vajtər niks šrajbn̩
und vəln ba dən blajbn̩
špɔx xamɔ́sxɔ al (h)agɔ́jəm gɔt
hɔt fargɔ́sn̩ zajn cɔrn̩ af di
sɔ́nəm. zej cu štrɔfn̩ mit negɔ́jəm
gɛgn̩ di cɔ́rəs fun ukrájnə un
k[hiləs]"k[ɔjdəš] umən kejn jɔ́vdu
kɔl ɔjvɛxɔ h'[adɔ́jnə] un mir
zɔln̩ zɔ́jxə zajn dən gɔ́jəl cɛ́dək
zɛn bəmhéjrə bəjəméjnə ɔ́mejn.

nu mir viln vajtər nit šrajbn̩
un mir vəln ba dəm blajbn̩
špɔx xamɔ́sxɔ al (h)agɔ́jəm gɔt
zɔl undzər sɔnəm šlɔgn̩ mit negɔ́jəm
rɔjəm un far di cɔrəs fun
ukrájne un umən zɔln̩ mir zɔjxə
zajn az undzər gɔjəl cɛdək zɔl
bəmhejrə kumən ɔ́mejn.

We will not write any more and
hereby we will stop. 'Pour out Thy
wrath upon the nations', God poured
his wrath upon [our] enemies [in order]
to punish them with heavy afflictions
for the sufferings of the Ukraine and
the holy community of Uman. 'So let
all thine enemies perish, O Lord' and
[may] we be graced [by the arrival] of
the just Redeemer speedily in our days!
Amen!

And so we will not write any further
and hereby we will stop. 'Pour out Thy
wrath upon the nations', may God
strike our enemies with heavy
affliction, and for the sufferings of
the Ukraine and Uman may we
live to be graced by the speedy
arrival of our Redeemer! Amen!

Judging by the extant texts, each of the two versions seems to have aimed at a slightly different readership. If we were to assume that its peculiar language was intelligible to Eastern Yiddish speakers of the period, MF1783 might be thought to have been written for all Yiddish readers. However, a few explanations of some basic geopolitical terms at the beginning may indicate that this version was written primarily for readers in Western and Central Europe, who were far less familiar with these terms and with the actual political situation in Eastern Europe at that time. The following explanation is found on the title-page:

אקריינא גרעניצט מיט רוסין אונד טאטרייא
ɔkrájnə grɛnəct mit rusṇ und tatár(y)jə
'The Ukraine borders Russia and Turkey.'

Similarly, the first paragraph of MF1783 gives a brief introductory description of the contemporary political situation in the Ukraine, including *inter alia* a clarification of the Eastern Yiddish term jevónəm :

אלי דען רוזישן גלויבן װעלבי גינעגנט װערדן יװנים
alə dən rúzišṇ(!) glɔjbṇ vélxə gənɛnt vɛrdṇ jevónəm
'all [people] of Russian [Orthodox] faith, that are called *yavonim*' (lit. 'Greeks')

It is hardly surprising that these explanations are not found in the Eastern version.

Both versions of *Mayse gdoyle min Uman* are significant monuments of the changing literary language of the second half of the eighteenth century. The Western version epitomizes the ever increasing restructuring of contemporary Western Yiddish and of the old literary language on the patterns of New High German. The Eastern version, on the other hand, offers what may be considered to be the earliest original work written entirely in modern Eastern Yiddish, and, retrospectively, one of the most significant qualitative achievements of the nascent modern literary language.

A linguistic examination of MF1783 and M[N1783] is offered in §§31 and 32. Two excerpts exemplifying some of the sharp linguistic contrasts and textual differences between the two main versions are offered in Appendix 8 (pp. 310-11). The first passage contains the prefaces that appear on the title-pages of each version; the second gives descriptions of one of the episodes reported in both texts.

31 The Language of the Western Version (Fürth, 1783)

The Western version is an important linguistic document that combines a number of dialectally distinct features. On the whole its language may most appropriately be characterized as a strongly Germanized Western Yiddish. Its spelling, morphology, and syntax exhibit the most cardinal features of restructuring of the old literary language and the spoken Western Yiddish on the orthographic and grammatical patterns of New High German. A number of genuine Western Yiddish forms nevertheless occur in lexicon, phraseology, and to a lesser degree morphology. Finally, in spite of the heavy façade of New High German (or *à la* New High German) usage, we find here a few distinctly Eastern Yiddish features. These apparently echo an original Eastern Yiddish version of this account.

31.1 Orthography

The spelling system of MF1783 represents a typical, for that time and place, combination of traits inherited from Old Literary Yiddish with conventions introduced from New High German.

31.1.1 Unstressed Vowels

Thanks to the socio-linguistically prestigious High German models of MF1783, the frequency of the orthographically represented unstressed vowels increased significantly, especially in posttonic position. The unstressed vowel ⟨ע⟩ ə of the masculine nominative definite article דער dər is systematically spelled out. Other pretonic vowels seem also to be more often represented, although such variations as גילאָפֿין ⟨gilofin⟩ ~ גלאָפֿין ⟨glofin⟩ for gəlofn̩ 'ran' (cf. 71, 47) and קאָנאַנין ⟨kanonin⟩ ~ קנאָנין ⟨knonin⟩ for kanónən 'cannon' (pl., 54, 97) show that the Old Yiddish convention of optional representation of the pretonic vowels was far from being abolished.

The posttonic vowels, including most of the shewas, are graphemically represented; e.g. מענשין mɛnčn̩ 'people' (25); שעכטין šɛxtn̩ 'slaughter; massacre' (26, 43, 44, 125); לייאָנין lejənən 'read' (3); קומין kumən 'come' (50, 91, 175); דערפֿיר dɛrfər 'villages' (179). However, the Old Yiddish convention of unspelling the posttonic vowel in covered syllables with final ⟨ר⟩ still prevails; e.g. העכשטר hɛxstər 'highest' (67); ווייבר vajbər 'women' (27), מוטר mutər 'mother' (125); פֿענסטר fɛnctər 'window' (108).

The adoption of the ⟨ע⟩ grapheme instead of the conventional ⟨א⟩ to represent the postdiphthongal ə vowels is apparently modelled on German; e.g. שרייען šrajən 'cry' (69, 72, 90, 117, 153); פֿפֿייער fajər 'fire' (186). Similarly, this spelling is occasionally adopted to represent a posttonic vowel or shewa; e.g. קינדער kindər 'children' (101, 124); לעבענדיג lébn̩dik 'alive' (169); אונטער untər 'down' (110).

31.1.2 Consonants

Among the most striking orthographic features of MF1783 are the introduction of double consonants and the massive use of the silent postvocalic ⟨ה⟩. Both were directly inspired by New High German spelling conventions. Double consonants—e.g. אללי alə 'all' (72, 89, 116, 169, 191) and זאללין zɔln̩ 'should' (3rd pers. pl., 158)—were apparently introduced also into some other contemporary Germanized Western Yiddish texts (cf. Reyzen 1930: 118 §49; Timm 1987: 255–6). The use of the postvocalic ⟨ה⟩ was restricted to a handful of lexical items in Old Yiddish texts (see Reyzen 1920: 114 §35; Shtif 1928: 36 §37; M. Weinreich 1958*a*: 111 §18). In MF1783 and in many other contemporary printed works (§28.1.3) the silent ⟨ה⟩ was often introduced; e.g. אוהן גליק unglík 'misfortune; calamity' (cf. modern Yiddish אומגליק umglík, 12); שוועהר švɛr 'difficult' (63); איהם im 'him' (43, 44); מעהר mɛr 'more' (51).

One orthographic 'foible' is also peculiar to other Yiddish texts printed at this time in the same printing shop in Fürth (e.g. *Ben hameylekh vehanozir* of 1783 and *Seyfer poykeyakh ivrim vehu seyfer goyroles*, to which this version is appended). The ⟨ב⟩ grapheme normally representing v (and until the seventeenth century the syllable-initial or syllable-final f; see Timm 1987: 67–8) is frequently used instead of the etymologically and orthographically expected ⟨ב⟩; e.g. אבר for אבר ɔbər 'but' (62); בשרייבן for בשרייבן bašrájbn̩ 'describe' (149); בלוט for בלוט blut 'blood' (120); לעבן for לעבין lɛbn̩ 'live' (141). There seems to be no phonological justification for this confusion between v and b in Western Yiddish dialects (see Timm 1987: 297–8 §35.3.2). Such frequent variation between ⟨ב⟩ and ⟨ב⟩ is uncharacteristic of Old Yiddish orthography. It is noteworthy, however, that a similar 'misspelling' with ⟨פ⟩ instead of the expected ⟨פ⟩ occasionally occurs, as in the case of שלעפֿין for שלעפֿין šlɛpn̩ 'drag' (134) and הויפֿט מאן for הויפֿט מאן hɔ́jptman 'marshal' (136). Could it be a hypercorrection 'once removed' or an overcompensation, namely that the printer slipped even further in his attempt to introduce and maintain the syllable-final allophone pf as in ⟨קאפּף⟩ 'head' (e.g. 187), whereby the chain of overcompensation may be summarized as [*šlɛpə → *šlɛpfən →] šlɛfən?

31.2 Phonology

On the phonological level a number of spellings of certain stressed vowels point to either the increasing impact of New High German or the conventional Western Yiddish vocalism.

31.2.1 *Vowels Introduced from New High German*

The massive introduction of New High German forms had an obvious impact on the graphemic representation of certain stressed vowels. However, in most cases the Old Yiddish spelling conventions can equally represent various dialectal or Germanized realizations of historically related stressed vowels. Hence the small number of phonologically unusual spellings; e.g. פֿאליר fɔlər 'full' (fem. dat. sing., 30; cf. NHG *voll*, St.Y. פֿולער fulər); וואלין vɔln̩ '[we] will; want' (68; cf. NHG *wollen*, St.Y. וועלן vɔln̩); קאמ(י)ן kɔ́mən 'come' (69, 166, 178; cf. NHG *kommen*, St.Y. קומען kumən); נור nur 'only' (78, 161;

cf. NHG *nur*, St.Y. נאָר ⟨nor⟩); װאָן ⟨van⟩ *van* 'when' (78; cf. NHG *wann*, St.Y. װען ⟨vən⟩).

In some cases the chosen spelling is 'phonetically' closer to its real or presumed New High German realization; e.g. ברינגן *bringən* 'bring' (59; cf. NHG *bringen*, St.Y. ברענגען *brɛngən*); ברינגטין *bringtn̩* 'brought' (133; cf. NHG *brachten*, SEY געברענגט *gəbrɛngt*). However, the large-scale inconsistency in the representation of stressed vowels betrays the writer's rather unsuccessful attempt to implement the non-native High German norm; e.g.:

ברינגן *bringən* (59) ~ ברענגין *brɛngən* 'bring' (86, 94, 104);

קאָמ(י)ן *kɔmən* (69, 166, 178) ~ קומין *kumən* 'come' (31, 34).

31.2.2 *Traits of Western Yiddish Vocalism*

The historical vowel **44** (NEY ej ‖ MEY ɔj ‖ SEY ɔj ‖ WY ā) is normally spelled with the conventional ⟨ו⟩ or ⟨וי⟩ graphemes. Only once is a distinctly Western Yiddish spelling used; i.e. לאָפֿין ⟨lafin⟩ 'run' (152), revealing that its underlying phonemic realization is the Western Yiddish lāfn̩ (cf. St.Y. לויפֿן lɔjfn̩). This spelling, although dialectal, was accepted for vowels **44** and **24** in some Old Yiddish texts from Western Europe (see §7.1.4). Because this spelling is exceptionally rare, we may attribute it to the printer. By contrast, the graphemic representation of these vowels with ⟨א⟩ is often found in *Ben hameylekh vehanozir* printed also in 1783 in the same printing shop in Fürth and in the booklet *Seyfer poykeyakh ivrim vehu seyfer goyroles* to which our text is appended.

Another, rather anachronistic, spelling is ⟨וי⟩ for vowel **52**. It was used to represent rounded vowels in older Yiddish orthography (cf. Timm 1987: 171–4). But in the eighteenth century this convention became obsolete (cf. Reyzen 1920: 113–14 §§32–3; Shtif 1928: 33 §11), and it is also quite unusual in this text. In spite of this, one word is consistently spelled with ⟨וי⟩; viz. שויל ⟨šuil⟩ 'Synagogue' (90, 91, 96, 98; cf. NEY šul ‖ MEY šıl ‖ SEY šil ‖ WY šūl ‖ šüil). It may be that this spelling testifies to the printer's or writer's effort to Westernize the underlying Southeastern Yiddish šil into Western Yiddish šūl or šüil. (On the diaphonemic realization of this vowel in Western Yiddish dialects see D. Katz 1983: 1026–8 §6.1.1–6.2.) This suggestion is supported by the similar orthographic treatment of the toponym Tituv/ Tetijev [títiəv/títəv/títəv or tátiəv (?)] spelled here טיטוב (27, 47). The writer or printer of this text had before him the Eastern Yiddish form of the place-name títəv, which apparently belongs to the same pattern of Yiddish toponyms as kítəv (for Katy) and gríbəv (for *Grzybow*; cf. Stankiewicz 1965: 163 §2.1). Other spellings of this name in the Eastern version are טוטיוב ⟨tutiuv⟩ (in M[N1783], 14, 560); טיטוב ⟨tituv⟩ (in Gurland's 1892 reprint of

MV1845, p. 68); טוטויב ⟨tutuiv⟩ and טיטשיוב ⟨titšiuv⟩ (in Dubnov 1929: 37, 51, apparently following MS1834; cf. also טעטיוב ⟨tetiuv⟩ in Skomorovski 1889: 33, which is apparently closer to the Slavonic form of this place-name, Tetijev).

31.2.3 *An Eastern Phonological Feature*

Only one case may be considered a possible phonological trait of Eastern Yiddish. The past participle gəvust 'knew' is spelled once with ⟨י⟩: גוויזט gəvist (66). This spelling, otherwise unusual for MF1783, may well echo the Southeastern dialect of the original Eastern Yiddish account, although the sentence in which it appears is not found in the parallel passage of the Eastern version. The occasional employment of ⟨י⟩ for vowel 51 is also found in some of the seventeenth- and early eighteenth-century Western Yiddish texts (e.g. *Simkhes hanefesh* (Frankfurt am Main, 1707)) where it apparently reflects its Midwestern Yiddish i realization.

31.3 Morphology

The reinstatement of the lost unstressed final vowels (deapocopation) and the frequent remodelling of many forms on the patterns of New High German are among the most striking morphological features of MF1783. (On the role of apocope in the history and structure of Yiddish see Sapir 1915; M. Weinreich 1973: ii. 132–3 §132.2; 176ff. §§142. 2–142. 22; King 1980: 397–403 §6.1; for analogous developments in German dialects cf. Lindgren 1953; Wells 1985: 113–14, 153–61.) In some cases the Germanized variants are far from dominant. However, the fact that they were introduced reveals the qualitative change in the grammatical and stylistic preferences of the anonymous author of this version.

31.3.1 *Forms without Apocope*

Because of the frequent, in some cases systematic, reinstatement of the unstressed final vowels, a whole range of new forms is introduced. A number of nouns are appropriately modified to comply with the underlying New High German norm; e.g. שטימי štimə 'voice' (30, 67; cf. St.Y. שטים štim); ערדי ɛrdə 'earth' (110, 119; cf. mod. Y. ערד ɛrd). The New High German pattern of plural formation is occasionally introduced; e.g.:

שטעטי štɛtə 'towns' (6; cf. mod. Y. שטעט štɛt);
טאגי tɛgə 'days' (130; cf. mod. Y. טעג tɛg);
שאפי šɔfə 'sheep' (pl., 26, 123; cf. mod. Y. שאף šɔf).

Similarly, the first-person singular present forms in most cases receive the unstressed final vowel; e.g.:

לאָזי ləzə (?) '[I] let' (62; cf. mod. Y. לאָז ləz);
קומי kumə '[I] come' (61; cf. mod. Y. קום kum);
האבי həbə (?) '[I] have' (81; 173; cf. mod. Y. האָב həb).

31.3.2 *Germanization and Western Yiddish Traits*

The Old Yiddish preterite is by and large 'rehabilitated' in our text, thanks to the systematic introduction of the weak and strong forms of the German imperfect; e.g.:

ווישטן vistn̩ (?) '[they] knew' (151); לויפֿטן ləjftn̩ '[they] ran' (29);
שלעפֿטן šlɛptn̩ '[they] dragged' (128); שרעקטין šrɛktn̩ '[they] scared' (178);
האטי hətə (?) '[he] had' (16); רופֿטי ruftə '[he] called' (67);
גינג ging '[he] went' (110); ליס lis '[he] let' (76, 108, 175);
קאם kɔm (?) '[he] came' (103).

In fact, the imperfect becomes the most frequently used, hence unmarked, past tense form, whereas the regular (periphrastic) past is seldom found in this version.

Other typical importations from New High German include the accusative of the third-person masculine pronoun (e.g. איהן in 'him', 138, 144, 154, 161, 182, 184, 188) and the subjunctive:

זאָלטין zoltn̩ (3rd pers. pl. past subj., 100; cf. NHG *sollten*, St.Y. זאָלן zoln̩ 'should');
זאָלי zoltə (1st pers. sing. pres. subj., 80; cf. NHG *solle*, St.Y. זאָל zol '(I) should');
מעכטין mɛxtn̩ (3rd pers. pl. past subj., 100; cf. NHG *möchten*,
    St.Y. וואָלטן געמעגט voltn̩ gəmɛgt 'could').

It is unclear to what extent the subjunctive was preserved in contemporary spoken Western Yiddish, although it could have been reintroduced from German. We know that the accusative and dative of the masculine pronoun merged in the spoken language into a unitary *im* (see Friedrich 1784: 187–8, s.v. *Ihm*).

The Western version is also marked by morphological instability. Quite often Germanization is partial and inconsistent. In many nouns, apocope remains intact; e.g. ארזאָך úrzax 'cause; reason' (12); שׁוּיל šul 'Synagogue' (90, 96, 98); שׁוועל švɛl 'threshhold' (114); שׁטראם štrɔs 'road, way' (46). In one episode (ll. 40–5), the colloquial איהם im 'him' (acc.) is repeatedly used. In the rest of the text it is cautiously avoided in favour of איהן in. As in Old Literary Yiddish the genitive case is formed with possessive pronouns; e.g. איר אויגן ir ɔjgn̩ 'her eyes' (83). Otherwise it is rarely used (cf. אן אנפֿאַנג איר

קומן ɔn ɔ́nfang ir kumən 'with their arrival', lit. 'at the beginning of their arrival', 33-4). Similarly, in sharp contrast to the imperfect, the introduction of subjunctive forms is far from systematic. Even such easily 'convertible' forms as un 'and' and iz 'is' remain unchanged in a few cases. Otherwise אונד and איזט prevail.

A number of distinctly Western Yiddish forms survived despite overall Germanization. The dative and accusative of the masculine definite article are merged into a unitary דען dən (cf. ll. 39, 113, 161, 167, where דען dən is used for dative). This usage undoubtedly reflects the spoken Western Yiddish of that period (see Friedrich 1784: 53-4 §2; Lincoff 1963: 54 §4.213). Similarly, in MF1783, the Western Yiddish negation pronoun ניקש niks 'nothing' (38, 64, 66, 147, 155, 192) and the negation adverb ניט nit (e.g. ll. 78, 89, 96, 135, 149), are consistently employed, whereas the Germanized adverb ניכט nixt is used only once (189). It seems that such forms as שוינט šɔjnt 'already' (60, 155) and זיך zix 'look!' (imperative, 83) were also characteristic of late eighteenth-century Western Yiddish.

31.3.3 *Traces of Eastern Yiddish Morphology*

Of special importance to the textual genealogy of *Mayse gdoyle min Uman* are the few Eastern Yiddish forms that can be traced in the Western version. A number of forms are conspicuously Eastern Yiddish; e.g. גווארין gəvɔ́rņ 'became' (pass. v. aux., 123); ברײנלי brájn(d)alə [female name] Brayn(d)ale (100); and possibly רוצחנים rɔcxɔ́nəm (or racxɔ́nəm?) 'murderers' (31; but note the spelling) and the reflexive פֿר שפרייטין זיך faršpréjtņ zəx 'spread (of crowd)' (35).

Moreover, some Eastern Yiddish forms of MF1783 are also found in the parallel passages of the Eastern version. The various forms of future auxiliary used in this version are either genuinely Western Yiddish (e.g. איר ווערט ir vərt 'you will', 86; איך ווער ix vər 'I will', 155) or are remodelled on the High German paradigm (זיא ווערדין zej vərdņ 'they will', 155). However, in its final passage, which is textually close to M[N1783], this edition twice uses the distinctly Eastern Yiddish וועלין (מיר) (mir) vəlņ '(we) will' (192; cf. above §30.3, Table 23). Similarly, the unstressed verbal prefix dər- was usually replaced by the Western Yiddish ar- (e.g. ארוועקט זיך arvékt zəx '[he] stirs', lit. 'wakes up', 92) or by its Germanized variant ər- (e.g. ער ליזין ərlejzņ 'to redeem', 11). Conversely, in the following sentence the original Eastern Yiddish aspect marker dər- seems to have survived:

זיא ווערדין וייטר ניט דער לעבין צו גיהן

zej vərdņ vajtər nit dərlɛbņ cu gejn

'They shall not live to go [any] further' (MF1783, 155-6);

אז זיא זאלן וייטער ניט דר לעבן צו גיין. Cf.

az zej zɔlṇ vajtər nit dərlɛbṇ cu gejn

'So that they shall not live to go [any] further' (M[N1783], 406).

Other Eastern Yiddish forms that can be traced to the parallel passages of M[N1783] are the plural form וועגין vɛgṇ 'carts' (MF1783, 46; cf. M[N1783], 33) and the distinctly Southeastern Yiddish ברונע brunə 'well' (MF 1783, 89; cf. M[N1783], ll. 111, 113, 118). In the Vilna (1845) edition of the Eastern version, ברונע was replaced by the Northeastern ברונעם brunəm.

It is remarkable that these Eastern Yiddish forms survived despite the radical abridgement and linguistic revision that the Western version underwent. Its anonymous author was undoubtedly fluent in contemporary Western Yiddish. Not only was he well aware of the lexical, grammatical, and stylistic differences between Eastern and Western dialects; he also consciously attempted to recast the whole account in the Germanized (hence 'literary') Western Yiddish of his time (see §26 on another Germanized Western Yiddish text). To cite just one example, a distinctly non-Eastern use of the adjective ɔrəm 'poor' (cf. NHG *arm* 'poor; unfortunate') occurs in MF1783 in one of the few sentences which are textually unprecedented in the extant editions of the Eastern version:

דיא ארמי יהודים הבן פֿון דען אלין ניקש גוויזט

di ɔrəmə jəhudəm hɔbṇ fun dən alṇ niks gəvist

'The poor Jews knew nothing about this' (66).

In modern Eastern Yiddish אָרעם ɔrəm 'poor' does not have the semantic value of 'unfortunate'. Instead, the adjective אומגליקלעך umglíkləx or the emphatic adverb נעבעך nɛbəx are used.

31.4 Lexicon and Phraseology

Despite the extensive Germanization in phonology and morphology, only a handful of lexical items are borrowed from German. Most of them belong to military terminology; e.g. איבֿר פֿאל íbərfal 'attack' (17; cf. NHG *Überfall*); גילעגנהייט gəlégṇhajt 'occasion' (21; cf. NHG *Gelegenheit*); אן רוקין ɔ́nrùkṇ '(military) approach' (28; cf. NHG *abrücken*); בנאבריכטין banáxrixtṇ 'reports' (167; cf. NHG *benachrichtigen; nachrichten*).

Two Eastern Yiddish terms related to the events described are used; i.e. קאזאקין kɔzákṇ 'Cossacks' (158, 163, 167); יוונים jəvɔnəm 'Russians', lit. 'Greeks' (14, 20, 56). Curiously enough, neither of them is found in the extant editions of the Eastern version. Conversely, the original Eastern

Yiddish terms are usually replaced in MF1783 by their Western Yiddish equivalents:

1 האַרמטאַ harmátə 'cannon' (M[N1783], 55, 133) →
   קאָנונין kanónən 'cannon' (pl., MF1783, 54, 97);
2 צאַרוונאַ carévnə 'the (Russian) empress' (M[N1783], 63) →
   קייסרין kéjsərən 'empress' (MF1783, 58);
3 יעניראל jənərál (M[N1783], 402) →
   יונראל junərál 'general' (MF1783, 153);
4 קאָמ(י)ס(א)ר kɔmisár 'commissary' (M[N1783], 60, 68, 222) →
   הויבט מאָן hɔ́jptman 'leader; marshal' (MF1783, 56, 65, 137);
5 ראָט הויז rɔ́thɔjz (M[N1783], 144, 152) →
   עצה הויז éjcəhɔjz 'city council' (MF1783, 107);
6 שטאָט štɔt '[the] city [of Uman]' (M[N1783], 34, 54, 72) →
   חזקה xazókə ~ חזקה xazókəs '[the] fortress [of Uman]' (MF1783, 48, 52, 72).

In contrast to some contemporary printed Western Yiddish texts, Fürth (1783) has a strikingly large number of lexical items of the Semitic component. Most of them were common to both Western and Eastern Yiddish. The following is a sample of some of these items:

הרגט hargət 'kills' (94);
הריגה harígə 'killing' (130);
חזקה xazókə 'fortress' (48, 72);
חיל xajəl 'army' (18, 61, 67);
חלילה xɔlílə 'heaven forbid' (adv.; 87);
טרפה trejfə 'nefarious' (189);
יללה jəlɔlə 'scream' (73);
מלחמה məlxɔmə 'war' (19);
מנוחה mənuxə 'rest' (60);
נפשות nəfašəs 'people; persons', lit. 'souls' (34, 52, 98);
נקמה nəkɔmə 'vengeance' (183);
ספר תורות séjfər tɔjrəs 'Torah scrolls' (118);
פ מסרת farmásərt 'betrayed' (112);
צרות cɔrəs 'troubles; sufferings' (72, 196);
רחמנות raxmónəs 'pity; compassion; mercy' (174, 175);
שונאים sɔnəm 'enemies' (21);
שעכטין šɛxtn̩ 'slaughter' (43, 44, 45; note the spelling);
תפיסה tfisə 'gaol; custody' (178).

Many larger phraseological units of Hebrew origin are incorporated. A few are formulaic expressions which would not otherwise pass in Yiddish. Most of their vocabulary, however, is synchronically part of the lexical fund of Yiddish (see nos. 7–8 below). Many larger units conform with the known lexical and phraseological patterns of Yiddish (see nos. 9–10). Even such a phrase as אֶחָת דָתוֹ לְהָמִית áxas dásɔj ləhómis or axəs dasə ləjɔməs 'his only law [= verdict] is death' (133), which is a direct quotation from the Bible (Esther 4: 11), may be viewed as an idiomatic expression in Yiddish (cf. Mark and Joffe 1966: 856). Similarly, many of the lexical items belong to the pan-Yiddish category of periphrastic verbs (or 'inherently analytic verbs'; see D. Katz 1987a: 172–7 §9.2; Wexler 1980) formed with the auxiliaries זײַן zajn 'be', האָבן hobn̩ 'have', וערן vərn̩ 'become', or טאָן tɔn 'do' (see nos. 11–14). As a result, the phraseological and, to some extent, the morpho-syntactic fabric of this version remains markedly non-Germanized. This, of course, is in sharp contrast to its grammatical and syntactic features (cf. §§31.3.1–2, 31.5) and to the general avoidance of Semitisms which is so characteristic of some contemporary Western Yiddish texts (cf. §27.2).

7 אונד פֿאַנגט זיא אללי לעבענדיג כמה וכמה אלפֿים
und fangt zej álə lébn̩dik kamə vəkamə alɔfəm
'and [he] catches all of them alive, a few thousand [altogether]' (168–9);

8 אונד ליס יהודים צו זאם רופֿין מכמה קהילות וישובים
und liz jəhudəm cuzám rufn̩ məkamə kəhiləs vəjəšuvəm
'and [he] summons the Jews from a number of communities and villages' (182–3);

9 אונד פֿיהרט זיא גבונדין מיט ענוים קשים
und firt zej gəbúndn̩ mit inujəm kɔšəm
'and [he] led them [while they were] bound and in much pain' (170–1; cf. also M[N1783], 194);

10 דיא הרוגים וואַרפֿטין זיא אויש דער שטאָד אויף אײן תחום שבת וויט
di harúgəm varftn̩ zej ɔjs der štɔt af ejn txum šabəs vajt
'They threw the dead (lit. killed people) out of the city in a *tkhum* [= maximal distance within which it is permissible to carry on] Sabbath' (127–8; cf. also M[N1783], 194);

11 זיך נוקם זײַן zəx nɔjkəm zajn 'revenge; take vengeance' (21);
זיך מציל זײַן zəx macl̩ zajn 'save oneself' (21);
אונד איצונד ביסטו עובר שבועה und icúnd bístu ɔjvər švuə
'and now you are breaking your sworn promise' (142);

12 רחמנות האבֿין raxmónəs hobn̩ 'condone; have mercy' (175);

13 טוט תפֿילה צו גאָט tut tfílə cu gɔt 'prays to God' (41);
האבֿין אײן הרג רבֿ געטאָן hobn̩ an (h)érəg rav gətɔn
'[they] committed many murders' (146);

14 כמה אלפֿים יהודים זײַן נהרג ווארדין
kámə alɔ́fəm jəhudəm zajn nɛrəg vɔrdn̩
'A few thousand Jews were killed' (74).

31.5 Syntax

The 1783 Fürth edition exhibits a remarkable receptivity to New High German word-order patterns. Whereas inconsistencies in Germanization are often found in phonology and morphology (cf. above §§31.2.1, 31.3.2), the High German syntactic rules are thoroughly implemented. There are no instances of double negation, and only once is the more 'colloquial' main consecutive clause with finite verb in first place used (cf. 100–2). As in Reuven Halevi's translation of *Ben hamelekh vehanazir* (Frankfurt am Main, 1769; cf. §27.3), the final position is assigned to the finite verb in subordinate clauses (see no. 1 below). Similarly, past participles and infinitives are more often placed in a clause-final position (see nos. 2–3). The only noteworthy exception is one sentence in which the infinitive is fronted. As in modern Eastern Yiddish, the fronted infinitive may be analysed as topic (see no. 4).

1 װיא גאנטי ימח"ש מיט דיא יהודים װאהל פֿערטיג װאהר גינג ער
  vi gontə jímaxšmɔj mit di jəhudəm vɔjl fártik vɔr ging ər

  איבר דען הויפֿט מאן װאש די שטאד אויף גימאלבט האט
  ibər dən hójptman vɔs di štɔt úfgəmaxt hot

  'When Gonta, may his name be erased, was done with the Jews, he set about the marshal who opened [for him] the [gates of the] city' (136–8);

2 דער הויפֿט מאן זאגט דוא שװעהרשט יא דוא װילשט מיך לעבֿין לאזין
  dər hójptman zɔgt du švɛrst jɔ du vilst mix lɛbn̩ lɔzn̩

  'The marshal says you did swear [that] you will let me live' (141);

3 װיא גאנטי ימח"ש דאש געלט װאל גהאט האט ליס ער
  vi gontə jímaxšmɔj dɔs gɛlt vɔjl gəhat hot lis ər

  זיא צום פֿענסטר ארונטיר װארפֿין
  zej cum fɛnctər arúntərvarfn̩

  'When Gonta, may his name be erased, got all the money, he let them [be] thrown [from] the window' (107–8);

4 לאהבין טוט מען איהן מיט אללר האנד שמעקיט װאסיר
  lɔbn̩ tut mən in mit álərhand šmɛkə[x]t[s] (?) vásər

  'They kept reviving him with all kinds of scented liquids' (187–8).

The syntactic organization of each of the two main versions of *Mayse gdoyle min Uman* epitomizes the strikingly different linguistic and stylistic orientations of late eighteenth-century works. Fürth (1783), symbolic of the West, systematically adopts the socio-linguistically more prestigious patterns of German word order. The Eastern version by contrast, is entirely based on modern Eastern Yiddish. In both, Old Literary Yiddish norms are abandoned. The final placement of the finite verb in subordinate clauses becomes obligatory in MF1783, whereas in the old literary language it had been less consistent. This word order is totally abolished in the Eastern version.

32 The Language of the Eastern Version [Novidvor, *c*.1783]

The Eastern version is written in what we may call modern Eastern Yiddish. Many major features of morphology, lexicon, and especially syntax that in the course of the nineteenth century became part and parcel of the modern literary language can be found in this text. Its earlier edition (M[N1783]) has only a few archaic features. Their scarcity and context suggest that these are mostly stylistic survivals. It seems only natural that these features of older literary style could not be totally suppressed or surmounted even in this vivid and linguistically authentic description of the tragic events of 1768. However, their number is so minimal that even if its author did occasionally attempt to use the archaic forms as 'more literary' variants, his efforts were remarkably marginal and unsuccessful. The Novidvor(?) (*c*.1783) edition (= M[N1783]) will serve as the basis for the present examination of the Eastern version.

32.1 Orthography

The orthography of Yiddish books printed in late eighteenth- and early nineteenth-century Eastern Europe still awaits a detailed study. The period, roughly between the 1770s and the 1830s, provides a variegated corpus of texts, which exhibit varying degrees of adherence to older Yiddish spelling conventions and to the orthographic features of New High German intro-duced via Yiddish books printed in Western Europe. Some of these texts introduce many new features especially devised for a more adequate (or more 'modern' or both) representation of Eastern Yiddish phonology, such as the representation of certain consonants—e.g. ⟨טש⟩ for č, ⟨ה⟩ for word-initial x—and diphthongs—e.g. ⟨וי⟩ for vowels 44 and 42, which had earlier been represented by ⟨ו⟩, ⟨וי⟩, and ⟨א⟩. These orthographic features often go hand in hand with dialectal and hypercorrect spellings of certain stressed vowels, which in fact reveal to the modern researcher the actual dialect of a given author, editor, or printer.

These Eastern Yiddish orthographic features are largely absent from M[N1783]. Its spelling system is almost entirely based on the older ortho-graphic conventions. The fact that it was printed in the traditional type-font (*mashkit*) apparently contributed to the somewhat archaic nature of its spelling. At least until the second decade of the nineteenth century, Old

Yiddish orthography usually showed strong resilience in Eastern Yiddish texts printed with this type-font.

32.1.1 Unstressed Vowels

In accordance with Old Yiddish conventions, most of the unstressed vowels remain orthographically unrepresented. This applies to pretonic as well as posttonic vowels. As in other late eighteenth-century Eastern Yiddish printed works, some of these vowels are occasionally represented in M[N1783].

32.1.1.1 Pretonic Vowels

In general, the unstressed vowels often remain orthographically unrepresented in M[N1783]. However, the vowels of the gə- prefixes are far more often spelled than in MF1783, and this trend may be seen to derive from Old Yiddish (cf. e.g. Goldwasser 1982: 42). Most of the pretonic vowels that are usually spelled in M[N1783] belong to the past-participle prefix; e.g. גישלאָגן gəšlɔgn̩ 'beat' (5); גיקאָנט gəkɔnt 'could' (11); גיפֿרעסן gəfrɛsn̩ 'ate' (pej., 142); גיקומן gəkumən 'came' (15, 31, 49, 54). At the same time this vowel remains unrepresented in many other instances; e.g. גשריגן gəšrign̩ 'shouted' (24, 82); גפֿירט gəfirt 'lead' (past part., 111). In some items the representation of this vowel is inconsistent; e.g.:

גוועזן gəvɛzn̩ (20, 56, 68, 129, 135) ~ גיוועזן gəvɛzn̩ 'was' (13, 99, 121, 138);
גנומען gənumən (16) ~ גינומען gənumən 'took' (27, 117, 121, 133, 151);
גבראַכט gəbraxt (12) ~ גיבראַכט gəbraxt 'brought' (122, 136).

In some gə- prefixes the vowel is represented; e.g. גישאַנק gəšank 'present' (41); גינאָד gənɔd 'mercy' (72); גיוויין gəvejn 'cry' (28, 37, 99). But this is not always the case, and we sometimes find spellings such as גשרייא gəšrej 'scream' (28, 98, 109) and פֿאָר גוויש far gəvis 'for sure' (39).

The variant spellings of the prefix ba- reveal competition between ⟨בי⟩ and ⟨ב⟩. This variation is inherited from Old Yiddish orthography—e.g. ביקומן bakúmən 'receive' (48) ~ בפֿעל bafél 'order' (62)—and the new spelling ⟨בא⟩ in which the vowel is represented by the ⟨א⟩ grapheme—e.g. באקומן bikúmən 'receive' (29). This spelling is less frequent in M[N1783].

As in Old Yiddish, the vowels of the prefixes with covered syllables with final r—i.e. dər and far—remain orthographically unrepresented; e.g. דר ערט dər(h)ɛrt 'detected (by ear)' (83); זיך דר וועקט zəx dərvɛkt 'became alert' (126); פֿר מאַכט farmáxt 'closed' (55); פֿר טריבן fartríbn̩ 'expelled' (18); פֿר גיסן fargísn̩ 'shed [blood]' (150). In pre-modern Yiddish both these prefixes were written as separate words. Each was thus equated, at least orthographically, with the preposition far and the masculine definite article dər, respectively. The non-obligatory unstressed vowel representation applied to these two forms as well. This is strongly evident in M[N1783], where the vowels of the definite article dər and of the preposition far often remain unspelled; i.e. ⟨דר⟩ and ⟨פֿר⟩. In general, most of the unstressed vowels of covered syllables (pre- and post-tonic alike) with a final r were often omitted in Old Yiddish (cf. Goldwasser 1982: 42; on the Old Yiddish spelling coventions of gə-, fer-, der-, and bə- prefixes see Timm 1987: 225–33 §20).

On the other hand, the pretonic vowels are often spelled in most lexical items belonging to either geopolitical terminology or private names; e.g.:

צארוונא carévnə 'the (Russian) empress' (62, 438); צאראוני caróvnə (612);
קאמיסר kɔmisár 'commissary' (60); קאמיסאר kɔmisár (68, 87, 89);
פּאלקאוניק pɔlkóvnik 'colonel' (425, 430); פּולקאוניק pulkóvnik (434);
מאסקוויטר mɔsk(ə)vítər 'Muscovites' (418, 428);
פּאן מארקאוסקי pan markóvskə 'pan Markowski' (85–6, 87–8).

However, in some cases, the pretonic vowel remains unrepresented; e.g. זליזנאק žələzn(j)ák(?), 'Zhelezniak' (46); טטארענטיש tótarəntiš(?) 'Tatars' (74); קאממסר kɔmisár 'commissary' (79).

32.1.1.2 *Posttonic Vowels*   As was often the case in Old Yiddish (cf. Timm 1987: 227–8 §19.3.6), in the vast majority of -ən suffixes the unstressed vowel and the shewa remain unspelled in M[N1783]. This applies to most of the infinitives (see no. 1 below), first- and third-person plural present forms (no. 2), and strong past participles (no. 3):

1 גדענקן gədɛnkən 'to remember' (2); הרגנן hargənən 'to kill' (71);
   לײנן lej(ə)n(ə)n 'to read' (2);

2 קומן (מיר) (אום) (mir) kumən (um) '(we are going to) die' (169; cf. 174);
   זענן zɛnən 'were' (31 and elsewhere);

3 גגאנגן gəgangən 'went' (21, 144) ~ גישטאנן gəštanən 'stood' (32);
   גנומן gənumən 'took' (16).

Similarly, the vowel is not represented orthographically in the plural marker -ən; e.g. מאנן manən 'men' (12). Cases in which the unstressed vowel of the -ən suffix was spelled are very rare; e.g. זענין zénən 'were' (170, 214); בעטלין bɛtlən 'to beg (for food, money)' (104). The shewa of the -n̩ suffixes (mostly with infinitives, strong past participles, and first- and third-person plural present forms) is generally unrepresented. However, there are quite often alternative spellings in which the shewa is represented by ⟨י⟩; e.g. אן גהויבין óngɛhɔjbn̩ 'began' (104); גיוועזין gəvɛzn̩ 'was' (317); טערקין tɛrkn̩ 'Turks' (229). In addition, the grapheme ⟨י⟩ is more often used in M[N1783] for posttonic vowels; e.g. שעפֿליך šéjfələx 'little sheep' (pl., 295); נעביך nébəx 'poor thing; oh dear!' (adv., 250); גרענין grɛnəc 'border' (341); גיקאוויט gəkɔvət 'put into chains' (p.p., 451).

Posttonic vowels are mostly unrepresented, especially in covered syllables with final r; e.g. ביינר bejnər 'bones' (217); קלוֹסטר klɔjstər 'church' (222, 227). Occasionally, however, they are represented by ⟨ʼ⟩ or ⟨ו⟩ graphemes; e.g. טאטיר tɔtər 'Tatar' (352); האַרמטום harmátəs 'cannon' (pl., 321);

32.1.2 *Consonants*

Only a few modifications are introduced in the otherwise conventional graphemic representation of consonants. The orthographic treatment of sibilants and shibilants largely continues the Old Yiddish convention according to which ⟨ש⟩ can be used for both and ⟨ס⟩ only for sibilants. Similarly, there is no systematic distinction between š and č such as had been introduced earlier in *Ben hameylekh vehanozir* (cf. §28.1.2). Nevertheless, the spelling of certain lexical items of the Slavonic component introduces the grapheme ⟨טש⟩ for č; e.g. האָטשה ⟨hotše⟩ for xɔčə 'at least' (308); מוטשין ⟨mutšin⟩ for mučən 'suffer' (481). The older spelling system is not sufficiently modified in order to represent the modern Eastern Yiddish combination šč; e.g. פּיינטצני ⟨pantcni⟩ for panščənə 'statute labour' (390). Alternative spellings of this word are given in the later editions. They include פּאַנטשינע ⟨pantšine⟩ pán(š)činə and the Polonized פּאַנשציזנע ⟨panšcizne⟩ pánšciznə (or pánščiznə; cf. modern Yiddish spelling פּאַנשטשינע). The Old Yiddish spelling of the syllable-final p is often preserved, and is even wrongly introduced sometimes; e.g. די קעפּף אראָפּף גינומן di kɛp arópgɛnumən '[they] cut off their heads' (361; cf. also 164, 204, 279). However, M[N1783] sometimes follows the contemporary Eastern Yiddish spelling practice whereby the syllable-initial f and the syllable-final p are represented by ⟨פֿ⟩ and ⟨פּ⟩ respectively; e.g. פֿערד fɛrd 'horse' (105); אָפּ טרעטן óptrɛtn̩ 'retreat; give up' (25, 564).

Another characteristic of contemporary Eastern Yiddish printed works is the ⟨טש⟩ grapheme for the post-vocal and post-liquid c; e.g. אַלטש alc 'continuously (adv.); everything (pron.)' (81, 143, 149, 245, 327, 527); עטש ɛc 'you!' (voc., 109, 439; cf. §11.1.3); קלאָטש klɔc '(butcher's) block' (188); אַל דאָש גוטש al dɔs gutc 'all the best' (greeting, 38). The last form is orthographically and possibly phonetically levelled with the others on the basis of its phonetic realization guc; hence [*guts → *guc →] gutc (on the form גוץ guc for St.Y. גוטס guts 'goods' see §15.1; cf. also such phonetic spelling as עלצטן ɛlctn̩ (← ɛltstn̩) 'to the superior', lit. 'to the oldest' (321)).

32.2 Phonology

Given the conservative nature of its orthography, M[N1783] has only a few spellings that would lend themselves to a significant evaluation of its phonological features. These suffice, however, for an approximate reconstruction of the underlying stressed-vowel system characteristic of the writer's (or printer's) dialect. These spellings comprise the evidence of h dropping, as well as the variant representations of some stressed vowels which point to Southeastern Yiddish. Other cases may not necessarily be exclusive to Eastern Yiddish texts of that period. However, given the extra-linguistic characteristics of this account, its other non-Northeastern dialectal features are more likely to be of Southeastern provenance.

32.2.1 *Loss of Functional* [h]

Two spellings clearly testify to the loss of the functional h:

1 האנטלאָפֿן hantlɔ́fn̩ 'ran away' (p.p., 20)
2 דר ערט dərért 'heard' (p.p., 84).

The first form is a hypercorrection with an inorganic h phoneme (cf. St.Y. אַנטלאָפֿן antlɔ́fn̩); the second is an orthographic omission of an etymo-logically expected h (cf. St.Y. דערהערט dərhért). Each represents one of the two possible effects of h dropping. The dialectal spread of the inorganic and that of the omitted h largely coincide (see Herzog 1965a: 220 §5.22; 221 Maps 5:100 and 5:101). The loss of stem-initial h in modern Eastern Yiddish has also been attested in the Southwestern regions of Northeastern Yiddish (cf. Veynger 1926: 189, 190, 191; 1929: 132). The heartland of this development was the Southeastern dialect area (cf. Veynger 1926: 196–8; U. Weinreich 1963: 344–8 §2.3, 352–3 §3.3).

32.2.2 *Stressed Vowels*

Graphemic representation of stressed vowels is the most important, and apparently the oldest, rule of Yiddish spelling. The only stressed vowel whose representation was non-obligatory was the interconsonantal a, which corre-sponds with the historical vowels 11 and 13 in all Yiddish dialects and with vowels 24 and 44 in Western Yiddish (see Joffe 1954: 105 ff.; on the ortho-graphic treatment of these vowels in Old Yiddish see Timm 1987: 93 ff. §1; 186 ff. §13; 194 ff. §14).

In M[N1783] there are many variant graphemic realizations of certain stressed vowels. But only a few of these are significant for a dialectological analysis of this text. Others derive from Old Yiddish spelling conventions. (See Table 24; the inventory does not include phonologically irrelevant representations.)

32.2.2.1 *Vowel Lowering before* [x]   Vowel 32 before x is systematically spelled with a ⟨ע⟩ grapheme in the case of געך gɛx for גיך gix 'quick'. This rare spelling reflects the lowering of front vowels before x and r that occurred in

Table 24 The graphemic inventory of stressed vowels in *Mayse gdoyle min Uman umin Ukrayne* [Novidvor,] *c.*1783

grapheme	vowels
⟨א⟩	11/12/13/41/42
⟨ו⟩	12/13/41/42/44/51/52
⟨וי⟩	42/44/54
⟨י⟩	31/32/51
⟨יי⟩	11/22/24/34/41
⟨ע⟩	21/25

most Eastern Yiddish dialect regions (see M. Weinreich 1965: 73 ff.; Herzog 1965*a*: 191–7 §5.13.5). In Southeastern Yiddish it resulted in the ε realization of neutralized vowels (see M. Weinreich 1965: 75, 77, 85 §(f)). The spelling ⟨ע⟩ is truly phonetic in this case. It corresponds to the allophonic realization of the neutralized vowel in Southeastern Yiddish. Analogous spelling becomes characteristic of some of the contemporary Eastern Yiddish printed works (e.g. SSh1796; see §15.2.3).

32.2.2.2 *Merger of Vowels* 11 *and* 34 A number of spellings reveal the merger of vowels 11 (NEY a ‖ MEY ă ‖ SEY a ‖ ɔ) and 34 (NEY aj ‖ MEY ā ‖ SEY a). Vowel 34 is spelled more phonetically in one lexical item where the ⟨א⟩ grapheme occurs; i.e. באלן for baln̩ 'bumps' (436; cf. St.Y. and NEY ביילן bajln̩, MEY baln̩). Conversely, the grapheme ⟨יי⟩ is occasionally used to represent vowel 11; e.g. שפייר דיך ניט špar dəx nit 'do not be stubborn; do not argue' (64; cf. conventional spelling שפארין šparn̩ 'to argue', 61); פיינטצני pánščənə or pánščinə 'statute labour' (390).

The phonological merger of vowels 11 and 34 could have taken place only in Southeastern Yiddish. In Mideastern Yiddish it would be an orthographic merger only (a vs. ā), because the phonological opposition remains intact. Vowel length was never marked in Yiddish orthography. But it is possible that to a Mideastern Yiddish speaker the grapheme ⟨יי⟩ was associated with the long ā realization in such frequent lexemes as וייב vāp (St.Y. vajb) 'wife' and מיין mān (St.Y. majn) 'my, mine', which stands in clear opposition to the short realization of vowel 11, usually spelled with ⟨א⟩ or zero (cf. MEY hănt ≠ hānt, spelled ה(א)נט ≠ היינט 'hand' vs. 'today'). On the other hand, the a realization of vowel 11 was socially more acceptable in Southeastern Yiddish, where this opposition was neutralized into (h)ant for both forms, hence ⟨האנט⟩ = ⟨היינט⟩.

32.2.2.3 *Merger of Vowels* 51 *and* 31 The spelling גווישט gəvist 'known' (p.p., 75, 226, 251; cf. St.Y. געוואוסט gəvust) can be found in some early eighteenth-century Western Yiddish texts (cf. above §31.2.3), where it is possibly associated with the Midwestern i realization of vowel **51**. This spelling could also have resulted from the orthographically inconvenient combination of three consecutive *vov* graphemes; i.e. ⟨וווֹ⟩. According to Dubnov's publication of the Sadilkov (1834) and Vilna (1845) editions of the Eastern version, this item was consistently spelled גיװישט ⟨givšt⟩ or גיװסט ⟨givst⟩ with an unusual zero representation of the stressed vowel. However, in our text the spelling גוװישט gəvist could certainly be motivated, or at least enhanced, by the Mideastern or Southeastern i realizations of vowel **51**. On the other hand, the name of one of the Cossack leaders, Shilo, is given as סולה ⟨sula⟩ (p. 12). The representation of š with ⟨ס⟩ is puzzling for a non-Northeastern text. It is clear, however, that the grapheme ⟨ו⟩ usually used for vowels **51** and **52** is here used for etymological i. The name was apparently pronounced šilə ~ silə or šilɔ ~ silɔ. In the later editions it is spelled with ⟨י⟩.

Another possible indication of the merger of vowels **51** (NEY u ‖ MEY ī ‖ SEY i | ī | i) and **31** (NEY i ‖ MEY ī ‖ SEY i | ī | i) into a unitary i is provided by the following lexical alternation. The preposition untər 'under' is sometimes used where hintər 'behind; at the back of' is semantically and etymologically expected; e.g. אונטר דר שטאָט untər dər štɔt 'close to the town; in the suburbs' (p. 3, ll. 52, 56; cf. St.Y. הינטער דער שטאָט hintər dər štɔt). This usage is also evident in other texts of the Eastern version. Both these forms could have become homophonic only in an 'h-dropping' dialect such as Southeastern Yiddish and the Eastern varieties of Mideastern Yiddish. The so-called h dropping is sufficiently attested in M[N1783] (see above §32.2.1). The substitution of untər for (h)intər in Eastern Yiddish is a well-known phenomenon, attested in a Yiddish quotation that appears in a collection of rabbinic responsa of 1640 (cf. Rubashov 1929: 138 no. 71; Mark 1971: 684 §16). It is possible, however, that this particular usage untər dər štɔt has a Slavonic analogue. The prepositions *pod* (Pol.), під (Ukr.), and под (Russ.), all primarily meaning 'under', can be used, mostly with various toponyms (names of cities, towns, regions, districts, etc.), as prepositions of place, meaning 'in the vicinity of; in the suburbs of' (cf. *pod Warszawą*, під Полтавою; под Москвой). But here untər is not used with a specific geographical name. Given the evidence of h dropping, as well as the corroborative evidence of other dialectal spellings, we may view this usage as a possible indicator of the merger of vowels **52** and **32**.

Parallel to this merger we may infer the convergence of vowels **52** (NEY u ‖ MEY ī ‖ SEY i|ī) and **32** (NEY i ‖ MEY ī ‖ SEY i|ī) into a unitary i.

32.2.2.4 *Vowels 12 and 13 Yield* [u]   Neither old nor modern Yiddish conventional spellings of vowels **12** and **13** (both yielding NEY ɔ ‖ MEY u ‖ SEY u) reveal much their Mideastern and Southeastern realizations. The graphemic representation of this vowel in M[N1783] is ⟨ו⟩ throughout. It may be, however, that the spelling קראָז kruž 'jug; pitcher' (p. 9), indicates that the ⟨אָ⟩ grapheme was apparently used to represent a stressed u vowel (cf. Old Polish *kruż* 'jug', Russ. кружка 'mug'; but cf. §32.3 no. 19).

32.2.2.5 *Possible Realizations of Vowel 25*　　In M[N1783] there is one, otherwise exceptional spelling of vowel 25 (NEY ε ‖ MEY ej ‖ SEY i|ej) with ⟨י⟩: ביטן bejtņ 'ask; beg' (p. 15; cf. St.Y. בעטן bɛtņ). This spelling of a stressed ε was somewhat archaic for the late eighteenth century. Our text has a few other outdated Old Yiddish spelling conventions (most notably ⟨ו⟩ for ɔ in הוט hɔt 'has' and הובן hɔbņ 'have'). The grapheme ⟨י⟩ is often used in the Eastern Yiddish *Seyfer khsidem* (Zholkve, 1776), where it apparently denotes the Southeastern merger of vowels 22 (NEY ej ‖ MEY aj ‖ SEY ej) and 25 into ej. However, in the case of ⟨ביטן⟩, M[N1783] does not employ one of its markedly archaic or older spellings (cf. above §30.2.1); rather, we have here a rare dialectal spelling modelled by analogy on such cases as שטיין štejn 'stand' (p. 20) with vowel 22, which converges with 25 only in Southeastern Yiddish (cf. §7.1.3). Another possible realization exclusively characteristic of the 'Podolian' variety of Southeastern Yiddish is i (bitņ; see U. Weinreich 1958b: 235–6, 240; 1958c: 230–1; Wolf 1976: 36–7 §3.4; D. Katz 1983: 1030 §8.1.2). Geographically, the i realization appears to be more realistic (cf. Herzog 1969: 62–4 §3.1 Map 3). Socio-linguistically, the ej realization of vowel 25 (common to both Mideastern and Southeastern dialects) was apparently more prestigious.

32.2.2.6 *The Stressed-Vowel System*　　Given the extra-linguistic factors, the Eastern version of *Mayse gdoyle min Uman umin Ukrayne* was probably either written by a speaker of Southeastern Yiddish or based on oral testimonies of survivors, who were most likely to be Southeasterners. Either way, it seems only natural to suggest that the underlying vowel system of this text is more likely to match the Southeastern dialect. This suggestion cannot be refuted on the grounds of the stressed vowel representation of M[N1783].

The first reconstruction offered in Table 25 is based strictly on the graphemic evidence of M[N1783]. The only assumption, which cannot be borne out by most Yiddish spelling systems, is the apparent loss of the long–short vowel opposition. Vowels given in square brackets could not be directly identified from their graphemic representations in the text. The second reconstruction is a radical interpretation of the dialectal spellings. The u realization of vowel 54, as well as the socially less prestigious ɔ and i realizations of vowels 11 and 25, are inferred as structurally (synchronically) the most probable phonemes of Southeastern Yiddish. The third reconstruction is a 'compromise' between the first two. Vowels that were not identified directly from the various dialectal spellings are accepted with the exception of the 'too radical' inferences of the phonemic value of vowels 11, 25, and 54.

Table 25 Reconstruction of the stressed-vowel system in *Mayse gdoyle min Uman umin Ukrayne* [Novidvor,] c.1783

(a) strictly on the graphemic evidence		
$i_{31/32/51/52}$		$u_{12/13}$
$ej_{22/24/25}$		$[\text{ɔj}_{42/44/54}]$
	$a_{11/34}$	
(b) radical reconstruction		
$i_{31/32/51/52/25}$		$u_{12/13/54}$
$ej_{22/24}$		$ɔj_{42/44}$
$ɛ_{21}$		$ɔ_{41/11}$
	a_{34}	
(c) compromise		
$i_{31/32/51/52}$		$u_{12/13}$
$ej_{22/24/25}$		$ɔj_{42/44/54}$
$ɛ_{21}$		$ɔ_{41}$
	$a_{11/34}$	

32.3 Lexicon

A significant increase in items of Semitic origin is characteristic of this and of other contemporary Eastern Yiddish texts (cf. §27.2). What appeared to be extraordinary for the otherwise heavily Germanized Western version (cf. §31.4 on MF1783) is of course the norm for the Eastern version. A large number of Semitisms became fully acceptable, and in many cases frequently used, in the Eastern version; e.g. שררה srɔrə 'lord' (p. 2); כלי זיין klɔzajən 'arms' (pp. 5, 8); מתנות matɔnəs 'presents' (p. 13); פריצים pricəm 'lords, landowners' (pp. 3, 9); תיכּף tejkəf 'at once, immediately' (pp. 8, 9, 14, 15); חלילה xɔlilə 'heaven forbid' (p. 6); עולם ɔjləm 'crowd; public' (p. 7); עצה האלטן ejcə haltn̩ 'consult' (pp. 2, 12).

However, simple verbs of the type גנבענען gánvənən 'steal' are still very rare. Most verbs derived from the Semitic component belong to the paradigm of periphrastic (or inherently analytic) verbs; e.g. פטור ווערן pɔtər vɛrn̩ 'get rid of' (40, 504); ניצול ווערן nicl̩ vɛrn̩ 'be saved' (260); זיך מיישב זיין zəx məjašəv zajn 'deliberate, reflect' (68); מרמה זיין məramə zajn 'deceive' (121). By contrast, only a few simple verbs are used; e.g. גיהרגת gə(h)argət 'killed' (207, 216, 280, 285); אויש הרגנן ójs(h)argənən 'kill, liquidate' (256); שעכֿטן šɛxtn̩ 'slaughter' (102); גישאַחטן gəšɔxtn̩ 'slaughtered' (541; note the 'naturalized' and 'semi-naturalized' spellings of the last two forms). It is possible that in some cases in which a parallel simple verb exists, the periphrastic form was preferred as a more 'literary' variant; e.g. זיך מיישב זיין zəx məjašəv zajn 'deliberate, reflect', rather than *יישובֿן זיך jišəvn̩ zəx 'deliberate, consider' (cf. 68).

The situation is somewhat different with regard to lexical items of Slavonic origin. On the one hand, these are found in the Eastern version, which is not the case in many contemporary works (e.g. BZ1771, SZ1776, VS[1783], AH1795). However, on the whole their number is still relatively small. The author of this work must have been aware of the traditional stylistic aversion to words of Slavonic origin (cf. §§7.2.2–3). Most of these lexical items belong to geopolitical and military terminology (see below nos. 2, 4, 12–15, 17, 20). Others are used for objects for which the author seems not to have been able to find a non-Eastern Yiddish equivalent (see nos. 1, 3, 10, 11, 16, 19). Finally we find a number of older Eastern Yiddish words (e.g. nos. 7 and 9, cf. M. Weinreich 1973: ii. 184 §144; 201 §151; 203 §151.1), and some well-established modern Eastern Yiddish lexical items (see nos. 5, 6, 8, 18). Of these, נעביך nɛbəx 'poor thing' and האטשה xɔčə 'although' were often acceptable in the older literary language (cf. §§5.1 and 7.2.2). Our text, however, introduces האטשה xɔčə as an adverb meaning 'at least'.

Lexical items of Slavonic origin

1 בראָם bram 'gate' (55, 82, 93),
   cf. Pol. *brama*;

2 דונצית dɔncəs 'Cossacks from the river Don area' (408, 440, 442, 445),
   cf. Russ. донец (sing.), донцы (pl.);

3 דיבות dibəs 'stocks' (423, 424, 447),
   cf. Ukr. диби;

4 האַרממאַ (h)armátə 'cannon' (55, 95, 133),
   cf. Ukr. гармата, Pol. *armata*;

5 האטשה xɔčə 'at least' (308),
   cf. Pol. *choć(by)*, Ukr. хоча (б);

6 גיהאַפֿט gəxapt 'caught' (95, 106, 128, 328),
   cf. Pol. *chapać* 'catch', Ukr. хапати;

7 יאַטקי קלאָץ játkə klɔc 'butcher's chopping block' (188),
   cf. Czech *jatka* 'slaughter house';

8 מוטשין זיך mučən zəx 'suffer; torture oneself' (481),
   cf. Ukr. мучитися, Pol. *męczyć się*;

9 נעביך nɛbəx 'poor thing; oh dear!' (adv., 214, 250, 358, 627, 634, 644),
    cf. Czech *nebohý* 'unfortunate, poor' (adj.);

10 פאלי pɔlə 'lap of a garment' (95),
    cf. Pol. *poła*, Ukr. пола;

11 פאלים paləs 'piles' (85),
    cf. Pol. *pal* 'pile', Ukr. паля;

12 פאלקאָוניק pɔlkóvnik 'colonel' (428, 430, 431),
    cf. Ukr. полковник;
    פולקאָוניק pulkóvnik 'colonel' (434),
    cf. Pol. *pułkownik*;

13 פאן pan 'lord, sire' (att., 85, 87),
    cf. Pol. *pan*, Ukr. пан;

14 פיינטצני pánščinə 'statute labour' (390),
    cf. Ukr. панщина, Pol. *pańszczyzna*;

15 פראווים pravəs 'rights; (Russo-Turkish) agreements' (341),
    cf. Pol. *prawa*, Ukr. права 'rights';

16 פרענגר prɛngər 'pillory' (480),
    cf. Pol. *pręgierz*;

17 צארוונא carévnə/carívne 'the (Russian) empress' (62, 334, 340, 438);
    צאראוני caróvnə (612),
    cf. Ukr. царівна 'royal princess', Russ. царевна;

18 גיקאווים gəkɔvət 'put into chains' (451),
    cf. Pol. *okuwać*, *skowany*; Ukr. кувати, оковувати;

19 קראז kruž 'jug' (235),
    cf. Old Polish *kruž* 'jug', Russ. кружка 'mug', but cf. also in Dutch *kroos* [krus]
    'mug; jug';

20 רוביל rubļ 'roubles' (98),
    cf. Pol. *rubel*, Ukr. рубель, Russ. рубль.

A number of these lexical items exhibit some of the major patterns of
morphological adaptation of the Slavonic component into modern Yiddish.
These comprise a compound noun with the main stress on the first component (יאַטקי קלאָין játkə klɔc 'butcher's chopping block', no. 7), an infinitive
and two past participles formed in two cases with a thematic vowel (מוטשין זיך
mučən zəx 'suffer', no. 8; גיהאָפט gəxapt 'caught' and גיקאָוויט gəkɔvət 'put
into chains', nos. 6 and 18), and many nouns with the plural marker -*s* (e.g.
פראווים pravəs 'rights; (Russo-Turkish) agreements', פאלים paləs 'piles', see
above nos. 2, 3, 11, 15).

The plural marker -*s* in words of Slavonic origin is usually represented by
⟨ות-⟩—e.g. האַרמטות harmátəs 'cannon' (pl., 365, 397); דיבות díbəs 'stocks'
(see above nos. 2, 3)—which is the conventional spelling of the plural
marker of the Semitic component; e.g. צרות cɔrəs 'troubles' (6), נפשות nəfašəs
'souls; people' (205). It is uncertain whether the two kinds of plural

marker—viz. ⟨ה׳־⟩ and ⟨(ע)ס־⟩ (both yielding -(ə)s)—are etymologically related. (For strong support of the Semitic origin of the s-plural see King 1990; for a different opinion see M. Weinreich 1973: ii. 277 §164.4.) The writer or printer of this work obviously preferred the quasi-etymological spelling. An analogous case appears to be pɔlákn̦ 'Poles' spelled three times as פאלקים ⟨polakim⟩ (100, 462, 465) and once as פאלקין ⟨polakin⟩ (337). It stands to reason that in the spoken language the actual plural morpheme was -n̦, not -əm (cf. St.Y. פאַלאַקן pɔlákn̦; it is noteworthy, however, that Marion Aptroot observes the form polējkəm in Jewish Dutch).

In some cases it is possible to specify from which co-territorial Slavonic language a given lexical item was introduced (see M. Weinreich 1973: ii. 198-9 §150). Apart from the older items (nos. 7, 9), there are forms that entered Yiddish from Ukrainian (e.g. nos. 3, 4, 8, 14), and others that entered from Polish (e.g. nos. 13, 16). However, in most instances the particular source language is uncertain. It is also unclear why the original plural form did not, as with all other items, yield a plural form in Yiddish (no. 1) or how the ultimately Russian царевна [carévna] 'royal princess' came to mean in our text 'the (Russian) empress' (no. 17), even though Catherine the Great certainly was a royal princess at the beginning of her career. Could it be that in the wake of the events of 1768 the empress (who reigned in 1762-96) was still referred to as 'the princess'?

32.4 Morphology

One of the most striking characteristics of the Eastern version is its essentially modern morphology. It has a limited stock of exceptional features, which stand out as remarkably archaic for this version. If the Eastern Yiddish account was written in the last three decades of the eighteenth century, these features would be surprisingly rare, and they may be explained either as a few survivals of the old literary language or in most cases as stylistically conditioned forms. Less surprising, though by no means less significant, is that most of these features were abandoned in the later Sadilkov (1834) and Vilna (1845) editions of the Eastern version.

All in all, this version presents us with the earliest coherent sample of modern Yiddish morphology employed in a literary monument. Among its most essential features, which subsequently formed the foundations of Modern Literary Yiddish, are the new plural and diminutive formation of nouns (see §§35.1 and 35.2), the restructured case system (§35.6), the modern network of functional words (§35.7), the morphologically differentiated future-tense and passive-voice auxiliaries (§35.9; cf. §28.3.34), and the more developed system of verbal aspect (§35.10). All these are discussed in Chapter 8. At present we shall focus on the few archaic features of M[N1783] and on their significance for the dynamics of linguistic change at one of its most advanced stages.

32.4.1 *Archaic Features*

A number of features found in M[N1783] stand in clear opposition to its overwhelmingly Eastern and modern language. Because of their scarcity and their subsequent irrelevance to Modern Literary Yiddish, these features cannot be qualified as other than 'archaic'. By contrast, such archaic features were still surviving in and in some cases were characteristic of many other late eighteenth- and early nineteenth-century literary texts.

The following is a list of archaic forms found in M[N1783]. The modern variants which replaced most of them in Sadilkov (1834) and Vilna (1845) editions are supplied. Only a few older forms remained unchanged in the later editions (see nos. 1.2, 1.4, 2.1, 5.1 below). Two others were omitted (see nos. 4.4 and 4.7).

[Novidvor] (*c.*1783)   **Sadilkov (1834) and Vilna (1845)**

1 Passive-voice construction

1. 1 אנטרונן [. . .] ווארן vɔrn̩ antrúnən   אנטרונין גיווארין antrúnən gəvɔrn̩
'escaped' (375–6);

1. 2 ווארן פֿר טריבן vɔrn̩ fartríbn̩   ווארין פֿר טריבין vɔrn̩ fartríbn̩
'exiled' (378);

1. 3 ווארן געהערט vɔrn̩ gəhɛrt   גיהערט גיווארין gəhɛrt gəvɔrn̩
'heard' (590);

1. 4 ווארן גיקוילט vɔrn̩ gəkɔjlət   ווארין גיקוילט vɔrn̩ gəkɔjlət
'(were) butchered' (618),

2 Periphrastic possessive

2. 1 אן דעם תוגר זיין ידיעה   אן דעם תוגר זיין ידיעה
ɔn dəm túgar zajn jədiə   ɔn dəm túgar zajn jədiə
'without the Turk's consent' (338);

2. 2 מיט גאט זיינר הילף mit gɔt zajnər hilf   [שם]'ה[רצה]י א[ם] mírcə((h)a)šɛm
'with God's help'   'God willing' (405),

3 Declinable possessive pronouns

3. 1 נאך אונזרן טויט nɔx undzərn̩ tɔjt   נאך אונזר טויט nɔx undzər tɔjt
'after our death' (170);

3. 2 אין דיינר ליבה תורה in dajnər libə tɔjrə   אין דיין תורה in dajn tɔjrə
'in your dear Torah'   'in your Torah' (652),

4 Genitive of possessive pronouns

4.1 דיין אויגן dajn ɔjgṇ   דייני אויגין dajnə ɔjgṇ
'Your eyes' (640);

4.2 זיין קינדר zajn kindər   זייני קינדר zajnə kindər
'his children' (160);

4.3 אין זיין צייטן in zajn cajtṇ   אין זייני צייטין in zajnə cajtṇ
'in his time' (591);

4.4 אונזר שונאים undzər sɔnəm   _____ 'our enemies' (486);

4.5 מיט אונזר אויגן mit undzər ɔjgṇ   מיט אונזרי אויגין mit undzərə ɔjgṇ
'with our eyes' (648);

4.6 זייר ביינר zejər bejnər   זיירע ביינר zejərə bejnər
'their bones' (196);

4.7 זייר שווערדן zejər švɛrdṇ   _____ 'their swords' (445);

4.8 זייר [. . .] נשמות zejər nəšɔməs   זיירע [. . .] נשמות zejərə nəšɔməs
'their souls' (566),

5 Third-person plural possessive pronoun

5.1 אירי גלידר irə glidər   אירי גלידר irə glidər
'their limbs' (153),

6 Short-form zajn 'are'

6.1 דיא יהודים וואש זיין אלי גיוועזן   די יהודים וואש זיינין אלי גיוועזין
di jidṇ vɔs zajn alə gəvezṇ   di jidṇ vɔs zajnən alə gəvezṇ
'all the Jews that were [. . .]' (123),

7 Accusative of the masculine definite article

7.1 דען הייבט מאן dən héjbtman   דעם הייבט מאן dəm héjbtman
'the [Turkish] commander' (dat., 324);

7.2 נאך דען תליון nɔx dən taljən   נאך דעם תליון nɔx dəm taljən
'after the hangman' (prep. c., 472);

7.3 אונטר דען הימל unter dən himḷ   אונטר דעם הימל unter dəm himḷ
'under the sky' (prep. c., 509);

7.4 דען זומר dən zumər   דעם זומר dəm zumər
'this summer' (acc., 542);

7.5 אין דען יאר in dɛn jɔr   אין דעם יאר in dɛm jɔr
'(during) this year' (prep. c., 584);

7.6 פֿר דען אלמעכֿטיגן גאט   פֿאר דעם אלמאכֿטיגן גאט
far dən alméxtikṇ gɔt   far dəm almáxtikṇ gɔt
'before God almighty' (658–9).

Most of these forms are so rare that we may safely consider them residues of the old literary language. This applies to the periphrastic possessive constructions (no. 2 above), the declinable attributive possessive pronouns (no. 3), and the forms אירי irə 'their' and זיין zajn 'are' (nos. 5 and 6). More frequent are the old passive-voice construction (no. 1), the genitive of possessive pronouns (no. 4), and the historical accusative of the masculine definite article (no. 7). Yet they too are markedly rare.

Some of these features—e.g. the old ('imperfective') passive-voice construction, the periphrastic possessive construction, and the declinable possessive pronouns—may still have been current in the spoken Eastern Yiddish of that period (cf. §28.3.2 Table 16, §28.3.2.2, §35.5.1). However, our text indirectly testifies to their apparent decline in spoken Southeastern Yiddish.

It is remarkable that all other archaic forms are proportionately more frequently used in the shorter *kine* appended to the main text of the account (493–658). This is hardly a coincidence. The anonymous author was apparently far more style-conscious when writing the more formal *kine*. The alphabetical arrangement into short paragraphs opening with Hebrew quotations and formulaic phrases and the less than successful attempt to write it in rhyme indicate that the *kine* was intended as a commemorative para-liturgical text. Stronger awareness of style and form in the *kine* apparently led to the significant increase in archaic forms (see nos. 1.2–4, 3.2, 4.1, 4.3, 4.5, 4.8, 7.3–6).

Insignificant as these features may be for the overall linguistic evaluation of the Eastern version, they illustrate a crucial aspect of the shift from the Old to the nascent Modern Literary Yiddish. Not only are the lexicon and morphology of M[N1783] directly based on Eastern Yiddish, but its syntax too is remarkably modern. It provides an early, possibly the earliest known, example of some of the major modern sentence types. Its word-order patterns almost fully agree with those of the modern literary language. The whole structure of the literary language had shifted towards modern Eastern Yiddish, and whatever traditional stylistic preferences survived were mostly restricted to the realms of morphology and lexicon. A number of archaic, mostly morphological features apparently continued to be perceived as more 'formal' and possibly more 'correct', or in some cases as stylistically more 'appropriate' variants. However, their actual incidence in this work is so marginal that even in the late 1820s and 1830s *Mayse gdoyle min Uman umin Ukrayne* would be considered one of the most significant works in modern Eastern Yiddish. Indeed, now that we have every reason to believe that the earlier edition appeared in the 1780s, it fully deserves the title of the most remarkable early monument of the nascent modern literary language.

8

Shift: A Comparative Analysis

33 Introduction

Eastern Yiddish works of the late eighteenth century were by and large conceived or presented within the semiotic matrix of conventional pre-modern Yiddish literature. However, the linguistic shift towards contemporary Eastern Yiddish is evident in all these texts. It transpired during the period in which Early New Yiddish was rapidly advancing towards its modern stage (taking the New Yiddish period as *c.*1800 to the present; see Table 30). Therefore, the significance of these works for the earliest history or the immediate pre-history of the modern literary language cannot be overlooked. Nevertheless, their language has remained virtually untouched by modern Yiddish scholarship, with the exception of Moyshe Markuze's *Eyzer Yisroel* (Poritsk, 1790), which has been discussed and analysed from linguistic, socio-cultural, and textological perspectives (see e.g. Prilutski 1917*a*; Reyzen 1923: 83–101; Tsinberg 1935: 185–203; Herzog 1965*b*; Roskies 1974*b*: 13–16; Shmeruk 1977; 1978: 187–97; 1981: 184–203). Other works that have often been singled out as the earliest known literary monuments of modern Eastern Yiddish are *Ben hameylekh vehanozir* (Zholkve, 1771; cf. Reyzen 1932: 178; Shtif 1932*a*: 36; Roskies 1974*b*: 4–5) and *Mayse gdoyle min Uman umin Ukraine* ([Novidvor], *c.*1783; cf. Reyzen 1920: 27; Shtif 1932*a*: 35–6). But the language of these two works has not been examined.

The fact that these texts have not been studied systematically is to the detriment of our general knowledge of the early stages of modernization of the literary languages and of the earliest history of Modern Literary Yiddish in particular. This chapter offers a comparative linguistic examination of these texts. Although each work represents a different degree of shift from the old literary language to Eastern Yiddish in a literary form, they will be treated as constituents of the same corpus. The two extremes are the earliest work written on the basis of Eastern Yiddish, *Ben hameylekh vehanozir* (Zholkve, 1771), and the first original book written entirely in Eastern Yiddish, the Eastern version of *Mayse gdoyle min Uman umin Ukrayne* (Novidvor(?), *c.*1783), which have been discussed separately in Chapters 6 and 7.

To begin with, these books will be analysed from the perspective of Eastern Yiddish dialects (§34). In most cases the adoption of some narrow dialectal features testifies to the direct impact of the Southeastern or Northeastern dialects on the literary language (§§34.1–2). In other cases the attempt to preserve certain grammatical features that were lost in the Northeastern dialect of some authors may be viewed as the first steps towards the eventual evolution of Modern Literary Yiddish as a supradialectal linguistic formation (§34.3).

Then the examination will focus on the ongoing restructuring of the literary language (§35). Within the broader context of the continuity of Yiddish as a literary language, each of these books participated in the linguistic shift from Old Literary towards nascent Modern Literary Yiddish. The Old Yiddish forms, morphological categories, and syntactic patterns were dwindling in some of the texts, and disappearing in others (the dynamics of change being summarized in §35.11). Subsequently a new literary language emerged. In nearly all cases it was based entirely on modern Eastern Yiddish.

In what follows, the references to AH1795, SZ1776, and VS[1783] are by line numbers as these texts are reprinted in the Appendices (pp. 312–19, 297–304, 305–9), to M[N1783] as the text is reprinted in Kerler 1988b (pp. 545–90). Some page references to parts of SZ1776 which were not reprinted are to the original edition. The references to BZ1771, B[L1798] and EP1790 are to the pages of the original editions. Page numbers provided in angle brackets refer to the passages from EP reprinted in Prilutski 1917a.

34 Eastern Yiddish Dialect Correlates

Most of the known late eighteenth-century Eastern Yiddish books were printed in the Southeastern region; in Zholkve (BZ1771, SZ1776), Poritsk (EP1790), and possibly Lemberg (B[L1798]; cf. Zfatman 1985: 162 no. 168). One was in all probability printed in Mideastern Novidvor (M[N1783]; cf. §30.2.1). Two others appeared in the Northeast: one in Shklov (VS[1783]), the other in Horodne (AH1795). Both pan-Eastern and particular Southeastern or Northeastern Yiddish features are either discernible or in many cases prominent on all levels of the linguistic structure of the extant texts. This section summarizes some of the major Eastern Yiddish dialectal features of the texts hailing from the Southeast (BZ1771, SZ1776, M[N1783], EP1790, B[L1798]) and the Northeast (VS[1783], AH1795). My contention is that the two Northeastern texts generally retain certain grammatical features that were obsolete in the Northeast dialect of the authors, but current in the Southeastern and Mideastern dialects.

34.1 The Southeastern Texts

Although M[N1783] was printed in the Mideastern region there seem to be no distinctly Mideastern Yiddish features in it. Given its immediate extra-linguistic background (see §32.2.2.6), supported by one possibly dialectal spelling (see §32.2.2.5), this work will be discussed together with all Southeastern Yiddish texts.

34.1.1 *Phonology*

All books printed in the Southeast and in one case in the Mideast have dialectal spellings such as טיט tit 'does' (e.g. B[L1798]; cf. NEY טוט tut), as well as hypercorrect spellings of the type זייא טרונקען ⟨zej trunken⟩ zej trinkən 'they drink' (e.g. EP1790). Both kinds of spelling testify to the Mideastern or Southeastern merger of the historical vowels *u_{51} and *i_{31} into a unitary i, and *$ū_{52}$ and *$ī_{32}$ into a unitary ī, which shortened to /i/ in Southeastern Yiddish. In some cases more localized Southeastern phonology can be traced. In EP1790, for example, the form דאװערט davərt or dɔvərt 'takes time' may be analysed either as the northern Southeastern av or as the usual Southeastern ɔv realization of historical vowel **54** in open syllables (cf. St.Y. דױערט dōjərt ‖ MEY dōvərt; see Herzog 1969: 76 §7.1.5, 78 Fig. 14).

In SZ1776 the dialectal spelling שידינג šɛdikṇ 'harm' can safely be interpreted as representing the Southeastern ej or i realization of vowel **25** (cf. NEY and MEY šέdikṇ ‖ SEY šéjdikṇ ~ šídikṇ; on the diaphoneme ej ‖ i in Southeastern Yiddish see M. Weinreich 1973: ii. 138–40 §133.6, iv. 188–9 §133.6; U. Weinreich 1958b: 235–6; Herzog 1969: 62–4 §3; D. Katz 1983: 1030 §8.1.2). Similarly, the older orthographic variation ⟨ɛ⟩ ~ ⟨i⟩ in such forms as ביט ~ בעט bɛt 'asks', with historical vowel **25** (cf. NEY bɛt ‖ MEY and SEY bejt), often led to the hypercorrect spelling of vowel **25** in such forms as װיט vət '[he] will' and װישט vəst '[you] will' (both in SZ). These instances point to i_{25} in the author's Yiddish.

Southeastern phonology can also be adduced for M[N1783] (cf. §§32.2.1–2 and 32.2.2.5). No specifically Southeastern phonological features can be recovered from the orthography of BZ1771 and B[L1798].

34.1.2 *Morphology*

Certain morphological features found in these texts are especially charac-teristic of Southeastern Yiddish. The pronominal adjectives derived from איל־ il—e.g. אילה ilə 'all; every'; אילץ ilc 'everything'; מיט אילם mit iləm 'with everything'—occur repeatedly in BZ1771 and B[L1798] and less frequently in M[N1783] and EP1790. These forms were also characteristic of the neighbouring varieties of Northeastern and Mideastern dialects. Their geographical heartland, however, was on Southeastern territory (cf. §7.2.1). The plural marker -s after stem-final r is another Southeastern feature. It is used in SZ1776 and BZ1771 (cf. §28.3.3.1), as well as in EP1790, where it becomes one of the regular patterns of plural formation (cf. below §35.1.2).

All the other morphological 'dialectalisms' are characteristic of both Mideastern and Southeastern Yiddish. The first- and third-person plural form זענען zɛnən 'are' is regularly used in BZ1771, SZ1776, M[N1783], and EP1790. This form is also systematically used in the Northeastern AH1795. On the other hand, the Northeastern variant זיינן zajnən seems to gain more acceptance in EP1790, though זענן zɛnən still prevails. Mideastern or Southeastern forms of past participles are employed in BZ1771 (see §28.3.3), EP1790, B[L1798], and less frequently in SZ1776 and M[N1783].

In three texts, SZ1776, M[N1783], and B[L1798], the second-person plural pronoun עטץ ɛc appears alongside the pan-Eastern Yiddish איר ir. In these texts both forms are used in a complementary distribution. The Mideastern or Southeastern form עטץ ɛc functions as a vocative, and appears only in direct or 'quoted', but not in reported, speech (cf. SZ, 163, 164; M[N], 109, 414; B[L], 17b, 24b, 40b). It is also frequently used together with the modal verb zɔln̩ 'should; ought' or with an imperative (SZ, 30b; M[N], 268, 346; B[L], 2a, 10a, 20b). On the other hand, איר ir is used as a general (i.e. unmarked) subject pronoun.

The consistent functional differentiation between עטץ ɛc (in modern Yiddish spelling עץ) and איר ir in SZ1776, M[N1783], and B[L1798] may well indicate that the same distinction existed in the spoken Southeastern Yiddish of that period. This suggestion is also supported by the fact that in Mideastern and Southeastern dialects the enclitic עץ ɛc usually appears in a close juncture with the preceding imperative (cf. Prilutski 1924a: 26–9 §§45–53; Herzog 1965a: 147 §4.55; 149 Fig. 4:80).

In B[L1798] the conventional spelling אים im 'him' is repeatedly replaced with עם əm (e.g. B[L], 16a–b), corresponding more directly with the Mideastern ejm or with the Northeastern əm/ɛm (cf. M. Weinreich 1973: ii. 140 §133.6; iv. 189 §133.6; Schaechter 1969: 289 §1.52). However, אים im (cf. Southeastern im) is on the whole the prevailing objective form of the third-person masculine singular pronoun in B[L1798].

With regard to the emergence of the prepositional case, we note that BZ1771, M[N1783], and EP1790 occasionally use די di for the singular feminine definite article after various prepositions (cf. below §35.5.3). These cases may indicate that the prepositional case had not yet been levelled in contemporary Southeastern Yiddish. However, judging by majority usage, it is clear that such levelling into a unitary דר dər for feminine (and דעם dəm for both neuter and masculine) was taking place in the literary language.

34.1.3 *Syntax*

One of the characteristic syntactic features of Mideastern and Southeastern Yiddish is the trend towards a more agglutinative word order, whereby the free verbal prefix is placed after the object. Mark (1946: 85; 1978: 381) observed that speakers of Mideastern and Southeastern Yiddish are strongly inclined to prefer this syntagm-final placement of the free prefix, whereas Northeasterners overwhelmingly favour the more analytic word order. The placement of the free verbal prefix still awaits further analysis, which may establish an important syntactic isogloss of modern Eastern Yiddish. All we can say at present is that Mark's observation is supported by the earliest Eastern Yiddish texts. The final placement of the verbal prefix is found only in the Southeastern texts, and it appears in each one of them; e.g.:

1 אונ וויא דער מלך קומט אין זיין הויז אריין [. . .]
un vi dər mejləx kumt in zajn həjz arajn
'and when the king comes into his home' (BZ, 44a);

2 ווען ער האט עשירות נעמט אים גאט זיין עשירות אוועק
vən ər hət ašírəs nɛmt im gət zajn ašírəs avɛ́k
'when he has wealth, God takes the wealth away from him' (SZ, 81–2);

3 ער וואשט דאם קינד אוים מיט קאלט וואסר
ər vašt dəs kind ɔ́js mit kalt vasər
'he washes the child in cold water' (EP, 9b);

4 איין אשה איז גגאנגן גאנץ פֿריא די בהמות טרייבן אין פֿעלד אריין
an išə iz gəgangən ganc fri di bəhéjməs trajbṇ in fɛld arájn
'a woman went early in the morning to drive the cattle into the field' (M[N], 21);

5 אזו האבן זיא גינומן איין הארמטי פֿון דעם שלאס אראפ
azɔj hobṇ zej gənumən an (h)armátə fun dəm šlɔs arɔ́p
'And so they brought [took] down a cannon from the castle' (M[N], 133);

6 בֿבֿא שלאגט זיינה אויגן אונטר
bɔ́və šlɔgt zajnə ɔjgṇ untər
'Bove averts his eyes (in embarrassment)' (B[L], 7a).

Like many other strong features of the Southeastern and Mideastern grammatical system (see below §34.3), the more agglutinative word order is linguistically more archaic. However, this is not the only word-order pattern. In these works the free verbal prefix is more often than not placed before the non-pronominal object.

A closely related morpho-syntactic peculiarity of Mideastern and Southeastern Yiddish is the postpositive adverb, which functions as a bound direction marker in the extended type of preposition group (for more details see §28.3.3.6). In two of the sentences cited above, vi dər mejləx kumt in zajn

hɔjz arajn (no. 1) and di bəhejməs trajbn̩ in fɛld arajn (no. 4), the form arájn
may be analysed as a postpositive adverb of this kind. Three types of closed
preposition groups, each with one of the postpositive adverbs אריין arájn
'inside', ארויש arɔ́js 'outside', and ארום arúm 'around; about', are often used
in EP 1790:

7 אריין שטאט דר אין קומט רשע דר איי ej dər rɔ́šə kumt in dər štɔt arájn
   'before this villain arrives in the town' (EP, ⟨36⟩);

8 ארוים סכנה דער אוים זענן זיי zej zɛnən ɔjs dər sakɔ́nə arɔ́js
   'they are out of danger' (EP, 9b);

9 ארום שטאט דער אום לאזן ניט מען זאל zɔl mən nit lɔzn̩ um dər štɔt árum
   'not to be allowed [to wander] around the town' (EP, 41a).

Closed syntagms of the type {אויש ɔjs 'out of' (prep.)} + {noun (location)}
+ {ארויש arɔ́js} are also found in BZ1771 and B[L1798]. However, the
preposition group of the type {אין in 'in' (prep.)} + {noun (location)} + {אריין
arájn} is used in all Southeastern texts. (On the constructions with a postpositive adverb see above §28.3.3.6 and cf. Kerler 1990: 292.) In BZ1771,
M[N1783], EP1790, and B[L1798] it becomes a productive morpho-
syntactic device to mark the direction implicit in the governing motion verbs.
Constructions with postpositive adverbs are not found in books emanating
from the Northeastern area.

34.2 The Northeastern Texts

Of the two books printed on Northeastern territory, VS[1783] can be clearly
identified as directly based on Northeastern Yiddish. A few Northeastern
features can also be traced in AH1795. It is none the less remarkable that
this work consistently employs the Mideastern or Southeastern form זענן
zɛnən 'are' (cf. §34.1.2, above). Moreover, all major grammatical conventions common to these two dialects (MEY and SEY) are fully preserved in
AH1795. It is possible, therefore, that its author was either sufficiently
conversant in Mideastern or Southeastern Yiddish or himself a native
speaker of one of these dialects.

34.2.1 Phonology

The most striking phonological feature attested in VS[1783] is the underlying absence of phonemic opposition between sibilants and shibilants. (On
this phenomenon in Northeastern Yiddish cf. U. Weinreich 1952a; 1963:
348–9 §2.4; 352–4 §3.4.) VS[1783] is a moralistic poem arranged in the
form of an alphabetical acrostic. However, the stanza that begins with the
letter ⟨ס⟩ opens with the word שוואך ⟨švax⟩ svax (?!) 'weak' (VS, 91; cf. St.Y.

švax). Other evidence of the neutralized opposition between sibilants and shibilants is the hypercorrect spelling פרנשה ⟨prnšh⟩ parnɔ́sə 'livelihood' (VS, 125) where the conventional etymological spelling requires פרנסה ⟨prnsh⟩. Even more revealing are the 'phonetic spellings' פֿאַלסע ⟨false⟩ falsə 'false' (pl., VS, 83, cf. St.Y. פֿאַלשע falšə); נארסר ⟨narsr⟩ nárisər 'foolish' (nom. sing., VS, 118; cf. St.Y. נאַרישער nárišər); פֿר לאסין ⟨fr losin⟩ farlɔ́sn̩ 'extinguished' (VS, 136; cf. St.Y. פֿאַרלאָשן farlɔ́šn̩); and סטרומין ⟨stromin⟩ strɔmən 'stream; flow' (VS, 152; cf. St.Y. שטראָמען strɔmən).

The spelling ⟨קריינק⟩ for krank 'sick' (cf. VS, 91) could be interpreted in a Southeastern text as a hypercorrection, since the historical vowels 34 (NEY aj ‖ MEY ā ‖ SEY a) and 11 (NEY a ‖ MEY ă ‖ SEY a ∼ ɔ) often merged in the Southeast into unitary a. However, in the context of Northeastern Yiddish this is simply a more phonetic representation of Northeastern vowel 11 before ng/nk (cf. Borokhov 1913: 22; Veynger 1926: 191; Wolf 1976: 39 §3.8; Timm 1987: 228 §19.3.7). Hence the underlying realization of ⟨קריינק⟩ in VS[1783] is krajnk (cf. Herzog 1965a: 209–10 §5.14.4).

The rhymes in this text are not very reliable, and in many cases they are far from precise; e.g.:

קערן kɛrn̩ 'investment' : צאָרין cɔrn̩ 'rage' (VS, 95–6);
הירטן hirtn̩ 'shepherds' (gen. pl.) : דאָרטן dɔrtn̩ 'there' (VS, 143–4).

In two instances the anonymous rhymester chose forms that are obviously not Northeastern; viz. the past participles גיפֿינן gəfinən (NEY/St.Y. gəfunən) 'found' and צו שפרינגן cəšpringən (NEY/St.Y. cəšprungən) 'exploded' in rhyming pairs:

דער שלינגן dəršlingən 'swallow': צו שפרינגן cəšpringən 'exploded' (VS, 5–6);
גיווינן gəvinən 'win': גיפֿינן gəfinən 'found' (past part., VS, 71–3).

These exceptional rhymes apparently testify to the author's familiarity with other varieties of Eastern Yiddish. This enabled him to utilize the Southeastern or Mideastern forms for rhyming purposes. (On an analogous case of non-native dialectal rhyming see §28.2 above.)

On the other hand, it is also possible that some rhymes sounded plausible only in Northeastern Yiddish, where the historical vowels 22, 24, 42, and 44 merged into unitary ej (cf. D. Katz 1983: 1031 §8.2), thereby making ej a somewhat better rhyme with ɛ:

עושר ejsər 'rich man': בעסר bɛsər 'better' (VS, 84–5;
   cf. St.Y. ɔjšər : bɛsər);
פֿר שטומן farstéjsn̩ 'hide': עסין ɛsn̩ 'eat' (VS, 134–5;
   cf. St.Y. farštéjsn̩ : ɛsn̩).

Phonological Northeasternisms are not found in AH1795. But with the sole exception of בצוואונגן bacvúngən 'subjugate' (inf., AH, 187; cf. NEY and St.Y. באַצוויינגען bacvíngən), where the ⟨ו⟩ grapheme corresponds with the non-Northeastern merger of vowels 31 and 51, no other markedly Mideastern or Southeastern spellings were found in AH1795. By comparison, such spellings are frequent in the Southeastern texts (cf. above §34.1.1).

34.2.2 *Morphology and Syntax*

Specifically Northeastern forms are not found in these books. The only possibly Northestern form is עם əm 'him' used once in AH1795 (cf. 31). Otherwise both books employ the more conventional literary form אים im.

The forms גיפֿינן gəfinən (NEY/St.Y. gəfunən) 'found' and צו שפרינגן cəšpringən (NEY/St.Y. cəšprungən) 'exploded' cited earlier are exceptions in VS[1783]. The consistent appearance of זענן zɛnən 'are' (cf. NEY זיינן zajnən) is the only distinctly non-Northeastern feature found in AH1795. Given that all other Southeastern morphological and syntactic features (cf. above §§34.1.2–3) are absent from these two books, we may conclude that they were by and large based on Northeastern Yiddish. In the case of VS[1783] this is also evident from the partial shift in gender (see §34.2.3), as well as from a number of features peculiar to the Northeastern grammatical system (see §34.3 below).

34.2.3 *Grammatical Gender*

One of the most salient features of Northeastern Yiddish is the loss of the neuter gender and the subsequent restructuring of its gender system (cf. Sapir 1915: 255; Shapiro 1939; Mark 1944b; Herzog 1965a: 101-15 §4.11; Wolf 1969; D. Katz 1983: 1030 §8.2). In VS[1783] we find a number of cases that directly reflect the Northeastern gender system. The possible shift from masculine to feminine is apparent from the variation דער טוט dər tojt ~ די טוט di tojt 'death' (VS, 4 and 80; cf. Herzog 1965a: 114-18 §4.12.2; Wolf 1969: 168-71 §4.13).

The Northeastern loss of the neuter gender is evident from the assignment of the masculine gender to the historically neuter nouns אום רעלט úmrɛxt 'injustice' (cf. דעם אום רעלט dəm úmrɛxt 'the injustice' (acc. sing.), VS, 48) and ביכל bixl 'booklet' (cf. זאל ער ליינן דעם ביכל zol ər lejnən dəm bixl 'may he read this booklet', VS, title-page). In other cases the historically neuter גיבאט gəbot 'commandment' (VS, 82, spelled ⟨גילבאט⟩) and רשעת rišəs 'malice' (VS, 90) acquire the feminine gender.

But the neuter gender as such did not totally disappear from VS[1783]. Besides the frequently used pronoun דאס dos 'this' (cf. VS, 24, 34, 46, 89, 109, 131), the attributive adjective retains its short (i.e. neuter-compatible) form before certain historically neuter nouns; e.g. דיין מוט וויליג האָרץ dajn mútvilik harc 'your wicked heart' (VS, 46); פֿרעמד גוטש frɛmd guts 'someone else's possessions' (VS, 112). Both these nouns, האָרץ harc and גוטש guts, were treated morpho-syntactically as neuters. Finally, the neuter gender was fully preserved in דאָש אייגין גוטש dɔs ejgn̩ guts 'your own possessions' (VS, 58).

On the other hand, the neuter is very much alive in AH1795. The only two instances of a possible Northeastern change of gender are רעכט rɛxt 'right' and ליכט lixt 'light', which appear in this text as feminine (AH, 235, 247; on ליכט lixt 'candle' as a historical neuter turned feminine in Northeastern Yiddish cf. Wolf 1969: 158 Map 4:5). In AH1795 אקסל aks͔l 'back' (cf. AH, 221) still appears as feminine. This is clearly a survival from Old Literary Yiddish. In all Eastern Yiddish dialects this noun has the masculine gender (cf. Schaechter 1969: 295 §3.21).

34.3 Grammar

The most important criteria for verification of the underlying dialectological basis of Modern Literary Yiddish are the following major grammatical features (cf. Birnbaum 1954: 71; Schaechter 1977: 39):

(1) the neuter gender;
(2) the accusative personal pronouns (1st and 2nd sing. and 3rd sing. fem.);
(3) the inflecting paradigm of the verbal reflexivity marker זיך zɔx;
(4) זיין zajn 'be' as one of the past-tense auxiliaries.

The actual dialectal boundaries in which each of these features was retained or lost may vary. However, in principle the whole historical Eastern Yiddish speech territory was divided into two major areas: Northern Yiddish (i.e. Northeastern dialect) on the one hand and Southern Eastern Yiddish (comprising both Southeastern and Mideastern dialects) on the other. All these features were lost in Northeastern Yiddish, and preserved in the Mideastern and Southeastern dialects.

The initial dialectal composition of nascent Modern Literary Yiddish was certainly not supraregional. The various dialectal differences between the Southeastern and Northeastern texts are in some cases transparent. These texts show, however, that the full (and in the case of VS[1783] principal) retention of these features is diachronically based on the historical continuity of Yiddish as a literary language. Synchronically, this retention is tantamount to the adoption of the grammar of Southeastern Yiddish as the principal dialectal basis of the nascent modern literary language.

Given the markedly Southeastern character of BZ1771, SZ1776,

M[N1783], EP1790, and B[L1798], it is hardly surprising that all these characteristic grammatical features were fully preserved in them. The only exception is the employment of האבן həbn̩ 'have' as a past-tense auxiliary of the transitive verb רינן rinən 'leak; run', found once in M[N1783]:

עש האט אזוו פיל בלוט גרונן דורך די טורן

əs hɔt azój fil blut gərúnən durx di tɔ(j)ərn̩

'so much blood ran through the gates' (M[N], 219-20).

(However, earlier (l. 178) the same verb appears with זיין zajn 'be'; cf. also Kerler 1990: 296.) This Northeastern type of shift in the past-tense auxiliary was marginally characteristic of some intransitive verbs in Southeastern Yiddish (cf. Wolf 1976: 44 §4.7).

The direct orientation to the spoken language also resulted in a dialectal impact on the two Northeastern texts. As we have seen, the Northeastern loss of the neuter gender is amply attested in VS[1783], and can be gleaned from a few cases in AH1795. Nevertheless, VS[1783] employs some nouns as morpho-syntactically or explicitly marked neuters, thereby preserving the neuter gender in principle. Moreover, AH1795 operates fully within the non-Northeastern three-gender system.

In VS[1783] the underlying Northeastern loss of accusative personal pronouns (1st and 2nd sing. and 3rd sing. fem.) can be seen in the apparently free variation between האט דיך בשאפן hət dix bašáfn̩ 'created you' (acc.) (VS, 47, 50) and האט דיר בשאפן hət dir bašáfn̩ 'created you' (dat.) (VS, 141). Furthermore, the accusative דיך dix (or dəx) was used after a dative governing verb העלפין hɛlfn̩ 'help' (VS, 113). An accusative form of the third-person feminine pronoun זיא zi is employed after a preposition; e.g. פֿר זיא far zi 'for her' (VS, 120; note that the expected 'correct' form in all three dialects would be פֿר איר far ir). But these cases notwithstanding, the anonymous versifier of VS[1783] did quite well in preserving clear morphological and syntactic distinctions between דיר dir 'you' (dat.; e.g. VS, 27, 57, 95, 97) and דיך dix 'you' (acc.; e.g. VS, 23, 29, 60, 121). Similarly, only זיא zi is employed as accusative (VS, 120). No traces of the Northeastern loss of accusative personal pronouns are found in AH1795.

With regard to the verbal reflexivity marker, VS[1783] normally employs זיך zəx as a general (uninflecting) marker, as in Northeastern Yiddish (cf. VS, 12, 17, 33, 84, 116, 118). Only in one case is the older second-person singular form דיך dəx preserved: דער מאן דיך dərmán dəx 'remind yourself [= remember, recall]' (imperative, 2nd pers. sing., VS, 22). However, in two other instances the Northeastern דער מאן זיך dərmán zəx was used (cf. VS, 34, 136). By contrast, AH1795 employs the inflecting non-Northeastern paradigm of the verbal reflexivity marker (e.g. AH, 208, 211).

Finally, the past-tense auxiliary זײַן zajn 'be' is never replaced by האָבן həbṇ 'have' in either of the Northeastern books.

The fact that most of the distinctly non-Northeastern grammatical features are preserved in the otherwise mostly Northeastern text, VS[1783], does not necessarily prove that its author was standardizing his literary language according to the grammatical patterns of Southeastern or Mideastern dialects. All these features could have been directly inherited from the old literary language. But it is clear that many essential grammatical features of Old Literary Yiddish were wholly replaced by their modern Eastern Yiddish equivalents (e.g. the future auxiliary, most of the functional words, the place of the finite verb in subordinate clauses). Why would the anonymous author pattern his literary language so systematically on his vernacular in some cases, yet attempt to preserve other archaic features that were equally obsolete in his spoken language?

The conservative inertia of literary usage can possibly account for the exceptional דער מאָן דיך dərmán dəx 'remind yourself [= remember, recall]' (imperative, 2nd pers. sing.), used once in VS[1783]. But it is less likely that the old literary language was solely responsible for the retention (although dialectally qualified) of the neuter gender and for the by and large systematic distinction between dative and accusative forms of personal pronouns. It cannot be proved that the anonymous author of VS[1783] was aware that these features were the norm in other Eastern Yiddish dialects. But it is not unreasonable to suggest that he was familiar with other Eastern Yiddish dialects—hence his employment, for rhyming purposes, of a few Southeastern or Mideastern forms (cf. above §34.2.1) which were otherwise in sharp contradiction to the major phonological features of the book.

One possible explanation is that the author perceived most of these grammatical features as 'more correct', for they were current in both the old literary language and all other Eastern Yiddish dialects. The other book, AH1795, was also probably written by a speaker of Northeastern Yiddish. However with regard to its dialectal composition, AH1795 may be considered the earliest example of a dialectologically neutral style. Its language is more interdialectal than any other Eastern Yiddish text of the period. AH1795 retains the neuter gender, the accusative forms of the personal pronouns, and even the inflecting paradigm of the verbal reflexivity marker; but at the same time it does not use distinctly Southeastern forms (other than זענען zɛnən 'are'), and its syntax does not exhibit the distinctly non-Northeastern patterns that can often be encountered in contemporary Southeastern books (cf. above §34.1.3).

Because of the ever increasing *rapprochement* between the spoken and the literary languages in the nineteenth and twentieth centuries, many Northeastern dialectal features gained acceptance in Modern Literary Yiddish. However, most of the grammatical features under discussion (with the exception of the verbal reflexivity marker) were fully accepted as patterns of literary usage by all writers whose native dialect was Northeastern Yiddish. As we have seen, the beginnings of this important development can be found in the late eighteenth century in the earliest known Northeastern Yiddish books.

35 The Emergence of Common Eastern Yiddish (Proto-Standard Yiddish)

Most of the new forms that replaced Old Yiddish equivalents are common to all Eastern Yiddish dialects. The introduction of a new paradigm of the future-tense auxiliary (§35.9) and the complete deletion of the genitive case (§35.6.1) are two striking examples. Moreover, the whole grammatical fabric of the literary language was drastically restructured via the systematic incorporation of many new structural features. Here too, most of the new features and categories are common to all Eastern Yiddish dialects; e.g. the new plural formation (§35.1), the morphology and semantics of diminutives (§35.2), the abstract noun formation (§35.3), the category of verbal aspect (§35.10), and the analogical placement of the finite verb in main and in subordinate clauses (cf. U. Weinreich 1958a: 383 §3.3).

The overall structural affinity of the major Eastern Yiddish dialects overshadows their differences. As a result, a new literary language, based primarily on Eastern Yiddish dialects, emerges as the legitimate heir and a new alternative to the old literary language. In the following sections we shall focus on some of the most essential morphological and morpho-syntactic changes that occurred in late eighteenth-century Eastern Yiddish books.

35.1 Plural Formation

In modern Yiddish the suffix -s is a regular plural marker for nouns ending in an unstressed vowel, and for those with final -n̩, -m, or -ər (cf. Mark 1978: 161–3 §§2–3; D. Katz 1987a: 54–6 §4.2.2). This marker was normally used in BZ1771 after masculine -ər and feminine -n̩ agentive suffixes (cf. §28.3.3.1). It is also found in SZ1776, and is systematically employed in EP1790; e.g.:

מעסרם mɛsərs 'knives' (SZ1776, 72);
וואקס גימערם váksgisərs 'waxers' (EP1790, 52b);

דאָקטערם dɔktərs 'physicians' (EP1790, 52b; cf. Herzog 1965b: 58 §3.2);

באָבעש bɔbəs 'grandmothers' and טאַטעש tatəs 'fathers' (EP1790, 109-10).

Lexical items with ultimate unstressed vowels automatically received this plural marker in M[N1783] (pp. 375-6; cf. §32.3) and in B[L1798]; e.g.:

טאַרבם tɔrbəs 'sacks' (B[L], 15a);

פאָלים pɔləs 'laps (of a garment)' (B[L], 19b).

The Eastern Yiddish fusion formula adopts the Slavonic nominative plural form with an open final syllable as a base to which the plural marker -s is added; e.g. באָלוואַן bɔlván 'dummy; moron' → באָלוואַנעם bɔlvánəs 'dummies; morons' (cf. Russ. болван in sing. and болваны in pl.). In some cases the Slavonic plural stem was adopted as the basis from which the singular was derived in Yiddish by means of back formation (cf. U. Weinreich's 1958a: 392 analysis of Yiddish בלינצע blincə 'crepe': blincə < blincə-s (pl.) < Ukr. blync-i in pl. < blynec in sing.). However, in other cases Yiddish adopted both the Slavonic singular and plural stems. So original Slavonic vowel deletion in the plural is fully preserved in such forms as קעלישעק kélišək '(glass) tumbler' and קעלישקעם kéliškəs '(glass) tumblers' (cf. Pol. kieliszek in sing. and kieliszki in pl.); טשערוואָנעץ čərvɔnəc 'gold coin' and טשערוואָנצעם čərvɔncəs 'gold coins' (cf. Russ. червонец in sing., червонцы in pl.). The mechanism for morphologically integrating these nouns in Yiddish is the suffixation of the Slavonic plural stem with the Yiddish plural marker -s (cf. M. Weinreich 1973: ii. 64, iv. 92; Stankiewicz 1985: 181 n. 6). Synchronically, however, this marker is analysed as -əs, and is operative for all etymologically Slavonic words and suffixes with a final closed syllable (cf. Zaretski 1929: 68 §151; Mark 1978: 164 §4; D. Katz 1987: 57, §4.2.3.1). Naturally, the marker -əs is found only in those texts in which lexical items of Slavonic origin were introduced, in M[N1783] and especially in EP1790, which is the earliest text to employ lexical Slavonicisms in abundance; e.g. הולטייעם hultájəs 'libertines'; שעניקאַרעם šɛnkárəs 'innkeepers' (EP, 51a). In M[N1783] we find the form דונציתּ dɔncəs 'Cossacks from the river Don area', in which the original Slavonic vowel deletion of the plural has been preserved (cf. Russ. донцы in pl., донец in sing.).

35.2 Diminutive Formation

Diminutive formation in these texts complies fully with the morphological patterns of Eastern Yiddish. The diminutive formants that can be found in the books under discussion are -ḷ (sing.)/-ləx/-lax (pl.) for the first diminutive and -ələ (sing.)/-ələx (pl.) for the second diminutive. Among others, the following forms of first diminutive were found in the extant texts:

אביסל abísḷ 'a bit' (adv.) (AH, 85; EP, ⟨30⟩);
ביכל bixḷ 'booklet' (VS, title-page; M[N], 1);
בעזימלאך bézimlax (bɛzəmləx) 'little brooms' (EP, 42a);
הינדל hindḷ 'chick' (B[L], 5a);
העמדיל hɛmdḷ 'shirt' (BZ, 26a; M[N], 233);
שיפל šifḷ 'small boat' (B[L], 19b);
פלעשל flɛšḷ 'flask' (B[L], 21b);
פערדיל fɛrdḷ 'horse' (EP, 49a; B[L], 22b);
קינדרליך kindərləx '(little) children' (M[N], 79, 191);
שווערד(י)ל švɛrdḷ 'sword' (B[L], 21b).

Some of these possibly function as expressive forms of endearment in M[N1783], B[L1798], and in EP1790 (see last three above). This usage is especially characteristic of Eastern Yiddish (cf. Stankiewicz 1985: 178–81 §2; D. Katz 1987a: 67 §4.3.5).

In modern Yiddish the first diminutive of masculine agentives is markedly pejorative (cf. D. Katz 1987a: 67–8 §4.3.6). Such 'diminutivization of contempt' is repeatedly employed by Markuze in his EP1790. Whenever he talks about incompetent physicians or people who pretend to be medics, he refers to them as דאקטערליך doktərləx (e.g. 5a, 49a). In modern Yiddish, the plural marker -ləx (/-lax) is suffixed to the plural of the noun, hence דאָקטוירימליך doktójrimləx (or doktójrəmlax).

Vestigial survivals of the alternative diminutive formant -(ə)xṇ and -čə (cf. Western Yiddish -jə ‖ -tjə, NHG -chen) can still be recovered from a handful of dialectal Eastern Yiddish forms, especially in the Southeastern dialect (cf. M. Weinreich 1973: iv. 246–7 §142.3; Herzog 1965a: 140 §4.3). Mendele Moykher Sforim used such diminutives as mɔjlx(ə)n 'little mouth' and kɛlx(ə)n 'thin voice' with -(ə)xṇ after stem-final l, whereas in modern Yiddish the suffix -əxḷ became the standard (cf. majlxḷ and kɛlxḷ in St.Y.). The New High German formant -chen was often used in contemporary Western Yiddish printed works. But neither the dialectal -(ə)xṇ nor the New High German -chen was introduced into these late eighteenth-century Eastern Yiddish books. This may well indicate that -(ə)xṇ was already a moribund suffix in the spoken language of that period and that the pan-Eastern Yiddish pattern of diminutivization was, in the case of Markuze's EP1790, strong enough to resist the introduction of New High German -chen into literary usage.

The second diminutive was rarely, if ever, used in the older literary language. The morphological second diminutive, which is the only possible diminutive formation for stems with a final -ן , is found in M[N1783], VS[1783], and EP1790; e.g.:

װינדלאך víndəlax 'diapers' (EP, 136a;
  cf. mod. Y. װינדלען vindlən 'diapers' → װינדעלעך vindələx '[tiny] diapers');
װינקליך vinkələx 'corners' (VS, 153;
  cf. mod. Y. װינקלען vinklən 'corners' → װינקעלעך vinkələx '[small] corners');
שעפֿליך šɛfələx 'lambs' (M[N], 296).

In modern Yiddish the proper second diminutive is morphologically, and in many cases also semantically, differentiated from the first diminutive; e.g. טאָפּ tɔp 'pot' → טעפּל tɛpḷ 'smaller pot' → טעפּעלע tɛpələx 'very small pot'. (On the 'two-tier' system of diminutivization in modern Yiddish see Landau 1896; Zaretski 1929: 61–3 §§127–34; M. Weinreich 1973: ii. 181 §142.3; 190; Mark 1978: 184–7; Birnbaum 1979: 238–40 §§64–78; D. Katz 1987a: 65 ff. §4.3.) Second diminutives were found only in EP1790 and B[L1798]; e.g.:

אביסעלע abísələ 'a little bit' (adv., EP, 136b);
הינדלה hindələ or híndalə 'little chick' (B[L], 5a);
הינדליך hindələx or híndalax 'little chicks' (B[L], 7b);
מיידלה mejdələ or méjdalə 'little girl' (EP, ⟨35⟩);
לעבֿליך lɛxələx or léxalax 'pores' (EP, 56a).

The emergence of the second diminutive was apparently supported by the structural impact of the co-territorial Slavonic languages upon Eastern Yiddish (cf. M. Weinreich 1973: ii. 190 §146; U. Weinreich 1958a: 380 §3.2). Its introduction into the literary language is a significant move towards the derivational patterns and the semantically differentiating system of spoken Eastern Yiddish.

35.3 Abstract Noun Formation

In modern Eastern Yiddish the suffix -kajt has become the most productive abstract noun formant. It has replaced -hajt, which became unproductive, and substantially restricted the productivity of the compound abstract noun formant -ikajt (cf. §28.3.3.2). This state of affairs is only partly echoed in BZ1771, where the morphological patterns of *taytsh* enforced the employment of the obsolete formant -hajt and the latter was sometimes artificially preserved in forms that were suffixed with -kajt in the spoken language (e.g. אָרעם הייט ɔrəmhajt (?!) 'poverty', 41a, but also אַרמקייט ɔrəmkajt, 12a).

However, in all the other texts only -kajt and less frequently -ikajt are found; e.g. אום זיניקייט umzínikajt 'foolishness' (SZ, 30b); מידקייט mídkajt 'fatigue' (SZ, 127); שטאַרקייט štárkajt 'strength' (AH, 60); נאַרעשקייט náraškajt 'stupidity' (EP, 103b); שאַרף קייט šárfkajt 'sharpness' (B[L], 11a); בייזקייט béjzkajt 'malice' (B[L], 11b). The formant -kajt is also found to be productive with Semitic component stems:

אזו איז איז עש אליץ פֿון פֿאַרנט ביז אן הינטרשטן דף אייטל חסידותקייט

azój iz əs alc fun fərṇt biz ɔn hintərštṇ daf ejtļ xsídəskajt

'and so each page of this book is sheer piety';

lit. 'and so this [book], from its first to its last page is pure piety' (SZ, title-page).

35.4 Pronominal Adjectives

The modern Eastern Yiddish pronominal adjectives azójn- and azélx- and the invariant azá(n), all meaning 'such', were introduced in some of the works. Usually the spelling remains etymological; e.g.:

אזו איינם azójnəm (dat. sing., SZ, 18b);
אזו איינ י azójnə (pl., SZ, 42, 170);
אזו איין azá(n)(?) (SZ, 102, 114; M[N], 98, 177; B[L], 1a);
איין זעלבן azélxṇ (dat. sing., BZ, 30b).

However, the phonetically integrated modern spelling may also be found in M[N 1783] and in B[L 1798]; e.g.:

אזוני azójnə (pl., M[N], 284);
אזעלבי azélxə (pl., M[N], 626; B[L], 24b).

These forms were directly introduced from spoken Eastern Yiddish. However, in these texts they are less frequently used than in the modern literary language.

35.5 Possessive Pronouns

A number of important morphological changes occurred in the Eastern Yiddish system of possessive pronouns. First, the attributive possessive pronouns (without the indefinite article) became indeclinable in all cases. In the old literary language they had usually declined after prepositions and in the dative (see Lincoff 1963: §5.2). As a result, the older form מיט זיינ י פֿרוא י mit zajnə frɔj 'with his wife' was replaced in Eastern Yiddish by מיט זיין פֿרוא י mit zajn frɔj (cf. §11.3.2.2). On the other hand, the historical genitive of personal pronouns was lost in modern Yiddish. It was subsequently reanalysed as a regular possessive pronoun; cf. the more archaic מיין העַנט majn hɛnt 'my hands' was changed to מייני העַנט majnə hɛnt (cf. §28.3.1.3). Finally, the third-person plural possessive pronoun איר ir, which was largely the norm in the old literary language, was replaced by זײער zejər (cf. §§5.4, 11.3.2.2, and 28.3.2.1).

35.5.1 The Declinable Possessive Pronouns

The declinable possessive pronoun can still be found in most of the books under discussion (cf. also §11.3.2.2). It is repeatedly used in B[L1798], but only occasionally in SZ1776 and EP1790 and twice in M[N1783]. It is found only once in AH1795 (at 233) and not at all in BZ1771 and VS[1783].

In B[L1798] declinable possessive pronouns are used mostly after a preposition and in conjunction with nouns that are clearly classifiable as objects of 'inalienable' possession (e.g. 'parts of the body'; cf. 9a, 10a, 18a, or 'close relatives'; cf. 3a, 4b, 7b, 25a). The few cases with declinable possessive pronouns found in SZ1776 and M[N1783] support the possibility that this usage was a morpho-syntactic device for marking 'inalienable' possession (cf. SZ, 25a §573; M[N], 170, 652).

It is not known whether the declinable possessive pronouns were used in this way in the spoken language of the period, which may be suggested by their frequency in B[L1798]. However, even in B[L1798] declinable possessive pronouns appear alongside the modern Yiddish use of the definite article as a marker of 'inalienable' possession; e.g. אין זײנר הנט in zajnər hant 'in his hand' (B[L], 10a) but also אויש דר האנט ojs dər hant 'from his hand' (B[L], 15b). Judging by all the other texts, declinable possessive pronouns were very uncommon in nascent Modern Literary Yiddish.

35.5.2 The Genitive of Personal Pronouns

The historical genitive of personal pronouns often occurs in BZ1771 and SZ1776 in free variation with the regular possessive pronouns. Genitive pronouns are considerably scarcer in M[N1783], EP1790, and AH1795. Given the fact that the genitive as a category ceased to exist within the case system of modern Eastern Yiddish (cf. below §35.6.1), we may safely assume that these forms are vestiges of Old Literary Yiddish. The decline of the older forms increases chronologically (see also §28.3.1.3). Statistically, the genitive of personal pronouns can be viewed as exceptional in M[N1783], EP1790, and AH1795. It is used only once in VS[1783] (at 143) and B[L1798] (17b).

Possibly as a consequence of the general disappearance of the genitive case, these forms were viewed by some writers as more 'literary' short forms of attributive possessive pronouns which do not inflect in number before nouns in the plural. This may be the socio-linguistic reasoning behind the continuous employment of the historical genitive personal pronouns in such works as BZ1771 and SZ1776 (§32.4.1), and their very survival in M[N1783], EP1790, and AH1795.

35.5.3 *Third Person Plural of Possessive Pronouns*

The replacement of the third-person plural possessive pronoun איר ir by the pan-Eastern Yiddish זייער ze(i)ער zejər is not complete in all these books (see also §§5.4, 11.3.2.2, and 28.3.2.1). The older form is still employed, mostly in free variation with zejər in BZ1771, SZ1776, and EP1790; but it is obsolescent in *Mayse gdoyle min Uman*, where it is found only once (M[N], 153), and in B[L1798]. It is fully replaced by זייער ze(i)ער zejər in VS[1783] and AH1795.

35.6 The Case System

The case system of modern Yiddish has been substantially restructured. The genitive case has become obsolete. The dative and accusative of the masculine definite article have merged, and a levelled prepositional case has developed. Although the relative chronology of the changing case system remains to be explored, it seems that all these structural changes are correlated. Thus the loss of the genitive case was compensated for by the possessive case and the emerging prepositional case. The loss of formal opposition between the dative and the accusative of the masculine definite article may have promoted the loss of the accusative of the neuter definite article after prepositions, hence the modern prepositional case. In the literary language the feminine definite article was also levelled in the prepositional case, a development that can be traced in the texts under discussion.

35.6.1 *The Loss of the Genitive*

Unlike the old literary language and contemporary Western Yiddish printed works, all these books clearly show the complete loss of the genitive case in Eastern Yiddish. The only genitive form that is found amounts to one of the very last vestiges of Old Literary Yiddish, e.g.

איך בדארף מיך זיינר ניט צו שעמן
ix badárf mix zajnər nit cu šɛmən
'I do not have to be ashamed of him' (B[L], 13a).

This usage in B[L1798] goes back, ultimately though not directly, to איך דרף מיך זיין ניט שעמן ix darf mix zajn nit šɛmən 'I do not have to be ashamed of him' in the original edition of *Buovo d'Antona* (Isni, 1541, stanza 200; see Joffe 1949).

35.6.2 *Merger of the Dative and Accusative Masculine Case Markers*

Given the dialectological evidence of eighteenth-century Western Yiddish (cf. Friedrich 1784: 53 §1; Lincoff 1963: 54 §4.211) and of modern Eastern Yiddish, we may safely assume that the accusative and dative forms of the masculine definite article became syncretic in both larger dialects, yielding דען dən in Western and דעם dəm in Eastern Yiddish. This is supported by the books under discussion. The authors of such texts as BZ1771, SZ1776, and AH1795 were apparently at pains to preserve דען dən, in order to sustain the old distinction between dative and accusative. However, their efforts resulted in various hypercorrections and an unfunctional variation. As a result, דען dən was often employed as dative and דעם dəm as accusative, while both were in many cases used with the same prepositions without any functional opposition (cf. §28.3.2.3). In Markuze's EP1790 the frequent use of the defunct accusative form דען dən may safely be attributed to the direct influence of New High German. However, the actual employment of this form is often unfunctional and at times hypercorrect (see Herzog 1965b: 53–5 §2.11).

The situation changes radically in M[N1783], VS[1783], and B[L1798], where דעם dəm becomes the norm for both accusative and dative, and דען dən is exceptionally rare. The latter was found only twice in B[L1798] (2b, 28b) and six times in M[N1783] (324, 479, 509, 542, 584, 657; cf. §32.4.1). Only דעם dəm was systematically employed in VS[1783].

35.6.3 *The Prepositional Case*

In modern Eastern Yiddish the formal distinction between accusative and dative cases (in masculine singular) was neutralized after prepositions. As a result, a new prepositional case developed. Morphologically it is based on the dative, and in the modern literary language all case and gender markers (i.e. all singular definite articles) were levelled on the analogy of their dative forms. In Eastern Yiddish dialects of the late nineteenth and twentieth centuries the actual situation with regard to the prepositional case was far less uniform. Vestiges of the neuter accusative case after prepositions may have survived in a relatively small Northeastern enclave in Mideastern Yiddish (see Herzog 1965a: 136 Fig. 4:51). Even less uniform is the dialectal treatment of the feminine singular definite article. Feminine accusative after prepositions was a regular dialectal feature of Mideastern and Southeastern Yiddish (see Herzog 1965a: 128 Fig. 4:42, 131–4 §4.22; Wolf 1969: 130–9 §§3.1–2). However, this dialectal usage of the feminine accusative can synchronically be viewed as the Mideastern and Northeastern variant of the feminine prepositional case, since prepositions did not attract the feminine dative in those dialects. In other words, whereas Southeastern Yiddish had {prep.} + {dəm} for masculine and neuter singular and {prep.} + {dər} for feminine singular, Mideastern and some varieties of Northeastern Yiddish had {prep.} + {dəm} for masculine and neuter singular and {prep.} + {di} for feminine singular.

The texts under discussion exhibit a high degree of levelling of the prepositional case. All singular neuter definite articles were levelled to דעם dəm (the variant usage of דען dən is in these cases a hypercorrection; cf. above §35.6.2). The only exception is found in EP1790; פֿון דאָס מקום fun dɔs mɔkəm 'from the place [= institution]' (EP, ⟨26⟩). This can be viewed as a rare dialectalism, or more likely as a hypercorrection based on the New High German distinction between accusative and dative cases depending upon the preposition.

With regard to the feminine singular definite article, the norm in most of these texts appears to be דר dər, as in Modern Literary Yiddish. The least consistent text is M[N1783], although in some cases the noun in question may be analysed as a morphologically unmarked plural (e.g. M[N], 178, 543). The variation דר dər ~ די di after prepositions is found only in Southeastern texts (see the footnotes to Table 26). However, even in these books the use of דר dər clearly prevails in most cases. (For ratios in M[N1783] see Table 26 nn. 1, 3, 7, 9.)

Among the prepositions found, the following are used in each of the specified books with dər as the historical dative case of the feminine definite article:

אויף af 'on'—BZ1771, SZ1776, M[N1783], VS[1783], EP1790, AH1795, B[L1798];
אויש ɔjs 'out; from'—BZ1771, M[N1783], EP1790, B[L1798];
אונטר untər 'under'—M[N1783], EP1790;
איבר ibər 'over'—M[N1783];
אין in 'in'—BZ1771, SZ1776, M[N1783], VS[1783], EP1790, AH1795, B[L1798];
ארום arúm 'around; about'—M[N1783];
ביי(א) ba 'at'—EP1790;
מיט mit 'with'—BZ1771, SZ1776, M[N1783], VS[1783], EP1790, B[L1798];
נאך nɔx 'after'—SZ1776;
פֿון fun 'from; of—BZ1771, SZ1776, M[N1783], EP1790, AH1795, B[L1798];
פֿר far 'for; before'—BZ1771, M[N1783], EP1790, AH1795, B[L1798];
צו cu 'to'—SZ1776, M[N1783], EP1790, AH1795, B[L1798].

Table 26 sums up the distribution of the masculine, neuter, and feminine singular definite articles after prepositions (in the case of M[N1783] and AH1795 the whole text was fully surveyed). The masculine and neuter forms of the definite article are represented in some of the texts by both variants דען dən and דעם dəm (cf. §35.6.2 above). In the table they are represented by a unitary morpheme דעם dəm, which was the only variant that existed in the spoken language of the period. The forms in brackets are those used less frequently in the texts. They are specified in the relevant footnotes.

Table 26 The prepositional case in late eighteenth-century Eastern Yiddish printed works

Preposition	masc./neut.		fem.	
	דעם dəm	דאָס dɔs	דר dər	די di
אויף af	+	−	+	(+)[1]
אויש ɔjs	+	−	+	−
אונטר untər	+	−	+	−
איבר ibər	+	−	+	(+)[2]
אין in	+	−	+	(+)[3]
ארום arúm	+	−	+	−
בײַ(א) ba	+	−	+	−
מיט mit	+	−	+	(+)[4]
נאָך nɔx	+	−	+	(+)[5]
פֿון fun	+	(+)[6]	+	(+)[7]
פֿר far	+	−	+	(+)[8]
צו cu	+	−	+	(+)[9]

[1] In BZ; in M[N] in 2 cases out of 15 (2:13).
[2] In M[N] in 1 case out of 2 (1:1).
[3] In BZ; in M[N] in 1 case out of 19 (1:18).
[4] In EP once.
[5] In SZ in a possessive case: nɔx di mutərs bridər 'after maternal uncles'.
[6] In EP (noticed once).
[7] In BZ; in M[N] in 1 case out of 5 (1:4).
[8] In BZ.
[9] In M[N] in 1 case out of 7 (1:6).

It is possible that in the Eastern Yiddish dialects of earlier periods (perhaps before the middle of the eighteenth century) there still existed an opposition between feminine accusative and dative after certain prepositions. This possibility is based on the evidence of BZ1771, where the accusative after the prepositions אין in 'in' and אויף af 'on' is usually used for the lative case while the dative is employed as locative; e.g.:

lative	locative
גיין אין דיא ערד אריין	מיט קיין זאך אין דר וועלט
gejn in di ɛrd arájn	mit kejn zax in dər vɛlt
'to go into the grave' (BZ, 14a);	'with anything in the world' (BZ, 11a);
גייט אויף דיא גאס	איך בין אויף דר הייך פֿון דען עולם
gejt af di gas	ix bin af dər hejx fun dən ɔjləm
'walks on the street'	'I am on the top of the world'
(BZ, 43a);	(BZ, 43a).

However, there is no such distinction in BZ1771 with the neuter definite articles. The formal opposition between {prep.} + {di} for lative and {prep.} + {dər} for locative was not maintained in SZ1776 (e.g. 53, 179–80, 218–19) and all later books.

Given the dialectal distribution of the prepositional case, it is not surprising that דר dər appears to be the regular form in such books as SZ1776 and B[L1798]. The occasional employment of די di after certain prepositions in M[N1783] may be explained by the fact that this text was printed in the Mideastern area. Both M[N1783] and EP1790 may also testify to the fact that the prepositional case of the feminine definite article had not yet been fully levelled to דר dər in contemporary Southeastern Yiddish. What is puzzling is that both texts printed in the Northeast, VS[1783] and AH1795, have only דר dər in the prepositional case.

The precise dialectological and socio-linguistic factors related to this development deserve a separate study; but it is apparent that all these books point towards an overall levelling of the prepositional case, a levelling that subsequently became one of the major grammatical hallmarks of the modern literary language.

35.7 Functional Words

In all the texts, the modern Yiddish functional words are systematically employed. The morpho-syntactic organization of these texts thereby became markedly Eastern Yiddish. However, in the earlier works, BZ1771 and SZ1776, the older functional words inherited from the old literary language continued to be used side by side with their new pan-Eastern Yiddish equivalents.

Thus the old relative pronouns (דר (דא)/ די (דא)/ דש (דא) dər (dɔ)/ di (dɔ)/ dɔs (dɔ) 'that; which' (masc./ fem./ neut.) and the old conjunction דז dɔs/ das 'that' are still used along with the new general relative pronoun וואס vɔs 'that; which' and the modern conjunction אז az 'that' in BZ1771 and SZ1776 (cf. §28.3.2.5). However, even here דז dɔs/ das is already markedly less frequent than אז az. (On the historical development of אז az 'that' see

Fridberg 1968.) And though דז dɔs/das is still current in EP1790, it was fully replaced by אז az in all other books from the 1780s and 1790s—viz. VS[1783], M[N1783], AH1795, and B[L1798]—except EP1790.

On the other hand, the old relative pronouns continued to be used occasionally in EP1790 and B[L1798]. In EP1790 this usage was sanctioned by the direct impact of New High German on its author. In B[L1798] it was directly inherited from Old Literary Yiddish. In both texts the occurrence of the old relative pronouns declined markedly in comparison with their use in BZ1771 and SZ1776. In all the other books, VS[1783], M[N1783], and AH1795, the old relative pronouns dər (dɔ)/ di (dɔ)/ dɔs (dɔ) 'that; which' (masc./ fem./ neut.) were entirely replaced by the new general relative pronoun וואָס vɔs 'that, which, who'.

Another important innovation is the frequent use of the final conjunction כדי kədej 'so that; in order to'. The older final conjunction דר וואָרטן dərvɔrtn̩ is still found in BZ1771, SZ1776, and VS[1783]. However, כדי kədej prevails in these books, and the occurrence of דר וואָרטן dərvɔrtn̩ is very rare in SZ1776 and VS[1783]. In all the other works only the new final conjunction is used.

Table 27 sums up the occurrence of the old and new functional words in the extant texts.

Table 27 Functional words in late eighteenth-century Eastern Yiddish printed works

	Final conjunctions		Subordinate conjunctions		Relative pronouns	
	old	new	old	new	old	new
	דר וואָרטן ‖ כדי		דז ‖ אז		דר/די/דש (דא) ‖ וואָס		
	dərvɔrtn̩ ‖ kədej		dɔs/das ‖ az		dər/di/dɔs (dɔ) ‖ vɔs		
BZ	+	+	+	+	+	+
SZ	+	+	+	+	+	+
VS	+	+	−	+	−	+
M[N]	−	+	−	+	−	+
EP	−	+	+	+	+	+
AH	−	+	−	+	−	+
B[L]	−	+	−	+	+	+

35.8 The Preterite

Although the preterite had disappeared from Western as well as Eastern Yiddish dialects at a much earlier stage (cf. Joffe 1940: 92–3; Lincoff 1963: 110–12 §7.4; Weinreich 1973: ii. 175–6 §142.1), it continued to play an important stylistic function in the narrative or 'epic' styles of Old Yiddish literature. Consequently, the third-person preterite forms of some strong verbs survived in the old literary language until very late. In the eighteenth century, as a result of the increasing impact of New High German, preterite forms of weak verbs were often introduced into Western Yiddish books (e.g. *Ben hameylekh vehanozir* (Frankfurt am Main, 1769); *Mayse gdoyle min k"k Uman* (Fürth, 1783); *Bove mayse* (Frankfurt an der Oder, 1796)).

By contrast, in Eastern Europe only the conventional third-person preterite forms of some strong verbs survived in works that were stylistically patterned on the Old Yiddish narrative or 'epic' styles—hence the repeated use of these forms in BZ1771, SZ1776, and B[L1798]. However, only a limited number of strong verbs appear in the preterite in BZ1771 (cf. §28.3.1.1), and in SZ1776 only the forms וואר vɔr 'was' and שפראך šprɔx (or šprax) 'spake' are found (e.g. 138, 146, 168, 187, 213, 229). The most extensive employment of the preterite is found in B[L1798]. The occurrence of many of these forms may perhaps be traced back to one of the earlier revisions of this book, its direct textual source. The repeated use of the preterite is one of the very few archaic features of B[L1798]; otherwise its grammar and phraseology are based almost entirely on modern Eastern Yiddish. The preservation of the preterite was in this case motivated by the conventional stylistic requirements of the Old Yiddish narrative genre.

In all other texts, VS[1783], M[N1783], EP1790, and AH1795, the preterite as a category was totally abandoned. The only exception is Markuze's EP1790, in which the form וואר vɔr 'was' is still occasionally used (see Herzog 1965b: 61 §5.2). However, this was the most frequently used form in Old Literary Yiddish, and it may have survived even in the spoken language of that period. Markuze himself apparently perceived this form as the Yiddish variant of the New High German imperfect (cf. NHG *war*). Another possible relic of the preterite is found in M[N1783]: האטן אן גיהובן hɔtṇ(?) ɔ́ngəhɔjbṇ '[they] began' (M[N], 362–3). This form is especially surprising, since M[N] has no other preterite forms, and האטן hɔtṇ(?) is not found in other texts. Whereas the historical past-subjunctive form העטן hɛtṇ 'would' (1st and 3rd pers. pl.) was still used in Eastern Yiddish and in these texts as conditional, there are no clear indications that האטן hɔtṇ(?) survived in the spoken or written languages of the period.

But it is clear that one of the major features of nascent Modern Literary Yiddish was the wholesale rejection of the Old Yiddish preterite. The general decline of the preterite is characteristic of most of the books under discussion (including EP1790 and especially M[N1783]).

35.9 The Future-Tense Auxiliary

The Eastern Yiddish paradigm of the future-tense auxiliary was already the norm in the earliest text, BZ1771. Subsequently the finite forms of the modal verbs װערן vɛrn̩ 'become' and װעלן vɛln̩ 'want' became formally distinguished from the respective forms of the future-tense auxiliary (cf. §28.3.3.4; on the historical development of the future-tense in Yiddish see Lincoff 1963: 143–6 §9.2). However, before the infinitive זײן zajn 'be', BZ1771 still occasionally employs the form װירט virt(?)/vɛrt as the third-person singular of the future-tense auxiliary. This usage was probably inspired by contemporary Germanized Western Yiddish books.

The second text, SZ1776, is far less uniform. It does not distinguish between the first-person singular forms of the future auxiliary and the verb װעלן vɛln̩ 'want' (e.g. 64, 68 142). This may in part be explained by the fact that in SZ the grapheme ⟨י⟩ is often interchangeable with ⟨ע⟩, thus ⟨װיט⟩ and ⟨װעט⟩ both representing vət '[he] will' (cf. 150, 156). However, this text often uses the older forms װערשט vərst, װערט vərt and װערן vərn̩ for the second- and third-person singular and for the first- and third-person plural of the future-tense auxiliary. The first two forms are less frequent than their Eastern Yiddish equivalents װעשט vəst, װעט vət. But it is obvious that SZ1776 has a 'mixed' paradigm in which the older (synchronically Western Yiddish) forms of the future-tense auxiliary compete with their Eastern Yiddish equivalents. Similarly, in EP1790 the New High German model reinforces the occasional use of װערט vərt as the second-person plural and third-person singular and of װערן vərn̩ as the second- and third-person plural of the future-tense auxiliary (see Herzog 1965b: 61 §5.5). However, these forms are clearly outnumbered by their Eastern Yiddish equivalents so that, statistically, the Eastern Yiddish paradigm of the future auxiliary may be viewed as the norm in EP1790.

Residues of the old future auxiliary are still found in one of the later texts, AH1795. Here װערן vərn̩ is used a few times as the third-person plural (66, 74, 94, 103, 122, 275, 287), and װערט vərt (44) as well as װער vər (AH, 206) were used, once each, for the third-person singular . But these are very rare exceptions. In all other cases װעלן vəln̩ (94 times) and װעט vət (145 times) appear throughout.

In all the other later books, M[N1783], VS[1783], and B[L1798], only the Eastern Yiddish future auxiliary is found.

As can be seen from Table 28, the Eastern Yiddish paradigm of the future-tense auxiliary was adopted in the earliest text (BZ1771). In a number of later printed works (SZ1776, EP1790, and AH1795) certain conventional Western Yiddish forms occasionally appear along with the prevailing Eastern Yiddish forms. In other texts (M[N1783], VS[1783], B[L1798]) the new

Table 28 The future-tense auxiliary in late eighteenth-century Eastern Yiddish printed works

	1st pers. sing.		2nd pers. sing.		3rd pers. sing.		1st and 3rd pers. pl.	
	old	new	old	new	old	new	old	new
	װער	װעל	װערשט	װעשט	װערט	װעט	װערן	װעלן
	vər	vəl	vərst	vəst	vərt	vət	vərṇ	vəlṇ
BZ	–	+	–	+	(+)	+	+	+
SZ	–	+	+	+	+	+	(+)	+
VS	–	+	–	+	–	+	–	+
M[N]	–	+	–	+	–	+	–	+
EP	–	+	–	+	(+)	+	(+)	+
AH	–	+	–	+	(+)	+	(+)	+
B[L]	–	+	–	+	–	+	–	+

Note: bracketed sign (+) designates minority usage.

future-tense auxiliary became the norm, and a full formal distinction between the finite forms of the modal verbs vɛlṇ 'want' and vɛrṇ 'become' and between the respective forms of the future-tense auxiliary was achieved.

35.10 Verbal Aspect

In Western Yiddish and in the old literary language a set of verbal prefixes and unstressed preverbs functioned as various *Aktionsart* markers. It may be possible to trace some beginnings of a more grammaticalized aspect system in the old literary language of the late seventeenth and early eighteenth centuries (cf. §7.3.7). If such a system did already exist in contemporary spoken Eastern Yiddish, it probably had some impact on Western Yiddish dialects as well. Yet, overall, one of the most essential structural differences between Western and Eastern Yiddish, and ultimately between the old and the modern literary languages, is the markedly 'Slavonicized' system of verbal aspect so essentially characteristic of the modern language. Most of the native stressed verbal prefixes and unstressed preverbs were reinterpreted in Eastern Yiddish as aspect markers, and were accordingly remodelled semantically and grammatically on the Slavonic type of aspect system (see U. Weinreich 1958a: 380–2; Wexler 1964). Here we are primarily concerned with the verbal aspect as such. A systematic examination of the modern Yiddish aspect and its correlations with other verbal categories warrants a separate monograph. (On the possible correlations between tense and aspect categories see Comrie 1976: 66–82; Dahl 1985: 129–53; various facets of verbal aspectology in Yiddish are analysed or discussed in

Schaechter 1951, 1952*a*, 1952*b*; U. Weinreich 1952*b*; Wexler 1964, 1972; Lockwood-Baviskar 1974; Mark 1978: 291-8; Aronson 1985; Taube 1987; Nath 1988; Rothstein 1990; Weissberg 1991.)

The only text in which the exclusively Eastern Yiddish type of aspect marking was not detected is VS[1783]. In other texts the extent to which the Eastern Yiddish aspect system was introduced is still limited. Whereas in BZ1771 (cf. §28.3.3.5) and M[N1783] aspectually perfectivized verbs can quite often be encountered, they are still relatively infrequent in SZ1776, EP1790, and AH1795. On the other hand, B[L1798] is possibly the earliest text with a decidedly Eastern Yiddish aspect system.

Prefixed verbs continue to function in VS[1783] as conventional *Aktionsarten*. The form הושט אוש גימאַכט host ɔ́jsgəmàxt 'you won over' (VS, 105; cf. NHG *aussmachen*) is not necessarily the perfective form of מאַכן maxn̩ 'make'. The imperative נעם אָפּ nɛm ɔ́p (VS, 58; cf. NHG *abnehmen*) retains the meaning 'take away' in this context. It therefore cannot be analysed as a markedly perfective 'take'.

At first glance the same may appear to be true of the following forms found in SZ1776: קערן אוש ɔ́jskɛrn̩ 'sweep out' (89; cf. NHG *auskehren*); אָן שרייבן ɔ́nšrajbn̩ 'write down' (190; cf. NHG *anschreiben*); אָפּ ווישן ɔ́pvišn̩ 'wipe off' (190; cf. NHG *abwischen*) and אָפּ וועגן ɔ́pvɛgn̩ (195; cf. NHG *abwiegen*) 'weigh'. However, the forms נעמט אָפּ nɛmt ɔ́p (206) and גיט אָפּ git ɔ́p (205) already function as aspectually marked (i.e. perfective) counterparts of נעמן nɛmən 'take' (e.g. 203) and געבן gɛbn̩ 'give' (e.g. 98, 194) respectively. Moreover, the modern Yiddish aspectual stem construction is found once in SZ1776 (cf. below §35.10.1), and an exclusively Eastern Yiddish type of prefixation is evident in the form אָן לייגן ɔ́nlejgn̩ 'pile on' (237; cf. Pol. *nałożyć*, Ukr. накладати). Although the aspectual forms in SZ1776 are very few, they clearly indicate that the underlying aspect system of this text is ultimately modelled on Eastern Yiddish usage. It is therefore possible that the above-mentioned conventional *Aktionsarten* had by then largely been reinterpreted in this text as perfective forms.

In AH1795 the aspectually marked forms can be contrasted with the verbs used in an earlier Western Yiddish translation of the same book entitled *Avkes roykhl taytsh apteyk* (Amsterdam, 1648). The most obvious perfective forms of AH1795 are usually represented in the Western Yiddish translation with simple (unprefixed) verbs. Thus the form בריט אים אָן bréjt im ɔ́n 'prepares him' (perf., 38; cf. Pol. *nagotować*, Ukr. наготувати) appears as ברענגט אים brɛngt im 'brings him' in the 1648 translation and אָן טרענקן ɔ́ntrɛnkən 'give to drink' (perf.) (AH, 229-30, cf. Pol. *napoić*, Ukr. напувати) as טרענקן trɛnkən 'give to drink'. These cases illustrate one of the major differences between the old literary and the modern literary language.

However, the marked perfectivity of the prefixed forms used in AH1795 and
other books can safely be identified if a given prefixed verb does not have an
exact morphological and semantic equivalent in New High German (cf.
Lockwood-Baviskar 1974: 30), but does have a Slavonic parallel. This pro-
cedure is objectionable in a strictly synchronic analysis of aspect in Yiddish,
but it may be used here for the detection of aspect, since the fundamentally
'aspectless' old literary language continued to play an important part in the
grammatical and stylistic make-up of the texts.

Many verbal prefixes were most likely to be calqued from Slavonic
languages as productive aspect markers (cf. U. Weinreich 1958a: 380–1;
Wexler 1964: 85; 1972: 89–90; Lockwood-Baviskar 1974: 33; Nath
1988). These have been examined in all the texts.

The following prefixes and preverbs were identified as markers of the
aspectual perfective ~ imperfective opposition in the extant texts:

אָן ɔn 'on' (cf. Pol. na-, Ukr. на-): M[N], SZ, EP, B[L], AH;
אוי(י)ש ɔjs 'out' (cf. Pol. wy-, Ukr. ви-): M[N], EP, B[L];
אָפ ɔp 'off' (cf. Pol. od-, Ukr. від-): SZ, M[N], B[L];
דר dǝr- (perf., resultative, cf. Pol. do-, Ukr. до-): BZ, M[N], B[L];
פֿ(אַ)ר far- (perf., resultative; cf. Pol. prze-, za-, Ukr. за-): EP.

The most frequently used verbal prefix is אוי(י)ש ɔjs. However, its productivity is by and large restricted to one text (B[L1798]). The most widely used
productive 'Slavonicized' verbal prefix functioning as aspect marker is אָן ɔn.
Its presence as *Aktionsart* or as an aspect marker was undoubtedly less
prominent in the old literary language. The fact that אָן ɔn is so popular in at
least two texts (M[N1783] and B[L1798]) may indicate that it was one of the
most productive aspect markers in certain Eastern Yiddish dialects of that
period (Southeastern Yiddish?).

Certain forms that have direct Slavonic parallels have been included in the
following list, even where their exact morphological and semantic equivalent was found in New High German (e.g. nos. 1.8, 2.1, 2.8–9, 3.3–4, 4.4
below). Given the persistent pressure of the Slavonic *Aktionsart* and aspect
systems upon Eastern Yiddish and upon most of our texts, it is reasonable to
assume that these forms were reanalysed as aspectually marked verbs.

In some cases it can be argued that the prefixed form functions primarily
as *Aktionsart* (e.g. nos. 1.4, 1.6, 1.9, 2.3, 4.3 below). These forms are not
only exclusively modelled on the Slavonic pattern, however, but are also
adopted as perfectives. So most of them are generally unacceptable in a dura-
tive construction in Eastern Yiddish (cf. Lockwood-Baviskar 1974: 24, 29).

The following list gives some aspectually marked verbs found in late
eighteenth-century Eastern Yiddish printed works:

1 **With the verbal complement** אָן ɔn

1. 1 ɔnbrejtn̩ 'prepare' (perf., cf. Pol. *nagotować*, Ukr. наготувати):
   בּרייט אים אָן brejt im ɔn 'prepares him' (perf.) (AH, 38);

1. 2 ɔ́ntrɛnkən 'give to drink' (perf., cf. Pol. *napoić*, Ukr. напувати):
   אָן טרענקן ɔ́ntrɛnkən 'give to drink' (perf.) (AH, 229-30);

1. 3 ɔ́nlejgn̩ 'pile up' (cf. Pol. *nałożyć*, Ukr. накладати):
   אָן גילייגט ɔ́ngəlejgt 'piled up' (SZ, 237);

1. 4 ɔ́nvarfn̩ 'throw about; pile up' (cf. Pol. *narzucić*, Ukr. накидати):
   אָן גיוואָרפֿן ɔ́ngəvɔrfn̩ 'piled up' (M[N], 194);

1. 5 ɔ́nšnajdn̩ 'cut, mow' (perf., cf. Pol. *nakrajać, nakosić*,
   Ukr. нарвати, накосити):
   אָן צו שנײדן ɔ́ncušnajdn̩ 'mow down' (B[L], 9a);

1. 6 ɔ́nɛsn̩ zəx 'eat one's fill' (cf. Pol. *najeść się*, Ukr. наїстися):
   זיך אָן גגעסן zəx ɔ́ngəgɛsn̩ 'ate his fill' (B[L], 5a);
   וועט זיך אָן עסן vət zəx ɔ́nɛsn̩ 'he will eat to his fill' (B[L], 16b);

1. 7 ɔ́nhɔdəvən 'feed; nurse' (perf., cf. Pol. *nahodować*,
   Ukr. нагодувати):
   אָן גיהאָדעוועט ɔ́ngəhɔdəvət 'nursed; fed to fill' (EP, 108b);

1. 8 ɔ́nštɔpn̩ 'cram, stuff' (perf., cf. Ukr. напхати, Russ. набивать,
   NHG *anstopfen*):
   אָן גישטאָפּט ɔ́ngəštɔpt 'stuffed' (EP, 108a);
   שטאָפֿן זיך אָן štɔpn̩ zəx ɔ́n, 'stuff themselves' (EP, 108a);

1. 9 ɔ́narbətn̩ 'make, cause' (perf., cf. Pol. *narobić*, Ukr. наробити):
   אײן הריגה אָן גיאַרבט an (h)aríɡə ɔ́ngəarbət 'performed many killings'
   (M[N], 177).

2 **With the prefix** אוֹ(י)ס ɔjs

2. 1 ɔ́jsrɛdn̩ 'utter' (cf. Pol. *wymówić*, Ukr. вимовити, NHG *aussprechen*):
   אויס גרעט ɔ́jsɡərɛt 'uttered' (B[L], 12a);

2. 2 ɔ́jshɛrn̩ 'hear out' (cf. Pol. *wysłuchać*, Ukr. вислухати):
   הערט אויס hɛrt ɔ́js '[he] hears out' (EP, ⟨p.34⟩);

2. 3 ɔ́jsšisn̩ 'shoot out' (cf. Pol. *wystrzelić*, Ukr. вистрілити,
   NHG *ausschießen*):
   אויס גישאסן ɔ́jsɡəšɔsn̩ 'shot out' (M[N], 54, 93);

2. 4 ɔ́jshargənən 'kill, exterminate' (cf. Pol. *wymordować*,
   Ukr. виморити, NHG *ausrotten*):
   אויס הרגנן ɔ́jshargənən 'kill, annihilate' (M[N], 256; B[L], 17a);

2. 5 ɔ́jsštɛxn̩ 'kill, annihilate', lit. 'pierce to death'; cf. Pol. *wykłuć*,
   Ukr. виколоти 'prick out', NHG *ausstechen*):
   אויס גישטאָכטן ɔ́jsɡəštɔxn̩ 'killed (a whole group of people) by
   piercing' (M[N], 231);

2. 6 ɔ́jslɛbn̩ 'live (through a certain period)' (cf. Pol. *wyżyć*):
לעבט קאם דש יאר אויש lɛbt kam dɔs jɔr ɔjs
'[he can] barely live through the year' (B[L], 19a);

2. 7 ɔ́jsklejdn̩ 'dress up' (cf. Ukr. вирядити,
note NHG *auskleiden* 'undress'):
קלייד אויש klejd(t) ɔ́js '[he] dresses [her] up' (B[L], 41a);

2. 8 ɔ́jstrinkən 'drink up' (cf. Pol. *wypić*, Ukr. випити, NHG *austrinken*):
טרינקט דש אויש trinkt dɔs ɔjs '[he] drinks it up' (B[L], 14a);

2. 9 ɔ́jstrikənən 'dry out' (cf. Pol. *wysuszyć*, Ukr. висушити;
NHG *austrocknen*):
טריקנט אויש triknt̩ ɔ́js 'dries out' (perf., BZ, 13a).

3 With the prefix אפ ɔp

3. 1 ɔ́pruən 'rest; relax' (cf. Pol. *oddychać*, Ukr. відпочити):
אפ רוא̇ן ɔ́pruən 'take a rest' (B[L], 22b);

3. 2 ɔ́pnɛmən 'take away (perf.)' (cf. Pol. *odebrać*, Ukr. відібрати,
cf. NHG *abnehmen*):
װען ער נעממ אפ vən ər nɛmt ɔ́p 'when he takes away' (perf.; SZ, 206);

3. 3 ɔ́pgɛbn̩ 'give' (perf., cf. Pol. *oddawać*, Ukr. віддати, NHG *abgeben*):
אפ געלט [. . .] װען ער גיט vən ər git [. . .] ɔ́p gɛlt 'when he returns the
money' (perf., SZ, 205);

3. 4 ɔ́pɛsn̩ 'eat' (perf.; cf. Pol. *odjeść*, Ukr. від'їсти, NHG *abessen*):
אפ גגעסן ɔ́pgəgɛsn̩ 'finished eating' (B[L], 13a).

4 With the prefix דר dər-

4. 1 dəršrajbn̩ 'describe [perf.]; provide an account'
(cf. Pol. *dopisać*, Ukr. дописати 'finish writing'):
דער שרייבן dəršrajbn̩ 'tell; describe in full detail' (M[N], 381);

4. 2 dərlɛbn̩ 'live to see; survive' (cf. Pol. *dożyć*, *przeżyć*, Ukr. дожити):
דר לעבן dərlɛbn̩ 'live [to do evil]' (M[N], 406);

4. 3 dərzɛn 'see [perf.]; notice' (cf. Pol. *dojrzeć*, Ukr. добачити):
דר זעה(י)ן dərzɛn 'see; notice' (BZ, 37b; M[N], 295; B[L], 32b);

4. 4 dərjɔgn̩ 'catch up with' (cf. Pol. *dognać*, Ukr. догнати,
NHG *erjagen*):
דר יאגן dərjɔ́gn̩ 'to catch up with' (B[L], 5b);

4. 5 dərštɛxn̩ 'pierce through' (cf. Pol. *dobić*, Ukr. добити 'beat up',
NHG *erschlagen* 'kill'):
דר שטעכ̇ין dərštɛ́xn̩ 'pierce through [to death]' (B[L], 11b).

5 With the prefix פֿ(א)ר far-

5. 1 farblɔ́nžən/ farblɔ́ndžən 'wander [perf.]; go astray'

(cf. Pol. *zabłądzić*, Ukr. заблудити, also NHG *verirren*):

פאר בלאָנזיט farblón(d)žət 'wanders (perf.) [→ arrives]' (EP, 49b).

35.10.1 *Stem Construction*

Another distinctive feature of the modern Yiddish aspect system is the so-called stem construction that developed into a special morpho-syntactic device to express instantaneous action (see Schaechter 1951, 1952a, 1952b; Mark 1978: 293–5 §4; Taube 1987; Aronson 1985; D. Katz 1987a: 156–9 §9.1.1; 167–9 §9.1.9). In the modern literary language it has two major productive patterns: {tɔn 'do'} + {indefinite article} + {verbal stem}, and {gɛbṇ 'give'} + {indefinite article} + {verbal stem}. The complete grammaticalization of this construction in the modern literary language apparently occurred before the middle of the nineteenth century. (See the many examples analysed by Taube 1987.)

The stem construction is not found in most late eighteenth-century Eastern Yiddish texts, though it may have been current in the spoken language of that period. This construction may have been felt to be too colloquial, and thus by and large inadmissible in literary usage. However, its existence in the spoken language of the eighteenth century is echoed in a few exceptional occasions where this construction was employed in SZ1776, M[N1783], and B[L1798].

The following forms are found:

1 האט אין שיין גגעבן ווי איין בליץ איבר זיין קאפ
hɔt a šajn gəgɛbṇ vi a blic ibər zajn kɔp
'and light appeared like a flash over his head' (SZ, 186);

2 הט אים איין האק גיגעבן מיט דר שווערד
hɔt im a hak gəgɛbṇ mit dər švɛrd
'and he hacked him with the sword' (SZ, 227);

3 איך האב איר איין שטורק גגעבן מיט דעם פֿוס
ix hɔb ir a štɔrk gəgɛbṇ mit dəm fus
'I kicked her with my foot' (M[N], 455);

4 טוט זיא אים איין קוש tut zi im a kuš
'she kisses him [swiftly]' (B[L], 7b);

5 אונ זיא טוט אים איין קוש אין מויל un zi tut im a kuš in mɔjl
'and she kisses him [swiftly] on [his] mouth' (B[L], 9b);

6 אונ ער טיט אים איין קוש un ər tut im a kuš
'and he kisses him [swiftly]' (B[L], 14b).

The reading of the first sentence is somewhat problematic. Its verbal phrase may be analysed either as האָט אײן שײן גגעבן hɔt a šajn gəgɛbṇ or alternatively as האָט גגעבן ווי אײן בליץ hɔt gəgɛbṇ vi a blic, in which case שײן

šajn 'light' is the subject. But it is clear that either way the choice of the verb gɛbņ was motivated by its auxiliary function in the stem construction marking instantaneous action. The fact that it translates the original Hebrew הכה hikkōh (literally 'struck') supports this suggestion.

The second example is a more conventional stem construction with gɛbņ, a special auxiliary. Judging by the context, it was used to express instantaneous action. The form האק hak is a specially derived verbal stem of האקן hakņ 'hack'. The same type of stem construction was found in M[N1783] (see no. 3 above). It may still be viewed as a simple combination of verb and complement; e.g. טוא דוא נאך איין פרוב tu du nɔx a pruv 'make another attempt' (M[N], 59). Such combinations were also occasionally used in Old Literary Yiddish (see Taube 1987: 13–14). The form שטאָרק štɔrk(?) could be either a noun (cf. modern Yiddish שטאָרך štɔrx 'jostle; kick') or the special verbal stem of שטאָרכן štɔrxņ 'jostle; kick'. In either case the construction describes, or alternatively marks, an instantaneous action.

In B[L1798] (see nos. 4–6 above) the stem construction is formed with the auxiliary tɔn 'do'. It is used only with קושן kušņ 'kiss'. The verbal stem קוש kuš is homonymous with the noun קוש kuš 'kiss'. There can be no doubt, however, that this construction is employed in B[L1798] as an aspectually marked syntagm. It is used only when the 'kissers' are in a hurry; otherwise the same action is usually expressed by an aspectually unmarked verb or by the so-called 'habitual aspect'; e.g.:

אונ זי קושט אים אין מויל
un zi kušt im in mɔjl
'and she kisses him on [his] mouth' (B[L], 10b);

אונ טוט אים קושן אין זיין מויל אונ ער קושט זי
un tut im kušņ in zajn mɔjl un ər kušt zi
'and [she] kisses him on his mouth and he kisses her' (B[L], 11a).

However, on the whole, stem construction did not become a regular feature in the texts under discussion. It seems not to have been fully accepted in the literary language until the early nineteenth century (e.g. in *Sipurey mayses* (Ostra, 1815) and *Shivkhey Besht* (Korets, 1816); on the language of *Shivkhey Besht* see Wolf 1976).

35.11 Old versus Modern Forms and Categories

A remarkable approximation to the spoken language was achieved in late eighteenth-century Eastern Yiddish books. In the earliest works, BZ1771 and SZ1776, modern Eastern Yiddish was accepted as a possible, and in some cases as the preferable, model of literary usage. In the later books the linguistic shift from the old literary language to nascent Modern Literary Yiddish was either imminent (in VS[1783] and EP1790) or almost complete (in M[N1783], AH1795, and B[L1798]). All these texts therefore point to an increasing *rapprochement* between the spoken and the literary languages.

At the same time, it is important to stress that all these books were written in the traditional semiotic framework of Old Yiddish literature. The usually anonymous authors certainly did not perceive themselves as daring linguistic innovators in the field of literary Yiddish. On the contrary, their work was directly associated with Old Yiddish literature and with the old literary language, which therefore continued to play an important part in the linguistic fabric of these books. This is primarily evident in the relatively limited choice of forms and in certain lexical items. In most of these works aspectually marked verbs and grammaticalized stem constructions are still inadequately or poorly represented (e.g. SZ1776, EP1790, AH1795). Slavonic component items that became fully acceptable in literary works from the early nineteenth century onwards were still by and large inadmissible in such remarkably Eastern Yiddish texts as VS[1783] and AH1795, and even in M[N1783] and B[L1798].

A final balancing of the evidence makes it clear that most of the Old Yiddish features are already on the defensive in the two earliest books. In some of the later works they are remarkably obsolescent. In others still they have become totally obsolete. Most of the archaic features may thus be viewed as disappearing vestiges of Old Literary Yiddish. Only in a handful of cases can the retention of older forms be explained either as stylistic convention or as a feature that might still have been current in late eighteenth-century Eastern Yiddish.

The most obvious case of a stylistically motivated retention of an archaic feature is the use of the preterite in such works as BZ1771, SZ1776, and B[L1798] (cf. above §35.8). It is clear that in these and also in some early nineteenth-century Eastern Yiddish texts the preservation of the preterite was motivated by the stylistic conventions of Old Yiddish narrative style. The periphrastic possessive construction {noun (= possessor) + possessive pronoun + noun} (cf. §28.3.2.2) may also have been considered a stylistically preferable archaism at the time. This construction was used in free variation with the regular possessive case in BZ1771, SZ1776, and EP1790, but is exceptionally rare in M[N1783] and B[L1798] and absent from VS[1783] and AH1795.

All other Old Yiddish features seem to follow a similar pattern of progressive disappearance. First they continue to be used alongside their Eastern Yiddish equivalents, in BZ1771 and SZ1776. In some cases the older forms are outnumbered even in those early texts (e.g. functional words, cf. §35.7, and possessive pronouns, cf. §35.5). They are seldom used in some of the later books, and have become totally obsolete in others. The eventual disappearance of the older paradigm of the future-tense auxiliary (cf. §35.9), the historical accusative form of the masculine definite article (cf. §35.6.2), and the old possessive pronouns (cf. §35.5) are cases in point.

The most striking disappearance of older patterns can be observed in the realm of syntax. Finite verbs may still occupy the final position in a subordinate clause in BZ1771 and SZ1776. In EP1790 this pattern was directly reinstated from New High German, but it is rejected in all the other books, where the place of the finite verb is the same in the main and in the subordinate clauses (with the exception of indirect questions). Similarly, in BZ1771 and SZ1776 past participles and infinitives are often placed in a clause-final position when this word order is at variance with the prevalent syntactic pattern of Eastern Yiddish. However, in all other texts (again with the sole exception of the Germanized EP1790), the actual placing of participles and infinitives complies with the syntactic and stylistic requirements of modern Eastern Yiddish.

Whatever stylistic prestige might have been ascribed to the various morphological and syntactic features of the old literary language initially, it was only a short time before the ever increasing pressure of the spoken language fully reshaped the grammatical make-up of the literary language.

The decline and eventual disappearance of many Old Yiddish morphological features was not strictly chronological. All these works represent the same period in the history of spoken Eastern Yiddish, and the extent to which an Old Yiddish feature may survive varies from text to text irrespective of whether it was printed in the 1770s, 1780s, or 1790s. Thus the recurring confusion between the historical dative and accusative forms of the masculine definite article in BZ1771 and SZ1776 is also characteristic of the later AH1795. The Eastern Yiddish future-tense auxiliary was more consistently used in BZ1771 than in SZ1776 and AH1795. The declinable attributive possessive pronoun becomes a regular means of expressing 'inalienable' possession in the latest book, B[L1798] (cf. §35.5.1). The overall decline of Old Yiddish morphological and morpho-syntactic features is summarized in Table 29.

Certain features that appear to be archaic from the viewpoint of Modern Literary Yiddish may still have been current in the various dialects of late eighteenth-century Eastern Yiddish. But it is impossible clearly to identify them solely on the basis of the texts discussed. These books primarily represent changes in the literary language, so they cannot be viewed as direct, unmediated documents of the contemporary spoken language. Nevertheless, it is plausible that the periphrastic possessive construction was

Table 29 Old Yiddish features in late eighteenth-century Eastern Yiddish books

Book	Relative pronouns	Conjunctions	Periphrastic possessive	Genitive of pronouns	Declinable pronouns	Future auxiliary
BZ1771	+	+	+	+	–	(+)
SZ1776	+	(+)	+	+	(+)	+
VS[1783]	(+)	(+))	–	(+))	–	–
M[N1783]	–	–	(+))	(+)	(+))	–
EP1790	(+)	(+)	(+)	(+)	(+)	(+)
AH1795	–	–	–	(+))	(+))	(+)
B[L1798]	–	(+))	(+)	+	+	–

Note: (+) indicates minority usage; (+)) less then four times in the given text.

still current in the Southeastern dialect as the more formal expression of possession. Its total absence from VS[1783] and AH1795 may also indicate that it was already obsolete in Northeastern Yiddish. Similarly, the construction {tɔn + infinitive} (cf. §28.3.1.2) may have been used, at least in the Mideastern dialect, as a marked analytic form of the habitual aspect. Its frequent occurrence in VS[1783] and in most of the Southeastern texts may also be ascribed directly to the continuing influence of Old Yiddish phraseology. Nor is it clear whether the functionalized employment of declinable possessive pronouns in SZ1776, M[N1783], and B[L1798] (in particular) is a sufficient indication that this form of 'inalienable' possession existed in contemporary spoken Southeastern Yiddish.

When compared both with contemporary Western Yiddish texts and with the Easternized re-editions and revisions of Old Yiddish texts, the books under discussion are all seen to be either principally or wholly based on the morphological, and in most cases also the syntactic, patterns of modern Eastern Yiddish. All three groups of texts are marked by various degrees of *rapprochement* between the literary and the spoken languages. In the West the increasing linguistic assimilation to German coincided with the radical Germanization of the literary language. In the East the traditional Old Yiddish works were in some cases systematically revised on the grammatical patterns of spoken Eastern Yiddish. The most significant development of the literary language in Eastern Europe was achieved in the late eighteenth-century books that were both written and published in Eastern Europe. Most of the older or archaic features that can still be found in these works are direct survivals from the old literary language. Their imminent and often complete disappearence was to be only a matter of time. Because of the persistent pressure of the spoken language, the grammatical make-up of the literary language was fundamentally restructured and linguistically modernized. From such works as VS[1783], M[N1783], AH1795, and B[L1798] it was but one step to Modern Literary Yiddish.

9

Synthesis

36 The Eighteenth-Century Origins of Modern Literary Yiddish

In the late eighteenth century, literary Yiddish in Eastern Europe underwent a rapid process of restructuring and realignment. It was increasingly modelled on the grammatical, phraseological, and (to a lesser degree) lexical patterns of modern Eastern Yiddish. This process is evident in two types of literary texts printed in Eastern Europe. The first consists of older Yiddish works which were linguistically re-edited or revised, marking the transition from the old literary to the nascent modern literary language (see Part II). The second comprises literary monuments primarily, or entirely, written in modern Eastern Yiddish (see Part III), which embody the shift to nascent Modern Literary Yiddish. Such works as *Ben hameylekh vehanozir* (Zholkve, 1771), *Seyfer khsidem* (Zholkve, 1776), and *Eyzer Yisroel* (Poritsk, 1790) contribute in one way or another to its changing grammatical and lexical norms. In other works, *Vikuekh yeytser tov im ben odem* (Shklov, c.1783), *Avkes roykhl* (Horodne, 1795), and the *Bove mayse* ([Lemberg], c.1798), the shift was near its completion. In *Mayse gdoyle min Uman umin Ukrayne* ([Novidvor], c.1783) we have the earliest known original work written entirely in modern Eastern Yiddish.

The extent of linguistic change was restrained in the Eastern re-editions of older Yiddish works. Even in its more advanced stages the Easternization of older Yiddish works was by and large limited to morphology (see §23). Syntactic changes, however significant in the Lemberg (1786) revision of the *Tsene rene*, were in most cases impeded by the underlying word-order patterns of the original Old Yiddish texts. To restructure these patterns too drastically would mean to constantly break up the syntagmatic organization of the original text. The involvement of the anonymous eighteenth-century style-editors in all these re-editions, including that of the *Tsene rene*, remains largely confined to the 'updating' of most of the morphological features.

The nature of linguistic change is strikingly different in the late eighteenth-century works written in modern Eastern Yiddish. Their grammar is based mainly on the contemporary spoken language. The few archaic features inherited from the old literary language are in many cases either statistically insignificant residuals or stylistically conditioned usages.

Most of these archaic features are restricted to morphology and lexicon. The fact that the author's stylistic awareness becomes primarily confined to morphology shows how fundamental the change in the literary language was (cf. §32.4.1). Only individual archaic forms, and to a lesser degree categories, can still be perceived as stylistically more 'correct' or 'literary' variants. However, in all works subsequent to the 1780s the drive to write in Eastern Yiddish by and large neutralizes a similar stylistic awareness in syntax. On the other hand, the archaic language of the traditional Old Yiddish literary works continues to exert certain grammatical and mainly stylistic pressures to which most of the conservative or 'archaic' features of the nascent Modern Literary Yiddish may be directly attributed (cf. Viner 1928: 87–8; 1940b: 291–2; Shmeruk 1978: 180).

It is only natural that there was a substantial interface between the two types of texts: that is, between the linguistically revised or updated re-editions (the 'transition-texts') and the works primarily written in Eastern Yiddish (the 'shift-texts'). The latter, as we have just seen, continued to be influenced by what were rapidly becoming the 'bookish' features of the old literary language still abundant in contemporary re-editions of older works. The most decisive linguistic revisions of the older traditional works, on the other hand, began to appear sometime after the 1820s. The Eastern re-editions of *Tsene rene* are a case in point. Those printed between the Lemberg (1786) and Yozefov (1845) editions introduced various systematic and significant changes (cf. Shmeruk 1981: 156–7). However, only the later, Yozefov edition presents a linguistically fully modernized text. Evidently, this delay can be explained by the virtual corpus growth of new Eastern Yiddish works that appeared between the 1780s and 1840s (see §37). It seems thus that whereas the first transition-texts began to appear as early as 1777, the actual completion of the process was achieved under the impact of books written in Eastern Yiddish (the 'shift-texts'). In other words, the new Eastern Yiddish printed works encouraged and endorsed the successful completion of the transition from the old to the nascent modern literary language in those older works whose popularity did not diminish throughout the nineteenth and early twentieth centuries.

Most of the late eighteenth-century Eastern Yiddish works are anonymous. It is even unclear whether someone called Mórdkhe (Mordechai) was the author of *Vikuekh yeytser tov im ben odem* (Shklov, c.1783), as suggested by the letters ⟨מרדכ⟩ printed in larger type-font on the title-page. In all the other books, with the exception of *Eyzer Yisroel* (Poritsk, 1790), the author is unnamed. This anonymity of most of the works supports their semiotic attribution to conventional Yiddish literature (cf. Zfatman 1983: i. 56–79; however, the whole issue of the supposed 'anonymity of the Old Yiddish literature' awaits further exploration). Anonymity in this case reveals that an attempt at radical linguistic modernization may occur somewhat earlier than the socio-cultural modernization that usually accompanies it. The need for change in the literary language, so evident from the texts encountered in this study, resulted directly from the ever increasing pressure of contemporary spoken Yiddish.

37 Periodization of Literary Yiddish

To suggest a periodization scheme means to try to make sense out of narrow linguistic, textual, or any other chronology. A proper attempt at categorizing and abstracting chronological data for purposes of defining periods of a language must be attuned to the major historical landmarks, and particularly to the significant shifts and changes manifest in the corpus both in quality and quantity. Periodization of a literary language is primarily concerned with essentially different types of written or printed texts from those providing supporting evidence for the historical reconstruction of the spoken language (see Tolstoj 1988: 43–5). Thus, in a handful of older printed books from the seventeenth century, we find a number of sporadic and otherwise unacceptable or suppressed forms of the modern Eastern Yiddish future-tense auxiliary (cf. §5.3). A number of other modern Eastern features can and should be gleaned from various older Yiddish works written, printed, or published by native speakers of Eastern Yiddish from the sixteenth century onwards (§§5.1–2). Moreover, in some rare cases we may even find exceptionally innovative texts providing early printed attestation of Eastern Yiddish (see §5.3 on *Tikuney tshuve erets Tsvi* ([Cracow], 1666) and §§6–7 on DtZ1723 and DkZ[1723]). However, unless the work in question is an exception that proves the rule, its dialectal features are nothing but occasional and for the most part rare 'slips of print'. Therefore, all these texts, important as they are for the history of the spoken language, remain insignificant from the viewpoint of the history of the literary language. For it is only when the single, discrete, and isolated dialectalisms become collectively manifest in a sizeable body of texts that one can start to speak of the beginning of a new era in the history of the literary language. A small but qualitatively significant corpus of such texts was printed during the last three decades of the eighteenth century. A substantial number of these works all but discarded the old literary language in favour of modified or early nascent Modern Literary Yiddish (see Chapter 8).

Most of the Eastern European printed works discussed and analysed in this study mark the very beginnings of a principally new era in the history of literary Yiddish. They, together with a substantial corpus of works printed in increasingly Germanized Western Yiddish, justify a more focused internal subdivision of the NEW YIDDISH period (which starts *c*.1700 according to M. Weinreich 1973, but *c*.1650 according to D. Katz 1988*c*; see §2.3.1) into EARLY NEW YIDDISH (*c*.1650 or *c*.1700 to 1800) and NEW YIDDISH proper (±1800 to the present; see Table 30). In retrospect, the late seventeenth and especially the eighteenth century appear to be the springboard for modernization, providing a number of its important precursors in the fields of literature (cf. Shazar 1978: xxvii–xxx), educational reform (see Aptroot 1989 on the Amsterdam Bible translations), historiography, and proto-ideological religious and secular aspirations. (On Glikl Hamil's memoirs of 1691–1715, see Landau 1901; Aptroot 1991: 44–5; Turniansky 1993*b*; on Amsterdam as an important new centre of Yiddish literature and publishing in the seventeenth and eighteenth century, see Fuks 1983 and Aptroot 1988; on popular Yiddish historiography of the period see Shazar 1978 and Fuks 1981.) As in all periodization schemes the dates provided cannot be more than rough approximations. It seems, however, that the most decisive developments from the viewpoint of the literary language surfaced sometime around the year 1800.

Table 30 Internal chronological division of New Yiddish based on the historical development of the literary language

Period	Chronology	Literary languages
Early New Yiddish	±1650–±1700	Old Literary Yiddish
	±1700–±1800	Germanized Old Literary Yiddish or
		Germanized Western Yiddish
		nascent Modern Literary Yiddish
New Yiddish	1800–present	Modern Literary Yiddish

37.1 From Early New Yiddish to the Early Modern Literary Language

When compared with contemporary works, Moyshe Markuze's *Eyzer Yisroel* (Poritsk, 1790) is a remarkable exception. Though hardly the best 'stylist' of his time, Markuze is the first known personality to consciously attempt to use modern Eastern Yiddish as a literary medium. As he repeatedly writes, he does so to enlighten and educate his potential readers on matters of private and public health. He often touches on general social issues, and is well aware of his image in the eyes of the contemporary reader (cf. Shmeruk 1977). Markuze's linguistic contribution to literary Yiddish is equally exceptional, for his is the earliest work in which a large number of new Eastern Yiddish features are introduced together with many elements of *daytshmerish* (Eastern Yiddish remodelled on the lexical, morphological, and syntactic patterns of New High German).

Given all the other Eastern Yiddish works of the late eighteenth century, Markuze's book is a remarkable precursor of the imminent modernization of the literary language in the nineteenth century. The authors whose works were printed in the early nineteenth century are in many cases well known to us; e.g. Eliezer Pavir, Mendl Lefin (b. 1749), Khaykl Hurvits (b. 1759), and Rabbi Nakhmen Bratslaver (b. 1772). Their linguistic and stylistic awareness is not only evident from their language, but is often expounded upon in their works or attested in other documents (e.g. on Pavir cf. Yaari 1960; on Lefin cf. Shmeruk and Werses 1969: 71; Werses 1983: 174; Fishman 1989: 66–96; on Hurvits cf. Unger 1929; Shtif 1932*a*: 33). The emergence of individual authors who consciously chose to write and publish in modern Eastern Yiddish was crucial for its further development as a modern literary language. Yet until the end of the eighteenth century, with the remarkable exception of Moyshe Markuze, there are no other known individual writers with, so to speak, modern literary or educational aspirations.

The first work written and printed by a known literary figure after Markuze's *Eyzer Yisroel* was Eliezer Pavir's *Gdules Yoysef* (Zholkve, 1801), a popular translation of the Hebrew play *Milkhome basholem* (Shklov, 1797). All known Eastern Yiddish texts from the late eighteenth century, although innovative and often modern in their language, nevertheless belong to the pre-modern period in the history of literary Yiddish.

Whether the modern period is said to begin with Markuze's *Eyzer Yisroel* of 1790 or with Pavir's *Gdules Yoysef* of 1801 is a matter of choice. It seems convenient, however, to link the actual beginning of the modern period with the year 1800. We do not know how popular Markuze's book was or whether it was ever reprinted (cf. Shmeruk 1977: 378). By contrast, Pavir's literary career was not restricted to *Gdules Yoysef*, which was subsequently reprinted more than forty times (see Reyzen 1932: 211–12). He also wrote such works as *Sipurey haploes* (Zholkve, 1807, and reprinted at least twenty-one times), an important modern adaptation of the old Yiddish *Mayse bukh* (cf. Zfatman 1985: 167–8 no. 175), and *Shivkhey haBesht* (Zholkve, 1817), one of three then contemporary Yiddish translations of the hagiographic collection about the founder of Hasidism, the Baal Shem Tov (see Yaari 1960, Shmeruk 1988: 241–2). Pavir's language was no less Germanized than Markuze's, and his style was possibly too 'literary' in the traditional sense (or by our standards excessively 'bookish'), and hence more archaic than other contemporary Eastern Yiddish works (cf. M. Weinreich 1928: 28; 1973: i. 9–10 §3.1; Roskies 1974*b*: 4–5). However, the lasting influence of some of his works, as well as the fact that he, 'the [official] scribe of the Holy Community of Zholkve' (cf. Zfatman 1985: 163 no. 175), was apparently the first professional (or quasi-professional) modern Yiddish author must not be underrated.

Other important contemporary works written in modern Eastern Yiddish include Mendl Lefin's translation of Proverbs, *Mishley* (Tarnopol, 1814), into 'Podolian' (Northeastern variety of Southeastern) Yiddish (cf. Shmeruk 1964b); two earlier Yiddish texts of *Shivkhey haBesht* (Ostra, 1815 and Novidvor, 1816; cf. Yaari 1935, 1964; Shmeruk 1988: 240–1), Nakhmen Bratslaver's bilingual (Hebrew and Yiddish) *Sipurey mayses* (Ostra, 1815; cf. Piekarz 1972: 151 ff.; Shmeruk 1988: 246–8); Khaykl Hurvits's *Tsofnas paneyakh* (Berditshev, 1817; cf. Shlosberg 1937; Lerner 1939), which is an extensive adaptation and reworking of J. H. Campe's *Kolumbus oder die Entdekkung von Westindien* (Tübingen, 1798); Moyshe Bloshtern's new translations of *Khoyves halevoves* (Sadilkov, 1820) and *Kav hayosher* (Sadilkov, 1821; cf. Roskies 1974b: 5, 9–10); and the anonymous satiric play *Di genarte velt* (c.1820s; cf. Viner 1940b; Shmeruk 1979b). Although much has been written about most of these works, they nevertheless await a comparative linguistic and stylistic evaluation. They signify the beginning of the modern period (c.1800), a new qualitative phase in the history of literary Yiddish. During the nineteenth and early twentieth centuries, Eastern Yiddish rapidly developed into a new literary language with radically modern literary, educational, ideological, and political functions. The linguistic origins of this period are found in the late eighteenth-century Eastern Yiddish works.

38 The Rise of Modern Literary Yiddish: Historical, Linguistic, and Socio-linguistic Perspectives

The radical change of literary language was effected before the need for this change was adequately articulated or even referred to. Prior to the nineteenth century, it is still premature, and in retrospect anachronistic, to speak of any modern type of public or literary concern, let alone debate, pertaining to the ways in which literary Yiddish should have been used or developed in Eastern Europe. By contrast, such debates were in full swing throughout the eighteenth century with regard to some of the modern national languages of Europe. (On modern literary German cf. Blackall 1978; on Slavonic literary languages cf. Tolstoj 1988; on modern literary Russian cf. Uspenkij 1985; but cf. Tolstoj 1988: 71 on the absence of grammars of national literary East Slavonic languages until mid-eighteenth century.) In this respect, modern Yiddish was still firmly in its pre-modern stage. However, *de facto*, the old literary language had been almost discarded by the end of the eighteenth century, and was becoming increasingly replaceable by a new type of literary language primarily based on spoken Eastern Yiddish.

The shift to nascent Modern Literary Yiddish appears to have resulted from two major factors. First, the traditional pan-European network of Yiddish speakers and readers in Western and Eastern Europe had collapsed. The old literary language, which had until then served the readers of Ashkenaz I and Ashkenaz II equally, was rapidly losing its *raison d'être*. Secondly, the earliest Eastern Yiddish books bear witness to the direct and constantly increasing pressure of the spoken language. Even the least re-edited older literary works were subjected to some linguistic Easternization and modernization (see Chapter 4). A radical change was in the making. The extent to which written Yiddish grammar was already restructured and its dialectal base changed in the final decades of the eighteenth century was unprecedented in the history of literary Yiddish.

The ever increasing approximation of the written to the spoken language at the expense of conventional models is perhaps the most salient feature of this change. (On analogous and often contemporary eighteenth-century developments in some of the other national languages of Europe, mostly the Slavonic languages, see Zhuravlev 1982: 195–7; Venediktov 1965: 4 ff., 16; Tolstoj 1978: 269 ff.; 1988; Vinogradov 1978: 198, 1982[3]: 10–13; Uspenskij 1985: 3–8.)

In this study linguistic change was evaluated from the perspective of the literary language. The fundamentally modern structure of late eighteenth-century spoken Eastern Yiddish was assumed on grounds of internal reconstruction (see Introduction §4.4.2). Many of the literary monuments also provide some of the earliest attestations of important features of spoken Eastern Yiddish (see Chapters 6–8). It would be methodologically improper, however, to use these literary monuments as direct, unmediated sources for diachronic research into Eastern Yiddish (for a different opinion on methodology cf. Samuels 1972: 4–6). Many questions concerning the relative chronology of certain phonological, morphological, and dialecto-logical developments in modern Eastern Yiddish call for further enquiry. By the late eighteenth century, however, the modern grammatical make-up of spoken Eastern Yiddish was strong enough to provide contemporary writers with ready and largely stable patterns of morphological and syntactic usage.

It has long been understood that diachronic analysis is essential to the elucidation of various states of synchrony. However, modern historical linguistics tends to emphasize the spoken language (notwithstanding the fact that the fundamentals of Saussurian linguistics were conceptually forged in the image of the function and structure of the printing press; see Harris 1987: 51–5). Literary monuments are for historical linguists an essential, but indirect, source for the reconstruction of the contemporary spoken language. Yet to view the literary language only as an intermediary for the investigation of the underlying spoken form is to ignore its structural specifics. It is time to recognize that a literary language assumes a reality of its own (cf. Harris 1990: 38–42). It has to be taken not only as a historical and cultural category, but also as a distinct linguistic formation, however close or distant its correlation with the contemporary spoken language may be (cf. Guchmann 1955, 1959, on the case of literary German; Vinogradov 1967 and Tolstoj 1988: 27–33 on methods and the conceptual framework of the Russian school of history of literary language; Jedlička 1967 and Vachek 1970: 96–100 on the work of the Prague School linguists in the field of literary and standard languages). It is well known that a *modern* literary language tends to provide more stability to usage, and is predisposed to the adoption of supradialectal norms and standardization (on the nexus literalization–standardization cf. Bartsch 1987: 250). However, the overall equilibrium between norm and variation also allows for its ongoing evolution.

The emergence of Modern Literary Yiddish raises a number of important issues regarding the linguistic and socio-linguistic mechanisms of change of a literary language. It is remarkable that a well-established older literary language, one that continued to be used until very late, was so rapidly disposed of in favour of a fundamentally new one by authors who worked in traditional, pre-modern genres. Was it done for practical motives, to facilitate the intelligibility and distribution of these works? Intelligibility can hardly be the only reason. Works in Old Literary Yiddish continued to be reprinted with either minimal or no changes at all until very late, perhaps until the 1840s. Diglossia between the spoken and the literary language does not necessarily lead to a drastic restructuring and modernization of the latter. Among other factors that may have contributed to the general drive towards the shift in literary Yiddish was the lower societal status assigned to the language by many of its native speakers. This also applies to the conventional literary form. To *consciously* change the grammatical norms of conventional Hebrew would be infinitely less tolerable.

Another important issue is the rise of modern Standard Yiddish. How did its codification occur? (For a revealing criticism of the notion of Standard English see Harris 1987: 115–23; for a recent practical treatment of Standard English see Hudson 1992: 39–57.) It is far too early, of course, to speak of such issues as norm and grammatical codification in late eighteenth-century Yiddish. It was not enough that professional or quasi-professional individual authors began to write and publish in modern Eastern Yiddish in the 1820s and 1830s. The modern press, the second vital component for a full-fledged development of a modern literary language, did not emerge until 1862. Nevertheless, 'middle-ground' usage was a remarkable 'natural' attribute of a considerable number of literary works written and printed prior to the 1860s. A comprehensive investigation of these works would reveal many early examples of interdialectal usage and uncover the acceptance of certain grammatical norms that became the hallmark of modern Standard Yiddish. The origins of many of the salient modern norms can be found in most of the late eighteenth-century Eastern Yiddish printed works (see §34). Northeastern authors attempted to retain archaic grammatical features (gender, case system, and past-tense auxiliary) that were lost or restructured in Northeastern, but not in Mideastern and Southeastern, dialects. The emergence of the 'literary' prepositional case can be traced in all these works, including those emanating from the Southeastern Yiddish area (cf. §35.6.3; on Northeastern Yiddish phonology as the basis of modern literary norm see D. Katz 1993b: 49–61 and 1994). The precise sociolinguistic and dialectal correlates of this remarkable development are open for further investigation, which will need to take into account the much larger corpus of works written and printed in Eastern Yiddish during the first half of the nineteenth century.

The specific orientations of Jewish traditional literacy, the lower social prestige assigned to the everyday language, and the complete absence of governmental forces in support of standardization all converge to render the emergence of Modern Literary Yiddish a remarkable event in the history of European literary languages. Yiddish may provide evidence for the claim that there are in 'natural' societies, unpopular as it may be to say this, centripetal forces which strive towards standardization. The actual rise of a modern literary language need not be the province of petty normative grammar or of powerful political groups if for literate societies it is just as natural a phenomenon of language as variation is to speech.

1. Two Versions of a Parable: *Simkhes hanefesh* (1707) and *Derekh Tomim* (1723)

דרך תמים	שמחת הנפש
Derekh tomim (Zholkve, 1723)	*Simkhes hanefesh* (Frankfurt am Main, 1707)

	דרך תמים		שמחת הנפש
1	**עש** שטיט איין איין משל. איין גנב		**משל** איין גנב האט
	האט איין גיבראבֿן איין שטיק		אין גיבראבֿן
	מויאר אין דעם חדר וואו דאש		אין דען
	אוצד פֿון דעם מלך איז דרינן		אוצר פֿון מלך
5	גילעגן. אזו האט דר גנבֿ גיזעהן		האט ער גיזעהן
	זילברני כלים שטיאן האט ער		זילברני כלים שטין האט ער
	גינומן דר פֿון אזו פֿיל דז ער		אן גינומן דער פֿון וו.אש ער
	האט קענען דר טראגן.		האט קענען דער טראגן
	דר נאך האט ער גיזעהן		דער נאך האט ער גיזעהן
10	גילדני כלים שטין האט ער		גילדני כלים שטין האט ער
	דיא זילברני כלים פֿון זיך		דיא זילברני כלים פֿון זיך
	גיטאן אונ האט זיך גינומן		גיטאן אונ׳ האט זיך גינומן
	גילדני כלים. דר נאך האט ער		גילדני כלים דער נאך האט ער
	גיזעהן שיני פערל האט ער זיך		גיזעהן שיני פֿערליך האט ער
15	גיטראבֿט וואש זאל איך אזו שווער		מיט זיך זעלבשטן גירעד בין
	גאלד טראגן איך וויל ליבר נעמן		איך ניט אין נאר איך זאל
	אזו שווער פערל		אזו שווער טראגן אן גאלד אזו
	דאש איז וויא		שווער פֿערליך זיינן דאך וויא
	פֿיל מאל אזו פֿיל ווערט אז		פֿיל מאל אזו פֿיל ווערט אונ׳
20	גאלד. אונ האט דאש גאלד		האט ווידר דיא גילדני כלים
	פֿון זיך גיטאן אונ האט גינומן		פֿון זיך גיטאן אונ׳ האט פֿערל
	דיא פֿעריל. דר נאך האט ער		גינומן דער נאך האט ער
	גיזעהן גרושי שטיק דימאנטן.		גיזעהן גרושי שטיק דימאנטן
	האט ער דיא פֿעריל פֿון זיך		שטין האט ער דיא פֿערל אוועק
25	גיטאן אונ האט דימאנטן גינומן.		גיטאן אונ׳ האט דימאנטן גינומן
	דאש האט גיווערט איין גאנצי		אזו האט ער גיוואלט דיא גאנצי
	נבֿם אין דעם וויא ער האט		נאבֿט. אין דעם
	דיא דימאנטן גינומן אזו		איז
	איז טאג גיווארן האט ער		דער טאג קומן האט ער
30	מורא גיהאט מן ווערט אים דר ווישן		מורא גיהאט מן ווערט אים דער ווישן
	אונ ווערט אום זיין חיות קומן		אונ׳ ווערט אום זיין חיות קומן
	אונ איז אוועק גילאפֿין פֿון אלים		אונ׳ איז דער פֿון גילויפֿן
	אונ האט גאר נישט מיט זיך		אונ׳ האט גאר ניקש מיט זיך
	גינומן. אזו אוך איז דער		גינומן. אזו אך דער
35	מענש וואש לאזט זיך ניט בנוגן		מענש לאזט זיך ניט בינינין

<table>
<tr>
<td>

האט ער צינן גיפֿעם וויל ער
זילבר האבן האט ער זילבר
וויל ער גאלד האבן אונ
דווקא די שענשטי קליידר
40   אונ פֿר ברענגט זיין צייט אין
הבֿלים אונ איז וויא איין גנבֿ
עד גנבֿת דיא דעה פֿון גאט
אונ גיט אלי זייני טאג
אין דער פֿינשטר
45   אורבלצינג קומט דר טאג
דער מענש איז ניט זיבֿר
צו איבר נעלֿטיגן
אום גריבֿט שטאארבט ער
אונ׳ לאזט אילץ הינטר זיך:
50

</td>
<td>

האט ער צינן גיפֿעם וויל ער
זילבר האבן האט ער זילבר
וויל ער גאלד האבן אונ׳
דווקא דיא שענשטי קליידר
אונ׳ אלי טאג וויל ער העלֿרן
שטאט פֿירן אונ׳ לויפֿט אונ׳
רענט אונ׳ זייני צייט אזו
אוועק ברענגט
אין הבל הבלים
אורבליצלינג קומט דער טאג
דער מענש איז ניט זיבֿער
איבר נעלֿטיג
אום גירילֿט שטאארבט ער
לאזט אליש הינטר זיך אונ׳
בלייבט איין גנבֿ ער גנבֿת
דיא דעה פֿון גאט אונ׳ גיט
אלי זייני טאג אין
דער פֿינשטר אונ׳ לויטר וויא טאג [. . .]

</td>
</tr>
</table>

2. Two Stories in Four Editions of *Kav hayosher* (1705, 1709, 1777, 1788)

קב הישר

Kav hayosher

(Zholkve, 1777)
([. . .] Novidvor, 1788)
(]. . .[only in Zholkve, 1777)

(Frankfurt am Main, 1705)
(Frankfurt am Main, 1709; *variae lectiones* at foot)

פרק כ״ה Chapter 25

	Zholkve/Novidvor	Frankfurt
1	עש שטיט אין ברכֿת כהנים	עש שטיאט אין ברכת כהנים
	(יברכך ה׳ וישמרך) שרייבן אונזרי	יברכך ה׳ וישמריך שרייבן אונזרי
	חכֿמים אין מדרש רבות פ׳ נשא	חכֿמים אין מדרש רבות פ׳ נשא
	יברכך ה׳ גאט ווערט דיך בענשן	יברכך ה׳ גאט ווערט דיך בענשן
5	מיט גרוש געלט וון דוא פֿרום	מיט גרוש געלט וען דוא פֿרום
	בישט וישמרך אונ גאט ווערט דיך	בישט. וישמרך אונ גאט ווערט דיך
	בהיטן פֿר מזיקים ומשחיתם ז[א]לן	בהיטן פֿר מזיקים ומשחיתים זאלין
	איבר דיר נישט צו ש[א]פֿן ה[א]בן	איבר דיר ניקֿש צו שאפֿין האבין.
	זאל מן דאך פֿר שטין וואש [הבן]	מֿז מען דאך פֿר שטין וואש אונזרי
10	אונזדי חכֿמים מיט דען פסוק גמיינט	חכֿמים מיט צו דרוש גימיינט האבן.
	מיינן מיר מתֿרץ צו זיין על פי	מיין מיר מתרץ צו זיין על פי
	∽	הגמרא וואש אין דיא מסכת חולין
	∽	שטיאט. דז טרעגר האבן איין מאל
	∽	איין גרוש פֿאם וויין גיטראגין [. .]
15	∽	אודר נאך איין פֿירוש קען מען
	∽	זאגין אויף דיזן מדרש רק וויל
	∽	איך איין מעשה שרייבן וואש
		גישעהין איז.
	ו[א]ש גשעהן איז	עם וואר איין מאלֿט איין עושר דער
	עש וואר אמאל איין עושר דר	וואר גאנין רייך אין געלט אין
20	וואר גנין רייך אין געלט [אונ זילבר]	זילבר כלים אונ׳ גאלד אונ׳
	אונ גאלד אונ אבֿנים טובֿות	אבֿנים טובות האט פֿיל סחורות
	אונ האט פֿיל סחורות	אונ׳ דער זעלביגר מאן איז איין
	אונ דר זעלביגר מאן איז אין	קארגיר מאן גיווען וואש מאן אין
	קארגר מאן גוועזן וואש מן אין	גאנצין עולם אזו איין קמצן ניט
25	גנצן עולם גפֿינט ניט אזו איין	גיווען אונ׳ איז קיין קמצן מאנטאג
	קמצן אונ איז קיין מאנטיג	אונ׳ דאנרשטאג ניט אין דיא
	אונ דאנרשטיג אין שול	שול אריין גאנגין דען ער האט
	אריין גגאנגן דען ער ה[א]ט	

2 וישמרך 3 רבות 4 בענשן 7 ביהיטן. זאלן 8 שאפֿן האבן 9 פֿרשטין
10 מיט דען דאש 14 גיטראגן 15 קאן מן 16 זאגן 18 גישעהין איז 19 עז
22 טובות, סחורות 23 איז 24 וואש מאן 25 גאנצן 26 איז 27 גאנגן

זיך גיפורלטן אין דיא הקדש
ביקם אריין צו וערלֿפֿין אין פֿפֿענינג.
ומכל שכן האט ער קיין
עני קענין פֿר זיך זעהין. איז
אין גרושר אכזר גיװעזין אונ'
אין רשע רק אן איין מצוה איז
ער נזהר גיװעזין די מצוה האט
אים מציל גיװעזן בעוה"ז אונ'
האט אים גיבראטֿט אויף עולם
הבא אונ' דיא מצוה האט אים
גיבראטֿט דז ער אין גרושר
װתרן גיװוארין אונ' דיא מצוה
איזט גיװעזן דז ער אין מוהל
איז גיװעזן אונ' האט אין טבע
אן זיך גיהאט װען שון אויף
צװאנצטיג דרייסיג מייל אין ברית
מילה איז גיװעזן אלזו איז
ער אויף זיין הוצאה גיצוגין אונ'
האט מל גיװעזין.
ויהי היום עז װאר אין מאל גינג
דער קארג מאן אויף דען מארק
קומט צו אים איין שד אין דיא
גישטאלט פֿון איין מענשן אונ'
זאגט צו אים מיין פֿריינט מיין
װייב איזט אין קינדפֿעט קומן אונ'
האט אין זון אזו ביט איך אייך
זאלט מיין קינד מל זיין אונ'
דיא ברית מילה איז איבר
מארגין דא שפראך דער מאן יוא
איך װיל מיין פֿֿערד נעמין אונ'
װיל דיר נאך פֿארין דען איר
װאוסט דען װעג בעסר אין אייער
היים. אונ' צום אנדרין טאג
דא פֿארט דער בעל ברית אויף
איין װאגין אונ' דער מוהל פֿארט
אים נאך אויף זיין גאויל אונ'
דער מוהל מיינט דז אים אליז
אין מענש. װיא ער אין עטליבֿי
מייל גפֿירט האט אין רעלבֿטן װעג
אין דיא לנד שטראז דער נאך
פֿירט אים דער משחית אויף אין

30
35
40
45
50
55
60
65

זיך גפֿארלטֿן[ז] אין די צדקה אריין
צו װארפֿן איין פֿענוג [פֿעניג]
ומכ"ש ה[א]ט ער קיין
עני קענין פֿר זיך זעהן אונ איז
אין גרושר אבֿזר גװעזן אונ
אין רשע רק אן איין מצוה איז
ער נזהר גװעזן די מצוה ה[א]ט
אים מציל גװעזן בעוה"ז אונ
ה[א]ט אים גבראטֿט אויף עה"ב
אונ די מצוה ה[א]ט אים
גבראטֿט דש ער אין גרושר
װתרן איז גװארן אונ די מצוה
איז גװעזן דש ער אין מוהל
איז גװעזן אונ ה[א]ט אין טבֿע
אן זיך גהאט װען שון
צװאנצטיג דרייסיג מייל אין ברית
איז גװעזן אזו איז
ער אויף זיין הוצאה גפֿארן אונ
ה[א]ט מל גװעזן
ויהי היום עש װאר איין מאל גינג
דר קארג[ר] מאן אויף דען מארק
קומט צו אים איין שד אין
גישטאלט פֿון איין מענש אונ
זאגט צו אים מיין פֿריינט מיין
װייב איז אין קינד בעט קומן אונ
ה[א]ט אים איין זון ביט איך
איר זאלט מיין קינד מל זיין
די ברית מילה איז איבר
מארגן דא שפֿראך דר מאן יוא
איך װיל מיין פֿֿערד נעמן אונ
דיר נאך פֿארן איר
װיישט דען װעג בעסר אין אייער
היים אונ צום אנדרן טאג
[דא] פֿארט דר בעל ברית אויף
איין װאגין אונ דר מוהל פֿארט
אים נאך אויף זיין פֿערד [= װאגן] אונ
דר מוהל מיינט דש איז אלין
איין מענש װיא ער אין עטליבֿי
מייל גפֿירט האט אין רעלבֿטן װעג
אין די לנד שטראז דר נאך פֿירט
אים דר משחית אויף אין הו[י]ל[ן]

---

34 איזט 33 גיװעזן 32 קענן פֿר, זעהן, איז 30 װערלֿפֿין 29 גיפֿארלטן

44 צװאנצטיג דרייסיג 42 איזט 41 דז 40 גיװארן 39 דז 35 גיװעזן

56 איזט 53 איז, קינדבעט קומן 49 מארק 48 עז 47 גיװעזן 45 איז

68 לאנד 65 דש איזט אלז 64 זיין פֿערד 63 װאגן 61 אנדרן 57 מארגן

הולכין בערג אונ' אין גרושין וולד
אין אזו איין ווענ וואו קיין מאל
איין מענש דא הין קומט. דא ווערט
דען מוהל דער שראקן דא פרענגט
ער אים וואו פירשט דוא מיך
אהין עם איז דאך קיין ווענ
אונ' שטעג אין דען וואלד
דא שפראך דעד משחית צו אים
איך האב איך אין איין קורצין
ווענ גפירט מיר קומין בלד אין
דאש דארף. אונ' וויא ער איין
וויניק פארט פאריט דא זיך ער
קעגין צוואנציג הייזר שטין ווארין
היפש גיבויאט. דא פירט דער
בעל ברית דען מוהל אין זיין
הויז אריין דא זילכט דער מוהל
דאז דער בעל הבית איז איין
עושר דא גאב ער זיין פערד אין
שטאל אונ' הייושט זיין משרת זאל
היא אונ' האביר געבין פר זיין
פפערד אונ' דער מוהל מיינט אליז
ער וואר צווישן ליטין אונ' וויש ניט
דז דאש לאויטר מזיקים זיין. אונ'
דער בעל הבית גיט אין הויז הין
אונ' ווידר אונ' דער מוהל גיט
אין דיא שטובן אריין. דא זילכט
ער אין גרוש עשירות אין דער
שטוב אונ' דיא קינדבעטרין לינגט
אין איין זילבר בעט אונ' גאלדיני
ציכן אין קוטין אונ' פערליך. דא
רופט דיא קינדבעטרן דען מוהל
צו זיך דען זיא וואר פרוא
דז זיא איין מענשין גיזעהן האט.
אונ' גאב אים שלום אונ' שפראך
מיין ליבר מאן איר זאלט וויישן
דז מיין מאן איז איין שד
ומשחית ער האט אייך פר פירט
היא אהער. גיב איך אייך איין
ראט איר זולט בייא אונש ניקש
עסין אונ' ניקש טרינקין אונ' קיין
מתנה ניט נעמין דא ווערט איר
ניצול ווערין פר דיא משחיתים

---

70 ב[א]רג אונ [= אין איין] גרושן וואלד
אין אזו איין ווענ וואו קיין מאל
קיין מענש אהין קומט דא ווערט
דער מוהל דר שראקן דא פרענגט
[=פראגט] ער אים וואו פירשטו מיך
75 אהין עז איז דאך קיין ווענ
אונ שטעג אין דעם וואלד
דא שפראך דר משחית צו אים
איך האב איך אין איין קורצין
ווענ גפירט מיר קומן ב[א]לד אין
80 דארף אונ וויא ער איין
ווינג פארט דא זיך ער
קעגן צוואנציג הייזר שטיין וואָרן
היפש גיבויאט פירט דר
בעל ברית דען מוהל אין זיין
85 הויז אריין דא זילכט דר מוהל
דז דר בעל ברית איז איין
עושר דא גאב ער זיין פערד אין
שטאל אונ הייושט זיין משרת זאל
היא אונ האבר געבן פר זיין
90 פערד אונ דר מוהל מיינט אז
ער איז צווישן ליט אונ ווי[ן]ש ניט
דז דש [= דא] לויטר מזיקים זיין אונ
דר בעה"ב גיט אין הויז הין
אונ הער אונ דער מוהל גיט
95 אין די שטובן אריין דא זילכט
ער אין גרוש עשירות אין דר
שטוב אונ די קינד בעטרין לינגט
אין איין זילבר[ן] בעט אונ גילדיני
ציכן אין קוטן אונ פעריל דא
100 רופט די קינד בעטר[י]ן דען מוהל
צו זיך דען זי וואר איין פרויא
דז זי פון איין מענש קומט
אונ שפר[א]ך מיין פריינד
[=פריינט] איר זאלט וויישן
105 דז מיין מאן איז איין שד

∞

גיב איך אייך איין
ראט איר זאלט בייא אונז ניט
עשן אונ טרינק[ן]ן אונ קיין
110 מתנה נעמן דא ווערט איר
ניצול ווערן פר די משחיתם

---

70 הולכן, גרושן וואלד   73 דער שראקן פראגט   75 עז איזט   78 קורצן   79 קומן, באלד
81 ווינינ, זילכט   82 קעגן   86 בעל הבית איז   89 געבן   90 פערד, אלז   91 ליטן
92 לויטר   96 עשירות   100 קינדבעטרין   102 דז, מענשן   105 דז, איזו   108 זאלט, אונז

אבר איר מוזט ווישן דז איך בין
אין מענש בין בעו"ה פון קליינר
ווייא אויף גיפֿאנגין גיוווארין און'
מוז בייא זיא בלייבן ע"כ ביט
איך זולטן מיין קינד מל זיין.
און' ביט זיא איך זולטן ניקש זאגין
פֿר קיינם דז איך האב איך מזהיר
גיוועזן און' האב איך מגלה גיוועזן
דז איר זיט צווישן שידים. וויא
דער מוהל הערט דיא ווערטר פֿון
דיא קידבעטרין דא דער שראק
ער זיער דא זאגט דיא
קינדבעטרין דער שרעקט זא ניט
נאר טואס איר וויא איך האב איך
ביפֿולין זאל איך ניקש גישעהין
איך מוז בעו"ה בלייבן בייא זיא.
אבר זיער עשירות און' זיער
מעשים זיינן הבל ורוה און' לאוטר
נריריא. און' איך בין איך מזהיר
זולטן מיין קינד רעלבט מל זיין
זוא גיט דער מוהל אויף דיא זיט
און' וואר אים אנגסט און בנג.
וויא עש צו ווייג דיא נלבט קאם
דא קומין צו פֿארין משחיתים אין
גישטאלט לייט און' זעצין זיך צום
טיש דא זאגט דער בעל ברית
צוא דעם מוהל ער זאל זיך וועשין
און' זאל זיך זעצין צום טיש עסין
און' דער מוהל מאבט זיך גלייך
אליו ער זיער מיד איז פֿון וועג
און זאגט אלי דיא אויש ריד
און' מאג ניקם עסין אינ' טרינקן
צו ווייג נאבט (אודר וואלבט נאבט)
ויהי ממחרת און' וויא עש צו מארגין
קאם דיא צייט אין דער שול אריין
צו גין דא אורין זיא און' מוז דער
מוהל וכרת עמו הברית זינגין און'
איז מל דאש קינד אליש וויא דער
סדר איז וויא נאך שול קומט

אבר איר מוזט ווישן דש איך בין
אין מענש איך בין בעו"ה פון קליינר
ווייש אויף גפֿאנגן גוווארן און
מוז דא בליבן ע"כ ביט
איך איר זאלט מיין קינד מל זיין
און ביט מיר איר ז[א]לט ניט זאגן
פֿר קיינם דש איך ה[א]ב איך מזהיר
גוועזן
דש איר צווישן שדים [זייט] וו[י]א[ן]
דר מוהל הערט די ווערטר פֿון די
קינד בעטרן דא דר שרעק [=שראק]
ער זיער דא זאגט די
קינד בעטרין דר שרעקט ניט
נאר טוט איר וויא איך האב אייך
בפֿולן זאל איך ניקש גשעהן
איך מוז בעו"ה בליבן בייא זי
אבר זיער עשירות און זיער
מעשים זענן הבל לון[ן]טר היברייא
[=איבריריא] איך בין איך מזהיר
איר זאלט מיין קינד רעלבט מל זיין
אזו גיט דר מוהל אויף די זייט
און ווער אים אנגשט און באנק
ווי עש איז גקומן די וואך נאלבט
דא קומן צו פֿארן משחיתים אין
גשטלט לייט און זעצן זיך צום
טיש דא זאגט דר בעל ברית
צו דען מוהל ער זאל זיך וועשן
און זיך זעצן צום טיש עשן
און דר מוהל מלבט זיך גלייך
אז ער זיער מיד איז פֿון וועג
און זאגט אין אויש ריד
ער מאג ניקש עשן און טרינקט
צו וואך נאלבט
ויהי ממחרת און וויא עש צו מארגן
קאם דיא צייט אין שול אריין צו
גין דא זענן זי מתפלל און דר
מוהל מוז ולברות זינגן און
איז מל דש קינד וויא דר
סדר איז וויא נאך שול קומט

114 אויף גיפֿאנגן גיוווארין 116 זאלט 117 זאלט, זאגן 121 ווערטיר 123 זיער
124 קינדבעטרין 125 טוט 126 ביפֿאל, גישעהן 128 זיער עשירות, אירי 129 לוטר
131 זאלט, יודשן 133 אנגשט, באנג 134 עז, וויל, נאלבט 135 קומן 136 זעצן
137 דא 138 צו, וועשן 139 זעצן 141 אלו, איזט 142 אויו 143 ניקש,
145 עז, מארגן 146 אין דער שול צו 147 אורין 148 זינגן 149 דש, אלו
150 איזט טרינקן

דא ביט אים דר קוואטר אויף לעקף	דא ביט אים דער גיפֿאטיר אויף
[=לעקוד] אונ בראנטוויין דעם מוהל	לעקולין אונ ברנט וויי דעם מוהל.
דא זאגט דר מוהל איך פֿאסט	דא זאגט דער מוהל איך פֿאשט
איין תענית חלום אבר דר מוהל	איין תענית חלום אבר דער מוהל
מוז דאך אהים גין צום קוואטר	מוז דאך אהים גין צום גיפֿאטיר
אין זיין הויז אבר ער פֿ[א]רלבט	אין זיין הויז אבר ער פֿערבלטיט
זיך צו עשן אונ צו טרינקן וויא	זיך צו עסין אונ׳ צו טרינקן וויא
זי אזו זיצן זאגט דר בעל	זיא זוא זיצין זאגט דער בעל
ברית רבותי דען מוהל צו גפֿאלן	ברית רבותי דען מוהל צו גיפֿאלין
וועלן מיר סעודות מילה אפֿ	וועלין מיר דיא סעודת מילה אפֿ
לינן ביז נאכט כדי ער זאל ג״כ	לינן ביז נאכט כדי ער זאל ג״כ
אויך מיט עשן [=עסן] אונ זיין כוונה	אויך מיט עסין אונ׳ זיין כוונה
איז נאר גוועזן דש דר מוהל	איז נאר גיוועזין דז דער מוהל
זאל וואש הנאה האבן	זאל וואש הנאה פֿון אין האבן
כדי דש ער זאל קענן	כדי דז ער זאל קענין אים
מזיק זיין אן זיין גוף אבר דר	מזיק זיין אן זיין גוף. אבר דער
בעל ברית וויש ניט אז דר	בעל ברית וויש ניט אליז דער
מוהל וויש דש ער צוויישן שדים	מוהל וויש דז ער צוווישן שדים
איז אונ וויש ניט דא [=דש] זיין	איז. אונ׳ וויש ניקש דז זיין
וייב עש אים מזהיר גוועזן אונ	וייב האט אים מזהיר גיוועזין. אונ׳
ווא עש אבינט איז גוווארן	וויא עם נון קומן איזט דז אבענט
דא זיך די לייט	ווער גיוואריׄ דאז זיך דיא לייט
וועשן אונ דר מוהל מלבט זיך	וועשין אונ׳ דער מוהל מאכט זיך
קראנק דען ער קאן קיין תירוץ	קראנק דען ער קען קיין תירוץ
אונ אוש ריד מער זאגן אונ וואר	אונ׳ אויז ריד מער זאגין. אונ׳
אים אנגשט אונ באנק ער מיינט	ווער אים אנגשט אונ׳ בנג ער
זיין ציים וער [=וואר] צו שטארבן	מיינט זיין ציים ווער צו שטערביין
פֿר גרוש פֿארבט אונ די	פֿר גרוש פֿארכט. אונ׳ דיא
משחיתם מאבן זיך לוסטיג אונ	משחיתים מאכין זיך לושטיג אונ׳
עשן אונ טרינקן וויא זי האבן	עשין אונ׳ טרינקן. וויא זיא האבין
אויף גגעסין גהאט דא זאגט דר	אויף געסין גיהאט דא זאגיט דער
בעל ברית צו דען מוהל איך קאן	בעל ברית צו דעם מוהל איך קאן
וואו[ל] דענקן ווארום איר האט ניט	וואול דענקין ווארום איר האט ניקש
גגעשן [=גגעסן] אדר גטרינקן [=גטרונקן]	גיגעסין אודר גיטרונקין
קומט מיט מיר אונ פֿרבט אייך	קומט מיט מיר אונ׳ פֿערכיט איך
ניט דא גינג דר מוהל	ניקש. דא גינג דער מוהל
מיט דען ב״ב בטריבטר הייט	ביטריבטר הייד מיט דען בעל ברית
	דא פֿירט אים דער בעל ברית
אין חדר וואו לוטר זילברני כלים	אין חדר וואו לאוטר זילבר כלים
שטין אונ זאגט נעמט מיט אויין	שטיאן אונ׳ זאגט נעמט מיר איין

155   160   165   170   175   180   185   190

152 לעקולין 154 תעניית 155 אהין, גיפֿאטר 158 זיצן 163 איזט, גיוועזין
165 דאו. קענן 167 אלו 169 איזט 170 גיוועזן 171 עז, אבנט 172 דז
175 זאנג 176 באנג 177 שטערבן 178 גרוש פֿורבט 180 טרינקן, האבן
181 זאנגט 183 דענקן. איר האבט 184 גיגעסן, גיטרונקן 185 פֿערבלט 187 ביטרבטר
היט. ברית 188 ברית 189 לויטר

כלי וועלבֿש אייך גפֿעלט   כלי וועלבֿיש אייך גיפֿאלט
דא ענ[ט]פֿרט דר מוהל איך האב   דא ענווורט דער מוהל אייך הב
אוך זעלבֿי שיני זילברני כלים   אך שיני זולבֿי זילברני כילים.
דא מאבֿט ער אין טיר אויף אונ   דא מאבֿט ער אין טיר אויף אונ'
195   פֿירט אים אין אין אנדר חדר   פֿירט אים אי' אין אנדר חדר
וואו גילדני כלים זענן אונ אין   וואו גאלדני כלים זיין אונ' אין
אײן חדר וואו לויטר דימנטן אונ   אײן חדר וואר לאויטר דימנט אונ'
אנדרי אבֿנים טובֿות אונ אליר   אנדרי אבנים טובת אונ' אליר
לייא גשמוקין דא זאגט דר בעה"ב   לייא גישמוקין דא זאגט דער בעל
200   נעמט אייך דען גרעשטן   הבית נעמט אייך דען גרעשטין
דימנט אדר גילדני כלי צו אין   דימנט אודר גולדן כלי צו אין
גדעבֿניש דא זאגט דר מוהל   גידעבֿניש. דא זאגט דער מוהל
איך ב[י]דאנקי מיך איך האב גינוגן   איך בידאנקי מיך איך האב גינוגין
אבנים טובֿות אונ פֿערליך   אבנים טובות אונ' פֿערליך. אונ'
205   דר נאך פֿירט אים דר בעל ברית   דער נאך פֿירט אים דער בעל ברית
אין אײן חדר וואו   אין אײן חדר אונ' אין דען חדר
לויטר שלוסלן [=שליסלן] פֿון   דא זיינן דריאן לאויטר שליסלן
אײזן אונ דש גאנצי חדר זיינן   פֿון אײן אונ' דאש גאנץ חדר
פֿיל [פֿול] מיט בונט שלוסלן [שליסלן]   זיינן פֿול מיט בונט שליסלן
210   גיהאנגן ווי דר מוהל אריין קאם   גיהאנגין ווי דער מוהל אריין קאם
אין דען חדר וואו די שליסל האנגן   אין דען חדר וואו דיא שליסלן
[=הענגן] דא פֿר וואונדרט ער זיך   הינגין דא פֿר וואונדרט ער זיך
זייר דא פֿראגט אין דר   זייר דא פֿראגט אים דער בעל
בעה"ב מיין ליבר פֿריינט איך האב   הבית מיין ליבר פֿריינט איך האב
215   אייך זעלבֿי חידושים גוויזן   אייך זולבֿי אוצרות גיוויזן פֿון
    זילבר אונ' גאלד אונ' אבנים

∽

אונ איר האט אייך ניט   טובות אונ' איר האט אייך ניט
פֿר וואונדרט אונ איבר די   פֿר וואונדרט. אונ' איבר דיא
שלוסל פֿר וואונדרט איר אייך   שליסלן פֿר וואונדרט איר אייך:
220   דא ענ[ט]פֿרט אים דר מוהל איך   דא ענטוואָרט אים דער מוהל איך
פֿר וואונדר מיך אלץ דא אײן   פֿר וואונדר מיך אליז דא אײן
בונט שלוסל העענגט זיך גלייך   בונט שליסלן הינגין זיבֿן גלייך
[=גלאך] [אויז] אז די שלוסל וואש   אויש אלז דיא שליסלן וואש איך
איך האב צו מיין הויז אונ חדרים   האב צו מיין הויז אונ' חדרים
225   אונ צו מיין קסטן וואו איך האב   אונ' צו מיין קיסטין וואו איך הב
מיין האב אונ גוט אונ וויזט   מיין האב אונ' גוטשט. אונ' וויזט
אים אן וועלבֿי [=וועלבֿן] נאגיל זי   אים אן וועלבֿין נאגיל זיא
הענגין דא שפֿראך דר בעה"ב   הענגין. דא שפראך דער בעל
צו אים איך וויל אייך זאגן   הבית צו אים איך וויל אייך זאגן
230   מיר אין דיזן דארף זיינן לויטר   מיר אין דיזן דארף זיינין לאויטר

192 ענטפֿרט, האב   193 זאלבֿי, כלים   195 אין   197 לויטר   198 טובֿות
200 בעל הבית, גרעשטן   202 גידעבֿנים   203 גינוג   204 טובות, פֿערליך   205 דר נאך,
ברית   207 זיין, דרינן לויטר   209 זיינן   210 גיהאנגן   211 שליסלן   212 הינגן
214 בעל הבית   215 זאלבֿי אוצרות   217 טובות   220 ענטפֿרט   221 אלז   222 הינגן
223 אויש אלי   225 קיסטן, איך האב   226 גוט, וויישט   229 זאגן   230 זיינן לויטר

משחיתים אונ׳ מיר זיינין דיא	משחיתֿים אונ מיר זיין די
ממונים איבר דיא לייט ווערלכֿי	ממונים איבר די לייט וועלכֿי
גרושי קאמצנים זיינין דיא האבין	גרושי קמצנים זענן די האבן
קיין מאכֿט איבר זיער האב אונ׳	קיין מאכֿט איבר זייער האב אונ
גוטשט אונ׳ זיא קענין קיין קיסטן	גוט אונ זי קענן קיין קסטן
אוף מאכֿין ביז מיר מוזין פֿראנט	אויף מאכֿן ביז מיר מוזן פֿאר
אוף מאכֿן אונ׳ זולכֿי לייט האבין	אויף מאכֿן אונ זעלכֿי לייט האבן
קיין רשות איבר זיער אייגיני קיסט	קיין רשותֿ איבר זייער אייגני קסטין
צו גין געלט ארויש נעמן צדקה	צו גין געלט ארוש נעמן צדקה
צו געבין אודר גמילות חסד צו טאן.	צו געבן אדר גמילותֿ חסד צו טאן
נוא וויל איר האט גומל חסד	נוא וויל איר הוט [=האט] גומל חסד
מיט מיר גיוועזן אונ׳ זייט צוועלף	מיט מיר גוועזן אונ זייט צוועלף
מייל מיט מיר אין ווילדן וואלד	מייל מיט מיר אין ווילדן וואלד
גיפֿארין דא שענק איך אייך דען	גפֿארין דא שענק איך אייך דעם
בונט שליסלן כדי איר זולט	בונט שליסל כדי איר זאלט
מאכֿט האבין איבר דען איירגין	מאכֿט האבן איבר דען אייערן
אונ׳ שווער אייך בייא גאט זולט	אונ איך שווער אייך בייא גאט זאלט
אייך ניקש פֿארכֿטין אונ׳ דער	אייך ניט פֿארכֿטן אונ דר
מוהל נאם דעם בונד שליסלין	מוהל נאם דען בונט שליסל
אונ׳ גיאט זיין וועג ווידר צו רוק	אונ גיט זיין וועג ווידר צו ריק
נאך זיין היים אונ׳ וויא ער איין	נאך זיין היים אונ וויא ער
היים קאם דא איזט ער גלייך אליז	אהיים קום דא איז ער גלייך אז
איין אנדריר מענש האט גרושי	איין אנדרר מענש האט גרוש
צדקה געבין אונ׳ האט פֿיל עניים	צדקה געבין אונ האט פֿיל עניים
נייאי קליידר גימאכֿט אונ׳ האט	נייאי קליידר גמאכֿט אונ האט
לאזין איין שול מאוירן אונ׳ טואט	לאזן איין נייאי שול מויארן אונ טוט
פֿיל גוטשט ביז זיינים טוט אונ׳	פֿיל גוטץ ביז זיין טוט אונ
איז נפטר בשם טוב גיווארין.	איז נפֿטר גווארן בשם טובֿ
נוא מיין איך דאש מיינט דער	נוא מיין איך דש מיינט דר
מדרש רבה יברכך ה׳ בממון גאט	מדרש רבה יבֿרכֿך ה׳ בממון גאט
ווערט דיך בענשין מיט געלט	ווערט דיך בענשן מיט געלט
ווערט דיר גרושין עושר געבין.	וועט דיר גרושר עושר געבן
ווערשט דוא וועלין זאגין וואש	ווערשטו וועלן זאגן וואש
העלפֿט מיך דאש געלט ווען מיר	העלפֿט מיך דש געלט ווען מיר
קיין מאכֿט דאריבר האבין דען	קיין מאכֿט דריבר האבן דען
דיא מזיקים האבין דיא שליסלן	די מזיקים האבן די שליסל
דריאבר דא ענטוורט דער מדרש	דריבר דא ענפֿרט דר מדרש
וישמרך מן המזיקין דאש איזט	וישמרך מן המזיקים דש איז
טייטש דיא ווערשט בהיט וועריז	טייטש דו ווערשט בהיט ווערן

231 זיינן 233 זיינן, האבן 234 איר האב 235 גוט 236 אויף מאכֿין, מוזן 237 אויף מאכֿן, זאלכֿי, האבן 238 רשותֿ, איבר איר 239 ארויז צו נעמן 240 געבן, גמילותֿ, טון 244 גיפֿארן 245 זאלט 246 האבן, אייעריגן 247 זאלט 248 פֿערכֿטן 249 דען בונט שליסלן 252 איז ער גלייך אלז 253 איין אנדרר 254 געבן 256 לאזן, מויארן 257 גוטש, זיינם טוט 258 איזט, בשם טובֿ גיווארן, 261 בענשן 262 גרושן, געבן 263 וועלן זאגן 265 האבן 266 האבן 267 דאריבר, ענטווארט 269 ווערן

	פֿר דיא מזיקין דיא וערשט יוא	270	פֿר די מזיקים דו וערשט יוא
	מאלט דאריבר האבין איבר דיין		מאלט האבן איבר דיין
	גוטשט. נוא איזט יוצא אויש דען		גוטין נוא איז יוצא אויש דען
	פרק דז איטלבֿר מענש זאל זעהין		פרק דש איטלבֿר מענש זאל זעהן
	מצות צו הלטין אונ' זאל זיך		מצות צו האלטן אונ
	איין ראייה נעמין פֿון דעם מוהל	275	איין ראייה נעמין פֿון דעין מוהל
	וען ער העט ניט מקיים גיוועזן		וען ער העט ניט מקיים גוועזן
	דיא מצוה אזו וער ער פֿר לארין		די מצוה אזו וער [ער] פֿר לארן
	גיוועזן אויף דיא וועלט דז ער		גווארן פֿון די וועלט דש ער
	קיין הנאה הט גיהאט פֿון זיינם		קיין הנאה הט גהאט פֿון זיין
	גרושין עשירות. אונ' העט קיין	280	גרושן עשירות אונ העט קין
	עולם הבא גיהאט. אונ' דורך		עולם הבא גהאט אונ דורך
	דער מצוה האט ער הנאה גיהט		דר מצוה האט ער הנאה גהאט
	איז איין גרושר ותרן גיווארין		איז אין גרושר ותרן גווארן
	אונ' זיך וואול גיטאן. אונ' האט		אונ' זיך וואול גטאן אונ
	זיינר נשמה וואול גיטאן.	285	זיין נשמה וואול גטאן:
	דז אנדרי לערנין מיר פֿון דעם		∞
	פרק דז קיין מענש גיהער קארג		∞
	צו זיין דען וער דא גאנץ קארג		∞
	איזט איז אונטר רשות פֿון דיא		∞
	מזיקים אונ' וער דא מילד איז	290	∞
	אונ' איז איין ותרין דער איז		∞
	אין רשות פֿון הק"בה בעוה"ז		∞
	והעוה"ב:		∞

271 האבן   272 גוט, אויש דען   273 זעהן   274 מצות, האלטן   275 איינן ראייה
נעמן   277 די, פֿר לארן   278 דאו   279 האט   280 גרושן עשירות   282 גיהאט
283 גרושיר, גווארן   286 דש, לערנין   290 איזט   291 איזט, ותרן, איזט   292 רשות

Frankfurt am Main, 1705   Novidvor, 1788
Frankfurt am Main, 1709

פרק ס"ט Chapter 69

	דער מענש זאל ווישן דיא מוטיר		דר מענש זאל ווישן די מוטר
	פֿון דיא שידים דיא דא הייסט	295	פֿון דיא שדים די דא היישט
	מחל"ת מיט אירי כיתות דיא		מחלת מיט אירי כיתות די
	ביווייזין זיך צו צייטין צו דיא		בוויזין זיך צו צייטן צו די
	לייט ביא העלין טאג אונ'		לייט ביא העלין טאג אונ
	צירין זיך מיט גישמוק אונ'		צירין זיך מיט גישמאק אונ
	אלירלייא צירונג אונ' זיינין גאנץ	300	אילירלייא צירונג אונ זענן גאנץ
	היפש פֿון גישטאלט אונ' איבר		היפש פֿון גישטאלט אונ איבר

294 מוטר   295 שדים די, היישט   296 מחלת   297 ביוויזין, צייטן, צוא   300 אילירלייא,זיינן

רידן אפֿט איין מענשן דז ער	רידן אופֿט איין מענשן דש ער
זאל מיט זיא צו טאן האבין אונ׳	זאל מיט זיא צו טאן האבן אונ
גוויגן קינדר פֿון מענשין דיא	גווינין קינדר פֿון מענשן די
זינין הלבי מענשן אונ׳ הלבי	זענן הלבי מענשן אונ הלבי
מזיקים אונ׳ זאלבֿי קינדר הייסן	מזיקים אונ זעלבֿי קינדר הייסן
משחיתים אין דיא תורה הקדושה.	משחיתים אין דר תורה הקדושה
אונ׳ בנים זרים אונ׳ ווער זיך	אונ בנים זרים אונ ווער זיך
ביהעפֿט צו איין זוא איין שדית	ביהעפֿט צו אזו איין שדית
דער נאך ווערט ער גישטראפֿט	דר נאך ווערט ער גישטראפֿט
דז דיא שידית אין ממית איז	דז דיא שידית איז אים ממית
אונ׳ זיין גאנצי משפחה ווערין	אונ זיין גאנצי משפחה ווערן
שטערבן אן זרע קיימא וויא	שטארבן אן זרע קיימא וויא
איך וויל איין מעשה שרייבין	איך וויל איין מעשה שרייבן
וואש קורצליך איז גישעהין אין	וואז איז גישעהן אין
אונזרי טאגין אין ק״ק פוזנא אין	אונזרי טאגן אין ק״ק פוזנא אין
יאר תמ״ב לפ״ק איז איין	יאר תמ״א ותמ״ב לפ״ק איז איין
גימאוירט הויז גיוועזן אין יידשי	גימוארט הויז גוועזן בק״ק פוזנא
גם צווישן אנדרי גימאוירטי הייזיר	אין דר גאס צווישן אנדרי גימורטי
אין דעם הויז איז גיוועזין איין	הייזר אין דען הויז היה גוועזן איין
היבשיר גימאוירטר קעליר דא הט	היפש גימוארטר קעליר דא הט
מן ניט קענין אריין גין אין דעם	מן ניט קענין אריין גיאן אין דעם
קעליר וועלבֿיר מענש איז אריין	קעליר וועלבֿר מענש איז אריין
גאנגין אין דעם קעליר דער איז	גינגנגן אין דעם קעליר דר איז
גישעדיקט גיוואריןאונ׳ מן הט	גישעדיקט גווארן אונ מן האט
ניט גיוואושט וואש עז ביטיט	ניט גיוואוסט וואש עש בטיט
אונ׳ איין מאל איז איין בחור	אונ איין מאל איז איין בחור
בייא העלין טאג אין דעם קעליר	בייא העלין טאג אין דעם קעליר
גיגאנגין אלזו איין קליני פֿירטיל	גיגאנגן אזו איין קליני פֿירטל
שעה נאך זיין אריין גין הט מן	שעה נאך זיין אריין גין האט מן
אים גיפֿונן דז דער בחור טוט	אים גיפֿונדן דז דר בחור איז טוט
איזט גילעגין אויף דיא טיר פֿון	גילעגן אויף די טיר פֿון
קעליר אונ׳ מן הט ניט גיוואושט	קעליר אונ מן האט ניט גיוואוסט
ווער אים ממית הט גיוועזן.	ווער אים ממית האט גיוועזן
אונ׳ איין פֿירטיל יאר דער נאך	אונ איין פֿירטיל יאר דר נאך
זיינין דיא חיצוניים דז זיינין	זענן די חצונים דש זענן
גיוועזין קינדר פֿון משחיתים	גוועזן קינדר פֿון משחיתים
וויטער אין פֿיר הויז גיצאנגין אונ׳	וויטר אין פֿיר הויז גינגן אונ
ווען מאן הט עסין צו גישטעלט	ווען מן האט עשין צו גישטעלט
צו קאבֿן אויף דעם הערד	צו קאבֿן אויף דעם הערד

Line numbers: 305, 310, 315, 320, 325, 330, 335, 340

302 אופֿט, מענשן   303 האבן   304 גווינין. מענשן   305 זיינן. מענשן   306 הייסן
309 שדית   310 גישטראפֿט   311 שידית, ממית   313 שטערבין און זרע   314 שרייבן
315 גישעהן   317 תמ״א תמ״ב   318 גימוארט   319 גימוארטי הייזר
320 גיוועזן   323 וועלבֿר   324 גאנגן   325 גיוואארן, האט
326 עש   329 גינגנגן, פֿירטל   330 האט   331 גיפֿונדן   332 גילעגן   333 האט
334 ממית   335 פֿירטיל   336 זיינן די, דאש זיינן   337 גיוועזן   338 פֿיר הויז, גיצאנגן
339 מן האט   340 קאבֿן

אודר אין אובין דא איזמ דאש עסין   אודר אין אובן דא איז דש עסין

פֿול גיוועזין מיט עש אונ׳ קומ דז   פֿול גוועזן מיט אש אונ קומ דז

מן הט ניט קענין עסין דז עסין   מן האט ניט קענן עסן דש עס

פֿר עש אונ׳ קומ עטליכֿי וואלין   פֿר אש אונ קומ עטלֿבֿי וואלֿן

345   דער נאך זיינין דיא משחיתים   דר נאך זענן די משחיתים

גיצאגין אין דיא שטוובין אונ׳   גיצוגן אין דיא שטובן אונ

האבין דאז צין פֿון דיא שענק   האבן דש צין פֿון די שענק

גינומין אונ׳ האבין אויף דיא   גינומן אונ האבן אויף די

ערד גיוווארפֿין אונ׳ דיא ליכֿטר   ערד גיוווארפֿן אונ די לייכֿטר

350   אונ׳ לאמפין גינומין אונ׳ אויף   אונ לאמפֿן גינומן אונ אויף

דיא ערד גישמיסין אונ׳ ווען   די ערד גישמיסן אונ ווען

מן זיך צו טיש גיזעצט הט אונ׳   מן זיך צום טיש גיזעצט האט אונ

הט אויף גיגעבין עסין האבין   האט אויף גיגעבן עסן האבן

דא דיא טיש צוועל מיט דאש   זיא די טיש צוועל מיט דש

355   עשין שפֿייז ארונטר אויף דיא   עשין שפֿייז ארונטר אויף די

ערד גיוווארפֿין אבר זיא האבין קיין   ערד גיוווארפֿן אבר זיא האבן קיין

כלי ניט צו בראכֿין אונ׳ האבין   כלי ניט צו בראבֿן אונ האבן

קיין מענש גישעדיקט אבר דיא   קיין מענש גישעדיקט אבר די

אין וואונר אין הויז האבין זיך   אין וואונר אין הויז האבן זיך

360   ניט קענין ביהלטין אונ׳ האבין   ניט קענן בהאלטן אונ האבן

טאג אונ׳ נאכֿט קיין רוא גיהט   טאג אונ נאבֿט קיין רוא גיהאט

ביז אלי דיא לייט האבין זיך   ביז אלי די לייט האבן זיך

מוזין אויש ציהן אויז דעם הויז   מוזן אויש ציהן אויז דעם הויז

דא איז איין גרוש גישרייא   דא איז איין גרוש גישרייא

365   גיוועזין אונ׳ האט איטליכֿם מענשין   גוועזן אונ האט איטליבֿן מענש

באנג גיטאן דש אזו אין הויז   באנק גיטאן דש אזו איין הויז

זאל חרוב שטין אין אזו איין   זאל חרב שטין אין אזו איין

קהילה קדושה וויא פֿוזנא איז   קהילה קדושה וויא פֿוזנא איז

דא האלטין דיא פרנסי הקהילה   דא האלטן די פרנסי קהילה

370   איין עצה אונ׳ שיקטן נאך מכשפים   איין עצה

עריליים וגם נאך גלחים וואש זיא

זיעיר שמות קענין אבר דיא

מכשפים קענין קיין פֿעולה טאן

    ∽

    ∽

    ∽

דא שיקטן זיא נאך איין בעל שם   דא שיקן זיא נאך איין בעל שם

375   דער הט גיהייסין ר׳ יואל בעל שם   דר האט גיהייסן ר׳ יואל בעל שם

איז איין גרושר חסיד גיוועזין   איז איין גרושר חסיד גוועזן

אונ׳ איין גרושר פֿועל גיוועזין   אונ איין גרושר פֿועל גוועזן

אין זיין זאבֿין. וויא נון דער ר׳   אין זיין זאבֿן וויא נון דר ר׳

יואל בעל שם אהין קאם נאך   יואל בעל שם אהין קאם נאך

380   פֿוזנא דא פֿינג ער אן תיכּף   פֿוזנא דא פֿאנג ער תיכּף

341 אובן. איז דש   342 גיוועזן   343 האט. קענן. דש   344 וואלֿן   345 זיינן   346 גיצאגן.

שטובן 347   האבן   348 גינומ. האבן   349 גיוווארפֿן   350 לאמפֿן. גינומן   351 גישמיסן

352 האט   353 האט. גיגעבן. האבן   354 דא זיא   355 עסן   356 גיוווארפֿין. האבן

357 צו בראבֿן. האבן   359 האבן   360 קענן ביהאלטן. האבן   361 גיהאט   362 האבן

363 מוזן אויז ציהן   364 איזט   365 גיוועזן. האט. מענשן   369 האלטן

372 איר שמות. קענן   374 שיקטן   375 האט גיהייסן   378 זאבֿן

משביע צו זיין דיא חיצוניים
דז זיינין דיא משחיתים אונ׳
מזיקים וואש זיא צו טאן האבין
אין דיזן הויז דען איר אורט פֿון
מזיקים גיהערין צו זיין אין וואלד
אודר אין דיא מדבר אודר וואו
זומפֿן זיין אונ׳ קיין מזיק הט
מאכֿט צו וואונן בייא ליטא דא
ענטווארטין זיא העטין דין ודברים
אונ׳ איין חזקה אן דעם הויז מן
זאל אין ביֿת דין זעצין וועלן זיא
טענה פֿירן פֿר דעם ביֿת דין
אונ׳ ווילין זיערי זכיות ווייזין.
דא זיינין דיינים פֿון פוזנא
גאנגין אין דעם הויז מיט ר׳ יואל
בעל שם אונ׳ האבין זיין גיזעצט
אין איינר שטוב. אלזו האבין
דז ביֿת דין גיהערט דיא תענות
פֿון דיא משחיתים אביר זיא
האבין קיינים גיזעהין דא פֿינגין
דיא משחיתים אן צו טענה דז
אין דעם הויז הט גיוואונט איין
יודישר גאלד שמיד אונ׳ דער
גאלד שמיד הט גיוואונט מיט
איין שידית אונ׳ הט קינדר מיט
איר גיהט אונ׳ מיר זיינין זיין
קינדר. אונ׳ דער גאלד שמיד
דער הט גאר ליב גיהאט אונזרי
מוטר דיא שידית אונ׳ ער הט
קיין שעה קעניין אן איר זיין אונ׳
זיין ליב איז ממש אן גינופֿט
גיוועזין אן דיא שידית איר ליב
אונ׳ הט ער איר ווילן גיטאן וואש
זיא הט גיוועלט אפֿילו וועןֿ
דער גאלד שמיד איז אין
שול גיוועזין הט ער מוזין זיין
טלית אונ׳ תפֿילין אב ליגין אונ׳
איז צו איר גינגין אונ׳ ער הט
מיט זיינים רעבֿטין ווייב איבל

משביע צו זיין די חצונים
דאש זענן די משחיתים אונ
מזיקים וואש זיא טואן האבן
385　אין דעם הויז דען איר אורט פֿון
מזיקים גיהערן צו זיין אין וואלד
אודר אין דיא מדבר אודר וואו
זומפֿן זענן אונ קיין מזיק האט ניט
מאכֿט צו וואונן בייא ליט דא
390　ענטפֿרן זיא האבן דין ודברים
אונ איין חזקה אן דעם הויז מן
זאל אין ביֿת דין זעצן וועלן זיא
טענות פֿירן פֿר דעם ביֿת דין
אונ ווילן אירי זכיות ווייזן:
395　דא זענן די דיינים פֿון פֿוזנא
גינגנ אין דעם הויז מיט ר׳ יואל
בעל שם אונ האבן זיך גיזעצט
אין איינר שטוב. אזו האבן
דש ב״ד גיהערט די תענות
פֿון דיא משחיתים אבר זיא
400　האבן קיינם ניט גיזעהן: דא פֿאנגן
די משחיתים אן צו טענן דש
אין דעם הויז האט גיוואונט איין
יודישר גאלד שמיד אונ דער
גאלד שמיד האט גיוואונט מיט
405　איין שדית אונ האט קינדר מיט
איר גיהאט אונ מיר זענן זיין
קינדר אונ דער גאלד שמיד
דר האט גאר ליב גיהאט אונזרי
מוטר די שדית אונ ער האט
410　קיין שעה ניט קענן אן איר זיין אונ
זיין ליב איז ממש אן גיקניפֿט
גוועזן אן די שדית איר ליב
אונ ער האט איר ווילן גטאן וואש
זיא האבן גוואלט אפֿילו וועןֿ
415　דר גאלד שמיד איז אין דר
שול גוועזן האט ער מוזן זיין
טלית אונ תפֿילין אפ ליגן אונ
איז צו איר גינגנן אונ ער האט
מיט זיינם רעבֿטן ווייב איבל

382 דאש זיינן　383 טון האבן　385 גיהערן　387 זומפֿן, האט　389 ענטפֿרטן.
העטן　391 ביֿת דין זעצן　392 פֿאר דעם ביֿת　393 ווילן אירי זכיות ווייזן　394 זיין
גיוועזין, פֿינגן　395 גאנגן　396 האבן זיך גיזעצט　397 האבן　398 דאש ביֿת דין, תענת　400 קיינם
זיינן　408 האט　401 דאו　402 האט　404 האט　405 האט　406 גיהאט,
תפֿילין, ליגן　413 האט　409 מוטר, שידית, האט　410 קעניין אונ איר　412 גיוועזן, שידית　417 טלית אוני
419 זיינם רעבֿטן, האט　418 גאנגן, האט　416-415 איז אין דער שול, האט, מוזן　414 האט גיוועלט

	גילעבט. אלזו הט זיין רעלבט	גילעבט: אזו האט זיין רעלבט
420	וייב גישפירט דז עם מוז ניט	וייב גישפירט דש עש מוז ניט
	אום זונשט זיין דאש איר מאן הט	אום זונשט זיין דש איר מאן האט
	ניט נוהג גיוועזן מיט איר אליז	ניט נוהג גוועזן מיט איר אז
	אין מאן מיט זיינער פראוי. אונ׳	אין מאן מיט זיין פרויא. אונ
425	אין מאלטן וואר פסח צו נאלבט	אין מאל וואר אום פסח צו נאלבט
	דא גיבט דער גאלד שמיד דען	דא גיבט דר גאלד שמיד דעם
	סדר דיא ערשטר נאלבט פון פסה	סדר דיא ערשטר נאלבט פון פסה
	וויא עש קאם דז מן זאל אפיקומן	וויא עש קאם דש מן זאל אפיקומן
	עסין דא ווארלבט ער אויז זיין	עסין דא ווארלבט ער אויז זיין
430	קיטל אונ׳ גינגז אין בית החיצון	קיטל אונ גינג אין בית החיצון
	אונ׳ זאומט זיך גאר לאנג דארטין	אונ זוימט זיך גאר לנג דארט
	דא גינג זיין פראוי פון טיש אונ׳	דא גינג די פרויא פון טיש אונ
	וויל זעהין וואש איר מאן אזו לאנג	וויל זעהן וואש איר מאן אזו לאנג
	טואט אין בית החיצון דא זילבט	טוט אין בית החיצון דא זעהט
435	זיא דורך אין שפאלט פון דיא	זיא דורך אין שפאלט פון די
	טיר אין בית החיצון אריין דא	טיר אין בית החיצון אריין דא
	זילבט זיא גליך אליז אין שין	זעהט זיא גליך אז אין שין
	שטוב אונ׳ איז פיל ליבט אונ׳ אוף	שטוב אונ איז פיל לעלבט אוף
	גישטעלט מיט זילבר אונ׳ גולדי	גישטעלט מיט זילבר אונ גילדני
440	כלים אונ׳ אין בעט איז דרינן	כלים אונ אין בעט דא דרינן
	גצירט מיט גאלדי בעט אונ׳	גצירט מיט אין גילדן בעט אונ
	אין נאקטיגי וייב וואר אין בעט	אין נאקטיגי וייב וואר אין בעט
	דיא איז גאר היפש גיוועזין אונ׳	די איז גאר היפש גוועזן אונ
	איר מאן ליגט ביא דעם וויב	איר מאן ליגט ביא דען וויב
445	וואש אין שדית איז גיוועזן דא	וואש אין שדית איז גוועזן דא
	דער שרעקט זיא אונ׳ הט מורא	דער שרעקט זיא אונ האט גרוש מורא
	וואש צו רידין אונ׳ גינג ווידר אין	וואש צי רידן אונ גינג ווידר אין
	אירי שטוב אונ׳ מוזט ווארטן ביז	אירי שטוב אונ מוזט ווידר ווארטן
	איר מאן איז גיקומן אויז דען	ביז איר מאן איז גיקומן אויז דעם
450	בית החיצון. אונ׳ דז וויב	בית החיצון אונ דאש וויב
	שוויגט שטיל אין גאנצי נאלבט	שוויגט שטיל אין גאנצי נאלבט
	אונ׳ נעמט זיך ניקש אן גענין	אונ נעמט זיך ניקש אן קעגן
	אירים מאן דען זיא הט גיזעהין	אירם מאן דען זיא האט גזעהן
	דז ער הט מיט אין שדית צו	דש ער האט מיט אין שדית צו
455	מאן. אונ׳ צו מארגנש גינג זיא	מאן אונ צו מארגנש פריא גינג זיא
	צו דעם שטאט רב דער האט	צו דעם שטאט רב דר האט
	גיהייסין הגאון ר׳ שעפטל סג״ל	גיהיישן הגאון ר׳ שעפטיל סג״ל
	אונ׳ קלאגט אים דז איר מאן	אונ קלאגט אים דש איר מאן
	בעו״ה פר פירט איזט מיט אין	בעו״ה פר פירט איז מיט אין

420 האט   421 עז   422 דאש, האט   423 אלו   424 פרויא   428 עז
431 זוימט זיך, דארטן   432 פרויא   434 בית החיצון   433 זעהן   436 בית החיצון
437 אלו   338–339 אוף גישטעלט   441 גיצירט   443 היפש גיוועזן   445 שידית
446 דר שרעקט, האט   447 צו רירן   450 בית החיצון, דאש   451 גענגן   453 אירם
מאן, האם גיזעהן   454 האט, שידית   457 גיהיישן   459 איז

שידית דא לאזט דער רב רופֿין
דען גאלד שמיד אונ׳ איז גוזר
בחרם אוף אים דז ער זאל
דעם אמת זאגין. דא איז דער
גאלד שמיד תכף מודה אונ׳ זאגט
דז זיך הט צו אים ביהעפֿט
איין שידית וויא ער זיך האט בייא
דעם פֿלום וואסיר גיוועשן. אלזו
שריב אים דער רב איין קמיע
דז זיך הט מוזין אב טאן פֿון
דעם גאלד שמיד דיא שידית
אונ׳ וויא נון דער גאלד שמיד
הט זעלין שטערבין איז דיא
שידית צו אים גיקומן מיט אירי
קינדר וואש זיא הט פֿון אים
גיהאט אונ׳ היבט אן צו וויינין פֿר
אים וויא ער זיא לאט מיט אירי
קינדר. אונ׳ פֿאלט איבר אים אונ׳
אונ׳ קישט אים אונ׳ איבר רעט
אים דז ער אויך זאל גערבין דז
זיא מעלבט לעבין קענין אונ׳ דער
גאלד שמיד פֿר שפרעלבט איר
איין קעלר אין זיינם הויז. אונ׳
דער נאך שטערב ער וויא עש וואר
עטליבי יאר דז איז זיך איין
מלחמה אין דיא מדינו פולין אונ׳
דיא מלחמה הט גיווערט פֿון דען
יאר ת״ח אונ׳ הט גיווערט ביז
שנת תי״ח איז דער גאלד שמיד
גישטארבן אונ׳ זיני קינדר מיט
אלי זייני יורשים אונ׳ איזונד
הט דער גאלד שמיד קיין יורשים
מער אלזו האבין דיא חצונים
איין טענה גפֿירט דז זיא זיינין
דיא יורשים צו דעם הויז. אלזו
האבין דיא לייט משיב גיוועזן וואש
דיא האבין אין הויז גיוואונט מיר
האבין דז הויז גיקאפֿט פֿון דיא
קינדר דעם גאלד שמיד אונ׳ איר
זייט משחיתים היישט קיין זרע

שידית דא לאזט דר רב רופֿן
דען גאלד שמיד אונ איז גוזר
בחרם אוף אים דז ער זאל
דעם אמת זאגן דא איז דר
גאלד שמיד תיכף מודה אונ׳ זאגט
דש זיך האט צו אים ביהעפֿט
איין שידית וויא ער זיך האט בייא
דען פֿלום וואשר גיוואשין: אזו
שריבט אים דר רב איין קמיע
דא האט זיא זיך מוזן אפ טאן פֿון
דעם גאלד שמיד די שדית
אונ׳ וויא נון דער גאלד שמיד
האט זעלן שטאַרבן איז דיא
שידית צו אים גיקומן מיט אירי
קינדר וואש זיא האט פֿון אים
גיהאט אונ׳ היבט אן צו וויינן פֿר
אים וואז ער לאט זיא מיט אירי
קינדר אונ׳ פֿאלט איבר אים
אונ׳ קושט אים אונ׳ איבר רעט
אים דש ער זאל אוך געבן דש
זיא מאבֿט לעבן קענן אונ דר
גאלד שמיד פֿר שפרעבֿט איר
איין קעלר אין זיינם הויז אונ
דר נאך שטאַרב ער וויא עש וואר
עטליבי יאר דא איז זיך איין
מלחמה אין די מדינות פולין אונ
די מלחמה הט גיווערט פֿון דען
יאר ת״ח אונ׳ הט גיווערט ביז
שנת תי״ח איז דר גאלד שמיד
גישטארבן אונ זייני קינדר מיט
אלי זייני יורשים אונ איזונד
הט דער גאלד שמיד קיין יורשים
מער אלזו האבין דיא חצונים
איין טענה גפֿירט דז זיא זיינין
דיא יורשים צו דעם הויז. אלזו
האבין דיא לייט משיב גיוועזן וואש
דיא האבין אין הויז גיוואונט מיר
האבין דז הויז גיקאפֿט פֿון דיא
קינדר דעם גאלד שמיד אונ׳ איר
זייט משחיתים היישט קיין זרע

460 שידית, רופֿן   463 אמת זאגן   464 תיכף   465 האט   466 שידית
467 וואשר   469 האט מוזן   470 שידית   472 האט זעלן שטערבן   473 שידית,
474 האט   475 וויינן   478 קושט   479 געבן   480 קענן   483 עז   485 מדינת פולין
486 האט   487 האט   488 שנת   490 אונ׳ איצונד   491 האט
492 האבן   493 זיינן   495 האבן, משיב   496 האבן   497 האבן דאש   499 היישט

ישראל אונ נאך איינש האבן	ישראל. אונ' נאך איינש האבין
די ליט גיטעגנת דש די שידית	דיא ליישט גיטעגנט דז דיא שידית
האט זיך מיט גוואלט בהעפֿט צו	הט זיך מיט גיוואלד בהעפֿט צו
דעם גאלד שמיד דש ער הט בעל	דעם גאלד שמיד דז הט בעל
כרחו מיט איר גוואנט: אזו האט	כרחו מיט איר גיוואונט. אלזו הט
מן איין פסק אויש גיגעבן דש די	מן איין פסק אויש גערבין דז דיא
משחיתים האבן קיין חלק אן דעם	משחיתים האבין קיין חלק אן דעם
הויז דען איר וואונונג איז אין די	הויז דען איר דירה איז אין דיא
מדבר אונ ניט אין איין אורט	מדבר אונ' ניט אין איין אורט
וואו ליט וואונן אונ נאך דען	וואו ליט וואונן. אונ' נאך דעם
פסק האט ר' יואל בעל שם	פסק האט ר' יואל בעל שם
משביע גוועזן דש די חיצונים	משביע גיוועזן דז דיא חיצוניים
האבן מוזן אפ ווייכֿן פֿון הויז אונ'	האבין מוזין אב ווייכֿין פֿון הויז אונ'
פֿון קעלר אונ האבן מוזן גין אין	פֿון קעלר אונ' האבן מוזן גין אין
ווילדן וואלד: נון גיהערט מן	ווילדן וואלד. נוא גיהערט מן
איין ראייה נעמן פֿון דער מעשה	איין ראייה נעמן פֿון דעם מעשה
דש ווען זיך איין בן אדם בהעפֿט	דז ווען זיך איין בן אדם ביהעפֿט
אן די כיתה פֿון לילי״ת אדר	אן דיא כיתי פֿון לילית אודר
מחלת דש זענן מוטר פֿון	מחלת דז זיינין דיא מיטור פֿון
די שדים אזו ווערט דען	דיא שידים אלזו ווערט דער
זעלביגר מענש אויש גיוווארצלט	זעלביגר מענש אויש גיוווארצלט
מיט זיין גיזינד אונ שטארבן	מיט זיני גיזינד אונ' שטערבין
אלי אוועק: דרום גוהערט איטליבֿר	אלי ווען דרום גיהערט איטליבֿר
גוואָרנט זיין דש זאל קיין זנות	גיוואָרנט זיין דז זאל קיין זנות
נאך גין גין דען מענבֿיש מאל קומט	נאך גין גין דען מענבֿיש מאל קומט
איין שידית אין גישטאלט איין זונה	איין שידית אין גישטאלט איין זונה
אונ' בהעפֿט זיך אן איין מענשן	אונ' ביהעפֿט זיך אן איין מענשן
דש דר מענש קומט אוועק פֿון דר	דז דער מענש קומט וועק פֿון דער
וועלט מיט זיין משפחה: דרום גיהער	וועלט מיט זיין משפחה דרום גיהערט
איטליבֿר מענש נזהר צו זיין דז	איטליבֿר מענש נזהר צו זיין דז
ער זיך זאל בהעפֿטן אן זיין וייב	ער זאל זיך ביהעפֿטן אן זיין וייב
אונ זאל ניט מוציא זרע לבטלה	אונ' זאל ניט מוציא זרע לבטלה
זיין אונ אוב ער שון מוציא זרע	זיין אונ' אוב ער שון מוציא זרע
לבטלה איז באונס אדר ברצון	לבטלה איז באונס אודר ברצון
זאל ער תיכף תשובה טאן ואז	זאל ער תיכף תשובה טאן ואז
טוב לו יהיה סלה:	טוב לו יהיה סלה:

500 · 505 · 510 · 515 · 520 · 525 · 530 · 535

500 האבן   504 האט   505 אויז גערבן   506 האבן   517 לילית   518 מחלת דאש זיינן   528 גיהער

501 דיא ליט גיטענגת, שידית   502 האט, מיט גיוואלט   503 דאש האט

512 האבן מוזן ווייכֿן   513 האבן מוזן

520 אויז גענוווארצלט   521 שטערבין   523 זנות

3. A Selection from Five Editions of the *Tsene rene* (1622, 1726, 1786, 1827, 1848)

צאינה וראינה

Tsene rene

H = Hanau, 1622
A = Amsterdam, 1726
L = Lemberg, 1786
V–G = Vilna-Grodno, 1827
Y = Yozefov, 1845

1   וימת הרן על פני תרח אביו . . . דען

2   זיין פֿאטר תרח האט ואר קויפֿט צלמים   H
       זיין פֿאטר תרח האט פֿר קויפֿט (צלמים)   A
       זיין פֿאטר תרח הט פֿר קויפֿט ע״ז   L
       זיין פֿאטר תרח האט פֿר קויפֿט אפ געטיר   V–G
       זיין פֿאטר תרח האט פֿר קויפֿט אפ געטר   Y

3   אונ׳ עבודה זרות אונ׳ אברהם איז איין
       אונ׳ (עבודה זרות) אונ׳ אבֿרהם איז איין
       אונ׳ אברהם איז איין
       אונ׳ אברהם איז איין
       אונ האט גיזעצט אברהם ער זאל

4   מאל גישטנדן דר בייא אונ׳ וען
       מאל דער בייא גישטאנדן אונ׳ וען
       מאל גשטאנן דר בי אונ וען
       מאל דער בייא גישטאנדן אונ וען
       אים פֿר קויפֿן דיא אפ געטיר אונ וען

5   איינר קומן אישט אונ׳ האט גיוואלט
       איינר איז גיקומן אונ׳ האט גיוואלט
       איינר גקומן איז אונ הט גוואלט
       איינר איז גיקומן אונ האט גיוואלט
       איינר איז גיקומן

6   קויפֿן דיא עבֿודה זרה דא פֿרוגט אברהם וויא
       קויפֿן דיא (עבֿודה זרה) דא פֿראגט אבֿרהם וויא
       קופֿן די ע״ז דא פֿרעגט אברהם וי
       קויפֿן איין אפ גאט דא פֿרעגט אברהם וי
       קויפֿן איין אפ גאט אזו האט אברהם אים גיפֿרעגט וויא

7

אלט בישטו דא אנטוורט ער פֿונפֿציג אודר

אלט בישטו דא ענטפֿרט ער פֿופֿציג אודר

אלט בישטו ענפֿרט ער פֿופֿציג אדר

אלט בישטו דא ענטפֿרט ער פֿופֿציג אודר

אלט בישטו האט ער אים גינפֿערט פֿופֿציג אודר

8

זעלטציג יאר דא זאגט ער וויא דיר

זעלֿציג יאר דא זאגט ער וויא דיר

זעלֿציג יאר זאגט ער וויי דיר

זעלֿציג יאהר דא זאגט ער וויי דיר

זעלֿציג יאר אזו האט אברהם צו אים גיזאגט וויי צו דיר

9

דו בישט נון אלט זעלֿטציג יאר אונ׳ דוא

דוא בישט נון אלט זעלֿציג יאר אונ׳ דוא

בישט אלט זכציג יאר אונ

דו בישט נון אלט זעכציג יאר אונ דו

דוא בישט אלט זעלֿציג יאָר אונ

10

ווילשטו דיך בוקין צו איינם דאש דא איין

ווילשטו דיך בוקן צו איינם דש דא איין

ווילשטו דיך בוקן צו אינם דא איין

ווילשטו דיך בוקן צו איינם דש דא איין

ווילשטו דיך בוקין צו איינים וואש איז איין

11

טאג אלט איז דא האט זיך דר זעלביג

טאג אלט איז דא האט זיך דער זעלביגר

טאג אלט איז דא האט זיך דר זלבגר

טאג אלט איז דא האט זיך דר זעלביגר

טאג אלט דען דיא אפ גאט האט עז ערשט היינט גימאלֿט גיווארין אזו

12

גישעמט אונ׳ איז בחרפה איין וועק גאנגן

גישעמט אונ׳ איז (בחרפה) איין וועק גיגאנגן

גשעמט אונ איז בחרפה אוועק גנאנגן

גישעמט אונ איז בחרפה אוועק גיגאנגן

איז יעניר אוועק גינאנגין בחרפה

13

איין מאלט קאם איין פֿרויא אונ׳

איין מאלט קאם איין פֿרויא אונ׳

איין מאל קאם איין פֿרוי אונ

איין מאל קומט איין פֿרויא אונ

איין מאל איז איין אשה גיקומן אונ

14

בראכט איין שיסל מיט זעמיל מעל אונ׳

בראלֿט איין שיסל מיט זעמיל מעל אונ׳

בראכט איין שיסל מיט זעמיל מעל אונ

האט גיבראכט איין שיסל מיט זעמל מעל אונ

האט גיבראלֿט איין שיסיל מיט זעמל מעל

15 זיא זאגט צו אברהם נעם דש מעל צו

זיא זאגט צו אבֿרהם נעם דש מעל צו

זי זגט צו אברהם נעם דאש מעל צו

זי זאגט אברהם נעם דש מעל צו

אײן

16 קרבן ואר דיא צלמים דא נאם אברהם דיא

(קרבן) פֿר דיא (צלמים) דא נאם אבֿרהם דיא

קרבן פֿר דיא ע״ז נאם אברהם די

קרבן פֿר אב גַעטר דא נעמט אברהם דיא

קרבן צו די אפ גַעטר האט אברהם גינומן דיא

17 שיסל מיט זעמיל מעל אונ׳ שטעלט זיא

שיסל מיט דעם זעמיל מעל אונ׳ שטעלט זיא

שיסל מעל אונ שטעלט זי

שיסל מיט זעמיל מעל אונ שטעלט זי

שיסיל מיט זעמל מעל אונ האט זי גישטעלט

18 ור דיא צלמים אונ׳ נאם אײן גרושן

פֿר דיא צלמים דא נאם אבֿרהם אײן גרושן

פֿר די ע״ז אונ נעמט אײן

פֿר דיא אפ גַעטר דא נעמט אברהם אײן גרושן

פֿר דיא אפ גַעטר אונ האט גינומן אײן גרוישן

19 שטעקן אונ׳ צו ברעכֿט אלי דיא צלמים

שטעקן אונ׳ צו ברעכֿט אלי דיא צלמים

שטעקן אונ צו ברעכט זי אלי

שטעקן אונ׳ צו ברעכט אלע אפ גַעטר

שטעקין אונ הט צו בראכֿין אלי אפ גַעטר

20 נייארט אײן גרוש פֿסל ליש ער שטין

נייארט אײן גרוש פֿסל לים ער שטין

נייארט אײן גרושן לאז ער שטין

נייארט אײן גרוישן בילד לאזט ער שטין

נאר אײן גרושן אפ גאט האט ער גילאזט שטין

21 אונ׳ גאב אים דען גרושן שטעקן אין

אונ׳ גאב אים דען גרושן שטעקן אין

אונ גיב אים אײן שטעקן אין

אונ גיט אים דעם גרושן שטעקן אין

אונ האט אים גיגעבן דעם שטעקין אין

22 דיא הנט דא תרח קאם דא זאגט ער

דיא הנט דא קאם תרח דער צו דא זאגט ער

די האנט דא קום תרח דא זגט ער

דער האנט דא קומט תרח דר צו זאגט ער

דר האנט איז תרח גיקומן אונ האט גיזאגט

23

צו אברהם ווער האט דש גיטאן דא זאגט

צו אבֿרהם ווער האט דש גיטאן דא זאגט

צו אברהם ווער הט דש גטאן דא זגט

צו אברהם ווער האט דש גיטאן דא זאגט

צו אברהם ווער האט דש גיטאן האט

24

אברהם איין פֿרויא האט גיבראכֿט זעמיל

אבֿרהם איין פֿרויא האט גיבראכֿט זעמיל

אברהם איין פֿרוי הט גברכֿט זעמל

אברהם איין פֿרויא האט גיבראכט זעמיל

אברהם גיזאגט איין אשה האט גיבראכֿט זעמל

25

מעל צו קרבן דא הבן זיך דיא צלמים

מעל צו קרבן דא האבן זיך דיא צלמים

מעל צו קרבן קרבן זיך האבן די ע״ז

מעל צו קרבן דא האבן זיך דיא אפ גֿעטר

מעל פֿר איין קרבן אזו האבן זיך די אפ גֿעטר

26

מיט אננדר גיקריגט איטליכֿר האט וועלן

מיט אננדר גיקריגט איטליכֿר האט וועלן

מיט אננדר גקירגט איטלכר האט וועלן

מיט אננדר גיקריגט איטליכר האט וועלן

מיט אננדר גיקריגט איטליכֿר הט גיוואלט

27

פֿאר עשין דא הוט דז גרעשטי פֿסל איין

פֿאר עסין דא הוט דאש גרעשטי (פסל) איין

פר עשן דא האט די גרעשטי איין

פֿאר עסין דא הוט דש גרעשטר בילד איין

פֿריער עסין אזו האט דר גרעסטער אפ גֿאט

28

שטעקן גינומן אונ׳ הוט זיא אלי צו

שטעמען גינומן אונ׳ האט זיא אלי צו

שטעקן גנומן און האט זי אלי צו

שטעקן גינומן און האט זיי אלי צו

גינומן איין שטעקין און האט זייא אלי צו

29

בראכֿין דא זאגט תרח אונ׳ האבן זיא

בראבֿין דא זאגט (תרח) אונ׳ האבן זיא

בראכן דא זגט תרח אונ׳ הבן זי

בראכֿין דא זאגט תרח האבן זיי

בראכֿין האט תרח גיזאגט צו אברהם האבן זייא

30

דען שכל אודר הבן זיא חית אין

דען שכֿל אודר האבן זיא חיותֿ אין

שכל אין

דען שכל אודר האבן זיא חיות אין

דען שכל אודר האבן זייא דען חיות אין

31

זיך דא זאגט אברהם ווען זיא יוא

זיך דא זאגט אבֿרהם ווען זיא יוא

זיך זגט אברהם ווען זי

זיך זאגט אברהם ווען זייא יוא

זיך האט אברהם גיזאגט אז זייא האבן יוא

32

קיין שכל הבין אוני וואָרום זאָלן מיר זיא דען

קיין שכֿל האבן אוני וואָרום זאָלן מיר זיא

קיין שכל האבן וואָרום זאל מיר זי

קיין שכל האבן וואָרום זאָלן מיר זיי

קיין שכל ניט וואָרים זאָלין מיר זייא

33

דינן דא נאם אין תרח זיין פֿאָטר אוני

דינן דא נאם אים תרח זיין פֿאָטר אוני

דינן נאם אים תרח זיין פֿאָטר אונ

דינן דא נעמט אים תרח זיין פֿאָטר אונ

דינן האט תרח אים גינומן אוני

34

גאב אין נמרוד אין דיא הנט דא זאגט

גאב אים (נמרוד) אין דיא הנט דא זאגט

גוט אים נמרוד אונ די הנט זגט

גיט אין צוא נמרוד אין דער האנט דא זאגט

האט אין גגעבן צו נמרוד אין דר האנט האט

35

נמרוד צו אברהם ווילשטו דיך בוקן צו

(נמרוד) צו (אבֿרהם) ווילשטו דיך בוקן צו

נמרוד צו אברהם ווילשטו דיך בוקן צו

נמרוד צוא אברהם ווילשטו דיך בוקן צו

נמרוד גיזאגט צו אברהם ווילשטו דיך בוקין צו

36

דעם פֿייאר דא איזט עש גוט ווילשטו דען

דעם פֿייאר דא איז עש גוט ווילשטו דען

דען פֿייאר איז גוט ווילשטו

דעם פֿיער איז גוט ווילשטו אבר

דעם פֿיער איז גוט און ווען

37

ניט דא וויל איך דיך לאזין ווערפֿן

ניט דא וויל איך דיך לאזין ווערפֿין

ניט וויל איך דיך לאזן ווארפֿן

ניט דא וועל איך דיך לאזן ווארפֿן

ניט וועל איך דיך היסין אריין ווארפֿין

38

אין דז פֿייאר וואר הרן דר בייא

אין דש פֿייאר דא וואר (הרן) דער בייא

אין פֿייאר אונ הרן איז דר בי

אין דעם פֿיער וואר הרן דער בי

אין דעם פֿייאר איז הרן דר בייא

39　　גישטנדן אונ' ער וואושט ניט וועם ער

גישטנדן אונ' ער וואושט ניט וועם ער

גישטאנן אונ ווישט [ניט] וועמן ער

גישטאאנן אונ ער וויש ניט וועמין ער

גישטאאנן אונ

40　　זאלט נאך העלפֿין אברהם אודר נמרוד ער

זאלט נאך העלפֿן אבֿרהם אודר נמרוד ער

זאל נאך העלפֿן אברהם אודר נמרוד ער

זאל נאך העלפֿן אברהם אודר נמרוד ער

האט זיך

41　　גידאכֿט זיך וויל זעהן ווערט אברהם

גידאכֿט זיך וויל זעהן ווערט אבֿרהם

גדכט זיך וויל זעהן וועט אבֿרהם

גידאכֿט זיך וויל זעהן וועט אברהם

גיטראכֿט איך וועל זעהן וועט אברהם

42　　הרויש גין דא וויל איך זאגן איך

הרויש גין דא וויל איך זאגן איך

ארוש גין וויל איך זאגן איך

ארויש גיין וועל איך זאגן איך

ניצל ווערין פֿון דעם פֿייאר וועל איך זאגין איך

43　　דין דעם גוט דעם אברהם דינט אבר

דין דעם גאט דעם אבֿרהם דינט אבר

וויל דעם גוט וואש אברהם דינן אבר

דין דעם גאט פֿון אברהם אבר

דין דעם גאט פֿון אברהם אבר

44　　ווערט אברהם דרינן בלייבן דא וויל

ווערט אבֿרהם דרינן בלייבן דא וויל

וועט אברהם דרינן בלייבן וויל

וועט אברהם דרינן בלייבן דא וועל

ווען ניט וועל

45　　איך דינן וואש דא נמרוד דינט אונ' דא

איך דינן וואש דא (נמרוד) דינט אונ' דא

איך זגן איך וויל דינן וועמן נמרוד דינט אונ

איך דינן וואש נמרוד דינט אונ דא

איך דינן וואש דא נמרוד דינט אונ אז

46　　נון אברהם וואר גאנץ הרויש גאנגן אויש

נון אבֿרהם וואר גנץ ארויש גיגאנגן אויז

ווי אברהם וואר גנץ ארוש גגנגן אוש

נון אברהם וואר גאנץ ארויש גיגאנגן אויש

אברהם איז ארויש גיגאנגן גאנץ פֿון

47

דעם פֿייאר דא פֿרעגט מן הרן

דעם פֿייאר דא פֿרעגט מן (הרן)

דעם פֿייאר פֿרעגט מן צו הרן

דעם פֿייאר דא פֿרעגט מען אן הרן

דעם פֿייאר הט מען גיפֿרעגט צו הרן

48

אברהמש ברודר אונ װעם דינשטו דא

אן אבֿרהם) זיין ברודר אונ װעם דינשטו דא

אברהם זיין ברודר װעמן דינשטו

נוא װעמין װילשטו דינן

װעמין דינשטו

49

אנטװורט ער דין װאש דא דינט

ענטפֿרט (הרן) איך דין װאש דא דינט

ענפֿרט ער איך דין װאש אברהם

ענטפֿרט ער איך װיל דינן דעם גאט

הט ער גיזאגט דעם גאט

50

אברהם דא האבן זיא אינן אין דש װיאר הינײן

אבֿרהם דא הבן זיא אים אין דז פֿייאר הינײן

דינט הבן זי אים אין פֿייאר אַרײן

פֿון אברהם דא האבן זייא אים אין דש פֿייער אַרײן

פֿון אברהם האט מען אים אין דעם פֿייאר אַרײן

51

גיװוארפֿן אונ' דיא גידערם זיין

גיװוארפֿן אונ' דיא גידערם זיין

גװוארפֿן אונ די גדערם זיין

גיװוארפֿן אונ דיא גידעריס זיין

גיװוארפֿין זענן אים זייני גידערים

52

אים װוארדן איין גישרומפפֿן אונ' איזט

אים װוארדן איין גישרומפֿן אונ' איז

אים איין גשרומפן אונ איז

אים װארן איין גישרומפּפֿן אונ איז

װוארין איין גשרימפן אונ ער איז

53

אזו גישטארבן דא איזט איין מלאך קומן

אזו גישטארבן דא איז איין מלאך גיקומן

גשטארבן איז גקומן איין מלאך

גישטאַרבן דא איז איין מלאך גיקומן

גישטאַרבן אזו איז איין מלאך גיקומן

55/54

אונ' האט אין הרויש טאן װוארפֿן ואר תרה || זײנם פֿאטר . . .

אונ' האט אים ארויש גיװוארפֿן פֿאר תרה || זיין פֿאטר . . .

אונ האט אים אַרוש גיװוארפֿן פֿר תרח || זיין פֿאַטר . . .

אונ האט אים ארויש גיװוארפֿן פֿר תרה || זיין פֿאַטר . . .

אונ האט אים ארויש גיװוארפֿן פֿון דעם פֿייאר פֿר זיין פֿאַטר תרח . . .

4. Two Narratives in Four Editions of *Simkhes hanefesh* (1707, 1718, 1723, 1796)

שמחת הנפש

Simkhes hanefesh

Shklov, 1796	Frankfurt am Main, 1707
	Sulzbach, 1718 = א
	Amsterdam, 1723 = ב
	[ ] appears only in Frankfurt am Main, 1707

	Shklov, 1796	Frankfurt am Main, 1707
1	מ שׁ ל איין גנב האט איין גבראבֿן	מ שׁ ל איין גנב האט אין גיבראבֿן
	אין דעם אוצר פֿון מלך האט ער	אין דען אוצר פֿון מלך האט ער
	גיזעהן זילברני כלים שטין האט	גיזעהן זילברני כלים שטין האט
	ער גנומן דר פֿון וואש ער	ער [אן] גינומן דער פֿן וואש ער
5	האט קענען דר טראגן דר נאך	האט קענען דער טראגן דער נאך
	הט ער גזעהן גילדני שטין	האט ער גיזעהן גילדני כלים שטין
	האט ער די זילברני כלים פֿון זיך	האט ער דיא זילברני כלים פֿון זיך
	גטאן אונ האט גינומן גילדני	גיטאן אונ׳ האט זיך גינומן גילדני
	כלים דר נאך האט ער גזעהן	כלים דער נאך האט ער גיזעהן
10	שיני פערליך האט ער מיט זיך	שיני פערליך האט ער מיט זיך
	זעלבשט גירעט	זעלבשטן גירעד [בין איך ניט
	איך זאל אזו שווער	איין נאר] איך זאל אזו שווער
	טראגן אן גאלד אזו שווער פערליך	טראגן אן גאלד אזו שווער פערליך
	זענן דאך פֿיל מאל אזו פֿיל	זיין דאך [וויא] פֿיל מאל אזו פֿיל
15	ווערט אונ הט ווידר די גילדני	ווערט אונ׳ האט ווידר דיא גילדני
	כלים פֿון זיך גטאן אונ האט פעריל	כלים פֿון זיך גיטאן אונ׳ האט פערל
	גנומן דר נאך האט ער גזעהן	גינומן דער נאך האט ער גיזעהן
	גרושי שטיק דימאנטן שטין הט	גרושי שטיק דימאנטן שטין האט
	ער די פֿעריל אוועק גטאן אונ	ער דיא פֿערל אוועק גיטאן אונ׳
20	האט די דימנטן גנומן אזו האט ער	האט דימאנטן גינומן אזו האט ער
	גטאן דיא גאנצי נאבֿט אין	גיוואלט דיא גאנצי נאבֿט. אין
	דעם איז דר טאג אן גקומן האט	דעם איז דער טאג אן קומן האט
	ער מורא גהאט מן ווערט אים	ער מורא גיהאט מן ווערט אים
	דר ווישן אונ וועט אום זיין	דער ווישן אונ׳ ווערט אום זיין
25	חיות קומן אונ איז דר פֿון	חיות קומן אונ׳ איז דער פֿן
	גילאפֿן האט גאר נישט מיט זיך	גילויפֿן האט גאר ניקש מיט זיך
	גנומן אזו אוך דר מענש לאזט	גינומן. אזו אך דער מענש לאזט
	זיך ניט בנוגן האט ער צין גפֿעם	זיך ניט בינוגן האט ער צינן גיפֿעם
	וויל ער זילבר האבן האט ער	וויל ער זילבר האבן האט ער

1 גנב -א, איין גיבראבֿן   2 אין דעם -ב   3 זילברי -ב   11 זעלבשט גירעט,   15 ווערהרט -ב

17 הוט ער -א   20 הוט -א, די דימאנטן.   21 די -א, גנצי   22 דר טאג -א,   23 גיהט -א

25 חיות -א, דר פֿן -א   26 גילאפֿן, אונ׳ האט -ב   27 דר מענש -א   29 זילברי -ב,

זילבר וויל ער גאלד האבן אונ׳
[דווקא] דיא שענשטי קליידר
אונ׳ אלי וויל ער העלֿברן
שטאט פֿירן אונ׳ לויפֿט אונ׳ רענט
אונ׳ זייני צייט [אזו] אוועק
ברענגט אין הבֿל [הבֿלים]
אורבליצלינג קומט דער טאג דער
מענש איז ניט זילֿבר איבר נעלֿטיג
אום גיריֿבֿט שטעארבט ער לאזט
אליש הינטר זיך אונ׳ בלייבט
אין גנבֿ ער גנבֿת דיא פֿה פֿון
גאט אונ׳ גיט אלי זייני טאג אין
דער פֿינשטער אונ׳ [לויטר] וויא טאג
[דער צו] אונ׳ גרושי דאגות דש
מאֿבֿט אליש פֿר [וויל ער אליש פֿר
איברגט] וויא מער אלו ער זיך
אין זאמליט וויא מער זורג ער
זיך אויף לאדן טוט. וועז ער אבר
זאלֿבֿש ניט טוט פֿר שפֿארט ער
צוויֿא ארלייא זורג בידארף ניט
צו זורגן דש אין צו קויפֿן אונ׳
אין צו זאמלן אונ׳ בידארף ניט צו
זורגן אלו ער עש פֿאר לירט.
מן האט אמאל אין פֿילסוף
גיפֿרעגט וויא קומט דש ווארום
זארגשטו ניט האט ער גענטפֿרט
איך טוא מיר ניט זאלֿבֿש אין
קויפֿן וועז עש זעלט פֿר לארן
ווערן אלו איך דריבר זורגן
זעלט.

---

30   זילבר וויל ער גאלד האבן און
    די שענשטי קליידר
    אונ אל טאג וויל ער העלֿבר
    שטאט פֿירן אונ לופֿט אונ ארבט
    אונ זייני צייט אוועק
35   ברענגט אין הבֿל
    פלוצים קומט דער טאג דר
    מענש איז ניט זעלֿבר איבר נעלֿטיגן
    אום גרעלֿבֿט שטעארבט ער אונ לאזט
    אלין הינטר זיך אונ בלייבט
40   אין גנבֿ ער גנבֿת די פֿה פֿון
    גאט אונ גיט אל זייני טאג אין
    דר פֿינשטער אונ וויא טאג
    אונ גרושי דאגות דאש
    מאֿבֿט אלו
45   וויא מער אלש ער
    אין זמלט וויא מער זארג ער
    זעלֿבֿיש אויף לאדן טוט וועז ער
    אבר דש ניט טוט פֿר שפֿארט ער
    צוויֿא ארלייא זארג בדארף ניט
50   צו זארגן דאש אין צו קויפֿן אונ
    אין צו זאמלן אונ בדארף ניט
    זארגן אלש ער עש פֿאר לירט
    מן האט אין פֿילוסוף
    גפֿרעגט וויא קומט דש ווארום
55   זארגשטו ניט האט ער גענפֿרט
    איך טו מיר ניט זעלֿבֿש
    קויפֿן וועז עש פֿר לארן
    ווערן אלש איך דריבר זארגן
    זעלֿט:

פ ע ש ה אמאל איז אין גרושר
עושר גיווען דער האט זיך
אמאל בידאֿבֿט אונ׳ גיזאגט ווש
האב איך פֿון אלי מייני ארביט
ווש ווערט מיך פֿון מיין געלֿט אונ׳
גוט העלֿפֿן וועז איך ווער שטארבן
ווש ווער איך פֿון דר פֿון נעמן

---

60   פ ע ש ה אמאל איז אין גרושר
    עושר גיווען דר האט זיך
    בדאֿבֿט אונ זאגט ווש
    האב איך פֿון אלי מייני ארביט
    ווש ווערט מיר מיין געלֿט אונ
65   גוט העלֿפֿן וועז איך וועז שטעארבן
    ווש ווער איך פֿון דר פֿון נעמן

---

31 די שענשטי -א   35 איז -א   36 אורביצלינג, דר טאג דר -א   38 שטעארבט   39 אלי
42 דר פֿינשטר   43 דז -א, דאו -ב   44 אליו -א, אלו -ב   46 זאריג -א, זארג -ב   47 זעלֿביש
אויף -ב   48 דש ניט טוט -ב   49 זאריג -א, זארג -ב   50 זארגן דאו -ב   51 אין צו זאמלן
52 זארגן -ב   53 פֿילוסוף -ב   54 דאו -ב   55 גיגענטפֿרט -ב   58 זארגן   61 דיר -א,
עושיר -ב   62 גזאגט -א, ב, וויש -א   64 ווזו   65 שטעארבן   66 ווש -א,
ווזו -ב, דר פֿון -ב

לעולם הבא איך מוז אליש
הינטר מיך לאזן. האבן דיא
ליוט צו אים גיזאגט ער זאל
מיט זיין געלט גומל חסד זיין
אונ׳ זאל צדקה געבן דאש
[ווערט זיין צדה לדרך זיין אונ׳]
בלייבט אים לעולם הבא. [דען
דאש עשירות האט קיין בישטאנד.]
אזו האט דער עשיר אויף זיך
מקבל גיוועזן ער וויל [יא] צדקה
געבן. אונ׳ האט אים איין שבֿועה
גיטאן ער וויל קיינם צדקה געבן
נייארט זאלבֿי ליוט דיא דיא נון גאר
קיין האפֿנונג אונ׳ בטחון האבן
אויף דער וועלט דער מיט ער
זיין צדקה וואל אן לינגט.
[נון עש האט זיך אמאל גיטראפֿן
דער עשיר איז פֿר דער שטאט
גאנגן] האט ער אן גיטראפֿן איין
ארים מאן זיצן אויף דען מישט
אונ׳ האט ניט איין שטיקלי
גאנצן ראק אן זיין לייב גיהאט.
אלז ער זיך האט קענן בידעקן.
אזו האט זיך דער עשיר גידאכֿט
אין זיינם זין דער ארים מאן
האט גיוויש קיין האפֿנונג מער
אויף דער וועלט אונ׳ פֿר לאנגט
דען טוט דער וויל ער זאלבֿן
צער ליידן מוז [האט ער גיוויש
קיין פֿר זיבֿרונג מער אויף דער
וועלט.] אונ׳ האט אים געבן
הונדרט גילדן. אזו האט זיך
דער עני פֿר וואונדרט אונ׳
שפֿריבֿלט צו אים ווארום גיבט
איר מיר אזו פֿיל געלט אליינטש
איר העט דאך פֿילי עניים דר
מיט קענן ביטיילן. אזו האט
דער עשיר אים דר צילט דיא
שבֿועה וואש ער גיטאן האט אלז
ער קיינם ניקש גיבט נייארט

לעוה״ב איך מוז אלז
הינטר מיר לאזן האבן די
ליוט צו אים גזאגט ער זאל
מיט זיין געלט גומל חסד זיין (70)
אונ זאל צדקה געבן דש

בלייבט אים לעוה״ב

אזו האט דר עשיר אויף זיך (75)
מקבל גוועזן ער וויל צדקה
געבן אונ האט איין שבֿועה
גיטאן ער וויל קיינם צדקה געבן
נייארט זעלבֿי ליוט די די נון גאר
קיין בטחון האבן (80)
אויף דר וועלט דר מיט ער
זיין צדקה וואול אן גלינגט
נון אמאל
איז דר עושר פֿר דר שטאט
גגאנגן האט ער אן גיטראפֿן איין (85)
ארים מאן זיצן אויף דעם מישט
אונ האט ניט איין שטיקל
גאנצן ראק אן זיין לייב גיהאט
אלז ער זיך האט קענן בידעקן
אזוא האט דר עושר גידאבֿט (90)
אין זיינם זין דר ארים מאן
האט גוויש קיין האפֿנונג מער
אויף דר וועלט אונ פֿר לאנגט
דען טוט דר וויל ער זעלבֿי
צער ליידן מוז (95)

אונ האט אים געבן
הונדרט גילדן אזו הט זיך
דר עני פֿר וואונדרט אונ
שפֿריבֿלט צו אים ווארום גיבט (100)
איר מיר אזו פֿיל געלט אליינט
איר העט דאך פֿיל עניים דר
מיט ביטיילן אזו האט דר עושר
אים דר צילט די שבֿועה
וואש ער האט גיטאן האט אלז (105)
ער קיינם ניט גיגעבן נייארט

---

67 לעוה״ב -א. אלו   68 הינטר מיר   69 גזאגט -א   71 דו -א. דאז -ב

78 גטאן -א   80 האפֿנונג -א   81 דער מיט -ב   82 וואל   85-83 נון אמאל איז ד(ע)ר עשיר פֿר ד(ע)ר שטאט גאנגן

86 אויף דעם מישט -ב   87 הוט -ב   90 דער -ב   91 אן זיינם זין -ב   92 גוויש -ב

101 אלינט -ב   102 פֿיל עניים -א. ב. דער -ב   104 עושר -ב   105 וואז -ב

דער קיין בטחון האט אויף דער

וועלט. האט דער עני ווידר צו

אים גירעט נעם דיין געלט

צו ריק [דוא נאר] דוא שוטה

דוא האשט קיין בטחון ניט דוא

פֿר זילֿברשט דיך אויף דיין געלט

אוני׳ איך פֿר זילֿבר מיך אויף

גאטש גינאד אוני׳ האף צו זייני

דר באארימקייט אלי שעה אוני׳

אלי רגע דען ער איז

בארם הערציג אויף אלי זייני

בישעפֿנים האשטו ניט גילייאנט

וואש דא שטיט גישריבן השי״י

מאכֿט אויף ריכֿטן דען ארמן פֿון

דער ערד אוני׳ פֿון מישט

דר היבט ער דען נוט

בידארֿפֿטיגן [בייא] גאט [איז

אליש מיגליך ער] קאן מיך רייך

מאכֿן אוני׳ פֿון דער צרה ארליזן

טרעט אב פֿון זאלֿבי נארישקייט אוני׳

פֿר לאז דיין שטות. אזו זאגט

דער עשיר צו דעם עני איז דש

מיין לון איך האב דיר וועלן

גוטש טון אוני׳ דוא פֿר געלשט

[עש] מיר מיט ביזן [דר קינן]

דוא לעשטערשט מיך אוני׳ האשט

מיך שוטה. אזו האט דער עני

צום עושר גיענטפֿרט דוא

מיינשט דוא טושט מיר גרושן

חסד אבר עש איז ניט אזו [ביז

טושטו מיר אלן] דוא זאגשט

איך בין מיך חיו מיאש פֿון דעם

עולם איך האב נאך גוטי

האפֿנונג צו גאט. עש איז קיינר

דער ניט זיין האפֿנונג האט

צו גאט נייארט דיא טוטי לייט

אבר ווייל דער מענש לעבט

האט ער זיין בטחון צו גאט.

האט דער עשיר גירעט וען דעם

נון אזו איז וויל איך גין אוני׳

וויל מיין געלט ביגראבן אויף

דר קיין בטחון האט אויף דר

וועלט האט דר עני ווידר צו

אים גירעט נעם דיין געלט

צו ריק דו שוטה

דו האשט קיין בטחון ניט דו

פֿר זילֿברשט דיך אויף דיין געלט

אוֹן איך פֿר זילֿבר מיך אוֹף

גאטש גנאד אוֹן האף צו זייני

דר בארמקיט אלי שעה אוֹן

אלי רגע דען ער איז

בארים הערציג אוף זייני

בשעפֿניש האשטו ניט גילייאנט

וואז דא שטיט גישריבן השי״י

מכֿט אוף ריכֿטן דעם ארמן פֿון

דר ערד און פֿון מישט

דר היבט ער דען נוט

בדארֿפֿטיגן גאט

קאן מיך רייך

מאכֿן און פֿון דר צרה דר לייזן

טרעט אפ פֿון זעלֿבי נאארישקייט

אוֹן פֿר לאז דיין שטות אזו זאגט

דר עושר צו דעם עני איז דז

מיין לון איך האב דיר וועלן

גוין טאן און פֿר געלטשט

מיר מיט ביזן

דו לעשטרשט מיך און היישט

מיך שוטה אזו האט דר עני

צום עושר גיענטפֿרט דו

מיינשט דו טושט מיר גרושן

חסד אבר עז איז ניט אזו

דו זאגשט

איך בין מיך חיו מיאש פֿון דען

עולם איך האב נאך גוטי

האפֿונג צו גאט. עז איז קיינר

דר ניט זיין האפֿונג הט

צו גאט נייארט די טוטי לייט

אבר ווייל דר מענש לעבט

האט ער איין בטחון צו גאט

האט דר עושר גיזאגט וען דש

נון אזו איז וויל איך גין און

וויל מיין געלט בגראבן אויף

110

115

120

125

130

135

140

145

דעם בית הקברות ביי דיא מתים
דיא האבן זיך מיאש פון דער
וועלט דען קאן איך מיין שבועה
האלטן אונ' האבן אך אזו גיטאן.
נון עש האט איין צייט לאנג
אן גישטאנדן דער עשיר האט
דען דלות ביקומן [אונ' האט
ניקש מער גיהאט צו צערן]
אונ' האט גרושן דוחק מוזן
ליידן אזו איז ער גאנגן אויף
דעם בית הקברות זיין אוצר
אויש צו גראבן דז ער זאל צו
לעבן האבן. אזו האבן אים עבין
דיא שומרים אן גיטראפן אונ'
האבן אים תפום גינומן אונ'
האבן אים גיבראכט אין דער
שטאט פאר דעם שר. אונ' דער
זעלביג שר איז גיוועזן דער
ארים מאן דער אויף דען מישט
איז גילעגן דעם ער האט וועלן
הונדרט גילדן געבן דען דר
זעלביג עני איז זער פרום
גיוועזן אונ' פון איינר הולי
משפחה אהער גיוועזן אזו האבן
דיא שטאט לייט אים צו איין
שר גימאכט. נון דיא וועלטריש
האבן דעם מאן פאר דעם שר
גיבראכט אונ' האבן גיזאגט
דעם מאן האבן מיר גיפונדן אויף
דעם בית הקברות ער האט
דעני מתים איר תכריכים
אב ציגן. אזו באלד האט דער
עני אים דער קענט אונ' האט זיך
[דאך] פרעמד קיגן אים גישטעלט
אונ' איז מיט אים שארף פר פארן
ווארום אלז ער זאלביש מעשה רע
האט וועלן טון [אונ' האט צו
אים גיזאגט דוא האשט דען פר
שולד.] אזו האט דער גיוועזנר
עושר אן גיפאנגן צו רידן מיין
הער חיי זאלבי שאלק האפטיקייט

דען בית הקברות ביי די מתים
די זיין זיך מיאש פון דר
וועלט דען קאן איך מיין שבועה
האלטן אונ האט אוך אזו גיטאן
נון עש האט איין צייט לאנג
אן גטראפן דר עושר האט
דען דלות בקומן

אונ האט גרוש דוחק מוזן
ליידן אזו איז ער גגאנגן אויף
דען בית הקברות זיין אוצר
אויש צו גראבן דר ער זאל צו
לעבן האבן אזוא האבן אים
די שומרים אן גיטראפן אונ
האבן אים תפום גינומן אונ
האבן אים גיבראכט אין דר
שטאט פר דען שר אונ דר
שר איז גווען דר
ארים מאן דר אופ דעם מיסט
איז גילעגן דען ער האט וועלן
הונדרט גילדן געבן דען דר
עני איז פרום
גוועזן אונ פון איין הולר
משפחה גוועזן אזו האבן
אים די שטאט לייט גמאכט
צו איין שר נון די שומרים
האבן דען מאן פר דעם שר
גיבראכט אונ האבן גיזאגט
דען מאן האבן מיר גיפונדן אופ
דעם בית הקברות ער האט
וועלן די תכריכים
אפ ציהן: אזו בלד האט דר
עני אים דר קענט אונ האט זיך
פרעמד קיגן אים גישטעלט
אונ איז מיט אים שארף פר פארן
ווארום אלק ער זעלביש מעשה רע
הט גיטאן

אזו הט דר
עושר אן גיפאנגן צו רידן מיין
הער חיי זעלבי שאלק האפטיקייט

150
155
160
165
170
175
180
185

---

148 בייא די -א   149 די זיינה זיך מיאש מיאש -א, די זייני זיך מיאש -ב   159 דאש -א, דש -ב
164 פר דעם -ב   168 דען, דער -א, ב   173 וועלטטריש -ב   178 וועלן דיא מתים איר תכריכים -א,
דיא מתים איר תכריכים -ב   179 אב ציהן -ב   180 דער קענט -א   182 פאר פארן -א
183 אלש ער זאלביש   184 מאן   187 עשיר -ב   188 חם ושלום -ב

	בייא מיר זיך ניט בפֿונדן ווערט	בייא מיר זיך ניט ביפֿינדן ווערט
190	אזו אונ' אזו איז עש מיט מיר	אזו אונ' אזו איז עש מיט מיר
	דר גנגן אונ' האם אים אליש	דר גאנגן אונ' האט אים אליש
	דר צילמ (מאלף ועד תיון)][אונ	דר צילמ מאלף ועד תיו אונ'
	איצונד האם ער וועלן זיין געלמ	איצונד האט ער וועלן זיין געלמ
	וואש ער ביגראבן האמ	לאנגן וואש ער ביגראבן האמ.
195	אזו היבמ דר שר צו אים אן צו	אזו היבמ דר שר צו אים אן צו
	רידן קאנשמו מיך ניט האם ער	רידן קענשמו מיך ניט. האמ ער
	גענפֿרמ ניין וואו הער זאל	גיענמפֿרמ ניין וואו אהער זאל
	איך מיין הער קענען זאגמ דר	איך מיין הער קענען. זאגמ דער
	שר ווידר צו אים איך בין דר	שר ווידר צו אים איך בין צו דער
200	עני וואש אויף דש מישמ איז	עני דער אויף דעם מישמו איז
	גוועזן דען דוא האשמ וועלן	גיוועזן דעם דוא האשמ וועלן
	הונדרמ גילדן געבן אונ הושמ	הונדרמ גילדן געבן אונ' האשמ
	צו מיר גזאגמ איך האב קיין	צו מיר גיזאגמ איך האב קיין
	האפֿונג אויף דר וועלמ אונ	האפֿנונג אויף דער וועלמ אונ'
205	האמ אים מאן האלזן אונ קושן	האמ אים מון דען האלזן אונ' קיסן
	אונ הם ביפֿולן מן זאל אים	אונ' האמ ביפֿאלן מן זאל אים
	זיין געלמ אויף גראבן אונ אים	זיין געלמ אויף גראבן אונ' אים
	ווידר געבן אונ האמ אים דר צו	ווידר געבן אונ' האמ אים דר צו
	גשפיזמ וויל ער גילעבמ	גשפיזמ דר וויל ער גילעבמ
210	המ	האמ.
	אוך בפֿינדן זיך פֿיל מאל	אך ביפֿינדן זיך פֿיל מאל
	אלז דעם עושר זייני קינדר דעם	אלזו דעם עושר זייני קינדר
	דלות האבן אונ דען אריס מאן	דלות האבן אונ' דעם אריס מאן
	זייני קינדר זיינן רייך דען דר	זייני קינדר זיינן רייך דען דער
215	עושר האמ קיין צדקה געבן האמ	עושר האמ קיין צדקה געבן האמ
	זיין געלמ קיין קיום דר	זיין געלמ קיין קיום. אונ' דער
	אריס מאן העמ גערן צדקה געבן	אריס מאן העמ גערן צדקה געבן
	ווען ער גהאמ העמ דז	ווען ער גהאמ העמ. דאש
	ביצאלמ גאמ זייני קינדר	ביצאלמ גאמ זייני קינדר.
220	נון וואארום זאל דר מענש	נון וואארום זאל דער מענש
	מרויארן ווען ער אום זיין געלמ	מרויארן ווען ער אום זיין געלמ
	קוממ אונ מראבמ נימ אלו גאמ	קוממ אונ' מראבמ ניט אלז גאמ
	קיינם אום זונשמ שמראפֿמ אונ	קיינם אום זונשמ שמראפֿמ אונ'
	זעלבֿש איז אלין למובה דער	זאלבֿש איז הכל למובה דער
225	מענש זאל זיך בדענקן	מענש זאל זיך [הוך] בידענקן
	אונ זאל זיין במחון צו גאמ שמעלן	אונ' זיין במחון צו גאמ שמעלן
	ווער צו גאמ מרוויארמ דר האמ	ווער צו גאמ מרוויארמ. דער האמ
	וואול גבוויאמ אונ איטלכן	וואל גיבוויאמ. אונ' איטליכם
	מענשן איז זיין גזר אן רי"ה	מעניש איז זיין גזר אם ראש

189 בפֿינדן -ב   191 דער גאנגן אלו -א, דער גאנגן אלו -ב   192 דער צילמ   194 וואו ער -ב

195 דער -א   201 וועלין -ב   204 האפֿנונג -א   205 מאן -א   206 ביפֿולן -ב

208 דער צו -א   212 עשיר -ב   212-213 דעם דלות -ב   215 עשיד -ב

224 זאלבֿש -א, איז אלו למובה -ב   227 דר האמ -ב   228 וואול -ב

השנה וויא פֿיל אלז ער דש יאר	וויא פֿיל אז ער דז יאר
גיווינן אודר פֿר לירן זאל.	גיווינן אדר פֿר לירן זאל
נון וזארום זאל דר מענש גרושן	נון וזארום זאל דר מענש גרושן
משא ומתן טון אוני לויפֿן אוני	משא ומתן טאן אוני לויפֿן אונ
רענן טאג אוני נאכֿט [זיך וויא	רייז טאג אונ נאכֿט
טון] אלז ער פֿר איבריגן וויל	אלז ער פֿר איבריגן וויל
ער קאן דאך ניט מער דר לאנגן	ער קאן דאך ניט מער דר לאנגן
אלז וויא זיין גזר גיווען איז	אלש וויא דר גזר איז גוועזן
אם ראש השנה. דיא גמרא זאגט	אן ראש השנה די גמרא זאגט
די דורות ראשונים האבן איר	די דורות ראשונים האבן איר
עיקר גימאכֿט פֿון תורה ומצות	עיקר גימאכֿט פֿון תורה ומצות
אוני האבן וויניק דער בייא	אוני האבן וויניק דער בייא
גיהאנדלים אזו האט השי"י הצלחה	גיהאנדלט אזו האט השי"י הצלחה
געבן אין איר וויניק משא ומתן	געבן אין איר וויניג משא ומתן
אוני איר תורה האט בישטאנד	אוני איר תורה האט אין בישטאנד
גיהאט אוני האבן איר פרנסה	גהאט אוני האבן איר פרנסה
בכֿבֿוד גיהט. אבר דיא דורות	אויך בכֿבֿוד גיהאט אבר די דורות
אחרונים האבן איר עיקר [פֿון]	אחרונים הבן איר עיקר
משא ומתן גימאכֿט אוני האבן	משא ומתן גימכֿט אונ האבן
וויניק גילערנט אזו האט ביידי	וויניג גלערנט אזו הבן ביידי
קיין בישטאנד גיהאט. [אך איז	קיין בישטאנד גיהאט אויך
בייא גרושי משא ומתן קיין הצלחה	בייא גרושי משא ומתן
זעלטן אלז עש גיראד אלז ניט]	זעלטן אלז ער גראט
מוז פליטה גין. דש קומט אליש	מוז פליטה גין דאש קומט אלש
וזייל ער הוכֿן שטאט פֿירן וויל	וזייל ער הוכֿן שטאט פֿירן וויל
וזער הוך שטייגט פֿאלט באלד	וזער הוך שטקיט פֿאלד באלד
נידר. דיא גמרא זאגט איין	נידר די גמרא זאגט איין
שפריך ווארט דש קעמיל [איז	שפריך ווארט דז קעמיל
גאנגן] האט זיך וועלן הערנר	האט זיך וועלן הערנר
מיט ברענגן אזו האט מן אים	מיט ברענגן אזו האט אים
דיא אורן דר צו אבגישניטן:	דיא אורן דר בייא אפ גישניטן:

230 דז יאר -א, דאו יאר -ב   232 דער מענש גרושי -ב   234 רענין -ב   236 דער לאנגן -ב
237 איז גוועזן -א   238 די גמרא -ב   239 דיא -א, די דורות הראשונים -ב   241 וויניג
242 גיהאנדלט   243 וויניג   244 האט אין בישטאנד -ב   245-246 אך בכֿבֿוד גיהט -ב
246 בכֿבֿוד -א   249 וויניג, אזו האבן ביידי   250-252 אך בייא גרושי משא ומתן זעלטן אלז ער, עז
אליז גיראד   253 ער מוז פליטה גין דז קומט אלי   257 דז, דאו קעמיל   258 הוט -א
259 הוט, האט מן אין   260 די -א, אב גשניטן -א, דער צו אב גישנידן -ב

5. A Selection from Two Yiddish Translations of *Ben hameylekh vehanozir* (1769, 1771)

ספר בן המלך והנזיר

Ben hameylekh vehanozir

Zholkve, 1771	Frankfurt am Main, 1769

הקדמת המחבר

	Zholkve, 1771	Frankfurt am Main, 1769
1	[. . .] אונ דש פֿאלק האבין גיאײלט	[. . .] דיא אונטר מאהנן
	צו גיין אין זיני שטעגין דען ער האט	מאהנן אפֿטין איהרן
	גרינג גמאכֿט פֿון זיא דען יאך פֿון זיין	קיניג נאך. דש אלזו
	דינשט אונ אילה טאג האט ער אײן	יא אין גאנצֿיש לאנד
5	גזאמלט זיין הויבט הערין אונ די	ניקם אלֿו אבֿגעטרייא.
	שטארקי פֿון זיין (חיילות) אונ מאכֿט	פֿרעמסן. זויֿפֿן. טאֿנצֿן.
	אײן מאל ציים צו זיין אילה הערין	אונ וואהל לושטן:
	אונ קנעכֿט דא ווארין אילה מיט אים	
	לוסטיג אונ גוט בהארצט טרינקין אונ	
10	פֿירין מיט אים דען ער ווֹאר דארט ני מער	
	אלז עשין אונ טרינקין אונ פֿול זעמין	
	אונ פֿיל זופֿין אונ די מאנין זענן	
	גקומן מיט שעבֿטונג אונ אפֿפֿערין אונ	
	די וויבר גיין אויש מיט פֿויקין אונ	
15	טאנצין:	

השער השני

	Zholkve, 1771	Frankfurt am Main, 1769
	[. . .] ב כ ל פֿר אל דיין גוט אונ	
	געלט זאלשט דוא דיר קופֿן פֿר	
	שטאנדיגהיט: וועשט דו דיין גוף	
	בקליידן מיט פֿרייד: אונ זולשט	
20	דיר ניט מערין פֿיל סחורה אודר	
	געלט: ווארום דר מיט וועשט דו	
	זיפֿצן אונ זארגין אוף דר וועלט:	
	ואיך אונ ווי איז דען ניט זיין	ואיך דז אלי פֿריידי
25	שמחה אײן טרוייארהײט וען ער מוז	טריבֿזאלן זיינד. דען דז
	גידענקין אוף אל די זאלֿבן וואש	ענד אלר פֿריידי זיינד
	אים האט אײן פֿרייד גיגעבן אז ער	טריבֿזאלן אונ׳ איזט קיני
	וועט דר נאך אײן טרוייארהייט דר	פֿריידי דיא ניכֿט אײני טרויר
	פֿון האבין אונ ער קען ניט פֿר	צור פֿאלֿגי האט.
30	זילֿרט זיין אז ער זאל מיט וועלֿבי	
	זאך אײן פֿרייד זעהן (רק) ער	

ווערט איינר דורך רייכטום
אונ' קינדער ערפֿרייאט.
איזט דיא פֿרייידי פֿר ניכטש
צו אכטן. געגן דיא דרויף
פֿאלגנדי טרויארינגקייט.
דאך דיא זעלבי ווידרום
צו פֿרליהרן. אהן פֿר
מיידליך. העננגט
דז ענד אונזרש לעבן.
קוואהל. אנגשט. פֿורכט.
אונ נאמ.

ווען זעהן פֿיל ארלייא זיפֿצונג
אונ טרוויארהייט ווען ער שוין זעהט
(שמחה) מיט געלט אונ קינדר
ווערט דאך זיין שמחה פֿר נישט
גיאכט קעגן די טרוויארהייט וואש
אים ווערט זיך פֿינן ווען דאש ווילן
ווערט פֿר לארין ווארן אין וועלכי
צייט. נוא ווען דאם אפ שיידן
אונ פֿר לירן דאש מוז פֿר גוויש
זיין איז וואול ריכט אונ בילך אז
קיין קלוגר מענטש זאל זיך ניט
פֿרייאין מיט קיין זאך אין אין דר
וועלט ווייל דאש איז צו ווישן אז
נאך אלים פֿון די זאכין ווערט

35

40

45

איין וועלט וויזר זאגטי.
לעבט איינר אין פֿאלקאמנשטי
צופֿרידנהייט. האט ער דען
דארויף פֿולגנדן פֿר דרום
צו בֿפֿרכטן.

איין וויסט אונ בייז דינג. אונ
דר חכם האט גיזאגט ווער דא וויל
גרייכן צו דעם תכלית פֿון דר זאך
וואש ער האט ליב אונ איז זאט
דר פֿון דר מוז זיך ווידר פֿארכטן
פֿר דעם תכלית פֿון דר זאך וואש
אים ווערט דער נאך דער צערנין
ווען עש ווערט פֿר לארין ווערין.

50

איין אנדרר זאגטי.
וויא יעמרליך איזט דעם
מענשן לעבן. לעבט ער
לאנג. וויא פֿילה פֿריינדי
פֿרליהרט ער אין זיינר
צייט. שטירבט איינר באלד
דאהין. וויא פֿיל מעהר האט
זיך זעלבשטן צו בקלאנגן:

אונ איין אנדרר חכם האט גיזאגט
אל די טעג פֿון מענטשין זענן
וויא טאג. ווען זי לאנג ברייט
זענין דא וועלין שטארבין אין דר
צייט זיין ליב האבר אונ גוטי
פֿריינט האט ער צו זיפֿצן אויף
זיא. אונ ווען זיא קורץ זענן
האט ער מער אויף זיך צו זיפֿצן.
אונ דר בעל משל האט גיזאגט:
אנוש דר מענטש איז גיפֿלאנצט
אונ גישטראפֿט אל זיין טאג.
ווייל ער ניט אלי צייט צו שלעק
אונ צו פֿלאג. ווען ער לעבט דא
האט ער צו טרוארין אז אין זיין
צייט וועלן זייני ליב האבר ווערין
פֿר לארין. אונ ווען ער ניט לנג
לעבט דא האט ער צו טרוייארן
אויף זייני יונגי יארן.

55

60

65

70

השער החמישי

בעת צור זעלביגן צייט פֿר
מעהרטי זיך דיא פֿינדשאפֿט

בעת אין דר זעלביגר צייט האט
גימעהרט דער (מלך) פֿינט צו

דעם קיניגם גענגין דיא פֿרומי
אונ׳ גלויביגי.

דאן ער בפֿירבטי זיין פרינץ
מעלבטי זיך צו איהן הלטין.
אונ׳ איהרן גלויבן אן נעהמן.
דער קיניג האטי איינין
פֿירשטן דען ער הירצליך
ליבטה. ער מאבטי איהם גרויש.
ער היהטי איהם אונ׳ זעצטי זיינן
שטול איבר אלי זיני אנדרי
פֿירשטן. וויילן זיך דער קיניג
אויף זיני אויף ריבטיגי טרייא
הײט פֿר ליזי. זא מוזטי אלזו אין
גאנצין קיניגרייך דורך איהם
גשעהן. ער וואר ביים קיניג אן
גנעהמר. אונ׳ וואורדי הערליבר
גהאלטין דאן אלי גרוויש.
דיא אנדרי פֿירשטן זאהין דש
איהם דר קיניג ליבר האטי דאן

זיא ווארן איהם פֿיינד. ניידיטן
איהם.
אונ׳ טראבטיטן נאך זיין לעבן.

ויהי עז בגאב זיך דער טאג
איינר דש דער קיניג לוסט צור
יאבט בקאם. ער ברופֿטי זיינן
טרייאן מארשאל דעם פֿירשטן
איהם צו בגלײדן. זיא רײטן
בײדי אויז דער שטראם אונ׳

טראפֿין איינן מאן אן.
דער עררי גינג אויף דעם פֿעלד
אויזר דעם וועגי:

האבין איטליבן (נזיר) אונ וואש
75 האט גהאלטין דען (דת) אדר וער
איין שיינה (בעל לשון) וואר.
ווארום ער האט זיך גיפֿארבטין
ווענגין זיין זון. פֿיליבט וועט ער
זיך נאך ציהן אונ וועט גיין אין
80 זייער גלויבין אונ עש וואר צו דען
(מלך) איין הער וואש ער האט אים
זייער ליב גיהאט אונ האט אים אויף
גהויבין זיין שטול מער אז דיא
הערין. אונ האט אים הויבן אונ
85 האט גפֿירט גאר דאש (מלבות)
דורך זיין הנט. דען ער האט
קענטו זיין בגליבט הארץ. אונ
וויא ער איז איין גוטר (בעל סוד)
דרום איז גיעהרט אונ גליבט אונ
90 בוויליגט גוועזין אין זיני אויגן
מער אז אילה זיני הע[רי]ן וואש
וואורין פֿר אים. אונ וויא דיא
הערין אונ דיא קנעבט פֿון (מלך)
הא[בין גזעהין זיין גרוויש (כבוד)
95 האט דאש גמיט גמיט פֿון (שנאה) אין
זייא גברענט [אונ] זיא האבין
אים פֿיינט גקרינן אונ גדאבטין
אים צו טייטין:

ויהי אונ עש וואר איין טאג דא
100 האט דר (מלך) גגלושט צו גיין
אין פֿע[לד] אריין צו יאגין איין
(חיי) אדר איין (עוף) דא רופֿט ער
ד[עם] מארשליק אונ גיאין
אל בײדי אויש דער (מחנה) ארויש.
105 וויא זיא רײטין ב[יי]א אנגדר
אויף דיא פֿערד אדר מויל אייזלין.
גפֿינן זיא איין מענטש דר וואר
פֿ[ר] אירט. דען עש וואר קיין
וויידי ארט צו פֿרעגין לייט אויף
110 דען וועג:

אמר זאגט דר מארשליק וער
בישט דוא גפֿיניגטר מאן אונ
וואָרום האשט דוא דיך אזו לנג
גזוימט אונ פֿון וואש פֿר איין פֿאלג
115 בישט דוא:

אמר ער אנטװארטי איך
בין אין מאן פֿאלר אנגשט
אונ׳ טריבזאלין. דער אין

שרייבי צייג עהנליך.
מיין קירפֿר איזט מאגר דען
איני ליניאל. מיין
גשטאלט איזט דונקלר
װעדר שװערצי.
איך בין שמעהלר דען
דער שפֿאלט איינר
פֿעדר. מייני הענדי זיינד
שװאבר. דען איני פֿעדר
קיילי. מייני שפֿייזי איזט
ביטרר דען גאל עפֿפֿיל. מיין
טראנק איזט זא אהן גשמאק
אלז דינטן װאשר. מיין ברויט
איזט פֿר הערטיט. גלייך דער
גומי:

אמר זאגט דער מאן איך בין װאש
דיא צייט האט מיך בצװונגין אונ
האב זיך גמעהרט אויף מיר מיין
טרויריג הייט. װען איך זאל זאט

120 זיין בין איך הונגריג אונ װען איך
זאל זיין הונגריג בין איך זאט.
מיין לעבין איז קירצר אז דיא
שרייב פֿעדר אונ מיין גוף איז
מעגריר אז איין װירע. אונ מיין

125 הארץ איז מער שװארץ אונ
טונקיל מער אז דאש שװארץ
װאשיר. אונ מיין טייל איז מער
ארם אז דיא שפֿאלט פֿון דער
פֿערד. אונ מיין הענט זענין

130 שלאפֿיר אז דאש רעריל אונ מיין
עסין איז ביטרר מער פֿון גאלשין.
אונ צייג גטראנק איז מער אום
גזאלצין אז טינט װאשיר. אונ דש
הארטיקיים פֿון ברויט איז מער אן

135 אננדר בהעפֿט אז איין גומא. אונ
הייבט אויף זיין קול אונ זאגט:

זמני מיין צייט איז װיא איין
פֿעדיר קורץ אונ ענג אויף מיין
הארץ. אזו מיין גזיבֿט איז פֿינצטר

140 אונ שװארץ: מיין לייב איז אזו
מאגר װיא פֿון איין שרייב פֿעדיר
דיא צייג. אונ מייני הענט זענין
אז איין רעריל מאגר אונ גמיין:
מיין עסין איז אזו ביטר אז עש

145 װאלטין עש ניט װעלין עסין דיא
הינט. אונ מיין גטראנק איז אזו אום
גזאלצין װיא דש װאשר פֿון טינט:

6. Title-page and a Selection from *Seyfer khsidem* (1776, 1806)

ספר חסידים

Seyfer Khsidem

Zholkve, 1776

ספר חסידים

תנו עינכם טוטין אייער אונן דעם (ספר הקדוש) וואש איז ארוש נקומן
וואש עש איז נאך אויף דער וועלט ניט נוועזן. איר ווערט דרינן
נפֿונן נרוש (מוסר) און (תוכחה): און נאנץ היפשה שיינה
מעשות אויך נרושה (דינים) וען מיר וועלן אלש ארויש שרייבן דאש (תועלת) פֿון דעם
(ספֿר) איז אום מינלך צו דר שרייבן דען וויא דר נאמן דר פֿון איז **ספר חסידים**
אזו איז עש אלין פֿון פֿארנט ביז אן הינטרשטן דף איטול חסידותקייט דש ספר
האט מחבר נוועזן **האיש הקדוש אלקי רבינו**
יהודה החסיד זצ״יל (זכותו יעמוד לנו וללל ישראל)
דז מיר זאלן קאנן האלטן אלין וואש אין דעם ספֿר שטיט
(בזכות) זה וועלן מיר זולכה זיין (לעלות לציות לויון ברנה)

נדפס פה ק״ק   זאלקווא

תחת ממשלת אדונינו המיוחם הנדול החסיד הדוכם וואודי ווילענסקו קארל
סטאנסלב ראדזוויל יר״ה:

בדפום האלוף התורי מהור״ר דוד במהור״ר מנחם מן זצ״ל. ומהור״ר חיים
דוד במהור״ר אהרן סנ׳ל וצ׳ל. ומהר״ר זאב וואלף במוהר״ר נרשון
סנ׳ל וצ״ל:

באותיות   אמשטרדם

בשנת   תקלי״ו   לפ״ק

Zholkve, 1776 [Zholkve, 1806]

יט   פֿיר אונ צוואנציג [1806: צוואנצוג] זאלן זענן מעכב די
1   תשובה [. . .] אײנער וואש איז חושד אײן גוטן יוד (*) [. . .]

כא   די פֿר צייטקי חסידים פֿלעגן אױף צו שרייבן זייערי חטאים
        אױף אין בריב [1806: אונ זאל דראן גידענקן כדי זי זאלן]
5   דרוף מתודה זיין אונ חרטה האבן דרוף אונ זאלן [1806: זאל]
        קענן רעלבט תשובה טאן דש מיינט דר פסוק (חטאתי נגדי
        תמיד) אױך האבן זי תמיד גדאבט יום המיתה אונ גיהנם ויום הדין
        דא איז אין זי אין גנאנגן גאט ליב צו האבן: אױך זאל מן דש
        שרייבן (ברמז) ניט ארױש צו שרייבן זייני חטאים תאמר ווערט
10   אײנער גפֿינן [1806: גפֿונן] דא ווענ ער אים הלטן פֿר אין רשע
        אבר ער מעג זאגן פֿר אין צדיק (**) זייני זינד כדי ער זאל אים
        לערנן וויא ער זאל דרוף תשובה טאן אונ ער זאל אים פֿרענגן
        סתם ווענ אײנר אזו עבֿירה טוט וואש פֿר אין תשובה זאל ער
        דרוף טאן: חאטשי תשובה אונ צדקה איז אומדאר [1806: אימר]
15   גוט אבר צווישן רייה אונ יום כפור איז צום בעשטין דען מאל
        אפֿילו אין יחיד אז ער טוט תשובה שלימה מיט זיין גאנצן [1806:
        גאנצן] הארץ איז אים השי״י מוחל ווי אין פסוק שטיט (דרשו את ה׳
        בהמצאו) אבר ווען רבים טאן תשובה אפֿילו אין מיטן יאר ווערן
        זיא גיענטפֿרט ווי אין פסוק שטיט (מי כה׳ אלהינו בכל קראנו
20   אליו) ״כ העלפֿט תשובה הן פֿון אין יחיד אונ פֿון רבים אונ יום
        סליחה ומחילה לכל ישראל דרום זאל איטלבֿר מענש תשובה טאן
        אונ ווידוי זאגן פֿר נאבֿט אי מן עשט אונ דר עיקר ווידוי איז מן
        זאל זאגן (אבֿל אנחנו חטאנו) דש איז טייטש פֿר וואר מיר האבן
        גזינדיקט אױף די עבֿרות וואש מן אין יום כפור האט מתודה
25   גיווענזן מעג מן איבר אין יאר ווידר מתודה זיין:

לג   בשעה אז דער מענש ווערט גיבאבן ווערט נגזר אוב
        ער זאל זיין אין גבור אודר שלאפֿ אוב ער זאל זיין אין
        עושר אודר ערום [1806: ארום] שין אודר מיאוס לנג אודר נידריג.
        אבר צדיק ורשע דש גיט מן דען מענשן אין זיין הנט וויל ער איז
30   ער אין צדיק אודר רשע ווי זייער קער צו ווינין דער חוטא אז
        ער האט זיך דען שלעבֿטן וועג בוחר גיווענזן זעה ווען זיין קינד
        קראנק [1806:קרענק] איז וויא פֿיל תעניות תחינות ובקשות ער
        טוט פֿר אים וואורין ער האט אים ליב מכ״ש אז ער קער דש צו טון
        פֿר זיין אייגין [1806: אייגנן] נפֿש אז ער זאל קומן לחיי
        עולם הבא:

לז   דאש איז די בעשטי יראה ווען עש טרעפֿט [1806: טראפֿט]
35   זיך אין חטא אים צו טאן אונ ער פֿארבֿט זיך פֿאר אין
        מענשן ניט דהינו קיין מענש קאן אים ניט ווערן. אונ קיין בושה
        איז אױך ניט דר ביי אונ ער פֿר לאזט דאך דען חטא דש היישט
        (יראת ה׳ טהורה) דען די יראה איז וואש ער פֿארבֿט זיך פֿר גאט.

(*) החושד בכשרים   (**) אבל מותר להגיד לאדם צדיק וצנוע

40 לח נצור   לשונך) אז דו שטראפֿשט לייטן זעה אז דו זאלשט

שטראפֿן מיט שכֿל: למשל אז דו שטראפֿשט זי אין

אזוני זאכֿן וואש איבר שכֿל איז דהיינו עש איז קיין מענשלכֿי

נאטויר ניט זו הוך צו גרייפֿן קומט דיר איין שאנד ארויש דען

ליט זאגן ער קאן דש אליין ניט מקיים זיין אבר וון ער שטראפֿט

45 נאך דעם שכֿל דהיינו וואש נאטורלך איז דא וערן זיין ריד מקובל:

נ צדיק   אוכֿל לשובֿה נפֿשו וגו') דער מענש זאל זעהן אז זיין

מעשים זאלן זיין שין ער זאל ניט עסין (אכֿילה גסה)

ניט מער וואש ער בדרף אונ זאל ניט חפֿן גשווינד ווי איין

פֿרעסר אונ זיין כוונה זאל ניט זיין מיט דעם עסן אז ער זאל

50 שטארק זיין נייארט זיין גוף זאל זיין שטארק גאט צו דינן:

ע הוי   זעה אז דו זאלשט חן הבן בייא לייטן אונ זאלשט דיך

מרחיק זיין פֿון רבנות די גדולה ברענגט דעם

מענשן אין דר ערד דען יוסף הצדיק איז פֿריאר גשטארבן פֿר אלי

זייני ברידר ווען דאך ער איז יונגר גוועזן פֿון זיי:

55 עו אל   ניט דוא זאלשט קיין ישראל שעלטן נייארט ביט גאט

אוף אים אז גאט זאל אים געבן איין גוטי דיעה אונ

זאלשט ניט אוף אים מוסר דין זיין דהיינו ווערשט זאגן גאט זאל

אן אים [1806: דיר] איין נקמה טון דען ווען מן [1806: ווען מן

איז] מקלל איין ישראל ווערן די קללות פֿר קערט אוף אים דו

60 זלשט [1806: זאלשט] ניט פֿיינט הבן דיין חבֿרת שונא דען זי

ווערן דיך [1806: זיך] איבר בעטין אונ דוא ווישט [1806: וועשט]

בלייבן איין שונא:

צח אוהב   האב ליב צו זאגן דש ווארט (תאמר) דהיינו תאמר

אז איך וויל טאן די זאך אודר וויל גיאן שפֿאציירן

65 וועט איין זינד ארויש קומן. אונ זאלשט פֿיינד האבן צו זאגן דש

ווארט (מה בכך) כלומר וואש נאך דר מער אז איך וויל דש טואן

אדר איך וויל גיאן שפֿאצירן אז ווערשט אזו טאן וועט דיך ברענגן

צו עבֿירות:

קב ואסור   עש איז איין איסור צו הרגגן איין לייו אוף דען

70 [1806: דעם] טיש וואש מן עשט דרויף אונ דר וואש

הרגט הייישט גלייך ווי ער הרגת אוף דעם מזבח (בשעת ברכֿת

המזון) זמל [1806: זאל] מן די מעסרם צו דעקן דען אוף דען

מזבח האט מ ניט בדארפֿט צו קומן קיין אייזן. מן טאר ניט שרייבן

אין איין ספֿר דר איז מיר שולדיג.

75 קכג שני   צווויי הרהורים האט דר מענש טאג אונ נאכֿט איינש

אוף איין אשה: דאש אנדרי אוף געלט אוף די צוווייא

ניט ער זיין לעבן. אוך האט ער הרהורים דאש זענן קנאה שנאה

גאווה תאווה אל [1806: אלין] די דאזיגי זענן מבֿטל זיא פֿון דער

תורה און עש שטיט (ולך ה' החסד כי אתה תשלם לאיש כמעשהו)

גאט איז גומל חסד מיט דעם מענשן דש איז וען ער האט קינדר

נעמט אים גאט זיין קינדר אוועק: ווען ער האט עשירות נעמט

אים גאט זיין עשירות אוועק: כדי אז ער זאל עולם הבא האבן:

קכז לא   ער זאל ניט עסין סיידן ווען ער הונגריק איז אוך ניט

טרינקן סיידן וואו [1806]: ווען] ער דארשטיג איז און

ווען אים גלוסט זיין צורך טאן זאל ער זיך ניט אויף האלטן וארום

עש איז אין סכנה ער בקומט די געלי זוכט און ווערט גשוואלן

אוך איז ער עובר אויף (בל תשקצו]():

קכח   רבי יעקב בר יקר פלעגט מיט זיין בארט [1806]: בארד]

אוש צו קערן דש שטויב פר דען ארון הקודש און ווען דש

קהל פלעגן צו גין צו דעם מלך צו טראגן שוחד האט ער זיין שיך

אפ גצוגן און האט מתפלל גוועזן אז גאט זאל זי חן געבן לפני

המלך.

קלט אם   ווען דו הערשט אז איין מלמד לערנט מיט זיין

תלמיד און זאגט אים פיר איין גראז [1806]: גרייז]

זאלשטו אים ניט מבזיש זיין נייארט זאלשט זאגן פר דען מלמדת

פרינט און ליב האבר אז זי זאלן אים אויש [1806]: אליש!] דען

גרייז פירן. אוך זאל זיך ניט ברימן איינר און זאל זאגן דר האט

מיך גיבעטן אז איך זאל געבן מיין טאבטער זיין זון פר איין וויב

דען ער האלט זיך בגאווה און יענר ווערט מבויש.

קמה כעם   בחיק כסילים ינוח) דר מענש מוז זיך זייער מרחיק זיין

פון (כעם) און ער זאל זיך גיוויינן אז ער זאל גאר

קיין כעם וויזן אפילו אויף אזו איין זאך וואש מען קער זיך דען צו

בייורן. דען אונזרי חכמים האבן גיזאגט ווער עש צערנט איז

ער איין חכם וועט זיך די חכמה פון אים אב [1806]: אפ] און דאש

לעבן איז גאר קיין [1806]: קיין] לעבן ניט און שטארבן

פר דר צייט [. . .]

[קנו] ואם   ווען דו זעהשט דרייא דורות וואש נאך און דר

[1806]: נאך אננדר] זיינן תלמידי חכמים דהיינו ער און

זיין זון און זיין אייניקל און דר נאך קומן פון זיא עמי הארצים

ארויש דש מאבט דש וויל זיא האבן משדך גוועזן מיט זו איין משפחה

וואש דרינן זיינן קיין תלמידי חכמים פר האנדן גראטן די קינדר

נאך ד[ין] [1806 =]: די] מוטרש ברידר זיינן אוך עמי הארצים דרום

זאל מן בעטין אז גאט זאל צו שיקן אין (זיווג) אים און זיין

קינדר מיט אזו איין לייט וואש הבן יראת שמים תורה וגמילות

חסדים.

[קסט] מעשה   אין מענש [1806]: איימענש] איז בייא נאבט

גריטן אליין און די לבנה האט גשיינט און

ער האט גזעהן אין גרוש חיל זענן גזעסן אויף וועגן און [אין]

מענשן האבן די וועגן גשלעפט און אז זי וארן מיד זייער [1806]: זייער]

זענן דיא לייט פון די וועגן אראפ גגנגן אונ די
וואש האבן גפֿירט זענן ארוף גגנגן אונ האבן ווידר גפֿירט אונ
דער וואש איז גריטן האט פֿיל דער קענט וואש זי זענן שון לאנג
גשטארבן האט ער זי גפֿראגט [1806]: גפֿרעגט] וואש דאש בטייט אז
זי [1806]: זיירי] די וועגן אזו ציהן האבן זיא געגנטפֿערט [1806]:
געגנטֿערט] מיר פֿלעגן זיך צו שפֿילן מיט נשים ובתולות איז אונזר
עונש אז מיר מוזן אונזרי [1806]: אונזר] ליבר מיד מאכן אז מיר
מוזן פֿאלן אנידר פֿר מידקט [1806]: מיידקייט] דר נאך אונ די
אוף [1806]: דר [נ]אך זיצן מיר אוף] די וועגן מוזין אוך אזו ציהן
ביז זיא זייר [1806]: זיערן] מיד ווערן אונ מן שלאנגט זי שלאנג
די וואש שלעפֿן דען דאש טוט מעשה בהמה ארבייטן מיט אים
דארטן ווא מיט אים אין בהמה אזו וועד דא מושל איז אוף לייטן
אוך ווען ער פֿיניגט זיין בהמה אין דר ארביט.

[קע] מעשה   איין חסיד האט מנדר גוועזן פֿון זיין קרובים
וועגן נאך דעם האט ער מנדר גוועזן פֿון אלי
נשמות ווען מן אים גפֿרעגט פֿר וואש ער דש טוט האט ער
גענטֿרט עש מאג זיין אז איך איין זכות האבן [1806]: האב] פֿון זיערט וועגן
דרום בין איך זיא אוך מזכה וואש איך בין מנדר צדקה פֿון
זיערט וועגן אוך ווער איין מעשה איינר וואר פֿאר ערט אין איין
וואלד ביא נאכט אונ די לבֿנה האט גלייכט איז נקומן אים
אנטקעגן איין מענש אונ ער האט דר קענט אז ער וואר מת האט
דר מענש גוואלט אנטלוֿפֿן פֿר פֿחד זאגט דר מת צו אים פֿארכֿט
דיך ניט איך וויל דיך ניט שידיגן [1806]: שעדיגן] איך זאג דיר פֿר
וואש איך בין (נע ונד) איבר איין פֿעלד וואש איך האב גינזלט
[1806]: גינזלת] מאכט מן מיך מיד אונ טרייבט מיך אין די וועלדר
אוך ווער איין מעשה איין נבֿרי נאך זיין טויט האט אים זיין קנעכֿט
גפֿונין [1806]: גפֿונן] אז ער וואר שטין ביא נאכֿט האט ער צו
אים גזאגט מן מאכֿט מיך זייר מיד וואש איך האב אים פֿעלד
גזלט [1806]: גגזלת] פֿון דעם פֿלוני דרום זאג דו מיין וייב אז
זי זאל אים אום קערן שפֿראך דר קנעכֿט צו אים ווען מען וויט
[1806]: וועט] מיר ניט גלויבן זאגט ער מורגן [1806]: מארגן] וויל
איך שטין אוף דעם ארט אונ דארטן ווילן [1806]: וועלן] זיא מיך
זעהן ביי איין בוים האט דער קנעכֿט אזו גיזאגט זענן אלי גנגגן
אונ האבן אים גפֿונדן [1806]: גפֿינדן] ביא דען זעלביגן בוים דר
נאך האבן זיא אים גזוֿלט [1806]: גזוֿלט] אין זיין קבֿר האבן זיא
אים ניט גפֿונן האט דר קנעכֿט גזאגט לאז מן אום קערן די גזילה
וועט ער מנוחה האבן:

[קפֿב] מעשה   איין חסיד האט אים איינר (מבֿייש) גיוועזן אונ
הט אים דברים רעים גירעט האבן דש קהל
גיזאגט צו דען חסיד מיר וערן אים איין (נזיפֿה) טאן. אונ אים
מחרים זיין הט ער דר חסיד ניט גיוואלט ליידן האבן דש קהל גזאגט
מיר וועלן טון ניט פֿון דיינט וועגן נייארט אז ער זאל דש אנדרן
ניט טאן. זאגט דער חסיד נעמט אייך (ראייה) פֿון מיר ווי איך

בין (סובל) זאלט עטין אויך זו טאן אז עטין ווערט הערן דש
לעשטרן אונ שעלטן פֿון איין רשע זאלט עטין שוויגן דען עש
שטיט זו ביי משה רבינו (ומשה עניו מאוד מכל אדם).

[רע] נכרית   איין נכֿרית איז גילוגן אין הינר בעט הט מן זי
גטראגן צו בגראבן דען די נכֿרים הבן גמיינט אז

זי וואר מת הט זי זיך אויף גזעצט אונ שפראך איך בין גוועזן אין
זו איין עולם הב איך גזעהן שרים ומלכים אין גיהנם [1806: אוך]
אויף אזוני וואש הבן גלעבט נאך הט זי גזאגט דר און דר ווייט די
צייט שטארבן זיין [1806: וויא די צייט גישטארבן זיין] אין גיהנם
אבר די יהודים האב איך גזעהן אין גן עדן אונ און אויף די וואש זי
הט גזאגט אז ווערן שטארבן אויף דר צייט איז זו גוועזן אוך האט
זי גזאגט איך האב גזעהן איין אשה יהודית איז אוך איר הנט הנט אוך איין
גרעלבט מיט חלב גיוועזן הט די נכֿרית זי גפֿרעגט פֿר וואש דש איז
הט די יהודית גיענטפֿרט [1806: גענפֿרט] איך הב איין מאל איין
ליכֿט אן גצונדין [1806: או צונדן] אן שבֿת דרום הט מן מיר
די בושה אן גטאן.

[שכד] עשיר   איין עושר פֿלעגט צו געבן דעם גבאי איין דער
הנט אריין צדקה אז ער זאל טיילין ארמי לייט

אונ דר עושר הט גיהאט איין ארמן ברודר אוך ארמי קרובֿים הט
איין חלם גיזאגט צו דעם עושר פֿון דיין צדקה קומט ארויש איין
צעקה דש איז דיין ארמי קרובֿים שרייאן אויף דעם גבאי אוך אויף
דיר דרום גיב ליבר דיין קרובֿים:

[שע] חסיד   איין חסיד האט זיך גיבאדן אין איין וואן אונ
[1806: דר] זיין ווייב איז נעבן אים גזעסין האט

איין שיין גגעבן וי איין בליק איבר זיין קאפֿ שפֿראך דש ווייב צו
אים וואש בטייט די שיין האט דר חסיד גיענטפֿרט [1806: גענפֿרט]
דש איז ווען גאט שרייבט אן די מעשים פֿון דעם מענשן אונ די
טינט וואש בלייבט איבריג אין דר פֿען ווישט ער אפֿ אן די
צדיקים אירי קעפֿ אן זו אייני צדיקים וואש אירי צייט איז צו
שטארבן. זו איז גוועזן די זעלבגי וואך איז דר חסיד גישטארבן:

[שצו] כתיב   ואשקולה להם אֵת הכסף) דש איז דר עזרה הסופֿר
האט גגעבן דש זילבר וואש האט גקערט צו דעם

ביֵת המקדש צו די (נאמנים) האט ער אפֿ גוואוגן אונ דש ווארט
(ואשקולה) שטיט דרינן איין איברגנה (וא"יו) דש וויזט אז (עזרא
הסופֿר) האט גיוואוגן דש זילבר אונ האט זיינש דריין גגעבן [1806: געבן]:

[תא] כל   ווען איינר אנטלייט געלט [1806: ביי] אזו אייני שרים
וואש גין אום בעלילה איז גלייך אז ער גזלת די

ישראל אפֿילו ווען ער אנטלייט אויף איין משכון דען דר (שר) וועט
זאגן גיב מיר ארוש דש משכון ניט וויל מיין יהודי תפֿום
נעמן דר נאך ווערן די יהודים מוזן די יהודים ליזן:

[תב] לעולם   אייביג זאל זיך דר מענש נוהג זיין ווען ער נעמט
בײַ זיין חבר געלט זאל ער צײלן דעשטוועגלײכן

205

פר קערטט ווען ער גיט זיין חבר אפ געלט זאל ער אים צילן דען
ווען ער גיט אדר נעמט אפ אן צאל קען ארוש קומן אײן חשד ווען
עש עפיש פעלט אונ תאמר האט אײן אנדרר אוועק גנומן.

[תסט] כי יש   עש יז פר הנדין [1806]: האנדן] אײן מזיק דר
מזיק דר הײשט אוף לשון (יון דר גוײ"ן) אונ ווען

210

מן האקט אוף אים מיט אײן שווערדט שאט אים נישט אבר אײן
אנדרר (דרגוײ"ן) קאן אים יוא ממית זיין מיט דר שווערדט: עש וואר
אײן מעשה אײן מלך זיין טאכטר איז בײ איר גלעגן אײן (שד) הט
זי גיהאט אײן (דרגון) אונ אוך וואר אײן דרגון וואש פלעגט עו לינן
מיט דר (מלכה) זעלבשט פלעגנט צו זגן [1806]: זאגן] דר וואש בײ דר

215

מלכה איז גלעגן אײך פארכטט מיך פר קײנם סײדן פר דעם (דרגון)
וואש איז גיבוארן ווארן [1806]: גבורן גוווארן] פון דעם מלך זיין
טאכטר. אונ דר זעלבגר וואש פון דר טאכטר איז גיבורן ווארדן
[1806]: גבורן גוווארן] הט אים פון דר מלך גילאזט אײן זעצן אין דר
(תפיסה). אמאל שפראך דר מלך צו אים וויל איך דיך לאזן פרײא

220

פון דר תפיסה אונ זלשט [1806]: זולשט] יענם (דרגוײ"ן) ממית זיין.
איז ער גינגנין [1806]: גגנגן] אונ הט גינומן אײן שווערדט אונ הט
זיך פר בארגן אונטר די מלכה איר בעט איז גיקומן דר (דרגוײ"ן)
צו לינן בײ דר מלכה שפראך ער איך שמעק אײנם וואש איך
פארכטט מיך פר אים אונ איז דאך גיגאנגן אין בעט צו דר מלכה

225

נאך דעם איז ער ארויש גיגאנגן [1806]: ארוש גגאנגן] אוישן בעט
[1806]: אושן בעט] איז דר אנדרר אײן פיר פון אונטרן בעט אונ
הט אים אײן האק גיגעבן מיט דר שווערד אונ הט אים גימאכט
[1806]: גמאכט] אײן וואונד שפראך ער גיב מיר דעם אנדרן האק
ווערט מיר נישט שאדן דען די (סגולה) איז זו. הט ער גיענטפרט

230

[1806]: גענטפרט] אײן מאל האט מיך מײן מוטר גיוואונן ניט צוויי מאל
דרום וויל איך דיך דש אנדרי מאל ניט שלאגן. נאך דעם איז
די זייל פון אים אוש גיגנגן אונ זיין פלייש איז גישוואלן ווארן
[1806]: גשוואלן גוווארן] ביז ער וואר פול דש גאנצי חדר אונ מן
הט ניט גיקענט אים ארויש [1806]: ארוש] ברעגגן אוש דעם חדר

235

הט דר מלך גיהײשן [1806]: גהיישן] אז מן זאל דעם באלקן אײן
ברעכן: אונ אים ארויש צו נעמן שטיקר האט מן גנצי [1806]: גאנצי]
וועגן מיט פלייש אן גילייגט [1806]: גלייגט] ביז מן הט
אים ארויש גיקומט [1806]: גנומן]. אונ די מלכה הט נט ניט
גזאגט פר דעם מלך אז דר (דרגוײ"ן) איז בײ [1806]: בײא] איר

240

גילעגן [1806]: גלעגן] זונשט העט גימוזט [1806]: גמוזט] דר מלך
שטארבן אבר די [1806]: דיא] מלכה הט [1806]: האט] נאך דעם קײן
הצלחה גיהאט [1806]: גהאט] אוך ווען דר (דרגוײ"ן) איז אין אײן שטאט
איז ער נט ניט מזיק אונ בלד ווי [1806]: ווי] ער ארויש [1806]: ארוש]
גיט זו [1806]: זוא] זאו] ווערט די שטאט אפ גיברענט [1806]: גברענט]

245

אונ פר אײן דונר אנטלופט ער אונ זעצט זיך ער צו אײן מענש אבר
דש איז דר כלל די מזיקים רײצן זיך נט ניט סײדן דר וואש מיט זי

[1806]: זיא [וויא] רייצט זיך דהיינו מיט זו איינם וואש ער אודר זיין
עלטרן הבן גישריבן [1806]: גשריבן [גשריבן] קמיעות אודר [1806]: אדר [אדר] זי
הבן גיבראכט [1806]: גבראכט (השבעות) אונ כישוף אודר (שאלת
חלום) דרום זאל מן זיך היטן פֿר די זאכן אונ ער זאל ניט זגן
[1806]: זאגן [זאגן] פֿון איין נפֿש וועגן טוא איך דש דר קינן [1806]: דר [דר]
קעגן [קעגן] פֿר קערצט ער זיין לעבן אונ זיין קינדרש לעבן נייארט דר
מענש קער זיך אלש [1806]: אלין [אלין] פֿר לאזן אויף גאט אונ וואש אים
קומט צו איין (סיבה) זאל ער ליבר גאט בעטן.

7. The Yiddish Text of *Seyfer vikuekh yeytser tov im ben odem* (c.1783)

ספר ויכוח יצ״ט עם בן אדם

Seyfer vikuekh yeytser tov im ben odem

Shklov, *c.*1783

ראשית חכמה יראת י׳
ספר ויכוח יצ״ט עם בן אדם
מעלת הצדקה

מאן בעי חיי בהאי עלמא דאתי
יקרא בזה הספר בלבא רעותא
הגם בעיתים מזומנים בשבתה וחד״שה
והבא לטהר אי״ע מסייעים לו ככה לעשותה :
ויבא לשלימ׳ השם לקיים התורה בכל פרטותיה :

ווער עש וויל קריגן צוויא וועלטין: זאל ער
לינן דעם ביכל וועט אים זיין הארץ
ווערין גישפאלטין: ער זאל לינן אופט אונ ניט
צו צייטין: אזו וועט ער זיך פר נעמין צו דינן
השי״י אוך גוט צו בגיין מיט לייטן :

נדפס פה ק״ק   שקלאוו

תחת   ממשלת האדון הגדול החסיד
יענעראל מאיאר קוואליר

סעמייאן גוורילאוויץ זאריץ
בדפום המשותפים הי״ה ה[ר]בני בני מוה[ר״ר]
צבי הירש בהרבני מוהר״ר ארי[ה]
ליב זצ״ל וחתנו הי״ה הרבני מוהר״ר שמואל
במוהר״ר ישכר בער סג״ל:

בשנת כי ממנו תוצאת חיים לפ״יק

Note: Only the Yiddish text of the poem is reprinted. The title-page is given in full. The printed text was divided into lines containing rhymes. Some of these exceed a single line in this reprint, but are counted as one line. The end of each line as it occurs in the original print is marked with ‖.

1 אוֹ דוּא מענש וויא זאלשטו לושטיק זיין אוּנ זינגן:

וויל || דוּא טושט מיט דיין געלט קלינגן:

דייני טעג טוען פֿון דיר || אוועק שפרינגן:

אוּנ דער טוט וועט דיך בצווינגן:

5 אוּנ דער || קבֿר וועט דיך דער שלינגן:

אוּנ דער בויך וועט || אין קבֿר ווערין צו שפרינגן: ||

ב בישקן וואנן וועשטו אין דייני זאבֿן שלומן:

וויא זאל || דיין הארץ אין דיר ניט ברומען:

דוּא וועשט דאך פֿון || טוט ניט ווערין אנטרונן:

10 פֿיליבֿט וועט מען דיר באלד || [. . .] אהין קומען:

אוּנ דוא האשט ניט מיט זיך וואש צו || נעמן:

גוויש וועשטו זיך דארטן שעמן: ||

ג געלט אוּנ גוטש טושטו קלייבן.

האטשי פֿון אום רעכֿט || זיך ניט צו פֿר מיידן

עניים ואביונים טושטו פֿון זיך פֿר || טרייבן:

15 דער מיט טושטו דייני יארן פֿר שניידן:

אוּנ פֿון || דיין וויב אוּנ קינדר זיך אפ שיידן:

ווער וויש וועמן דיין || גוטש וועט בלייבן: ||

ד דייני הענגט טושטו אוּף דיין חברת גוטש פֿאר שפרייטן ||

20 אוּנ נעמשט בייא אים אוועק זיין גוטש נייטן:

בעשר וואלט איך || זיין ווען דוּא וואלשט אים טייטן צ [!]

דער מאן דיך וויא באלד || וועט מען דיך אין קבֿר גוט בהאלטן:

וויא זאלשטו זיך ניט || בעראטן:

דאש איז אלטש מעשה שטן: ||

25 ה הוך אין דייני אוּגן טוט דיך דער שטן האלטין: ||

כדי דוּא זאלשט מיט דיין חבֿר קריגן אוּנ שטרייטן:

דער || מיט ברינגט ער דיר בייז אין אלי דייני זייטן:

זעלברט || טוט ער פֿון דיר שפאטט:

ער טוט דיך פֿר טרייבן פֿון דיין || לושטיגין גארטין:

30 אוּנ נאך דיין טוט וועט ער נאך דיר בעטין || אוּף דיר איין משפט דארטן: ||

ו ואול טושטו דיין גוף צירין:

דייני קליידר מיט גאלד || סמעלירין:

הארעש טושטו זיך פֿירן:

דער מאן זיך אז || דוּא וועשט דאש אלטש פֿאלירן [!]:

35 דעם גוף וועט מען ארויש || טראגין פֿון אלי טירן:

אוּנ די נשמה טושטו בישמירן: ||

ז זים טושטו עסין:

דעם גוף מאחשטו פֿעטין

אוּנ צו ליגין || אפ גוטע בעטין.

40 וויא באלד וועט מען דיין גוף מעסטין ||

אוּנ אין דער ערד וועט מען דיך טעטן

אוּנ אלי וועלן איבר || דיין קבֿר טרעטין: ||

ה הן טושטו דיר ביין חבר מאבין

און אין זיין ‖ ניטין טושטו אים שוואבין:

און דער נאך טושטו פון ‖ אים לאבין:

דיין מוט וויליג האריץ טוט דאש דיר שאפין: ‖

וויל דוא גלובשט ניט אן דיין בשעפר וואש האט דיך בשאפין ‖

און ער וויש דאך דעם אום רעבט פון אלי דייני זאבין: ‖

ט טראכטין זאלשטו אין דיין שלאף און וואבן:

פון וועגשט ‖ וועגין האט דיך דיין בשעפר בשאפין:

דוא מיינשט ‖ אז דוא זאלשט דעם גוף תענוגים אן טאן ער זאל גשמאק ‖ שלאפין:

נאיירט זאלשטו די נשמה רייניקין

מיט תורה און ‖ מעמט וויא גים גאלד צו מאבין:

און וואל זיא צו דער קוויקין ‖

אבר דוא טושט זיא נאך ארגער בפלעקין: ‖

י יוא עש איז רעבט פר דיין איגין גוטש צו שטיין:

וועז ‖ דיין חבר האט דיר אום רעבט גיטאן מאגשטו בייא ‖ אים דער גיין:

נעם אף דאש איגין גוטש אבר ניט מיין

האב ‖ אין בטחון אוף השיי ב"ה ער שפיזט דעם וואָרים הינטרן ‖ שטיין:

פשיטא דיך וועז דוא וועשט אין זיין גיבאט זיין רייז: ‖

און וועז דוא וועשט אין זיין וועג גיין [:] ‖

כ כבוד איז דיין בגער דיין חבר זאל דיר טעטין

וועז ער ‖ גיט דיר ניט כבוד טושטו אים טרעטין

וויא קומשטו צו ‖ כבוד דוא שטינקנדיקר טראפין

בייא דיין לעבין שטינקשטו ‖ צו ציטן

אבר נאך דיין טוט וועשטו שטינקן פון אלי דייני ‖ זייטין

דיין וייב און קינדר וועלין ניט קאנן צו דיר צו טרעטין ‖

און וועלין שטיין פון ווייטן: ‖

ל לעקר טושטו דיין חבר אין זיין הנדל שאפט גיפינן: ‖

האטשי זיך נישט צי פר דינן

נישמער דער חבר זאל נישט ‖ גיוינין:

אבר דוא נאר וועז השיי ב"ה וועט אים מצליח זיין ‖ דרינן

פון דיא זעלביגן לעבר וואש דוא האשט אים גיפינן: ‖

וועט אים פיל גוץ פון דעם ארויש קומען:

און דוא וועשטו נאר ‖ מער שוער האריץ בקומן: ‖

מ מארגין וועשטו השיי גיבאט טאן אזו טושטו דינה ‖ רייד פר טראגין:

און איינטגין [!] טאג טושטו טראבטן פר דיין ‖ גוף [!!]

און היינטיגן טאג טושטו טראבטן פר דיין גוף און וייב ‖ און קינדר אוך זיא

ניט צו פר זאגין:

דוא נארשער מענש וויא ‖ זאלשטו ניט זארגין:

דיא טוט פון מענשן איז דאך פר בארגין: ‖

פיליבט וועשטו היינט שטארבין און וועשט ווערין בגראבין ‖

און דיא גילבאט [!] פון השיי וועשטו ניט קאנין טאן מארגין: ‖

נ נארין טושטו דיין חבר מיט פֿאלסע [!] אונ זיסע ווערטר ||

וויזט זיך פֿר אים גלייך אז דוא בישט איין גוטער פֿריינט || איין גרושר עושר

85

כדי זאלשטו פֿון אים איין הקפֿה || בקומען בעשר

גיט ער דיר איין סך געלט אז דוא זאלשטו אים || געבן וואלוולה סחורה שפעטר:

נעמשטו זיין בלום אונ געלט || אונ טושטו זיך תענוגים אן אונ פֿר שטעקסט

מיט זיין || געלט אלי דיינע לעבֿר

טושט הולֿע שדולים אונ גישט גרושי || נדנן דיינע טעכטר:

קאן דאש השיי ליידן דער הולֿר || בשעפֿר:

90

דיא רשעת וואש דוא טושט דיין חבר דאש דוא || בישט זיין שעכטר [:]

ס שוואך אונ קריינק טוט דיין חבר ווערין

וויא ער טוט די || ביזה שמועה הערין:

אזו קומט ער צו דיר צו קערין:

איך || ביט דיך ברודר מיינר יארין ניט צו פֿר שטערין

95

איך שיינק || דיר דעם ריוח גיבֿ [!] מיר מיין קערן

אונ דוא ענטפֿרשט צו אים || מיט קריג אונ צארין

איך וועל דיר ניט געבן אפֿילו פרוטה אחת || אונ וועל אין לי שווערין:

ע ער האט מיט דיר קיין ברירה ניט

וויל דוא גילשט אים || זייער דיק

100

אזו קומט ער צו דיר בעטנדיק

איין טייל שענק איך || דיר אוף אייביג

אונ איין טייל אוף לאנגי ציטן בליב מיר שולדיק ||

נישמר דעם טייל וואש בייא דיר גאנץ איז גיב מיר צוריק

אזו || ווערשטו לוסטיק

105

דוא מיינשט דוא הושט דיין זאך אוש גימאכט || שפילנדיק

עש איז ניט אזו האשטו זיך גיפֿלאבֿטן איין גראבֿע || שטריק:

וועשט פֿר פֿאלין אין כף הקלע אוף אייביק [:] ||

פ פֿון ליים בישטו ווארין גיקנעטין

ווארום זאלשטו זיך דאש || אין הארצין ניט האלטן:

דיין איינן גוטש איז אוך ניט || דיין פֿון פֿייער אונ פֿון אנדרי הזיקות צו פֿר טרעטין:

110

וועשט אויש || שפֿיאן פֿרעמד גוטש וואש דוא טושט דער מיט דיין גוף || פֿעטין

אזו טוא האפ צו השיי בֿ"ה אונ טוא אים בעטין:

ער || זאל דיך אין דיין כשר געלט העלפֿין:

ער זאל דיר געבֿין [!] דיין || בדערפֿנם אין אלי דיינה ציטן [:] ||

115

צ צער אונ טרהה האשטו תמיד איבר דיין בדערפֿניש || פֿון דיין וויב אונ

קינדר אונ דיין גוף:

טאג אונ נאבֿט || שלאנגשטו זיך אפ פֿון עסין אונ טרינקען אונ שלאפֿן:

דער וויל || מאג צו טאג איבר דעם דוא וועשטו שוואך אונ שלאף

דוא נארסר [!] || מענש וויא נעמשטו זין דיין זין צו דער מאניך דעם ||

סוף אונ דוא טראבֿשט תמיד פֿארן גוף זייער שארף:

120

אונ || אוף דער נשמה פֿר געשטו אונ ווען דוא יוא זיא דער מאנשט אזו

טראבֿשטו פֿר זיא נאר שלאף: ||

ק קנאה בריינגט דיך צו שנאה אז דוא זאלשט מיט דיין ‖ חבֿר קריגין אונ שטרייטן

וואש מיגליך איז צו פֿר שעמין ‖ אים פֿר לייטן:

אונ פשיטא [!] איין ווארט ניט צו פֿר שווייגן ‖

125

אונ וואש דוא קאנשט טושטו אים זיין פרנסה [!] שלאגין

בישט ‖ דער ווידר השי״י ער האט גיבאטן

אז דוא זאלשט דעם חבֿר גון ‖ טאן קיין זאך ניט צו פֿר זאגין

אונ דוא טושט פֿר קערט טושט ‖ אים ביז אונ וואש מיגלך אים צו פֿר זאגין:

אוי בשעת יום ‖ הדין דיין נשמה זעלבׂרט וועט אויף דיר עדות זאגין:

130

דיא זינד ‖ וואש עש היינגט אן דיין חבר וועט השי״י ניט פֿר טראגין:

דאש ‖ וועשטו אויף דיין אכסל אייביק טראגין: ‖

ר ריין ווען דוא בישט [יוא ?] פֿון גזילות אונ אנדרי אום רעבֿט ‖

אונ צדקה וגמילות חסדים טושטו ניט פֿר געסן:

דאך ‖ איז רעבֿט דיין געלט ניט צו פֿר שטוסן

135

הארעם טושטו זיך ‖ פֿירן אונ וואל צו עסין

דער מאן זיך דיין ליבֿט וועט ווערין ‖ פלוצלינג פֿר לאסין [!]:

אונ אין קבר וועט מען דיך פֿר שליסין: ‖

ש שוויג שטיל דוא מענש הער צו מיינע רייד וואש איך ‖ וועל דיר ראטין:

וועשטו אזו טאן אונ וועשטו פֿון מיינע ריד ‖ ניט שפאטין:

140

וואל וועט זיין דיין גוף אונ דיין נשמה אונ ‖ פשיטא קיין ביז וועט דיר ניט שאטין

צו ווישן אז דער בשעפֿר ‖ האט דיר בשאפֿין דער ווארטין

אז דוא זאלשט טאן אלי זיינה ‖ גיבאטן:

די ער האט גיגעבין דורך משה רבינו ע״ה דער ‖ ווארהפֿטיגר אונזר הירטן:

וואל וועט זיין דיין נשמה אונ גוף ‖ דא אונ דארטן: ‖

145

ת תענוגיא [! =תענוגים] מאגשטו דיר אן טאן נאר נאר מיטן מאס

אוך אין ‖ אנדרי מידות אזו זיך צו ביגיין נאר אויף גאוה גאר פֿר ‖ געם:

דעם עני צדקה צו געבין אויף זיין בדרפֿנם:

אונ וען ער ‖ קומט אין דיין הויז בעט אים ברודר טרינק אונ עם:

אוך ‖ מיטן עושר גומל חסד צו טאן אונ ניט צו פֿרענגין פֿר וואש: ‖

150

וואר האפֿטיג צו ריידן מיט דיין חבר אונ ווען דיין חבֿר וועט ‖ דיר איבל ריידן

דאך זאלשט אים ניט מביֿיש זיין אונ צו האלטן ‖

דעם צונג הינטרן שלאם:

ווען דוא וועשט אזו טאן וועט דיר השי״י ‖ בגליקן דיין ווערק אין הויז אונ אין גאם:

פֿון דיינה ‖ ווינקליך וועט סטורמן [!] גון וי פֿון אפֿולע פֿאם:

154

אונ וואול וועט ‖ זיין דיין נשמה אונ גוף אויף דיזה וועלט אונ

אויף יענה וועלט ‖ גאר אן מאם: ‖‖

8. The Title-pages and One Episode of *Mayse gdoyle* in Eastern and Western versions

מעשה גדולה

Mayse gdoyle

Eastern version	Western version
[Novidvor, *c*.1783]	Fürth, 1783

מעשה גדולה מר ק"ק אומן

במדינת אקריינא

השייך לפולין

הנעשה בשנת תק"ל לפ"ק:

אקריינא גרעניצט מיט רוסין
אונד טאטרייא

מעשה גדולה

מן אומן ומן אוקריינא

ד א ש ביכליין פֿון אומן אונד
גאנצין אקריינא זאל איטליכר
מענש לייאנין אונד זאל זיך
צו הערצן נעהמן. דיא גרווזי
צרה. ווז גאט צו גשיקט
האט אויף גאנץ אקריינא אין
יאר תק"ל: פֿיל שטעטטי זיין
נהרג ווארדן דורך מיתות משונת
אונד גרוזי יסורים.
גאט זאל ווייטר אונש היטן פֿון
אלין ביזן. אונד זאל אונז
נקמות ווייזן. אן דיא שונאים.

ביכל פֿון אומן אונ
אוקריינא זאל איטלכר מענש
לייגן אונ זאל גידענקן וואש
פֿר אײן גרושה צרה גאט האט
גשיקט אויף אומן אונ אויף
אוקריינא אונ אויף באלטי אונ
אויף אך אנדרי שטעטט מן הט
גישלאגן מיט מכות אלזריות:

דרום קער מן צו בעטן גאט אז
ער זאל שון מער קיין צרות ניט
צו שיקן אונ זאל אויך גער אונ'
באלד אײן נקמה טאן אן אונזר
שונאים אונ זאל אונש גער
אונ באלד אויש לייזן אויש דעם
ביטרן גלות במהרה
בימינו אמן:

אונד זאל אונז אויז דען
ביטרן גלות ער ליזן במהרה
בימינו אמן:

בשנת בישראל הודיעתיהו
נאמנה לפֿ"ק

Eastern version [Novidvor, c.1783]	Western version Fürth, 1783

Eastern version [Novidvor, c.1783]

דר נאך האבן
זיא גיהאפט איין (בתולה) איין
שיינה איר פאטער האט גהיישן
הקדוש רבי משה אזו האבן זיא
אן גהובן צו ריידן אז זי זאל
זיך שמאדן אזו האט זיא אן
גיהובן צו ריידן מיט גרויש גשרייא
עטץ אומה טמאה וויא רעמ עטץ
מיך אן צו איין ביזה דיעה איר
קענט מיך ניט ניימן ליברשט
ווייל איך אום קומן אזו הט מן זיא
גפירט צו דר ברונה מן האט איר
גוויזן וויא פיל הרוגים ליגן
דרינן אונ האבן גיטאן זייער
מעסר שארפן צו קולין אטייל
זאגן מען זאל זי לעבדיגר הייט
אין דר ברונה אריין ווארפן אזו
האט זי גזאגט איך טוא מיך פר
דעם טוט ניט פארכטן איך טוא
תיכף מיין האלז אויש שטרעקן
צום קולן אונ איר מוטר איז
גישטאנ[ן] דר בייא נעביך אזו
הט זיא גשריגן מיין ליבה טאכטר
פר געש ניט אן אונזר ליבן גאט
אזו האבן דיא פוחזים זיא גינומן
אונ האבן זיא אריין גיוווארפן
לעבדיגר הייט אין דער ברונה

Western version Fürth, 1783

אין בתולה וואהר דא. איהר
שוינהייט וואהר צו זוכין אין
דער וועלט. זיא וואלטין זיא
גערין מאנם זיין. וואן נור ניט
איר סדר וועהר אן איין יהודא
זיך ניט מטמא צו זיין. זיא
רעדין זיא אן דאש זיא זיך מימר
דת זיין זאלי מיט אלליר גוואלד.
זיא זאגט אבר מיין נשמה האבי
איך איבר ענטפארט צו גאט
ברענגש מיך נור אום. זיא
שארפין דאש מעסיר. פר איר
אויגין. אונד זאגין. זיך וואן
דוא ניט פאלגנשט צו שנידין
מיר דיין פלייש מיט דיזען
מעסיר זיא ענטוואָרט אבר.
איר אומה שפלה וטמאה. איר
ווערט מיך דא צו ניט ברענגין.
אלליש איך מימר דת זאל זיין
חלילה. שעלבט מיך נור מאלט
מיט מיר וויא איר וועלט. זיא
בינדין זיא אונד ווערפין זיא
אין איין ברונע. זיא שטארבט

9. The Short Midrash 'Ten Signs of Messiah' in
Avkes roykhl (1795)

אבקת רוכל

Avkes roykhl

Horodne, 1795

ספר
אבקת רוכל

דש ספֿר האט מחבר גוועזן הרב רבינו
מכיר דער רבי פֿון רש"י :
אין דעם ספֿר איז נכֿלל כמה דברים דהיינו
די (אותות ומופֿתֿים) וואש וועלן
גשעהן איי (משיח) וועט קומן אונ ווי מען קאן
ניצול ווערן פֿון (חבֿלי משיח) אונ אויך כמה
זאכֿן בעניׁן (דין ועונש גיהנם) (ושכֿר עולם
הבא) אונ נאך אנדרי זאכֿן וויא איר וועט גיפֿינן
איטליכֿש אין זיין (חלק) פֿר טײלט :

נדפס פה ק"ק
הורודנא

נדפֿם בדפֿוס חדש אשר הוקם על ידי
ה"ה הראש והקצין מוהר"ר
ברוך במו' יוסף ז"ל מ"ם :
מקהילתנו יצ"ו :

בשנת   תקנ"ה   לפֿ"ק

Note: Only the first part of *Avkes roykhl* (Horodne, 1795), the one containing the eschatological midrash 'Ten signs of Messiah', is reprinted. The title-page is given in full. The original lines of the book are preserved. Original page numbers from 1a to 6a are marked in the left-hand margins.

ספר הראשון

יכלול   אין דען ערשטן ספר איז כולל דיא אותׁות

ומופׁתים אונ מלחמות אונ די צרות וואש וועט

גשעהן אי משיח וועט קומן אונ ווי מען קאן ניצול ווערן דר

פֿון אונ דש ווערט צו טיילט אויף צוויי חלקים:

החלק הראשון   דאש ערשטי חלק איז אים צען

ציילן וואש וועט גשעהן אז משיח וועט קומן

יתברך   שמו של הקב״ה. גלובט איז גאטש נאמן ער

האט אוש דר ווילט ישראל פֿון שבעים אומות

אונ ער בגערט זי מזכה צו זיין אונ האט זי גגעבן די תורה אונ

האט זי מאכֿן הערן דיא עשרת הדברות:

אונ   קענגן די עשרת הדברות האבן אונזרה חכמים

גיצײלט צעהן מעלות: אונ די גרינגרה מעלה ברענגט

צו דר העבֿרי מעלה ביז מען קומט צו דר העלׁשטי מעלה דש

איז (רוח הקדוש) דען הקב״ה איז דר העלׁשטער איבר אלי:

די ערשטי מעלה איז (זהירות) דש איז אין מענש מוז זיין

גווארנט פֿון אין חטא אונ פֿון אין זאך וואש ברענגט צו אין

עבֿירה אונ די מעלה ברענגט צו דר אנדרי מעלה פֿון (זריזות)

דש איז אין מענש זאל זיין גפֿרישט צו טאן מצות אונ לערנן

תורה אונ מעשים טובים. אונ דש ברענגט צו (נקיות) דש

איז מען זאל זיין לויטר אונ ריין פֿון כל חטאים ופשעים וֹמכל

טומאות אונ דש ברענגט צו (טהרה) דש איז מען זאל זיין

טהור פֿד הקב״ה אונ (נקי כפים) אונ דאש ברענגט צו

(קדושה) דאש איז מען זאל זיין קדוש וטהור פֿר הקב״ה אונ

דאש ברענגט צו (יראת חטא) דש איז מען זאל זיין אין ירא

שמים אונ גליבט צו הקב״ה. אונ דאש ברענגט צו (חסידות)[[] דאש

איז מען זאל זיין אין חסיד אונ מען זאל גומל חסד זיין לׁכֿל

הברׁיות: אונ דאש איז גורם צו (רוח הקודש) דש איז די

שכֿינה איז אויף אים שורה דש איז די העלׁשטי מעלה איבר אלי מעלׁות:

שכר   דר שכׁר פֿון די צעהן מעלׁות איז וועןּ ער איז אין

(זהיר) איז עם הקב״ה מצֿיל פֿון כל צרה וצֿוקה

וֹממֹשׁחית ופֿרֹענֹיֹות: אונ וועןּ ער איז אין (זריז) במצוה

מאלׁט אים הקב״ה ברׁיט זיין הרץ אונ דר לײַבֿט זײַן אויגן אין

דר תורה. אונ וועֹן ער איז אין (פֿרוש) מאלׁט אים

הקב״ה פֿר זיין גליבטן קנעלׁבט: אונ וועֹן ער איז אין (נקי)

צו ברעלׁבט הקב״ה זיין פֿיינד פֿר אים. אונ וועֹן ער איז אין

(טהור) ווערט ער גרופֿן דר ליב האבר פֿון הקב״ה אונ וועֹן

ער איז אין (קדוש) ברײַט אים הקב״ה אן צו עולם הבא:

אונ אז ער איז אין (עניו) מאלׁט אים הקב״ה פֿר שטיין

סודות התורה אונ עפֿנט אונ זיין אוצֿרות פֿון חכמה אונ אז

ער איז אין (חסיד) מאלׁט הקב״ה אויף אים רֹואֹן דעם רוח

הקודש אונ רעט אים וֹי אים צו כל נביאים אונ קענגן די עשרת

הדברות אונ די צעהן מעלׁות וועט הקב״ה טאן צעהן ציילׁן

אי משיח ווערט קומן הקב״ה זאל אונז מקרב זיין די גאולה אמן

45

האות הראשון דר ערשטער צייכן איז הקב״ה וועט אויף
ריכטן דרי מלכים אונ זיי וועלן לייקנן אן הקב״ה
אונ וועלן זיך ווייזן גלייך זיי גלייבן אן הקב״ה אונ וועלן פר
אירין דען עולם אונ וועלן מבלבל זיין כל הבריות אונ די אומות
וועלן לייקנן אן זייער גריכט: אונ אוך די פושעי ישראל וואש

50

זענן מיאש פון דר גאולה וועלן אוך לייקנן אן הקב״ה אונ אוף
דעם דור זאגט דר פסוק (ותהי האמת נעדרת) די בעלי אמת
וועלן זיך איין זאמלן עדרים עדרים כתות כתות אונ וועלן
אנטלופן אונ וועלן זיך איין זאמלן אין דיא היילן אונ גריבר
פון ערד. אונ וועלן ווערן איין גטאן די גבורים אונ וועלן בטל

2a

ווערן די וואר הפטיני לייט אונ וועלן בהאלטן ווערן דיא שערי
חכמה אונ דר עולם וועט ווערן פר ענדרט אונ אין דר צייט
וועט ניט זיין צווישן ישראל קיין מלך און קיין נביא אונ קיין
ראשי ישיבות אונ קיין חסידים ובעלי השם אונ וועלן פר
שלאסין זיין די שערי שמים אונ שערי פרנסה אונ אין דר צייט

60

אז משיח וועט זיך בווייזין מיט זיין שטארקייט וועט דער
עולם פאלין גייאנדיג מחמת גרושה צרות וגזירות וואש וועלן
גזר זיין די דרי מלכים אונ זי וועלן גזר זיין מען זאל לייקנן
אן גאט ב״ה אונ אן דר תורה אונ ביח המקדש און הקב״ה וועט
גזר זיין אז דש מלכות הרשעה זאל זיין ניין חדשים פון איין

65

עק וועלט צו דר אנדרר אונ וועלן גזר זיין גזירות קשות אונ דר
מם וואש ישראל גיבן ווערן גטאפילט זיין פון איין גילדין ביז
צעהן אונ ווער עש וועט ניט האבן צו געבן וועט מען אים דעם
קאפ אפ שניידין: אונ דיא ניין חדשים וועלן זיך בניאן איין
גזרה שווערר אז די אנדרי אונ אוך וועלן קומן מענושן פון עק

70

וועלט וואש זענן זייער מיאום אונ ווער עש וועט זיי זעהן וועט
שטארבן פר פחד אונ ווערן ניט בדארפן מלחמה צו הלטן נאר
פון פחד וועט מען שטארבן אונ איטליכר וועט האבן צווי קעפ
אונ זיבן אוגן אונ וועלן ברענן אז פלאם פייר אונ גרינג זיין
אז דיא הערשן אונ דיא קינדר פון ישראל ווערן זיך פארבלטן אונ

75

וועלן שרייאן ווי ווי ווי וואש וועלן מיר טאן אונ די עלטרן וועלן זי
ענטפרן אצונד האפן מיר צו דר גאולה:

האות השני דר אנדרר צייכן וועט זיין הקב״ה וועט
ברענגן איין היין היין איין היין אויף דר וועלט פון דר זון אונ
מיני קדחת אונ חלאים רעים אונ דבר אונ מגפה אונ וועלן שטרבן

80

פון די [אומות] אלף אלפים אלי טאג אונ אל די רשעים פון
ישראל וועלן שטארבן ביז דיא אומות וועלן וויינן וויא צו אונז
וואו וועלן מיר זיין אודר אנטלופן אונ וועלן זיך גראבן איטלכר
איין קבר בי זייער לעבן אונ וועלן חשק האבן צו שטרבן אונ

2b

וועלן זיך בהאלטן אין די פעלין אונ צווישן דערנר: אז זי זאלן

85

זיך אביסל אפ קילין אונ וועלן קומן אין היילן אונ גריבר פון ערד

אונ דר וועשט וועלן פֿרעגן ווי וועלן די צדיקים טואן פֿר דר היין
הקבֿ״ה וועט זייא מאבֿן איין רפֿואה אויש דר היין. אויף דעם
האט בלעם הרשע גזאגט (אוי מי יהיה משומו אל) [ ]:

האות השלישי דר דריטר צייכֿן הקבֿ״ה וועט מאבֿן
90 נידרן טויא פֿון בלוט אונ עש וועט זיך ווייזן פֿר
די אומות ווי וואשר אונ זי וועלן טרינקן דר פֿון אונ דיא רשעי
ישראל וואש זעגן זיך מיאש פֿון דר גאולה וועלן אויך טרינקן
אונ וועלן שטאַרבן: אונ דיא צדיקים וואש האלטן אן דר אמונה
פֿון הקבֿ״ה ווערן ניט גשעדיקט זיין אונ אין דען גאנצן עולם וועט
95 זיין דם דרייא טאג אז דר פסוק זאגט (ונתתי מופֿתֿים בשמים
ובֿארץ דם אש ותֿמרותֿ עשן):

האות הרבֿיעי דר פֿירדר צייכֿן הקבֿ״ה וועט מאבֿן
נידרן איין טויא פֿון רפֿואה צו די בינונים אונ זי
וועלן טרינקן צו היילן די קרענק פֿון דר טויא פֿון בלוט:

100 **האות** החמישי דר פֿינפֿטר צייכֿן הקבֿ״ה וועט מאבֿן די
זון פֿינצטער דרייסיג טאג אונ די לבֿנה צו בלוט נאך
דעם וועט מאבֿן הקבֿ״ה שיין אונ ווי צום ערשטן אונ די אומות
ווערן זיך שעמן אונ ווערן זין פֿארבֿרגטן אונ וועלן ווישן אז דאש
איז אלש פֿון ישראל וועגן אונ טייל וועלן זיך בסתֿר מגייר זיין:

105 **האות** הששי דר זעקסטר צייכֿן הקבֿ״ה וועט מאבֿן
קינגן דאש מלבֿותֿ הרשעה אויף דר גאנצר וועלט
אונ עש וועט אויף שטיין איין נייאר מלך אין רום אונ וועט
קיניגן אין רום אויף דר גאנצר וועלט ניין חדשים אונ וועט מחריבֿ
זיין מדינותֿ אונ וועט צערנן איבר ישראל אונ וועט אויף זיא
110 וואַרפֿן גרושן מס אונ ישראל וועלן זיין אין דר צייט אין איין
גרושה צרה מחמתֿ פֿיל גזירותֿ וואש וועלן זיך בניאן אלי טאג
אונ ישראל וועלן זיך מינרין אונ קיינר וועט זי ניט העלפֿן נאך

3a דיא ניין חדשים וועט זיך בוויין משיח בן יוסף אונ זיין נאמן
איז נחמיה בן הושיאל [!] מיט שבט אפֿרים אונ מנשה אונ בנימין
115 אונ טייל פֿון שבֿט גד אונ כל ישראל וועלן הערן פֿון כל המדינותֿ
אז ער קומט משיח וועלן זיך איין זאמלן איין טייל פֿון איטליבֿר
מדינה אונ פֿון איטליבֿר שטאט אחד מעיר ושנים ממשפחה אונ
משיח בן יוסף וועט אן רייצן איין מלחמה מיט מלך אדום
אונ וועט דעם מלך אדום בי קומן אונ וועט הארגנן פֿון זייא
120 הויפֿן וויש אונ וועט הרגנן דעם מלך אדום אונ וועלן חרובֿ מאבֿן
רום אונ וועלן אויש ציהן איין שיף פֿון כלים פֿון בית המקדש
אונ וועט ברענגן קיין ירושלים אונ ישראל ווערן הערן אונ זיך
איין זאמלן צו אים אונ דר מלך פֿון מצרים וועט שלום מאבֿן מיט
אים אונ וועט הרגנן אלי מדינותֿ וואש ארום ירושלים זענן ביז
125 (דמשק אונ אשקלון) אונ זי וועלן הערן דיא גאנצי וועלט אונ וועט
פֿאלן אויף זיי איין גרושה אימה:

האות   השביעי דר זיבטר צייכן הקב״ה בעל נפלאות
וועט טואן אין מופֿת אויף דר וועלט דען עש איז
פֿר הנדן אין שטאט רום אין שטיין איז גשניצט אין
130
גשטאלט פֿון אין בתולה יפֿת תואר און זיא איז ניט גשניצט
גוווארן דורך אין מענש נאר דורך גאט ב״ה און זיא זיא קומן די
שלעכטסטי פֿון די אומות און דר היצן זיך און לינן בייא איר און
הקב״ה היט דיא זרע אין דען שטיין און וועט בשאפֿן דר פֿון
אין קינד און דר שטיין וועט צו שפֿאלטן ווערן און וועט ארוש
135
קומן אין גשטאלט פֿון אין מענש און זיין נאמן וועט זיין
(ארמילוס השטן) זיין לענג וועט זיין צוועלף איילן און דיא
בריט צוועלף איילן און דיא אויגן אז אין דום גרוש און וועלן
זיין טיף און רוט און די האר פֿון קאפ אז גאלד פֿארב די פֿים וועלן
זיין גרין און וועט האבן צווי קעפ און וועט קומן צו אדום און וועט
140
זאגן איך בין משיח און בין אייער גאט באלד וועלן זי גלייבן
אן אים און וועלן אים מאכן קיננגן איבר זייא און וועלן זיך

3b
בהעפֿטן אן אים און וועלן פֿון עשו און וועלן קומן צו אים און ער
וועט גיין און וועט זאגן אין נעמן אלי מדינו׳ און וועט זאגן צו די קינדר
עשו ווא׳ איז די תורה וואש איך האב אייך גגעבן דא וועלן זיי
145
ברענגן די ספֿרי פסולים וועט ער זאגן דש איז אמת וואש האב
איך גיגעבן און וועט זאגן צו די אומות גלייבט אן מיר אז איך
בין אייער משיח דא וועלן זי באלד גלייבן אין דר צייט וועט
ער שיקן צו משיח בן יוסף און צו כל ישראל און וועט זאגן צו זיי
ברענגט מיר אייער תורה און זאגט עדות אז איך בין גאט זו
150
באלד וועלן זי זיך פֿארבֿרטן און וואונדרן אין דר צייט וועט אויף
שטיין משיח בן יוסף מיט דרייסיג טויזנט גבורים פֿון שבֿט
אפֿרים און וועלן ברענגן אין ספֿר תורה און וועלן ליינן דיא
עשרת הדברות (אנכֿי ה׳ אלהיך לא יהיה לך אלהים אחרים על
פניֿ) (] [) וועט ער זאגן אייער תורה איז גאר נישט נייארט קומט און
155
זאגט אויף מיר עדות אז איך בין גאט אז ווי זי האבן גטאן
אלי אומות זו בלד וועט זיך שטעלן קיגן אים משיח בן יוסף און
וועט זאגן צו זיין קנעכֿט פֿאנגט אים און און בינט אים זו באלד וועט
אויף שטיין משיח בן יוסף און די דרייסיג טויזנט מאנן וואש
זענען מיט אים און וועלן מיט אים מלחמה הלטן און וועלן הארגנן
160
פֿון אים און וועלן מיט אים מלחמה האלטן. און וועלן הארגנן פֿון
אים צווי הונדרט טויזנט מאנן זו וועט דער ארמילוס הרשע [=הרשע] זייר
פֿר דריסונגן און וועט אין זאמלן אלי חיילות פֿון די אומות צום
טאל (חרוץ) און וועט מלחמה האלטן מיט ישראל און ישראל וועלן
הארגנן פֿון זי הויפֿן וויש און ישראל וועלן אויך אביסיל גמארט
165
ווערן און משיח בן יוסף וועט נהרג ווערן דא וועלן קומן מיט די
מלאכֿים און וועלן אים אוועק נעמן און וועלן אים בהאלטן מיט די
אבֿות זו בלד וועט צו גיין דש הרץ פֿון ישראל און דר ארמילם
הרשע וועט זאגן ניט וויש אז משיח בן יוסף איז נהרג גוווארן זישט
וועט ער פֿון ישראל ניט איבר גלאזט אין (שריד ופליט) אין דר
170
צייט וועלן די אומות ישראל פֿר טרייבן פֿון זייער מדינות

4a אונ וועלן זי ניט לאזן וואוינן מיט זייא אונ וועלן זאגן זעהט דש
מבוזה אונ שפל פאלק האבן אן אונז מורד גוועזן אונ האבן זיך
גימאבט אײן מלך אונ עש וועט זיין אויף ישראל אײן גרושה צרה
וואיש נאך ניט גוועזן זינט די וועלט שטײט. אין דר צייט וועט
175 זיך שטעלן (מיכאל) דר (שר הגדול) אויש צו קלויבן די רשעי
ישראל זוא באלד וועלן אנטלויפן כל ישראל אין די מדברות אונ
וועט עש וועט מסופק זיין אין דר גאולה וועט וועט צו שטײן צו די
אומות אונ וועט וועט זאגן די גאולה וואיש מיר האבן צו איר איז משיח
נהרג גוווארן אונ ווער עש וועט האבט ניט אויף דר גאולה דר וועט
180 מבזיש ווערן אונ וועט צושטײן צו די אומות אין דר צייט וועט
הקב״ה לייטרן די ישראל אז וועי זילבר אין דר טעפשט אונ די איבר
בלײבונג פון ישראל די (קדושים וטהורים) וועלן זיין אין דר
(מדבר יהודה) אונ וועלן עסין בלעטר אונ גראז מיט דעם וועלן
זיי אײן קיום האבן אין דר צייט וועלן שטארבין אלי (רשעי
185 ישראל) וואש זענן ניט ראוי צו דר גאולה אונ ער וועט קומן
(ארמיל״ים הרשע) אונ וועט מלחמה האלטן מיט מצרים אונ וועט
זי בצוואונגן אונ וועט זיך אום קערן קיין ירושלים חרוב צו מאבן
דאש אנדרי מאל אבר אבר גאט וועט אים ניט העלפן דר צו:

האות השמיני דר אבטר צייבן ער וועט זיך שטעלן
190 מיכאל המלאך אונ וועט בלאזין שופר דרײ מאל
די ערשטי תקיעה וועט זיך בווייזן (משיח בן דוד אונ אליהו
הנביא) () [ ] צו די צדיקים וואיש זענן אנטלאפן קיין מדבר יהודה נאך
פינף אונ פירצינ טאג וועט הקב״ה זייא שטארקן דש הרצ פון די
שלאפי אונ זי וועלן הערן כל ישראל וואיש זענן איבר גיבליבן אין
195 דר גנצי וועלט דען קול שופר וועלן זייא וויישן אז הקב״ה האט
גידענקט זיין פאלק צו גוטן אונ אז דיא גאולה קומט אונ וועלן זיך
אײן זאמלן אונ וועלן אלי קומן אונ פון דעם קול וועלן זיך פרבלטן
אלי אומות אונ וועלן פר קרענקט ווערן אונ ישראל וועלן זיך
שטרקין אקעגן צו גיין אונ משיח בן דוד אונ אליהו הנביא אונ

4b די ישראל וואיש האבן זיך ווידר קערט פון מדבר יהודה אונ כל
ישראל וועלן קומן קיין ירושלים אונ וועט גיין אויף שטפלן
פון בהמ״ק וואיש איז איבר גבליבן אונ וועט דארט זיצן אונ ער
וועט הערן ארמיל״ים הרשע אז עש איז אויף גשטאנן אײן מלך
צו ישראל וועט ער זאגן ביז וי לאנג נאך וועט דער (אומה שפילה)
205 אזו טאן זו באלד וועט ער אײן זאמלן אלי חיילות פון די אומות
אונ וועד קומן מלחמה האלטן מיט משיח דש מאל וועט הקב״ה
דעם משיח ניט מאבן בדארפן מלחמה צו הלטן נייארט ער וועט
זאגן זעין דיך אן מיין רעבטי הנט אונ משיח וועט זאגן צו ישראל
שטעלט אייך וועט וועלן איר זעהן פון גאט וואש ער וועט
210 אייך טאן היינט זו באלד וועט הקב״ה מלחמה האלטן מיט זיי
אונ הקב״ה וועט לאזן נידרן פייאר אונ שוועבל פון הימל אונ אויך
גרושה שטיינר זוא באלד וועט וועט ארמילום הרשע שטארבין ער אונ
זיין גאנצ חיל אדום אונ אין דר צייט וועלן ישראל האבן זייער
גרושה נקמות:

האות   התשיעי דר ניונטיר צייכֿן וועט מיכֿאל בלאזן איין   215

תקיעה גדולה דא וועלן צו שפאלטן ווערן די קבֿרים

פֿון ירושלים אונ הקב״ה וועט מחיה מתֿים זיין אונ משיח אונ

אליהו הנבֿיא וועלן גיין אונ וועלן לעבֿדיג מאכֿן משיח בן יוסף

אונ משיח בן דוד אונ וועט גיין פֿון וועגן ישראל וואש זענן פֿר שפרייט

אין אלי לענדר זו באלד וועלן אלי אומות זי ברענגן צו טראגן   220

אויף דר אקסל צו גאט ב״ה:

האות   העשירי דר צעהנטר צייכֿן וועט מיכֿאל בלאזן די

דריטי תקיעה וועט הקב״ה אויש ציהן פֿון אונטרן

סמבטיון אונ אנדרי לענדר אל די די שבֿטים אונ די בני משה גאר

אן צאל אונ די ערד וועט זיין אז דש גן עדן אונ אונטר זי וועט   225

ברענגן אז פֿלאם פֿייאר אונ זי וועלן ניט לאזן קיין דר נערונג צו

די אומות אונ אויף דר צייט אז דיא שבֿטים וועלן אוש גיין וועלן זי

ארום רינגלין די (עני כבֿוד) אונ הקב״ה וועט גיין פֿר זי אונ

ער וועט עפֿן זי עפֿֿנן קוואלן פֿון (עץ החיים) אונ וועט זיא אן   5a

טרענקן אזו ווי עש שטיט אין ישעיה: הקב״ה זאל אונז מזכה   230

זיין צו זעהן די גאולה במהרה אונ דש בית המקדש אונ זאל אן

אונז מקוים ווערן ווי עש שטיט איך וועל ווידר קערן דאש ווידר

קערונג פֿון גצעלטן פֿון יעקֿב אונ זיינ רואונג וועל איך דר ברמן

אונ עש וועט גבויאט ווערן דיא שטאט ירושלים אויף איר אורט אונ

דש בית המקדש וועט גבויאט ווערן ווי די רעכֿט איז אונ זאל אן   235

אונז מקוים ווערן די נחמות וואש די נבֿיאים האבן גזאגט במהרה

בימינו אמן סלה:

וכנגד   אונ קעגן די צעהן צייכֿן וועט הקב״ה גרונד

פֿעסטן ירושלים מיט צעהן ארליי אבֿנים טובֿות

דהיינו (רובֿין) (פריזנד) (גאר פֿונקל) (יאכֿצונג) (אונקיל)   240

(יאשפֿ) (שמראק) (ספֿיר) (פֿערלמוטר) אונ גאלד איז צעהן:

אונ הקב״ה וועט מוסף זיין אין (בית המקדש) נאך צוויי ארליי

אבֿנים טובֿות (כדכֿוד) אונ (אקדה) אונ קעגן דיא וועט

הקב״ה אום קערן צעהן זאכֿן וואש איז אפ גגאנגן אין אנדרן

בית המקדש דהיינו דעם ארון אונ כרובֿים אונ (שמן המשחה)   245

(עצי המערבֿֿה) (אורים ותומים) אונ (רוח הקודש) אונ נאך

פֿינף אנדרי זאכֿן הקב״ה וועט מוסיף זיין די ליכֿט פֿון דר

זון דריי הונדרט אונ דריי אונ פֿֿיֿרֿצֿיֿג מאל אזו פֿֿיֿל ווי די שיינט

איצונד אונ די צדיקים וועט הקב״ה אויך אזו דר לייכֿטן ווי די

זון: אונ נאך וועט הקב״ה אום קערן די (כתֿרים) וואש ישראל   250

הבן גהאט אז זי הבן תורה מקבל גוועזן אונ דר נאך האבן זי

פֿר לורן זי אז ווי הבן דש עגל גמאכֿֿט אונ ישראל וועלן גיין אן

גצירט מיט פֿיקן אונ וועלן שפֿילן אונ טאנצן : אונ די ברכֿה וועט

זיין אויף דר תבֿואה דש איז צעהן זאכֿן: אונ קעגן די צעהן

וועט הקב״ה געבן צעהן ארליי גאולות אונ נחמות וואש הקב״ה   255

האט דיא ישראל צו גזאגט דש ערשטי איז דז משיח וועט קומן ווי

אין פֿסוק שטיט (הנה מלכֿך יבֿֿא לך) דש איז דיין מלך המשיח

5b

וועט צו דיר קומן דש אנדרי הקב״ה וועט אײן זאמלן ישראל פֿון
דר גאנצר וועלט ווי עש שטײט אין ירמיה (הנני מביא אתﬗﬞם

260

מארץ צפֿון וקבצתים מירכתי ארץ בם עור ופיסח) וואש איז עור
ופיסח דש בטײט דש הקב״ה וועט מאכן לעבדיג איטלﬔn צדיק
ווי ער איז גוועזן ביי זיין לעבן דהיינו אז ער איז גוועזן בלינד
וועט ער אוף שטײן בתהיית המתים בלינד: אונ ווען ער איז

265

גוועזן קרום וועט ער אויף שטײן קרום אונ דעשט גלייﬡﬞ וואש
פֿר אײן מום כדי אז אײנר זאל דר קענן דען אנדרן אז מען זאל
ניט מיינן דאש זענן גאר אנדרי מענשן אונ דר נאך וועט זיי
הקב״ה הײלין זײַערה מומין: דש דריטי איז תחיית המתים
ווי עש שטײט אין דניאל (ורבים מישיני עפֿר יקיצו) דש איז

270

טײטש אונ פֿיל פֿון די וואש שלאפֿן אין דר ערד וועלן אוף וואﬦﬞن
דש פֿירדי איז דש בנין בית המקדש אז ווי ער האט עש
גזעהן יחזקאל אין דר נבֿואה. דש פֿינפֿטי דש ישראל וועלן
קיניגן פֿון אײן עק וועלט צו דר אנדרר ווי עש שטײט דש פֿאלק
וואש וועט דיך ניט דינן וועט פֿר לורן ווערן פֿון דר וועלט. אונ
כל העולם וועט וויבדר קערן צו גאטש תורה אונ דינים: ווי עש

275

שטײט אין פסוק איך וועל אום קערן כל אומות זי ווערן ריידן
אײן לוימר לשון אונ וועלן אלי אין רופֿן אן גאטש נאמן: דש זעקסטי
הקב״ה וועט מאכן אל די פֿינד פֿון זיין פֿאלק אונ
וועט אן זיי טאן נקמותﬗﬞ ווי עש שטײט אונ איך וועל טאן נקמות
אן אדום דארﬤﬞ מיין פֿאלק ישראל: דש זיבנטי הקב״ה וועט אפ

280

טון פֿון ישראל אל די קרענק אונ וויטאﬡﬞ: וויא עש שטײט אונ
ער וועט ניט זאגן ישראל וואש רוען אין ירושלים איﬤﬞ בין קראנק
דען דש פֿאלק וואש וועט זיצין דרינן האט אים גאט פֿר טראנן די
זינד: דש אﬖﬞטי הקב״ה וועט דר לענגרן די טעג פֿון ישראל אז
דר עץ החיים: דען עש שטײט אין פסוק אז די טעג פֿון דען עץ

285

החיים וועט זיין די טעג פֿון מיין פֿאלק: אונ שטײט ער וועט
אײן גשלונגן ווערן דער טוט אונ גאט ב״ה וועט אפ ווישן די

6a

טרעהרין פֿון אל דעם פנים: דש ניינטי הקב״ה וועט זיﬤﬞ
אנטפֿלעקן צו ישראל פנים אל פנים אונ כל ישראל ווערן זיין
נבֿיאים: דש צעהנטי הקב״ה וועט אפ טון דען יצר הרע אונ אלי

290

ביזי זאﬔﬞ פֿון ישראל ווי אין פסוק שטײט אונ איﬤﬞ וועל איﬤﬞ
געבן אײן נייא הערץ אנו [!] אײן נייא גמוט וועל איﬤﬞ געבן צו
איﬤﬞ אונ איﬤﬞ וועל אוֿ טון דש שטײנדיגי הרץ פֿון איﬤﬞ אונ וועל
איﬤﬞ געבן אײן הרץ פֿון פֿלײש דש מיינט מן אײן גוט הרץ
אמן:

BIBLIOGRAPHY

AKHUNZYANOV, E. M. (1978), 'O genezise literaturnogo yazyka', in O. N. Trubachev et al. (eds.), *Vostochnoslavyanskoe i obshchee yazykoznanie* (Nauka: Moscow), 201-8.

ALTBAUER, M. (1965), 'The Yiddish Rimes of Kh. N. Bialik: A Manifestation of the Trend Toward Standard Yiddish', in U. Weinreich (1965), 182-4.

APTROOT, M. (1988), 'Dutch Impact on Amsterdam Yiddish Prints', in D. Katz (1988a), 7-11.

—— (1989), 'Bible Translation as Cultural Reform: The Amsterdam Yiddish Bibles (1678-1679)' (Oxford D. Phil. thesis).

—— (1991), 'Northwestern Yiddish: The State of Research', in Kerler (1991), 41-59.

ARONSON, H. I. (1985), 'On Aspect in Yiddish', *General Linguistics*, 2: 171-88.

BACH, A. (1961), *Geschichte der deutschen Sprache*, 7th edn. (Quelle & Meyer: Heidelberg).

BALABAN, M. (1912-1916), 'Die Krakauer Judengemeinde-Ordnung von 1595 und ihre Nachträge', *Jahrbuch der jüdischliterarischen Gesellschaft* (Frankfurt), 10 (1912): 296-360; 11 (1916): 88-114.

—— (1935), *Sabatizm w Polsce*, offprint from M. Schorr *festschrift*, separate pagination (Warsaw).

—— (1936), *Historia Żydów w Krakowie i na Kazimierzu 1304-1868*, vol. 2, (Krakow).

BARNET, V. (1976), 'Yazykovaya norma v social'noj kommunikacii', in Filin and Gorshkov (1976), 47-69.

BARTAL, I., MENDELSOHN, E., TURNIANSKY, Ch. (1993) (eds.), *Studies in Jewish Culture in Honour of Chone Shmeruk* (The Zalman Shazar Center for Jewish History: Jerusalem).

BARTSCH, R. (1987), *Norms of Language, Theoretical and Practical Aspects*, (Longman: London and New York).

BEEM, H. (1954), 'Yiddish in Holland: Linguistic and Sociolinguistic Notes', in U. Weinreich (1954), 122-33.

—— (1975), *Resten van een Taal. Woordenboekje van het Nederlandse Jiddisch*, 2nd edn. (van Gorcum B.V.: Assen/Amsterdam).

BEN-SASSON, H. (1976a) (ed.), *A History of the Jewish People* (Weidenfeld and Nicolson: London).

—— (1976b), 'The Social Ideals of Jewry at the end of the Middle Ages', in Ben-Sasson (1976a), 691-723.

BERNFELD, Sh. (1926), *Sefer hadmaot. Meoraot hagzerot veharedifot vehashmadot*, iii (Eschkol: Berlin).

BERNSHTEJN, S. B., SMIRNOV, S. B., and VENEDIKTOV, G. K. (1978) (eds.), *Nacional'noe vozrozhdenie i formirovanie slavyanskikh literaturnykh yazykov* (Nauka: Moscow).

BERNSHTEYN, M. V. (1975), 'Di yidishe drukerayen in Ukrayne', *Yivo bleter* (New York), 45: 9–46.

BESCH, W., KNOOP, U., PUTSCHKE, W., and WIEGAND, E. (1983) (eds.), *Dialektologie. Ein Handbuch zur deutschen und allgemeinen Dialektforschung* [= *Handbuch zur Sprach- und Kommunikationswissenschaft*, 1] (Walter de Gruyter: Berlin & New York).

BESTEN, H. den, and MOED-VAN WALRAVEN, C. (1986), 'The Syntax of Verbs in Yiddish', in H. Haider and M. Prinzhorn (eds.), *Verb Second Phenomena in Germanic Languages* [= Publications in Language Sciences, 21] (Foris Publications: Dordrecht, Holland; Riverton, USA), 111–35.

BICKEL, Sh., and LEHRER, L. (1958) (eds.), *Shmuel Niger bukh* (Bibliotek fun Yivo: New York).

BIN-NUN, J. (1973), *Jiddisch und die deutschen Mundarten. Unter besonderer Berücksichtigung des ostgalizischen Jiddisch* (Max Niemeyer: Tübingen).

BIRNBAUM, S. A. ([1918]), *Praktische Grammatik der Jiddischen Sprache für den Selbstunterricht. Mit Lesestücken und einem Wörterbuch* [*Die Kunst der Polyglottie*, 128] (Vienna and Leipzig).

—— (1926), 'Dialekt un literatur loshn', *Filologishe shriftn* (Vilna), 1: 89–92.

—— (1953), 'Fun daytshmerizm biz der heyl in der midber yehude', *Yidishe shprakh* (New York), 13: 109–20.

—— (1954), 'Two Problems in Yiddish Linguistics', in U. Weinreich (1954), 63–72.

—— (1979), *Yiddish: A Survey and a Grammar* (University of Toronto Press: Toronto and Buffalo).

—— (1987), 'Etymology: davenen', in D. Katz (1987*b*), 11–14.

BLACKALL, E. A. (1978), *The Emergence of German as a Literary Language 1700–1775*, 2nd edn. (Cornell University Press: Ithaca and London).

BLOOMFIELD, L. (1933), *Language* (Holt, Rinehart and Winston: New York).

BOROKHOV, B. (1913), 'Ufgabn fun der yidisher filologye', in Niger (1913*a*), 1–22.

—— (1915), 'Di geshikhte fun der yidisher literatur', reprinted in Borokhov (1966), 178–221.

—— (1926), 'Ber Borokhovs plan far a geshikhte fun yidish' (published by Shmuel Niger in) *Filologishe shriftn* (Vilna), 1: 21–8.

—— (1966), *Shprakh-forshung un literatur-geshikhte*, gezamlt un tsunoyfgeshtelt fun Nakhmen Mayzl (Peretz: Tel Aviv).

BREUER, M. (1989) [M. Broyer], 'Nedudei talmidim vehakhamim—akdamot leperek mitoldot hayeshivot', in M. Ben-Sasson, R. Bonfil, and J. Hacker (eds.), *Culture and Society in Medieval Jewry, Studies Dedicated to the Memory of Haim Hillel Ben-Sasson* (Zalman Shazar Center: Jerusalem), 445–68.

BYNON, Th. (1977), *Historical Linguistics* (Cambridge University Press).

CAHAN, Y. L. (1931), *Yidishe folksmayses* (Yidishe folklor bibliotek: New York and Vilna).

—— (1938), *Yidisher folklor*, unter der redaktsye fun Y. L. Kahan (Filologishe sektsye, komisye far folklor, Yivo: Vilna).

—— (1975), *Yidishe folkslider un melodyes*, tsunoyfgenumen un fun dos nay aroysgegebn durkh Maks Vaynraykh (Bibliotek fun Yivo: New York).

CARMILLY-WEINBERGER, M. (1977), *Censorship and Freedom of Expression in Jewish History* (Sefer-Hermon Press and Yeshiva University Press: New York).

COMRIE, B. (1976), *Aspect. An Introduction to the Study of Verbal Aspect and Related Problems* (Cambridge University Press).

DAHL, Ö. (1985), *Tense and Aspect Systems* (Basil Blackwell: Oxford).

DAN, J. (1974), *Hasipur haivri biyemei habeinayim* (Keter: Jerusalem).

—— (1975) *Sifrut hamusar vehadrush* (Keter: Jerusalem).

DAWIDOWICZ, L., ERLICH, A., ERLIKH, R., and FISHMAN, J. (1964) (eds.), *For Max Weinreich on his Seventieth Birthday. Studies in Jewish Languages, Literature, and Society* (Mouton: The Hague).

DEROY, L. (1956), *L'Emprunt linguistique* (Société d'Édition 'Les Belles Lettres': Paris).

DEVITT, A. J. (1989), *Standardizing Written English: Diffusion in the Case of Scotland 1520-1659* (Cambridge University Press).

DINSE, H. (1974), *Die Entwicklung des jiddischen Schrifttums im deutschen Sprachgebiet* (J. B. Metzler: Stuttgart).

DRESNER, A. (1981), 'Scholem-Alejchems "Jidische folksbibliotek"', *Zeitschrift für deutsche Philologie (Sonderheft Jiddisch)*, 100: 186-94.

DUBNOV, Sh. (1909), 'Razgovornyj yazyk i narodnaya literatura pol'sko-litovskikh evreev v XVI i pervoj polovine XVII veka', *Evrejskaya starina* (Petrograd), 1: 7-40.

—— (1929), 'Der tsveyter khurbn fun Ukrayne (1768). Di folks-khronik "Mayse gdoyle min Uman umin Ukrayne"', *Historishe shriftn fun Yivo* (Warsaw), 1: 27-54.

—— (1953), *Di velt geshikhte fun yidishn folk*, vii: *Geshikhte fun yidn in eyrope zint dem onheyb fun bazetsn zikh bizn sof 18tn y[or]'h[undert]* (Alveltleker yidisher kultur-kongres: Buenos Aires).

ELBAUM, J. (1990) [Y. Elboym], *Ptihut vehistagrut, hayecira haruhanit-hasifrutit bePolin beshilhei hamea hashesh-esre* (Hebrew University, Magnes Press: Jerusalem).

ERIK, M. (1926), *Vegn altyidishn roman un novele, fertsnter-zekhtsnter yorhundert* [Druk: 'Brandes i Kaweberg' Kowel] ('Der veg tsum visn', Farlag Meyer Rayz: Warsaw).

—— (1928), *Di geshikhte fun der yidisher literatur fun di eltste tsaytn biz der haskole-tkufe* (Kultur-lige: Warsaw).

—— (1935), 'Di yidishe literatur in Rusland in der biz-reform-epokhe 1800-1861', in M. Erik and A. Rozentsvayg, *Di yidishe literatur in XIX yorhundert. Ershter bukh: 1800-1881* (Ukrmelukhenatsmindfarlag: Kiev).

ETTINGER, Sh. (1972), 'Haidamacks', in *Encyclopaedia Judaica* (Keter: Jerusalem), vii. 1132-3.

—— (1976), 'The Jewish Community in Western and Central Europe', in Ben-Sasson (1976a), 777-89.

EVEN-SHMUEL, Y. (1954), *Midreshei geula. Pirkei haapokalipsa hayehudit mihatimat hatalmud vead reshit haelef hashishi* (Massada: Jerusalem and Tel Aviv).

FALK, F. (1961), *Das Schemuelbuch des Mosche Esrim Wearba: Ein biblisches Epos aus dem 15. Jarhundert*, Einleitung und textkritischer Apparat von Felix Falk, aus dem

Nachlass herausgegeben von L. Fuks, i: *Einleitung und Faksimile der editio princeps, Augsburg, 1544*; ii: *Textkritischer Apparat* (van Gorcum: Assen).

FALKOVITSH, E. (1940), *Yidish: fonetik, grafik, leksik un gramatik* (Der emes: Moscow).

—— (1966), 'Idish', in V. Vinogradov *et al.* (eds.), *Yazyki narodov SSSR* (Nauka: Moscow), i: 599-629.

—— (1984), 'O yazyke idish', in Shapiro *et al.* (1984), 666-720.

FAUCHER, E. (1984), *L'Ordre pour la clôture: essai sur la place du verbe en allemand moderne* (Presses Universitaires de Nancy: Nancy).

FEVRE, L., and MARTIN, H. (1984), *The Coming of the Book: The Impact of Printing 1450-1800*, trans. by David Gerard, ed. by Geoffrey Nowell-Smith and David Wootton (Verso Editions: London).

FILIN, F., and GORSHKOV, A. (1976) (eds.), *Problemy normy v slavyanskikh literaturnykh yazykakh v sinkhronnom i diakhronnom aspektakh* (Nauka: Moscow).

FISHMAN, D. E. (1991), 'Mikoyakh davnen af yidish: a bintl metodologishe bamerkungen un naye mekoyrim', *Yivo bleter* (New Series, New York), 1: 69-92.

FISHMAN, J. A. (1971), *Sociolinguistics. A Brief Introduction* (Newbury House: Rowley, Mass.).

—— (1973) 'The Phenomenological and Linguistic Pilgrimage of Yiddish: Some Examples of Functional and Structural Pidginization and Depidginization', *Kansas Journal of Sociology*, 9: 127-36 [page references to Fishman (1991), 189-201].

—— (1976), 'Yiddish and Loshn Koydesh in Traditional Ashkenaz: On the Problem of Societal Allocation of Macrofunctions', in A. Verdoodt and R. Kjolseth (eds.), *Language in Sociology* (Éditions Peeters: Louvain), 39-47.

—— (1977) (ed.), *Advances in the Creation and Revision of Writing Systems* (Mouton: The Hague).

—— (1980), 'Attracting a Following to High-Culture Functions for a Language of Everyday Life: The Role of the Tshernovits Conference in the "Rise of Yiddish" ', *International Journal of the Sociology of Language*, 24: 43-73.

—— (1981), 'The Sociology of Jewish Languages from the Perspective of the General Sociology of Language: A Preliminary Formulation', *International Journal of the Sociology of Language*, 30: 5-16.

—— (1985a) (ed.), *Readings in the Sociology of Jewish Languages* (E. J. Brill: Leiden).

—— (1985b), 'The Sociology of Jewish Languages from a General Sociolinguistic Point of View', in Fishman (1985a), 3-11.

—— (1989), *Language and Ethnicity in Minority Sociolinguistic Perspective* (Multilingual Matters: Clevedon, Philadelphia).

—— (1991), *Yiddish: Turning to Life* (John Benjamins Publishing Company: Amsterdam/Philadelphia).

FLEISS, P. M. (1912), 'Das Buch Simchath Hanefesch von Henele Kirchhain aus dem Jahre 1727. Reimuntersuchung als Beitrag zur Kenntnis der jüdisch-deutschen Mundarten' (Inaugural-Dissertation der philosophischen Fakultät der Universität Bern zur Erlangung der Doktorwürde).

FRAKES, J. C. (1989), *The Politics of Interpretation: Alterity and Ideology in Old Yiddish Studies* (State University of New York Press: Albany).

FRIDBERG, M. (1961), 'Slozhnopodchinyonnoe predlozhenie v idish-tajch XVI–XVIII vv. (k voprosu o vliyanii semiticheskikh i slavyanskikh yazykov na sintaksicheskij stroj idish)', in *Voprosy sintaksisa romano-germanskikh yazykov* (Leningrad University: Leningrad), 79–98.

——(1968), 'Èvolyuciya sredneverkhnenemeckikh soyuzov "daz" i "als" v idish i vozniknovenie soyuza "vos". (K voprosu o vliyanii slavyanskikh yazykov na sintaksicheskij stroj idish)', *Vestnik Leningradskogo Universiteta*, 22: 147–58.

FRIEDBERG, B. (1950), *Toldot hadfus haivri bePolania, mireshit hivasdo bishnat 1537 vehitpathuto ad zmaneinu*, 2nd edn. (Tel Aviv).

——(1951), *Bet Eked Sfarim. Bibliographical Lexicon* (4 vols., Tel Aviv).

FRIEDRICH, C. W. (1784), *Unterricht in der Judensprache, und Schrift. zum Gebrauch für Gelehrte und Ungelehrte* (Chr. Gottf. Ragoczy: Prenzlau).

FUKS, L. (1965), *Das altjiddische Epos Melokîm-bûk*, i: *Einleitung und Faksimile der editio princeps, Augsburg, 1543*; ii: *Hebräische und aramäische Quellen, textkritischer Apparat, und Glossar* (van Gorcum: Assen).

——(1981), 'Menachem Man ben Salomo Halevi und sein jiddisches Geschichtswerk "Sche'erit Jisrael"', *Zeitschrift für deutsche Philologie (Sonderheft Jiddisch)*, 100: 170–86.

——(1983) 'Amsterdam, a yidisher literatur tsenter in 17tn un 18tn yorhundert', *Di goldene keyt* (Tel Aviv) 115: 183–94.

GASTER, M. (1934) (ed.), *Ma'aseh Book: Book of Jewish Tales and Legends*, translated from the Judaeo-German by Moses Gaster (Jewish Publication Society of America: Philadelphia).

GITLIC, M. M. (1940), 'K voprosu o specifike i putyakh razvitiya evrejskogo yazyka (idish)', *Yazyk i myshlenie* (Akademiya Nauk SSSR: Moscow and Leningrad), 9: 47–56.

GLINERT, L. (1993) (ed.), *Hebrew in Ashkenaz: A Language in Exile* (Oxford University Press: New York and Oxford).

GOLDBERG, D. (1986), 'Nekudat hamifgash bein dialekt leharuz beyidish', *Ha-Sifrut* (Tel Aviv), 35–6: 220–7.

——(1993) (ed.), *The Field of Yiddish Studies in Language, Folklore, and Literature*, Fifth Collection (Northwestern University Press and The Yivo Institute for Jewish Research: Evanston, Illinois).

GOLDWASSER, M. (1982), *"Azhoras Noshim": a Linguistic Study of a Sixteenth Century Yiddish Work* [= Working Papers in Yiddish and East European Jewish Studies, 33] (Yivo: New York).

GUCHMANN, M. (1955) [M. Gukhman], *Ot yazyka nemeckoj narodnosti k nemeckomu nacional'nomu yazyku*, Part 1: *Razvitie nemeckoj narodnosti* (Akademiya Nauk SSSR: Moscow).

——(1959), *Ot yazyka nemeckoj narodnosti k nemeckomu nacional'nomu yazyku*, Part 2: *Stanovlenie nemeckogo literaturnogo nacional'nogo yazyka* (Akademiya Nauk SSSR: Moscow).

——(1968), 'Some General Regularities in the Formation and Development of National Languages', in J. A. Fishman (ed.), *Readings in the Sociology of Language*

(Mouton: The Hague), 766–79.

GUCHMANN, M. (1977), 'Sootnoshenie social'noj differenciacii i drugikh tipov var'irovaniya literaturnogo yazyka', in Yarceva and Guchmann (1977), 41–60.

GUGGENHEIM-GRÜNBERG, F. (1950), Die Sprache der Schweizer Juden von Endingen und Lengnau (offprint from Israelitisches Wochenblatt für die Schweiz, Zürich).

——(1954), 'The Horse Dealers' Language of the Swiss Jews in Endingen and Lengnau', in U. Weinreich (1954), 48–62.

——(1964), 'Überreste westjiddischer Dialekte in der Schweiz, im Elsaß und in Süddeutschland', in Dawidowicz et al. (1964), 72–81.

——(1969), 'Endinger Jiddisch', in Herzog et al. (1969), 8–15.

GURLAND, Kh. (1847), Lekoroys hagzeyroys al Yisroel [= Lekorot hagzerot al Yisrael] (Przemyśl).

——(1886), Lekoroys hagzeyroys al Yisroel [= Lekorot hagzerot al Yisrael] (Eisig Gräber: Przemyśl).

——(1892), Lekoroys hagzeyroys al Yisroel [= Lekorot hagzerot al Yisrael], published by D. Kahane (Odessa).

HARKAVY, A. (1928), Yiddish–English–Hebrew Dictionary (Hebrew Publishing Company: New York).

HARRIS, R. (1980), The Language-Makers (Duckworth: London).

——(1981), The Language Myth (Duckworth: London).

——(1987), The Language Machine (Duckworth: London).

——(1990), 'On Redefining Linguistics', in H. Davis and T. Taylor (eds.), Redefining Linguistics (Routledge: London and New York), 18–52.

HARSHAV, B. (1990), The Meaning of Yiddish (University of California Press: Berkeley, Los Angeles, Oxford).

HENZEN, W. (1954), Schriftsprache und Mundarten. Ein Überblick über ihr Verhältnis und ihre Zwischenstufen im Deutschen, 2nd edn. (Francke Verlag: Bern).

HERZOG, M. I. (1965a), The Yiddish Language in Northern Poland: Its Geography and History [= International Journal of American Linguistics, 31, no. 2, Part III] (Indiana University Research Center in Anthropology, Folklore, and Linguistics: Bloomington, Ind., and The Hague).

——(1965b), 'Grammatical Features of Markuze's "Sejfer Refues" (1790)', in U. Weinreich (1965), 49–62.

——(1969), 'Yiddish in the Ukraine: Isoglosses and Historical Inferences', in Herzog et al. (1969), 58–81.

——(1974), 'Yiddish', reprint from Encyclopaedia Britannica, 15th edn., 'Germanic Languages' (Macropaedia), 25–6.

——(1978), 'Yiddish', in H. Paper (ed.), Jewish Languages—Theme and Variations, Proceedings of Regional Conferences of the Association for Jewish Studies held at the University of Michigan and New York University in March–April 1975.

HERZOG, M., RAVID, W., and WEINREICH, U. (1969) (eds.), The Field of Yiddish: Studies in Language, Folklore, and Literature. Third Collection (Mouton: The Hague).

——KIRSHENBLATT-GIMBLETT, B., MIRON, D., and WISSE, R. (1980) (eds.), The Field of Yiddish: Studies in Language, Folklore, and Literature. Fourth Collection

(Mouton: The Hague).

HILEY, Sh. (1990), 'Ibern onheyb fun Ashkenaz un yidish', *Oksforder yidish*, 1: 107-14.

HIRSCHFELD, H. (1926), *Literary History of Hebrew Grammarians and Lexicographers* (Oxford University Press: London).

HUDSON, R. (1992), *Teaching Grammar: A Guide for the National Curriculum* (Blackwell: Oxford and Cambridge, Mass.).

HUTTON, C. M. (1984), 'Normativism in Yiddish—Definitions and Categories' (MA essay, Department of Linguistics, Columbia University, New York).

——(1987), 'Negation in Yiddish and Historical Reconstruction', in D. Katz (1987*b*), 27-37.

——(1993), 'Normativism and the Notion of Authenticity in Yiddish Linguistics', in Goldberg (1993), 11-57.

IZRAELSON, Y. (1929), 'Nosn-Nete Hanover, zayn lebn un literarishe tetikayt', *Historishe shriftn fun Yivo* (Warsaw), 1: 1-26.

JEDLIČKA, A. (1967), 'O prazhskoj teorii literaturnogo yazyka', in Kondrashova (1967), 544-56.

——(1976), 'Problematika normy i kodifikacii literaturnogo yazyka', in Filin and Gorshkov (1976), 16-39.

——(1983), 'Entwicklungstendenzen der Literatursprache aus vergleichender Sicht', in D. Nerius (ed.), *Entwicklungstendenzen der deutschen Sprache seit dem 18. Jahrhundert*, Linguistische Studien, Reihe A, Arbeitsberichte 111 (Akademie der Wissenschaften der DDR: Berlin), 50-60.

JELLINEK, A. (1938), *Beit hamidrash* (6 vols., 3rd edn., repr. 1969 by Wahrman Books: Jerusalem).

JOFFE, J. A. (1928), 'Der slavisher element in yidish', *Pinkes fun amopteyl fun Yivo* (New York), 3: 235-56; 4: 296-312.

——(1934), 'Di ershte oysgabe fun "Kav hayosher"', *Yivo bleter* (Vilna), 7: 78-87.

——(1940), 'Hundert un fuftsik yor yidish', *Yivo bleter* (New York), 15: 87-102.

——(1949), *Elia Bachur's Poetical Works: Reproduction of Bovobuch 1st edn., 1541* (Judah A. Joffe Publication Committee: [New York]).

——(1954), 'Dating the Origin of Yiddish Dialects', in U. Weinreich (1954), 102-33.

——(1964), 'Der genitiv in yidish', *Yidishe shprakh* (New York), 24: 19-23, 52-6.

KAHAN-NEWMAN, Z. (1988), 'The Discoursal "iz" of Yiddish', in Y. Tobin (ed.), *The Prague School and its Legacy in Linguistics, Folklore, and the Arts* (John Benjamins: Amsterdam/Philadelphia), 73-90.

——(1990), 'Another Look at Yiddish Scribal Language', in Wexler (1990), 35-46.

KALMANOVITSH, Z. (1937), 'Yoysef Perls yidishe ksovim, literarisher un shprakhiker analiz', in *Yoysef Perls yidishe ksovim* gefunen in der Tarnopoler Perl-bibliotek Yisroel Vaynlez (Bibliotek fun Yivo: Vilna).

KATZ, Dovid (1982), 'Explorations in the History of the Semitic Component in Yiddish' (Ph.D. thesis, 2 vols., Department of Hebrew and Jewish Studies and Department of Phonetics and Linguistics, University College, London).

KATZ, Dovid (1983), 'Zur Dialektologie des Jiddischen', in W. Besch *et al.* (1983), 1018-41.

——(1985), 'Hebrew, Aramaic and the Rise of Yiddish', in Fishman (1985a), 85-103.

——(1986), 'Hayesod hashemi beyidish: yerusha miyemei kedem (metodot veefsharuyot)', *Ha-Sifrut* (Tel Aviv), 35-6: 228-51 [see also D. Katz 1991b].

——(1987a), *Grammar of the Yiddish Language* (Duckworth: London).

——(1987b) (ed.), *Origins of the Yiddish Language* [= *Winter Studies in Yiddish*, i; supplement to *Language & Communication: An Interdisciplinary Journal*] (Pergamon Press: Oxford).

——(1988a) (ed.), *Dialects of the Yiddish Language* [= *Winter Studies in Yiddish*, ii; supplement to *Language & Communication: An Interdisciplinary Journal*] (Pergamon Press: Oxford).

——(1988b), 'Origins of Yiddish Dialectology', in D. Katz (1988a), 39-55.

——(1988c), 'Protolanguage Theory: The Case of Yiddish', paper placed before the seminar on Topics in Linguistics and Philology, St Hugh's College, Oxford, 17 May.

——(1990), 'Di eltere yidishe leksikografye: notitsn iber mekoyres un metodn', *Oksforder yidish* (Oxford), 1: 161-232.

——(1991a), 'The Children of Heth and the Ego of Linguistics: A Story of Seven Yiddish Mergers', *Transactions of the Philological Society* (Basil Blackwell: Oxford), lxxxix, 1: 95-121 [see also D. Katz 1993c].

——(1991b), 'Der semitisher kheylek in yidish: a yerushe fun kadmoynim', *Oksforder yidish* (Oxford), 2: 17-95.

——(1991c), 'A Late Twentieth Century Case of "katóves"', in Kerler (1991), 141-63.

——(1993a), *Tikney takones, fragn fun yidisher stilistik* (Oksforder Yidish Press: Oxford).

——(1993b), 'The Phonology of Ashkenazic [Hebrew]', in Glinert (1993), 46-87.

——(1993c), 'East and West, "khes" and "shin" and the Origin of Yiddish', in Bartal *et al.* (1993), 9*-37* [see also D. Katz 1991a].

——(1994), 'Di naye gilgulim fun alte makhloykesn: di litvishe norme un di sikhsukhim vos arum ir', *Yivo bleter* (New Series, New York), 2: 205-57.

——(1996), 'Tsvelf shites, zeks hundert yor: di yidishe lingvistik', *Yerushalaymer Almanakh* (Jerusalem), 26: 225-57.

KATZ, J. (1978), *Masoret umashber, hahevra hayehudit bemocaei yemei-habeinayim* (Mosad Bialik: Jerusalem).

KERLER, D.-B. (1988a), 'East Meets West: the Dialectal Climate of Two Early Eastern European Yiddish Prints', in D. Katz (1988a), 69-84.

——(1988b), 'The Eighteenth Century Origins of Modern Literary Yiddish' (Oxford D.Phil. thesis).

——(1990), 'Di haskholes fun der moderner literatur-shprakh (1771-1798)', *Oksforder yidish* (Oxford), 1: 271-316.

——(1991) (ed.), *History of Yiddish Studies* [=*Winter Studies in Yiddish*, iii] (Harwood Academic Publishers and OCPHS).

KING, R. D. (1968), *Historical Linguistics and Generative Grammar* (Prentice-Hall: Englewood Cliffs, NJ).

——(1980), 'The History of Final Devoicing in Yiddish', in Herzog *et al.* (1980), 371–430.

——(1987), 'Proto Yiddish Morphology', in D. Katz (1987*b*), 73–81.

——(1990), 'On the Origins of the 's-'plural in Yiddish', in Wexler (1990), 47–53.

KIRKNESS, A. (1975), *Zur Sprachreinigung im Deutschen 1789–1871. Eine historische Dokumentation.* Forschungsberichte des Instituts für deutsche Sprache, Bände 26.1–26.2 (TBL Verlag Gunter Narr: Tübingen).

KON, P. (1936), *Di haskhole fun yidishn druk-vezn un di ershte yidishe zetser in Grodne un Vilne* (Kletskin: Vilna).

KONDRASHOVA, N. A. (1967) (ed.), *Prazhskij lingvisticheskij kruzhok*, sbornik statej (Progress: Moscow).

KOSOVER, M. (1958), 'Yidishe maykholim (a shtudye in kultur-geshikhte un shprakhforshung)', in Mark (1958*a*), 1–145.

——(1967), 'Yidishe glosn in der rabonisher literatur', in Shtarkman (1967), 232–61.

KUKENHEIM, L. (1951), *Contribution à l'histoire de la grammaire grecque, latine et hébraïque à l'époque de la Renaissance* (E. J. Brill: Leiden).

LANDAU, A. (1896), 'Das Deminutivum der galizisch-jüdischen Mundart', *Deutsche Mundarten*, 1: 46–58.

——(1901), 'Die Sprache Memorien Glückels von Hameln', *Mitteilungen der Gesellschaft für jüdische Volkskunde* (Hamburg), 7: 20–68.

——(1924), 'Miluyim tsu M. Vaynraykhs "Shtaplen" ', *Yidishe filologye* (Warsaw), 1: 55–61.

——(1927–1929), 'Di slavishe elementn un hashpoes in yidish', *Filologishe shriftn* (Vilna), 2: 199–214, 3: 615–16.

LEHISTE, Ilse (1988), *Lectures on Language Contact* (MIT Press: Cambridge, Mass., and London).

LEIBOWITZ, N. (1931), 'Die Übersetzungstechnik der jüdisch-deutschen Bibelübersetzungen des XV. und XVI. Jahrhunderts, dargestellt an den Psalmen', *Beiträge zur Geschichte der deutschen Sprache und Literatur*, 55: 377–463.

LEITH, D. (1983), *A Social History of English* [Language and Society Series] (Routledge & Kegan Paul: London, Boston, Melbourne, and Henley).

LERNER, R. (1937), 'Der genezis fun genitiv-posesiv', *Afn shprakhfront* (Kiev), 2nd ser., 1: 126–49.

——(1939), 'Tsu der geshikhte fun der literarisher shprakh onheyb 19-tn yorhundert', *Afn shprakhfront* (Kiev), 2nd ser., 3: 165–90.

LIBERMAN, Kh. (1952), 'Bamerkungen tsu Shloyme Nobls artikl: "r[eb] Yekhiel Mikhl Epshteyn—a dertsyer un kemfer far yidish in 17tn yorhundert" ', *Yivo bleter* (New York), 36: 305–19.

——(1980), *Oyhel RoKHL* (2 vols., Empire Press: New York).

LIFSHITS, Y. (1876), *Yidish-rusisher verter bikh* (Zhitomir).

LINCOFF, B. (1963), 'A Study in Inflectional Morphologic Development: Old and

Middle Yiddish' (Ph.D. diss., New York University) [= University Microfilms International: Ann Arbor, Mich., 1981].

LINDGREN, K. B. (1953), *Die Apokope des mittelhochdeutschen -e in seinen verschiedenen Funktionen* (Annales Academiae Scientiarum Fennicae: Helsinki).

LIPSCHITZ, E. (1944), *Doyres dertseyln, materyaln tsu der geshikhte fun yidn in mitlalter un in der nayer tsayt (362-1848)* (Matones: New York).

LITINSKI, M. N. (1894), 'Tsu der geshikhte fun yidn in Podolyen. Nokh eyn dokument tsu gzeyres Gonte in Ukrayne', *Der hoyzfraynd* (Warsaw), 3: 188-91.

—— (1895), *Seyfer koyroys Podolia* (Odessa).

LOCKWOOD, W. B. (1968), *Historical German Syntax* (Clarendon Press: Oxford).

LOCKWOOD-BAVISKAR, V. (1974), *The Position of Aspect in the Verbal System of Yiddish* [= Working Papers in Yiddish and East European Jewish Studies, 1] (Yivo: New York).

—— (1975), *Negation in a Sample of 17th century Western Yiddish* [= Working Papers in Yiddish and East European Jewish Studies, 14] (Yivo: New York).

MAHLER, R. (1971), *A History of Modern Jewry, 1780-1815* (Vallentine, Mitchell: London).

MAITLIS, J. (1958), *The Ma'aseh in the Yiddish Ethical Literature* (Shapiro, Vallentine & Co.: London).

—— (1978), *Midrash lePirkei Avot beyidish kameyit leAnshl Levi* [Eng. title: *An Old Yiddish Midrash to the 'Chapters of the Fathers'*], edited from the manuscript with an Introduction and Annotations (Publications of the Israel Academy of Sciences and Humanities: Jerusalem).

MARK, Y. (1944*a*), 'A farglaykh tsvishn fir iberzetsungen fun koheles', *Yidishe shprakh* (New York), 4: 1-16.

—— (1944*b*), 'Di litvishe yidn un der neytraler min', *Yidishe shprakh* (New York), 4: 83-94.

—— (1944*c*), 'Di prepozitsye "in"', *Yidishe shprakh* (New York), 4: 129-35.

—— (1946), 'Der verter-seyder in poshetn zats', *Yidishe shprakh* (New York), 6: 84-105.

—— (1954), 'Undzer litvisher yidish', in M. Sudarsky *et al.* (eds.), *Lite* (New York), i. 429-72.

—— (1958*a*) (ed.), *Yuda A. Yofe bukh* (Yivo: New York).

—— (1958*b*), 'Yidish-hebreyish un hebreyish-yidishe nayshafungen', in Bickel and Lehrer (1958), 124-57.

—— (1959), 'In farteydikung fun shtumen alef', *Yidishe shprakh* (New York), 19: 1-16.

—— (1967), 'Tsu der geshikhte fun der yidisher literatur-shprakh', in Shtarkman (1967), 121-43.

—— (1971) (ed.), *Groyser verterbukh fun der yidisher shprakh*, iii (Komitet farn groysn verterbukh fun der yidisher shprakh: New York).

—— (1978), *Gramatik fun der yidisher klal-shprakh* (Alveltlekher yidisher kultur-kongres: New York).

—— (1980) (ed.), *Groyser verterbukh fun der yidisher shprakh*, vi (Komitet farn groysn verterbukh fun der yidisher shprakh: New York and Jerusalem).

—— and JOFFE, J. A. (1966) (eds.), *Groyser verterbukh fun der yidisher shprakh*, ii (Komitet farn groysn verterbukh fun der yidisher shprakh: New York).

MASHBITZ, D. (1970), 'The Emergence of Modern Yiddish in Literature: Mendl Lefin's Translation of Ecclesiastes of 1819' (MA essay, Columbia University, New York).

MATRAS, Y. (1991), 'Zur Rekonstruktion des jüdischdeutschen Wortschatzen in den Mundarten ehemaliger "Judendörfer" in Südwestdeutschland', *Zeitschrift für Dialektologie und Linguistik*, 58.3: 265–93.

MIESES, M. (1924), *Die Jiddische Sprache. Eine historische Grammatik des Idioms der integralen Juden Ost- und Mitteleuropas* (Benjamin Harz: Berlin and Vienna).

MILLER, D. N. (1987), 'Transgressing the Bounds: On the Origins of Yiddish Literature', in D. Katz (1987b), 95–103.

——(1991), 'Literary History and the Politics of Allusion', in Kerler (1991), 93–102.

MINKOV, N. B., and JOFFE, J. A. (1942), 'Alt-yidishe literatur', in *Algemeyne entsiklopedye*, supplementary volume: *Yidn III* (Dubnov Fond: Paris), 5–63.

MOSKOVICH, W. (1984), 'An Important Event in Soviet Yiddish Cultural Life: The New Russian-Yiddish Dictionary', *Soviet Jewish Affairs* (London), 14: 31–49.

—— and WOLF, M. (1981), 'The Great Dictionary of the Yiddish Language: Designs and Prospects', in *Zeitschrift für deutsche Philologie* (*Sonderheft Jiddisch*), 100: 55–78.

NATH, H. (1988), 'A Comparative Study of Aspect in the Russian and Yiddish Verb' (MA thesis, Columbia University, New York).

NIGER, Sh. (1913a) (ed.), *Der Pinkes. Yorbukh far der geshikhte fun der yidisher literatur un shprakh, far folklor, kritik un biblyografye* (Kletskin: Vilna).

——(1913b), 'Shtudyes tsu der geshikhte fun der yidisher literatur. Di yidishe literatur—un di lezern', in Sh. Niger (1913a), 138–85.

——(1928), 'Der yikhes fun der yidisher literatur', in *Tog* (New York), 25 May and 1, 17, and 24 June [page reference to Niger (1959), 11–34].

——(1932), 'R[eb] Nakhmen Braslaver un zayne mayses', Foreword to Y. Spivak, *R[eb] Nakhmen Braslaver* (Kletskin: Vilna) [page references to Niger (1959), 111–77].

——(1944), 'Vegn dem onheyb fun der nayer yidisher literatur', *Di Tsukunft* (New York) [page references to Niger (1959), 209–79].

——(1948) (ed.), *Kidesh hashem, a zamlung geklibene, oft gekirtste barikhtn, briv, khronikes, tsavoes, ufshriftn, legendes, lider, dertseylungen, dramatishe stsenes, eseyen, vos moln oys mesires nefesh in undzer un oykh in friyerdike tsaytn*, gezamlt un redaktirt fun Sh[muel] Niger (Cyco farlag: New York).

——(1959), *Bleter geshikhte fun der yidisher literatur*, tsunoyfgeshtelt fun H. Leivik (Alveltlekher yidisher kultur-kongres: New York).

NOBLE, Sh. (1943), *Khumesh-taytsh. An oysforshung vegn der traditsye fun taytshn khumesh in di khadorem* (Bibliotek fun Yivo: New York).

——(1951), 'R[eb] Yekhiel Mikhl Epshteyn—a dertsiyer un kemfer far yidish in 17tn yorhundert', *Yivo bleter* (New York), 35: 121–38.

332 BIBLIOGRAPHY

NOBLE, Sh. (1952), 'A tshuve Kh[ayim] Libermanen', *Yivo bleter* (New York), 36: 319-21.

——(1958), 'Yidish in a hebreyish levush', in Bickel and Lehrer (1958), 158-75.

——(1964), 'Hebreyizmen in dem yidish fun mitl-ashkenaz in 17tn yorhundert', in Dawidowicz *et al.* (1964), 411-501.

OL'KHOVIKOV, B. A. (1985), *Teoriya yazyka i vid grammaticheskogo opisaniya v istorii yazykoznaniya. Stanovlenie i èvolyuciya kanona grammaticheskogo opisaniya v Evrope* (Nauka: Moscow).

PAPER, H. (1954), 'An Early Case of Standard German in Hebrew Orthography', in U. Weinreich (1954), 143-6.

PELTZ, R. (1981), 'Dehebraization as an Issue in the Language Planning Efforts of the Soviet Yiddish Linguistics' (MA essay, Linguistics Department, Columbia University, New York).

PIEKARZ, M. (1964) [M. Pyekazh], 'Vegn "yidishizm" in sof fun 17tn yorhundert un der ershter helft fun 18tn yorhundert', *Di goldene keyt* (Tel Aviv), 49: 168-80.

——(1972), *Hasidut Braslav; prakim behaiei meholela uvikhtaveia* (Mosad Bialik: Jerusalem).

PRILUTSKI, N. (1917*a*), 'A yidishist fun 18 yorhundert', in *Noyakh Prolutskis zamlbikher far yidishn folklor, filologye un kulturgeshikhte*, ii: 1-56;

——(1917*b*), *Der yidisher konsonantizm* [= *Yidishe dialektologishe forshungen*, i] (Warsaw).

——(1920*a*), *Dialektologishe paraleln un bamerkungen* [= *Yidishe dialektologishe forshungen*, iii] (Warsaw).

——(1920*b*), *Tsum yidishn vokalizm, etyudn* [= *Yidishe dialektologishe forshungen*, iv] (Warsaw).

——(1924*a*), *Mame-loshn; yidishe shprakhvisnshaftlekhe forarbetn* [= *Yidishe dialektologishe forshungen*, v] (Kultur-lige: Warsaw).

——(1924*b*), 'Ile, ilts, ilemen ukh[doyme]', *Yidishe filologye* (Warsaw), 1: 220-1.

——(1931), 'Biblyologishe notitsn', *Yivo bleter* (Vilna), 1: 220-31; 408-25.

——(1932), 'Vi azoy di rusishe tsenzur hot gebalebatevet in der "Bove-mayse", biblyologisher notits', *Yivo bleter* (Vilna), 3: 354-70.

REKHTMAN, M. (1952), '"Di shnayders" oder "di shnayder"? "Di lerers" oder "di lerer"?',*Yidishe shprakh* (New York), 12: 43-7.

REMENIK, H. (1971), 'Grunt-etapn fun der nayer yidisher literatur (tsu der frage vegn periodizatsye)', *Sovetish heymland* (Moscow), 1: 165-73.

REYZEN, Z. (1920), *Gramatik fun der yidisher shprakh, Ershter teyl* (Sh. Shreberk: Vilna).

——(1923), *Fun Mendelson biz Mendele. Hantbukh far der geshikhte fun der yidisher haskole-literatur mit reproduktsyes un bilder* (Warsaw).

——(1931*a*), 'Tsu der geshikhte fun yidisher haskole-literatur', *Yivo bleter* (Vilna), 1: 193-207 [page references to Reyzen 1965].

——(1931*b*), 'Naye arbetn tsu der geshikhte fun yidisher haskole-literatur', *Yivo bleter* (Vilna), 1: 367-89 [page references to Reyzen 1965].

——(1932), 'Tsu der geshikhte fun der yidisher folks-literatur', *Yivo bleter* (Vilna),

5: 240-59 [page references to Reyzen 1965].

——(1965), *Yidishe literatur un yidishe shprakh* [= *Musterverk fun der yidisher literatur*, 24] (Literatur-gezelshaft bam Yivo in Argentine: Buenos Aires).

ROBINS, R. H. (1967), *A Short History of Linguistics* (Longmans: London).

ROSENFELD, M. N. (1978), 'The Origins of Yiddish Printing', in D. Katz (1987*b*), 111-26.

——(1988), Personal communication, letter dated: 16.05.1988, London.

ROSKIES, D. (1974*a*), 'Yidishe shraybshprakhn in nayntsntn yorhundert', *Yidishe shprakh* (New York), 33: 1-11.

——(1974*b*), 'Ayzik-Meyer Dik and the Rise of Yiddish Popular Literature' (Ph.D. diss., Brandeis University).

ROSMAN, M. (1981), Introduction to *Sipurei hagzerot bishnot TH"aH veTH"aT* [= *Texts on the Massacres of the Years 1648-1649*], Ben-Zion Dinur Center for Research of Jewish History, 'Kuntresim', 19 (Hebrew University: Jerusalem).

ROTHSTEIN, R. A. (1990), 'Yiddish Aspectology' [Review of Schaechter 1951], in Wexler 1990: 144-53.

RUBASHOV, Z. (1929), 'Yidishe gviyes eydes in di shayles-utshuves fun onheyb XV biz sof XVII y[or]"h[undert]', *Historishe shriftn fun Yivo* (Warsaw), 1: 115-96 [see also Shazar 1971].

SAMUELS, M. L. (1972), *Linguistic Evolution. With Special Reference to English* [Cambridge Studies in Linguistics, 5] (Cambridge University Press).

SAND, I. (1965), 'A Linguistic Comparison of Five Versions of the "Mayse-Bukh" (16th-18th centuries)', in U. Weinreich (1965), 24-48.

SAPIR, E. (1915), 'Notes on Judeo-German Phonology', *Jewish Quarterly Review*, 4: 231-6 [page reference to Edward Sapir, *Selected Writings in Language, Culture, and Personality* (University of California Press: Berkeley, Los Angeles, London, 1985), 252-72].

SCAGLIONE, A. (1981), *The Theory of German Word Order from the Renaissance to the Present* (University of Minnesota Press: Minneapolis).

SCHAECHTER, M. (1951), 'Aktionen im Jiddischen: Ein sprachwissenschaftlicher Beitrag zur Bedeutungslehre des Verbums' (Ph.D. diss. University of Vienna) [= University Microfilms International: Ann Arbor, Mich. 1986].

——(1952*a*), 'Di tushteygers in der yidisher shprakh', *Yiddishe shprakh* (New York), 12: 83-9.

——(1952*b*), 'Di shtam-konstruktsye', *Yiddishe shprakh* (New York), 12: 11-17.

——(1969), 'The "Hidden Standard": A Study of Competing Influences in Standardization', in Herzog *et al.* (1969), 284-304.

——(1977), 'Four Schools of Thought in Yiddish Language Planning', *Michigan Germanic Studies*, 3.2: 34-66.

——(1986), *Laytish mame-loshn: observatsyes un rekomendatsyes* (Yidish-lige: New York).

SCHISCHA, A. (1986), '"Ben hamelekh vehanazir" umetargemo leyidish; hatirgum vegoralo', *Alei Sefer* (Bar-Ilan University: Ramat Gan), 12: 111-23.

SCHNEIDER, D. (1988), 'Is there a Mystical Dialect in Modern Yiddish Drama?', in D.

Katz (1988a), 105–19.

SCHOHETMAN, B. (1972), 'Uman', in *Encyclopaedia Judaica* (Keter: Jerusalem), xv. 1527–8.

SCHOLEM, G. (1973), *Sabbatai Sevi: The Mystical Messiah 1626–1676*, trans. R. J. Zwi Werblowsky, Bolingen Series, 93 (Princeton University Press: Princeton).

SHAPIRO, M. (1939), 'Der gramatisher min in yidish', *Afn shprakhfront* (Kiev), 2nd series, 3: 111–63.

—— SPIVAK, E., and SHULMAN, M. (1984) (eds.), *Rusish–yidisher verterbukh; Russko-evrejskij (idish) slovar'* (Russkij Yazyk: Moscow).

SHATZKY, J. (1926), *Simkhes hanefesh, yidishe lider mit notn fun Elkhonon Kirkhan. Fotografisher iberdruk fun der ershter un eyntsiker oysgabe velkhe iz dershinen in Fyorda in yor 1727*, mit a kultur-historishn araynfir fun dr. Yankev Shatski (Max N. Maisel: New York).

—— (1928), 'Dray hundert yor "Tsene rene"', *Literarishe bleter* (Warsaw), 31; repr. in J. Shatzky, *In shotn fun over* (Tsentral farband fun poylishe yidn in Argentine: Buenos Aires, 1947), 69–76.

SHAZAR, Zalman (1971), 'Gviot-edut belashon yidish besheelot-utshuvot mithilat hamea hahamesh-esre ad sof hamea hashva-esre', in Z. Shazar, *Urei dorot, mehkarim vehe'arot letoldot Yisrael badorot haahronim* (Mosad Bialik: Jerusalem), 239–319 [see also Rubashov 1929].

SHLOSBERG, B. (1936), 'Etyudn vegn der yidisher shraybshprakh in der ershter helft 19-tn y[or]"h[undert]', *Yivo bleter* (Vilna), 10: 49–55.

—— (1937), 'Khaykl Hurvitses seyfer "Tsofnas Paneakh"', *Yivo bleter* (Vilna), 12: 546–58.

SHMERUK, Ch. (1964a), 'Di mizrekh-eyropeyishe nuskhoes fun der "Tsene rene" (1786–1850)', in Dawidowicz *et al.* (1964), 334–320.

—— (1964b), 'Vegn etlekhe printsipn fun Mendl Lefins Mishley iberzetsung', *Yidishe shprakh* (New York), 24: 33–52.

—— (1972), 'Yiddish Literature', in *Encyclopaedia Judaica* (Keter: Jerusalem), xvi. 788–833.

—— (1977), 'Moyshe Markuze fun Slonim un der moker fun zayn bukh "Oyzer Yisroel"', in Sh. Werses *et al.* (1977), 361–82.

—— (1978), *Sifrut yidish: prakim letoldoteha* [Publications of the Porter Institute for Poetics & Semiotics, Tel-Aviv Univ., *Literature, Meaning, Culture*, 5] (Mif'alim universitayim: Tel Aviv).

—— (1979a), 'Sefer "Derekh Tamim"—sefer musar bilti yadua beyidish miPolin mithilat hamea hayod-het', *Alei sefer* (Bar-Ilan University: Ramat Gan), 6–7: 121–8.

—— (1979b), 'Nusah bilti yadua shel hakomedia haanonimit "Di genarte velt"', *Kiryat sefer* (Jerusalem), 54: 802–16.

—— (1981), *Sifrut yidish bePolin, mehkarim ve'iunim historiyim* (Hebrew University, Magnes Press: Jerusalem).

—— (1980), *Sholem Aleikhem: madrikh lehayav uleyecirato* [Publications of the Porter Institute for Poetics & Semiotics, Tel-Aviv Univ., *Literature, Meaning, Culture*, 11]

(Hakibuc Hameuhad: Tel Aviv).

——(1986), *Ha'iurim lesifrei yidish bameot hatet"zayin-hayod"zayin, hatekstim, hatmunot venim'aneihem* [Yiddish—Texts and Studies Series] (Akademon Press: Jerusalem).

——(1988), *Prokim fun der yidisher literatur-geshikhte* (Hebrew University and Peretz farlag: Tel Aviv).

——(1990), 'Yidishe literatur un kolektiver zikorn: di Khmelnitski-gzeyres', in *Oksforder yidish* (Oxford), 1: 357-82.

——and WERSES, Sh. (1969) (eds.), Perl, Y. *Maasiyot veigrot micadikim umianshei shlomenu* (Publications of the Israel Academy of Sciences and Humanities: Jerusalem).

SHTARKMAN, M. (1967) (ed.), *Shloyme Bikl yoyvl-bukh, Ateres Shloyme, tsu zayn 70stn geboyrntog* (Matones: New York).

SHTIF, N. (1919), Bal-Dimyen, *Humanizm in der elterer yidisher literatur. A kapitl literatur geshikhte* (Kultur-lige, Kiev).

——(1928), 'Tsu der historisher antviklung fun yidishn oysleyg', *Di yidishe shprakh* (Kiev), 8-9: 33-60.

——(1929), 'Di sotsyale diferentsiatsye in yidish. Di hebreyishe elementn in der shprakh', *Di yidishe shprakh* (Kiev), 17-18: 1-22.

——(1932a), 'Afn shvel funem nayntsntn yorhundert. Di iberkerenish in der yidisher shrift-shprakh sof 18-tn onheyb 19-tn y[or]"h[undert]', *Afn shprakhfront* (Kiev), 29-30: 1-40 [also reprinted in Ch. Turniansky (1993a), 21-69].

——(1932b), 'Afn shvel funem nayntsntn yorhundert. Di slavizirung fun yidish', *Afn shprakhfront* (Kiev), 32-3: 27-66.

SHULMAN, E. (1913), *Sfas yehudis-ashkenozis usifruso: mikeyts hameyo hates-vov vead keyts shnoys hameyo hayud-khes* (Levin: Riga).

SHY, Hadassah (1990), 'Di reshtlekh fun yidish in Shopflokh', *Oksforder yidish* (Oxford), 1: 333-55.

SKOMOROVSKI, S. (1889), 'Di gzeyre fun Gonte in Uman un Ukrayne', *Di yidishe folks-bibliotek* (Kiev), 2: 32-41.

SORKIN, D. (1988), *The Transformation of German Jewry, 1780-1840* (Oxford University Press: New York and Oxford).

SOSIS, Y. (1926), 'Tsu der sotsialer geshikhte fun yidn in Lite un Vays-rusland', *Tsaytshrift* (Minsk), 1: 1-24.

SPIVAK, E. (1934), 'Vegn dehebreyizatsye un vegn dem hebreyishn "element" in yidish (tsum kh[aver] Shtifs shteln di frage)', in *Afn shprakhfront* (Kiev), 2: 3-22.

——(1939), *Naye vortshafung* (Melukhe farlag far di natsyonale minderhaytn in USSR: Kiev).

STANKIEWICZ, E. (1965), 'Yiddish Place Names in Poland', in U. Weinreich (1965), 158-81.

——(1985), 'The Slavic Expressive Component of Yiddish', in D. Segal, W. Moskovich, and M. Taube (eds.), *Slavica Hierosolymitana*, vii (Hebrew University, Magnes Press: Jerusalem), 117-87.

VAN STRAALEN, S. (1894), *Catalogue of the Hebrew Books in the Library of the British*

Museum Acquired During the Years 1868–1892 (London).

STRANG, Barbara M. H. (1970), *A History of English* (1989 repr., Routledge: London and New York).

SÜSSKIND, N. (1953), 'Batrakhtungen vegn der geshikhte fun yidish', *Yidishe shprakh* (New York), 13: 97–108.

TAUBE, M. (1987), 'The Development of Aspectual Auxiliaries in Yiddish', *Word*, 38: 13–25.

——(1994) 'On Factivity, Emotivity and Choice of Conjunction in Yiddish', *Studies in Language*, 18.1: 113–25.

THOMAS, G. (1991), *Linguistic Purism* (Longman: London and New York).

TIMM, E. (1987), *Graphische und phonische Struktur des Westjiddischen unter besonderer Berücksichtigung der Zeit um 1600* (Max Niemeyer: Tübingen).

——(1988), with the assistance of Hermann Süss, *Yiddish Literature in a Franconian GENIZAH: A Contribution to the Printing and Social History of the Seventeenth and Eighteenth Centuries* [Yiddish—Texts and Studies Series] (Akademon Press: Jerusalem).

TOLSTOJ, I. I. (1978), 'Literaturnyj yazyk u serbov v konce XVIII—nachale XIX veka', in S. B. Bernshtejn *et al.* (1978), 269–328.

——(1988), *Istoriya i struktura slavyanskikh literaturnykh yazykov* (Nauka: Moscow).

TSHERIKOVER, A. (1932), 'Di geshikhte fun a literarishn plagiat—ver iz geven der emeser mekhaber fun "Kav hayosher"?', *Yivo bleter* (Vilna), 4: 159–67.

TSINBERG, Y. (1929), 'Oys der alt-yidisher literatur', *Filologishe shriftn* (Vilna), 3: 173–84.

——(1935), *Di geshikhte fun der literatur ba yidn*, vi [= *Alt-yidishe literatur fun di eltste tsaytn biz der haskole-tkufe*] (Tomor: Vilna; page references to 1943 edn., Shklarski: New York)

——(1936), *Di geshikhte fun der literatur ba yidn*, vii [= Part I: *Berliner haskole*; Part II: *Khsides un ufklerung*] (Tomor: Vilna).

TURNIANSKY, Ch. (1971), 'Nusah maskili shel "Tsene rene", ktav-yad bilti-yadua shel Herc Homberg', *Ha-Sifrut* (Tel Aviv), 2: 835–41.

——(1977), 'Iberzetsungen un baarbetungen fun der "Tsene rene"', in Sh. Werses *et al.* (1977), 165–90.

——(1985a), *Sefer masa umeriva ler[eb] Aleksander ber[eb] Yitskhok Papen hofen (1627)* [= Eng. title: *Sefer massah u'merivah by Alexander ben Yitzhak Pfaffenhofen*] (Hebrew University, Magnes Press: Jerusalem).

——(1985b), 'Hatirgumim harishonim shel sefer Hayashar leyidish', *Tarbic* (Jerusalem), 54: 567–620.

——(1988), 'Letoldot ha"taytsh-khumesh"—"khumesh mit 'khiber'"', in *Iunim besifrut, dvarim sheneemru beerev likhvod Dov Sadan bimlot lo shmonim vehamesh shana* (Israel Academy of Sciences and Humanities: Jerusalem), 21–58.

——(1989), 'Yiddish "Historical" Songs as Sources for the History of the Jews in Pre-Partition Poland', in *Polin*, 4: 42–52.

——(1992), 'Bashraybungen fun gesheenishn in Glikl Hamels zikhroynes', *Di goldene keyt* (Tel Aviv), 35–40.

——(1993a) (ed.), *Di yidishe literatur in nayntsetn yorhundert, zamlung fun yidisher literatur-forshung un kritik in ratn-farband*, opklayb un forvort Khone Shmeruk (Magnes Press: Jerusalem).

——(1993b), 'Vegn di literatur-mekoyrim in Glikl Hamels zikhroynes', in Bartal *et al.* (1993), 153-77.

UNGER, M. (1929), 'Khaykl Hurvitses yikhes briv', in *Filologishe shriftn* (Vilna), 3: 83-8.

USPENSKIJ, B. A. (1985), *Iz istorii russkogo literaturnogo yazyka XVIII—nachala XIX veka* (Izdatel'stvo Moskovskogo universiteta: Moscow).

VACHEK, J. (1967), 'Pis'mennyj yazyk i pechatnyj yazyk', in N. Kondrashova (1967), 535-43.

——(1970), *The Linguistic School of Prague: An Introduction to its History and Practice* (Indiana University Press: Bloomington, Ind., and London).

VENEDIKTOV, G. (1965), 'K voprosu o nachale sovremennogo bolgarskogo literaturnogo yazyka', in *Istoriya slavyanskikh literaturnykh yazykov* [Akademiya Nauk SSSR, kratkie soobshcheniya Instituta slavyanovedeniya, 43] (Nauka: Moscow), 3-16.

VEYNGER, M. (1913), *Yidisher sintaksis* (Warsaw).

——(1926), 'Vegn yidishe dialektn', *Tsaytshrift* (Minsk), 1: 180-209.

——(1929), *Yidishe dialektologye* (Vaysrusisher melukhe-farlag: Minsk).

VINER, M. (1928), 'Di rol fun shprakh-folklor in der yidisher literatur (fun etyudn tsu a monografye vegn Shloyme Etinger)', *Shriftn* (Kiev), 1: 73-129 [repr. in Erik (1940a) and with addenda in Ch. Turniansky (1993a), 71-110].

——(1940a), *Tsu der geshikhte fun der yidisher literatur in XIX yorhundert: etyudn un materyaln* (Ukrmelukenatsmindfarlag: Kiev).

——(1940b), *Di genarte velt: komedye fun an umbakantn avtor inem tsveytn yortsendlik funem nayntsntn yorhundert*, unter der redaktsiye mit an araynfir fun M. Viner (Der emes: Moscow).

VINOGRADOV, V. V. (1967), *Problemy literaturnykh yazykov i zakonomernostej ikh obrazovaniya i razvitiya* (Nauka: Moscow).

——(1978), *Istoriya russkogo literaturnogo yazyka. Izbrannye trudy* (Nauka: Moscow).

——(1982), *Ocherki po istorii russkogo literaturnogo yazyka XVII-XIX vekov*, 3rd edn. (Vysshaya shkola: Moscow).

WALETZKY, J. (1980), 'Topicalization in Yiddish', in Herzog *et al.* (1980), 237-315.

WATERMAN, J. T. (1966), *A History of the German Language—with Special Reference to the Cultural and Social Forces that shaped the Standard Literary Language* (University of Washington Press: Seattle and London).

WEINREICH, M. (1923), *Shtaplen. Fir etyudn tsu der yidisher shprakhvisnshaft un literatur-geshikhte* (Wostok: Berlin).

——(1927), *Shturemvint, bilder fun der yidisher geshikhte in 17tn yorhundert* (Tomor: Vilna).

——(1928), *Bilder fun der yidisher literaturgeshikhte fun di onheybn biz Mendele Moykher Sforim*, (Tomor: Vilna).

——(1940a), 'Yidish', in *Algemeyne entsiklopedye*, supplementary volume: *Yidn II*

(Dubnov Fond: Paris), 23–90.

WEINREICH, M. (1940b), 'Yidishe filologye', in *Algemeyne entsiklopedye*, supplementary volume: *Yidn II* (Dubnov Fond: Paris), 101–8.

——(1950), 'A vort friyer funem redaktor', in N. Stutshkov, *Der oytser fun der yidisher shprakh* (Yivo: New York), ix–xvi.

——(1953), 'Roshe-prokim vegn mayrevdikn yidish', *Yidishe shprakh* (New York), 13: 35–69 [repr. with addenda as M. Weinreich (1958b)].

——(1955), 'Ikrim in der geshikhte fun yidish (II)', *Yidishe shprakh* (New York), 15: 12–19.

——(1956), 'Yiddish, Kanaanic, Slavic: the Basic Relationships', in *For Roman Jakobson* (Mouton: The Hague), 622–32.

——(1958a), 'Bney hes un bney khes in Ashkenaz: di problem—un vos zi lozt undz hern', in Bickel and Lehrer (1958), 101–17.

——(1958b), 'Roshe-prokim vegn mayrevdikn yidish', in Mark (1958a), 158–94.

——(1960), 'Old Yiddish Poetry in Linguistic-Literary Research', *Word*, 16: 100–18.

——(1965), 'On the Dynamics of Yiddish Dialect Formation', in U. Weinreich (1965), 73–86.

——(1973), *Geshikhte fun der yidisher shprakh—bagrifn, faktn, metodn* (4 vols., Yivo: New York).

——(1980), *History of the Yiddish Language*, trans. Shlomo Noble with the assistance of Joshua A. Fishman (Yivo and University of Chicago Press: Chicago and London) [Eng. trans. of M. Weinreich 1973, i and ii].

WEINREICH, U. (1952a), '"Sabasdiker losn" in Yiddish: a Problem of Linguistic Affinity', *Word*, 8: 360–77.

——(1952b), 'Tsurik tsu aspektn', *Yidishe shprakh* (New York), 12: 97–103.

——(1953), *Languages in Contact. Findings and Problems* (Mouton: Hague).

——(1954) (ed.), *The Field of Yiddish, Studies in Language, Folklore, and Literature* (Linguistic Circle of New York: New York).

——(1955), 'Yiddish Blends with a Slavic Element', *Word*, 11: 603–10.

——(1958a), 'Yiddish and Colonial German in Eastern Europe: The Differential Impact of Slavic', in *American Contributions to the Fourth International Congress of Slavists*, Moscow, Sept. 1958 (Mouton: The Hague), 369–421.

——(1958b), 'A Retrograde Sound Shift in the Guise of a Survival: an Aspect of Yiddish Vowel Development', in D. Catalán (ed.), *Miscelánea Homenaje a André Martinet, Estructuralismo e historia* (Biblioteca Filológica, Universidad de La Laguna), ii: 221–67.

——(1958c), 'Di klangike struktur fun a podolyer reydenish', in Mark (1958a), 221–31.

——(1958d), 'Nusah hasofrim haivri-yidi', *Leshonenu* (Jerusalem), 22: 54–66.

——(1959), 'On the Cultural History of Yiddish Rime', in J. Blau, A. Hertzberg, P. Friedman, and I. Mendelsohn (eds.), *Essays on Jewish Life and Thought*, Presented in Honor of Salo Wittmayer Baron (Columbia University Press: New York), 423–42.

—— (1963), 'Four Riddles in Bilingual Dialectology', in *American Contributions to the Fifth International Congress of Slavists*, Sofia, Sept. 1963 (Mouton: The Hague), 335–59.

—— (1965) (ed.), *The Field of Yiddish: Studies in Language, Folklore, and Literature*, Second Collection (Mouton: The Hague).

—— (1972), 'Yiddish Language', in *Encyclopaedia Judaica* (Keter: Jerusalem), xvi. 788–833.

WEINRYB, B. D. (1972), *The Jews of Poland. A Social and Economic History of the Jewish Community in Poland from 1100–1800* (Jewish Publication Society of America: Philadelphia).

WEISSBERG, J. D. (1991), 'Der Aspekt in abgeleiteten jiddischen Verben. Dargestellt anhand der korrelierenden Konverben "iber-" und "ariber-". Eine kontrastive jiddisch–deutsch–slawische Darstellung', *Zeitschrift für Dialektologie und Linguistik*, 58.2: 175–95.

WELLS, C. J. (1985), *German: A Linguistic History to 1945* (Clarendon Press: Oxford).

WERSES, Sh. (1983), 'Hanusakh hamekori habilti-yadua shel igrot Shmuel Yankev Bik el Tuvia Feder', *Kiryat sefer* (Jerusalem), 58: 170–87.

WERSES, Sh., ROTENSTREICH, N., and SHMERUK, Ch. (1977) (eds.), *Sefer Dov Sadan, kovec mehkarim mugashim bimlot lo shiv'im vehamesh shana* (Hakibuc Hameuhad: Jerusalem).

WEXLER, P. (1964), 'Slavic Influence in the Grammatical Functions of Three Yiddish Verbal Prefixes', *Linguistics*, 7: 83–93.

—— (1972), 'A Mirror Image Comparison of Languages in Contact: Verbal Prefixes in Slavicized Yiddish and Germanicized Sorbian', *Linguistics*, 82: 89–123.

—— (1974a), *Purism and Language: A Study in Modern Ukrainian and Belorussian Nationalism (1840–1967)* (Indiana University Press: Bloomington, Ind.).

—— (1974b), 'The Cartography of Unspoken Languages of Culture and Liturgy (Reflections on the Diffusion of Arabic and Hebrew)', *Orbis*, 23: 30–51.

—— (1980), 'Periphrastic Integration of Semitic Verbal Material in Slavicized Yiddish and Turkish', in Herzog *et al.* (1980), 431–73.

—— (1981a), 'Jewish Interlinguistics: Facts and Conceptual Framework', *Language*, 57: 99–149.

—— (1981b), 'Ashkenazic German: 1760–1895', *International Journal of the Sociology of Language*, 30: 119–30.

—— (1987), *Explorations in Judeo-Slavic Linguistics* (E. J. Brill: Leiden).

—— (1990) (ed.), *Studies in Yiddish Linguistics* (Max Niemeyer: Tübingen).

WILLER, J. (1915), 'Żargon żydowski na ziemiach polskich', in *Encyklopedya Polska*, ii. 3.1: 397–424.

WOLF, M. (1969), 'The Geography of Yiddish Case and Gender Variation', in Herzog *et al.* (1969), 102–215.

—— (1976), 'Di shprakh fun dem "seyfer Shivkhey Bal-Shem-Tov"', *Yidishe shprakh* (New York), 35: 32–48.

YAARI, A. (1934), 'Sefer Ben hamelekh vehanazir beyudit', *Kiryat sefer* (Jerusalem), 10: 376–78.

——(1935), 'Shlosha tirgumim shel "Shivhei haBesht" leyudit', *Kiryat sefer*, 12: 129-31.

——(1936), 'Tirgum yudi bilti yadua shel "Hovot haLevavot"', *Kiryat sefer*, 13: 398-401.

——(1937), 'Shlosha tirgumim shel "Igeret ba'alei hayim" leyudit ashkenazit', *Kiryat sefer*, 14: 394-401.

——(1940), 'Beit dfusa shel harabanit Yehudit Rozaniis(h)', *Kiryat sefer*, 17: 95-108.

——(1960), 'R[eb] Eliezer Pavir umif'alo hasifruti', *Kiryat sefer*, 35: 499-520.

——(1964), 'Shtey mahadurot yesod shel 'Shivhei haBesht'', *Kiryat sefer*, 39: 242-72, 394-407, 552-62.

YARCEVA, V., and GUCHMANN, M. (1977) (eds.), *Social'naya i funkcional'naya differenciaciya literaturnykh yazykov* (Nauka: Moscow).

ZARETSKI, Ayzik (1926), *Praktishe yidishe gramatik far lerers un studentn* (Shul un bukh: Moscow).

——(1927), *Grayzn un sfeykes, kapitlen stilistisher gramatik* (Kultur-lige: Kiev).

——(1929), *Yidishe gramatik*, nay-ibergearbete oysgabe (Kletskin: Vilna).

——(1931), *Far a proletarisher shprakh* (Tsentralfarlag: Kharkov and Kiev).

ZFATMAN, S. (1974), *Demonologia besifrut yidish—homer letargil* (Hafakulta lemad'aei haruah, hahug leyidish: Jerusalem).

——(1983), 'Hasiporet beyidish mireshita ad "Shivhei haBesht" (1504-1814)' [Eng. title: 'Yiddish Narrative Prose, from its Beginnings to "Shivhei ha-Besht" (1504-1814)'] (Ph.D. thesis, 2 vols., Hebrew University, Jerusalem).

——(1985), *Hasiporet beyidish mireshita ad 'Shivhei haBesht' (1504-1814)*, *bibliografia mueret* [Eng. title: *Yiddish Narrative Prose, from its Beginnings to "Shivhei ha-Besht" (1504-1814), Annotated Bibliography*] (Research Projects of the Institute of Jewish Studies, Monograph Series 6, Hebrew University: Jerusalem).

——(1987), *Nisuei adam vesheda* [Eng. title: *The Marriage of a Mortal Man and a She-Demon. The Transformations of a Motif in the Folk Narrative of Ashkenazi Jewry in the Sixteenth-Nineteenth Centuries*, Yiddish—Texts and Studies] (Akademon Press: Jerusalem).

ZHIRMUNSKY, V. (1936), *Nacional'nyj yazyk i social'nye dialekty* (Khudozhestvennaya literatura: Leningrad).

——(1940), 'O nekotorykh voprosakh evrejskoj dialektologii (po povodu "Evrejskogo dialektologicheskogo atlasa" Belorusskoj Akademii Nauk)', *Yazyk i Myshlenie* (Moscow and Leningrad), 9: 135-45.

ZHURAVLEV, V. K. (1982), *Vneshnie i vnutrennie faktory yazykovoj èvolyucii* (Nauka: Moscow).

GENERAL INDEX

WORD INDEX